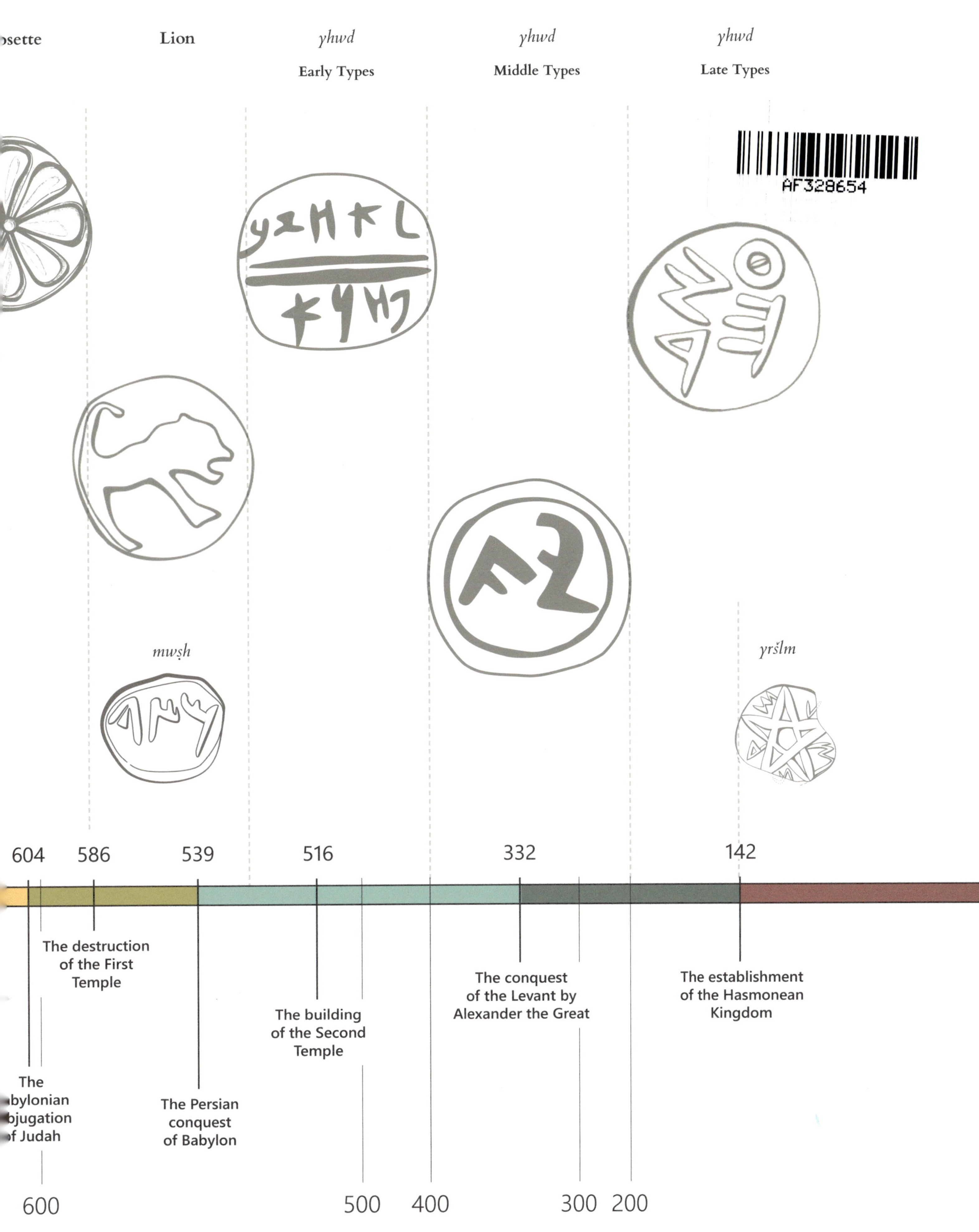
osette
Lion
yhwd
Early Types
yhwd
Middle Types
yhwd
Late Types
AF328654
mwṣh
yršlm
604
586
539
516
332
142
The destruction
of the First
Temple
The building
of the Second
Temple
The conquest
of the Levant by
Alexander the Great
The establishment
of the Hasmonean
Kingdom
The
Babylonian
subjugation
of Judah
The Persian
conquest
of Babylon
600
500
400
300
200

Age *of* Empires

TEL AVIV UNIVERSITY
SONIA AND MARCO NADLER INSTITUTE OF ARCHAEOLOGY

MOSAICS | STUDIES ON ANCIENT ISRAEL

NO. 2

Executive Editor Oded Lipschits

Managing Editor Tsipi Kuper-Blau

Editorial Board Ran Barkai

Erez Ben-Yosef

Israel Finkelstein

Yuval Gadot

Dafna Langgut

Guy D. Stiebel

Graphic Designer Nurit Rozenfeld

Age *of* Empires

The History and Administration of Judah
in the 8th–2nd Centuries BCE
in Light of the Storage-Jar Stamp Impressions

ODED LIPSCHITS

CO-PUBLISHED BY
EISENBRAUNS | UNIVERSITY PARK, PENNSYLVANIA
AND EMERY AND CLAIRE YASS PUBLICATIONS IN ARCHAEOLOGY | THE INSTITUTE OF ARCHAEOLOGY, TEL AVIV UNIVERSITY

THIS BOOK WAS PUBLISHED
WITH THE SUPPORT OF THE ISRAEL SCIENCE FOUNDATION

Mosaics: Studies on Ancient Israel

Cover illustration: Schematic drawing of four-winged *lmlk* stamp
impression (drawn by Yulia Gottlieb)

Library of Congress Cataloging-in-Publication Data

Names: Lipschits, Oded, author.
Title: Age of empires : the history and administration of Judah in the
8th–2nd centuries BCE in light of the storage-jar stamp impressions / Oded Lipschits.
Other titles: Mosaics (Makhon le-arkhe'ologyah 'a. sh. Sonyah
u-Marḳo Nadler) ; no. 2.
Description: University Park, Pennsylvania : Eisenbrauns ; [Tel Aviv,
Israel] : Emery and Claire Yass Publications in Archaeology, The
Institute of Archaeology, Tel Aviv University, [2021] | Series:
Mosaics: studies on ancient Israel ; no. 2 | Includes bibliographical
references and indexes.
Summary: "Examines the administrative system and function of
stamp impressions on storage jars in ancient Israel, illustrating
the history of Judah during six centuries of subjugation to the
empires that ruled the region"—Provided by publisher.
Identifiers: LCCN 2021006341 | ISBN 9781646021604 (hardback)
Subjects: LCSH: Stamp seals—Judaea (Region)—History. | Judaea
(Region)—History. | Judaea (Region)—Antiquities.
Classification: LCC CD5354 .L563 2021 | DDC 929.90933/49—dc23
LC record available at https://lccn.loc.gov/2021006341

Eisenbrauns is an imprint of The Pennsylvania
State University Press.
The Pennsylvania State University Press is a member of
the Association of University Presses.

It is the policy of The Pennsylvania State University Press to use
acid-free paper. Publications on uncoated stock satisfy the minimum requirements of American National Standard for Information
Sciences—Permanence of Paper for Printed Library Material,
ANSI Z39.48–1992.

In memory of my mother,
Yehudit Lipschits
The seal of her love is imprinted upon my heart

Contents

Preface

This book is the outcome of research conducted in recent years at Tel Aviv University on the history of Judah as a vassal kingdom under the consecutive imperial rules of Assyria (from 732 to the 630s BCE), Egypt (the final third of the 7th century BCE) and Babylon (604–586 BCE). Judah continued to exist as a Babylonian province (586–539 BCE), as a Persian province (539–333 BCE), and as a province under consecutive Macedonian, Ptolemaic and Seleucid rules (333–167 BCE) until the Hasmonean revolt.

The research began with many years of collecting, cataloguing, classifying and publishing the *yhwd* stamp impressions on storage-jar handles from the Persian and early Hellenistic periods. Since 2007, I have collaborated with Prof. David S. Vanderhooft (Boston College) in the publication of numerous articles dealing with these stamp impressions and their significance for the administration and history of the province of Yehud.[1] We co-edited an issue of the *Tel Aviv* journal in which numerous stamped handles were first published (2007), and we summarized our research and conclusions in a corpus published in 2011 (Lipschits and Vanderhooft 2011).

In 2007, following this research and with Israel Science Foundation support (ISF Grant No. 588/08, 2008–2010), Prof. Tallay Ornan (The Hebrew University of Jerusalem) and I began to research the stamp impressions bearing the image of a lion. Together, and with extensive help from Dr. Ido Koch, then one of my students, we collected data on all handles stamped with lion impressions known at that time, most of which were uncovered in the Ramat Raḥel excavations. After the classification and cataloguing of all these stamp impressions and following a thorough study into the various lion symbols and their meaning, we embarked upon the publication of a concluding study (Lipschits

and Ornan 2010). In 2010 we held a colloquium, in which scholars presented various lion-stamped handles and discussed new insights, along with accompanying studies, and in which initial ideas were raised about the time frame of this system and its place within the long uninterrupted practice of stamping impressions upon storage-jar handles (Lipschits and Koch 2010). We have summarized our research and conclusions in a detailed corpus (Ornan and Lipschits, forthcoming [a]) and in an article (Ornan and Lipschits [b]).

Through the research into *yhwd* and lion stamp impressions it became clear to me that these were the continuation of a protracted administrative tradition, which had already begun in the First Temple period. As part of the endeavor to publish the results of the excavations at Ramat Raḥel—both the findings of Yohanan Aharoni's early excavations and those of the new expedition, led by my Tel Aviv University colleague Prof. Yuval Gadot, Prof. Manfred Oeming (Heidelberg University) and myself[2]—I began research into the stamped storage-jar handles of the late First Temple period. This research could not have been conducted without the cooperation of Dr. Omer Sergi and Dr. Ido Koch, two students of mine who distinguished themselves in the Ancient Israel Studies program in the Department of Archaeology and Ancient Near Eastern Cultures at Tel Aviv University. Since then, they have each completed their Ph.D. and have become scholars in their own right. Ido wrote his M.A. thesis on rosette-stamp impressions under the guidance of Prof. Nadav Naʾaman and myself, and Ido and I have co-authored papers on these stamp impressions and on their contribution to our understanding of the final years of the Kingdom of Judah (Koch 2008; Koch and Lipschits 2010; 2013). I also worked with Ido on numerous examples of "private" stamp impressions,

---

1. Vanderfhooft and Lipschits 2007; Lipschits and Vanderhooft 2007a; 2007b; 2007c; 2009; 2014; 2020; Lipschits *et al.* 2007; Lipschits *et al.* 2008; 2009b; Stern, Lipschits and Vanderhooft 2007; Vanderhooft and Lipschits 2007; Vanderhooft, Richey and Lipschits 2019.

2. For an overview of the excavations and findings from this important site, see Lipschits *et al.* 2017. For the results of Aharoni's excavations, see Lipschits, Gadot and Freud 2016. The stratigraphic and architectural finds of the renewed excavations have been published in Lipschits, Gadot and Oeming 2020; the finds will appear in Lipschits *et al.*, forthcoming.

including the ones stamped on storage-jar handles found at Ramat Raḥel. Omer collected, catalogued and prepared for publication the abundance of *lmlk*-stamped handles from Ramat Raḥel, as well as the handles incised with concentric circles. In a study that began as an M.A. seminar at Tel Aviv University and continued with two articles, the three of us developed new insights into the typology and chronology of the *lmlk* stamp impressions and the relationship between these stamp impressions and the "private" ones (Lipschits, Sergi and Koch 2010; 2011; see also Lipschits 2012a). In these articles we summarized the importance of the *lmlk* and the "private" stamp impressions for an understanding of the history of the Kingdom of Judah as a vassal of the Assyrian Empire. My next step was to gather information regarding the concentric-circle incisions on storage-jar handles. I sought to study how these incisions, engraved on storage-jar handles after the vessels were already in use, in some cases next to—or even on top of—*lmlk* and "private" stamp impressions, were related to the long sequence of impressions that were stamped into the clay when still soft, as part of the storage-jar production process.

Completing the thread of the studies that serve as the backbone of this book is an M.A. thesis written by Ms. Efrat Bocher under my guidance, on the *yršlm* stamp impressions dating from the 2nd century BCE (Bocher 2012). Efrat and I wrote a summary article about these stamp impressions, their importance and their significance for understanding the history of Judah at the beginning of the Hasmonean period (Bocher and Lipschits 2011; 2013). The *yršlm* stamp impressions conclude the long tradition of stamp impressions on storage-jar handles. With their date firmly anchored to the 2nd century BCE, they are contemporaneous with the late *yhwd* stamp-impression types. Understanding when the system ended was essential to an understanding of its function. These investigations, which began in 2011, were supported in part by an Israel Science Foundation grant (No. 150/11).

While all this was going on, I participated in another Tel Aviv University study, conducted between 2007–2009, in collaboration with Dr. Omer Sergi, Prof. Yuval Gadot and Dr. Avshalom Karasik (the Laboratory of Computerized Archaeology in the Institute of Archaeology of the Hebrew University of Jerusalem, and currently the Director of the Artifacts Treatment and Laboratories Department in the Israel Antiquities Authority). The purpose of this research, which was supported by the Ancient Israel Foundation (the "New Horizons" project), was to create, on the basis of mathematical criteria, a detailed typology of the oval storage jars uncovered in various Iron Age strata from a variety of sites in Judah and to delineate the chronological and geographic distribution of the types. Based on this typology, new information was gleaned, independent of historical and other considerations (Sergi *et al.* 2012). This information provides an important contribution to an understanding of the various storage-jar production processes in Judah, to the study of the administrative system that used some of these storage jars, and consequently, to our understanding of the development of the Kingdom of Judah, of the processes that the various stamp-impression systems underwent and of the changes in the administration and economy of Judah during the Iron Age.

Following a very long process of research and study, I realized that the painstaking cataloguing and typological classification of all the finds—thousands of impressions stamped onto storage jars in Judah from the end of the 8th to the 2nd century BCE—and their publication have generated typological, chronological and historical discussions of the various types. The publication of a summarizing book that assembles all the information, defines this unique Judean phenomenon, and presents the typological, chronological and historical discussion and conclusions in a focused and systematic manner was the natural outcome of this process.

This book is therefore the culmination of many years of research, with colleagues and students accompanying me along the way. Each of them shepherded one of its parts, and each has made a significant contribution between these pages. I would like to single out Prof. David S. Vanderhooft, Prof. Tallay Ornan, Prof. Yuval Gadot, Dr. Omer Sergi, Dr. Ido Koch, Ms. Efrat Bocher and Dr. Avshalom Karasik for their contributions and for the parts of the journey that we traveled together. I hope that the overall picture presented here will be to their satisfaction.

During the years of research on the stamp impressions, I worked concurrently on the publication of Yohanan Aharoni's excavations in Ramat Raḥel, and I co-directed the renewed excavations at the site together with Prof.

Yuval Gadot and Prof. Manfred Oeming. Ramat Raḥel, where the greatest number of handles bearing stamp impressions of all types, periods and distinctive classes has come to light, can thus be called the "capital" of stamp impressions on storage-jar handles. In each of the six excavation seasons numerous stamp impressions came to light. The work on the publication of these stamp impressions was an integral part of the research. In addition to those already mentioned, I benefitted from the significant help of my students Boaz Gross and Nitsan Shalom in publishing the lion stamp impressions and some of the *yhwd* stamp impressions. Boaz, who wrote his M.A. thesis on the Ramat Raḥel garden, advanced the petrographic analysis of the storage-jar handles stamped with the lion emblem and their possible place of production, under the guidance of Prof. Yuval Goren (then head of the Laboratory for Comparative Microarchaeology at the Institute of Archaeology of Tel Aviv University, and now in Ben-Gurion University of the Negev). This research provided an important contribution to the dating of the lion stamp impressions to the 6th century BCE (the period of the Babylonian exile) and to the understanding that these stamp impressions serve as a "bridge" between the stamp impression types known from the late First Temple period to those of the early Second Temple period.

Dr. Liora Freud, the Ramat Raḥel expedition registrar, played an important role in preparing the stamp impressions found in the excavations for publication. Liora, who wrote her M.A. and Ph.D. dissertations, under my guidance, on the Ramat Raḥel pottery assemblages from the end of the First Temple period and from the Persian period, gathered all the findings and managed the processes of drawing and photographing the stamp impressions, of pottery restoration and of storage. At any given moment she knew where to find each and every stamped handle, drawing or photograph, and she served as the central link in the team's ability to conduct the research and to prepare the data for publication. As for Prof. Yuval Gadot, who managed the fieldwork and later led the research and the publication of the finds, he played a crucial role in the linking of finds to their stratigraphic context. Yuval's mastery of the data, his readiness to share with me his broad understanding of the overall picture of the excavations and of the other finds discovered and the contexts of each find, his friendship

and his unfailing willingness to assist me in whatever I needed all play a significant role in the development and conclusions of this research.

Colleagues and friends from Tel Aviv University helped at various stages of the research and publication. Prof. Nadav Naʾaman provided useful advice and guidance; Prof. Israel Finkelstein prodded and encouraged me; Prof. Yuval Goren provided cooperation regarding the identification of the sites of manufacture of the storage jars and in the research of Tel Socoh, their probable place of origin; and Prof. Ran Zadok provided answers to all my linguistic and prosopographic questions

Other colleagues and friends helped with the publication of new stamp impressions, with additional information and with good advice. Noteworthy among them are Prof. Ronny Reich (Department of Archaeology of the University of Haifa), Prof. Ephraim Stern (ז"ל) and Prof. Amihai Mazar (Institute of Archaeology of the Hebrew University of Jerusalem), Dr. Itzhak Magen and Mr. Benny Har-Even (Archaeology Department of the Civil Administration in Judea and Samaria), Dr. Hillel Geva (Israel Exploration Society), Prof. Shimon Gibson (University of North Carolina) and Prof. André Lemaire (Sorbonne, Paris), Prof. Jeffrey R. Zorn (Cornell University) and Prof. Aaron Brody (Badè Museum of Biblical Archaeology, Berkeley).

Over the years I received much help from the Israel Antiquities Authority staff in offices, in storerooms and in the field. The ability to examine the finds in museums and storerooms and to receive all the necessary information was imperative for every step in this research. In particular, I would like to extend thanks to Dr. Hava Katz, Ms. Pnina Shor, Dr. Orit Shamir, Dr. Michael Sebbane, Ms. Dvora Ben-Ami, Ms. Alegre Savariego, Dr. Gerald Finkielsztejn, Dr. Donald T. Ariel, Dr. Zvi Greenhut, Prof. Gideon Avni, Mr. Alon De Groot, Dr. Uzi Dahari, Mr. Baruch Brandl and Dr. Jon Seligman.

I received extensive help from the following institutes and individuals: Israel Museum: Ms. Michal Dayagi-Mendels, Dr. Eran Arie and Dr. Haim Gitler; Eretz Israel Museum, Tel Aviv: Prof. Cecilia Meir and Ms. Ziva Shimon; Badè Institute for Biblical Archaeology at the Pacific School for Religion: Dr. Aaron Brody and Ms. Catherine Peinter; La Sapienza University, Rome: Prof. Giovanni Garbini and Prof.

Maria Julia Amadasi. At Tel Aviv University's Institute of Archaeology, I was greatly aided by photographers Mr. Pavel Shrago and Mr. Sasha Flit, by Mr. Itamar Ben-Ezra, who prepared the maps, by Ms. Yulia Gottlieb and Ms. Rodika Pinchas, who prepared many of the drawings. Yulia also digitized some of the figures and was always willing to lend a hand throughout the book's production. I am grateful to Yafit Wiener, Shimrit Salem and Debora Menahem of the Restoration Laboratory, who carefully pieced together and restored the vessels from Ramat Raḥel.

The Hebrew version of this book, published in Jerusalem in 2018 by Yad Izhak Ben-Zvi, was written in Heidelberg University, Germany, under the auspices of the Faculty of Theology and with the support of the Alexander von-Humboldt Foundation. I would like to extend my sincere gratitude to Prof. Manfred Oeming for his hospitality and friendship. The data in this English edition of the book has been updated to include all the known and published material up to early 2019, as well as many of the unpublished stamp impressions, bringing the total number of stamp impressions discussed in this book from 2,969 in the 2018 Hebrew version to 3,282 in this English version. The indexes of the English edition were compiled by Sean Dugaw, who also meticulously checked the bibliography. The editorial, design and production department of our partners, Penn State University Press, provided useful input throughout the publication process.

I wish to extend my heartfelt thanks to Tsipi Kuper-Blau of the Institute of Archaeology of Tel Aviv University, who not only edited the manuscript with great talent and expertise, but restructured it, improved it beyond recognition, and at times helped me understand what I had intended to write. Nurit Rozenfeld designed the book with special talent and creative flair, and made sure that everything beyond the written word would be clear and accessible. Without Tsipi and Nurit the book now before you would not have been sent to press.

Last but not least: my family. Yael, Or, Tal, Naʿamah and Ido not only stored in our home many of the stamped handles mentioned in this book and welcomed many of the research partners as well, but were an inseparable part of the Ramat Raḥel excavations. They themselves even found, with great exuberance and excitement, some of the stamp impressions mentioned and discussed here. The fact that my family members can distinguish between the various types of stamp impressions and appreciate their singularity, taking true interest in the subject and enthusiastically discussing the significance of these finds with me, turned my research into a true "family project." For this I thank them.

Oded Lipschits | Tel Aviv University

Ido Lipschits after finding a *yhwd*-stamped handle in the Ramat Raḥel excavations, summer of 2009 (photo by the author)

Introduction

The Importance of the Stamp-Impression System
for an Understanding of the History and Administration of Judah
in the First and Second Temple Periods

Storage jars were widely used throughout the ancient world and throughout history. This type of pottery vessel, which appeared in many shapes and sizes, served an important function in the transportation and storage of liquid agricultural products, such as wine and oil—products that played a pivotal role in the agriculture, economy, commerce and diet of ancient Near Eastern peoples.

Among these vessels are the oval storage jars, characteristic of Judah during the Iron Age II. They have a straight (or slightly inward tilting) neck, a rounded base and wide rounded shoulders. Four thick and wide handles, set beneath the shoulder, were presumably used for tying and securing the storage jar during transportation and for stabilization during storage. These vessels, also known as "*lmlk* storage jars" or "royal Judahite storage jars," are quite large, typically reaching 50–60 cm in height, with an average diameter of ca. 42 cm and an average volume of ca. 45 liters. They were probably used for the transportation of oil and wine over short distances from the production areas of these agricultural products to their storage sites.

Oval storage jars are known from the onset of archaeological research in Jerusalem and the Shephelah in the late 19th century, and their typological development has been the subject of several studies. While much attention has been given to the stamp impressions that appeared on the handles and occasionally the upper body of these storage jars from the late 8th century BCE onward, these stamp impressions have never yet been treated as a unified topic, a component of a single system operating in Judah over the centuries. Most studies focused on the publication of specific stamped handles from archaeological excavations or the antiquities market, or on the investigation of certain families of stamp-impression types, the symbols characterizing some of these types, or stamp impressions characteristic of specific sites or particular historical periods.

The stamping of impressions on storage-jar handles was a well-known phenomenon throughout the ancient Near East from prehistoric times onward and was relatively widespread in the second and first millennia BCE. In most cases, a few impressions were made by the same seal or a similar one, and they were restricted to a specific geographical location and chronological period—and perhaps to a singular function. These early systems are generally a local phenomenon, limited in time and distribution and lacking continuity. It is difficult—and at times impossible—to interpret such phenomena. Some of these stamp impressions may be a manufacturer's label. In some cases, they may serve as evidence for palace or temple administration or for national or private commerce. They may distinguish between marked storage jars and similar unmarked ones. In other cases, the stamping of the handle may be an indication of the jar's ownership and its attribution to a certain administrative system, the significance of which is not always clear.

An overall consideration of the phenomenon of stamp impressions on storage-jar handles—not restricted to a specific period, site, type of impression, or technical aspect—yields a surprising conclusion, which has not received sufficient attention: at the end of the 8th century BCE, the stamp impressions in Judah became—for the first time in world history—a widespread administrative phenomenon. This is evident in the appearance of an abundance of similar stamp impressions during the same period, in the recovery of numerous stamp impressions created by each seal and in the widespread distribution of the stamped jars within a specific territory. Most importantly, there is evidence of administrative continuity in the use of these stamp impressions, with numerous types developing and evolving one from the other over a period of 600 years. The administrative system of impressions stamped on storage-jar handles can be defined as a specifically Judahite development of a phenomenon that was already familiar from earlier times. This system characterizes the economy and administration of Judah from the end of the 8th century BCE until the second half of the 2nd century BCE.

An administrative system based on stamped storage jars is not a new phenomenon *per se*. All the characteristics of this system are known in the ancient Near East, in numerous and diverse places and over long periods of time. What is unique to Judah, however, is the scope, diversity, continuity and consecutive nature of the storage-jar administration over a period of 600 years. This timespan coincides with the period that Judah served as a vassal kingdom and a province under the mighty empires that ruled the ancient Near East. The system is significant for an understanding of the history of the Kingdom of Judah under the imperial rules of the Assyrian, Egyptian and Babylonian empires, and later, the history of Judah/Judea as a province under the rule of Babylon and Persia and of the Ptolemaic and Seleucid dynasties.[1]

The first stamp impressions employed in Judah as part of a large and established system, probably already in the last third of the 8th century BCE, were the early types of *lmlk* stamp impressions. Despite its early date, this system is outstanding in the quality of its seals and the standardization of its storage jars. It is notable for its large number of stamp types (= seals, 11 in total), for its numerous stamped handles (723 originating in archaeological excavations and surveys), and for its widespread distribution within the Kingdom of Judah. Each stamp impression consists of three elements: a symbol (either a four-winged scarab or a two-winged sun disk), the denotation of possession (*lmlk* = "belonging to the King") and a place name (*ḥbrn* [Hebron], *swkh* [Socoh], *zyp* [Ziph], or *mmšt* [?]). In Lachish, 378 handles were found bearing early types of *lmlk* stamp impressions (ca. 52% of all handles with these types found in archaeological excavations), suggesting that this site was the main storage-jar collection center when the early system was in operation.

In its later stage (probably at the end of the 8th century BCE), this system overlaps with that of the "private" stamp impressions. The latter generally display two rows of writing, usually separated by a line, consisting of a private name and patronym, sometimes with the word "son" between them and almost always devoid of decoration. The system of "private" stamp impressions consists of 45 types (= seals) known to us from the 183 stamped handles uncovered in excavations or archaeological surveys. It should be noted that the distribution of "private" stamp impressions is similar to that of the early types of *lmlk* stamp impressions and that the 72 such handles uncovered at Lachish constitute ca. 39% of all the jar handles attributed to this system. I argue that the "private" stamp impressions constituted

---

1. The storage-jar administration system was not the only administrative-economic system operating in Judah at the time. For the fiscal bullae, which were apparently part of the royal taxation system, see below, p. 134.

Stamp impressions of various types

an *ad hoc* system that operated in Judah for only a brief period—within the framework of the preparations to withstand the Sennacherib campaign—alongside the already familiar method of *lmlk* stamp impressions. The system of "private" stamp impressions ceased to exist after Sennacherib's campaign, but it was not the last *ad hoc* system of stamp impressions on storage-jar handles to operate in Judah when the need arose.[2]

At the beginning of the 7th century BCE the system of "late" *lmlk* stamp impressions began to operate in Judah. It was a continuation of its predecessor in almost every aspect. The storage jars were of the same type, and the seals maintained the same basic concept of three elements: a symbol (now only the two-winged sun disk), the denotation of possession (*lmlk*) and the place name (one of the same four names: Hebron, Socoh, Ziph and *mmšt*). There is, however, a notable decline in the use of writing: several types lack the place name, in others the word *lmlk* is absent, and in some types only the symbol

remains. Whereas handles bearing all types of the earlier *lmlk* system of stamp impressions were uncovered under the Assyrian destruction levels of Sennacherib's 701 BCE campaign and the earlier handles continued in use in sites not destroyed in that campaign, not a single handle of the later system was found under destruction layers dated to 701 BCE. This suggests that storage jars with these later types of stamp impressions were not yet in use. It may be concluded, therefore, that the handles marked with these later types were produced only after Judah had begun to recover from the massive destruction wreaked by this campaign.

In the later system of *lmlk* stamp impressions, the number of types (= seals) declined (to eight), and there are fewer handles bearing stamp impressions of these types (490 stamped handles found in excavations and archaeological surveys). Their distribution is also more restricted, with an acute decline notable mainly in the sites of the Shephelah. It seems that the massive blow

---

2. It is argued below that the *mwṣh* and the *yršlm* stamp-impression systems were also *ad hoc* systems.

struck by Sennacherib in the Shephelah and the region's severance from Judah until at least early in the final third of the 7th century BCE are the main reasons for the division between the earlier and later systems of *lmlk* stamp impressions. The main collection centers associated with the later system are Jerusalem (ca. 180 handles)[3] and Ramat Raḥel (133 handles), with 64% of all handles stamped with late types found in these two sites. Only four jar handles with the late *lmlk* stamp impressions were discovered at Lachish, all from unclear archaeological contexts. In the entire Shephelah only 21 handles with late *lmlk* stamp impressions were found.

Concentric circles incised on storage-jar handles merit discussion in this book, even though they are technically not stamp impressions, because, to my mind, they served to adapt the storage jars with late *lmlk* stamp impressions (which probably existed in the first third of the 7th century BCE) to a new system of rosette stamp impressions (in all likelihood existing in the last third of the 7th and in the early 6th centuries BCE). About half of these incisions appear on handles previously stamped by *lmlk* seals, incised near—and sometimes even on—the stamp impressions, while the others were incised on similar storage-jar handles that lack any *lmlk* stamp impression. Excavations and archaeological surveys yielded 305 handles with concentric circle incisions. The main collection centers were now Jerusalem (which yielded 162 incised handles), Ramat Raḥel (40 handles), Gibeon (33 handles) and Mizpah (17 handles). In total, 212 of these 305 handles (ca. 69% of all the finds) were unearthed in Jerusalem and its vicinity, and 75 additional incised handles were found in the Benjamin region (ca. 25% of the total finds); i.e., 94% of all handles with concentric circle incisions were found around Jerusalem.

The rosette-stamped storage jars are the last of the series of systems that used stamped storage jars during the monarchic period of Judah. This system began to operate in the second half—perhaps even the final third—of the 7th century BCE and was in use until the destruction of Jerusalem. The rosette stamp impressions contain a symbol without any text. In this they resemble the concentric circle incisions, which, indeed, could

perhaps be viewed as schematic representations of rosettes. In terms of numbers, this system was similar to or slightly smaller in scope than the system of late *lmlk* stamp impressions and that of concentric circle incisions, which operated in the beginning and the middle of the 7th century BCE. In total, 290 handles with rosette stamp impressions were uncovered in excavations and archaeological surveys, stamped with 28 seals. The main collection centers were Jerusalem (which yielded 108 handles with rosette stamp impressions) and Ramat Raḥel (57 handles). A total of 172 stamped handles was found in Jerusalem and its vicinity (ca. 59% of all the finds). Only 19 rosette-stamped handles were found throughout Benjamin (ca. 6.5%), demonstrating that this region had lost its significance. The Shephelah, on the other hand, regained some stature: it is represented by 71 handles (ca. 24.5% of all the finds), with 30 uncovered in Azekah and 24 uncovered in Lachish.

The stamped storage-jar administration that existed in Judah at the end of the First Temple period, when the Kingdom of Judah was a vassal of the successive empires of Assyria, Egypt and Babylon, did not cease after the destruction of Jerusalem. A new system of stamp impressions on storage jars now began in Judah. Lion stamp impressions of a variety of types were stamped onto the handles, and sometimes onto the bodies, of storage jars that were similar in shape to the ones previously stamped with rosette stamp impressions. Like in the case of the rosettes, a single central iconographic motif was used, without any text. Most types depict a lion pacing either to the right or the left; one type depicts a lion standing on its hind legs. This system is dated to the 6th century BCE. The Shephelah no longer played a role, and storage jars with these stamp impressions were concentrated mainly in Ramat Raḥel and Jerusalem. Ten sub-types (= seals) of stamp impressions were identified in this system. In total, 136 stamped handles are known, 73 of which were found at Ramat Raḥel (ca. 54% of all the finds) and 31 in Jerusalem (ca. 23%). Nebi Samwil occupies a prominent place for the first time (13 handles), and, in total, 128 stamp impressions on jar handles or the

---

3. Most of the handles from Jerusalem with *lmlk* stamp impressions were published in a way that does not make it possible to identify the stamp-impression types. The estimate here is therefore based on the ratio between known early- and late-type stamp impressions (Lipschits, Sergi and Koch 2011: 30).

bodies of the jars were found in Ramat Raḥel, Jerusalem and the Benjamin region (94% of all the finds).

An additional system of stamp impressions on storage-jar handles from the 6th century BCE is known, consisting of the place name *mwṣh* (Moẓa), written in one or two rows with three or four letters. Of this system, which operated concurrently with the lion stamp-impression system, only a few stamp impressions and seals are known, and it has a limited geographic and chronological distribution. I propose that this system was established in an effort to overcome a specific problem of supply to the Babylonian governor, who settled in Mizpah immediately after the destruction of Jerusalem. This would account for the high concentration of *mwṣh*-stamped jar handles in Mizpah—30 out of a total of 43 stamped handles (ca. 70% of the finds). Isolated stamped handles were found at a few sites, including Jerusalem (four handles), Gibeon (four handles) and Jericho (two handles). Only one *mwṣh*-stamped handle was found at Ramat Raḥel, indicating that this was the only system of stamp impressions in which this site did not play a central role.

The use of storage jars bearing stamp impressions continued into the beginning of the Persian period, the main change evident in the total disappearance of iconography from the seals. In the course of the subsequent 250 years, storage jars with stamp impressions written mostly in Aramaic appeared in Judah, marked with the name of the province: *yhwd* (with four letters), *yhd* (in defective spelling), or even *yh* with two letters, sometimes with a ligature of these two letters in an emblem-like form. Only in some types, attributed to the early Persian period, does one see vestiges of the earlier tradition of personal names of the seal bearers (or their representatives), at times even with their title: פחוא (in Aramaic), i.e., governor. In total, 647 stamp impressions have been found (mostly on handles), classified into 17 types and 51 sub-types (= seals) that were in use in this system. Throughout the Persian period and early Hellenistic period, Ramat Raḥel was the main collection center of storage jars bearing these stamp impressions: 372 handles were uncovered (ca. 57.5% of all the finds).

A chronological breakdown of the known corpus of *yhwd* stamp impressions into early types (165 stamped handles, dating from the late 6th through the 5th century BCE), middle types (338 stamped handles, dating from the 4th–3rd centuries BCE) and late types (144 stamped handles, dating from the 2nd century BCE) makes it possible to study the history and track the changes in the administration and economy throughout the periods of Persian, Macedonian, Ptolemaic and Seleucid rule over Judah. The *yhwd* system continued to exist until the beginning of the Hasmonean period, when the use of stamp impressions on storage-jar handles came to a complete halt.

The final chapter in the history of Judah's stamped-jar systems is that of the *yršlm* stamp impressions. This family is characterized by the return of iconography: a pentagram is engraved in the center of the seal with five letters inserted between its vertexes, reading *yršlm*, an abbreviation of the name of the capital of the Hasmonean kingdom. Archaeological and epigraphic research have determined that these stamp impressions were contemporaneous with the end of the *yhwd* stamp-impression system and should be dated to the mid-2nd century BCE, when the Hasmonean kingdom was becoming firmly established. After this period, the use of stamp impressions on storage jars was discontinued and this ancient phenomenon disappeared. I contend that the *yršlm* stamp impressions—like the "private" and *mwṣh* stamp impressions—constituted an *ad hoc* administrative system, which aimed to consolidate the Hasmoneans' rule in Jerusalem in its formative stage, within their efforts to establish the city as their administrative center and capital. Eight *yršlm* types (= seals) are known in total, and 104 storage-jar handles have been uncovered to date in excavations and archaeological surveys. In Jerusalem, 58 handles were discovered (ca. 56% of all the finds), and at Ramat Raḥel, 33 handles were found (ca. 32%). A total of 93 *yršlm*-stamped handles were found in the immediate environs of Jerusalem (ca. 89.5% of all the finds).

My thesis in this book is that the phenomenon of impressions stamped onto storage jars was an administrative feature that continued throughout the period of Judah's subjugation to the great empires—Assyria, Egypt, Babylon, and Persia, followed by the

Ptolemaic and Seleucid dynasties.[4] We have no knowledge of such a system prior to Judah's subjugation, and shortly after the establishment of the Hasmonean kingdom it ceased to exist. Administrative systems of this kind continued to operate throughout this period, regardless of Judah's status as a subjugated kingdom or province. My assumption is that it was part of the administration involved in collecting agricultural products, mainly wine and oil, and that these products were sold and exchanged for precious metals, which were Judah's currency for paying taxes.

In Chapter 1, I describe the emergence of the practice of using seals to stamp impressions upon storage jars in the ancient Near East. This serves as a background for my claim (Chapter 2) that the development of this phenomenon as a systematic practice is unique to Judah in this period. The typology and chronology of these jars are delineated in broad strokes in Chapter 3. In Chapter 4, I offer a detailed discussion of the various types of stamp impressions, their characteristics and their distribution, outlining all the data on such impressions in the various periods. In Chapter 5, I define the time period in which the systems existed in the Kingdom of Judah (I do not deal with the time period of the systems in the Babylonian and Persian periods, since this has been extensively discussed; see Lipschits and Vanderhooft 2011). This serves as a foundation for the basic interpretation of the use, function and characteristics of the system, as presented in Chapter 6. This chapter introduces an (admittedly somewhat speculative) reconstruction of the purpose of the stamp-impression system in Judah and its *modus operandi*. Chapter 7 offers a detailed discussion on the significance of all the data introduced in the book for an understanding of the history of Judah, its economy and its administration from the late Iron Age through the Hellenistic period. In this discussion, I demonstrate how these stamp impressions can contribute to our understanding of the history of this long and important period in which Judah was first a vassal kingdom and then a province under the rule of the great regional powers.

---

4. As early as 2001, Ephraim Stern wrote a comment along these lines (Stern 2001: 174–175). Although he repeated this understanding of the system in an additional remark in the En-Gedi excavation report (Stern 2007c: 140–141), he did not develop this idea further. These two general remarks, however, show his understanding of the need for a comprehensive view of the phenomenon, instead of focusing on specific types that represented it in specific periods.

1

Storage-Jar Stamp Impressions in the Ancient Near East

Various types of seals existed throughout ancient history: they served a role in royal administration and household management, had commercial and legal functions, served as symbols of status and were used as objects of ritualistic, artistic and at times religious significance.

The seal represented the authority and power of government. Seals were likely made of precious materials and were worn hanging from a chain around the neck or set into a finger ring. They were manufactured with precision and on a high artistic standard, with great importance attached to the name of the seal bearer and to the symbols engraved on them. They were generally used for sealing documents— either clay tablets written in cuneiform script or clay bullae sealing leather or papyrus scrolls[1]—or for sealing goods. The clay bullae would be tied onto threads or onto the locks of boxes, containers or bags, or would seal the ceramic covers on various vessels. In all these cases, the main purpose of the seal was to protect the sealed object and to ensure that it reached its intended destination in its original condition, to protect the privacy of a personal missive or the full quantity and quality of the goods sent.

Obviously, the seal impressions on storage jars could not have served a protective function, as they were imprinted prior to the firing of the vessel. Therefore, stamping handles or the upper part of the body of storage jars during its production was not common. This is despite the fact that marking or engraving different symbols on storage-jar handles or on the upper part of their bodies seems like an easy task in pottery production, either as a potter's mark or as a sign of the client who ordered the vessels. These storage jars, which were mostly designated for the storage of liquid agricultural products, such as oil or wine, and for transportation over short distances, were an integral part of ancient agricultural economy, both on the royal and domestic levels. They served as the "bridge" between sites, where agricultural produce was manufactured, and consumers, playing a dual role in transportation and storage.

---

1. Biblical and ancient literary evidence generally refers to the sealing of documents. See, in particular, 1 Kings 21:8; Jer 32:10–11, 14, 44; Esther 8:2, 8, 10.

The marking of storage jars can be understood as part of production, administration and commercial systems. During production, the jars could be marked while the clay was still soft or "leather-hard."[2] Unlike seals used for legal, commercial, or economic purposes, those intended for storage-jar administration were sometimes made carelessly, out of cheap raw material available at hand. Some were perhaps intended for marking a specific series of jars within a given time frame and would have been simply carved out of wood or bone and discarded after use. In such cases, the act of stamping the impression upon the storage jar was presumably what was important, with far less attention attached to the engraved name or symbol. Thus, it is sometimes impossible to identify the details on the stamp impression, to read the letters, or to decipher the meaning of the symbol. In many cases, when the potter smoothed the juncture where the handle was attached to the jar—by dampening the spot with water and wiping it with a wet cloth or with his fingers—he would blur or even partially obliterate the stamp impression.

Marking, engraving and stamping seal impressions or rolling cylinder seals on the handles, the upper body, or the lid of storage jars are practices known from prehistoric times throughout the Fertile Crescent,[3] and from the 2nd and 1st millennia BCE they are found in greater quantities. In most cases, however, only a few solitary stamp impressions were made with the same seal, or a concentration of similar or identical stamp impressions was uncovered in one place. Such finds reflect short-term activity, perhaps serving a specific function. None of these are suggestive of an organized system of administration, operating for a long period with extensive distribution in a specific territory. Even in instances in which numerous identical stamp impressions or numerous vessels stamped with a variety of seals were uncovered (e.g., Pullen 1994; Emberling and McDonald 2003), it is always a limited distribution of individual seals with a relatively small number of stamped handles, contained within a specific area and, in particular, a lack of continuity of these stamp impressions over time. These are usually local phenomena, restricted in distribution and lacking chronological continuity.

In the Southern Levant too, the practice of marking storage jars—by stamp impressions, finger impressions,[4] or engravings—has been identified from early periods. The marking of storage jars was known already in the Early Bronze Age[5] and became widespread in the Middle Bronze Age.[6] Here too, however, the phenomenon of stamping numerous storage-jar handles with the same seal is unknown.[7] Some storage-jar stamp impressions are known from the end of the Late Bronze Age and the early Iron Age, reflecting cultural, religious and ritual influences of the surrounding cultures. In all these cases, there is no evidence for more than one handle stamped with each seal. This suggests that these storage jars were not produced locally, but were imported from afar, presumably for consumption of their contents.[8]

---

2. The term "leather-hard" refers to the stage at which the external part of the vessel's body or handle, exposed to the sun, has begun to dry and harden, while its internal part is still soft. At this stage the seal can be easily pressed into the material and will leave a clear and legible impression.

3. See, e.g., Buchanan 1967; Buchanan and Moorey 1984 [cf. Aruz 1992]; Emberling and McDonald 2003: 18, 20–21; Weippert 2010: 372.

4. Kang and Garfinkel's claim (2015) that finger impressions from the early 10th century BCE should be viewed as evidence of Judah's royal administration is unlikely. Many such impressions uncovered in the Shephelah date from the Late Bronze Age. Like other markings and impressions on cooking pots (Maeir 2010; Shai, Ben-Shlomo and Maeir 2012), these should be interpreted as potter's marks, rather than as part of the royal administration that later used *lmlk* stamp impressions. Most of these potter's marks consist of a single thumbprint, and indeed, this is the most common type found at Khirbet Qeiyafa (95% of all the handles uncovered there), and many similar ones were uncovered at nearby Tel Azekah and Tel Beth Shemesh. The distribution of finger impressions on clay ware seems to be associated with production centers, rather than with any kind of central authority. On the use of potter's marks to identify the artisan or to indicate the vessel's contents, see Donnan 1971; Wood 1990; Papadopoulos 1994. On the distinction between potter's marks and other signs on pottery, see Hirschfeld 2008.

5. For cylinder-seal impressions on storage jars, see Ben-Tor 1978 (esp. pp. 40–45, with further literature).

6. On this subject, see Keel 1995: 119. For an additional stamp impression from this period on a storage-jar handle from Tall al-ʿUmayri, see Eggler, Herr and Root 2002: No. 53; Eggler and Keel 2006: 338–339, No. 48. For handles impressed with cylinder seals, see Beck 2004: 1526–1527, with further literature.

7. Four identical stamp impressions discovered in Jericho are notable; see Rowe 1936: 235, S.5.

8. Thus, for example, stamp impressions made by Egyptian seals were found at Bethany (Saller 1957: 195 and Pl. 111:d) and at Tell el-Farʿah South (Chambon 1984: Pl. 80:10). Egyptian influence is evident in a stamp impression from Shiloh on a handle of a collared-rim storage jar (Brandl 1993: 215–216), as well as in an impression on a storage-jar handle found in Tall al-ʿUmayri (Eggler and Keel 2006: 320–321, No. 14, with further

The phenomenon of stamping storage-jar handles is also known in the Kingdoms of Israel and Judah. Stamped storage jars, and in particular storage-jar handles on which the impression includes inscriptions with private names, began to appear during the Iron Age IIA. Three identical stamp impressions from Tel Dan, bearing the name לעמדיו, are known from the beginning of the Iron Age IIB (Biran 1988: 16–17; 1994: 199–201; 1995: 9). To this period one can probably also attribute a single stamped storage-jar handle uncovered at Samaria; beneath the depiction of a griffin and a seraph, it bears an illegible and unidentifiable inscription (probably the seal owner's name) (Ben-Dor 1946: 81; Crowfoot, Crowfoot and Kenyon 1957: 89). Two storage-jar handles with an identical stamp impression, reading לזכר/יו, one found at Tel Dan and the other at Bethsaida, are attributed to this period.[9] Four stamped storage-jar handles were found at Megiddo; although their date is uncertain, the assemblages in which they were found contained mainly Iron II pottery (Sass 2000: 409–411).[10] Another stamp impression from Megiddo depicts a bird turning to the left (Brandl 2002: 427). Parallels, although not made by the same seal, were found at Tel ʿAmal (Levy and Edelstein 1972: 344–345; Keel and Uehlinger 1998: 268) and Tell el-Farʿah North (Amiet 1996: 29). To this corpus, which is associated with local or royal administration and economy, one should add five stamp impressions on

handles of "hippo" storage jars from Tel Reḥov (Keel and Mazar 2009: 63*–64*, Figs. 3–4), a single stamped handle found at Tell Abu al-Kharaz (Fischer 1998: 214, Fig. 2; Eggler and Keel 2006: 278–279, No. 3) and three found at Tell Deir ʿAllā (Franken and Ibrahim 1977–78: 73, Pl. 30:3; Franken 1989: Nos. 15, 64; Eggler and Keel 2006: 400–403, Nos. 20–21, 23).

In this period stamp impressions on storage-jar handles were no more widespread in Judah than in Israel or elsewhere in the ancient Near East. Additional handles with stamp impressions from Judah include a find from the Ophel excavations in Jerusalem with the inscription לחנה.ב/ת.עזריה ("[belonging] to Hannah, daughter of Azariah")[11] and one uncovered at Tel Goded in which the last part of the name מכא/… survived, with perhaps a floral decoration to the left of the letter *aleph* (Bliss 1900c: 221, No. 9, Pl. 7:9; Bliss and Macalister 1902: 120–121, No. 26, Pl. 56:26). Only in the late Iron Age (7th–6th centuries BCE)—alongside the main systems of stamp impressions on storage-jar handles (discussed below)—did various local and separate groups of stamp impressions, characteristic of specific local, short-term administrations, emerge in Judah and its environs. One such group is of five handles of *lmlk* storage jars bearing a stamp impression of a horse galloping to the left (Barkay 1992b).[12] These handles were found at Jerusalem, Tel Azekah, Tell en-Naṣbeh (biblical Mizpah), En-Gedi and Tel Goded.[13] It

---

literature). Storage-jar handles engraved with Cypro-Minoan markings were found at Ashkelon and dated to the Late Bronze and early Iron Ages (Cross and Stager 2006: 129 and Nos. 12–17). Stamp impressions with motifs associated with the moon god of Harran were found at Hazor (Yadin *et al.* 1960: Pls. 76:8, 162:4) and Tell el-Farʿah South (Chambon 1984: Pl. 80:7). Stamp impressions that have been attributed to rituals were found at Jericho (Sellin and Watzinger 1913: Pl. 42f), Megiddo (Loud 1948: Pl. 164:10) and Tell el-Farʿah South (Chambon 1984: Pl. 80:8). To this group one might add stamped jar handles found at Bethel (Kelso 1968: 88, 359 and Pl. 114:11), Jericho (Sellin and Watzinger 1913: Pl. 42e, g) and Tell en-Naṣbeh (McCown 1947: 154 and Fig. 35:1). A stamp impression on the rim of a large pithos was found at Tel Dan (Biran 1980: 175), and five sherds of collared-rim storage jars with stamp impressions on the outer part of the neck were found at Saḥāb (ca. 12 km southeast of Amman) (Ibrahim 1978: Pl. 20; 1983: 48–49 and Fig. 5; Eggler and Keel 2006: 260–263, 266–267, Nos. 5–9, 13). One stamped storage-jar handle, dated to the late Iron Age I or the early Iron Age II, was found at Dhiban, in the center of the Kingdom of Moab (Mussell 1989: Figs. 9, 17, 18; Eggler and Keel 2006: 148–149, No. 3), and two handles from this period bearing stamp impressions were found at Tall al-ʿUmayri (Eggler, Herr and Root 2002: Nos. 62, 70; Eggler and Keel 2006: 342–343, 348–349, Nos. 57, 64).

9. For the Tel Dan handle, see Biran 1994: 255, 258; No. 23677/1, Locus 7129, Stratum II, Area B. For the Bethsaida handle (Israel Antiquities Authority, unnumbered), see Avigad and Sass 1997: 246, No. 669.

10. The stamp impressions depict an animal standing on four legs and turning to the left. In three cases a symbol of a crescent or a star appears above the animal and a nursing whelp under it. Two of these stamp impressions were made by the same seal.

11. Ben-Dov (1982: 36) read תמר.ב/ת.עזריה ("to Tamar, daughter of Azariah"); Avigad (1987) read לחנה.ב/ת.עזריה ("to Hannah, daughter of Azariah") (Mazar and Mazar 1989: 18; Nadelman 1989: 131, 133); Lemaire (1995: No. 37) read לחבה.ב/ת.עזריה ("to Habah, daughter of Azariah").

12. For the galloping horse motif on seals and impressions in the Southern Levant, see Buchanan and Moorey 1988: 23–25.

13. Avigad and Barkay 2000: 250–251; Bliss and Macalister 1902: 122, Pl. 56:33; McCown 1947: 154, Fig. 35:6; Stern 2007d. Barkay's attribution of these stamp impressions to the corpus of "private" stamp impressions (1992a) is difficult to accept, both because these impressions are later than the "private" ones (most of which were in use before 701 BCE; see below) and because they do not include the seal holder's name, a central feature in the "private" stamp impressions (in which the ornamental element is secondary and usually absent).

seems that they characterized a targeted and exceptional activity of the administration, which existed alongside the main storage-jar system with stamp impressions. The storage-jar handles with the לנרא stamp impression from En-Gedi should also be dated to the late 7th or early 6th century BCE.[14] It too seems to reflect a short-term local use for a specific administrative purpose. Some 22 or 25 stamp impressions on storage-jar handles from Tell el-Kheleifeh, bearing the inscription לקוסענל/עבד.המלך ("[belonging] to Qosʿanal/servant of the king"), should probably also be dated to this period (Vanderhooft 1995: 153; Avigad and Sass 1997: 389–390, No. 1051, with further literature). This group of stamp impressions is also unusual: stamped storage-jar handles are not widespread in Edom and are not characteristic of the administration there (Vanderhooft 1995: 151–154);[15] the phenomenon should, instead, be related to processes that took place in Judah during the Egyptian and Babylonian rule throughout the region (see discussion below).

This survey indicates that from prehistoric times throughout the ancient Near East the marking of storage vessels—generally by a stamp impression on the jar handle—was widespread, and the Kingdoms of Israel and Judah were no exception. In this regard, the emergence of *lmlk* stamp impressions and the various systems of stamp impressions on storage jars at the end of the 8th century BCE is nothing new. The phenomenon is, however, rare, appearing only sporadically in history. It is therefore no exaggeration to say that the large numbers of storage jars bearing stamp impressions in the Kingdom of Judah and later in the smaller province of Yehud, along with their distribution and the continuous nature of the system, all point to a phenomenon unparalleled in any other time or place throughout history.

The scholarly interpretation given to this phenomenon suggests that such a system—which seems so essential for administration and economy—is not sufficiently understood (Buchanan and Moorey 1988: 19; Millard 2009: 31). A plethora of scholarly interpretations has been offered over the years for the markings and impressions on storage-jar handles, and indeed, it is reasonable to assume that the variety of stamp impressions on storage jars of different types and sizes and in different places over millennia served a variety of purposes (Bikaki 1984: 42; Papadopoulos 1994: 478). The many different accounts—some unlikely[16]—given for the administrative and economic systems that utilized stamped storage jars point to the difficulty in reconstructing these systems.[17] Some stamp impressions may be interpreted as potter's trademarks; others may be evidence of palace or temple administration or of royal or private trade. They may be intended as a means of distinguishing the marked storage jars from similar unmarked ones. In other cases, the handle marking may indicate ownership of the storage jar and of its contents, and may point to its belonging to a certain administration system, the *modus operandi* and scope of which are not always clear.

A common scholarly assumption is that the markings were often related to the storage-jar manufacturing process and that this was a "potter's trademark."[18] In some cases this assumption can be accepted, not only regarding the potter's identity (Nordquist 1987: 63), but as an indication of its location (Vitelli 1977: 30; Zerner 1986: 69). However, given the vast quantities of storage-jar sherds uncovered in archaeological excavations throughout the ancient Near East, the paucity of stamp impressions on storage jars in general, and on handles in

---

14. Stern 2007e; Parayre 1993: 37–38; Avigad and Sass 1997: 252. See also van der Veen 2014: 153–161, with further literature.

15. Noteworthy is the stamped handle uncovered at Umm el Biara קוסג[בר?] / מלך א[דם?] (Bennett 1966; Weippert 2010: 374–376, with further literature), and the stamp impressions found in Buṣeirah (Bennett 1975: 15 and Pl. B7; see also Lemaire 1975b; Puech 1977: 18–19, No. viii, Pl. C6, Fig. 7; Layton 1991; Eggler and Keel 2006: 108–111, Nos. 10, 14, with further literature).

16. An example is the suggestion that markings assisted blind users, although what type of assistance that might have been is unclear (Vitelli 1977: 23).

17. I do not include cases of clearly decorative markings on the upper body of vessels; see Ben-Tor 1978: 95. This phenomenon already existed in the Southern Levant, as well as elsewhere in the ancient Near East, during the Early Bronze Age (see, e.g., Ben-Tor 1978: 89; Lapp 1989, with further references and parallels).

18. See, e.g., Vitelli 1977: 27. Åström collated the potter's marks from the Early, Middle and Late Bronze Ages in Cyprus (1966: 149–192); see there for an in-depth discussion of the phenomenon.

particular,[19] makes this explanation unlikely.[20] It is also difficult to accept the explanation proposed by several scholars (e.g., Åström 1966: 189; Frankel 1975: 38)—at times based upon ethnographic parallels (Donnan 1971)—that some of these markings were intended to identify vessels made by different potters, including itinerant potters, and fired together in the same kiln. After all, potter's marks appear on common widespread types of pottery that are typical of the site where they were found. Moreover, in most cases, there is no evidence of a variety of local potters or of numerous itinerant potters; the local ceramic traditions are known, accepted and familiar; and the main workshops continued to manufacture their standard variety of vessels over long periods.

Other scholars have suggested that the stamp impressions were intended to mark the type of product in the jar (see, especially, Stewart 1988) or its quality (Mazzoni 1984: 488; cf. Bikaki 1984: 42–43). This too is unlikely, as the impressions were stamped on the vessel at the pottery production site and, moreover, only on a limited number of vessels. Sometimes the stamp impression appears twice on the same handle or on different handles of the same storage jar; in other cases, a single seal was stamped onto different types of vessels.[21] It seems that the type of product within the storage jar was indicated by incisions or by ink writing on the vessel, a practice known already from early periods, but mainly from the Hellenistic period (Tal 2006: 313, with further literature).

It can be assumed that already from the Early Bronze Age, the use of stamp impressions on ceramic vessels was commonly intended to identify the vessels and to verify its ownership (Boardman 1972: 13). Although this phenomenon has numerous parallels from throughout the ancient world (Papadopoulos 1994: 483, with further literature), the relatively small quantity of ceramic vessels with bodies or handles marked by stamp impressions indicates that this was not a widespread or commonly accepted custom, but was used in special cases or for specific reasons to indicate ownership of the vessel itself or of its contents (Pullen 1994: 45). That being the case, the vessel was marked, in the course of production, with the seal of its designated owner (or of his representatives), either with the purpose of guaranteeing the authenticity of the contents (Pullen 1994: 43) or in order to signify the owner (Papadopoulos 1994: 483; Tal 2006: 313). In any event, the vessels marked with stamp impressions were not designated for permanent storage in one location or for long-term storage, for this would make it superfluous to mark them. It is reasonable to assume that stamped vessels were designated for transport from some place to another, perhaps on a regular basis. In the case of agricultural produce (likely the contents of these storage jars), transportation and storage were probably carried out annually; in this case, marking the handle or body of the storage jar permanently would have made sense. If indeed the marked vessels addressed the needs of some administrative or economic mechanism, this would explain why, generally speaking, the archaeological excavation of a site does not uncover large quantities of storage jars stamped with a single seal, but instead exposes various—sometimes even numerous—types (Pullen 1994: 45).

On the assumption that the seals themselves were the private property of officials (whether belonging to the royal administration or a private economic, administrative, or commercial system),[22] the transportation of the storage jars to and from the storehouses would point to the amassing of agricultural products in designated storage areas and their

---

19. I do not refer here to improvised markings on jars, such as various incisions and finger impressions—but note that even these markings are exceedingly rare.

20. The number of potter's marks is extremely small, when one takes into consideration the total amount of pottery. For example, in the Ayanis Citadel above Lake Van, eastern Turkey, of a total of 2,787 sherds collected between 1989–1997, only 179 (ca. 6.5%) bore such marks (Derin 1999: 81). In Ebla, where numerous storage jars were gathered from a large geographic area, only a few stamp impressions on pottery were uncovered (Mazzoni 1984: 488). The percentage of ceramics uncovered in excavations in Israel with various markings, ranging from incisions to seal impressions, is also extremely low. The suggestion that it was a standard mark made by potters on vessels created in their workshops is, therefore, unlikely.

21. Wiencke 1969: 505; Pullen 1994: 43–44. For cases in which two *lmlk* stamp impressions appear on the same storage jar, or even on the same handle, and cases in which *lmlk* stamp impressions appear alongside "private" ones, see below, p. 104.

22. See Renfrew 1972: 387–388. The notion that the seals were the property of individuals arose in a modern world of literacy.

redistribution from there (Renfrew 1972: 287–288, 389–390; Bikaki 1984: 63). It can further be assumed that the marking of a limited number of storage jars out of many similar vessels that were left unmarked was intended to single out these storage jars. A reasonable conclusion would be that the stamped storage jars served as a component of a taxation system and were either designated to transfer a portion of the agricultural produce to distinct locations or, conversely, to be sent empty to other production sites, from where they would be transported full to the same storage location as the other, unmarked, storage jars. In such scenarios, the seal owners would likely be middlemen or officials, and not necessarily the recipients of the goods (Pullen 1994: 45–46). In any case, it should be borne in mind that the storage jars could have been used repeatedly for several, and perhaps many, years. We may speculate that in some cases, sherds were found at sites that did not serve as storage locations, but were locations of secondary use: perhaps the place where the agricultural produce was manufactured or where agricultural surpluses were traded or bestowed as gifts.

2

The Jar-Stamping Phenomenon in Judah

The uniqueness of the phenomenon of impressions stamped on storage jars, especially on handles, that developed in Judah is all the more salient when one considers the infrequency of this practice in the ancient Near East from prehistoric times. In no other period and in no other region did the practice coalesce into an organized system that functioned for such a long period (approximately 600 years), with so many stamped storage-jar handles (ca. 3,300) and with such an enormous variety of types and seals. Furthermore, throughout these six centuries the storage jars were manufactured in the same royal center and maintained an almost constant form. It is even more remarkable that almost all the stamped jar handles were found within the borders of Judah—both from when it was a large kingdom and from when it was a significantly smaller province. The vast majority of the stamped handles were found in one or two known collection centers, which continued to serve in this capacity throughout almost the entire duration of the system. A few isolated stamped handles were found at small agricultural sites near the main collection centers—sites where the agricultural products were processed and prepared and where occasionally, a stamped jar must have broken during the processing of the agricultural product, and its sherds discarded there. A few stamped handles, of all types, were found in secondary administrative centers—presumably sites that received surplus produce. The recovery of some stamped storage-jar handles in storage rooms of elite private homes, mainly in Jerusalem, suggests that some of the surplus was sold or traded.

We may conclude that not only was the phenomenon of stamped storage-jar handles an administrative feature unique to Judah, with no parallels in any other ancient Near Eastern kingdom or province, but that it preserved consistent elements over a long period. All the components of the system—the site where the jars were manufactured, the vessels' physical attributes, the technique and method of stamping, the sites of agricultural production and the collection centers—continued to exist uniformly, with very few modifications. The gradual development of the various components of the system can be traced, and, in some cases, the circumstances leading to this development can be established.

The main conclusion to be drawn is that the system that developed in Judah did not involve any actual technical, administrative, or economic innovation. Storage jars and the practice of stamping impressions on them are known from prehistoric times. The filling and collection of storage jars were practices integral to every agricultural economy in the ancient world, and the system that developed in Judah was no different. What is unique to this system is its grand scale, its uniformity and its enduring nature. The Judahite system adopted familiar components of the economy, trade and administration of the ancient world and incorporated them into a uniform method, deceptively simple in its components, but complex and sophisticated in its breadth and manner of operation. It is a system that operated on an unparalleled scale for an unprecedented length of time.

The uniformity in the shape of storage jar, their production in the same workshop, the method of stamping the jars, their distribution within the borders of Judah and the system's *modus operandi* all require the postulation of an administrative system with clearly defined roles, which remained in operation over a long period of time. Its purpose, in all likelihood, remained constant throughout its 600 years of existence. This was an original Judahite development: there are no parallels and no source from which the officials could have copied this method.

The question that therefore arises is: why did this system develop in Judah alone and not in any of the neighboring kingdoms?

In my opinion, the answer to this question is three-fold: it has to do with the historical reality of the second half of the 8th century BCE, with the geographical features of Judah and with its economic potential. Most of the large kingdoms in the region of Syria and the Southern Levant—and particularly the Aramaic kingdoms and the Kingdom of Israel—were destroyed by the Assyrians in a swift process that took place mainly during the reign of Tiglath-pileser III (745–727 BCE). The Assyrians annexed the areas of these kingdoms to their empire, divided the region into provinces, deported large populations and replaced them with exiles brought from far-flung regions of the empire. The various provinces were ruled by appointed Assyrian governors, who resided in the central administrative city of each province. The provincial economies were fully subjugated to the empire, and the governors used the existing economies to exact as much tax as possible (Lipschits 2018a: 115–118, with further literature).

Only a few kingdoms survived the Assyrian Empire's wave of expansion and conquest. These were mainly the kingdoms along the Mediterranean coast, where Assyria had clear economic and strategic interests, and the small inland kingdoms—Ekron, Judah, Ammon, Moab and Edom. After their subjugation, these small kingdoms were required to be loyal and pay tribute to Assyria. Each found its own way to store agricultural produce and to reach the annual quotas, which presumably assumed the form of a specific quantity of silver and gold.[1] The economies of these kingdoms prospered as a result of their integration into the imperial economic system. Moreover, the need to meet the fixed annual quotas required improving and streamlining the local production systems. The security and political stability they enjoyed during the 7th-century *Pax Assyriaca* and the opening of new markets throughout the empire, which became a single trade zone, were all contributing factors.[2] Even if the ultimate Assyrian objective was to maximize profit from the vassal kingdoms and to amass wealth and luxury products in Assyria,[3] it

---

1. For the empire's taxation of its vassal kingdoms as an incentive for the development of their economies, see Frankenstein 1979: 273; Sherratt and Sherratt 1993: 366, 370; Hopkins 1997: 29; Bedford 2005: 72–73.

2. See Finkelstein and Ussishkin 2000: 602; Na᾽aman 2001: 275. For the prosperity of Ekron under Assyrian rule, see Gitin 1989: 48; 1995: 61; Finkelstein and Singer-Avitz 2001: 253. For the development of the Negev during the *Pax Assyriaca*, see Na᾽aman 1987; 1995: 113–114. For the prosperity of Edom, see Na᾽aman 1993: 118; 1995: 114; Knauf 1995: 98; Finkelstein 1995: 137; cf. Vieweger and Häser 2007: 165. Elat, however, argued that it was not the Assyrians who encouraged the region's trade and economies (1977: 87–88), and Faust (2011; 2015; Faust and Weiss 2005; 2011) contended that the relative prosperity was the result of trade with the Phoenicians, who consumed the agricultural surpluses produced inland. Schloen (2001: 141–147) also argued that the Assyrians were not interested in developing conquered areas economically, but only in taking what could be confiscated or taxed. These scholars do not draw a sufficient distinction between those kingdoms that were conquered and became Assyrian provinces and the vassal kingdoms that were integrated into the economy and trade of the Assyrian Empire. At the same time, they were forced, due to onerous taxation, to develop their own economies and, specifically, to maximize their agricultural economic potential. For detailed discussion, see pp. 132–134.

3. For the Assyrians and their interest in luxury products, see Tadmor 1975: 37.

provided the vassal kingdoms with the potential to attain stability and development, hitherto impossible under the hegemony of the great territorial kingdoms that had ruled the region until the early 730s BCE. It also dictated the economic and commercial order and largely limited the ability of the small kingdoms located in the southern and western peripheries to develop their potential (Lipschits 2018a: 118–127).

The economic foundation of Judah, a small and poor mountainous kingdom, was its agricultural crops, mainly olives and grapes, which were processed into valuable products—olive oil and wine. The kingdom was forced to ramp up production in order to meet the additional cost of the tribute to Assyria. Agricultural areas that were previously untapped or did not reach their maximum potential were probably developed for this purpose. Much of this agricultural development may have taken place in the royal estates, which belonged to the Judahite monarchy and had been relatively free of settlement and intensive agricultural work. These were located in the vicinity of Jerusalem—the Rephaim Valley (the biblical "Valley of the King")[4] or around Moẓa[5]—or in more distant areas of the kingdom—around Hebron, the Elah Valley and the Shephelah.[6] Following the kingdom's subjugation to Assyria, its economy and administration were also forced to undergo a rapid process of increased sophistication, uniformity and development. It seems that as a part of this process Ramat Raḥel was established as the administrative center where agricultural produce was amassed and stored in jars.[7] Technological changes and improvements in this period are also evident in the agricultural production installations in Judah (Faust and Weiss 2005; Katz 2008: 55–59). Significant change also took place in the ceramic culture of Judah, which progressed from small-scale unstandardized manufacture

in local workshops to mass production in central workshops of standardized vessels, which were then distributed throughout the kingdom (Zimhoni 2004b: 1705; Katz 2008: 52–53, with further literature). The emergence and widespread distribution of the *shekel* weight was another innovation in the economy of Judah, one that unified measurements and established a consistent standard in the system of commerce (Katz 2008: 75–79, with further literature).

All these changes, which took place in the late 8th century BCE following the subjugation of Judah to Assyria, reveal a shift to a centralized royal economy, which improved agricultural production and transportation and served as a catalyst for the standardization of the economic and commercial systems (Lipschits 2018a). They could not have taken place without governmental initiative and implementation. The timing of these processes and their continuity over time, after Judah had lost its independence and had become a province, indicate that they are linked to the imperial government and to Judah's need, whether as a kingdom or as a province, to find sufficient resources to pay tribute to the ruling empire.[8]

The king of Judah and his ministers had to develop a method of administration in order to collect a fixed quota of wine and oil. As described above, this was a simple, yet original, method that capitalized on the existing infrastructure of storage-jar production and wine- and oil-production centers and developed a system for the collection of products in order to pay the royal tribute. The core component of this system was the storage jars, in which the expensive liquids were transported. An understanding of these storage jars is essential in order to understand the system as a whole and in order to place it within its historical setting. Chapter 3, therefore, presents a typology of these vessels.

---

4. On the identification of the "Valley of the King," see Lipschits and Naʾaman 2011: 75–77. On settlement periods in the valley and on its 7th-century BCE zenith, see Gadot 2015.

5. Greenhut and De Groot 2009; Greenhut 2006. On the identification of this site in the Babylonian and Persian periods in the nearby site of Khirbet Mizzah, see Finkelstein and Gadot 2015: 227–229, with further literature.

6. See: Katz 2008: 169–178; Lipschits and Gadot 2008: 89–90; Lipschits 2015: 238–240; Gadot 2015; see also discussion below, pp. 123–127.

7. See Lipschits *et al.* 2017: 30–74. Ramat Raḥel was not the only administrative center in Assyria's network of vassal kingdoms that exhibited magnificent architecture, uncharacteristic of the region, and that displayed ornamental stone capitals (known as proto-Aeolic capitals). Regional administrative centers with similar architectural features were built next to the royal capitals of Moab and Ammon; see Lipschits 2009b: 17–24.

8. The system that utilized storage jars was not the only administrative system in Judah. For a discussion of other systems, some presumably contemporaneous, operating to accommodate the exigencies of the royal tributary regime, see discussion of fiscal bullae on p. 134.

3

The Stamped Judahite Storage Jars

Origins and Characteristics

Storage-jar handles bearing stamp impressions were first found in 1870 in Warren's excavations in Jerusalem. In 1900, some 70 such handles were uncovered in excavations of the four tells of the Shephelah (Tel Azekah, Tell eṣ-Ṣafi/biblical Gath, Tel Goded and Tel Maresha), conducted by Bliss and Macalister. However, it was only when actual storage jars, and not just their handles, were uncovered at Lachish that these vessels—which were described as "oval storage jars" and became known as "*lmlk* storage jars" or "royal Judahite storage jars"— became a cornerstone of every typological or historical discussion dealing with Judah in the second half of the Iron Age.[1]

The oval storage jars were first defined and dated by Tufnell in the publication of the Lachish excavations (1953: 315–316, Pls. 28:1, 5, 11; 95:484). Numerous sherds of this type of storage jar were found in the Level III destruction layer, which she dated to Sennacherib's campaign (701 BCE).[2] She observed the unique, easily identifiable, composition and appearance of the sherds: their distinctive color is reddish-brown with many small white inclusions, the quality of the clay is very high, and the jars were fired at high temperature, which imparted extremely good durability.[3] They are uniform in form and size: these oval storage jars, 50–60 cm in height, with an average diameter of 42 cm and an average capacity of 44 liters (see discussion below), have wide rounded shoulders, a short and straight neck, sometimes curved slightly inward, a thickened and round rim and a rounded base. Four double-ridged loop handles were attached to the body of the jar just below the shoulder (Fig. 3.1).[4]

---

* This chapter is based on Sergi *et al.* 2012; Lipschits *et al.* 2010, with further literature.

1. See Tufnell 1953: 312–316; Ussishkin 1977: 56–57; 2004b: 2141–2142; Naʾaman 1979b; 1986; Vaughn 1999b: 81–169.

2. The date of Level III was confirmed by Ussishkin's renewed excavations at Lachish (Ussishkin 1977: 54–57; 2004b: 2141–2142). Ussishkin accepted Naʾaman's historical restoration (1979b; 1986), which attributed the storage-jar manufacture and the *lmlk* stamp-impression system to Hezekiah's preparations prior to Sennacherib's 701 BCE campaign.

3. This material composition and quality is unique to the *lmlk* storage jars and differs from other storage jars found in the same destruction layer (Zimhoni 2004a: 1795; cf. Mazar and Panitz-Cohen 2001: 94).

4. Tufnell 1953: 315–316; cf. Mazar and Panitz-Cohen 2001: 93–94; Zimhoni 2004a: 1795.

Fig. 3.1: *lmlk*-type storage jar from Tel Azekah

Zimhoni further developed the typology of the Iron Age pottery uncovered in the various Levels at Lachish. Only a few jars exposed at the site bore *lmlk* stamp impressions, but she classified many vessels as "*lmlk* storage jars" on the basis of their similar shape and clay composition, even if they did not bear stamp impressions.[5] Most of the other storage jars recovered from Lachish Level III differed in their attributes and their clay—which was light yellowish-brown with small gray inclusions—and none were stamped. Zimhoni called these vessels "*lmlk*-like storage jars."[6] She identified sherds from both storage-jar groups in earlier Lachish layers—Levels IV and V, dated to the 9th and early 8th centuries BCE respectively. The earlier type she defined is similar to the *lmlk* storage jars in overall shape, but is smaller and has only two handles. The clay is reddish-brown, with relatively large white inclusions, in contrast to the later *lmlk* jars.[7]

Storage jars similar to the ones found in Lachish—both *lmlk* and *lmlk*-like—were found throughout the Kingdom of Judah (Fig. 3.2), in contemporaneous settlement strata dated to the late 8th century BCE, and especially in sites destroyed along with Lachish in 701 BCE. Although not all displayed the same typological differences as defined in Lachish (see, e.g., Mazar and Panitz-Cohen 2001: 94), Zimhoni's typology was accepted by many scholars.

A petrographic examination of 118 storage-jar handles—some bearing *lmlk* stamp impressions, some unstamped, some with concentric circle incisions and some with rosette stamp impressions—led to an interesting and unequivocal conclusion: all the storage jars that served a role in the royal administrative system of Judah in the late 8th century BCE, along with storage jars that may or may not have been part of this system and later *lmlk* jars, were manufactured at the same site, located in the Shephelah—presumably Tel Socoh (Khirbet ʿAbbâd).[8] This conclusion had a major impact on the research and on our understanding of the origin, purpose and significance of these storage jars.[9]

---

5. For example, only one storage jar out of seven found at Lachish was stamped (Ussishkin 2004b: 2133–2144), and of 14 complete or almost complete storage jars found at Tel Batash, only three bore *lmlk* stamp impressions (Mazar and Panitz-Cohen 2001: 94).

6. Zimhoni called the first type, bearing *lmlk* and/or "private" stamp impressions on its handles, "Group III: SJ-1" (2004a: 1794–1796, Figs. 26.6, 26.7, 26.8:1,3) and the second type, the *lmlk*-like storage jars without impressions, "Group III: SJ-2" (Figs. 26.8:2,4,8, 26.9, 26.10:1,3).

7. Zimhoni classified these storage jars as "Group V–IV: SJ-7" (2004b: 1687 and Fig. 25.10:7).

8. Mommsen, Perlman and Yellin 1984; Gunneweg, Perlman and Meshel 1985: 272–278; Yellin and Cahill 2003; 2004. Goren and Halperin (2004) demonstrated that the clay of the *lmlk* storage jars originated in the Elah Valley and suggested Socoh as their possible site of manufacture. Most of the rosette-stamped storage jars were also produced with the same clay and in the same place, with only a few manufactured with clay originating in the Jerusalem area (cf. Mommsen, Perlman and Yellin 1984: 106–107; Yellin and Cahill 2003).

9. See, for example, Naʾaman's (1979b) proposal and his later (1986) amendment following research on the origin of the storage jars.

Fig. 3.2: *lmlk* storage jars
from Tel Azekah

Storage jars of earlier types were uncovered at other sites in the Shephelah and the Beersheba–Arad Valleys, with settlement strata dating from the 9th and the first half of the 8th century BCE (Fig. 3.3).[10] These findings indicated that the storage-jar manufacture had begun earlier than previously believed and had continued into the 7th century BCE and even later.[11] It became clear, therefore, that the *lmlk* storage jars were just one component in a long sequence of storage-jar development and that they are not characteristic of all Iron Age storage jars in Judah, a phenomenon of longer duration and greater complexity than previously assumed. These findings highlighted the need to distinguish between the study of the typology of the storage jars, the study of stamp impressions on specific jar types and the study of the administrative mechanism in which these stamp impressions served a central role.

Seymour Gitin (1990) was the first to take this direction in his research. Calling this storage-jar type the "oval store jar" to reflect the focus on typology rather than on the *lmlk* seals, Gitin noted a continuum in the development of storage jars from the second half of the 9th to the early 6th century BCE. The focus of his research was on the types that preceded the *lmlk* storage jars.[12] At this point, this type of storage jar was still interpreted as a Judahite phenomenon, as it was clear that the *lmlk* storage jars with stamp impressions played a role in the administration of the Kingdom of Judah. The discovery of storage jars at Tel Gezer, which is within the borders of the Kingdom of Israel and was destroyed by Tiglath-pileser III some 30 years before the Sennacherib campaign, as well as the finds at Tel Batash (biblical Timnah) did not change this interpretation. Scholars sought to provide explanations about how, when and under what historical circumstances the *lmlk* storage jars reached Gezer or Tel Batash from Judah. Vaughn, for example, broadened the overly narrow chronological boundary that had become established in the research of the *lmlk* storage jars, and he was the first to argue that this type of storage jar is Judahite, but should not be identified solely with Hezekiah's preparations for

---

10. E.g., Arad Strata VIII–X (Aharoni and Aharoni 1976: 83; Herzog *et al*. 1984: 12–21 and Figs. 13:1, 2; 19:1; 22:18); Gezer Stratum VIA (Gitin 1990: 122–124); Tel Batash Stratum IV (Mazar and Panitz-Cohen 2001: 93–94, Pls. 81:9–10; 83:2, 21; 86:12); and Tell eṣ-Ṣafi Temporary Stratum IV (Shai and Maeir 2003: 109–110). See also Vaughn 1999b: 138–140.

11. Storage jars similar in shape and clay composition were found in Lachish Level II (Zimhoni 2004a: 1799–1800 and Fig. 26.44:1–2), Tel Batash Stratum II (Mazar and Panitz-Cohen 2001: 95–96 and Pls. 35:1–3; 46:1, 3, 4, 6–7, 9–10) and elsewhere.

12. An early type of storage jar, similar to one identified by Gitin in Gezer, was also identified at Tel Batash by Mazar and Panitz-Cohen (2001: 93).

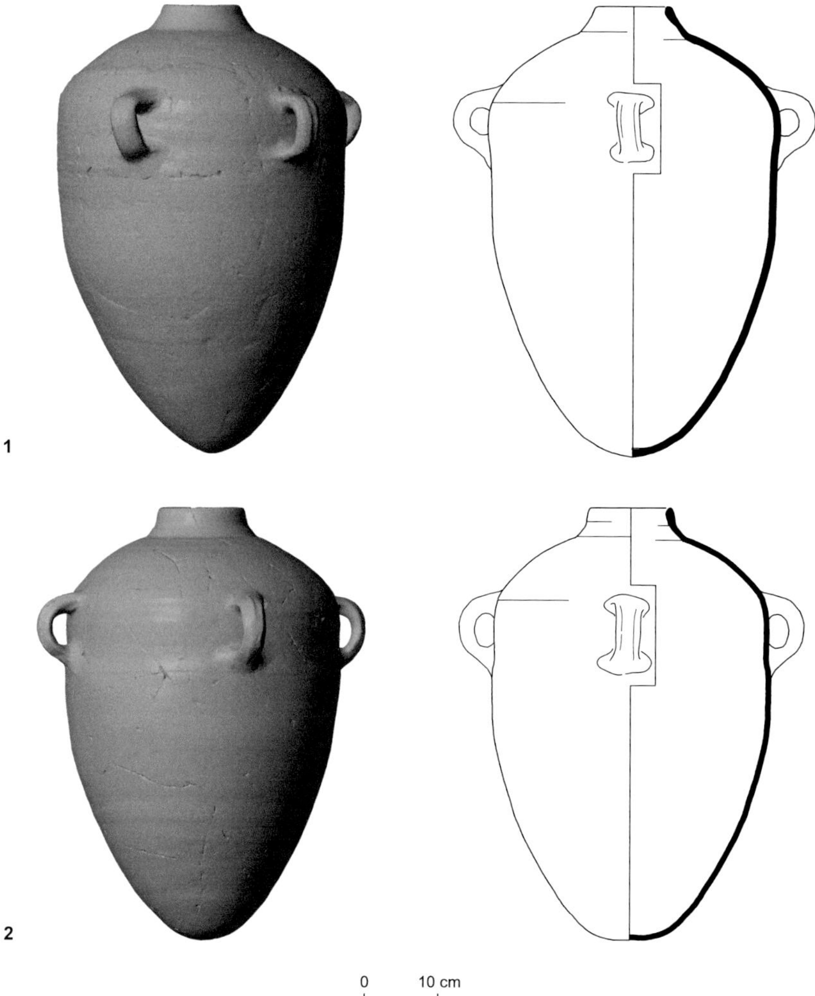

Fig. 3.3: Early types of *lmlk* storage jars
(Sergi *et al.* 2012: 77, Fig. 8):
1) Tel ʿIra Stratum VII
2) Tel Beersheba Stratum II

Sennacherib's military campaign (Vaughn 1999b: 138–140). Following Gitin, he argued that the types heralding the appearance of the *lmlk* storage jar were already to be found in the 9th century BCE and had developed in the 8th century and continued into the 7th century BCE, with minor changes.

The excavations in Tell eṣ-Ṣafi/Gath generated a major change in the scholarly perception of the origin of the storage jars. Jars similar to the early *lmlk* storage jars were uncovered, and they too were securely dated to the second half of the 9th century BCE.[13] Consequently, Shai and Maeir proposed a new type preceding the *lmlk* storage jars and termed it the "pre-*lmlk* jar" (Fig. 3.4). In their opinion, these types had already emerged at the end of the 10th century BCE[14] and their distribution was restricted to the Shephelah and eastern Philistia.[15] During the 8th century BCE, the *lmlk* storage jar developed from the pre-*lmlk* type and became the most common storage jar

---

13. Two types of storage jars parallel to the ones found in Gezer Stratum VIA (Shai and Maeir 2003: 109–110) were identified in Tell eṣ-Ṣafi Temporary Stratum 4, the destruction of which was dated to the second half of the 9th century BCE. Shai and Maeir compared these jars to similar types found at Gezer (Stratum VIA), Tel ʿEton (Strata I–II), Beth Shemesh (Temporary Stratum IV; finds not yet published), Tel Ḥalif (Strata VIA–VIB), Tell el-Ḥesi (Stratum VIIIA), Arad (Strata IX–X) and Beersheba (Stratum V).

14. Shai and Maeir 2003: 119. Herzog and Singer-Avitz (2004), in contrast, supported the attribution of Lachish Level V to the first half of the 9th century BCE.

15. It should be stressed that the pre-*lmlk* storage jar appeared mainly in Shephelah sites, in Gezer and in Tell eṣ-Ṣafi/Gath; see discussion below.

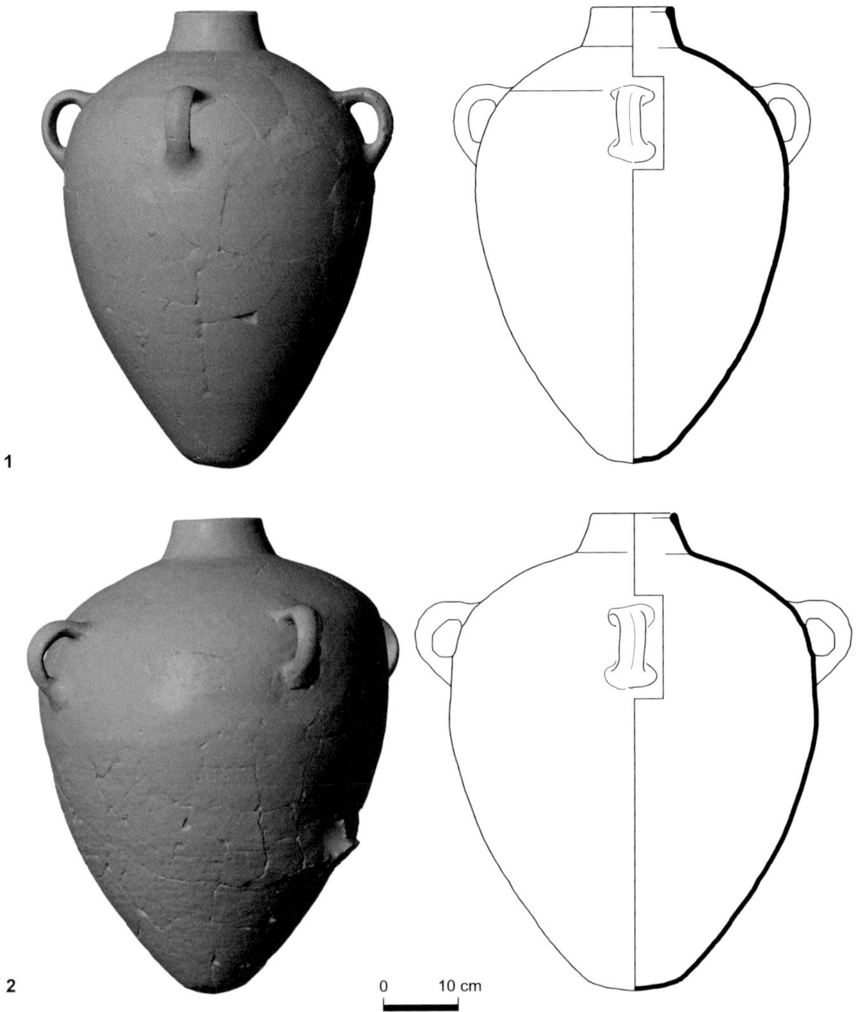

Fig. 3.4: Two early types of *lmlk* storage jars from Tell eṣ-Ṣafi/Gath (Sergi *et al.* 2012: 80, Fig. 11)

in Judah, continuing to be manufactured in the 7th century BCE. Shai and Maeir's observation makes it clear that the phenomenon of the various types of pre-*lmlk* storage jars was not unique to the Kingdom of Judah, but characterized the entire Shephelah region, transcending the political borders between Philistia, Israel and Judah.

Against this backdrop, Gitin published another article (2006) about the storage-jar phenomenon, in which he cemented the connection between the early storage jars (from Beersheba, Arad, Gezer, Tel Batash and Tell eṣ-Ṣafi) and the *lmlk* storage jars known from the late 8th century BCE. Stressing the heterogeneity of the early jars in terms of shape and clay composition (following Mazar and Panitz-Cohen 2001: 97), he posited that the *lmlk* storage jars constituted a specific point in time on the spectrum of storage-jar development (Gitin 2006: 506). He was also the first to propose a typology of the storage jars on the basis of their development, and, based on a comprehensive examination of the finds from sites in the Shephelah, the Negev and eastern Philistia, he defined six sub-types of the oval storage jars (SJO 1–6), each with several variants (Gitin 2006: 510–521). Types SJO 3 and SJO 4 are the ones that served the administrative system that utilized *lmlk* stamp impressions at the end of the 8th century BCE. The first of these (SJO 3) continued, with several variants, until the late 7th or early 6th century BCE, while the second (SJO 4) is characteristic mainly of Judahite sites in the late 8th century BCE but did not continue to develop after that.

A New Typology of the Oval Storage Jars

In 2012, Sergi, Karasik, Gadot and I suggested a detailed typology of the oval storage jars in Judah from various Iron Age strata and from a variety of sites in Judah (Sergi *et al.* 2012). This new computer-generated typology, based upon mathematical criteria, made it possible to plot the chronological and geographical development of the various types. The research utilized a system that performs high-resolution 3D scanning of archaeological finds, enabling their morphological analysis.[16] We selected 110 complete or almost complete oval storage jars, in which a significant part of their profile (including the shoulder and part of the body) was preserved,[17] and performed a 3D scan. They were studied as a single group, with their provenance, stratigraphic affiliation and chronological attribution not considered relevant for the typology. Like Gitin's research, our study included small storage jars similar in body shape to the large ones, as well as storage jars from the 7th–6th centuries BCE, some with rosette stamp impressions. The classification and typology were based upon objective morphological parameters alone, with no intrusion of extraneous information.[18]

On the basis of the data obtained, we classified the storage jars into six sub-types (Sergi *et al.* 2012: 72–81). Three of these were determined to be standard in shape, size and volume, and therefore, it is not surprising that all the *lmlk* impressions and most of the rosette impressions were stamped on two of these sub-types. Four chronological stages in the development of the storage jars were discerned: 1) the late 9th century BCE (Tell eṣ-Ṣafi Stratum A3);[19] 2) the mid-8th century BCE (prior to the Gezer Stratum VI destruction and Beth Shemesh Stratum III);[20] 3) the end of the 8th century BCE (Lachish Level III and its equivalents); and 4) the late 7th and early 6th century BCE (Lachish Level II, City of David Stratum X, Tel ʿIra Stratum VI, Arad Stratum VI and En-Gedi Stratum V).

The typology obtained through the computerized scanning and the attribution of these types to clear chronological stages, sealed by well-defined destruction layers, made it possible to trace the development of the storage jars. The conclusion that emerges is that early in their development—at the end of the 9th century BCE and perhaps even prior to that—there were three types of storage jars, differing in features and capacity. These types continued to exist in the 8th and 7th centuries BCE. At the same period, already in the 9th century BCE, the type that would ultimately become the prototypical storage jar—and would become the standard and most common of the family in terms of the number of types and the length of its existence—also began to develop (Fig. 3.5). It became more dominant in the mid-8th century BCE, and at the end of this century it was chosen as the type of jar to bear *lmlk* stamp impressions. In the 7th century BCE, a new, previously unknown, type of storage jar developed, and it was on this type that rosettes were stamped in the late 7th and early 6th centuries BCE. Throughout this time period, the non-uniform types did not disappear, and it can be assumed that different types of jars served different purposes. While the standard storage jars were used (and sometimes stamped) by the royal administration in the late 8th, 7th and early 6th centuries BCE, the non-standard types were probably part of the economic and commercial systems operating outside the kingdom's administration—although their quantity declined in

---

16. This scanner enables a faster and more precise measurement of the entire vessel surface. The 3D model obtained enabled an in-depth study of the vessel's morphology, including the degree of symmetry and uniformity it exhibits, a calculation of its volume and, crucially, the classification and typology of the various types. See, e.g., Karasik, Smilansky and Beit-Arieh 2005; Karasik and Smilansky 2006; 2008; 2011; Gilboa *et al.* 2004.

17. Of the 110 storage jars studied, 36 are from Lachish, 12 from Tel ʿIra, 11 from Gezer, 10 from Tell eṣ-Ṣafi, nine from Tel Batash, eight from Tel Beth Shemesh, seven each from Tel Arad and the City of David (Jerusalem), four from En-Gedi, two each from Beersheba and Tel Malḥata, and one from Khirbet Titura. An additional storage jar of unknown origin was selected, in order to study its relation and similarity to the other jars.

18. For a detailed review of the methodology and the parameters studied, see Sergi *et al.* 2012: 67–68.

19. For the date of Tell eṣ-Ṣafi Stratum A3, see Maeir 2004; 2008; cf. also Maeir 2012.

20. For the destruction of Gezer Stratum VI, see Gitin 1990: 16–18; Dever 1998: 181–187; Finkelstein 2002: 285–286. For the destruction of Beth Shemesh Stratum III, see Bunimovitz and Lederman 2009: 136; Finkelstein and Piasetzky 2010.

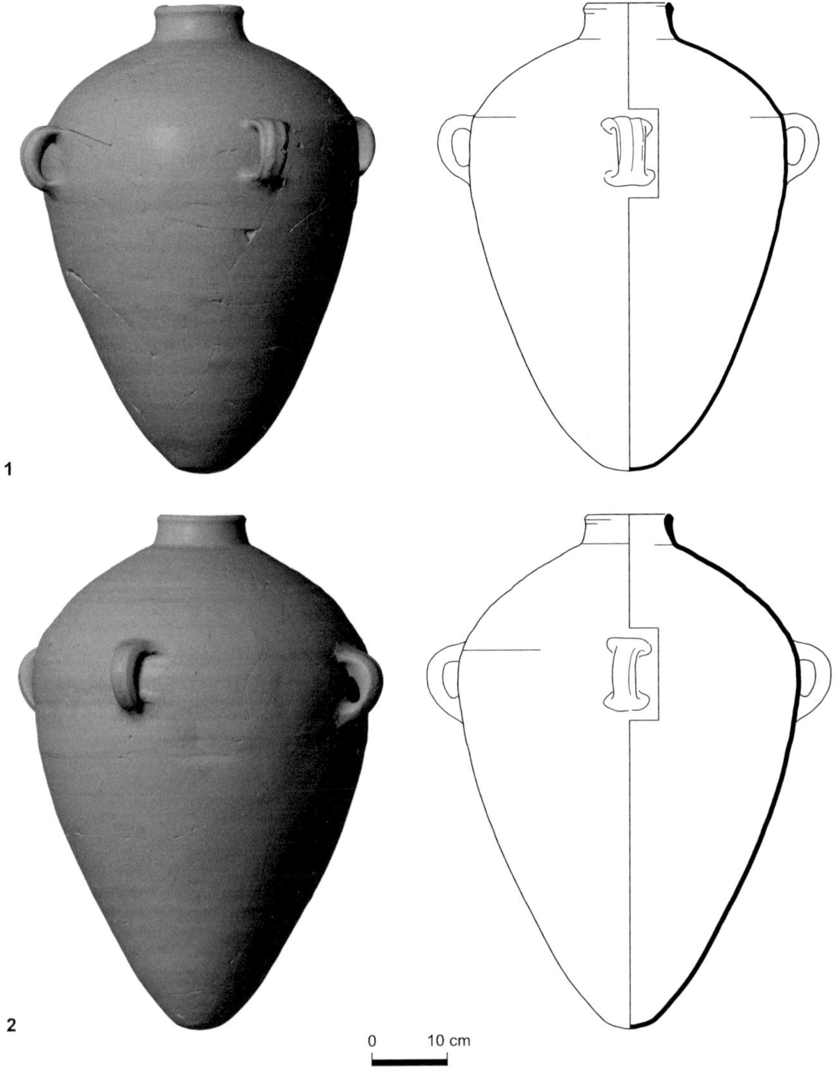

Fig. 3.5: Two standard *lmlk* storage jars from Lachish (Sergi *et al.* 2012: 75, Fig. 6)

the 8th–7th centuries BCE, while the number of uniform storage jars increased.[21] The royal administrative system presumably placed great importance on the uniformity of jar shape and capacity, whereas the non-standard storage jars displayed variability in size, and consequently, in capacity. The uniformity exhibited in the standard storage jars might have been a requisite of the royal administration, or should perhaps be attributed to the skilled workmanship of the potters employed or to the attention that was paid to each and every storage jar.

Our research into the geographical distribution of the storage jars within the Kingdom of Judah in the late 8th, 7th and early 6th centuries BCE is by necessity limited. Numerous storage jars have been uncovered in the Shephelah in destruction layers emanating from both the Assyrian (701 BCE) and Babylonian (586 BCE) campaigns. In the hill country, in contrast, in sites that were not

---

21. Interestingly, despite variations in neck length and slant, shoulder width and body diameter, all the storage jars have the same rim and neck diameter. This suggests that throughout the centuries, storage jars served a similar function—perhaps one of transportation and storage—that might have required a specific aperture for the proper sealing of goods.

destroyed in the Assyrian campaign, one finds storage jars mainly in the 586 BCE destruction layers. The archaeological finds thus offer a distorted picture of the historical reality: it is reasonable to assume that the paucity of 8th-century BCE storage jars uncovered in hill country sites does not mean that they were absent from these sites. It is more likely that they had been replaced over the years by new storage jars, belonging to later, 7th century BCE, types—types that were, indeed, found in destruction layers from the early 6th century BCE. The inevitable conclusion is that the distribution of 8th-century BCE storage jars does not, in fact, reflect the historical reality, but stems from the limitations of archaeological research. At this point, we must bear in mind that absence of proof is not necessarily proof of absence.

What we can conclude is that the picture demonstrates the centrality of the Shephelah as the source for the early types of storage jars, and that in its early stages, this was not limited to any specific geopolitical entity and was not restricted to the Kingdom of Judah. It also provides evidence of the centrality of Lachish in the late 8th century BCE. Indeed, as transpires from the study of the *lmlk* stamp impressions too, Lachish was undoubtedly the most significant Judahite center for the storage-jar administrative system during this period. At this stage, the Beersheba–Arad Valleys played a marginal role in the administrative system of Judah. Within this region, Tel ʿIra exhibited the largest number of storage jars and the greatest variety of types, suggesting that this site was an important commercial or administrative center in the region. However, the fact that the storage jars uncovered there belong to the types that exhibit little uniformity, coupled with the paucity of stamp impressions uncovered at this site, suggest that it was not part of the royal administrative system related to the *lmlk* storage jars. This system was primarily based in the Shephelah and, as far as can be determined, included the central hill country.

The most important observation to be drawn from the typological development of the storage jars is that the early 9th-century BCE types and those continuing into the 8th century BCE lack uniformity in proportions and vary widely in capacity. These are the jars referred to as the "pre-*lmlk* storage jars" (even though they continued to exist even after the emergence of the so-called "*lmlk*

storage jars" in the late 8th century BCE). It seems that the manufacture of non-uniform storage jars during that period was intended to meet a variety of needs and characterized all the Shephelah sites, not just the Kingdom of Judah. There is no evidence that these jars were intended to serve the Judahite royal administrative system, in particular, or that they were manufactured especially for this system.

The culmination of the process of "standardization" of storage-jar types is evident in the classic *lmlk* storage jars, which are mainly concentrated in Lachish Level III, but appear in the destruction layers in other Shephelah sites as well. It seems that at some point in the late 8th century BCE, the administrative system of Judah selected an existing type of storage jar for its needs, that this type consequently underwent a process of "standardization" in order to achieve uniformity, and that some of these storage jars were stamped. A process of standardization in the dimensions and proportions of storage jars underscores the assumption about an overall process of standardization in the Kingdom of Judah in the 8th century BCE. These jars have been found alongside other types of storage jars (termed by Zimhoni "*lmlk*-like") that are less uniform in diameter and capacity than the stamped storage jars. This indicates that the production of storage jars that were not intended for the Judahite administrative system and were perhaps used for other purposes continued during this period. It continued even after Sennacherib's campaign and until the destruction of Judah in the early 6th century BCE. The storage jars prevalent in the final days of the Kingdom of Judah—some of which bore rosette stamp impressions—continued the typological development from the late 8th century BCE and manifest the same tradition of manufacture.

The study of the storage jars also shows that Zimhoni's definition of *lmlk* and *lmlk*-like storage jars is no longer tenable. The "pre-*lmlk*" type proposed by Shai and Maeir must also be rejected as the various storage-jar types have been shown to coexist, the main difference between the types being the degree of their uniformity and standardization. Moreover, these storage jars should not be defined as "Judahite," because for long periods in the course of their development, they were not linked to the borders or administrative system of Judah.

Capacity

In this section, I argue that contrary to the generally accepted scholarly view, there was no precise system of liquid capacity measurements with set proportions, but instead, there were vessels of fixed shapes and sizes, designated for specific uses—in ritual and administration (see also Lipschits *et al.* 2010). The need for accuracy in measurements is in fact a later, post-Hellenistic, construct, and the attempt to determine the precise liter equivalence of biblical measurements is an imposition of our own modern preconceptions on the ancient world. Having established this, I will then show that the biblical בת (*bat*, usually appearing in Old Testament translations as *bath* and considered by scholars as a fixed measure for liquids) is in fact equivalent to the capacity of the standardized Judahite storage jar.

The Biblical Liquid Measurement Systems

At the heart of the liquid measurement system postulated by many scholars was the *bat*, divided into 6 *hîn* and 72 *lōḡ*.[22] Some scholars have also suggested that the *iśśārôn* is a liquid volume measurement, defined as one-tenth of a *bat* (Zapassky, Finkelstein and Benenson 2009: 53, 58). Our data regarding the liquid measurement system during the biblical period is based on the analysis of three main sources: the biblical text, epigraphic discoveries and archaeological finds. Of the three sources, the biblical text is the most important for the reconstruction and understanding of the First Temple liquid measurement system, and most scholars assume that biblical references testify to fixed measurements of liquid volume. A close analysis of the text reveals, however, that what scholars have termed "measurements"[23] are in fact vessels that were part of the official Temple cult—mostly in use during the Second Temple period.

The *hîn* is mentioned in the Bible 22 times, in all cases in association with the Temple cult and post-dating the First Temple period.[24] From the biblical references it seems that the *hîn*, probably an Egyptian loanword,[25] was a vessel for oil or wine that was used for cult purposes. The *hîn* does not occur in the Deuteronomistic history or in epigraphic sources, so there is no evidence of its use in the administration or economy of the First or Second Temple periods. Besides, there is no reference for interpreting the *hîn* as a sixth of a *bat* on the basis of the references in Ezekiel (cf. Cooke 1936: 504; Stern 1962: 854; Rattray 1991: 896), mainly because the only thing one can learn from these texts is that the *hîn* was a well-known container for cult use (Ezek 46:6; cf. Block 1998: 673), for libations (Lev 23:13; cf. Noth 1974: 171) and for concocting ointments (Exod 30:24; cf. Noth 1966: 238; Propp 2006: 471–472). One can also use a half *hîn* (Num 15:10; 28:14), a third *hîn* (Num 15:6,7; 28:14; Ezek 46:14) or a quarter *hîn* (Exod 29:40; Lev 23:13; Num 15:4, 5; 28:5, 7, 14). It may be speculated that it was a special vessel, probably small and open, with fixed shape and size,[26] and on which measurements of a quarter, a third and a half could have been marked.[27] In any case, it seems that this vessel had a limited use within the Temple cult.

The *lōḡ* is mentioned five times in the Bible, all in the same chapter in Leviticus (14:10, 12, 15, 21, 24) (Milgrom 1991: 846; cf. Cohen 1975: 60–61). The *lōḡ* is not a measurement but an oil vessel in the Temple cult, that can be lifted for waving (Lev 14:12, 24) or be used for pouring (14:15). It seems that just like the *hîn*, the *lōḡ* was also an open vessel used mainly in cult, on which measurements of a quarter, a third and a half could have been marked (Milgrom 1991: 846; Cohen 1975: 60–61).

---

22. See, e.g., de Vaux 1961: 200–201; Stern 1962: 851–852; Zapassky, Finkelstein and Benenson 2009: 58; Kletter 2009: 362; 2014: 22.

23. See, e.g., Albright 1943: 58–59; de Vaux 1961: 200–201; Scott 1970: 350–351; Ussishkin 1978: 87, n. 9; Heltzer 1989; 2008; Ephʿal and Naveh 1993; Zapassky, Finkelstein and Benenson 2006; 2009; Kletter 2009.

24. Exod 29:40 (twice); 30:24; Lev 19:36; 23:13; Num 15:4, 5, 6, 7, 9, 10; 28:5, 7, 14 (three times); and Ezek 4:11; 45:24; 46:5, 7, 11, 14.

25. On this, see, e.g., Ellenbogen 1962: 68; Muchiki 1999: 243.

26. For data on the uniformity of measurements in Judah in the First Temple period, with known deviations of 5% and even 10%, see Kletter 2009.

27. Kletter (2014: 27) insists that a quarter, a third and a half of a *hîn* were by necessity measures of known quantities and that otherwise, there was apparently no alternative but to break a vessel in order to pour out its exact quantity of liquids. This ignores the reality described in the biblical texts in which a specific quantity of liquid was poured from a vessel, on which measurements were probably marked, without the need to break the vessel. The inscription on the upper part of an alabaster vessel mentioning "1 *hîn* and half a *lōḡ* and a quarter of a *lōḡ*" (Aḥituv 2005: 242–243) supports the possibility that the *hîn* was a receptacle of known size and that either all or a certain proportion of its contents could be used.

Leviticus 14 is well dated to the post-exilic period, and there is no evidence that the *lōḡ* was used within the administration or economy during the First or Second Temple periods.

The *issārôn* was not known as a liquid volume measurement, and there is no evidence for its use within the administration or economy of the Kingdom of Judah during the First Temple period (Powell 1992: 904). It is mentioned 33 times in the Bible, all in post-exilic texts in the Pentateuch.[28] In all cases it refers to service in the Temple and is a dry measure of capacity, usually relating to quantities of semolina, which was mixed with oil in order to prepare burnt offerings (Kletter 2009: 362).

The *kōr* is mentioned eight times in the Old Testament; six as a dry measure of capacity for semolina and for wheat and barley flour (1 Kings 5:2, 11; 2 Chron 2:9, 27:5). 1 Kings 5:11 describes how "Solomon gave Hiram twenty thousand *kōr* of wheat as provisions for his household, and twenty *kōr* of pure oil." Scholars have used this verse as a source in order to understand Ezekiel's prophecy (Ezek 45:14): "Concerning the ordinance of oil, the *baṯ* of oil, ye shall offer the tenth part of a *baṯ* out of the *kōr*, which is a *ḥōmer* of ten *baṯ*; for ten *habbattim* are a *ḥōmer*." This verse describes a utopian future, when "you shall have honest balances, an honest *ephah*, and an honest *baṯ*" (v. 10), when the prophet is mixing the liquid and dry measures on purpose in order to emphasize that "the *ephah* and the *baṯ* shall be of the same measure, the *bath* containing one tenth of a *ḥōmer*, and the *ephah*

one tenth of a *ḥōmer*; the *ḥōmer* shall be the standard measure" (v. 11). On the basis of this verse, the *baṯ* was reconstructed by some scholars as a tenth of a *kōr*, and some have calculated the relative measures of the *hîn* and the *lōḡ*.[29] However, I accept the assumption that the Book of Ezekiel reflects the reality of the exilic or post-exilic period, primarily of the Temple cult, and not the First Temple reality of the administration and the economy.[30] Besides, it is important to note that in the Septuagint version of 1 Kings 5:11 and in Josephus' *AJ* (8.57), it says that Solomon gave Hiram "twenty thousand (χιλιάδας) *bath*s of fine oil";[31] the data presented above suggests that this version is preferable.[32]

On the basis of archaeological and epigraphic finds, further liquid capacity measurements have been suggested. Based on Arad Letter 2, which reads (lines 4–5) ‏ו/מלא.החמר.יין‎ ("fill the *ḥōmer* with wine"), Aharoni ascribed the *ḥōmer* measurement to the liquid volume measurement system (perhaps in accordance with the prophecy in Ezek 45:15).[33] Contra this view, the enormous volume of this shipment should be emphasized (220 liters, according to Aharoni),[34] as should the lack of a designated recipient. The term *ḥmr* could alternatively be translated as *ḥemar* = young wine.[35] According to several scholars, the *ḥōmer* was used to define the features or quality of the wine shipment mentioned in line 2 of the letter, and not its measurement (Lemaire 1977: 44–45; Mittmann 1993: 43–45; Dobbs-Allsopp *et al.* 2004: 14), just as the word ‏חמץ‎ (leavened bread) in

---

28. Exod 29:40; Lev 14:10, 21; 15:6, 9; 23:13, 17; Num 15:4, 6, 9; 28:9, 12 (twice), 13 (twice), 20 (twice), 21, 28 (twice), 29; 29:3 (twice), 4, 9 (twice), 10, 14 (twice), 15 (twice), 40.

29. Rattray 1991. Although there is no information on the *kōr* in the Bible or elsewhere, Kletter (2014: 29) still considers it to be a liquid measure as well and calculates its place within the system of these "measurements."

30. The earliest biblical scholars (Skinner 1895; Redpath 1907: xv, 214) viewed the prophecy in Ezekiel 45 as continuing previous prophecies, whose date is "in the twenty-fifth year of our exile, at the beginning of the year, on the tenth day of the month, in the fourteenth year after the city was struck down, on that very day, the hand of the Lord was upon me, and he brought me there" (Ezek 40:1). Some scholars (e.g., Torrey 1970) argued that the last collection of prophecies in Ezekiel (Chapters 40–45) had nothing to do with the prophet himself (but cf. Haran 1979: 46). The prevalent view in the research today (Laato 1992: 189–196; Tuell 1992; also Block 1998: 495, with further literature) is that the earlier layers of Ezekiel reflect the end of the exilic period and that the book itself was edited during the Persian period at the earliest (for a more conservative approach, see Greenberg 1983: 12–17). For a later dating of Ezekiel 45, see Wagenaar 2003.

31. In the *Peshitta* the word "twenty thousand" (χιλιάδας) was preserved.

32. Fritz 1996: 61, n. 25. On the other hand, Montgomery (1951: 136) and Mulder (1998: 217–218), who relied on Wevers (1950: 308), argued that the Masoretic version is the original one, whereas the translations include the later version, also reflected in 2 Chronicles 9, which exaggerates Solomon's wealth (see also Cogan 2001: 229).

33. Aharoni 1981b: 16, followed by Aḥituv 2005: 85. See also Pardee 1978: 297–298; and Stern 1962: 852.

34. According to Ezek 45:11, the *baṯ* equals the *'ēp̄āʰ* and the *'ēp̄āʰ* equals a tenth of the *ḥōmer*.

35. See Deut 32:14; Ps 75:9; and cf. Walsh 2000: 199–200. Lemaire (1977: 162–163) suggested that the reference was to a wine made of grape skin residue (a kind of mead; see also Ruth 2:14). See Cross 2008: 341, and compare to the Shiqmona storage-jar inscription (Cross 1968: 227).

line 7 details the features or quality of the bread mentioned in line 4 (Mittman 1993: 45; cf. Aharoni 1981b: 16). This parallels the definition of the quality or features of the wine in Letter 1, lines 9–10: מיין/האגנת.תתן ("from the wine of the krater you shall give") (see discussion in Aḥituv 2005: 85; Dobbs-Allsopp *et al.* 2004: 11–12).

On the basis of another Arad ostracon, Aharoni ascribed an additional measurement—the מעשר (tithe)—to the liquid measurement system. In Letter 5 (lines 10–12), Aharoni reconstructed: אשר.י./[שלח]/לך.את.המע/[שר].ב[תים]111 בטרם ("…who [will send] to you the ti[the], 3 *baths* before…") (Aharoni 1981b: 20). Some scholars considered this reconstruction (if correct) to be evidence for a measure of a tenth of a *bat* (e.g., Aḥituv 2005: 95). However, the reconstruction of ישלח ("will send") and [שר]/המע ("the tithe") is not certain and should not serve as the basis for the addition of another liquid measure, one that is unattested elsewhere.[36] Aharoni also associated the *issārôn* with the tithe on the basis of a find from Beersheba. In the basement of a Stratum II structure a small jug was uncovered, bearing an inscription that was evidently incised before firing. The inscription reads חצי למלך ("half [belonging] to the king," cf. Aharoni 1975a: 160, 162 and Fig. 7). The meaning of this inscription is not clear, and Aharoni argued that it refers to a half of the *iss*ārôn, since, in his view, "the *iss*ārôn is the most common measure" (Aharoni 1975a: 160). Because the volume of this jug was measured and found to be 1.2 liters, Aharoni calculated that the *issārôn* would be ca. 2.4 liters (Aharoni 1975a: 160). Extrapolating from the *issārôn* to the *bat* measure, he calculated the volume of the *bat* to be 24 liters.[37] Aharoni's suggestion is unlikely, as the *issārôn* measurement does not appear on the חצי למלך jug from Beersheba and because there is no mention in the Old Testament of the *issārôn* as a liquid measure.

Like the *lōḡ*, the *issārôn* is only mentioned in the priestly literature and always as a dry measure of capacity in association with semolina. The *issārôn* is connected to the dry measures of the *'ēpā*[h] and the *ḥōmer*, and therefore, its interpretation as a tenth of a *bat* is problematic, as is any attempt to reconstruct the measurement of the *bat* on the basis of this reconstruction of the *issārôn*.[38]

The *bat*

This short review demonstrates that in First Temple period Judah, vessels of fixed shapes and sizes were designated for specific purposes—in ritual and apparently in the administration and economy too. Of these, the *bat* was the main and most important vessel for liquids, and since we have much information about it, we can describe it and refer to it as a fixed measure. The *bat* is mentioned 13 times in the Bible, always as a fixed measure for liquids of various kinds: water, wine, or oil. According to 1 Kings 7:26, the "molten sea" in the Temple court held 2,000 *battim* (cf. 2 Chron 4:5, "three thousand *battim*");[39] and 1 Kings 7:38 specifies that the ten copper basins in the Temple contained 40 *battim* each. According to Isaiah 5:10, "ten acres of vineyard shall yield but one *bath*, and a *ḥōmer* of seed shall yield but an *'ēpā*[h]." Ezekiel 45:10 mentions "a just *bat*" as a liquid measure, together with "just balances" for weighing means of payment and "a just *'ēpā*[h]" for dry measure. Ezra 7:22 mentions 100 *battim* of wine and 100 *battim* of oil. In 2 Chron 2:10 one learns the difference between these measurements of dry and liquid products: "I will give for your servants, the hewers that cut timber, twenty thousand *kōr*s of crushed wheat, twenty thousand *kōr*s of barley, twenty thousand *battim* of wine and twenty thousand

---

36. See Pardee 1982: 38; Dobbs-Allsopp *et al.* 2004: 20. Aharoni has suggested another reading (1981b: n. 1): אשר.י./[שלח].לך.אתה.מע/[בה] . This reading, however, is problematic, since, as Aharoni himself states, a settlement called '[ ]*bh* is unknown.

37. In this context, Aharoni (1975a: 162) pointed to a sherd found next to the temple in Arad, on which חצי was inscribed (Aharoni 1981b: 114). While the engraving is complete, we do not know whether it was executed when the vessel was complete (as in the case of the Beersheba find). If not, the word on the sherd may be associated with the Ugaritic term *ḥṣt* (= luck), and the ostracon may have been used for casting lots (Dobbs-Allsopp *et al.* 2004: 104, with further literature).

38. While in some places the *issārôn* is a measurement for semolina (and see above), elsewhere a tenth of the *'ēpā*[h] is used to measure semolina (Lev 5:11; 6:13; Num 28:5) and the same measurement is used for flour (Num 5:15). The ratio between the *issārôn* and the *'ēpā*[h] can be seen here. However, all the occurrences appear in the priestly literature and therefore cannot be considered as evidence for the economy and administration of the First Temple period.

39. The Septuagint version of Kings has no reference to the capacity of the molten sea, and Josephus (*AJ* 8.3:5) describes its capacity as 3,000 *battim*, like the Book of Chronicles. On this subject, see literature and discussion in Hognesius 1994; Byl 1998, with further literature.

battim of oil." In light of the occurrence in Ezekiel, it is acknowledged in the scholarship that the capacity of the *bat* equaled the capacity of the *ʾêp̄āʰ* (cf. Dobbs-Allsopp *et al.* 2004: 123), but it is not clear whether the Ezekiel standardization reflects the First (or Second) Temple period reality.

These biblical references point to the centrality of the *bat* in the administration and economy in the First Temple period. The *bat* was apparently a well-known fixed measure of liquid capacity, with which it was possible to estimate the capacity of much larger vessels, containing thousands of *battim*, as well as those containing dozens of *battim*. However, there is no evidence for subdivisions of the *bat* as we have for the *lōḡ* and *hîn*. This suggests that the *bat* was a closed and presumably quite large vessel, which could not be marked with subdivisions and from which fixed amounts could not be poured. There is no evidence in the Bible for the precise capacity of the *bat* or for how fixed measures of liquid volume measures were determined in ancient times. I suggest below, on the basis of the archaeological finds and ancient Near Eastern parallels, that the *bat* was not a fixed and precise measurement of volume (see also Lipschits *et al.* 2010). The *bat* was, in my opinion, the name of the well-known Judahite oval storage jar. As aforementioned, this type of storage jar began to be manufactured in Judah in the 9th century BCE, and from the late 8th century BCE, its production became standardized and its size became uniform and constant by ancient standards.[40] It was in this period—when the storage jar became part of the administrative system of storage jars and some of the handles were stamped by seals—that this storage jar received its name: the *bat*.

Attempts to Reconstruct the Capacity of the *bat*

Several attempts have been made, on the basis of epigraphic finds and biblical references, to reconstruct the system of liquid volume measurements in the First Temple period. Early scholars suggested that the *bat* measure equaled the capacity of the *lmlk*/oval/Judahite storage jar.[41] Among them was Inge, who dealt with the differences between the measurements of a Lachish storage jar inscribed (before firing) בת.למלך ("*bat* [belonging] to the king" = a royal *bat*?) and those of the other *lmlk* storage jars (Inge 1941: 107). Despite this, he estimated that the capacity of the בת למלך storage jar equaled that of the stamped *lmlk* storage jars: ca. 44 liters. Inge assumed that the *lmlk* inscription in the royal stamp impressions was an abbreviation of the measure itself—[בת] למלך—and he was the first to suggest that the *bat* was in fact the name of the storage jar itself (Inge 1941: 108–109). This proposal was harshly criticized by Albright (1943: 58–59, n. 7) and was rejected in the research.

Most of the scholars who dealt with this subject assumed the capacity of the *bat* to be about 20, 22, or even 24 liters.[42] The genesis of this "scholarly tradition" appears in a footnote in Albright's Tell Beit Mirsim excavation report (1943: 58–59, n. 7). In this note, Albright discussed a post-firing incision on a sherd that reads בת (*bat*) (Fig. 3.6)[43] and compared it to the upper part of the Lachish בת למלך storage jar (Fig. 3.7).[44] Diringer insisted that while this jar resembles

---

40. On this subject, see above, pp. 17–24; cf. Mazar 1990: 509; Zimhoni 1997: 171; 2004b: 1706.

41. Barrois 1931: 212; Inge 1941: 109; Lemaire 1977: 157. Lemaire, relying upon a single complete storage jar that was found in Gibeon and whose capacity was measured by Pritchard (1964: 25) as 45 liters, contended that this was the capacity of the *bat* measure. Lemaire also cited de Vaux (1961: 202–203), but de Vaux did not actually claim that the *bat* measured 45 liters, and in any case, he based his estimation on a much later find from Qumran; it therefore does not withstand critical analysis.

42. Albright 1943: 58–59, n. 7; Segrè 1945: 357–358; Scott 1958; de Vaux 1961: 202; Stern 1962: 854; Aharoni 1981b: 13; Heltzer 1983: 161; 1989: 197; 2008: 71*; Mittmann 1991: 66; 1993: 47; Powell 1992: 902; Zapassky, Finkelstein and Benenson 2009. Busink (1970: 327, n. 611) estimated that the capacity of the *bat* was 23 liters (and see a similar note of Hognesius 1994: 357), Powell (1992: 161) and Ahituv (2005: 84, 216) estimated it as 24 liters, and Kletter (2009: 363) as 19.22 liters.

43. Albright 1932a: 78 and Fig. 12:1; 1943: 58, n. 7; Pl. 60:2. Contrary to Sukenik's opinion (in Albright 1943: 58), it is unclear whether the inscription is complete (Dobbs-Allsopp *et al.* 2004: 133). This sherd may be compared to one found in Gezer, inscribed after firing with the inscription ...בת... (Dever, Lance and Bullard 1986: Pl. 62) or a sherd from Hazor, inscribed בת/ה (Yadin *et al.* 1960: 71–72, Pl. 169:3; Reg. No. A382/1, Area A, Locus 151, Stratum VIII—9th century BCE; but see recently Sass 2005: 85–86). Since in all these cases, it is unclear whether the inscription is complete (*ibid.*; Dobbs-Allsopp *et al.* 2004: 133, 165), they cannot be used to determine the measurement of the *bat*.

44. Diringer 1953: 356–357 and Pl. 49:1; Locus 1078: H17, No. 7066. In this context, Avigad's (1953) reading of בת.למלך on a storage-jar handle incision from Tell en-Naṣbeh (McCown 1947: 168, Pl. 57:21) should be mentioned, although his reading was not accepted (except by Heltzer 1989: 197).

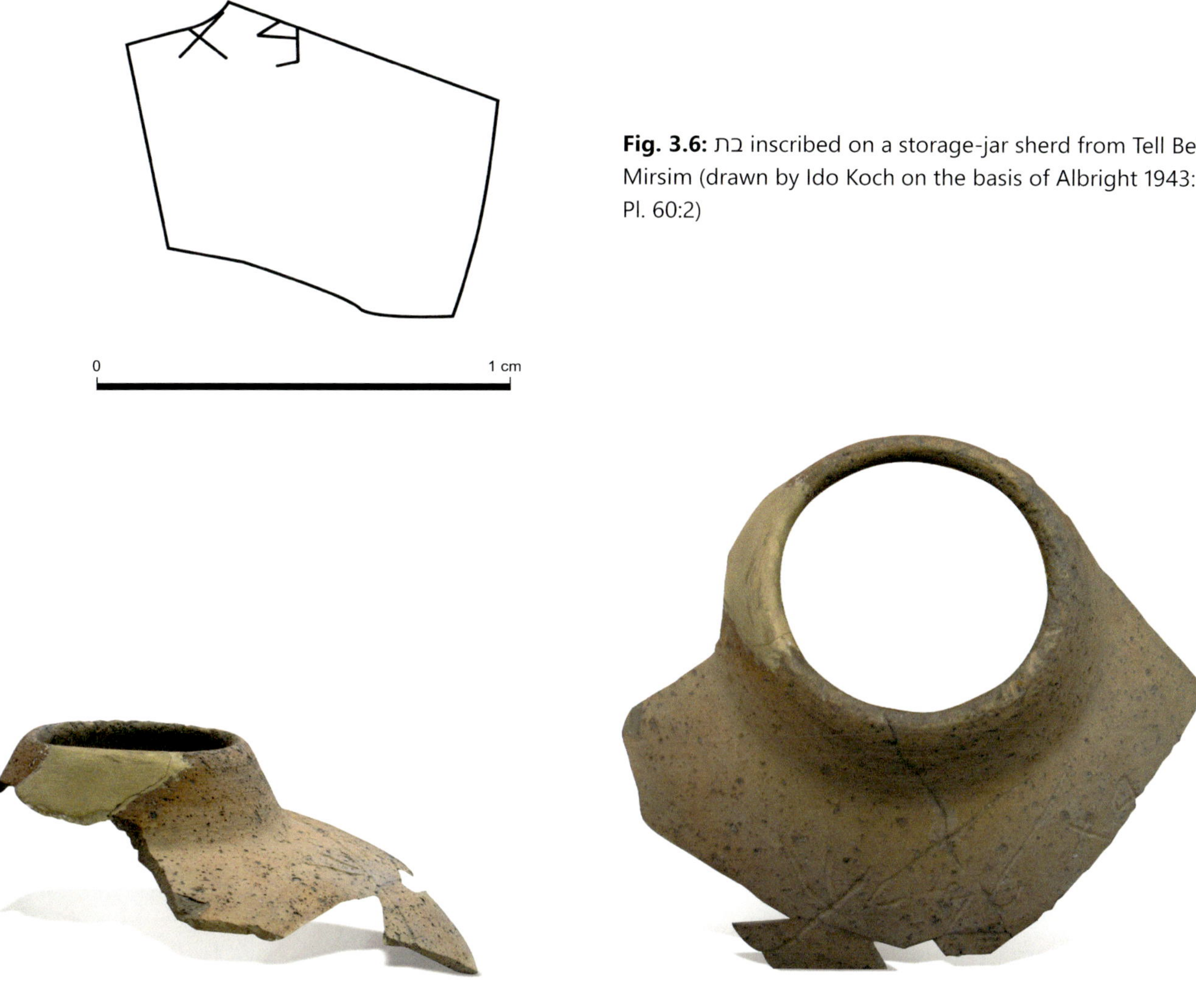

Fig. 3.6: בת inscribed on a storage-jar sherd from Tell Beit Mirsim (drawn by Ido Koch on the basis of Albright 1943: Pl. 60:2)

Fig. 3.7: בת למלך storage jar from Lachish (photo by S. Guil; courtesy of Dr. J.N. Tubb and Dr. R.L. Chapman of the British Museum; after Lipschits *et al.* 2010)

the *lmlk* storage jar in shape, they are not identical. He claimed that it was impossible to measure the capacity of the fragmented jar and thus to reconstruct the value of the *baṯ lmlk* measurement (Diringer 1953: 356). His views, however, did not stop Albright from attempting to calculate the volume of the Lachish storage jar bearing the בת למלך inscription on the basis of the rim diameter and to extrapolate from this that the *baṯ* equals half the capacity of the average *lmlk* storage jar (44 liters), or 22 liters. Unfortunately, Albright's calculations are highly speculative and based on incorrect and only partial data. The shape of the Lachish storage jar cannot be determined by its rim alone, and it is impossible to determine the ratio between this vessel and the *lmlk* storage jars.[45]

It seems to me that the claim that the *baṯ* measurement is 22 liters does not withstand critical analysis, but

---

45. In this assumption, Albright also endorsed Germer-Durand's (1909–10) assessment of some stone vessels in the Notre Dame Museum in Jerusalem as proving that the *baṯ* equaled 21.25 liters (Albright 1943: 58–59, n. 7). Cf. Lipschits *et al.* 2010: 461–462.

surprisingly, despite these reservations, this estimate of the *bat* measure has become entrenched in the research, with many scholars treating it as almost axiomatic. Even in several recently published papers that reexamined the liquid measurement system of the First Temple period,[46] the basic assumption was that the *bat* was the basic liquid volume measure in the First Temple period and equaled approximately 20 liters (22.4/22.5 liters in Zapassky, Finkelstein and Benenson 2009: 53; 19.22 liters in Kletter 2009: 363). They made several even more problematic assumptions: that the volume of the *lmlk* storage jar was a matter of interest to the administrative system and that the manufacturers of storage jars had the ability to calculate their volume (and consequently, the capacity of the liquids stored in them) to produce a series of storage jars of uniform volume.[47] This runs counter to the findings of Ussishkin, who measured the Lachish storage jars and found differences between them of up to 12.05 liters in capacity (2004b: 2145).[48] He concluded that the *lmlk* stamp impressions do not necessarily attest to uniform measurements and do not guarantee the quantity of liquid in the storage jars. Conversely, Zapassky, Finkelstein and Benenson (2009) assumed that the use of an official system of royal stamp impressions, taken in conjunction with biblical and other sources on measuring and weighing goods in the final period of the Kingdom of Judah, necessarily indicate a high degree of standardization. They therefore surmised that there must have been a simple calculation method to determine storage-jar capacity in Judah. To examine this possibility, they scanned seven storage jars with *lmlk*-stamped handles using advanced technological means and measured illustrations of five additional storage jars in order to create three-dimensional computerized models.

These models demonstrated that jar capacity varies between 7–10%, while their circumference varies by only 1–2%. They concluded that the potters preferred to achieve uniformity of shape rather than of volume (Zapassky, Finkelstein and Benenson 2009: 61). Their mathematical calculations showed that if the form was uniform, the volume could be relatively easily calculated by a simple arithmetic formula. The underlying assumption of Zapassky, Finkelstein and Benenson (2009: 54) was that uniformity in the capacity of *lmlk* storage jars was crucial for both the potters (the storage-jar manufacturers) and the consumers (the recipients of the stored agricultural commodities). They further assumed that the ancient potters could control jar height and shape to a degree of accuracy that did not deviate by more than 34% and that their skill enabled them to accurately achieve the required capacity (2009: 54, 60).

However, Zapassky, Finkelstein and Benenson were surprised to find that the actual variation between storage jars was 10.4%, and they therefore admitted the dissonance between the "need for accuracy" and the potters' abilities.[49] They proposed that the administrative system developed a calculation method to overcome this problem—again based on the assumption that the royal administration had a need to ascertain the precise quantity of liquid in the vessels. To a certain extent this continues the conjecture raised by Eph'al and Naveh (1993) that the central authority monitored commercial measurements by placing standard vessels at the city gates: the "Jar of the Gate" found at Tel Kinrot and the "Stone of the Gate" found at Deir ʿAllā.[50] Eph'al and Naveh argued that because the *lmlk* storage jars were not uniform, it was their contents that were measured before they were filled, by means of an approved standard measuring storage jar

---

46. See, e.g., Zapassky, Finkelstein and Benenson 2006; 2009; Benenson 2009; Kletter 2009.

47. See Zapassky, Finkelstein and Benenson 2009, continuing their 2006 article. In the first article they dealt with calculating the capacity of simple cylindrical vessels from the Negev region in the Iron Age, while in the second they discussed *lmlk* storage jars from the late 8th century BCE.

48. These differences in the capacity of storage jars in Judah were used by Aznar (2005: 233) to suggest that they stem from the employment of various craftsmen by Hezekiah, in an effort to increase storage-jar production in the northern Shephelah to meet the kingdom's increasing needs.

49. The basic assumption about the need for accuracy is apparently not well founded. Even in weights, where accuracy is presumably particularly important for economics and commerce, there is a 5% deviation (Kletter 1998: 80–82, 139–140; 2009: 358), and a 10% deviation was not considered unusual in Egypt's economy and commerce (Janssen 1975; 1988: 14–15). Cf. Powell 1992: 899.

50. The gate system proposed by Eph'al and Naveh is not a fixed and clearly-defined system of measurement: it is based upon two storage-jar sherds, one stone and one non-provenanced weight (see also Kletter 1998: 147–148; 2009: 360). For the Deir ʿAllā vessel, see Hoftijzer and van der Kooij 1976: 275. While it is possible that officials indeed checked the capacity of commercial vessels used by city merchants, this does not constitute evidence of a fixed system of measurement.

(Eph'al and Naveh 1993: 62). Zapassky, Finkelstein and Benenson (2009) presented a computational solution according to which storage-jar contents were measured by a hypothetical algorithm that enabled calculation of their contents despite their great variation in volume. In their opinion, storage-jar capacity could be measured on the basis of external dimensions and this algorithm had to be a simple one, based on linear measurement and subtraction of a constant.[51]

The significance of this formula is that it was possible in ancient times to calculate the volume of a storage jar in *issārôn*s with an average accuracy of 96–97%, by adding half of the horizontal circumference of the jar to half of its vertical circumference and subtracting two *cubits*. The authors proposed this formula because it takes into account two parameters, rather than just one (Zapassky, Finkelstein and Benenson 2009: 65).

Was Precision Essential to the Ancient Administration?

In addition to the problematic underlying assumption discussed above, the method of calculation leads to several inaccuracies in the predictive power of the system, with even slight calculation errors leading to the addition or subtraction of significant quantities from the volume.[52] Zapassky, Finkelstein and Benenson do not deal with the question whether accuracy was, in fact, a desired goal. There is no treatment in this article or others of the need for accuracy in calculating the quantity of the products within unequal storage jars, which varied by as much as 10% in volume.[53] It seems that the underlying assumption

itself is a product of modern thinking, which does not correspond to the reality of the ancient world.[54]

Hundreds of *lmlk* storage jars were used to store agricultural commodities in the royal administrative system. In my opinion, in these large numbers the average volume of the storage jars cancels out the 10% deviation. Was the discrepancy in volume even a factor for the royal administration? Did they need to know the precise volume of the liquid in each of the hundreds of storage jars? These questions are not addressed by Zapassky, Finkelstein and Benenson (see Kletter 2009: 358).

The problem of discrepancies in volume among the administrative system's storage jars is directly related to the בת למלך storage jar from Lachish. The difference between the dimensions of this vessel and the other *lmlk* storage jars was already noted by Diringer, who, after Inge (1941: 107), noted that it resembles but is not identical to the *lmlk* storage jar (1953: 356). Zimhoni, who accepted the assumptions of Inge and Diringer, suggested that this was a two-handled, rather than four-handled, jar and classified it into a different group from the *lmlk* or *lmlk*-like storage jars (Group SJ3).[55] Her claims, however, are problematic. In terms of typology, while the fragmentary בת למלך jar is indeed smaller than the "typical" *lmlk* storage jar, its full shape cannot be reconstructed and therefore its attribution to the royal *lmlk* storage-jar group cannot be ruled out. In addition, the number of handles cannot be determined from the measurements of the rim and half the shoulder. Furthermore, the distinction between *lmlk* jars and "*lmlk*-like" jars on the basis of size and color alone is untenable (Zimhoni 2004a: 1794–1796; cf. Gitin 2006: 508–509; Sergi *et al.* 2012: 83–85). On

---

51. In presenting the algorithm, the scholars used the *bat* as the basic ancient liquid volume measure, to which they added—without justification—the *issārôn*. For the measure of length, they used the *finger* and the *cubit*. Based on these guidelines they suggested two possible formulae: $V(a) = P(f)–16f$ or $V(a) = L(f)–19f$, where $V(a)$ equals the storage-jar volume in *issārôn*s; $P(f)$ equals half of the jar's horizontal circumference; and $L(f)$ equals half of the jar's vertical circumference. The significance of these equations lies in their ability to calculate storage-jar volume (in *issārôn*s) by measurement of its circumference or height and subtraction of a constant. Although these equations are fairly accurate in predicting volume (96–97%), the authors admit that the 16f and 19f constants are not "meaningful." Moreover, this calculation is "risky" because it relies solely on either $P(f)$ or $L(f)$. Thus, if even a slight error creeps into one of the measures, this will directly impact the calculated volume. These difficulties led the authors to propose a third formula, which included an additional variable—2c (= two cubits): $V(a) = P(f) + L(f) – 2c$. The use of this formula requires three stages: 1) measurement of the length P (the horizontal circumference) and L (the vertical circumference) in fingers; 2) subtraction of 2 cubits; and 3) the sum in *fingers* is approximately the volume in *issārôn*s.

52. For a more comprehensive critique, see Lipschits *et al.* 2010: 464–465.

53. This was the case in the Hellenistic and Roman periods too; see review in Lipschits *et al.* 2010: 466, with further literature.

54. Powell 1992: 899–900; Kletter 2009: 361–362. Benenson's response (2009: 366) that "our arguments are simple and come from classroom mathematics" only serves to strengthen this point.

55. See Zimhoni 2004a: 1797; cf. Gitin 2006: 519, 521, Type SJO 6.

these grounds, we cannot rule out the inclusion of the Lachish בת למלך storage jar in the corpus of royal Judahite storage jars.

The Lachish בת למלך storage jar was measured again at the British Museum in London,[56] revealing that it is even smaller than the other *lmlk* jars than previously assumed. Its rim diameter is 7.3 cm, while the rim diameter of the *lmlk* storage jar ranges from 8.2 to 9.4 cm.[57] In all other aspects, however—shape, material and body proportions—the בת למלך storage jar bears the standard features of the oval storage jars. It thus seems that one cannot accept the conclusions of Albright, Diringer, Zimhoni and others, who excluded it from the group of *lmlk* storage jars on the basis of its rim diameter. Moreover, on the basis of Gitin's typology (2006), storage jars are now generally classified according to shape, rather than measurements. The Lachish בת למלך storage jar, of which only the rim and the upper part of the shoulder survived, cannot be definitively classified, but it undoubtedly belongs to the family of Judahite storage jars. On these grounds, we may return to the proposal made by Inge (1941: 109) that the biblical *bat* was the storage jar itself. This conclusion is in keeping with the biblical evidence and the epigraphic finds, according to which units of oil or wine were counted according to the storage jars containing them and not by any fixed unit of volume.

The Biblical *bat* as the *lmlk* Storage Jar

The widely used storage jar of the late 8th and the 7th centuries BCE, especially the type selected as the official version of the storage-jar administrative system, was ubiquitous throughout Judah and was the preferred

storage jar for private individuals too. This storage jar continued to be used until the final days of the kingdom and even after its destruction. This uniformity is manifest in the ceramic finds, as well as in the biblical evidence and epigraphic finds. In none of its biblical mentions is the *bat* divided into sub-units, and unlike other vessels such as the *kad* and the *nēbel*, it is never described as a transport vessel.

From the epigraphic finds we also learn of the existence of liquid measuring units, but not of a system of measures. In some cases, wine or oil are mentioned without any reference to a measure or vessel. Parallels are noted in Akkadian and Ugaritic,[58] and in some cases there are references to כד (jar) or just כלי (vessel) of liquids (*KTU* 4.269). Scholars tended to fill in the missing information of liquid measures, based on what they learned from the biblical text. However, as discussed above, these measures did not in fact exist in the administration in the First Temple period. For example, the ostracon found at Tel Qasile that reads למלך אל[ף] שמן ומאה [א]חיהו ("[belonging] to the king: one thousand oil and one hundred. Aḥiyahu") was interpreted by Benjamin Mazar as referring to 1,100 *lōḡ* of oil.[59] This has no basis in the biblical text or the epigraphic finds, and it seems that Mazar's interpretation is anachronistic and does not reflect the administrative reality of the First Temple period. Two ostraca found in Kenyon's Jerusalem excavations feature the word שמן/שמנים (oil/oils), again without mention of a measure or vessel.[60] One reads שמנם 7 50 / 1 1 1 1 שברם ("50 and 7 oil, 4 fractions"). The other also mentions the word שמן (oil), apparently with a hieratic number next to it that did not survive. In the last line, eight vertical lines survived, ostensibly referring to an additional item; here too it is likely to refer to oil. On the reverse, there are two words reconstructed as

---

56. Shlomo Guil examined this storage jar in May 2009. I would like to thank Dr. Jonathan N. Tubb and Dr. Rupert L. Chapman of the British Museum for permitting the examination of this storage jar and for the additional assistance they provided. See also Lipschits *et al.* 2010: 467.

57. Of 120 storage jars measured, only four had a rim diameter that was smaller than 8 cm and no *lmlk* jar with a rim diameter smaller than 7.5 cm. Six additional *lmlk*-like jar rim diameters from the Beth Shemesh excavations range between 9.3 and 10.6 cm—a deviation of 1.3 cm, with the average being much larger than the rim diameter of the Lachish בת למלך jar. I am grateful to Prof. Shlomo Bunimovitz and Dr. Zvi Lederman, co-directors of the Tel Beth Shemesh excavations, for granting me permission to measure the jars.

58. E.g., the reference to תלת שמנ, "three [storage jars of] oil" (*KTU* 4.41.2) or מאית ין, "one hundred [storage jars of] fine wine" (*KTU* 4.213.11). See also Dobbs-Allsopp *et al.* 2004: 213.

59. See Maisler 1950–51: Pl. 37a; 1951: Pl. 11a; for interpretation, see Maisler 1951; Dobbs-Allsopp *et al.* 2004: 403.

60. Lemaire 1978: Pls. B23, D, E; Dobbs-Allsopp *et al.* 2004: 212–214, 216–218. Lemaire (1978: 159) dated the ostracon to the late 8th or early 7th century BCE, while Cross (1962: 40) dated it to the late 7th or early 6th century BCE.

גת.פרח (*gt.prḥ*), which may represent the origin of the shipment of oil (Dobbs-Alsopp *et al.* 2004: 217, 218). On another ostracon from the same assemblage the word נבל (*nēbel*) was reconstructed before the word יין ("wine"; Dobbs-Alsopp *et al.* 2004: 211–212). The expression נבל יין is well known from the ostraca found in Samaria;[61] this therefore suggests that the reference is to a shipment of wine arriving at Jerusalem from one of the production centers in its environs (Heltzer 2008: 70*).

Heltzer argued that these numbers refer to the fixed volume measurements of the vessel called *nēbel*. However, in all cases in which a number accompanies the word *nēbel* they denote the number of vessels (Stern 1962: 855). In this case, it may be assumed that the volume of the *nēbel* was known and fixed, or that at the very least, the vessel was uniform in shape and size, as in the case of the *lmlk* storage jars. An ostracon uncovered in Ashkelon points to a similar picture in Phoenician and Philistine coastal cities: wine, beer and oil were counted according to the number of vessels, as in the ostracon from Jerusalem.[62]

In the late 7th and early 6th centuries BCE, quantities of oil apparently continued to be counted by vessels of a fixed volume. In the Arad ostraca the oil was measured by number of vessels,[63] while the wine was measured according to the number of *battim*.[64] The most common formula in the Arad ostraca was: ב/ .ין יין (wine and the letter *bet*, followed by one diagonal line and a number of vertical lines). According to Aharoni, the letter *bet* was an abbreviation for the word *bat*, and the vertical lines marked the number of *battim*.[65] Following Aharoni,

Gibson suggested that all the lines—both the diagonal attached to the *bet* and the vertical lines—indicated the number of *battim* (Gibson 1971: 51–52), whereas Naveh viewed only the diagonal line adjacent to the *b* as referring to the number.[66]

Similarly, the letter *bet*, followed by a diagonal line, appears on a complete storage jar from Lachish Level II (Ussishkin 1978: 85–87 and Fig. 29), which led Ussishkin to argue that the capacity of this storage jar (20.85–21.15 liters) equals the *bat* measure.[67] To this jar one should add the בת למלך storage jar discussed above, as well as a storage jar from Tel Miqne Stratum I, with the word בת inscribed after firing (Aḥituv 2005: 317). The capacity of this latter jar is 32 liters, and it is unlikely that in the 7th century BCE, at a time when the borders between Judah and its neighbors were open for free movement, volume measurements would differ so greatly between two adjacent cities.

In light of the above-mentioned biblical and epigraphic evidence, Koch, Shaus, Guil and I suggested identifying the biblical *bat* with the Judahite storage jar (Lipschits *et al.* 2010). There is no other candidate mentioned in the Bible that could refer to this vessel, and in the context of wine and oil, the *bat* is mentioned as a vessel rather than as a measure, with no other vessel mentioned alongside it.[68]

In the investigation of any period of antiquity, we run the danger of projecting the values and conventions of our own times onto the period under study. In many cases, historical reconstructions involve anachronisms—in which

---

61. The resemblance between the Samaria ostraca and the Jerusalem ostracon is further strengthened by the mention in the latter of the oil-production site (*gt.prḥ*) and the mention of the wine- or oil-production site in the former.

62. Cross 2008, and see, e.g., Ostraca 1.5, 1.7 and 1.10.

63. Thus, for example, Letter 10 reads: יין ב/נ.[]מ[.אמתיים.ושמנ/... (and see Aharoni 1981b: Letter 10, line 3; Letter 14, line 3; Letter 17, line 4).

64. Aharoni 1981b: Letter 1, line 3; Letter 2, line 2; Letter 3, line 2; Letter 4, line 3; Letter 7, line 22; Letter 8, line 5; Letter 9, line 3; Letter 10, line 2; Letter 11, line 3; Letter 61, line 2.

65. Aharoni 1981b: 17; see also Dobbs-Allsopp *et al.* 2004: 10.

66. Naveh 1992: 52–53; see, further, Aḥituv 2005: 84. Since Naveh considered the *bat* to represent a fixed and known volume, he suggested interpreting the vertical lines as expressing the *hîn*, which was generally understood as a sixth of a *bat*. Naveh's assumption is problematic, for if we accept the letter *bet* as an abbreviation of the word *bat*, there is no evidence in any text for an abbreviation of the word *hîn*. Furthermore, as mentioned above, a measure called *hîn* is not known from any First Temple period sources, and there is no evidence for its existence as a liquid measure in Judah in this period.

67. Ussishkin 1978: 87, n. 9. Kletter (2009: 363) erroneously presented this vessel as a container upon which the word בת was inscribed, and following Ussishkin, he used it as an argument for determining the maximum size of the *bat*.

68. The *bat* as an official container for wine and oil may parallel two other liquid containers, also used in the daily life and economy of Judah at the end of the First Temple period: the *nēbel* and the *kad* (and see further discussion in Lipschits *et al.* 2010: 470–472).

the characters and background originate in the Iron Age, but their nature and relationships are grounded in the modern reality of the scholars investigating them. Many scholars, for example, impose characteristics of modern measurement systems upon their reconstructions of ancient liquid capacity. Furthermore, in doing so, they often use amorphous terms in biblical literature, without drawing any distinction between early and late or between relevant and irrelevant. Thus, a system of liquid capacity measures consisting of *baṯ*, *kaḏ*, *nēḇel*, *hîn*, *lōḡ*, *issārôn* and *ḥeṣy* is a patchwork of terms without any textual or archaeological evidence to anchor it in the First Temple period. While the *hîn* and the *lōḡ* were used as liquid containers, their only proven association is with ritual service in the Second Temple period; the *issārôn* and the *ḥeṣy* were used as dry measures and not for liquids; the *baṯ*, the *kaḏ* and the *nēḇel* are each mentioned separately and in their own respective contexts, never in relation to any other vessel and always accompanied by a numeral. Therefore, associating the latter three vessels with each other or with any other vessel and postulating a single system for them does not reflect the First Temple period reality.

Another anachronism is the use of mathematical formulae to meet the central administrative authority's "need for accuracy" in the capacity of the storage jars that it manufactured. This is based on the assumption that accuracy was crucial to the administration, but this assumption is unwarranted: the use of hundreds of very similar *lmlk* storage jars cancels out the approximate variation of 10% among jars. Furthermore, not a single piece of biblical or epigraphic evidence suggests that there was a need for accuracy—a need that in fact constitutes the very basis for the theoretical existence of a liquid volume measurement system.

The focus should therefore be on the biblical text and the epigraphic evidence, and in both these fields the *baṯ* denotes a storage vessel that served for the storage and shipping of wine and oil. The conclusion must be, in my opinion, that the *baṯ* is, in fact, the Judahite storage jar itself, and indeed, this conclusion is supported by the find in Lachish of two storage jars with the word בת inscribed upon them.

Conclusions

The various types of oval storage jars began to appear in the Shephelah mainly in the late 9th and the 8th centuries BCE. At first they were typically non-uniform in shape and size, and only in the mid-8th century BCE did more uniform storage jars begin to develop out of the non-standard types, probably as part of the transition from domestically- and locally-made pottery to a more centralized and larger royal production in specialized workshops. I have suggested above that it is these uniform storage jars that are denoted by the biblical term *baṯ*.

This transition presumably reflects the main stage in the expansion of Judah to the Shephelah, as well as the establishment of the Kingdom of Judah's administration in this area, while exploiting its economic possibilities— probably olive-oil production, in particular. At this stage, storage jars were probably manufactured in a central workshop (at Tel Socoh?) under the royal administration, and the stamping of some of these storage jars commenced. There is no doubt that at this stage the storage jars constituted part of the royal administration and economy of Judah and that this storage-jar administration continued to exist, with changes and modifications, throughout the subsequent centuries. The manufacture of jars also continued, and although their center of production gradually moved to the environs of Jerusalem at the end of the First Temple period, after the destruction of the capital, these storage jars continued to be used by successive Judean administrations until the 2nd century BCE (see below, Chapters 6 and 8).

4

Main Stamp-Impression Types: Typology, Corpus and Distribution

In this chapter, I briefly describe each of the main types and sub-types of the stamp impressions, providing details about the number of handles found to date and their distribution. This chapter serves as the "database" for the research, providing the basis for discussion on the dating of the various types, the role of the Judahite system and the purpose and *modus operandi* of the storage-jar administration in Judah. It also presents a preliminary survey of the development process of the system and the position of each type within this process. These topics are discussed in greater detail in later chapters.

lmlk Stamp Impressions

The *lmlk* stamp impressions (Fig. 4.1) are oval (average length: ca. 30 mm; average width: ca. 22 mm),[1] and most contain three basic components (Fig. 4.2):

- The word למלך (*lmlk*, meaning "[belonging] to the king")[2] appears in Hebrew letters at the top of the stamp impression.

- A royal emblem appears under the word *lmlk*, in the center of the stamp impression. There are two main types of emblems, each with numerous variants.[3]

---

1. The vast majority of stamp impressions, of almost every type, were quite uniform in size, with deviations of 1–2 mm. Only one type, bearing a four-winged scarab emblem, is a bit larger and differs from the other *lmlk* types (and see discussion below).

2. In this book I propose that the storage jars were sent empty to the royal estates, where they were filled with oil or wine and sent on to the collection centers. The word *lmlk* indicates that the product belongs to the monarchy. See Fox 2000: 222.

3. Most scholars assumed that these emblems represented the Kingdom of Judah and therefore appeared next to the word *lmlk*; see Keel and Uehlinger 1998: 248–273; Avigad and Barkay 2000: 243; Hudon 2010: 31–32, with further literature. Ornan's view (2005: 231–232) that the symbols selected for the *lmlk* seals were divine emblems, rather than royal, is unlikely. She considered the four-winged scarab to be the traditional symbol of the Judahite god and the winged sun disk, which replaced it, to have been adopted as the symbol of the god in Judah under Assyrian influence, when Assyria emerged as the most important and central power in the region. For a different view, see Mazar 1990: 507. Ornan drew a comparison with the Kingdom of Samʾal, where the winged sun-disk symbol was adopted to represent the local god, alongside his "traditional" symbol of the chariot yoke.

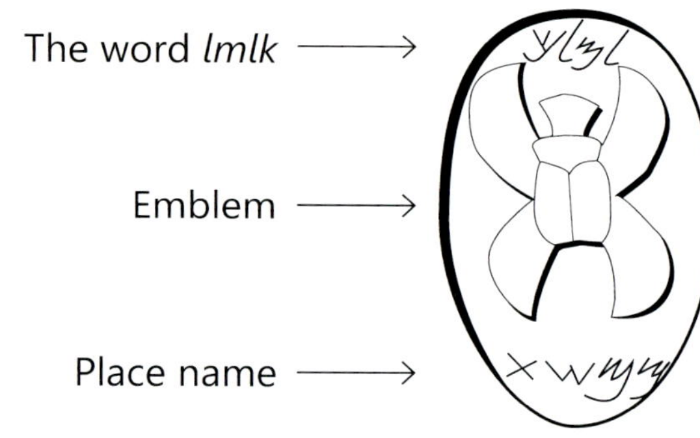

Fig. 4.1: A four-winged *lmlk* stamp impression from Ramat Raḥel (Sergi 2016: 295, No. 16)

Fig. 4.2: The components of *lmlk* stamp impressions

One is a four-winged scarab,[4] generally assumed to have originated in ancient Egypt and to have arrived in the region via Phoenician mediation. The other is a winged sun disk, often believed to have originated in ancient Near Eastern cultures in general and in Assyrian art in particular.

- The name of one of four places (probably royal estates) usually appears at the bottom of the stamp impression, under the royal emblem:[5] *ḥbrn* (Hebron, always spelled with four letters), *zp/zyp* (Ziph, spelled with two or three letters), *swkh* (Socoh, always spelled with four letters), and *mmšt* (probably Mamshit, always spelled with four letters).

Over the years, many different typologies have been proposed for the *lmlk* stamp impressions.[6] It was clear to all that each type of stamp impression was formed by a different seal, stamped into the clay of the storage jar while still soft. Most scholars divided the types (= seals) into two main groups on the basis of the royal emblem in the center—whether a four-winged scarab or a two-winged sun disk—with further division based on the inscriptions above and below the emblem.

The generally accepted typology, upon which the discussion below is based, was suggested by André Lemaire (1981). His initial distinction is based on the royal emblem: "four-winged scarab" (marked with the Roman numeral I) or "two-winged sun disk" (marked with the Roman numeral II). Among the first group of the four-winged types, Lemaire further distinguishes two types of script quality—informal (cursive) script (marked by the letter "a") or official (lapidary) script (marked by the letter "b"). A further sub-division is based upon the site name appearing on the stamp impression: Hebron (marked by the letter "H"), Ziph ("Z"), Socoh ("S") and *mmšt* ("M").

---

4. Keel and Uehlinger argued that the *lmlk* emblems reflected Egyptian cultural influence on the Syro-Israel region and that they were accepted in Judah through the attribution of the solar aspects to the deity, rather than through the agency of Israelite refugees fleeing their destroyed kingdom. See Keel and Uehlinger 1998: 276, cf. Tushingham 1970; 1971; Younker 1985: 175. On the appearance of the beetle scarab in the Bible, on its biblical name and on the significance of its appearance on the *lmlk* seals, see Lubetski 2000; Swanson 2002: 464–469.

5. For a discussion of these site names and their identification, see pp. 138–142.

6. See, e.g., Diringer 1941: 91–101; Lapp 1960: 15, Fig. 1; Welten 1969: 36–44; see also Grena 2004: 59–72.

The Four-Winged Scarab Types

Seven sub-types of the four-winged scarab stamp impressions have been defined (Fig. 4.3):

- HIa and HIb are two four-winged types in which the name *ḥbrn* (Hebron) appears beneath the royal emblem and the word *lmlk* above it—one using the informal cursive script and the other the official lapidary script.

- MIa and MIb are two four-winged types in which the name *mmšt* appears beneath the royal emblem and the word *lmlk* above it—one in cursive script and the other in lapidary script.

- ZIa and ZIb are two four-winged types in which the name *zp/zyp* (Ziph) appears beneath the emblem and the word *lmlk* above it—one in cursive script and the other in lapidary script.

- Interestingly, only one four-winged sub-type with the name *swkh* (Socoh) has been found, in the official lapidary script (SIb). Thus, sub-type SIa,

with the name written in cursive script, remains a theoretical construct.

This means that there were two systems of seals with the four-winged scarab. One system (Ib) consisted of four seals that employed the official script. While they were similar in width to the other *lmlk* seals, they were 35–36 mm in length—ca. 20% longer than the average. The uniformity in size of the four stamp impressions of this seal type attests to their production as a series, probably by the same craftsman and at the same time. The second system (Ia) consisted of only three seals, also uniform in size. As mentioned above, this series did not include a seal with the place name Socoh.

In the discussion below, I introduce the possibility of a chronological distinction between the two series of four-winged seals, with the set of four seals written in the official set (Ib) preceding the set with the cursive script (Ia). For some unknown reason, a seal with the place name Socoh was not required at this time (see, further, pp. 104–105).

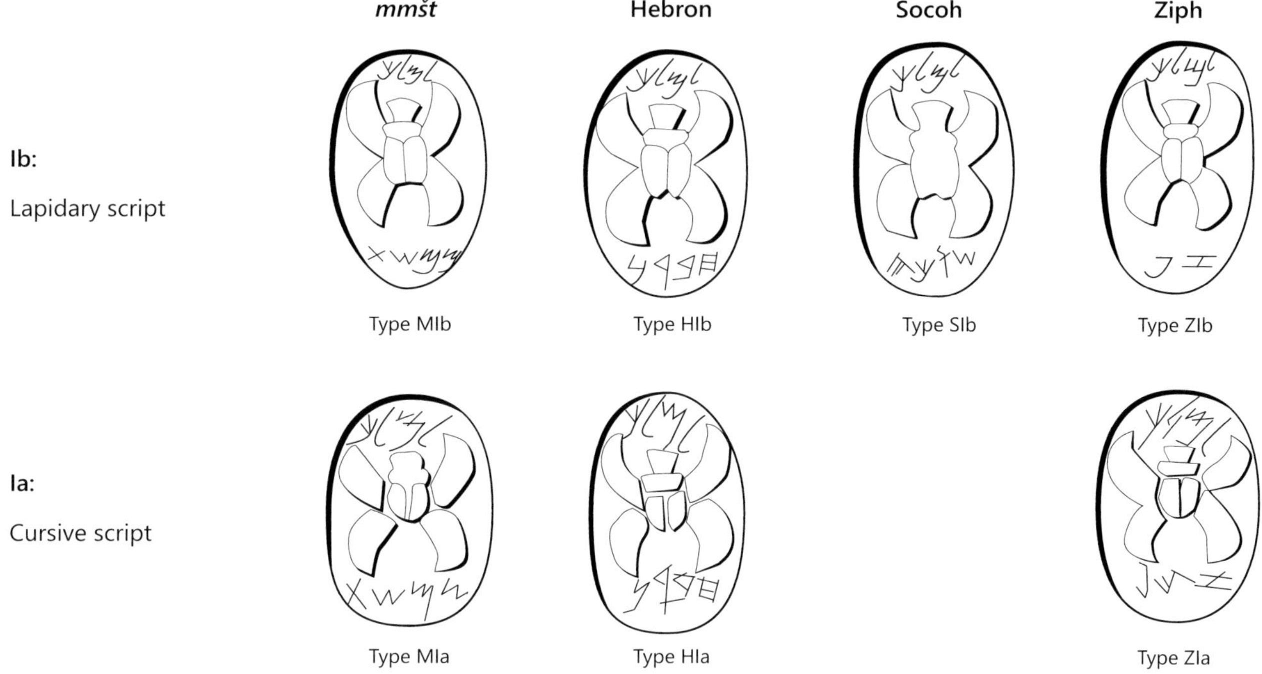

Fig. 4.3: The sub-types of the four-winged *lmlk* stamp impressions (based on Lipschits, Sergi and Koch 2010: 12, Fig. 1; drawn by Ido Koch)

The Two-Winged Sun-Disk Types

The stamp impressions with the two-winged sun disk in their center (indicated by the Roman numeral II; Fig. 4.4) are divided into three types:

- Type IIa denotes stamp impressions with the word *lmlk* above the two-winged sun disk and the place name—Hebron (H), Ziph (Z), Socoh (S), or *mmšt* (M)—written under the emblem as a single word.

- Type IIb denotes stamp impressions with the word *lmlk* above the two-winged sun disk and the place name appearing beneath the emblem, split into two, separated by the "tail" of the two-winged sun disk.

- Type IIc denotes stamp impressions lacking the word *lmlk* and with the site name appearing above the two-winged sun disk.

Like the four-winged stamp impressions, the two-winged stamp impressions were also divided into four sub-types based on the site names: Hebron (marked with the letter H), Ziph (Z), Socoh (S) and *mmšt* (M).

Lemaire identified another type of two-winged stamp impression with the *lmlk* inscription at the top, but without a site name under the emblem (his Type XII). An additional type that he posited on the basis of a single stamp impression from Ramat Raḥel—Type OII, with a two-winged sun disk in its center and without any inscription[7]—has recently been disproven following a reexamination, which revealed a *lmlk* inscription above the emblem (thus ascribing it to his Type XII). The same holds true for a Jewish Quarter stamp impression (Avigad and Barkay 2000: 261, No. 27), also mistakenly classified as Type OII, but shown to belong to Type XII. The inevitable conclusion is that Type OII does not exist and should be omitted from the list of *lmlk* stamp-impression types.[8]

Fig. 4.4: A two-winged *lmlk* stamp impression (Type HIIa) from Ramat Raḥel (Lipschits *et al.* 2017: 45, Fig. 48 [photo]; 44, Fig. 44 [drawing])

---

7. This stamp impression was first published by Aharoni (1962: Pl. 29:9).

8. This was also the conclusion of Lipschits, Sergi and Koch (2010). On this subject, see Ussishkin's incorrect criticism (2011: 221) and my clarification (Lipschits 2012a: 4 and n. 1).

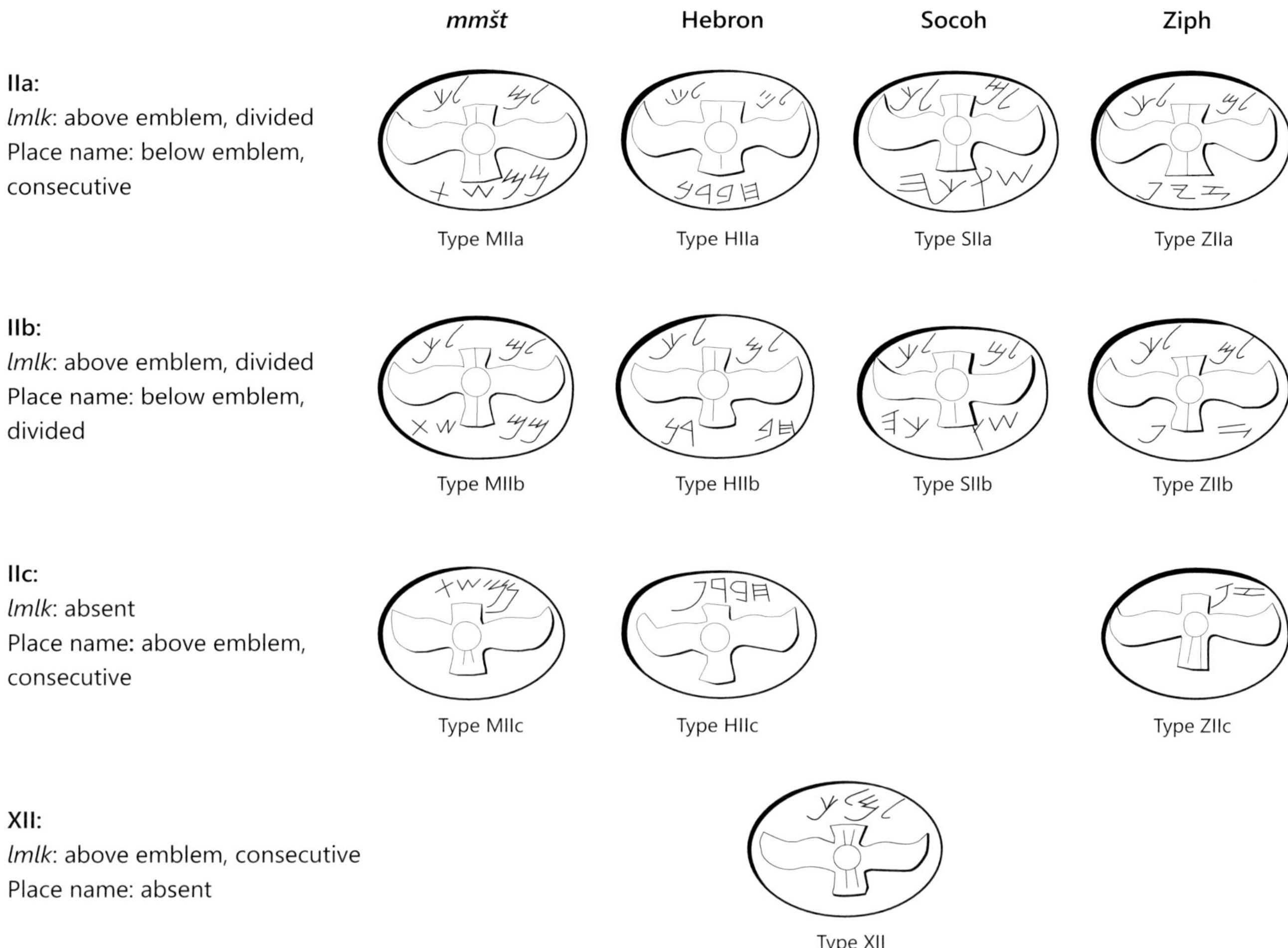

Fig. 4.5: The sub-types of the two-winged *lmlk* stamp impressions (based on Lipschits, Sergi and Koch 2010: 12–13, Figs. 1–2; drawn by Ido Koch)

In total, 12 sub-types (= seals) of two-winged stamp impressions are known to us (Fig. 4.5). These include the following:

1. A series consisting of four seals of similar size and quality, bearing the two-winged emblem, the word *lmlk* above it in paleo-Hebrew script, divided between the two sides of the upper part of the winged-sun disk. The place name appears under the emblem with three or four consecutive letters: HIIa (Hebron), SIIa (Socoh), MIIa (*mmšt*) and ZIIa (Ziph).

2. A series of four seals of similar size and quality, with the word *lmlk* divided into two by the upper part of the winged-sun disk and the place name similarly divided into two by the lower part of the emblem: HIIb (Hebron), SIIb (Socoh), MIIb (*mmšt*) and ZIIb (Ziph, spelled *zp* with two letters, one letter in each side of the lower part of the emblem).

3. A series of three seals with the place name above the winged-sun disk, instead of the word *lmlk*. HIIc bears the place name Hebron in a continuous word above the emblem, but not centered. The

letters *ḥet* and *bet* are located above the right wing of the emblem, and the letters *reš* and *nun* appear above the apex. In MIIc, the place name *mmšt* appears in a continuous word above the emblem—again off-center, with the two letters *mem* above the right wing of the sun disk, the *šin* above the emblem's apex and the letter *taw* above the left wing. In ZIIc, the place name Ziph (spelled with two letters—*zp*) appears above the right wing of the two-winged sun disk. In this series of two-winged stamp impressions too, no SIIc type of stamp impressions with the name Socoh have yet been found, and this place is absent from two different sets of *lmlk* seals.

4. A "series" consisting of only one seal with the word *lmlk* above the two-winged emblem and no place name below it. As aforementioned, this sub-type is called Type XII in Lemaire's typology.

In total, 19 seals (or sub-types) of the *lmlk* system are known to us, divided into six main groups, two with the four-winged scarab and four with the two-winged sun disk. This typological distinction is crucial to the discussion on the dating, function, features, symbolism and historical significance of the *lmlk* system.

When considering the corpus and the distribution of storage-jar handles stamped with *lmlk* seals, it is important to distinguish between the ones that were uncovered in archaeological excavations or surveys and have been published in scientific publications, as opposed to the hundreds of *lmlk* handles of uncertain provenance, which were improperly published or are in the possession of collectors or dealers.[9] The corpus assembled below consists of 1,574 *lmlk*-stamped handles, all found in archaeological excavations or surveys and published in

a manner that permits us to determine their number—if not necessarily their typological classification.[10]

The greatest concentration of handles bearing *lmlk* stamp impressions was discovered around Jerusalem—slightly to its north and its south, between the Benjamin region to the north and the Rephaim Valley and Ramat Raḥel to the south. In total, 780 *lmlk* handles (ca. 50% of all the finds) were discovered here. The greatest number of *lmlk* handles uncovered in any hill country site was found in Jerusalem and Ramat Raḥel: some 302 in Jerusalem (ca. 19% of all the finds) and 224 in Ramat Raḥel (ca. 14%). Many were also found in the Benjamin region: 92 in Gibeon (ca. 6%) and 88 in Mizpah (ca. 5.5%). The number of finds in each of these four sites is significantly greater than in all the other sites together, suggesting that Jerusalem and Ramat Raḥel were the main collection centers of the storage jars that had been filled with produce. An examination of the typology of the stamp impressions in all the other sites points to a diversity and a very small number of stamped jars from each type. This suggests that some sites (mainly Gibeon and Mizpah, but probably also Khirbet el-Burj and Tell el-Fûl) were regional collection centers and maybe also secondary administration centers to which stamped storage jars were occasionally brought—sometimes over long periods—but that there was no systematic or significant concentration of stamped jars there. Most of the other sites throughout the Judean Hills, where a few stamped handles have been and continue to be discovered, were small agricultural sites where wine and oil were probably produced and where the stamped storage jars were presumably transported to be filled.[11]

Table 4.1 presents the number of *lmlk*-stamped handles found at each site in the Judean Hills and the

---

9. The discussion below focuses on the former since the latter group of *lmlk* handles is of no archaeological or historical significance and cannot contribute to the typological debate.

10. The corpus of *lmlk* stamp impressions compiled by Vaughn (1999b: 185–197) consists of 1,716 handles, but if one subtracts the 355 handles of unknown origin, it contains 1,361 *lmlk*-stamped handles of known origin. The discrepancy between our figures and the ones presented by Vaughn stems from the discovery of additional *lmlk* handles since his publication, the revised publications of various sites, in particular Ramat Raḥel, and the reexamination of some of the relevant data. The *lmlk* stamp-impression corpus assembled by Grena (www.lmlk.com/research/index.html) consists of 2,251 *lmlk* handles, of which 725 are from private collections and a few are of uncertain origin. Several dozen additional handles that appear in his corpus are mentioned in various publications, but the information provided there is too general for inclusion here. Other handles were excluded after we examined them and determined their identification to be erroneous, their number to be wrong, or their publication to be incorrect.

11. The site of Mordot Arnona, approximately 700 m to the northeast of Ramat Raḥel, is a unique, very small and still not well understood farmstead with 33 different stamped and incised jar handles (as of the summer of 2019).

Table 4.1: Distribution of *lmlk* stamp impressions in the Judean hill country

Area	Site	Number of Stamped Handles	References
Judean Hills	Jerusalem	302	The information about *lmlk* stamp impressions from Jerusalem is partial because many are as yet unpublished and others only partially published[i]
	Ramat Raḥel	224	164 *lmlk*-stamped handles were uncovered in Aharoni's 1954–62 excavations, though he reported only 145; for full publication of *lmlk* stamp impressions from Aharoni's excavations, see Sergi 2016; 60 additional *lmlk*-stamped handles uncovered in renewed excavations (2004–2010); see Sergi, forthcoming (b)
	Mordot Arnona	21	Neria Sapir: personal communication
	Hebron	14	Abel (1938: 346) mentioned a *lmlk*-stamped handle as a surface find from Tel Hebron. Ofer (1986; 1988) reported five handles from Tel Rumeida; Kletter (2002: 142) reported eight other handles; cf. photos published by Grena (http://www.lmlk.com/research/lmlk_hebron.htm)
	Beth-Zur	11	Sellers (1933: 52–53) reported 13 handles from Beth-Zur (Khirbet Tubeika), but did not publish them; Grena collected his field sketches and photos and found only ten stamped handles, publishing nine photos (http://www.lmlk.com/research/lmlk_zur.htm)
	Rogem Gannim	4	Greenberg and Cinamon 2006: 231–232
	Additional sites	10	Including Moẓa (2); Mamila (3); Umm Tuba (4); Khirbet Rabud (1)
Total from Judean Hills		586	
Benjamin region	Gibeon	92	Pritchard (1959: 18–26) reported 80 *lmlk*-stamped handles from el-Jib (Gibeon); Vaughn (1999b: 190, n. 27) reported 12 others excavated at the site but they were not published, thus totaling 92 stamped handles (it is not clear why Vaughn calculated 95 handles); all photos of these 92 stamp impressions were published by Grena (http://www.lmlk.com/research/lmlk_gibeon.htm)
	Mizpah	88	McCown (1947: 161) reported 86 *lmlk*-stamped handles from Tell en-Naṣbeh (Mizpah), only 14 of which were fully published, with drawing or photo (McCown 1947: Pl. 56:1–14); Grena reported another two stamp impressions, published photos of all 88 (http://www.lmlk.com/research/lmlk_nasbeh.htm)
	Kh. el-Burj	23	Weinberger-Stern 2015 (first comprehensive publication of this site); cf. information gathered by Vaughn (1999b: 191, n. 32)
	Tell el-Fûl	13	Albright (1933: 10) reported five *lmlk*-stamped handles, not published; Sinclair (1960: 32, Pl. B16:2, 3, 6–8) reported another five; Lapp (1981: 111) reported three additional handles found at this site
	Nebi Samwil	4	Magen (2008: 41) reported a "number" of *lmlk* stamp impressions found in construction fills in Nebi Samwil; he published photo showing several stamped storage-jar handles, four with two-winged stamp impressions
Total from Benjamin region		220	
Total		806	

i   Wilson and Warren 1871: 152, 274; Warren and Conder 1884: 156, 534; Sayce 1893: 30; Clermont-Ganneau 1900; Macalister and Duncan 1926: 188, Fig. 202:1, 13–14; 190, Fig. 204; Duncan 1931: plate facing p. 141; Barkay 1985: 429–440; Nadelman 1989: 131; Avigad and Barkay 2000: 247, 252; Franken and Steiner 1990: 127–131; Shoham 2000b: 75; for City of David *lmlk* stamp impressions published without typological data, see Steiner 2001: 126–130; 12 more (still unpublished) were excavated by N. Szanton and J. Uziel in Area C of the eastern slope, above the Gihon Spring, and nine (still unpublished) were found in Area U, east of the entrance to Warren's Shaft, excavated by O. Chalaf and J. Uziel (personal communication); 11 were discovered in the Western Wall Plaza excavations (Weksler-Bdolah and Kisilevitz: personal communication). For summary of data, see Vaughn 1999b: 185–189; Cahill 2003; Barkay and Vaughn 2004: 2167, Fig. 29.18.

Benjamin region where more than a single stamp impression was found.

From the beginning it was clear that the Shephelah played a central role in the production of *lmlk* storage jars, as is evident from the many storage jars uncovered at Lachish and other sites in this area, especially those dating before 701 BCE. To date, 695 handles bearing *lmlk* stamp impressions (ca. 44% of all the finds) have been found at sites in the Shephelah. As discussed below, in the period leading up to Sennacherib's campaign, the Shephelah in general, and Lachish in particular, served as the production and collection centers of the stamped storage jars. The fate of the Shephelah in the wake of Sennacherib's campaign, highlighted by the Lachish excavations, accounts for the

great difference between the number of storage jars discovered at various sites in the Shephelah dating from before and after 701 BCE. It is, in fact, the *lmlk* storage jars themselves that provide the most compelling evidence for the destruction and abandonment of the Shephelah and the dramatic decline in its administrative and demographic status in the wake of Sennacherib's campaign.[12]

The centrality of the Shephelah in the *lmlk* stamp-impression system means that new stamped handles—particularly the ones with *lmlk* and "private" stamp impressions—are continually being discovered there. Table 4.2 presents the updated data from central sites in the Shephelah and from those where a significant number of stamp impressions was uncovered.

Table 4.2: Distribution of *lmlk* stamp impressions in the main Shephelah sites

Site	Number of Stamped Handles	References
Lachish	413	Barkay and Vaughn 2004: 2151–2159
Beth Shemesh	127	57 *lmlk* stamp impressions were unearthed at Tel Beth Shemesh (Vaughn 2016; Lipschits 2019a); some 70 additional handles were found during salvage excavations east of the Iron Age fortified part of the city, probably in and near the industrial area (personal communication); none have been published yet
Tel Goded	39	Bliss (1900c: 207) and Bliss and Macalister (1902: 206–207) reported 37 *lmlk*-stamped handles, only partially published; Bliss published illustrations of eight handles (1900a: Pl. IV:1–8)
Azekah	26	17 *lmlk*-stamped handles were found in the 1899–1900 excavations (1899b: 103–105; 1899c: 184–186; 1900b: 12–13; Bliss and Macalister 1902: 107); in the renewed excavations (2012–18), nine *lmlk*-stamped handles were uncovered
Socoh	24	Over ten *lmlk*-stamped handles were found at Kh. ʿAbbâd (Tel Socoh), but none were published (Vaughn 1999b: 192, n. 38); Lipschits and Amit (2011) published four other stamped handles found at the site, and ten other handles were found in the new excavations, conducted by Goren (Tel Aviv University), and in a survey by Tsur (2015)
Maresha	19	Bliss and Macalister (1902: 107) uncovered 17 *lmlk*-stamped handles; Kloner (1993: 952) found two more; not a single stamp impression has yet been fully published
Tel ʿErani	16	Yeivin (1959: 270; 1961: 9) reported 13 *lmlk* stamped handles, only two of which were published (Yeivin 1961: Pl. II); Vaughn (1999b: 192, n. 35) noted that three additional handles were found at the site, but did not provide further details
Tel Batash	15	Mazar and Panitz-Cohen 2001: 190–195
Tel eṣ-Ṣafi/Gath	7	Bliss and Macalister (1902: 107) found six *lmlk*-stamped handles; another was found in the renewed excavations, but has not yet been published, although a photo appears in the excavation project website (http://gath.files.wordpress.com/2007/07/lmlk-swkh-handle-safi-2007.jpg)
Other sites	9	For details and further literature, see Lipschits, Sergi and Koch 2011: 10
Total	**695**	

---

12. See, e.g., Naʾaman 1993: 117–120; 1994b: 247–250; Dagan 2004: 2682; Finkelstein and Naʾaman 2004; Lipschits, Sergi and Koch 2011: 16–17; Lipschits 2019a.

The predominance of Lachish is undisputed: of the total 695 *lmlk* handles found in the Shephelah, 413 such handles were uncovered at the site (59.5% of the *lmlk* handles found in the region and ca. 26% of all the *lmlk*-stamped handles found throughout the country). In contrast to the hill country, where there were two main collection centers (Jerusalem and Ramat Raḥel) and two additional, significant local collection and administrative centers (Mizpah and Gibeon), in the Shephelah, Lachish was the only significant collection center in the period preceding Sennacherib's campaign. Beth Shemesh was probably the main production and collection center in the area of the Soreq Valley, with some 127 stamped handles (18% of the *lmlk* handles found in the region), and seven other sites have revealed a significant number of *lmlk* handles, most notably Tel Goded (39 handles), Azekah (26), Socoh (24), Maresha (19), Tel ʿErani (16), Tel Batash (15) and Tell eṣ-Ṣafi (Gath) (nine stamped handles). They all appear to be regional collection centers or secondary administrative centers to which full storage jars were transported from time to time, probably as surpluses or as part of the occasional trade of storage jars. Many other sites in which only isolated *lmlk* stamped handles were found may have been agricultural processing sites, where an occasional storage jar would have broken.

Another observation, which seems to gain momentum as more data is collected, is the centrality of the Elah Valley in the *lmlk* and "private" stamp impression systems, and particularly, the role played by Tel Socoh. An exceptional concentration of *lmlk* stamp impressions of late types found at Tel Socoh, which represent a continuation of the *lmlk* impressions' early types and of the "private" stamp impressions, may point to the site's continued occupation even after Sennacherib's campaign or, at the very least, to its rapid reconstruction. This is in sharp contrast to all other known sites in the Shephelah, including nearby Tel Azekah, which apparently was not resettled during the first half of the 7th century BCE after its destruction by Sennacherib. The continuity observed at Tel Socoh is also notable in comparison to the southern Shephelah and the environs of Lachish, as well as to the northern Shephelah and the area around the Soreq Valley.

The exceptional history of Tel Socoh may stem from its importance as the *lmlk* storage-jar production center and from the kingdom's need for continuous manufacture of these storage jars in order to pay tribute to the imperial government (Lipschits and Amit 2011: 182–184).

Until recently, approximately ten handles with *lmlk* stamp impressions were known from Tel Socoh, none of which had been properly published or classified typologically (Lipschits, Sergi and Koch 2011: 30, Table 2; 34, n. 22). The publication of six newly-found stamped handles from Tel Socoh and its close environs, including two "private" and four *lmlk* stamp impressions (Lipschits and Amit 2011: 182–185), along with the ten stamped handles uncovered in Goren's 2012 excavations and Tsur's 2015 survey of the site, confirms the important role played by Socoh within the production system of the stamped storage jars.

No other area or site in the Judean kingdom was so significant in the *lmlk* stamp-impression administrative system, in terms of the number of stamped handles or the distribution of types uncovered. Table 4.3 presents the *lmlk*-stamped handles data from the peripheral areas in the Kingdom of Judah, from two central sites to its west (further discussed below) and from sites beyond the borders of Judah.

As mentioned above, 1,574 handles with various types of *lmlk* stamp impressions were collected and documented for the purpose of this research.[13] This is the largest group of handles with stamp impressions (about 50% of all the stamped handles produced in Judah over 600 years). The number of *lmlk* stamp impressions is more than double the number of *yhwd* stamp impressions (648 known impressions), even though the latter system operated for some 350 years, six times longer than the estimated length of operation of the *lmlk* system. The abundance of *lmlk*-stamped handles also has direct historical, geographical, economic and political implications, and it attests to the importance of the Shephelah and to its wealth in comparison to the hill country—the area to which Judah was reduced following Sennacherib's campaign, and even more so, after a short recovery, following the destruction of Jerusalem.

---

13. Many additional *lmlk* handles were not included in this count, as they were not found in clear archaeological contexts. The data in this study was last updated in the summer of 2019 and does not include stamped handles that were excavated and found since then.

Table 4.3: Distribution of *lmlk* stamp impressions in the Beersheba–Arad Valleys, Judean Desert and additional sites beyond the borders of Judah

Area	Site	Number of Stamped Handles	References
Beersheba–Arad Valleys	Arad	9	Aharoni 1981a; Grena published photos of these stamp impressions on his website (http://www.lmlk.com/research/lmlk_arad.htm)
	ʿAroer	6	Thareani 2010: 214 and Pls. 48:2, 106:2, 188:1, 193:8
	Tel Beersheba	2	Aharoni (1973: 76–77, Pl. 32:2) reported one four-winged *lmlk* impression (thus an early type) stamped on a pithos handle; another *lmlk* stamp impression, originatingd in the Old City market (Bir es-Sabaʿ), is not included here; see Grena (http://www.lmlk.com/research/lmlk_corp.htm)
	Tel ʿIra	1	Aharoni 1958: Pl. 16D
Total from Beersheba–Arad Valleys		18	
Jordan Valley and Dead Sea area	En-Gedi	1	Stern 2007c: 139, Photo 4.7.11; see also Lipschits, Sergi and Koch 2010: 14
	Jericho	1	Sellin and Watzinger 1913: Pl. 42
	Qumran	2	De Vaux 1973: 2–3; Magen and Peleg 2007: 24–28
	Kh. es-Samrah	1	Cross and Milik 1956: 8, Photo 2; cf. Lipschits, Sergi and Koch 2010: 15–16, n. 20
Total from Jordan Valley and Dead Sea area		5	
Beyond Judah's borders	Gezer[i]	37	
	Ashdod	1	Dothan 1971: Pl. XCV:4
	Tel Miqne	3	See information collected by Grena (http://www.lmlk.com/research/lmlk_corp.htm)
	ʿEn Tut	8	Finkielsztejn and Gorzalczany 2010
	Mount Meiron	1	Meyers and Meyers 1990: 126 and Pl. D:1
Total from beyond Judah's borders		50	
Total		**73**	

i   Gitin (1990: 17, n. 16) noted that: "The number of *lmlk*-stamped handles from R.A.S. Macalister's (PEF) excavations has always been problematic, as Macalister did not publish an accurate record of his finds. H.D. Lance's documentation provides a minimum number of 31. … With the six examples from J.D. Seger's Phase II excavations, the minimum total number from Gezer is 37." See also Macalister 1912: 209–210. Lance examined the *lmlk* stamp impressions from the Gezer excavations housed in the Istanbul Archaeological Museum, but did not publish them. He noted that "it appears that the minimum total of stamps from Gezer would be 31," but that "it may easily run as high as 50, judging from [Albright's notes]" (Lance 1971: 330, n. 70). However, Albright (1953: 46) did not have additional data about the Gezer stamp impressions, and it seems that he did not have accurate data about the number of stamp impressions found in Judah. He thus cannot be relied upon for the number of Gezer stamp impressions. Of the 37 stamp impressions definitely found in Gezer, only two were fully published (Macalister 1912: Fig. 361:1; Dever, Lance and Bullard 1974: Pl. 41:8; see also Lance 1967: 45, Fig. 6). Grena compiled photographs of 14 stamp impressions from Gezer: http://www.lmlk.com/research/lmlk_gezer.htm.

A word of caution is in order here. As a result of the massive destruction wreaked by Sennacherib on sites in the Shephelah, a great wealth of material culture was trapped beneath the destruction level. The abundance of stamped and unstamped storage jars therefore accurately reflects their intensive use and proliferation in the region at the end of the 8th century BCE. We cannot, however, ascertain the quantity of the stamped and unstamped storage jars in sites that were not destroyed—especially the ones in the hill country, which continued to exist, without interruption, for many years and in which pottery vessels gradually went out of use through wear and tear and were disposed of and replaced by new vessels. In light of this reality, one cannot take at face value a comparison between the finds uncovered in destruction levels emanating from Sennacherib's campaign and the finds recovered from sites that were spared from this campaign. Both the nature and the quality of the finds are inherent handicaps that affect the historical evaluations and reconstructions based on the archaeological findings.

To conclude, one discerns two clear chronological phases within the system of *lmlk* stamp impressions, enabling us to divide the finds into early and late types. Methodologically, the distinction between early and late types requires the meticulous examination of the emergence of the various types and sub-types in the destruction layers attributed to 701 BCE.[14] All sub-types found sealed beneath this destruction layer are defined as early types. The stratigraphic attribution of a certain handle to Lachish Stratum III or to a parallel stratum proves that it was in use prior to this period, and it can therefore be defined as an early type. Sub-types for which not even a single stamped handle was found in the 701 BCE destruction layer can be defined as late types. Handles with these types of stamp impressions were either found only in sites that existed without interruption throughout the 8th–7th centuries BCE or in sites first established in the 7th century BCE. Of course, the finding of specimens at such sites does not automatically classify them as late types. However, their total absence from the 701 BCE destruction layers, which contain such a large and representative concentration of stamped handles, when considered in conjunction with their discovery only in sites that existed during the 7th century BCE, constitutes strong circumstantial evidence that may anchor the determination of the later arrival of these types and thus merit their classification as late. As will be shown below (pp. 103–114), the early *lmlk* stamp impressions include all the four-winged types (Ia and Ib) and the two-winged Type IIa, while the late types include all the other two-winged impressions. The fact that all the late types come from families of seals that exemplify late development and, to some extent, even display the degeneration of some features of earlier seals further buttresses this circumstantial evidence into an established and reasonable assumption. We therefore deem this evidence sufficient to justify our claim that these types were manufactured after Sennacherib's campaign. Furthermore, it is proof that the practice of stamping *lmlk* seals on storage-jar handles continued in the 7th century BCE as well. Of course, the finding of even a single stamped handle in a clear pre-701 BCE archaeological context would suffice to rescind the classification of that particular type as a late type.

As seen in Table 4.4, the vast majority of *lmlk* impressions of the early types—from before Sennacherib's campaign—was uncovered in the Shephelah (Fig. 4.6), whereas the Shephelah disappears almost completely from the distribution of the late types of *lmlk* stamp impressions, which are found almost completely in the hill country (Fig. 4.7). This trend continues and becomes even more acute in the distribution of concentric circle incisions (see below). Although the Shephelah experienced a certain degree of recovery at the end of the First Temple period, as indicated by the number of rosette stamp impressions (see below), it never regained its former stature in subsequent systems of stamp impressions.

---

14. For discussion of the research methodology and a detailed presentation of its results, see Lipschits, Sergi and Koch 2010; 2011; Lipschits 2012a; Finkelstein 2012; and see below, pp. 103–114. The first to view *lmlk* storage-jar development as part of a long and continuous process, commencing in the late 8th century BCE and continuing until the destruction of the Kingdom of Judah, was Ji, who also noted that while use of the four-winged scarab ceased after Sennacherib's campaign, the two-winged sun-disk emblem continued to be used until the last third of the 7th century BCE (Ji 2001: 21a). The division between "pre-Sennacherib" and "post-Sennacherib" *lmlk* stamp impressions was also suggested by Grena (2004: 337), who based his observation on 13 stamped handles found in clear 7th-century BCE archaeological contexts (in Jerusalem, Arad, Lachish, Tel Batash and Ḥorvat Shilḥa).

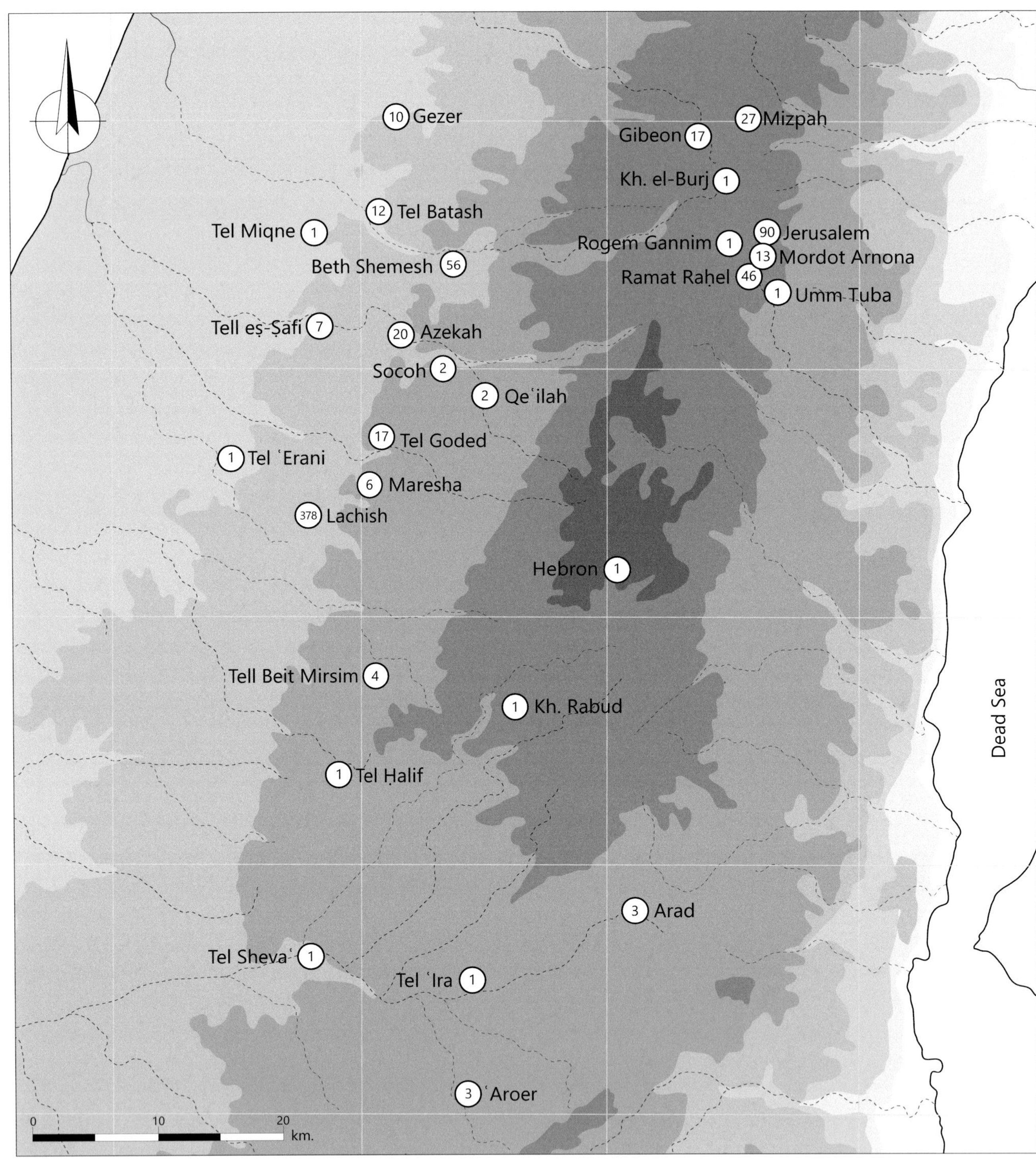

Fig. 4.6: Distribution of early types of *lmlk* stamp impressions

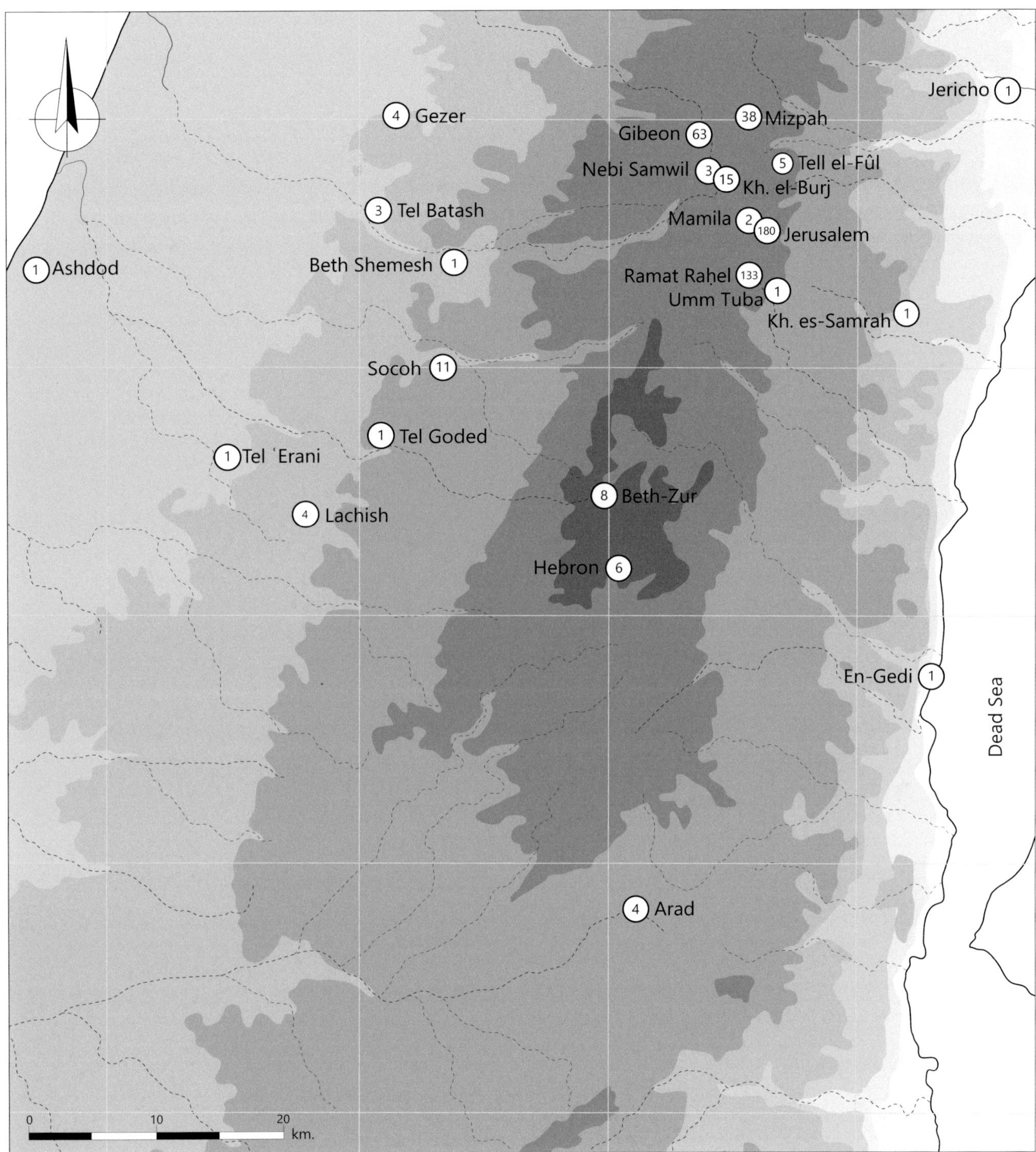

Fig. 4.7: Distribution of late types of *lmlk* stamp impressions

Table 4.4: Distribution of early and late types of *lmlk* stamp impressions[i]

Area	Site	Early *lmlk*	Late *lmlk*	Unidentified *lmlk*	Total	
Jerusalem and its environs	Jerusalem	Ca. 90	Ca. 180	32	302	**Total from Jerusalem environs:**
	Ramat Raḥel	46	133	45	224	**Early *lmlk*:** ca. 151
	Mordot Arnona	13	3	5	21	**Late *lmlk*:** ca. 319
	Mamila	0	2	1	3	**Unidentified *lmlk*:** 88
	Rogem Gannim	1	0	3	4	**Total: ca.** 558
	Umm Tuba	1	1	2	4	
Judean Hills	Hebron	1	6	7	14	**Total from Judean Hills:**
	Beth-Zur	0	8	3	11	**Early *lmlk*:** 2
	Khirbet Rabud	1	0	0	1	**Late *lmlk*:** 14
						Unidentified *lmlk*: 10
						Total: 26
Benjamin region	Mizpah	27	38	23	88	**Total from Benjamin region:**
	Gibeon	17	63	12	92	**Early *lmlk*:** 45
	Tell el-Fûl[ii]	0	5 (13?)	8 (0?)	13	**Late *lmlk*:** 124
	Khirbet al-Burj	1	15	7	23	**Unidentified *lmlk*:** 53
	Nebi Samwil	0	3	1	4	**Total:** 222
	Moẓa	0	0	2	2	
Shephelah	Lachish	378	4	31	413	**Total from Shephelah:**
	Beth Shemesh	56	1	Ca. 70	Ca. 127	**Early *lmlk*:** 506+
	Tel Goded[iii]	17+	1+	21	39+	**Late *lmlk*:** 21+
	Tel Batash	12	3	0	15	**Unidentified *lmlk*:** 168
	Tel Azekah	20	0	6	26	**Total:** 695+
	Tel Maresha	6	0	13	19	
	Tel ʿErani	1	1	14	16	
	Socoh (Kh. ʿAbbâd)	2	11	11	24	
	Tell Beit Mirsim	4	0	0	4	
	Khirbet Qeʿilah	2	0	0	2	
	Tel Ḥalif	1	0	0	1	
	Tel Zayit	0	0	2	2	
	Tell eṣ-Ṣafi	7	0	0	7	
Beersheba–Arad Valleys	Tel Beersheba	1	0	1	2	**Total from Beersheba–Arad Valleys:**
	Arad	3	4	2	9	**Early *lmlk*:** 8
	Tel ʿIra	1	0	0	1	**Late *lmlk*:** 4
	ʿAroer	3	0	3	6	**Unidentified *lmlk*:** 6
						Total: 18
Jordan Valley and Dead Sea area	En-Gedi (Tel Goren)	0	1	0	1	**Total from eastern fringe:**
	Jericho	0	1	0	1	**Early *lmlk*:** 0
	Qumran	0	0	2	2	**Late *lmlk*:** 3
	Khirbet es-Samrah	0	1	0	1	**Unidentified *lmlk*:** 2
						Total: 5
Beyond Judah's borders	Gezer	10	4	23	37	**Total from beyond Judah's borders:**
	Ashdod	0	1	0	1	**Early *lmlk*:** 11
	Tel Miqne	1	0	2	3	**Late *lmlk*:** 5
	ʿEn Tut	0	0	8	8	**Unidentified *lmlk*:** 34
	Mount Meiron	0	0	1	1	**Total:** 50

i   The data in this table is based on the classification of Lipschits, Sergi and Koch 2011: 30.

ii   On the difficulties of identification and attribution of the *lmlk* stamp impressions from Tell el-Fûl, see Lipschits, Sergi and Koch 2011: n. 5.

iii On the difficulties in identification and locating the types of stamp impressions from Tel Goded, see Lipschits, Sergi and Koch 2011: 33, n. 17.

"Private" Stamp Impressions[15]

The stamp impressions usually termed "private" are either oval or round (impressions made with a square or rectangular seal are rare) (Fig. 4.8). They come in a wide range of dimensions, but on average are 10–15 mm in height and 15–20 mm in length. Although they exhibit great variety, they generally contain four components (Fig. 4.9):

- An upper field containing a private name written in paleo-Hebrew script, usually interpreted as the seal owner's name;

- A lower field with an additional private name written in paleo-Hebrew script, usually interpreted as the seal owner's patronym;

- A divider consisting of one or two lines engraved across the length of the seal to separate between the upper and lower fields;

- A rounded frame (bezel), circumscribing the seal around its margins.

Most "private" stamp impressions do not contain any figurative elements, and the names appear without any additional titles. Only in very few cases does the word בן ("son of") appear between the two names, either at the end of the first or the beginning of the second line. Interestingly, a few names of officials were stamped by more than one seal (Lipschits, Sergi and Koch 2010: 22–27).

Handles with "private" stamp impressions were first discovered in Bliss and Macalister's excavations of four

Fig. 4.8: A "private" stamp impression from Ramat Raḥel, bearing a *lmnḥm/ywbnh* inscription (Koch and Lipschits 2016: 343, No. 2)

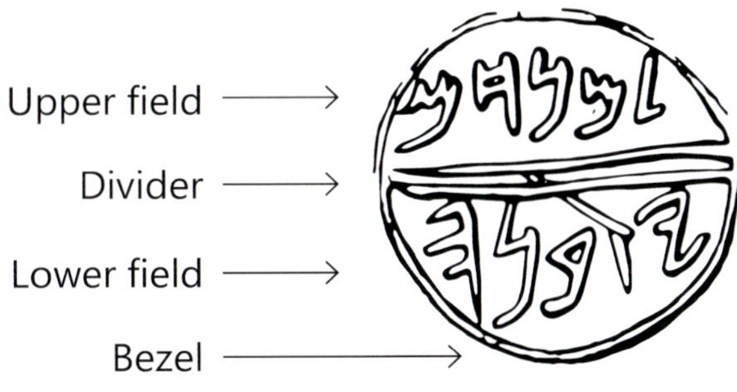

Fig. 4.9: The components of the "private" stamp impression in Fig. 4.8 (based on Aharoni 1962: Fig. 14:3)

---

15. Some scholars suggested calling this group "official" stamp impressions (see Vaughn 1999b: 110–117) because the people whose names appeared on these seals were clerks and office holders in the royal administration. However, since their personal name usually appeared without mention of their official title, I prefer the term "private," which is the most commonly accepted term in the literature.

sites in the Shephelah (Bliss and Macalister 1902: 119–122, Pl. 56:20–33). Since then 183 jar handles bearing this type of stamp impression have been discovered within the Kingdom of Judah.[16] These handles generally have two ridges along the handle, and they resemble the *lmlk* storage-jar handles in material and shape.

The affinity between the "private" and *lmlk* stamp impressions was better understood following the Lachish excavations, where handles of both types were found in the same assemblages (Diringer 1949: 71, 73, Figs. 2, 3). A handle uncovered in the Ramat Raḥel excavations bears both a *lmlk* and a "private" impression (Aharoni 1962: 16–17, Pl. 6:2). Complete storage jars with two handles bearing "private" stamp impressions and two bearing *lmlk* stamp impressions were found in the renewed excavations at Lachish (Ussishkin 1976: 1–3, Figs. 1–4). Handles bearing both a "private" stamp impression and concentric circle incisions were also recovered (Avigad and Barkay 2000: 247–248, No. 51).

In addition to the "private" stamp impressions on storage-jar handles, numerous seal impressions were found on bullae,[17] with the same four components: an upper field containing a private name, usually interpreted as the seal owner's name; a lower field with another private name, usually interpreted as the seal owner's patronym; a divider consisting of one or two lines; and a rounded frame (a bezel). There is no congruity between the seals appearing on the bullae and the ones on storage jar handles, and they apparently belonged to distinct administrative systems managed by different personnel.

To date, 45 types (= 45 seals) of "private" stamp impressions have been uncovered. Some variations occur, such as abbreviations or different spellings of the same name. In some cases, the name of the same individual appears on several seals, with both the private name and the patronym, indicating that at least some officials must

have had more than one seal. In total, 32 names of individuals are known. The 45 seals that were in use in the "private" stamp-impression system can be divided into three groups:[18]

1. Twenty-two types of "private" stamp impressions were found at Lachish (Table 4.5), mainly in the Stratum III destruction layer, including three types that were defined as surface finds: *lnḥm/ʿbdy*, *ltnḥm/ mgn* and *lšlm/ʾḥʾm*.[19] One type, *lsmk.b/n.spnyhw*, was also defined as a surface find in Lachish, but a stamp impression of the same type (= the same seal) was found at Tel Goded, which does not include 7th-century BCE settlement layers. Two other types, *lmšlm/ʾlntn* and *lnḥm/hṣlyhw*, were also found on the surface at Lachish, but stamp impressions of the same type were also found in the City of David, Gibeon, Mordot Arnona and Ramat Raḥel (sites without 701 BCE destruction layers). In view of the above, we cannot determine conclusively that these stamp impressions were from the late 8th century BCE. However, as most of the "private" stamp impressions from Lachish originated in Stratum III, and especially since no "private" stamp impression was found in Lachish Stratum II or in any clear 7th-century archaeological context in Judah, we can assume with high probability that these stamp impressions too originated in Stratum III and should be dated to the 8th century BCE.

2. Fourteen types of "private" stamp impressions were found in Shephelah sites that were destroyed in 701 BCE (Tel Goded, Tell Beit Mirsim, Beth Shemesh, Tell eṣ-Ṣafi, Azekah, Maresha, Tel Burna and Batash; Table 4.6).[20] Even if there was a short-term effort to reconstruct and resettle these sites after the destruction of Sennacherib's campaign (Finkelstein and Naʾaman 2004), the area as a

---

16. For all the information regarding these stamp impressions from Judah, Israel and its environs until the 1990s, see Avigad and Sass 1997; Vaughn 1999b. For a more updated catalogue, see Lipschits, Sergi and Koch 2011; and see below, Table 4.8.

17. A bulla is a small clay token generally intended for the sealing of documents or of sacks or cases of merchandise. For an updated compilation of information regarding the bullae from the First Temple period in the Israel and Judah, see Gurvin 2010.

18. This classification is crucial for the dating of the production and use of the "private" stamp impressions to the period preceding Sennacherib's campaign (i.e., before 701 BCE). For the significance of the dating for an understanding of the role of the "private" stamp impressions in the history of Judah, see pp. 105–106.

19. Cf. Ussishkin 1996: 57–59; Barkay and Vaughn 1996a; Vaughn 1999b: 96–98, Table 3 and Appendix II on pp. 198–216.

20. Compare this to the data gathered by Vaughn 1999b: 97–98 and Table 4.

Table 4.5: Types of "private" stamp impressions found at Lachish

No.	Type	Number of Stamped Handles	Additional Sites with This Type	References
1	ʾḥzyh/w.tnḥm	1	Beth Shemesh (1); Tell en-Naṣbeh (1); Ramat Raḥel (1)	Ussishkin 2004b: 2137, No. 78, Fig. 29.16:1; Barkay and Vaughn 1996b: 44–46, No. 17, Figs. 20–21; McCown 1947: 162, Pl. 57:10; Lipschits 2008
2	ʾḥʾ/tnḥmⁱ	1	–	Ussishkin 2004b: 2138, No. 91
3	hwšʿ/ṣpn	4	Gezer (1); Khirbet ʿAbbâd (Socoh) (1); Tel Goded (3)	Diringer 1953: 341, Pl. 47B:3; Barkay and Vaughn 2004: 2160; Macalister 1912: 211, Fig. 360; Vaughn 1999b: 200, No. 23; Bliss and Macalister 1902: 119–122, Pl. 56:20,30
4	yhwḥyl/šḥr	1	Umm Tuba (1)	Ussishkin 2004b: 2137, No. 80, Fig. 29.14:4; Zubair ʿAdawi, personal communication; http://www.antiquities.org.il/Article_heb.aspx?sec_id=25&subj_id=240&id=1495&hist=1
5	yhwḥl/šḥr	1	Ramat Raḥel (1); Socoh (1)	Ussishkin 2004b: 2137, No. 79; Aharoni 1962: 44, Fig. 31:2, Pl. 27:2; Lipschits and Amit 2011: 183
6	krmy/ypyhw	2	Jerusalem (1)	Diringer 1953: 341, Pl. 47B:7; Vaughn 1999b: 203, No. 55
7	lmnḥm/ywbnh	4	Gibeon (1); Ramat Raḥel (1); ʿAdullam (1); Khirbet ʿAbbâd (Socoh) (2)	Diringer 1953: 341, Pl. 47B:6; Barkay and Vaughn 1996b: 36–38, Nos. 7–9; Pritchard 1959: 28, Fig. 10:7, Pl. 11:7; Aharoni 1962: 17–18, Fig. 14.3, Pl. 6:4; Vaughn 1999b: 204, Nos. 60, 62; Tsur 2015
8	mšlm/ʾḥmlk	12	–	Diringer 1953: 341, Pl. 47A:4; Ussishkin 2004b: 2137, No. 81, Fig. 29.14:2; Barkay and Vaughn 2004: 2162–2163
9	lmšlm/ʾlntn	1	Gibeon (2)	Diringer 1953: 341; Barkay and Vaughn 2004: 2162; Pritchard 1959: 28, Fig. 10:5,6, Pl. 11:5,6
10	lnḥm/hṣlyhw	1	Gibeon (1); Jerusalem (1); Ramat Raḥel (1); Mordot Arnona (1)	Diringer 1953: 341, Pl. 47B:3; Pritchard 1959: 27, Fig. 10:2, Pl. 11:2; Nadelman 1989: 131; Aharoni 1964: 61; Neria Sapir: personal communication
11	lnḥm/ʿbdy	13	Tel Goded (1); Naḥal ʿArugot (1); Mordot Arnona (3)	Diringer 1953: 341, Pl. 47A:10,11; Barkay and Vaughn 2004: 2163; Bliss and Macalister 1902: 120; Hadas 1983; Neria Sapir: personal communication
12	lnrʾ/šbnʾ	1	Beth Shemesh (1); Jerusalem (1); Azekah (1)	Ussishkin 2004b: 2138, No. 84, Fig. 29.16:2; Vaughn 1999b: 208, No. 130; Avigad and Barkay 2000: 247–248, No. 51; the stamp impression from Azekah has not yet been published
13	lsmk.b/n.ṣpnyhw	3	Tel Goded (1); Jerusalem (1)	Diringer 1953: 341, Pl. 47B:8,9; Bliss and Macalister 1902: 120, Pl. 6:25; Vaughn 1999b: 209, No. 140
14	lʿbd/y	1	–	Diringer 1953: 341, Pl. 47A:8
15	ṣpn.ʿ/zryhw	5	–	Diringer 1953: 341, Pl. 47A:1,2; Barkay and Vaughn 2004: 2164
16	lṣpn/ʿzr	3	–	Tufnell 1953: 110; Barkay and Vaughn 1996b: 44, No. 14, Fig. 17; Ussishkin 2004b: 85, Fig. 29.16:3
17	lšbn/ʾ.šḥr	3	Tell en-Naṣbeh (3); Ramat Raḥel (3); Mordot Arnona (2); Azekah (1)	Diringer 1953: 341, Pl. 47B:1; Barkay and Vaughn 2004: 2164; McCown 1947: 160–162; Aharoni 1964: 60; Neria Sapir: personal communication
18	šbnyh/ʿzryh	1	Tel Goded (1); Mordot Arnona (1)	Diringer 1953: 341; Barkay and Vaughn 2004: 2161; Bliss and Macalister 1902: 120; Neria Sapir: personal communication
19	lšwk/y.šbn/ʾ	2	–	Diringer 1953: 341, Pl. 47B:2
20	lšlm/ʾḥʾ	1	Arad (1); Beth Shemesh (1); Jerusalem (1); Kh. Rabud (Debir) (2); Ramat Raḥel (1); Tel Goded (2)	Ussishkin 2004b: 2138, No. 90; Vaughn 1999b: 214, Nos. 195, 196, 197, 201, 214; Kochavi 1974: 18, Pl. 4:3–4; Ben-Dor 1948: 66–67
21	lšlm/ʾḥʾm	4	Khirbet Qeʿila (1)	Diringer 1953: 341, Pl. 47B:2; Barkay and Vaughn 1996b: 38–41, No. 10, Figs. 11, 13; Hizmi and Shabbtai 1991: Fig. 188
22	ltnḥm/mgn	7	Gibeon (1); Ramat Raḥel (1); Tell ʿErani (1); Tekoa (1)	Diringer 1953: 341, Pl. 47A:7; Ussishkin 2004b: 2138, Nos. 86, 87, Fig. 29.16:4; Pritchard 1959: 28, Fig. 10:8, Pl. 11:8; Aharoni 1964: 32; Vaughn 1999b: 215, No. 217; Ofer 1993: 95

i   As they are stamped on the same jar, Vaughn (1999b: 97, n. 56) considered this stamp impression and the previous one (No. 1 in this table) to belong to the same person.

whole was not resettled and did not become part of Judah again in the first decades of the 7th century BCE (Dagan 2001: 207–212; Koch and Lipschits 2010: 18–21; Lipschits 2019a; see also discussion below). Thus, the storage jars stamped with these seals must have been manufactured and used prior to Sennacherib's campaign.

3. Nine types of "private" stamp impressions were found in sites not destroyed in Sennacherib's campaign (Table 4.7). Handles stamped with these seals were found only in sites in the hill country and not in the Shephelah.

The typological division outlined above makes it possible to date, with high probability, 36 types (= seals)

Table 4.6: Types of "private" stamp impressions found in Shephelah sites destroyed by Sennacherib

No.	Type	Site and Number of Stamp Impressions	Sites without Evidence of Destruction by Sennacherib	References
23	ʾlyqm.nʿ/r.ykn	Beth Shemesh (1); Tell Beit Mirsim (1)	Ramat Raḥel	Grant and Wright 1939: 80; Vaughn 1999b: 199; Albright 1932a: Nos. 623, 860; Aharoni 1964: 33, Fig. 37:6, Pl. 40:4
24	lbky/šlm	Beth Shemesh (1)	Ḥorvat Shovav	Grant and Wright 1939: 82; Vaughn 1999b: 200; Rahmani 1969: 82, Pl. 20:1
25	bnʾy/yhwkl	Maresha (1); Tell eṣ-Ṣafi (2) Beth Shemesh (1); Ramat Raḥel (1); Tell Beit Mirsim (1)	–	Bliss and Macalister 1902: 121, Pl. 56:27; Vaughn 1999b: 200; Aharoni 1964: 33
26	lḥsdʾ/yrmyh	Beth Shemesh (1)	–	Grant and Wright 1939: 80; Vaughn 1999b: 201
27	lkslʾ/zkʾ	Beth Shemesh (2)	–	Grant and Wright 1939: 84; Barkay and Vaughn 1996b: 33–34, Nos. 4–5, Figs. 3–4
28	mnḥm/wyhbnh	Beth Shemesh (1)	Ramat Raḥel	Grant and Wright 1939: 81–82; Aharoni 1956: 145
29	mnḥm/ybnh	Tel Goded (1)	Jerusalem	Bliss and Macalister 1902: 120; Avigad and Barkay 2000: 249–250
30	lʿzr/ḥgyⁱ	Azekah (1)	Gezer	Bliss and Macalister 1902: 121; Macalister 1912: 211
31	lʿzr/ḥgy	Tel Burna (1)	–	Shai et al. 2014: 129–130; name identical to Type 30, but impression made by different seal
32	lṣdq/smk	Beth Shemesh (1); Azekah (1)	–	Grant and Wright 1939: 83; the stamp impression from Azekah has not yet been published
33	lšpn.ʾ/bmʿṣ	Azekah (1); Tel Batash (1); Tell eṣ-Ṣafi (2); Mordot Arnona (1); Jerusalem (1)	Jerusalem	Bliss and Macalister 1902: 121; Mazar and Panitz-Cohen 2001: 194, No. 10; Vaughn 1999b: 211, Nos. 156, 158, 160; Avigad and Barkay 2000: 249; Neria Sapir: personal communication
34	ṣpn/ʿzr	Beth Shemesh (1)	–	Grant and Wright 1939: 80–81
35	šbnyhw/ʿzryhw	Tel Goded (3)	–	Bliss and Macalister 1902: 120
36	ltnḥ/m.ngb	Beth Shemesh (2)	Gibeon; Jerusalem; Ramat Raḥel	Grant and Wright 1939: 83; Barkay and Vaughn 1996b: 46–48, No. 24, Fig. 19; Pritchard 1959: 28, Fig. 10:3, Pl. 11:3; Vaughn 1999b: 216, No. 234; Aharoni 1964: 44, Fig. 31:1, Pl. 27:3

i   Vaughn (1999b: 98; 210) erroneously noted that this stamp impression was found at Tel Goded, but it was found at Azekah (Lipschits, Sergi and Koch 2010: 25; Shai et al. 2014: 30, n. 14). Vaughn (1999b: 201) also included the Gezer stamp impression in this group, although Gezer was not destroyed in Sennacherib's campaign (Reich and Brandl 1985).

of "private" stamp impressions (out of the 45 known types) to the late 8th century BCE. Of the nine other types, found only in the hill country, five bear names (personal name of the owner and the patronym) that also appeared on stamp impressions uncovered in Lachish Stratum III. If they belonged to the same individual, they too can be dated to the late 8th century BCE.[21] Four names—*hwš ʿm/ḥgy*, *ḥšy/ʾlšm ʿ*, *lṣmḥ/ʾlšm ʿ* and *ʾḥmlk/ʿmdyhw*—appear on storage-jar handles found at Ramat Raḥel, Jerusalem and Umm Tuba. These handles were recovered from fills with no clear stratigraphic context (Aharoni 1962: 18–19; Nadelman 1989: 131; Shoham 2000a: 82), and these names have no equivalents in Lachish Stratum III or in any other Shephelah destruction layer. Since there are very few such types and the vast majority are dated with high probability to the end of the 8th century BCE, we may assume that all the storage jars with "private" stamp impressions were manufactured and used prior to Sennacherib's campaign and the destruction of the Shephelah sites in 701 BCE (see Vaughn 1999b: 97–98).

In contrast to the *lmlk*-stamped handles, no handle stamped with a "private" seal was found in any archaeological context clearly dating from the 7th century BCE.[22] The dating of the "private" stamp impressions can therefore be restricted to the late 8th century BCE. The picture that emerges, then, is that after Sennacherib's 701 BCE campaign, "private" seals were no longer stamped on storage jars.[23]

Most of the "private" stamp impressions were found in the Shephelah. As shown in Table 4.8 and Fig. 4.10, of the 183 "private" stamp impressions of known origin, uncovered in excavations or archaeological surveys, 125 were discovered in the Shephelah (ca. 68%), with 72 of those found at Lachish (ca. 39% of the total corpus and 57.5% of the finds in the Shephelah). It seems that, with the exception of Beth Shemesh and Tel Goded, which may be secondary administrative centers, the "private" stamp impressions were concentrated primarily in Lachish. Only 54 handles with "private" stamp impressions were found in the hill country and Benjamin region (29.5%). Not only is the hill country considerably less well represented in the corpus of "private" stamped storage-jar handles, but Jerusalem (with 13 "private" stamped handles—7% of all the finds) and Ramat Raḥel (with 19 stamped handles—10.5% of all the finds) are only marginally represented in the "private" stamp-impression system.

Another observation that should be taken into account is that from over half the types (= seals) of "private" stamp impressions (24 types) only one or two stamped handles were found. For nine types, three or four stamped handles were found; for nine other types, five to ten handles were found, and only three types were represented by more than ten stamped handles. The logical inference that the "private" stamp impression system did not operate on a large scale, both from the geographical and chronological aspects. Seal use was specific and localized, not part of a large-scale administrative system.

It is clear from the above that even though the system of "private" stamp impressions operated concurrently with the early phase of the *lmlk* stamp-impression system, the two systems differed in function and in storage-jar distribution. This is significant in terms of the administration and history of these systems (see below, pp. 103–114).

---

21. Only one of the "private" stamp impressions found in Ramat Raḥel and Jerusalem was recovered from a clear context. This stamp impression, bearing the name *lyhwḥyl/šḥr*, was found under the palace courtyard in Ramat Raḥel, and was therefore dated by Aharoni (1962: 44) to the 8th century BCE, just like the two Lachish impressions with the same name.

22. Contrary to Barkay (1995) and Vaughn (1999b: 209), we believe that the stamp impression with the name *nrʾ*, appearing on a storage-jar handle found in En-Gedi (Stern 2007e: 161), is not part of the "private" stamp impression system. Chronologically, the earliest settlement at Tel Goren (En-Gedi) is dated to late in the 7th century BCE (Stern 2007e: 162)—long after the "private" stamp impression system had ceased to operate in Judah. Furthermore, there is no evidence for the identification of Nera from En-Gedi as *lnrʾ/šbnʾ* or *lnry.b/n.šbnyhw*, whose stamp impressions were found throughout Judah (e.g., Vaughn 1999b: 209). For one thing, all the "private" stamp impressions include the patronym's name as well, and for another, the shape of the two-winged stamp impressions from Judah in the late 8th–early 7th centuries BCE does not resemble the *nrʾ* stamp impression from En-Gedi. The two-winged *lmlk* emblem—the sun disk with "tail" and upper horns—does not appear on the En-Gedi stamp impression. Furthermore, the features of the En-Gedi stamp impression resemble those of late 7th–6th-century impressions (Parayre 1993: 37–38), further weakening an 8th-century dating. In light of the discussion of the 7th-century BCE *lmlk* stamp impressions and the process whereby the royal emblems were "stripped" of their epigraphic elements, this impression should perhaps be viewed as a kind of amalgamation of a "private" stamp impression with a central component of a royal stamp impression.

23. On the significance of this dating for the history of Judah, see pp. 159–165.

Table 4.7: Types of "private" stamp impressions found only in hill country sites not destroyed in Sennacherib's campaign

No.	Type	Number of Stamp Impressions and Site of Discovery	References
37	*hwš'm/ḥgy*	Jerusalem (1)	Nadelman 1989: 131
38	*ḥšy/'lšm'*	Jerusalem (1)	Shoham 2000a: 82, No. P2
39	*lḥšy/'lšm'*	Ramat Raḥel (1)	Aharoni 1962: 18–19, Fig. 14:4, Pl. 6:1
40	*lyhwḥyl/šḥr*	Jerusalem (1); Ramat Raḥel (2)	Tushingham 1985: Pl. 69:13; Aharoni 1962: 44, Fig. 31:2, Pl. 27:2; 1964: 32–33, Fig. 37:1, Pl. 40:1
41	*lnr'/šbn'*	Ramat Raḥel (1)	Aharoni 1962: 16, Fig. 14:2, Pl. 6:2
42	*lnry.b/n.šbnyhw*	Jerusalem (1)	Avigad and Barkay 2000: 248–249, No. 54
43	*lṣpn/'zryhw*	Ramat Raḥel (1); Gibeon (1)	Pritchard 1959: 28, Fig. 10:4, Pl. 11:4; Aharoni 1962: 44
44	*lṣmḥ/'lšm'*	Ramat Raḥel (1)	Lipschits 2011a
45	*'ḥmlh/'mdyhw*	Umm Tuba (1)	http://www.antiquities.org.il/article_Item_ido.asp?sec_id=25andsubj_id=240andid=1495andmodule_id

Table 4.8: Distribution of "private" stamp impressions in Judahite sites: summary[i]

Area	Site	Number of Stamp Impressions	
Shephelah	Lachish	72	**Total from Shephelah: 125**
	Beth Shemesh	18	
	Tel Goded	12	
	Socoh/Khirbet 'Abbâd	7	
	Tell eṣ-Ṣafi/Gath	4	
	Azekah	4	
	Tel Burna	1	
	Tel Batash	1	
	Khirbet Qe'ilah	1	
	'Adullam	1	
	Tel 'Erani	1	
	Maresha	1	
	Tell Beit Mirsim	2	
	Ḥorvat Shovav	1	
Judean Hills and Benjamin region	Ramat Raḥel	19	**Total from Judean Hills and Benjamin region: 54**
	Jerusalem	13	
	Mordot Arnona	8	
	Gibeon	7	
	Mizpah	4	
	Umm Tuba	1	
	Tekoa	1	
	Khirbet Rabud (Debir)	1	
Other areas	Naḥal 'Arugot	1	**Total from beyond Judah's borders: 4**
	Arad	1	
	Gezer	2	
Total		**183**	

i   Vaughn included 261 stamped handles in his corpus of "private" stamp impressions (1999b: 198–218), but 24 of these are unidentified and 77 are of unknown origin. Most other stamp impressions in this corpus correspond to the ones gathered here, albeit with minor differences in several readings of impressions and a few new findings published in recent years. More than 250 handles were counted and 56 types defined in Grena's Internet corpus of "private" stamp impressions (http://www.lmlk.com/research/lmlk_pers.htm), but this includes many handles of unclear origin and context.

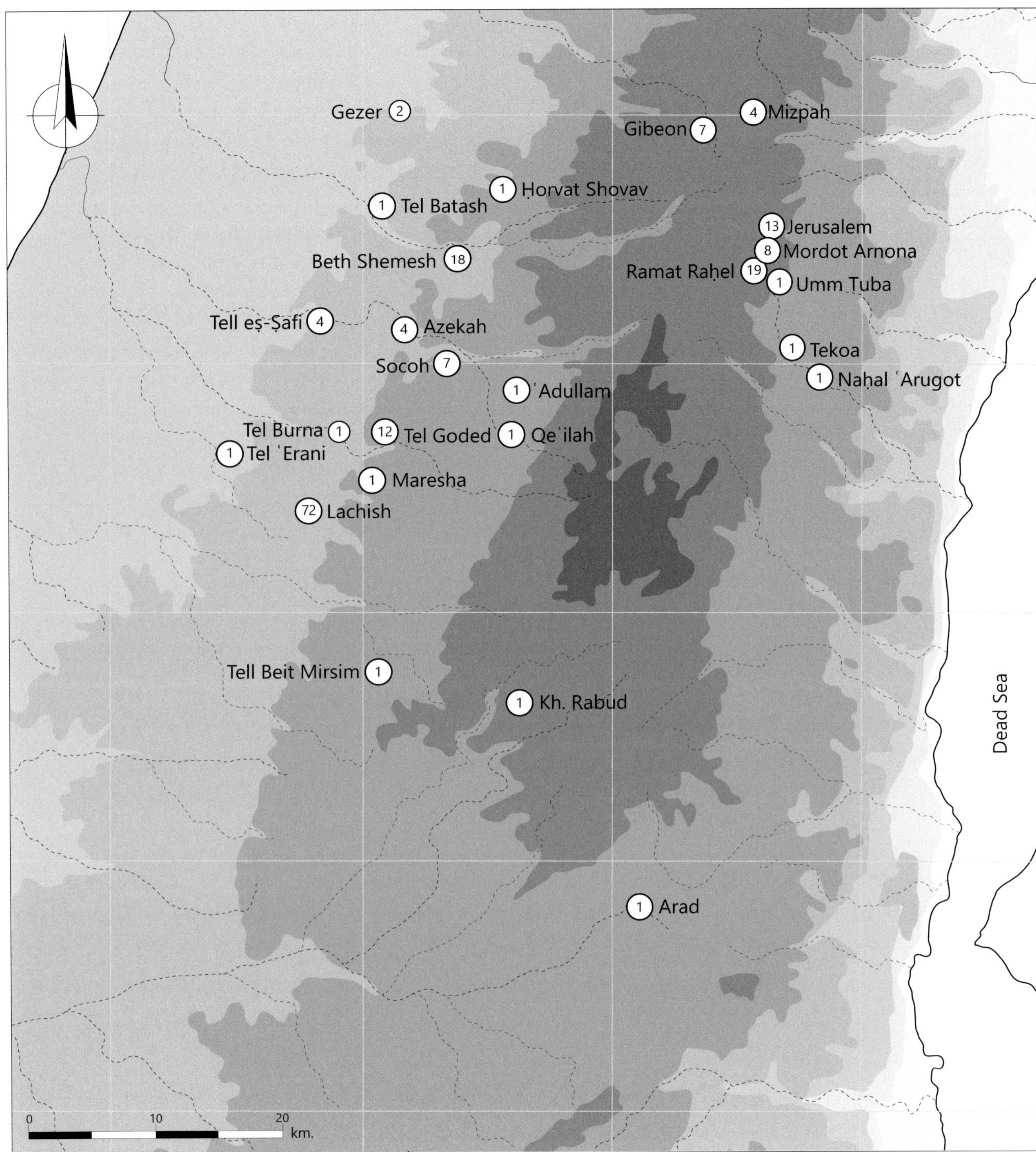

Fig. 4.10: Distribution of "private" stamp impressions in Judah

Concentric Circle Incisions

Rather than being stamped onto storage-jar handles, concentric circles were incised onto the handle around a central point sometime after the firing of the vessel, and in some cases, many years after the storage jar had already been in use (Fig. 4.11).[24] The series of concentric circle incisions are discussed here because, in approximately half the cases, they were engraved on the same handle as *lmlk* stamp impressions (e.g., Fig. 4.12). In the other cases, they were engraved on otherwise unmarked handles of the same type of storage jar. The incisions were apparently formed by two compass-like instruments, creating a constant diameter (see also Grena 2004: 95).

The incisions had to be carried out on a horizontal surface, and therefore they were always engraved on the upper part of the handle, presumably when the storage jar was standing upright. When the handle bore a *lmlk* stamp impression, the circles were incised next to it; when the *lmlk* impression was stamped high on the handle, the circular incision was at least partly engraved on top of the *lmlk* impression itself. This was a continuation of the storage-jar administrative system in Judah, as attested not only by the use of the same type of storage jar and by the appearance of so many circular incisions alongside *lmlk* stamp impressions on the same handles, but also by the limited distribution of the incised jar handles, which were found only within the Kingdom of Judah, in a very similar pattern to the series of late *lmlk* stamp impressions.

As for the typology of the concentric circle incisions, no specific types can be defined, because these were not stamped into the soft clay by different seals that can be identified with specific features, but were rather incised by the same or a similar tool. The differences between the incisions stem from the position where the central leg was placed on the handle, from the force applied while moving the lateral leg, from the number of turns executed, from the inclusions and other interferences in the clay, and from the location of the circles vis-à-vis the ridges along the upper part of the handle. The central hole is usually deeper than the circles, probably because it was used twice: first for the inner circle and then for

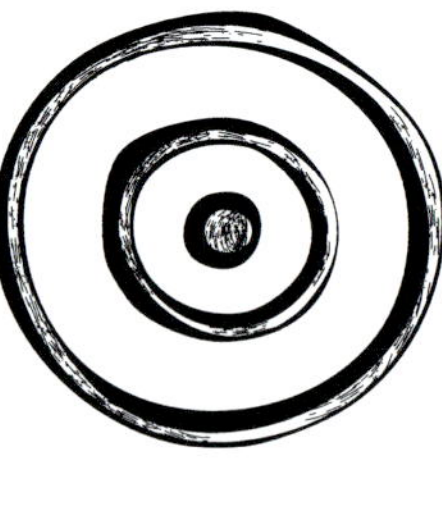

Fig. 4.11: Incision of concentric circles on a storage-jar handle from Ramat Raḥel (Sergi and Koch, forthcoming)

24. The possibility that these incisions were carried out only by skilled artisans (Ussishkin 2011: 223) is unlikely.

 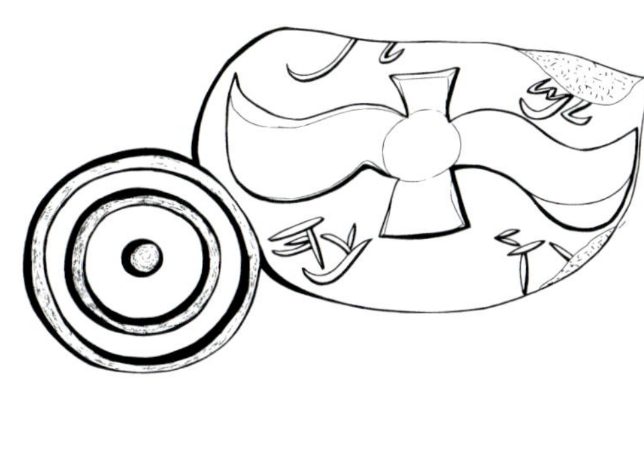

Fig. 4.12: A storage-jar handle bearing a concentric circle incision and a *lmlk* stamp impression, from Ramat Raḥel (Sergi 2016: 325, No. 103)

the outer one. The direction of movement does not appear to have been fixed and depended mainly on the location of the central hole, the inclination of the handle and the engraver's technical abilities in overcoming the ridges on the outer part of the handle. As a result of all these factors, the circles were generally not uniform in depth and the circle was sometimes left incomplete (mainly because of the differences in height between the ridges and the grooves). In rare cases (seven out of 278 incised handles), only one circle was incised, probably because the location of the central point made it difficult or impossible to incise a second one.

Since the first concentric circle incision was found in Warren's excavations south of the Temple Mount (Wilson and Warren 1871: 152), 305 handles of storage jars bearing such incisions have been uncovered in excavations and archaeological surveys, mainly within the Kingdom of Judah.[25] Of these, 140 concentric circle incisions (ca. 46% of all the finds) were engraved next to *lmlk* stamp impressions—generally (with only two exceptions) with

the two-winged sun disk (usually of the later types among the two-winged *lmlk* stamp impressions; see already Grena 2004: 95), and on three handles, they were incised next to "private" stamp impressions. In all the other 162 cases (ca. 53% of the finds), the incised handle did not bear any stamp impression (Shoham 2000b: 75–77; Avigad and Barkay 2000: 246–248; Stern 2007c: 139–141; and see discussion below).

The fact that these incisions appear on *lmlk* storage-jar handles and, moreover, next to *lmlk* stamp impressions, coupled with the fact that their distribution was limited to the Kingdom of Judah, indicates that these incisions served the royal administration of Judah. Since they were engraved on storage-jar handles after the firing of the vessel (and therefore after its impression with the *lmlk* seal, which was applied when the clay was still soft), this would mean that it cancelled, replaced, or adjusted the *lmlk* stamp-impression system with a new administrative system. The appearance of about a half of the concentric circle incisions by themselves on storage-jar handles with

---

25. This number does not include incised handles that did not originate in excavations or surveys and handles of unknown origin. Grena's Internet corpus contains 288 handles with concentric circle incisions (http://www.lmlk.com/research/lmlk_circ.htm), but despite the clear overlap in most cases between the corpus presented here and Grena's, in some cases the source of information is unclear and a few handles are of unknown provenance.

no *lmlk* stamp impressions suggests that this was an independent administrative system that initially coexisted with the *lmlk* stamp-impression system and later perhaps replaced it.

Of all the handles with concentric circle incisions, 287 (ca. 94%) were found in the environs of Jerusalem, between the Benjamin region in the north and Ramat Raḥel, the Rephaim Valley and Bethlehem in the south (Table 4.9; Fig. 4.13). In Jerusalem proper 162 incised handles were found (ca. 53%). Ramat Raḥel maintained its status as a secondary collection center with some 40 incised handles (ca. 13% of the finds). Of great importance is the fact that 75 incised handles (ca. 24.5%) were found in the Benjamin region to the north and west of Jerusalem (mainly in Gibeon, Mizpah, Khirbet el-Burj, Moẓa and Tell el-Fûl). Two additional handles were found at Beth-Zur and one at Hebron, both in the southern hill country; three were found at En-Gedi, one at Jericho and one at Arad. Although the number of incised handles found at Gezer and Tell Beit Mirsim is unknown, it is clear that this administrative system was concentrated in the hill country area, mainly around Jerusalem, and that it hardly even existed beyond this limited area.

This has already been noted by Ji in the only research to date that has focused on concentric circle incisions (Ji 2001). Noting that this system was located mainly in the hill country region, Ji deduced that it must have begun after Sennacherib's campaign and the serious blow it inflicted upon the Shephelah. He associated this system to the reign of Manasseh and suggested that the new king had replaced Hezekiah's two-winged sun disk with the symbol of the heavenly circle (Ji 2001: 13b–14a).

Table 4.9: Distribution of handles with concentric circle incisions

Area	Site	Number of Handles				Number of Circles		References
		Incisions next to *lmlk* stamp impression	Incisions next to "private" stamp impression	Incisions without stamp impression	Total	One	Two	
Jerusalem environs and Judean Hills	Jerusalem	82	3	77	162	5	157	See summary in Lipschits, Sergi and Koch 2011: 31–35[i]
	Ramat Raḥel	11		29	40	1	39	Aharoni 1956: 144, Pl. 25:3; 1962: 20, Pl. 7, 48, Pl. 30:1; 1964: 34, Pl. 39:5; Sergi and Koch, forthcoming
	Mordot Arnona[ii]			4	4	1	3	Neria Sapir: personal communication
	Rogem Gannim			4	4		4	Greenberg and Cinamon 2006: 232
	Bethlehem	1			1		1	Welten 1969: 190
	Kh. er-Ras			1	1		1	Barkay 1985: 408
	Beth-Zur	1		1	2		2	Sellers and Albright 1931: 7; Sellers 1933: 53, Fig. 44, upper left
	Hebron	1			1		1	Emmanuel Eisenberg: personal communication
Total from Jerusalem environs and Judean Hills		96	3	116	215	7	208	

Table 4.9 (continued)

Area	Site	Number of Handles				Number of Circles		References
		Incisions next to *lmlk* stamp impression	Incisions next to "private" stamp impression	Incisions without stamp impression	Total	One	Two	
Benjamin region	Gibeon	18		15	33		33?	Pritchard 1959: 20–21[iii]
	Mizpah	17			17	1	16	McCown 1947: 159, Pl. 56:1, 3
	Kh. el-Burj	1		14	15		15	Weinberger-Stern 2015: 155–158, Pl. 51
	Tell el-Fûl	2		2	4		4	Sinclair 1960: 32, Pl. 16b:1,4,6,8; Lapp 1981: 111
	Moẓa			5	5		5	De Groot and Greenhut 2002: 14
	Ras el-Harube			1	1		1	Barkay 1985: 408
Total from Benjamin region		38		37	75	1	74	
Shephelah	Lachish	2		2	4		4	Diringer 1941: 99; 1953: 343
	Tel Azekah			4	4		4	Bliss 1899c: Pl. 6:11–12; in the new excavations, two additional incised handles were discovered, not yet published
	Tel Goded	1			1		1	Bliss 1900a: Pl. 6:1
	Tell Beit Mirsim				?			Albright 1932b: 88, Fig. 15; number of incisions unknown
	Tel Batash			1	1		1	Mazar and Panitz-Cohen 2001
	Gezer				?			Macalister 1912: 210; number of incisions unknown
Total from the Shephelah		3		7	10		10	
Other areas	En-Gedi	1		2	3		3	Stern 2007c: 149
	Jericho	1			1		1	Bartlett 1982: 538–539
	Arad	1			1		1	Aharoni 1981b: 144
Total from other areas		3		2	5		5	
Total		140	3	162	305	8	297	

i Three incised handles were found in Warren and Wilson's excavations (Wilson and Warren 1871: 152, 474; Warren and Conder 1884: 156, 534; Sayce 1893: 30), one in Clermont-Ganneau's excavations (Clermont-Ganneau 1900; Barkay 1985: 440, No. B/9) and six in Macalister and Duncan's excavations (Macalister and Duncan 1926: 188, Fig. 202:1,13–14; 190, Fig. 204; Duncan 1931: plate opposite p. 141, Photo 180; Barkay 1985: 429). In total, 32 incisions were found in Kenyon's excavations (Barkay 1985: 441–444; Franken and Steiner 1990: 127–131), 19 incisions in Mazar's excavations of the Western Hill (Avigad and Barkay 2000: 247, 252, note only 18 incisions listed, contrary to the number in the text), 31 incisions in Shiloh's City of David excavations (Shoham 2000b) and 12 incisions in Mazar's Ophel excavations (Nadelman 1989: 131). According to Barkay (1985: 432–439), 15 handles were found in Broshi's excavations, 12 in Bahat and Broshi's excavations, one handle with an incision in Margalit, Lenn and Fixner's excavations and one handle with a concentric incision in Gibson's excavations. Seven handles were found in Fr. Godfrey's collection and four at Mount Zion. One stamp impression was found in the Mamila excavations (Amit 2009: Fig. 11D). Eleven incised handles were discovered in the Western Wall Plaza excavations, three with incisions alongside *lmlk* stamp impressions (S. Weksler-Bdolah and S. Kisilevitz: personal communication). Two additional handles with incisions next to *lmlk* stamp impressions were excavated by Szanton and Uziel in Area C of the eastern slope, above the Gihon Spring (not yet published), and three similar handles were found in Area U, east of the entrance to Warren's Shaft, excavated by Chalaf and Uziel (personal communication, not yet published).

ii One of the incised handles from Mordot Arnona was incised twice—with two concentric circles. The first, on the central part of the handle, includes a very rude incision of the inner circle, causing a peeling of the outer surface. The incision of the outer circle is very shallow and incomplete. Perhaps because of the problem with the central incision, another circle was incised on the very right edge of the handle, this time much more complete, with a deeper incision on the upper part. This circle is partly covered by white patina. On the basis of this handle we conclude that the outer circle was incised first, followed by the inner circle.

iii Pritchard referred to numerous handles or handle fragments with circular incisions, but presented only 15 examples in the excavation report.

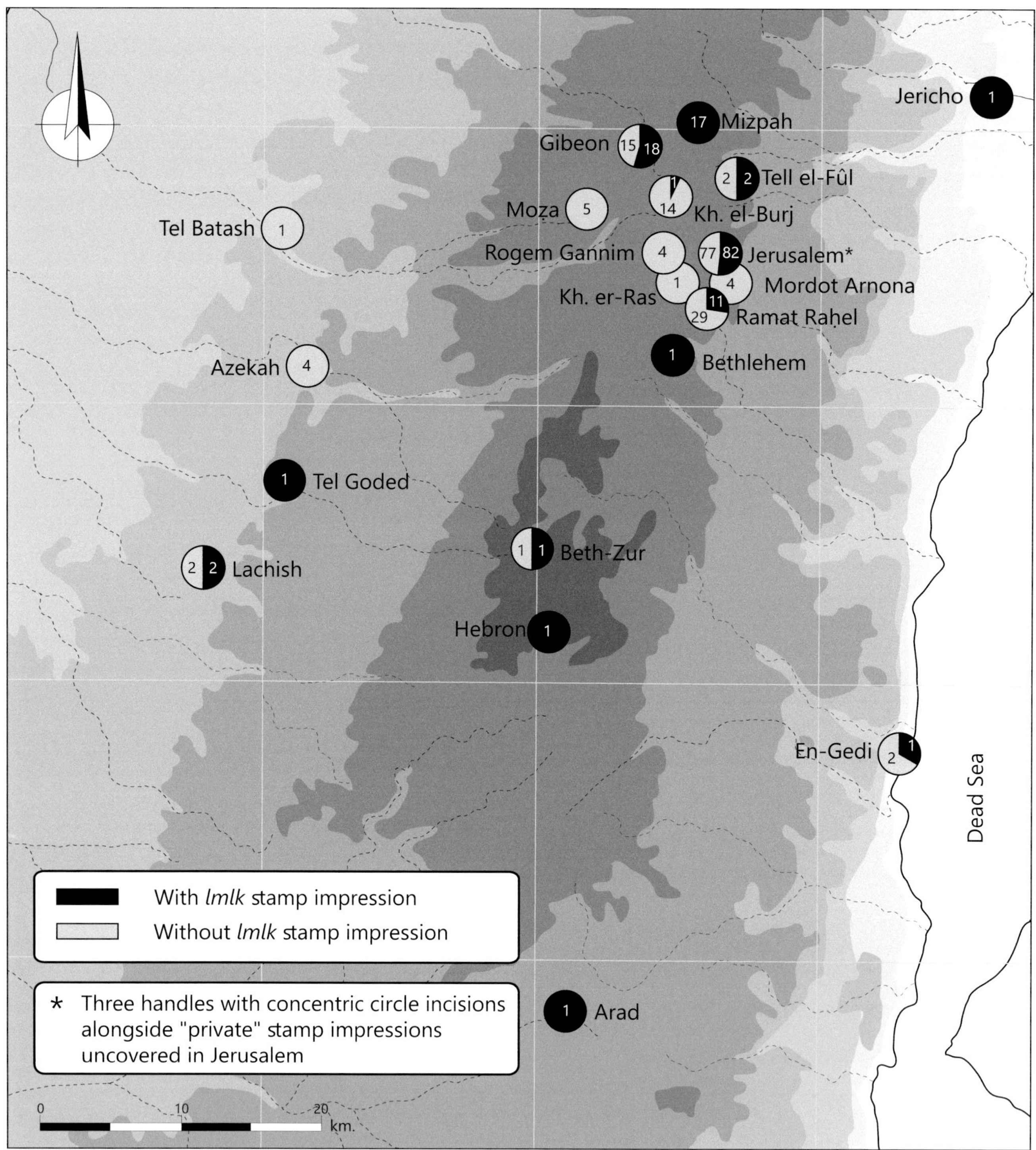

Fig. 4.13: Distribution of handles with concentric circle incisions

Rosette Stamp Impressions

Rosette-stamped handles are always rounded and bear a single rosette motif (Fig. 4.14). The storage jars on which rosette impressions were stamped differed slightly from the ones used for *lmlk* and "private" stamp impressions and for concentric circle incisions. The vessel used for rosette stamp impressions is slightly more elongated and with different body proportions. This type (Fig. 4.15) is characteristic of the settlement layers in Judah at the end of the First Temple period (Ussishkin 2004c: 110; Sergi *et al.* 2012: 83–85). Most of the handles with rosette stamp impressions were found in undated or mixed assemblages. In fact, Koch (2008) found that only 30 handles were uncovered in clear archaeological and stratigraphic contexts, usually in destruction layers from the early 6th century BCE.[26] The main conclusion from this is that the rosette stamp-impression system ceased to be used during the Babylonian destruction of Judah

(586 BCE), but it does not provide any indication as to when the system began to be used—at some point in the late seventh century BCE (see below, pp. 116–120).

As aforementioned, these stamp impressions are always rounded. In a few types, a frame was engraved along the edges. The size of the seal was uniform (13–18 mm in diameter, with few exceptions). Typically, most of the types and most of the impressions have eight or 12 petals (Koch 2008: 36; Koch and Lipschits 2010: 14–15), with only a few deviations (rosettes with 6, 7, 10, 11, 15, or 16 petals), which appear to be exceptional types.

In none of the rosette stamp impressions is there any writing or other addition to the motif. This symbol was adopted by the Judahite administrative system in the late 7th century BCE and is extremely rare among the seals of this period (Kletter 1995: 219–222; 1999: 36–37). Several scholars suggested that it originated as a royal symbol related to divinity, like the symbols selected for

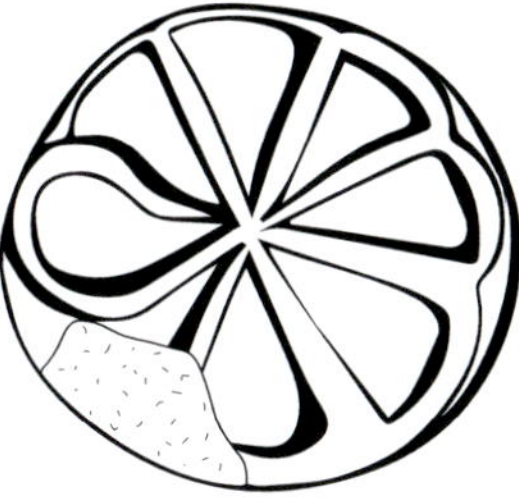

Fig. 4.14: A handle with a rosette stamp impression from Ramat Raḥel (Koch, forthcoming)

---

26. Koch (2008: 15) enumerated the following: seven handles from the City of David (Cahill 2000b: 96), six from Tel Batash (Cahill 2001: 197), at least three from Kenyon's City of David excavations (Steiner 2001: 127–130), two from Ramat Raḥel (Koch 2016), four from Tel ʿIra (Cahill 1999: 360), four from Lachish (Diringer 1953: 341), one from Tel Malḥata (Kochavi 1974: 23) and three from En-Gedi (Mazar, Dothan and Dunayevsky 1966: 33).

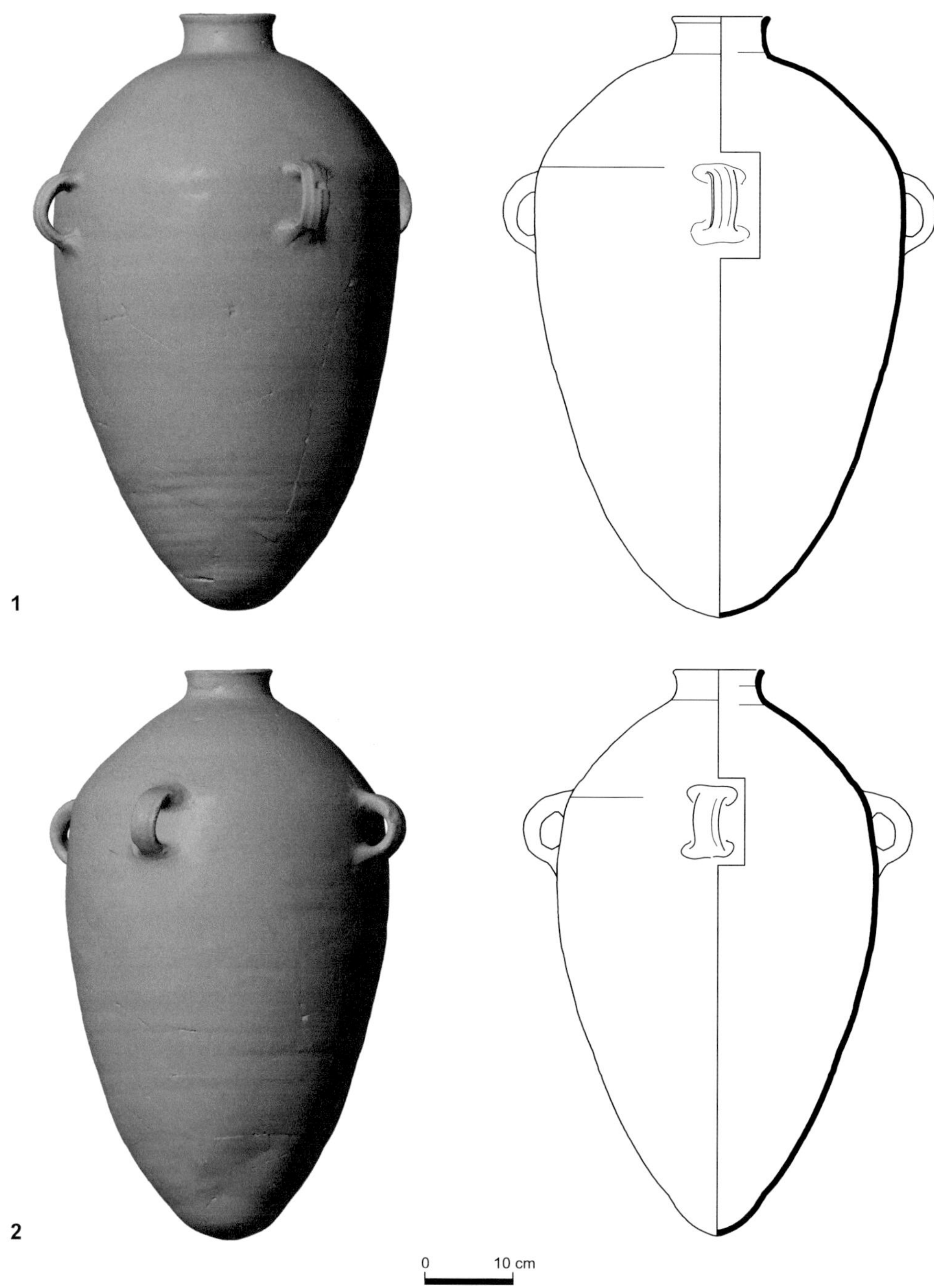

Fig. 4.15: Two rosette-stamped storage jars of types typical of Judah at the end of the First Temple period (Sergi *et al.* 2012: 78, Fig. 9)

use in the earlier *lmlk* stamp-impression system.[27] Others, however, contended that the rosette emblem was used by private individuals operating under the aegis of the royal household.[28] The choice of the rosette emblem to be used in the Judahite storage-jar administration at the end of the First Temple period stemmed from two main developments characterizing Judah at that time (see, in detail, Koch 2008: 65–67): on the one hand, the Assyrian tendency towards aniconism in the first millennium BCE had a strong impact on its vassal kingdoms in the 7th century BCE, and on the other hand, some vassal kingdoms tended to imitate Assyrian artistic motifs.[29] The choice of the rosette to mark royal storage jars may have been part of an effort to "erase" iconographic symbols and to replace the previous divinity symbol, the winged sun disk, with a geometric motif with no overtly "idolatrous" significance. It was related to the vegetal symbolism prevalent in Judah during the 7th century BCE, especially its second half (Uehlinger 1993: 225; Keel and Uehlinger 1998: 360). Nonetheless, the ruling elite of the Assyrian vassal kingdoms, including Judah, adopted Assyrian artistic motifs: the Assyrian government officials in the various provinces naturally adopted the imperial imagery, and the vassal kings followed suit (Postgate 1992: 257–260; Mazzoni 2000:

49–53). Judah was no different: the winged sun-disk emblem was adopted by the Judahite royal family as a result of Assyrian influence,[30] and indeed, the choice of the rosette symbol, not widespread in Judah, rather than a more prevalent vegetal motif (such as the lily symbol), should be viewed as an adoption of Assyrian cultural motifs and symbols. We do not, however, know the full significance of this motif as a royal symbol: was it related to divinity or devoid of any divine significance? Moreover, like other motifs throughout the ancient Near East, it is possible that the interpretation of the rosette motif in Judah diverged from its original meaning. The question of its meaning must therefore remain unresolved (on this, see Koch 2008: 21–52).

Initial efforts to establish a typology were based on the number of petals.[31] Barkay (1985: 446) extended the typological framework to include stylistic remarks, such as the "frame of pearls" circumscribing the rosette. The first comprehensive attempt to establish a typology of rosette stamp impressions was carried out by Cahill (1995: 233–241), who defined 29 types (= seals) on the basis of a wide variety of features, including: diameter of the rosette; number of petals; petal length; petal width; diameter of the central point; and diameter of the stamp impression. Her typology consists of five

---

27. Albright, in an editor's note to Mendelson's article (1940), interpreted the rosette as a royal symbol, associating it with the winged-rosette emblem on the seals of Hittite kings. Cahill concurred, considering the rosette symbol to be an expression of an affinity between the king and the head of the kingdom's pantheon and thus accounting for its distribution among the peoples of the ancient Near East. She argued that after Assyria had gained control over the southern Levant, and following the destruction of the Kingdom of Israel, the Judahite kings adopted the rosette as a royal symbol. See Cahill 1995: 250–251; 1997: 68.

28. Kletter (1995: 219–222, 225; 1999: 36–37) argued that the evidence from Judah makes it unlikely that the rosette was a royal symbol, since there is no clear connection in Judah between the rosette emblem and the kingdom, and this symbol hardly appeared among the contemporary stamp impressions and certainly did not enjoy widespread distribution like the symbol chosen for the *lmlk* stamp impressions. He argued that the use of numerous seals indicates that there must have been several private workshops and not a central one, as in the case of the *lmlk* stamp impressions. However, as Cahill and others have already argued, the monarchy was strongly associated with the rosette symbol as early as the second millennium BCE, and this association grew ever stronger in the days of the Neo-Assyrian empire in general, and during the dynasty of Sargon II in particular. Furthermore, Kletter's argument in favor of a "private" use of this system now seems untenable, as most of the rosette-stamped storage jars, like the other stamped vessels, were manufactured at a single center in the Shephelah (perhaps Socoh?). The variety of types appears to have been part of the system's regular functioning: it produced new storage jars to replace the ones that had been broken, delivered or sold, and this does not necessarily indicate "private" uses of the system itself. On this, see Koch 2008: 65–67.

29. Ornan 2004: 115. Evidence from the late 7th century BCE points to the "stripping" of iconographic symbols from the Judahite glyptic and to a preference for vegetal symbols. While it is true that even earlier, Judahite seals had fewer decorative elements than parallels from neighboring kingdoms, epigraphy was preferred over iconography in the seventh century BCE. Notable in their absence are previously prevalent symbols, such as the scarab or the seraph; see Sass 1993: 213, 214; Avigad and Sass 1997: 46.

30. Ornan 2005: 233–234; see also the above discussion of the *lmlk* emblems. According to Ornan, this divine symbol, known throughout the ancient Near East, was adopted for Judahite administrative use only after the consolidation of Assyrian rule in the Southern Levant.

31. E.g., Aharoni's typology (1955: 169; 1962: 48; 1964: 35, 63), which was also adopted by Mazar (Mazar, Dothan and Dunayevsky 1963: 48; 1966: 33).

Fig. 4.16: Examples of the main types of rosette stamp impressions (Koch 2016: 376, No. 3, 380, No. 20, 384, No. 32)

main types, each divided into sub-types.[32] Koch presented an updated typological analysis, based on Cahill's typology but noting several problems in her classification (Koch 2008: 18–19). He identified four main types, divided into 24 sub-types,[33] which were stamped with 28 seals.[34]

In Type I, the rosette is stamped very lightly and its petals consist of two elements: an inner core—the body of the petal—and an outer contour. The petals are drop-shaped, with slanted edges, and pointed, while the outer lines are broad ridges surrounding the core.[35] Type II is also stamped very lightly, but with a notable difference: the petals lack an outer frame. They are drop-shaped with slanting edges and sharp points. Type III rosettes are lightly stamped, but the petals appear broader and fleshier (Cahill terms them "crude"): the petals are short, do not reach the central point, and they vary in form. Type IV, also lightly stamped, has a schematic form of long narrow petals, reaching the central point.

This revised typology of Koch (2008) offers an understanding of the way the rosette stamp-impression system functioned: a third of the stamp impressions belong to one of the three main sub-types—IA8, IIA8 and IIIA12 (Fig. 4.16)—which have the broadest distribution, reaching diverse regions within the Kingdom

---

32. Cahill used her typology in numerous publications of rosette-stamp impressions and in the analysis of these impressions. See Cahill 1999; 2000a; 2000b; 2001; 2003; see also Fox 2000: 236–237.

33. Cahill's Types IIC and IID, for which there is no stratigraphic information and whose shape does not resemble any of the other rosette types (such as Type V, which is dated to the Persian period), were removed by Koch from the rosette typology (2008: 27–29, 32–33).

34. Koch 2008: 20–36. Each of the four sub-types (IA12, IB12, IIA12 and IIC8) was stamped with two seals (Koch 2008: 31–32). There are many possible reasons for the existence of multiple seals for a single type: a seal might have been created to replace its lost or damaged counterpart, or perhaps similar seals were created in advance for one or two officials. It is also possible that similar seals were created by accident. At any rate, the close similarity between the seals indicates that the general message and symbol was of importance, rather than the shape.

35. This is Cahill's Type A (1995: 231).

of Judah.[36] The other types with widespread distribution may have "revolved" around the main types and served as a kind of secondary system. Although an internal chronology among the various types cannot be determined, it may be assumed, on the basis of this typology, that this sophisticated administrative system operated over a long period. Furthermore, the large number of seals in use—greater than the number of seals used for the *lmlk* system—is an indication of the complexity of the system (Koch and Lipschits 2010: 16).

The first nine handles with rosette stamp impressions were discovered in the Tel Azekah excavations in 1898–1899 (Bliss and Macalister 1902: Pl. 56:35z–43z), and to date, some 290 such handles have been unearthed in archaeological excavations and surveys (Table 4.10; Fig. 4.17).[37] The clear majority of the stamped handles (197, ca. 68%) were found in the hill country, with 108 (ca. 37% of the finds) discovered in Jerusalem itself and 57 (19.5% of the finds) in Ramat Raḥel. No other hill country site produced a significant number of handles with rosette stamp impressions. In the Shephelah, 71 rosette-stamped handles (24.5% of the finds) were found, with Azekah,

where 30 stamped handles were found (ca. 10.5% of all the finds and 42% of the finds in the Shephelah), as the main rosette center in the region. Lachish regained its position as a significant center in the stamp impression system, with 24 stamped handles (ca. 8% of all the finds and 34% of the finds in the Shephelah). For the first time, a significant number of stamped handles appeared in En-Gedi (11, ca. 4% of the finds), demonstrating its affiliation with the Judahite administrative system, perhaps as a royal estate (Lipschits 2000; see also Katz 2008: 250–251).

When compared to the distribution of handles with *lmlk* or "private" stamp impressions or incised with concentric circles, the distribution of the handles bearing rosette stamp impressions points to major changes that took place in the storage-jar administrative system in Judah. An understanding of these changes is crucial to an understanding of the history of the Kingdom of Judah between the late 8th and the early 6th century BCE, its administrative system, the fate of the various regions within the kingdom, and the role played by its main administrative centers (see below).

Table 4.10: Distribution of rosette stamp impressions (continued on p. 66)[i]

Area	Site	Number of Handles	References
Jerusalem and its environs	Jerusalem	108	Koch 2008: 6–7[ii]
	Ramat Raḥel	57	Aharoni 1955: 168–169; 1956: 147; 1962: 21, Figs. 15:9–11, 48, Pl. 30:5–6; 1964: 35, 63 and Pl. 41:1–12; Koch 2016; forthcoming
	Rogem Gannim	3	Greenberg and Cinamon 2006: 232
	Jason's Tomb	1	Rahmani 1969
	Tomb in Reḥov Shmuel ha-Navi	1	Cahill 2000b: 104
	Khirbet er-Ras	1	Cahill 2000a: 54–55, Photo 12.5
	Manaḥat	1	Edelstein, Milevski and Aurant 1999: 54–56, Photo 4.11.23
Total from Jerusalem and its environs		172	

---

36. These three sub-types appear in Jerusalem and Ramat Raḥel, and each appears in one of the central Shephelah sites (IA8 and IIIA12 in Tel Azekah; IIA8 in Lachish) and in one of the Negev sites (IA8 in Arad; IIA8 in Tel ʿIra; IIIA12 in Tel Malḥata). See Koch 2008: 34.

37. In recent years the corpus of rosette stamp impressions has grown, but most recent discoveries have not yet been published. The number of stamp impressions is therefore an estimate. Cahill (1995: 230) defined a corpus of some 250 rosette stamp impressions, but she included types that do not belong to the late Iron Age rosette stamp-impression system. The most updated corpus, which includes 244 stamp impressions, was assembled by Koch (2008) and summarized by Koch and Lipschits (2010: 11–13).

Table 4.10 (continued)

Area	Site	Number of Handles	References
Benjamin	Tell el-Fûl	4	Albright 1933: 10; Sinclair 1960: 32–33, Pl. 16B:7,9; Lapp 1981: 112, Pls. 28:5, 29:4
	Khirbet al-Burj	4	Weinberger-Stern 2015: 158–160, Pl. 52
	Moẓa	4	De Groot and Greenhut 2002: 17; Greenhut 2006: 247–248[iii]
	Nebi Samwil	3	Magen and Dadon 1999: 64[iv]
	Gibeon	2	Pritchard 1961: 20, Fig. 46:77,109
	Mizpah	2	Zorn 1994: 81
Total from Benjamin		19	
Northern Judean Hills	Beth-Ẕur	5	Sellers 1933: 52, 53, Photo 44
	Nebi Daniel	1	Ofer 1993: 95
Total from the Judean Hills		6	
Shephelah	Lachish	24	Diringer 1953: 344, Pl. 53:1–4; Aharoni 1975b: 107; Ussishkin 2004b: 2138, Nos. 92–93
	Tel Azekah	30	Bliss and Macalister 1902: Pl. 56:35z–43z; 21 rosette stamp impressions were discovered in the new excavations at the site, not yet published
	Socoh	5	Ofer 1993: 93–95; Lipschits and Amit 2011: 183; Tsur 2015
	Tel Burna	1	Cahill 2000b: 104
	Tel 'Erani	1	Cahill 2000b: 104
	Ramat Beth Shemesh (Site 15-12/02/5)	1	Milevski 2005: 19–20; Dagan 1992: 127
	Tel Batash	6	Cahill 2001: 197
	Beth Shemesh	1	Boaz Gross: personal communication
	Tell eṣ-Ṣafi	1	Boaz, Maeir and Schneider 1998
	Gezer	1	Macalister 1912: 211, Fig. 361:5
Total from the Shephelah		71	
Eastern fringe	En-Gedi	11	Mazar, Dothan and Dunayevsky 1963: 48; 1966: 33, Pl. XIX:1–6; Stern 2007c: 143, 145, Pl. 4.7.2.1
	Vered Yeriḥo	1	Stern 2007c: 144
Total from the eastern fringe		12	
Beersheba–Arad Valleys	Tel 'Ira	4	Cahill 1999: 360
	Arad	3	Cahill 2000b: 104
	Tel Malḥata	3	Kochavi 1970: 23
Total from the Negev		10	
Total		**290**	

i   To the stamp impressions found in the Kingdom of Judah or near its border, the ones found in Beth Shean should be added. For their publication, see Koch and Lipschits 2010: 26.

ii The corpus of rosette stamp impressions includes 58 stamped handles from the City of David: 37 were reported by Cahill (2000b: 85), three more were excavated by Szanton and Uziel in Area C of the eastern slope, above the Gihon Spring (not yet published) and 18 (14 on complete rosette jars) were found in Area U, east of the entrance to Warren's Shaft, excavated by Chalaf and Uziel (personal communication, not yet published). Ten additional rosette stamp impressions were found in the Ophel (Macalister and Duncan 1926: 188, Fig. 202:6,7; 189; 190, Figs. 204, 205; Nadelman 1989: 132–134, 140, Photos 170–172), and six were excavated in the Western Hill (Cahill 2003). For additional handles found in various excavations throughout the city, see Lux 1972: 191 (Lutheran Church of the Redeemer); Tushingham 1985: 23, 297–298, 361, Fig. 9:23,40–42,46 (Armenian Garden); Barkay 1985: 438 (House of Caiaphas); Cahill 2000b: 90 (Armenian Garden and western city wall; Mamila). In addition, Barkay (1985: 431, 441–444) counted 14 rosette-stamped handles found in Kenyon's excavations, now housed in the British School of Archaeology in Jerusalem. A few appear in Steiner 2001, but with insufficient detail.

iii Greenberg and Cinamon (2006: 235) report five handles with rosette stamp impressions found in Moẓa, but in his Ph.D. dissertation (2006), Greenhut reports only four.

iv Rosette stamp impressions from this site were not fully published, and the information was taken from a photo published by Magen and Dadon.

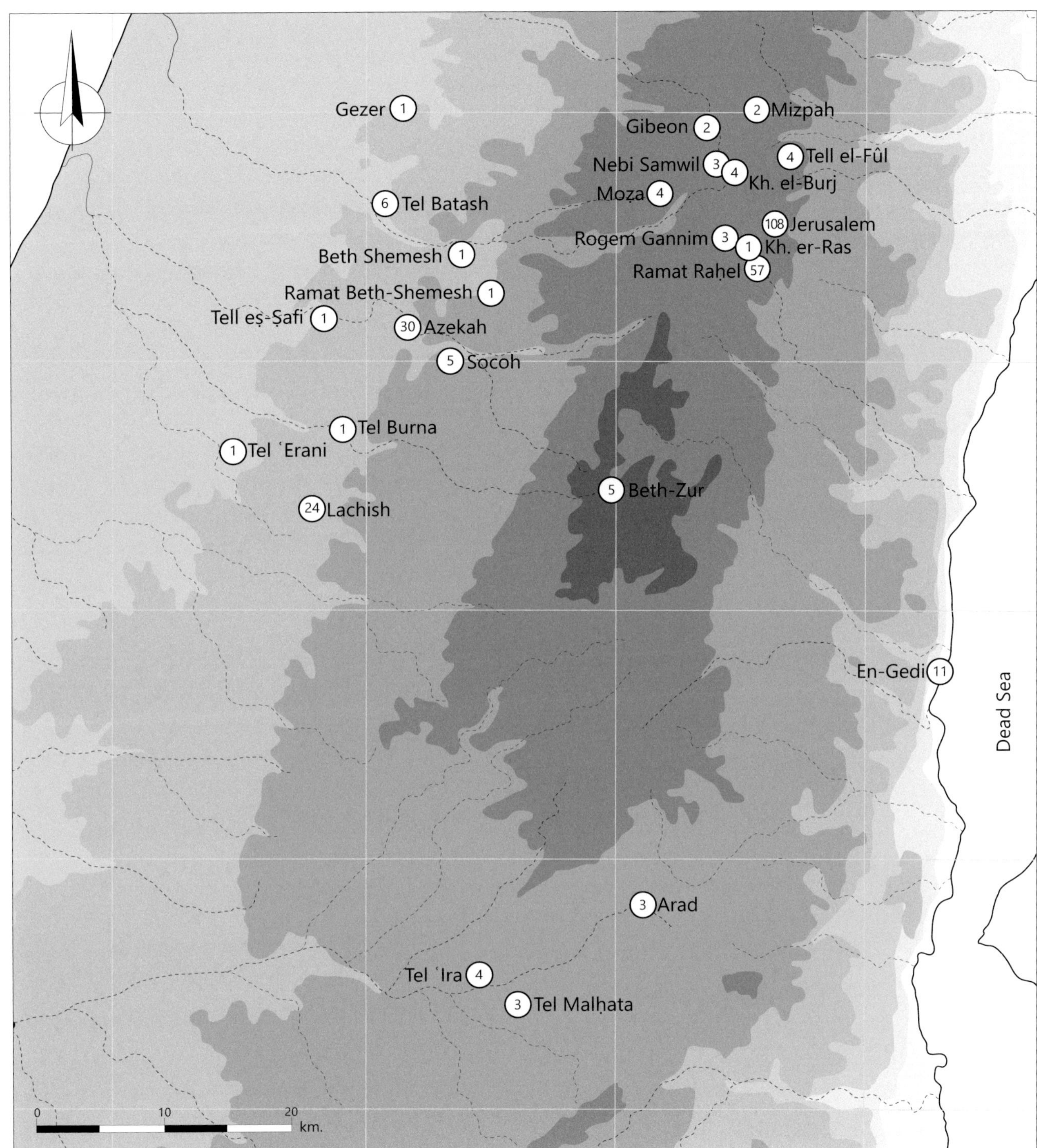

Fig. 4.17: Distribution of rosette stamp impressions

Lion Stamp Impressions

The storage jars bearing lion stamp impressions on their handles or sides (Fig. 4.18) are very similar in shape to the rosette-stamped storage jars, but their clay and firing are of lower quality. In some cases, their handles have two ridges and are made of reddish-brown clay, reminiscent of late Iron Age storage-jar handles. Some handles have one ridge and are made of a yellowish clay that bears a resemblance to Persian period storage-jar handles with *yhwd* stamp impressions. These storage jars, with or without lion stamp impressions, were not uncovered in any destruction layer from the end of the First Temple period. Even at Ramat Raḥel, where most of the handles with lion stamp impressions were discovered, not a single handle was found in fills used as courtyard and building foundations from the first and second construction phases. On the other hand, 11 handles with lion stamp impressions were uncovered in the renewed excavations, in the fill covering the foundation trenches and the garden in the western part of the site. These findings demonstrate that the lion stamp impression system began after the second building phase at Ramat Raḥel, i.e., not before the early 6th century BCE.[38] The dating of the lion stamp impression system to the period following the rosette stamp impressions of the late 7th–early 6th century BCE and preceding the *yhwd* stamp impressions that began in the late 6th century BCE is further bolstered by petrographic analysis of the storage jars (Gross and Goren 2010), by paleo-magnetic research (Millman 2014; Ben-Yosef *et al.* 2017) and by the study of the lion symbol (Sass 2010; Ornan 2010; Lipschits 2011f: 62–63). All this evidence suggests—contrary to the view that was prevalent for a long time that the lion

Fig. 4.18: A handle with a lion stamp impression from Ramat Raḥel (Bocher, forthcoming)

---

38. See Gadot 2010. Aharoni (1962: 34) already discussed this phenomenon.

stamp impressions should be dated to the late 6th–early 5th century BCE and that they constitute evidence for the first phase of Persian rule in Judah[39]—that they in fact began earlier within the 6th century and provide evidence for the Babylonian rule in the province of Judah (Lipschits 2011f: 68–71; Lipschits and Ornan 2010; Ornan and Lipschits, forthcoming [b]). This dating has far-reaching implications for the reconstruction of the history of Judah following the destruction of the First Temple (see below).

Lion stamp impressions on storage-jar handles have been known for over 100 years, since the discovery of the first one in Jericho (Sellin and Watzinger 1913: 159, Pl. 42n). Most lion stamp impressions discovered in Judah are simple; the seals appear to be of low quality, as is the carving of the image of the lion. The lion is depicted in profile, standing, crouching, or pacing to the right or left. Most of the seals are round or slightly elliptic; one type is square with rounded corners and another is somewhat rectangular. The latter is of exceptional quality and artistic level. It depicts a lion turning to the left while standing on its two hind legs and raising its two front legs to the sides (Fig. 4.19). Beneath its front left leg there are two objects, which were generally interpreted as an incense altar, but have now been identified as the profile of a human head and an adjacent palm of a human hand (Sass 2010: 14).

Until the early 1970s, lion stamp impressions were not studied as an independent phenomenon. Stern was the first to compile a comprehensive corpus based on all the evidence available in the late 1960s, discussing the typology, distribution, origin, stratigraphy and chronology of these stamp impressions, as well as their symbolic significance (Stern 1971a; 1971b; 1982: 210–212). Stern's corpus consisted of 66 lion stamp impressions, 45 of which (ca. 68% of all the finds) were found in the Ramat Raḥel excavations. Six additional stamp impressions from his corpus were found in Jerusalem, five in Tell en-Naṣbeh, five in En-Gedi, two in Gibeon and one each in Jericho, Moẓa and Shechem. On the basis of their distribution, Stern identified the clear Judahite nature of the lion stamp impressions: only one of the 66 stamp impressions was found beyond the borders of Judah.

Fig. 4.19: A stamp impression showing a lion standing on its hind legs on a handle found at Nebi Samwil (Type 8; Magen and Har-Even 2007: 54, No. 31)

---

39. See Stern 1982: 210–213; 2001: 541. Cf. Ariel and Shoham 2000: 141; but see already Williamson's arguments (1988: 60–64).

Today, with the publication of most of the excavations conducted since the 1960s until recent years, some 136 handles with lion stamp impressions have come to light. Of these, 73 are from Ramat Raḥel (ca. 53.5% of all the finds),[40] 31 from the City of David (ca. 23%),[41] 13 from Nebi Samwil (ca. 9.5%), five from En-Gedi,[42] five from Tell en-Naṣbeh,[43] three from Rogem Gannim,[44] two from Gibeon,[45] two from Khirbet er-Ras[46] and one each from Jericho (Sellin and Watzinger 1913: 159, Pl. 42n), Moẓa (Stern 1971b: 8 and n. 15) and Shechem (Campbell and Wright 2002: 25, Fig. 14).

This distribution shows that like the Beersheba–Arad Valleys and the southern hill country, the Shephelah is not represented at all, with the vast majority of lion stamp impressions uncovered in central hill country sites and only a few in sites far north of the borders of the province of Judah. Ramat Raḥel is the undisputed center of this system with over half the finds. This is an unprecedented concentration of stamped handles in one place, in comparison to any other historical period in which handles were stamped. To this one should add the fact that 117 of the 136 lion stamp impressions (ca. 86% of all the finds) were uncovered in only three sites—Ramat Raḥel, the City of David and Nebi Samwil. The seven lion-stamped handles discovered in Mizpah and Gibeon bring this number to 124 (ca. 91%). In all the other sites beyond this small circle around Jerusalem, the number of stamp impressions uncovered is insignificant; moreover, none of them offered more than a single stamp impression of any one type. One may deduce, therefore, that Ramat Raḥel was the main or only collection center in the system of lion stamp impressions, with Jerusalem and Nebi Samwil as secondary administrative centers where stamped jars were shipped from time to time.

All the sites in which lion stamp impressions were discovered were settled at the end of the Iron Age, and rosette stamp impressions were found in them as well. Not all continued to exist in the Persian period. The Benjamin region in particular shows a large decline in this period, with hardly any *yhwd* stamp impressions uncovered there (Lipschits and Vanderhooft 2011: 57). This further strengthens the connection of the system of the lion stamp impressions to the late Iron Age and highlights the changes that took place between the lion stamp-impression system of the 6th century BCE under imperial Babylonian rule and the *yhwd* stamp-impression system, which began at the end of this century, when Judah came under imperial Persian rule. In addition, a comparison of the distribution of lion stamp impressions to that of the earlier rosette stamp impressions points to a major decline in the status of Jerusalem (ca. 37% of the rosette stamp impressions were uncovered there, compared to only ca. 23% of the lion stamp impressions) and to a significant rise in the status of Ramat Raḥel (ca. 20% of the rosette stamp impressions, compared to ca. 54% of the lion stamp impressions). A comparison of the distribution of the lion stamp impressions to the early types of the subsequent *yhwd* stamp impressions shows a continuation of the same trend: about 77% of the early *yhwd* stamp impressions were discovered in Ramat Raḥel, whereas Jerusalem further declined in importance (ca. 10.5% of the corpus). Nebi Samwil, Jericho and En-Gedi also continued to be part of this system, but with only two or three stamp impressions uncovered in each site.

Stern (1971b: 9–10) defined three main types of lion stamp impressions: the first includes a lion walking to

---

40. Lipschits 2010: 17. Aharoni documented 45 handles found with lion stamp impressions, but published only 14 in full. When his Ramat Raḥel excavations were being published, an additional 11 handles were noted in his lists, bringing the total to 56 (Lipschits and Koch 2016). To this one should add 14 handles found in the renewed Ramat Raḥel excavations (Lipschits, forthcoming), bringing the current number of handles with lion stamp impressions to 70.

41. Duncan (1931: 142) reported six handles with lion stamp impressions; Ariel and Shoham (2000: 141) reported an additional 23 handles.

42. For the lion-stamped handles from En-Gedi, see Stern 2007b: 253, Photo 5.6.3.1.

43. See McCown 1947: 154, Fig. 35:2,3,4,5. Note that McCown's Nos. 1 and 6–7 are not lion stamp impressions, as opposed to Stern's classification (1971b: 7).

44. Barkay found the first lion-stamped handle from Rogem Gannim (1985: 387), and two additional ones were found in Greenberg and Cinamon's excavations (2006: 234, Fig. 3, D1, D2).

45. Two handles with lion stamp impressions were found in the Gibeon water pool; see Pritchard 1961: 20, Fig. 46:533,556.

46. Yuval Gadot: personal communication.

the right or to the left in various positions; the second is a lion standing on its hind legs, with the forepaws outstretched to the sides, with an object—that he interpreted as an altar—nearby; the third type depicts a bull's head with a solar orb between its horns.[47]

The new corpus of lion stamp impressions made it possible, for the first time, to identify the main features of the lion stamp impressions and to define the various types. Although the study of these stamp impressions is still ongoing, this detailed typology makes it possible not only to define the characteristics of the distribution of each type, but also to identify the main sites where they occur. Eight main types, with two notable sub-types, are identified (Fig. 4.20). This means that ten seals with a lion motif were used (Lipschits 2010; Ornan and Lipschits, forthcoming [b]):

1.   Lion bending forward (13 known stamp impressions);

2.   Lion and solar disc (10 known stamp impressions);

3a. Lion striding to the left (13 known stamp impressions);

3b. Lion striding to the left (seven known stamp impressions);

4.   Schematic lion facing left (nine known stamp impressions);

5a. Schematic lion facing right (15 known stamp impressions);

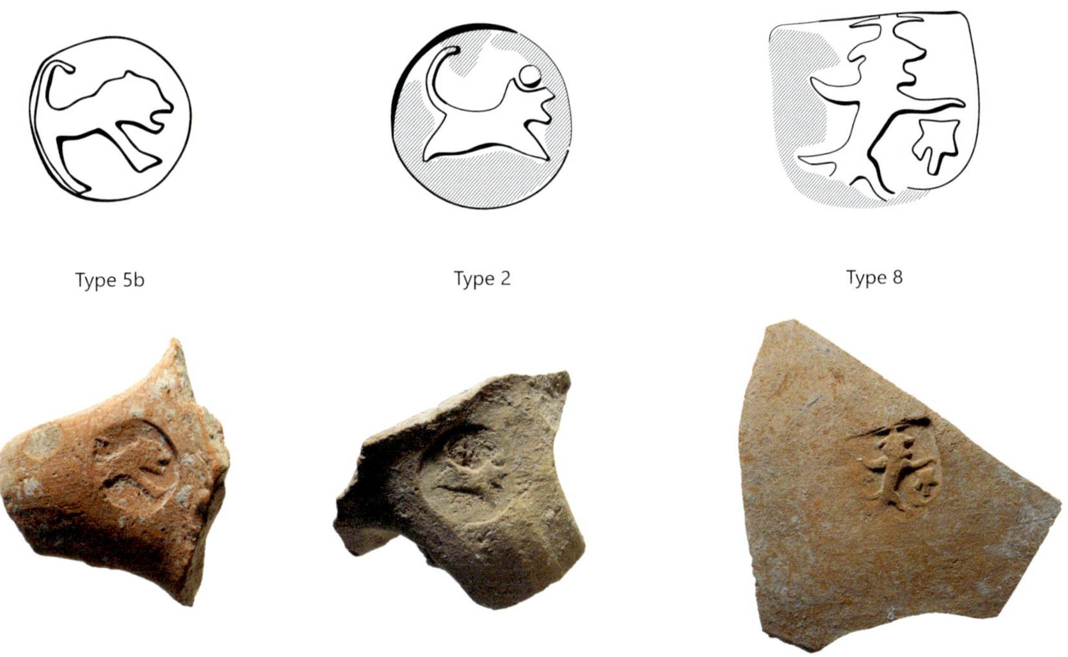

Fig. 4.20: Various types of lion stamp impressions from Ramat Raḥel (Lipschits and Koch 2016: 390, No. 1; 397, No. 20; 404, No. 42)

---

47. This definition follows Aharoni 1962: 10, 34.

Table 4.11: Distribution of lion stamp impressions according to type

Type		Ramat Raḥel	Jerusalem	Nebi Samwil	Tell en-Naṣbeh (Mizpah)	En-Gedi	Rogem Gannim	Gibeon	Khirbet er-Ras	Jericho	Shechem	Other sites	Total
1	Lion bending forward	12					1						13
2	Lion and solar disk	10											10
3a	Lion striding to left	11	2										13
3b	Lion striding to left	6				1							7
4	Schematic lion facing left	5	1		1	1		1					9
5a	Schematic lion facing right	5	3	7									15
5b	Schematic lion facing right	10	9	3					1	1	1		25
6	Lion striding to right	1		1		1	1						4
7	Lion bending forward— square stamp impression	5	4			1							10
8	Standing lion	5	1	1					1	1			9
	Unidentified	3	11	1	4	1	1						21
Total		73	31	13	5	5	2	2	2	1	1	1	136

5b. Schematic lion facing right (25 known stamp impressions);

6. Lion striding to the right (four known stamp impressions);

7. Lion bending forward—notable for its square shape (10 known stamp impressions);

8. Standing lion (nine known stamp impressions).

Table 4.11 shows the distribution of the various types according to site (Fig. 4.21), in cases where identification was possible.

All the types are represented at Ramat Raḥel, in most cases by a large number of items. Jerusalem is represented only in six of the ten sub-types, and only in one (Type 5b) does it have a clear majority (with nine of the 25 stamp impressions of this type). Only four sub-types were found at Nebi Samwil, and only in one (Type 5a) does it have a clear majority (with seven of the 15 stamp impressions of this type). Both these types were found in relatively large quantities, and a significant number of these stamp impressions were also found at Ramat Raḥel (five Type 5a stamp impressions and ten of Type 5b). On these grounds and given the large number of lion stamp impressions in general found at Ramat Raḥel, we postulate that this was the main collection center of lion-stamped storage jars, which functioned along with small production centers, such as Rogem Gannim and Khirbet er-Ras, and secondary administrative centers, such as Nebi Samwil, Tell en-Naṣbeh and En-Gedi. In my opinion, we cannot determine the status of Jerusalem in this period. We do not know whether the types uncovered there are early or late within the 6th century BCE, and we have not been able to relate this finding to other

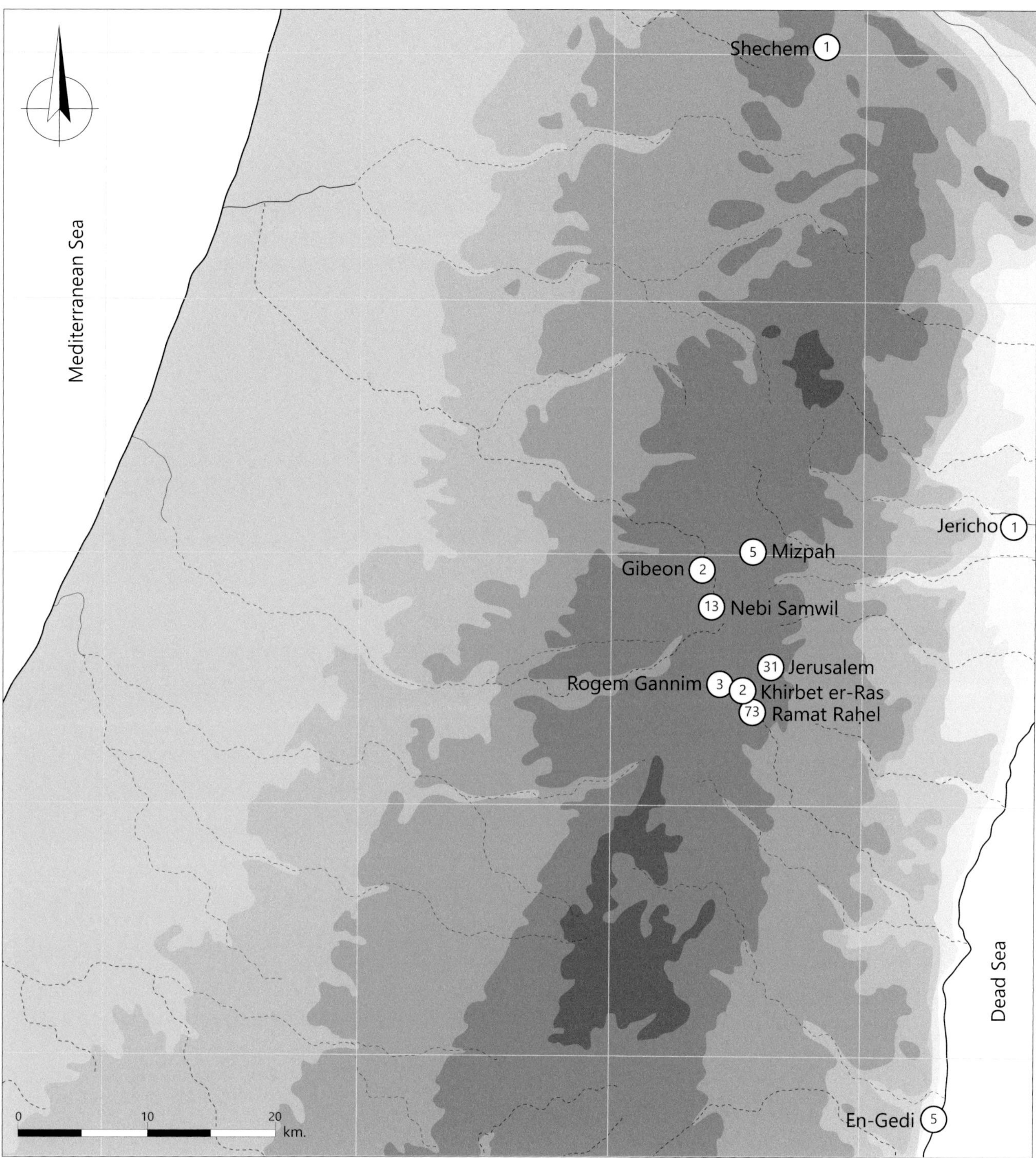

Fig. 4.21: Distribution of lion stamp impressions

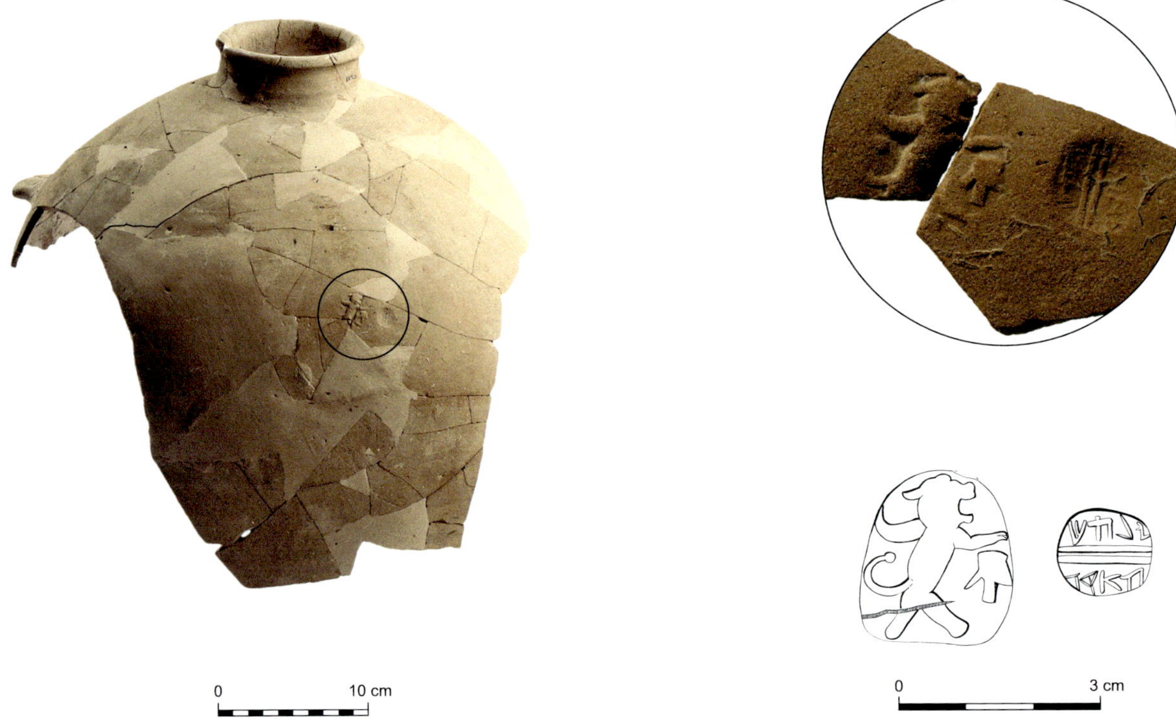

Fig. 4.22: A storage jar from Ramat Raḥel with a lion stamp impression alongside a "private" stamp impression (Lipschits and Koch 2021: 52, Fig. 4.14:1; 76, No. 3)

evidence that would shed light on the city's history in the period after 586 BCE and before the establishment of the Second Temple in the late 6th century BCE.[48]

In my opinion, the lion stamp impressions reflect the administration in the province of Judah under Babylonian rule after the destruction of Jerusalem, a direct continuation of the period during which Judah was a vassal kingdom first of Assyria and then of Babylon. The same storage-jar types were stamped in the same production centers, with the focus gradually shifting from the Shephelah to the environs of Jerusalem. Most of these storage jars continued to be collected in the same administrative center at Ramat Raḥel. The change in the symbol used reflects a new period, in which the administrative area of Judah was reduced and no longer included the Beersheba–Arad Valleys, the southern hill country, or the Shephelah. At the same time, the importance of the Benjamin region declined.

This understanding of the administrative and economic history of Judah leads to the conclusion that there was administrative and economic continuity between the First and Second Temple periods. It demonstrates that while the Babylonian exile was a period of darkness in the history of Judah, characterized by heavy destruction, by an unprecedented demographic crisis and by the exile of much of the societal elite and Jerusalem's population, it was also a period that served as a transition between the material culture, administration and economics of the 7th century and those of the 5th century BCE.

---

48. For the historical significance of the lion stamp-impression system, see pp. 172–177.

mwṣh Stamp Impressions

The type of storage jar on which *mwṣh* stamp impressions were stamped was defined by Wampler as the successor of the *lmlk* storage jar. It was slightly wider in its lower part and beginning to exhibit the "sack" shape so typical of the Persian period storage jar (Wampler 1947: 9, 137; cf. Stern 1982: 103; Zorn, Yellin and Hayes 1994: 169). This was the first type to be produced only in the Jerusalem area, providing the first—although not surprising—evidence that their production in the Shephelah ceased following the Babylonian destruction, when Judah became a Babylonian province (Zorn, Yellin and Hayes 1994: 175–182).

The *mwṣh* stamp-impression system is unusual in the paucity of handles uncovered, in their limited distribution, in the very small number of seals presumably used, and in its short duration. These stamp impressions (Fig. 4.23) bear no symbol that could be interpreted as representing a divinity or king, no mention of the kingdom's highest authority (*lmlk*), and no name of province (*yhwd*) or governor. Nothing but a place name (*mwṣh*) appears on these stamp impressions. All

these factors suggest that the system served a different function than its predecessors.

The *mwṣh* stamp impressions are oval or round and can be classified into four types, probably produced by four seals (Naveh 1970: 58–59; Zorn, Yellin and Hayes 1994: 170–174). Type A2—which is oval in shape, with the place name spelled defectively as *mṣh* on a single line—served to stamp 38 impressions (all on jar handles, most uncovered in Tell en-Naṣbeh). Two other seals, Types B and C—both circular, the former written in plene spelling on two lines and the latter in defective spelling on one line—have yielded one stamp impression each, both on the body of a storage jar. Of the fourth (Type A1, distinguished from A2 on palaeographic grounds), three stamp impressions were uncovered, all on handles: two in Tell en-Naṣbeh and one in Jericho.

Forty-three *mwṣh* stamp impressions are known (Table 4.12; Fig. 4.24): 40 on storage-jar handles and three on the body.[49] Thirty were found in Tell en-Naṣbeh, the only site to produce three of the four known types (McCown 1947: 165–167, Pl. 56:15–28, Fig. 38:5, 11). With the exception of Jericho, where the two stamp impressions uncovered were produced by

Fig. 4.23: A jar handle with a *mwṣh* stamp impression from Tell en-Naṣbeh (photo courtesy of the Badè Museum, Pacific School of Religion)

---

49. See Naveh 1970: 58–59; Zorn, Yellin and Hayes 1994: 164–165, Table 1.

Table 4.12: Distribution of *mwṣh* stamp impressions according to type (Zorn, Yellin and Hayes 1994)

Site	Type A1	Type A2	Type B	Type C	Total
Mizpah	2	27	1		30
Gibeon		4			4
Jerusalem		4			4
Jericho	1	1			2
Ramat Raḥel				1	1
Ṣuba		1			1
Unknown		1			1
Total	**3**	**38**	**1**	**1**	**43**

different seals, the other sites each exhibited a single type. [50]Four stamp impressions produced by the same seal (Type A2) were discovered in Gibeon and four in Jerusalem;[51] one stamp impression was found at Ramat Raḥel and one at Ṣuba.[52]

Many early scholars agreed that this group of stamp impressions should be dated to the 6th century BCE,[53] a period when Mizpah was the center of Babylonian rule in Judah (Lipschits 2005: 109–112). Examination of the archaeological contexts of these handles supports this view.[54] One should recall the main distinguishing feature of the *mwṣh* stamp impressions: they bear only a place name, without any symbol or any mention of the province (*yhwd*) or governor. This led to the view that the *mwṣh* stamp impressions were evidence of a royal estate that supplied produce to the governor residing in Mizpah just after the destruction of Jerusalem.[55] The incised inscription המצה.שעל, appearing on a storage-jar handle acquired from the antiquities market, may support this view,[56] according to which the stamp impressions indicated the origin of the agricultural products—probably wine or oil—brought to Mizpah (see also Cross 1969: 22*–23*; Graham 1984: 56).

---

50. Sellin and Watzinger 1913: 158; Bartlett 1982: 542, Fig. 220.5, Pl. 3b; Kenyon and Holland 1982: 113. The handle discovered by Sellin and Watzinger was found on the terraces at the foot of the tel and was probably dumped from one of the buildings in the northeastern part of the tel (Zorn, Yellin and Hayes 1994: 168). The handle discovered by Kenyon was found in a thick sediment layer covering the remains of a late Iron Age building, where a refuse pit had been dug in the Roman period (Zorn, Yellin and Hayes 1994: 168).

51. For the stamp impressions found at the City of David, see Ariel and Shoham 2000: 143–144. Two handles with *mwṣh* stamp impressions were found in a Stratum IX context, considered the earliest stage of the Persian period. One came from a Persian period fill excavated above an Iron Age floor, and the other from a filled-in quarry together with 90% Iron Age pottery. Two other handles came from later contexts or without a clear stratigraphic context (see also Zorn, Yellin and Hayes 1994: 169). For the *mwṣh* stamp impressions in Gibeon, see Pritchard 1959: 27, Figs. 10.1, 11.1; 1964: 20, 130, Fig. 51.6. Since no Persian period *yhwd* stamp impressions were found in Gibeon (Lipschits and Vanderhooft 2011: 57), the recovery of *mwṣh* stamp impressions here suggests that this system is earlier. Furthermore, two of the *mwṣh*-stamped handles were found in the basement of a building together with mainly Iron Age pottery (and see Zorn, Yellin and Hayes 1994: 168). An additional handle was discovered in a water reservoir, along with pottery dated mainly to the period between the Iron Age and the Persian period. One handle was found in an unclear context in the upper layer of a refuse pile.

52. Aharoni 1964: 18; Zorn, Yellin and Hayes 1994: 168. The *mwṣh*-stamped handle from Ramat Raḥel was uncovered along with additional Persian period stamp impressions and pottery attributed by Aharoni (1964: 19, 23) to the 6th century BCE, one sherd that he ascribed to the Iron Age and numerous sherds from the Persian–Hellenistic transition.

53. McCown 1947: 6, 202; Cross 1969: 24*; Naveh 1970: 61–62; Stern 1982: 207–209; Zorn, Yellin and Hayes 1994: 169. For a review of scholarly opinions, including some who dated the stamp impressions to the Persian period, mainly on the basis of palaeographic considerations, see Zorn, Yellin and Hayes 1994: 174–175.

54. Zorn, Yellin and Hayes (1994: 167) showed convincingly that two *mwṣh*-stamped handles were discovered in a cistern along with black-figure Greek pottery dated to ca. 530 BCE. As the cistern went out of use around this period, the stamped jars should be dated to the Babylonian rule. Six stamped handles were discovered near the wall connecting the site's northern gate to an early gate, which, according to Zorn, Yellin and Hayes (1994: 167), was built at the beginning of the Babylonian period. Fifteen additional stamped handles were discovered within an extremely small (ca. 15 m) radius at the southwest of the site. Two long warehouses were built here on top of the wall dated to the Iron Age, and the *mwṣh* storage jars may have been stored in or near these warehouses. McCown (1947: 202) already made a similar argument.

55. Avigad (1958b: 129; 1972b: 7–9), after considering several other possibilities, favored the notion of royal estate; he was followed by Stern (1982: 207–209), Tadmor (1983: 131–132) and Zorn, Yellin and Hayes (1994: 183). See also Graham 1984: 56.

56. For this, see Avigad 1972b: 5–9. For the meaning of the name and for the geographical context, see Avigad 1972b: 6–7. For the appearance of the name שעל on late First Temple period bullae, see Avigad 1986a: 56, and nn. 72–74. See also Bullae 79, 123, 164, 175.

The writing on the *mwṣh* seals was in the official Aramaic script, unlike the First Temple period impressions, in which Hebrew was exclusively used (Lipschits and Vanderhooft 2011: 63–65). According to Naveh (1970: 58–62), lapidary Aramaic script appeared only in the Persian period; he therefore dated the *mwṣh* script to the 5th–4th centuries BCE, contemporary to the script on *yhwd* seals. Lipschits and Vanderhooft demonstrated that the *mwṣh* script is earlier, and they concur with scholars who date it to the 6th century BCE (2011: 62–73, with further literature).

From the onset there was general scholarly agreement about the identification of the letter *mem*, which appears in initial position (McCown 1947: 165). Avigad (1958b: 129) correctly observed that it had been written so as to appear in mirror image on the impression, a familiar phenomenon in Persian period stamp impressions, while agreeing that the writing is typical of the Aramaic script of the 5th–4th centuries BCE. He further correlated the absence of the letter *waw* in most of these stamp impressions with its absence in many *yhwd* stamp impressions. Moreover, where it does appear, it corresponds to the Aramaic script of the Persian period. The letter *ṣade* also corresponds to the Aramaic script and is characteristic of the Phoenician script in the Persian period (Avigad 1958b: 130). The main issue under debate was the identification of the final letter. Badè considered it to be *pe*, thus reading the word as *msp*— in his opinion, an abbreviation for *msph* (Mizpah), where most of the handles bearing these stamp impressions were found (Badè 1932; Zorn, Yellin and Hayes 1994: 162). Ginsberg (1948) identified the final letter as *he*, reading the inscription as *msh*, but agreeing with Badè that this was an abbreviation of the name Mizpah.[57]

Only later did the association of the *mwṣh* stamp impressions to Moẓa became established. Given all the system's features and on the basis of this understanding of the name, we suggest that the system of *mwṣh* stamp impressions functioned as a temporary *ad hoc* system, in order to bring supplies to the Babylonian governor

residing in Mizpah, perhaps in the province's early days before the system had become well established or for a certain period in the 6th century BCE when Judah was a Babylonian province (Lipschits 2005: 118–146). In this respect, the *mwṣh* stamp-impression system resembles that of "private" stamp impressions, which was also a short-term adaptation of the *lmlk* system in preparation for Sennacherib's campaign, intended to manage supplies mainly to the Shephelah and especially to Lachish. Both these systems operated for a short well-defined period, developing out of a specific need and against the backdrop of well-established systems of stamp impressions on storage jars, systems that continued after these *ad hoc* systems had fulfilled their function and ceased to exist.

This would explain why almost all the *mwṣh*-stamped handles were impressed by a single seal and would account for the exceptional concentration of handles with this stamp impression in a single place—Tell en-Naṣbeh, a site that did not play a significant role in any of the previous systems. It would also explain why so few handles with such impressions were uncovered at Ramat Raḥel and Jerusalem—the major centers of all the stamp-impression systems that operated in Judah before and after the destruction of the First Temple, including that of the lion stamp impressions, which presumably operated alongside the *mwṣh* system during the Babylonian rule in Judah. The distribution of *mwṣh* stamp impressions shows that they had been concentrated in a single collection center and only a few had been distributed. As mentioned, with the exception of Gibeon and Jerusalem, each with four stamped handles, and Jericho, with two, the other sites yielded only one stamped handle each.

The theory that the *mwṣh* stamp impressions represent a wine- or oil-production facility belonging to the royal estate and supplying products to the governor in Mizpah would explain why most stamp impressions were found in the province's capital.[58] We may assume that Moẓa's

---

57. Surprisingly, Albright argued (in a cited suggestion to Badè) that the reference was to the feast of the unleavened bread and suggested that these marked vessels were the containers for the wine needed at this feast. Cf. McCown 1947: 167.

58. Zorn, Yellin and Hayes (1994: 166) argued that the *mwṣh* stamp impressions were restricted to the Benjamin region. This is unlikely, because, as mentioned above, apart from Mizpah, four identical stamp impressions were found in Jerusalem and Gibeon, and several impressions were uncovered at Ṣuba and Ramat Raḥel, which are not located in the Benjamin region. The distribution of the *mwṣh* stamp impressions was probably restricted to the vicinity of the Babylonian governor, who ruled from Mizpah after the destruction of Jerusalem and whose immediate environs served as a gathering place for the people remaining in Judah (Jer 40:7–41:18); and see Lipschits 1999b; 2005: 109–112.

status as royal estate served as the basis for several traditions that were upheld for centuries to come.

M. Sukkah 4:5 states:

> How is the commandment of the willow branch fulfilled? There was a place below Jerusalem and it was called Moẓa. They would go down there and gather branches of willow from there; and come to prop them standing up against the altar [in the Temple]; and their tops would lean over the altar.

PT Sukkah 18b states:

> What is Moẓa? Memetzia. Says Rabbi Tanchuma, Colonia was its name." BT Sukkah 45a states: "We have learned—the place was [actually] called Colonia. And the author of our Mishna, why then did he call it Moẓa? Since it was exempt from the royal tax, it was called Moẓa [taken out]. The commentator Rashi explains in this vein: Colonia—בֶּן חוֹרִין (a free man) from the king's tax.

It is generally assumed that royal estates in Judah and Israel continued to exist for centuries, even after the imperial ruler was replaced (Naʾaman 1981; Lipschits 2000: 31 and n. 1 for further literature). Perhaps it was due to this status that Moẓa ultimately became the place of residence of veteran Roman soldiers (Josephus, *AJ* 7.6.6), leading to the change of its name to Colonia.

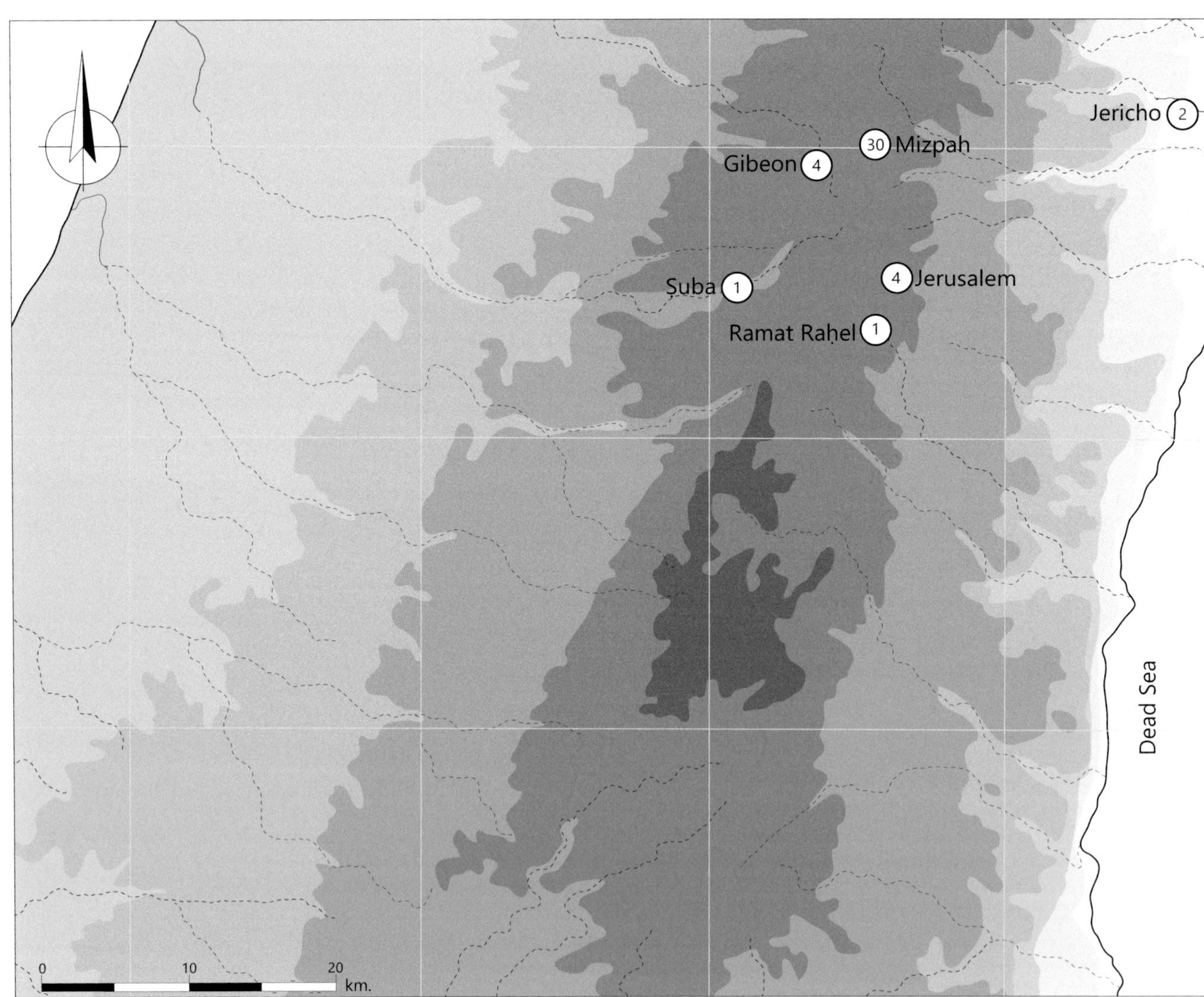

Fig. 4.24: Distribution of *mwṣh* impressions

yhwd Stamp Impressions

The *yhwd* stamp-impression system consists of 17 main types, stamped with more than 50 seals over a period of some 400 years, from the late 6th century BCE until the second half of the 2nd century BCE. These stamp impressions (Fig. 4.25) are characterized by a complete absence of iconography, following some two centuries in which the main component of the stamp impressions was iconographic. Furthermore, there is a transition to Aramaic script (at least until the late types, in which there is a return to Hebrew), and the name of the province appears in the center of the stamp impressions in plene (*yhwd*) or defective (*yhd* or *yh*) spelling. The stamp impressions from the early Persian period also bear the title *phw'* ("the governor" in Aramaic) and some private names of governors.

Until recently no restorable *yhwd* storage jars were uncovered that would enable us to place them within the typology of stamped storage jars. That changed when a pit containing 33 storage-jar handles with *yhwd* stamp impressions was uncovered in the Ramat Raḥel excavations (Lipschits 2011f; Lipschits and Vanderhooft, forthcoming). The pit also contained a large pottery assemblage from the early Persian period, including 15 complete or almost complete storage jars, each with four handles. Stamp impressions were found on eight storage jars: one with two handles marked with different stamp impressions (Fig. 4.26), several with one stamped handle and six with stamp impressions on their bodies, in some cases with two different stamp impressions on the same storage jar.[59] The *yhwd* storage jars strongly resemble the rosette-stamped storage jars of the late Iron Age, but with early Persian influences evident in their shape and in the low quality of their clay and production. Many were irregular in shape, with air bubbles and wrinkles in their body, shoulder, or rim, probably the result of the low-quality production process, including overcrowding in the kiln.

The *yhwd* stamp impressions can be divided into three main chronological groups:[60] early, middle and late.

Fig. 4.25: A *yhwd* stamp impression on a handle from Ramat Raḥel (Lipschits and Vanderhooft 2021: 103, No. 18)

---

59. All the finds from the Babylonian-Persian Pit in Ramat Raḥel are detailed in Lipschits *et al.* 2021.

60. See detailed discussion in Vanderhooft and Lipschits 2007; Lipschits and Vanderhooft 2011: 81–252.

Fig. 4.26: A storage jar from the Babylonian-Persian Pit at Ramat Raḥel, with a different *yhwd* stamp impression on each of two handles

The Early Types

This group includes 12 types stamped by 15 seals[61] and is dated to the late 6th and 5th centuries BCE (Fig. 4.27). All the seals are round or oval, engraved in Aramaic lapidary script and only in a few cases in cursive Aramaic. In nine of these types the name of the province יהוד (*yhwd*) appears in plene spelling; three types include the title פחוא and two governors אחיב and יהעזר are mentioned by their names and titles. Nine early types bear private names (one with the patronym too) and in seven the two rows of text are separated, generally by a single line, but in a few cases with a double-line field divider. All these features are shared with stamp impressions from the end of the First Temple period and with the *mwṣh* stamp impressions, and the continuity with late Iron Age practices is evident. The 12 types of stamp impressions in this group are characterized by great variety (Fig. 4.27),[62] suggestive of an administrative system that had not yet been consolidated and firmly established.

Even though most of the stamp impressions of this group were not found in clear stratigraphic contexts, there is archaeological support for their early dating. Several

handles uncovered in the City of David excavations and bearing *yhwd* stamp impressions of the early types were clearly attributed to Stratum 9, dated to the Persian period, and in some cases to the early stages of this stratum. A storage-jar handle stamped *yhwd/ḥnnh* (Type 4; see, e.g., Fig. 4.28) was found together with a *mwṣh* stamp impression in the early phase of Stratum IX, and a handle bearing a *lʾhyb/phwʾ* stamp impression (Type 1) was found in the second phase of this stratum. These two stamped handles were found at a lower level than the late types of *yhwd* stamp impressions exposed in the second and third phases of Stratum IX (De Groot and Ariel 2005). The importance of this find lies in the absence of late *yhwd* stamp impressions from the early stages of the Persian period. This runs counter to the findings from the Jewish Quarter excavations, where only late types of *yhwd* stamp impressions were found (together with *yršlm* stamp impressions) in clear Hellenistic period assemblages (Geva 2005). These findings show that *yhwd* stamp impressions of the early and late types did not coexist and that there was probably a considerable time gap between them.

For the distribution of the early types of *yhwd* stamp impressions, see below, Fig. 4.31 on p. 86.

---

61. A new type (= seal) of the early types was recently published; see Vanderhooft, Richey and Lipschits 2019.

62. Of one of these 12 types (Type 9) we have only a single stamped handle; of three types (Types 2, 5 and 8) we have two stamped handles; of two types (3 and 11) we have four exemplars. Of Type 4 we have six finds; of Type 7 we have eight stamped handles; of Type 12 we have 14 stamped handles; of Type 1 we have 18 stamped handles; of Type 10 we have 24 exemplars; and of Type 6 there are 80 stamped handles.

Fig. 4.27: Typology of the *yhwd* stamp impressions: the early group (based on drawings by D.S. Vanderhooft; Lipschits and Vanderhooft 2011: 18)

Fig. 4.28: A storage jar from the Babylonian-Persian Pit at Ramat Raḥel, bearing a *yhwd*/*ḥnnh* stamp impression on its body (impression in Lipschits and Vanderhooft 2021: 95, No. 1; 52, Fig. 4.14:2)

The Middle Types

This group consists of three main types (with several sub-types) stamped by at least 16 seals (Fig. 4.29). Dating from the 4th and 3rd centuries BCE, these stamp impressions exhibit great uniformity in characteristics. There are no private names and no title *pḥw'*. The letter *waw* disappears from the spelling of the name of the province, which from now one appears only in defective spelling—with three letters (*yhd*) or two (*yh*). In contrast to the early types, which were mainly round or oval, most of the middle types are rectangular, sometimes with rounded corners, and the *yh* stamp impressions are round and enclosed within a bezel. Palaeographic changes are also evident, presumably influenced by the Hebrew script (see Lipschits and Vanderhooft 2011: 62–73; Vanderhooft 2011). Although only a few letters in these types can be examined palaeographically, stylistic changes are evident

here too, especially in the letter *he*, which diverges significantly from the lapidary Aramaic form, and generally appears in the form of three lines joining a single vertical line, the direction of which frequently changes. The letter was sometimes written in mirror image and sometimes appears upside-down. The letter *he* in these stamp impressions is not Aramaic and seems to reflect Hebrew influence.

The middle types of *yhwd* stamp impressions should be dated to the 4th–3rd centuries BCE on the basis of the palaeographic changes in the script in Judah at that time (Lipschits and Vanderhooft 2011: 62–73; Vanderhooft 2011) and on the grounds that the early types are dated to the beginning of the Persian period and the late types are securely dated to the 2nd century BCE. The dating of the middle types is supported by the *yhd* coins,[63] on which the name of the province was written in three letters and which are palaeographically equivalent to the

---

63. Meshorer 2001: 2–6, No. 1; 10–11, No. 9; 198, No. 12, Pl. 2:12; cf. also the letter *he* in Nos. 2–6, 9–10, 13, 15–18.

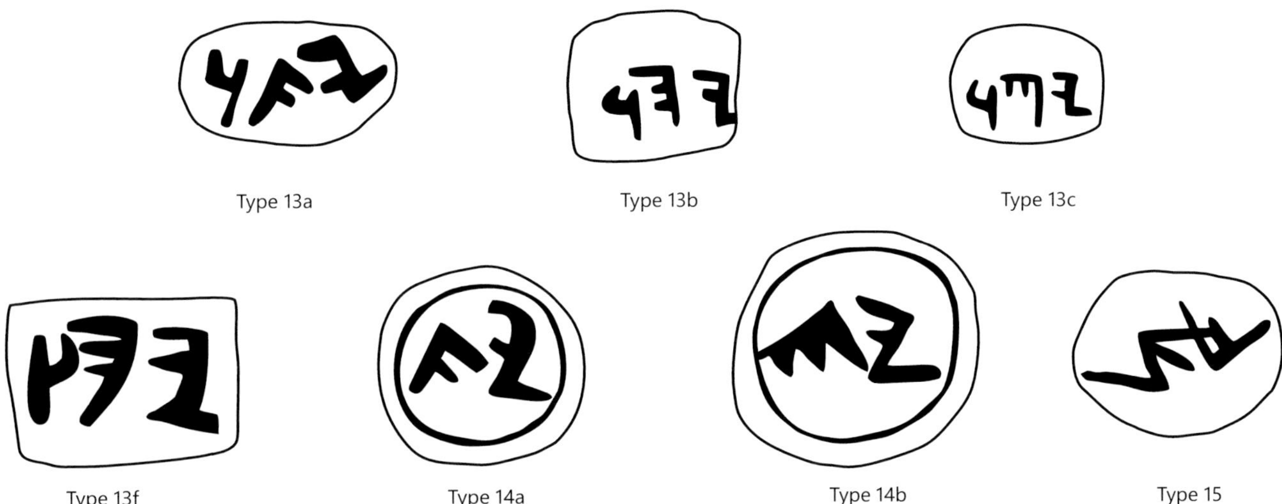

Fig. 4.29: Typology of *yhwd* stamp impressions: the middle group (based on drawings by D.S. Vanderhooft; Lipschits and Vanderhooft 2011: 20)

three-letter *yhd* stamp impressions. Meshorer dated these coins to before the Macedonian conquest, and their attribution to the late Persian period is generally accepted today (Barag 1986–87: 6, with further literature; Naveh 1998: 92). The practice of abbreviating the names of provinces to only two letters is accepted in south Levantine coins of the 4th century BCE: *yd* for Judah, *šmr*, *šm*, *šn*, or *š* for Samaria, *ʾn* for Ashkelon and *ʿz* for Gaza. This serves as supporting evidence for the dating of the middle group of *yhwd* stamp impressions.[64]

For their distribution, see below, Fig. 4.32 on p. 87.

The Late Types

This group contains two main types of stamp impressions, stamped by at least 21 seals (Fig. 4.30). In one type the province name is written as a ligature of two letters (*yh*).[65] Seven variants of this type are known, most showing the ligature within a square frame and a few without a frame.

In several cases the letters were engraved directly onto the storage-jar handle (Lipschits and Vanderhooft 2011: 595–656). The other type features at least 14 variants of round stamp impressions, all with the province name in defective spelling *yhd*, in Hebrew script, with the additional letter *ṭet*.[66] As is evident from the finds from the City of David, the Jewish Quarter and Ṣuba, and as observed by Cross and Avigad, most of the late types of *yhwd* stamp impressions were uncovered in archaeological contexts dated to the 2nd century BCE—perhaps even to its later half. The same holds true for the stamp impressions on jar handles from el-ʿAzariya and Ramat Raḥel.[67] Their discovery in the same contexts as *yršlm* stamp impressions, along with the absence of any early types of *yhwd* stamp impressions in these ceramic assemblages and stratigraphic contexts, support a late dating for these stamp impressions.

For the distribution of the late types of *yhwd* stamp impressions, see below, Fig. 4.33 on p. 88.

---

64. For the coins from Judah, see Meshorer 1982: Pl. 56:1, from Samaria, see Meshorer and Qedar 1999: 17; from Ashkelon and Gaza, see Meshorer 1982: Pl. 56:1; Meshorer and Qedar 1991: 14. The difference between the two-letter abbreviation of the province name on stamp impressions—*yh*—and its abbreviation on coins—*yd*—is interesting; a similar distinction exists in these abbreviations in the province of Samaria.

65. This reading follows Aharoni's suggestion (1956: 149); see Ariel and Shoham's review of various suggestions (2000: 152–154).

66. On the reading of the letter *ṭet* and its identification, see Cross 1968: 231; Avigad 1974: 52–54. This reading is accepted by most scholars; see Avigad 1960. For the meaning of this letter, see Lemaire 1991: 140.

67. See Ariel and Shoham 2000: 153; De Groot and Ariel 2005; Geva 2000a; 2005; Reich 2003; Finkielsztejn and Gibson 2007; Cross 1969: 22*; Avigad 1974; cf. Barag 1986–87: 18–19.

Type 16

Type 17

Fig. 4.30: Typology of *yhwd* stamp impressions: the late group (based on drawings by D.S. Vanderhooft; Lipschits and Vanderhooft 2011: 20)

Discussion

The *yhwd* corpus as a whole consists of 647 stamp impressions (Table 4.13), compared to the 582 that were published in the 2011 corpus.[68] The present corpus includes an additional 37 stamp impressions to the early types, bringing the total number to 165 (ca. 25.5% of the entire corpus of *yhwd* stamp impressions).[69] The number of new stamp impressions of the middle types is less meaningful: 26 new stamp impressions (8.5% of the 312 stamp impressions included in the 2011 corpus) bring the total number of stamp impressions of the middle types to 338 (ca. 52% of all the *yhwd* stamp impressions). Only two stamp impressions of the late types were added to the 2011 corpus, bringing the total number to 144 stamp impressions (ca. 22% of the total corpus).

From Ramat Raḥel we have 372 *yhwd* stamp impressions (57.5% of the corpus). The second most prominent site producing stamp impressions is the City of David, with 136 stamped handles. Combined with the finds from the Western Hill and its vicinity (27 stamped handles, all belonging to the late types), the finds from Jerusalem constitute 25% of the corpus. Most finds from Jerusalem belong to the late types of the 2nd century BCE (86 stamp impressions). By way of contrast, Jerusalem produced only 15% of the early and middle types (76 out of 503 stamp impressions), whereas Ramat Raḥel produced 67.5% (339 of the 503 stamp impressions). Among the other sites, only six have a significant number of stamped handles (between 7 and 19, mostly of the middle types; and see below). In conclusion, the two main sites in the stamped-jar administrative system yielded 534 out of 647 stamp impressions (82.5%).

Of the finds from Ramat Raḥel, 34% (127 stamp impressions) belong to the early types, dated to the late 6th and 5th centuries BCE; 57% (212 stamp impressions) belong to the middle types, dated to the 4th–3rd centuries BCE; and only 9% (33 stamp impressions) belong to the late types, dated to the 2nd century BCE. For a breakdown of the distribution of the finds according to early, middle and late groups, see Table 4.13.

The 127 early stamp impressions from Ramat Raḥel represent 77% of the total 165 stamp impressions of the early types. With the exception of the City of David, which yielded 17 early stamp impressions, nine of which are of a single type (Type 1), at all other sites (mainly small production centers), only one to three stamped handles were found. This is a clear indication that Ramat Raḥel served as the center of the system in the early

---

68. The 2011 corpus was published in Lipschits and Vanderhooft 2011; see further references there. Additional *yhwd* stamp impressions have been found since the compilation of this corpus, especially in Ramat Raḥel, and an updated corpus has recently been published in Lipschits and Vanderhooft 2020. The numbers in this chapter are updated to the summer of 2019, including one surprising and unpublished find of a *yhd* stamp impression (Type 13) from Beth Shemesh (Boaz Gross: personal communication), and especially the 41 unpublished new stamp impressions from Ramat Raḥel; Lipschits and Vanderhooft, forthcoming.

69. It is noteworthy that among the new finds there is only one stamp impression of Types 1–5, probably the earliest stamp impressions from the early Persian period, still presenting some of the characteristic monarchic era "private" stamp impressions of the late 7th and 6th centuries BCE. Most of the new finds (29 stamp impressions, four already published) are of Type 6. This type has the largest number of all the early types (55 stamped handles of Type 6 were published in the 2011 corpus, 48 of them discovered at Ramat Raḥel). Before the new publication, Type 6 comprised 43% of all the early types, but after the publication of the new stamp impressions the total rose to about 48.5% of the early types (80 out of 165). Seventy-three of the Type 6 stamp impressions were discovered at Ramat Raḥel (91% of the finds belonging to this type).

Persian period; its status thus continues from the lion stamp-impression system of the Babylonian period, with a clear decline during the subsequent periods of the *yhwd* system.

Of the 165 stamp impressions of the early types, 80 (almost half) belong to Type 6; 24 are of Type 10; 18 are of Type 1; and 14 are of Type 12. Thus, 136 stamped handles (about 83% of the early types) belong to four types, and 115 of these come from Ramat Raḥel. Four other types (Types 2, 3, 8 and 9) are not attested at Ramat Raḥel, and these are represented by only nine stamped handles—isolated finds in a variety of sites, usually small production centers.

From these updated data, it transpires that Ramat Raḥel was the definitive center of this phase of the storage-jar administration, best represented by four or five stamp types in this early phase. The City of David is best represented by a single type (Type 1; possibly reflecting a single event of transporting jars), but otherwise seems to have played a relatively less important role in this phase of the jar administration.

The 212 stamp impressions from Ramat Raḥel belonging to the middle types represent 62.5% of the total of 338 stamp impressions belonging to this phase. This is a statistically meaningful decline compared to the 77% of early types, reflecting a decline in the status of

Table 4.13: Distribution of *yhwd* stamp impressions according to early, middle and late groups

Site	Early Types	Middle Types	Late Types	Total
Ramat Raḥel	127	212	33	372
City of David	17	59	59	135
Jerusalem—Western Hill	0	0	27	27
Tell en-Naṣbeh (Mizpah)	1	18	0	19
Nebi Samwil	3	13	0	16
Gezer	2	1	5	8
En-Gedi	3	7	0	10
Jericho	2	16	0	18
Rogem Gannim	2	5	0	7
Khirbet Nisya	1	1	1	3
Bethany	0	0	2	2
Binyanei Haʾuma (Jerusalem International Convention Center)	1	0	1	2
Ḥusan	0	0	1	1
Tel Ḥarasim	2	0	0	2
Tell el-Fûl	0	0	1	1
Ramot Forest	0	0	1	1
Khirbet Moẓa	0	0	1	1
Belmont Castle	1	0	0	1
Battir	0	0	1	1
Khirbet ʿAlmit	0	0	1	1
Beth Shemesh	0	1	0	1
Tell Nimrin	1	0	0	1
Kadesh-Barnea	0	1	0	1
Tel Jemmeh	0	1	0	1
Babylon	1	0	0	1
Ṣuba	0	0	1	1
Unknown	1	3	9	13
Total	**165**	**338**	**144**	**647**

Ramat Raḥel in the administrative system. In this phase, during the late Persian and early Hellenistic periods, Jerusalem became somewhat more important in the system, with 59 stamped handles (17.5% of all the stamp impressions of the middle types), most of them belonging to a single type (Type 14 with 40 stamped handles). Three other sites became more significant in this phase: Tell en-Naṣbeh (18 stamped handles, eight of Type 13 and ten of Type 14), Nebi Samwil (13 stamped handles, 11 of them of Type 14) and Jericho (16 stamped handles, 13 of them of Type 14). These three sites thus yield 14% of all the finds in the middle phase, suggesting that they developed into secondary administrative sites, perhaps receiving jars from time to time from the province's central administration—which was presumably still at Ramat Raḥel.

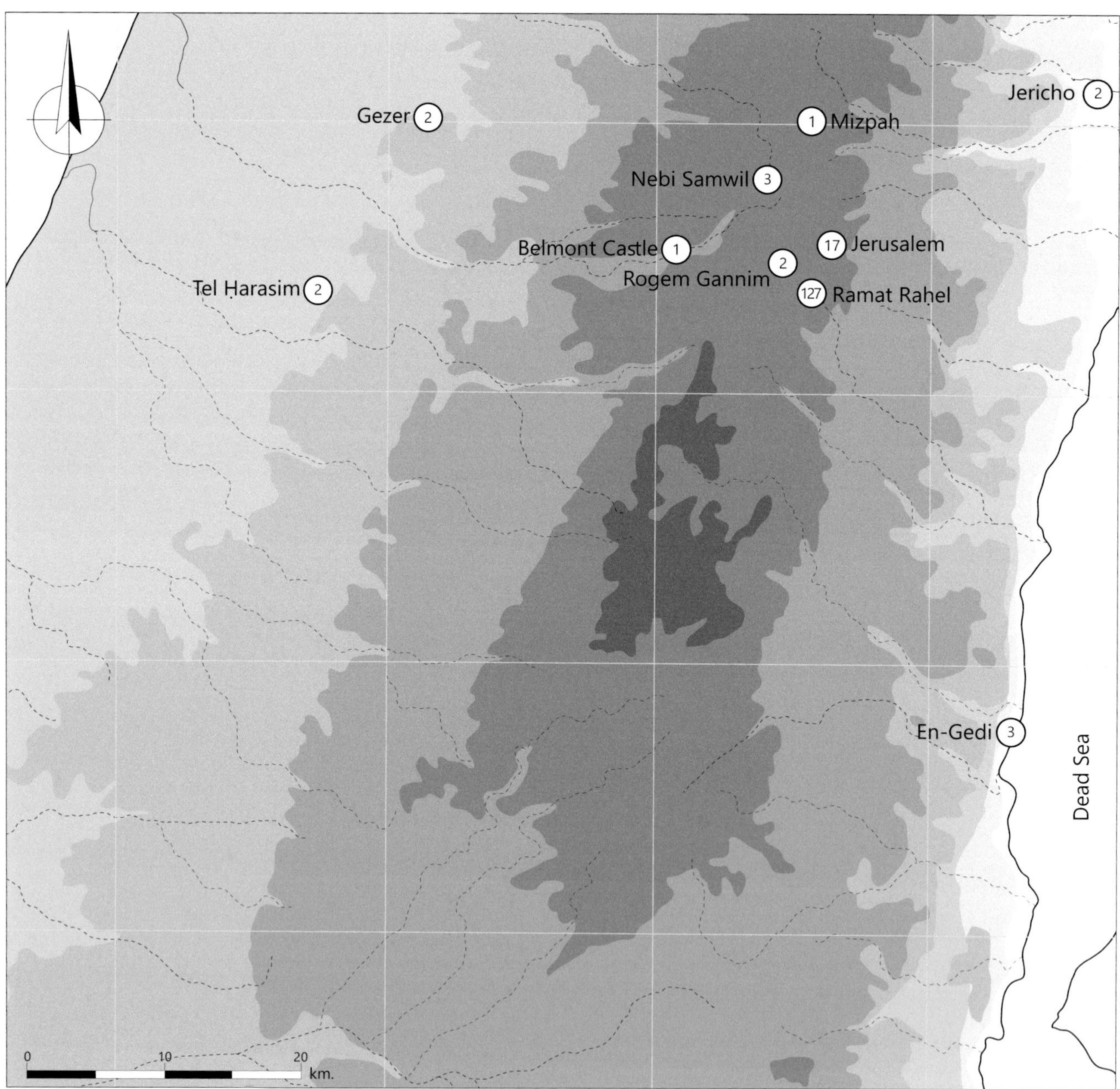

Fig. 4.31: Distribution of the early types of *yhwd* stamp impressions

The 33 stamp impressions from Ramat Raḥel belonging to the late types represent 23% of the corpus of 144 stamp impressions and are mainly of two types: three belong to Type 16 and 30 to Type 17 (*yhd-ṭ*). These numbers suggest that the centrality of Ramat Raḥel in the administrative system declined in the late Persian and early Hellenistic periods and that the site became far less important in the 2nd century BCE.

During the 2nd century BCE, however, Jerusalem became the main center of the administration, with 86 stamped handles (ca. 60% of the corpus). A third of the finds in Jerusalem come, for the first time, from the Western Hill, a clear indication of the growth of the city in this period. Ramat Raḥel is still represented by one type (Type 17) with 30 stamped handles out of 89 belonging to this type. A total of 119 stamped handles with late types

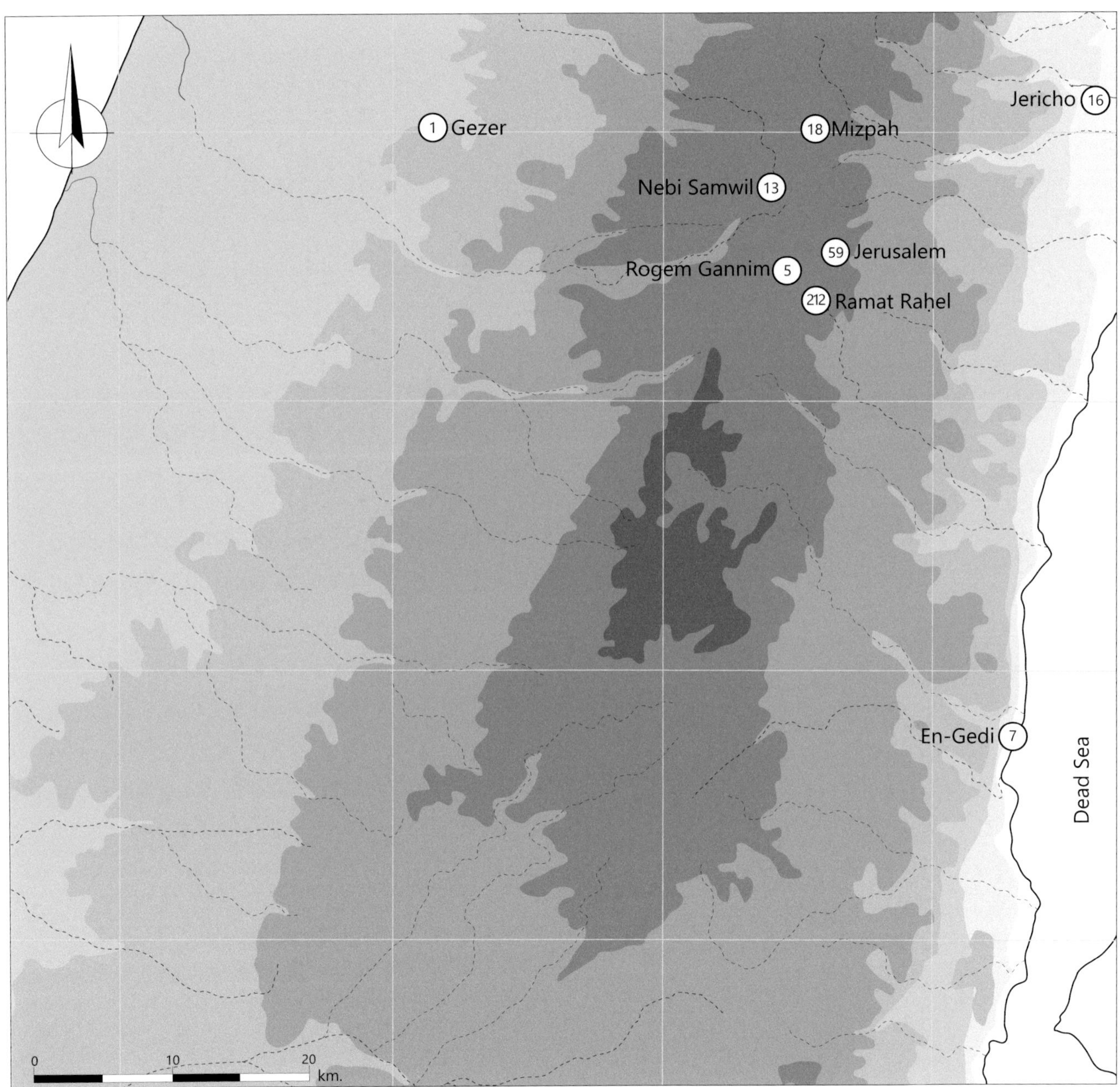

Fig. 4.32: Distribution of the middle types of *yhwd* stamp impressions

(ca. 82.5% of the entire corpus) were found in Jerusalem and Ramat Raḥel, and no other site is well attested in this period (although Gezer has five stamped handles of these types—two of Type 16 and three of Type 17).

This analysis of the *yhwd* stamp impressions in Judah during the Persian, Ptolemaic and early Seleucid periods points to continuity in the storage-jar administrative system—not only during the Babylonian–Persian transition but throughout the Persian period and into the early Hellenistic period. The main changes took place not at the beginning of this period but in the middle—probably in the early 4th century BCE—with the consolidation of the system. This is crucial for an understanding of the history of Judah in the Persian period and of the continuity that existed in the transition from the Persian to the Hellenistic period.

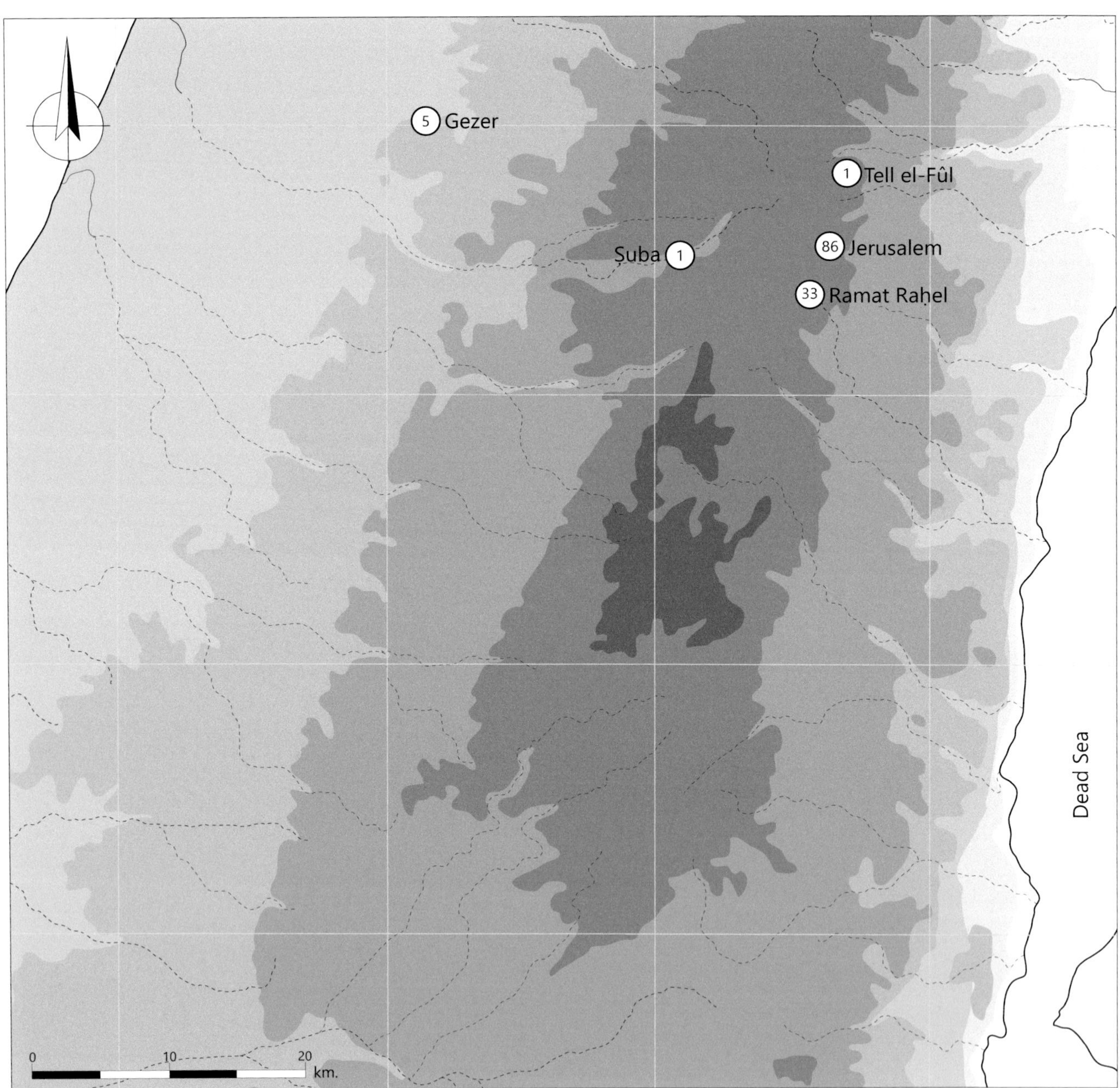

Fig. 4.33: Distribution of the late types of *yhwd* stamp impressions

yršlm Stamp Impressions[70]

The most notable feature of the *yršlm* stamp impressions is the reappearance of iconographic elements. The seals, which are rounded in shape, have two components: a pentagram and five letters in ancient Hebrew script, reading *yršlm* ("Jerusalem"), between the points of the pentagram (Fig. 4.34). Only 104 handles with *yršlm* stamp impressions have been uncovered, the number of types (= seals) is quite small, and the system was probably in use for only a short period.

Not all the *yršlm* stamp impressions were stamped on storage jars: one *yršlm* stamp impression was discovered on a cooking pot from Tel Yarmouth, and four were found on jugs uncovered in the City of David and the Jewish Quarter.[71] This suggests that this system served a completely different function than the previous ones, and, coupled with the use of the pentagram and the *yršlm* inscription, served as the basis for various scholarly suggestions regarding the use and function of these stamp impressions.[72] The dating of the *yršlm* stamp-impression system was also the subject of scholarly debate. Following the excavations at Gezer, Macalister was the first to suggest a date in the 3rd century BCE for the *yršlm* stamp impressions (1907: 264), a suggestion rejected by many scholars, who dated

Fig. 4.34: A handle from Ramat Raḥel with a *yršlm* stamp impression (Bocher, forthcoming)

---

70. This section is based on Efrat Bocher's M.A. research (Bocher 2012), as well as on the summary of Bocher and Lipschits (2013).

71. For references, see Table 4.14 below.

72. Albright (1926: 101) was the first to argue that storage jars with *yršlm*-stamped handles were designated to transport contributions to the Temple. He based this claim on the (erroneous) reading of the inscription on the stamp impressions as *šlmyh* and on his assumption that he was a priest and one of the treasurers whom Nehemiah had assigned to oversee the treasures of the Temple (Neh 13:13). Lapp (1963: 33–35) argued that the stamp impressions were clerically used by Ptolemy III and the High Priest Onias II, as this symbol was mentioned both in Qumran writings and in the pseudo-epigraphic literature. Other scholars suggested that they were used for collecting taxes on behalf of the Greek polis authorities (e.g., Aharoni 1956: 149–150). Cross (1969: 20*–21*) contended that the stamp impressions noted where the grapes were grown, a suggestion supported by Avigad (1974: 58) and Stern (1982: 207). Christoph (1993: 193–196) argued that stamp impressions with ancient Hebrew script differ from those with Aramaic writing and therefore do not constitute a continuation of the previous stamp-impression systems. He considered the function of the *yršlm* stamp impressions to be commercial rather than administrative. Ariel and Shoham (2000: 161) posited that since this is the first mention of a city, rather than a province, on the impressions, the storage jars were either stamped in or designated for Jerusalem. Geva (2007: 101) argued, on the basis of their limited area of distribution, that they were designated for administrative use in the Jerusalem region and were related to the Hasmonean revolt and the new-found independence in the region.

them earlier, to the post-exilic period (Sukenik 1933–34: 6; Albright 1926: 101; Duncan 1931: 140; Vincent 1956: 614). During the Ramat Raḥel excavations Aharoni returned to Macalister's dating and suggested attributing the *yršlm* stamp impressions to the early Hellenistic period. Garbini dated them to the 3rd–2nd centuries BCE,[73] a dating accepted by Avigad, who believed that the Jewish Quarter excavations supported a pre-Hasmonean dating.[74] Following the Tell el-Fûl excavations, N. Lapp claimed that the *yršlm* stamp-impression system was later than Avigad's dating, and she placed it in the second half of the 2nd century BCE.[75] Avigad acquiesced, agreeing on a Hasmonean period date for the *yršlm* stamp impressions. Based on the publication of the final reports of the Jewish Quarter excavations, Geva has dated these impressions to the first stage of the Hasmonean state.[76]

Due to the paucity of finds, the quality of the seals and impressions, and the complexity of the symbol and script, no detailed typology was developed until Bocher's 2012 research.[77] She classified the *yršlm* stamp impressions into six main types and two additional sub-types, formed by eight seals (Fig. 4.35):[78]

A. These stamp impressions are large (1.9–2.1 cm) and slightly elliptical, lacking a dot in the center of the pentagram. The pentagram's vertexes are asymmetrical, relatively thick and sometimes cut off by the external frame of the seal. The letters appear in mirror image (back to front) and are aligned clockwise. Sixteen specimens are known, originating from the various excavations at Jerusalem and Ramat Raḥel.

B. These are large (1.9–2.0 cm) and slightly elliptical, with a central dot. The edges of the pentagram are thick, relatively coarse and slightly convex. Some of the pentagram's edges cross the circular frame of the seal. The letters appear in mirror image and are aligned clockwise. Nine stamp impressions are attributed to this type; they were uncovered in Jerusalem, Ramat Raḥel, Naḥal Yarmouth and Merah el-Juma'.

C. These stamp impressions are round (1.7–1.8 cm on average), with a central dot. The vertexes are symmetrical and delicate and generally do not cross the external frame of the stamp impression. The letters appear in mirror image and are aligned clockwise. Eleven stamp impressions can be attributed to this type, found in Jerusalem, Ramat Raḥel and Khirbet Ḥamdan.

C1. Although similar to Type C, stamp impressions 1/5954 from the Jewish Quarter and L142 from the City of David are smaller, both in diameter and in the distance between the edges of the pentagram. These impressions are sunken, rather than

---

73. Aharoni (1956: 149–150) claimed that the production of the *yršlm* stamp impressions began after the establishment of the Greek *polis* in Jerusalem. Garbini (1962: 68) dated them to the 3rd–2nd centuries BCE on the basis of the Hellenistic pottery, especially lamps, found together with the stamped handles. Following Aharoni and Garbini, Lapp (1963: 35) suggested dating the *yršlm* and the group of late *yhwd* stamp impressions *ṭet+yhd* to the reign of Ptolemy III. Lapp's dating was accepted by most scholars, who dated the stamp impressions to the 3rd–2nd centuries BCE. See Stern 1982: 207; Richardson 1968: 16–17; Cross 1981: 68*; Reich 2003: 258.

74. Avigad 1974: 57–58; 1976a: 27; 1980: 77. Two jug handles with *yršlm* stamp impressions were found in the Jewish Quarter excavations (Areas A and F). Avigad (1974: 58) argued that similar jugs, uncovered in Area E (Locus 745), should be dated to the 2nd century BCE. Lapp (1968: 72) uncovered similar vessels at Beth-Zur in Strata I and II, which are dated to the 2nd century BCE. Based on his hypothesis of a stratigraphic gap in the Jewish Quarter at precisely this period, Avigad claimed that these stamp impressions should be dated to the pre-Hasmonean period.

75. N. Lapp believed (1981: 112) that the site was at its peak in the latter half of the 2nd century BCE and that the *yršlm* stamp impressions should therefore be dated to this period.

76. Avigad 1983: 77; Geva 2007. A similar opinion was expressed by Lipschits and Vanderhooft (2007a: 111–112; 2011: 593–595) and accepted by Bocher (2012; Bocher and Lipschits 2011: 200–201).

77. Aharoni (1955: 170–171, Drawing 18) was the first to attempt to characterize the letters between the points of the pentagram, but he did not develop a comprehensive typology. Lapp (1963) defined only two types for the 44 stamp impressions known to him. Richardson (1968: 14), on the basis of a stamp impression found at Tel Yarmouth, disputed Lapp's basic typology and contended that additional criteria should be added to it, but he did not present a detailed typology for the *yršlm* stamp impressions either. Nor did Ariel and Shoham (2000: 162) develop a clear typology for the *yršlm* stamp impressions; they argued that the stamp impressions themselves were of insufficient clarity.

78. For a detailed discussion of the *yršlm* stamp impressions and a survey of the history of their research, see Bocher 2012; she also discusses the possibility of additional seals in this system. For a summary of the typology of these stamp impressions, see Bocher and Lipschits 2011: 202–203.

Fig. 4.35: Typology of *yršlm* stamp impressions (based on Bocher 2016: 448, Fig. 27.1)

protruding, and the letters appear in the correct direction.[79]

D. This type is slightly smaller (ca. 1.6 cm in diameter) and has a dot in the center of the pentagram. The pentagram's edge are symmetrical, and all vertexes reach the external frame of the seal. All letters were written in negative, except for the letter *yod*, which was most likely engraved in negative on the seal, and therefore appears in the correct direction in the impression. The letters are aligned clockwise. Five stamp impressions belong to this type; all were found either at Jerusalem or at Ramat Raḥel.

D1. This unique impression is quite similar to Type D, but is sunken and the letters appear in positive. It was found in the Ophel excavations in the upper part of the City of David.[80]

E. A single example of this type was found, at the City of David. This is the largest of the *yršlm* stamp impressions (2.4–2.6 cm in diameter), it is slightly elliptical, and the pentagram does not have a dot in the center. The pentagram's edges are large and thick, some reaching the circular frame of the seal. Despite its large area, the letters are small; they are written in negative and are aligned clockwise.

F. This is a round type, prepared in a relatively crude manner, rendering most of the stamp impressions of this type illegible. It is ca. 1.8–1.9 cm in diameter and does not have a dot in the center of the pentagram. The pentagram's edges are coarse and thick, and most cross the circular frame of the seal. The letters are written in negative and are aligned clockwise. The letter *lamed* in this type is unique; it is upside-down, its acute angle facing the center of the

pentagram. Six of the known stamp impressions can be attributed to this type, all found in the various excavations at Jerusalem and Ramat Raḥel.[81]

The corpus of *yršlm* stamp impressions consists of only 104 handles (Table 4.14; Fig. 4.36), ca. 88% of which were uncovered in Jerusalem (58 handles) and Ramat Raḥel (33 handles). Only one *yršlm*-stamped handle was found in each of the other sites, with the exception of Gezer, where two handles were uncovered. A concentration of almost all the stamp impressions in two central collection sites is almost unheard of among the many varieties of the *yhwd* stamp-impression system. The only other type to exhibit such a concentration is the late *yhwd* Type 17 (Fig. 4.32), which is dated to the same period as the *yršlm* stamp impressions.[82] All the other types of stamp impressions from the Persian and Hellenistic periods exhibited more diversity in secondary administrative sites and in sites of production.

The distribution of the *yršlm* stamp impressions points to a decline in the status of Ramat Raḥel: the number of handles uncovered suggests that it had now become secondary to Jerusalem. Indeed, this is in keeping with the change that Ramat Raḥel underwent during the 2nd century BCE: the administrative center that had existed since the late 8th or early 7th century BCE was destroyed, and with it, all the luxurious buildings and the royal garden. A Jewish village was erected above it, as indicated by the numerous finds exposed here—the many ritual baths and the columbarium. A Hasmonean citadel may have been situated adjacent to it (Lipschits *et al.* 2011: 37; 2017: 119–126). The distribution of the *yršlm* stamp impressions in the City of David and the Ophel (43 handles with stamp impressions) and the Western Hill (ten handles) points to the growing importance of the Western Hill

---

79. The "sunken" aspect of this stamp impression, as well as that of Type D1 (below), suggests that the symbol and letters appeared in relief on the seal. However, given the low quality of the *yršlm* stamps in general and of these types in particular, it is unlikely that such a seal, requiring much work, would have been prepared. A more reasonable possibility is that the sunken impressions were created by means of another impression, perhaps after the storage jar in question had broken and the handle bearing the impression had been detached from the vessel. When such a "seal" is used, the resulting impression would be sunken, not in negative, and would be identical to another type. These unique stamp impressions were found only in excavations in Jerusalem.

80. For the method of its manufacture, see Type C1 (above).

81. Two such handles, found in City of David Area E1 (Reg. Nos. 6070 and 9072), belong to the same storage jar—the only example of a *yršlm* storage jar with two stamped handles.

82. Lipschits and Vanderhooft 2011: 658. For the historical and administrative significance of this phenomenon, see pp. 182–185.

Table 4.14: Distribution of *yršlm*-stamped handles

Area	Site	Number of *yršlm*-Stamped Impressions	References
Jerusalem and its environs	Jerusalem	58	Macalister and Duncan 1926: 188, Fig. 5, Pl. 203:7; Crowfoot and Fitzgerald 1929: 68; Duncan 1931: 140–141, Pl. 140; Amiran and Eitan 1973: Pl. 42:5; Avigad 1974: 56; 1983: 78, Pls. 54–55; Ariel and Shoham 2000: 161–163, Pls. 123–144; Reich 2003: 256–257, Pls. 7.1–7.2
	Ramat Raḥel	33	Aharoni 1956: 149–150, Fig. 18, Pl. 25:3; 1962: Pl. 31.1; 1964: 20; Bocher and Lipschits 2011; 2013; Lipschits *et al.* 2006; 2009a
	Mamila	1	Amit 2009: 94–104, Pl. 103 (F)
	Bethany	1	Saller 1953: 6; 1957: 12–13, Fig. 36, Pl. 111
Total from Jerusalem and its environs		93	
Shephelah	Gezer	2	Macalister 1912: 209, Pl. 359
	Yarmouth	1	Richardson 1968: 12–13, Figs. 1–2
	Naḥal Yarmouth	1	Farhi 2001: Photo 262
	Azekah	1	Bliss and Macalister 1902: 122–123, Pl. 54:56
Total from the Shephelah		5	
Benjamin	Tell el-Fûl	1	Lapp 1981: 113–122, Pl. 1:31, Photo 186
	Mizpah	1	McCown 1947: 164
Total from Benjamin region		2	
Samaria	Khirbet Burnat	1	Torgë and Gendelman 2008: 5, Fig. 5:15
Total from Samaria region		1	
Stamp impressions of unknown origin or unpublished		3	
Total		**104**	

in the 2nd century BCE, which was settled for the first time since the Babylonian destruction.[83]

In conclusion, it seems that the *yršlm* stamp impressions, securely dated to the beginning of the Hasmonean period, constitute the final system in the 600 years of operation of such systems in Judah. The choice of the Hellenistic symbol, which protects the capital, was a conscious decision to merge with the West, while the return to the use of ancient Hebrew writing in the symbols of authority embodies the nationalism prevalent at the time, reflecting a deep desire to restore the kingdom's splendor. The affinity between the *yršlm* stamp impressions and the late types of *yhwd* stamp impressions suggests that both systems were in use during the early Hasmonean period; archaeologically, however, it is difficult to determine whether or not these stamp-impression systems operated in conjunction. Historically, one may assume that the *yršlm* stamp-impression system

was also an *ad hoc* system formed at the onset of the Hasmonean period, on the basis of the already existing system, in order to ensure organized supply of produce to the rebels and their leaders. Alternatively, it is possible that when the rebellion subsided and the new country's administration could develop, the *yršlm* stamp-impression system—like the lion stamp-impression system of the early 6th century BCE—was introduced in order to collect taxes on behalf of the renewed capital.

Historically, this administrative system should probably be dated to the days of Simon Maccabaeus, under whose leadership Judea achieved independence (142 BCE), and who established and consolidated the kingdom and was largely responsible for its economic development (Rappaport 1995: 63). It would seem that the use of stamp impressions on storage jars ceased when the minting of coins began during the period of John Hyrcanus.

---

83. Reich 2003: 259. For a similar phenomenon, see Lipschits and Vanderhooft (2009), who also address the appearance of the later *yhwd* stamp impressions here.

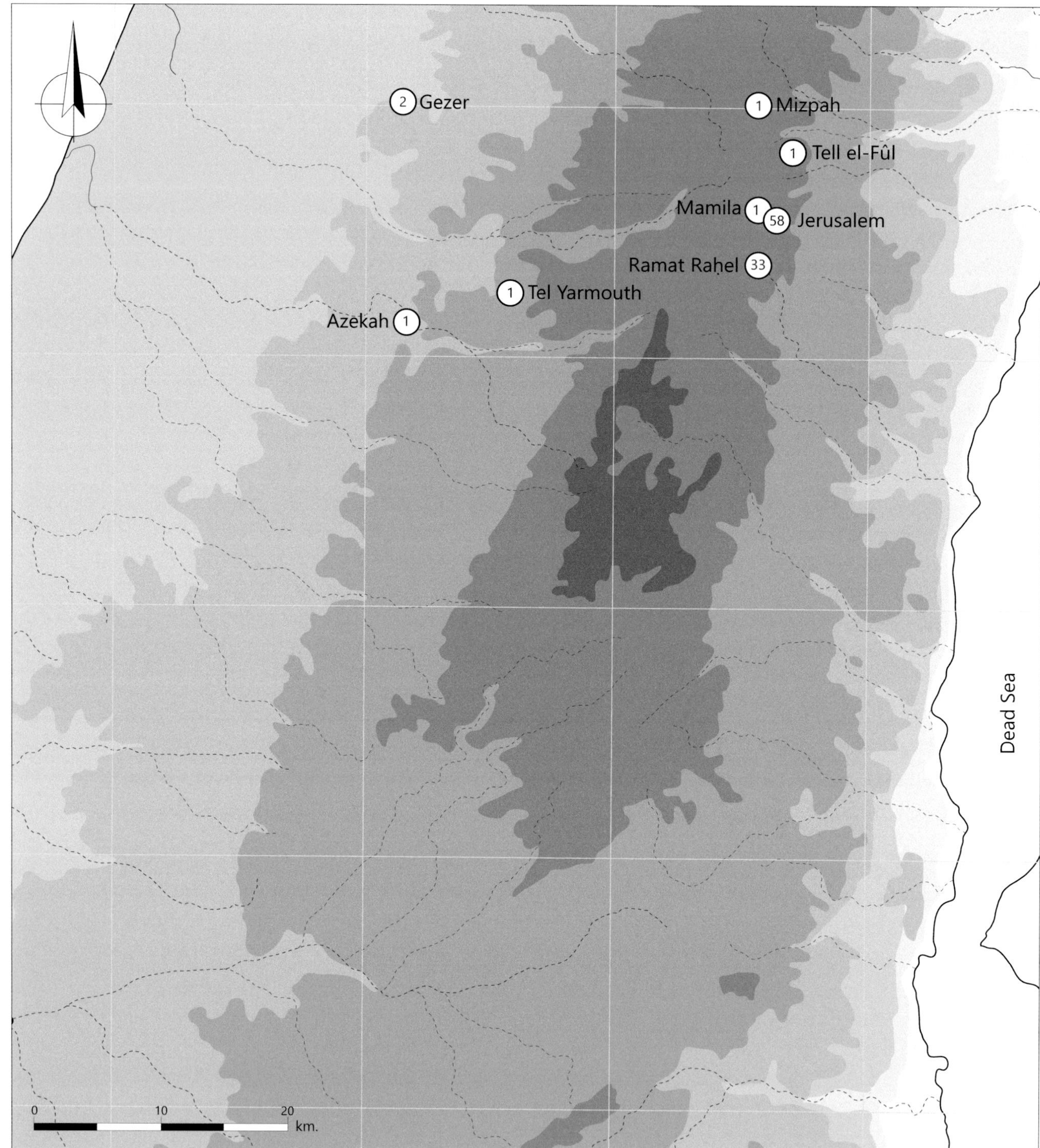

Fig. 4.36: Distribution of *yršlm*-stamped handles

Summary

For 600 years, impressions were stamped onto the handles and bodies of storage jars in Judah (for a summary of the distribution of the various types and systems, see Tables 4.15 and 4.16). These storage jars were part of an administrative system that produced and amassed agricultural products and operated without interruption despite the momentous political and historical upheavals that Judah suffered during this period.

Postscript: Script and Symbols on the Stamp Impressions from Judah

Two main and unrelated progressions can be traced in the script and symbols appearing on the various stamp impressions. At first, in the days of the Kingdom of Judah, the impressions bore a component of Hebrew script along with a symbol in their center. The transition to concentric circle incisions represents the beginning of a long period during which writing was absent (evident in the rosette and lion stamp impressions) and the focus was on a central iconographic element. With the transition to the Persian period, the use of symbols disappeared from the stamp impressions, and these became solely epigraphic—with a decisive Aramaic influence. Hebrew gradually returned to the seals from the late 4th century BCE and during the 3rd century BCE. Only after the Hasmonean revolt, in the mid-2nd century BCE, did iconography once again become a central component in the *yršlm* stamp impressions, with the Hebrew script alongside it.

Table 4.15: The number of stamped handles and the number of types in the various systems

System	Number of Stamp Impressions	Number of Types (= Seals)	Number of Impressions per Seal[i]
Regular Stamp-Impression Systems			
Early *lmlk* stamp impressions	723	11	66
Late *lmlk* stamp impressions	490	8	61
Unidentifiable *lmlk* stamp impressions	361		
Total *lmlk* Stamp Impressions	1,574	19	83
Concentric circle incisions	305	–	–
Rosette stamp impressions	290	28	10
Lion stamp impressions	136	10	13.5
Early *yhwd* stamp impressions	165	14	12
Middle *yhwd* stamp impressions	338	16	21
Late *yhwd* stamp impressions	144	21	7
Ad hoc Stamp-Impression Systems			
"Private" stamp impressions	183	45	4
mwṣh stamp impressions	43	6	7
yršlm stamp impressions	104	8	13
Total	3,282 (3,139)[ii]	167	16

i   The figures are rounded to whole numbers.

ii Handles with *lmlk* or "private" stamp impressions alongside concentric circle incisions were counted twice. The actual number of handles (when one factors out the 140 concentric circle incisions that occurred alongside *lmlk* stamp impressions and the three that appeared alongside "private" stamp impressions) is given here in parentheses.

Table 4.16: The distribution of the various series of stamp impressions

Area	Site	Regular Systems											Ad hoc Systems			Total[i]
		Early *lmlk*	Late *lmlk*	Unidentified *lmlk*	Total *lmlk*	Concentric Circle Incisions	Rosette	Lion	Early *yhwd*	Middle *yhwd*	Late *yhwd*	Total *yhwd*	"Private"	*mwṣh*	*yršlm*	
Jerusalem and its environs	Ramat Raḥel	46	133	45	224	40	57	73	127	212	33	372	19	1	33	819 (808)
	Jerusalem	Ca. 90	Ca. 180	32	302	162	108	31	17	59	86	162	13	4	58	840 (755)
	Mordot Arnona	13	3	5	21	4	0	0	0	0	0	0	8	0	0	33
	Other sites	2	3	8	13	6	7	4	4	5	8	17	1	1	2	51 (50)
Total from Jerusalem and its environs		151	319	90	560	212	172	108	148	276	127	551	41	6	93	1,743 (1,646)
Benjamin region	Mizpah	27	38	23	88	17	2	5	1	18	0	19	4	30	1	166 (149)
	Gibeon	17	63	12	92	33	2	2	0	0	0	0	7	4	0	140 (122)
	Nebi Samwil	0	3	1	4	0	3	13	3	13	0	16	0	0	0	36
	Khirbet el-Burj	1	15	7	23	15	4	0	0	0	0	0	0	0	0	42 (41)
	Tell el-Fûl	0	5	8	13	4	4	0	0	0	1	1	0	0	1	23 (21)
	Moẓa	0	0	2	2	5	4	0	0	0	0	0	0	0	0	11
	Other sites	0	0	0	0	1	0	0	1	1	2	4	0	0	0	5
Total from Benjamin region		45	124	53	222	75	19	20	5	32	3	40	11	34	2	423 (383)
Southern Judah Hill Country	Hebron	1	6	7	14	1	0	0	0	0	0	0	0	0	0	15 (14)
	Beth-Zur	0	8	3	11	2	5	0	0	0	0	0	0	0	0	18 (17)
	Other sites	1	0	0	1	0	1	0	0	0	0	0	2	0	0	4
Total from Southern Judah Hill Country		2	14	10	26	3	6	0	0	0	0	0	2	0	0	37 (35)
Shephelah	Lachish	378	4	31	413	4	24	0	0	0	0	0	72	0	0	513 (511)
	Beth Shemesh	56	1	ca. 70	127	0	1	0	0	1	0	1	18	0	0	147
	Tel Goded	17	1	21	39	1	0	0	0	0	0	0	12	0	0	52 (51)
	Tel Batash	12	3	0	15	1	6	0	0	0	0	0	1	0	0	23
	Azekah	20	0	6	26	4	30	0	0	0	0	0	4	0	1	65
	Maresha	6	0	13	19	0	0	0	0	0	0	0	1	0	0	20
	Tel ʿErani	1	1	14	16	0	1	0	0	0	0	0	1	0	0	18
	Socoh	2	11	11	24	0	5	0	0	0	0	0	7	0	0	36
	Tell eṣ-Ṣafi	7	0	0	7	0	1	0	0	0	0	0	4	0	0	12
	Other sites	7	0	2	9	0	3	1	2	1	0	3	5	0	2	23
Total from the Shephelah		506	21	168	695	10	71	1	2	2	0	4	125	0	3	909 (906)
Total from the Beersheba–Arad Valleys		8	4	6	18	1	10	0	0	0	0	0	1	0	0	30 (29)
Eastern periphery	Jericho	0	1	0	1	1	0	1	2	16	0	18	0	2	0	23 (22)
	En-Gedi	0	1	0	1	3	11	5	3	7	0	10	0	0	0	30 (29)
	Other sites	0	1	2	3	0	1	0	0	0	0	0	1	0	0	5
Total from the eastern periphery		0	3	2	5	4	12	6	5	23	0	28	1	2	0	58
Total from sites outside Judah		11	5	34	50	0	0	1	2	2	8	12	2	0	3	67
Unknown origin									1	3	9	13	0	1	3	17
Total		723	490	363	1576	305	290	136	163	338	144	647	183	43	104	3,284 (3,139)

i   Handles with *lmlk* or "private" stamp impressions alongside concentric circle incisions were counted twice. The actual number of handles (when one factors out the co-occurrence) is given here in parentheses. Since most of the incised handles were found in Jerusalem and they include 85 concentric circle incisions alongside *lmlk* stamp impressions and three alongside "private" stamp impressions, the number of stamped handles from Jerusalem is 755 and not 840. In Ramat Raḥel only 11 handles were incised with concentric circles alongside *lmlk* stamp impressions, and consequently, the number of stamped handles is 808 and not 819. The total number of stamp impressions and incisions is, thus, 3,277 and the number of actual stamped/incised handles is 3,139.

5

The Chronology of the Stamped Storage-Jar Systems in the Kingdom of Judah

With our growing understanding of the archaeology of the late Iron Age, the chronological boundaries of the various types of stamp impressions have become clear. Many storage-jar handles bearing *lmlk* stamp impressions were recovered from Lachish Level III, which was destroyed in 701 BCE, providing a *terminus ante quem* for this system. It is now clear that the unstamped prototypes of the *lmlk* storage jars appeared as early as the late 9th and early 8th centuries BCE, and that typologically, the standardization of the stamped types occurred during the 8th century BCE. Theoretically, therefore, the *terminus post quem* for the *lmlk* stamp-impression system is the beginning or middle of the second half of the 8th century BCE.

Not a single handle with concentric circle incisions was discovered in any destruction layer dated to Sennacherib's campaign. It is clear, therefore, that this system post-dates 701 BCE and that the beginning of the 7th century BCE is its *terminus post quem*. However, the close affinity between the systems of concentric circle incisions and of *lmlk* stamp impressions (sometimes appearing on the same jars or even on the same handles and displaying a similar geographical distribution),

coupled with the absence of handles with concentric circle incisions from the destruction layers of the early 6th century BCE (only a very small number were uncovered in this context and in sites where these few finds can be accounted for), indicate that this system went out of use long before the Babylonian destruction, presumably before the last third of the 7th century BCE.

No rosette-stamped storage jars and no jars typical of this late 7th-century BCE type were found in the 701 BCE destruction layers. It is clear, therefore, that the type of jar on which these impressions were stamped had not yet developed at this stage and that the rosette seals were a later development. Moreover, as discussed below, handles with rosette stamp impressions were not found in the fill from the early building phase at Ramat Raḥel, but only on the floors of the second building phase. Thus, theoretically, the *terminus post quem* for the rosette stamp-impression system is the beginning of the last third of the 7th century BCE. Many rosette-stamped handles were discovered in the 586 BCE destruction layers. This, coupled with their absence in later strata, provides a *terminus ante quem* for the system.

No storage jars with lion, *mwṣh* or *yhwd* stamp impressions were found in any late First Temple period destruction layers, but only in those of the Babylonian and Persian periods. It thus seems that 586 BCE is the *terminus post quem* for these systems. However, as discussed below, no storage jars bearing lion or *mwṣh* stamp impressions have been recovered from clear Persian period contexts, so archaeologically, these systems must have preceded the Persian period settlement layers. The *yhwd* stamp impressions are typical of Persian and Hellenistic period settlement layers. The appearance of the name of the province in Aramaic on some types, at times with the title *pḥw'* (Aramaic for "governor"), and the fact that most of the stamped types were written in Aramaic suggest that the Persian period is the *terminus post quem* for this system. Several factors indicate that it came to an end during the Hasmonean period, in the mid-2nd century BCE: the degeneration of some types of *yhwd* stamp impressions and the abbreviation of the name of the province to three letters (*yhd*), two letters (*yh*) (a phenomenon also known on coins), or even a ligature of *yh*; the shift from Aramaic to Hebrew script in some late *yhwd* types; the finding of late types in clear 2nd-century BCE archaeological contexts, including the Western Hill of Jerusalem; and their frequent recovery alongside storage-jar handles bearing *yršlm* stamp impressions. After the mid-2nd century BCE, locally manufactured storage-jar handles with stamp impressions ceased to appear in Judah.

The conclusion from the above is that there was a long and continuous development of stamp impressions on storage-jar handles in Judah, beginning in the second half of the 8th century BCE, with the emergence of *lmlk* stamp impressions, and ending in the 2nd century BCE, with the disappearance of the late *yhwd* and the *yršlm* stamp impressions. This conclusion runs counter to the view of various scholars that storage-jar production and the stamping of their handles took place during very short periods in the history of Judah. It also rejects the view that the main stamp-impression systems arose within the framework of the preparations in Judah to withstand Sennacherib's campaign (the *lmlk* stamp impressions in 704–701 BCE) or the Babylonian campaign (the rosette stamp impressions in 588–586 BCE). These explanations do not provide a unified theory that addresses the phenomenon in general and do not account for the other stamp-impression systems.

Within this general time frame—the late 8th century to the 2nd century BCE—we must pinpoint the precise period of each system and determine whether there was a chronological gap or overlap between systems. This should not be based solely upon the archaeological data, but should take into account historical, iconographic, typological and palaeographic considerations as well. It requires an analysis of the dating and development of the storage jars themselves, and relies upon broad archaeological considerations of dating strata in the key settlement sites in Judah. It necessitates an understanding of the different fates that befell the various regions of Judah, especially after the heavy destruction wreaked by the Assyrian campaign in 701 BCE and by the Babylonian campaign in 588–586 BCE, and it calls for an interpretation of the function and role of the administrative systems of stamped storage jars in the various periods.

This chapter presents the data and considerations necessary to pinpoint the precise chronology of each of the stamp-impression systems.

The Chronology of the *lmlk* Stamp Impressions

History of Research: Open Questions and New Directions

In the first half of the 20th century, the dating of Lachish Levels III and II served as the basis for scholarly views regarding the chronology of the various types of *lmlk* stamp impressions. In 1937 Starkey dated the Level III destruction to 597 BCE and the Level II destruction to 586 BCE, a dating accepted by Inge and Harding. Consequently, in 1941, Diringer dated the emergence of the *lmlk* stamp impressions to the late 8th–early 7th centuries BCE and argued that they were in use throughout the 7th century BCE, during the successive reigns of Hezekiah, Manasseh and Josiah.[1]

Diringer was the first to classify the stamp impressions uncovered at Lachish into three groups (1941: 91–101). Class I included those four-winged stamp impressions that appeared less stylized and schematic, Class II included the four-winged impressions with a more formal and square script and Class III included all the two-winged stamp impressions. Albright (1943: 74) accepted this typology, dating the first group to the days of Hezekiah, the second to the reign of Manasseh and the third to the reign of Josiah and the last kings of Judah.[2] At this stage, the iconographic transition from the four-winged scarab to the two-winged sun disk (called the "flying scroll") was attributed to the religious and cultic reforms of Josiah and served to corroborate the dating of these stamp impressions to his reign (Albright 1943: 74; cf. Diringer 1949: 74–75).[3] As the four-winged scarab symbol was identified as having originated in Egypt, the replacement of the "scarab" with the "scroll" was perceived as the rejection of a foreign deity and of foreign ritual in favor of an abstract representation of a winged "Scroll of the Law."[4]

The scholarly trend changed in the second half of the 20th century when Tufnell assigned the destruction of Lachish Level III to Sennacherib's campaign (701 BCE) (Tufnell 1953: 55–58; 1959: 97–103; cf. 1950: 76–79),[5] a dating confirmed by Ussishkin's 1974–1994 excavations at Lachish (Ussishkin 1977). As numerous *lmlk* storage jars were found in a sealed archaeological context under the Level III destruction layer and as Lachish revealed the largest quantity of stamped storage-jar handles to be discovered at a single site and in a single stratum, most scholars in the past 40 years have assumed that the storage jars should be dated to an extremely short period at the end of the 8th century BCE.[6]

On archaeological grounds, there was no reason to limit the date of the stamped storage jars to the few years during which Hezekiah prepared for the anticipated Assyrian campaign against Judah. Indeed, Ussishkin did not let historical considerations encroach upon the interpretation of the archaeological findings, and he argued that on the basis of the findings alone, one could not determine whether all the types of stamped storage jars were manufactured during the reign of Hezekiah or whether some were produced prior to his accession to the throne and continued to be used during his reign. He acknowledged that since Tel Lachish had been abandoned after the 701 BCE destruction, it was impossible to determine whether stamped storage jars were

---

1. Starkey 1937a: 235–236; 1937b: 175–177; Inge 1938: 251–255; Harding 1943: 9–10. Cf. Diringer's dating of the storage jars (1941: 106; 1949: 85–86). Albright (1943), Lapp (1960) and Cross (1969) accepted Diringer's viewpoint, with Cross (1969: 21*–22*) limiting the duration of the stamp impressions to the second half of the 7th century BCE, to the period of Josiah's rule alone.

2. Albright's dating was accepted by Diringer (1949: 84–86). In this context it should be noted that most scholars in the 1950s and 1960s accepted the assumption that the four-winged stamp impressions preceded the two-winged stamp impressions, supported by the paleography (Diringer 1949: 85–86; Lapp 1960: 21; Cross 1969: 20*–22*). Nevertheless, Lapp (1960: 18) admitted that there is no stratigraphic justification for a chronological distinction between the four- and two-winged stamp impressions, basing his distinction on paleographical grounds only.

3. Given the dating of the stamp impressions to the days of Josiah, Tushingham (1970; 1971) identified each of the *lmlk* emblems as a symbol of one of the kingdoms, associating the scarab with the Kingdom of Israel and the sun symbol with the Kingdom of Judah. In his view (1971: 33–35), both symbols were used by Josiah, who considered himself the true king of a united Israel. After the conclusive dating of the *lmlk* stamp impressions to the late 8th century BCE, Tushingham modified his theory to argue that it was Hezekiah who used the dual-symbol system (1992: 61–64): the Judahite symbol, according to Tushingham, was used only in Jerusalem proper, while the Israelite symbol was used throughout his kingdom to represent the unity between the Judahite locals and the Israelite refugees from Assyrian exile. See also Fox (2000: 222), who suggested that the word *lmlk* was intended to unite the two symbols—the "Israelite" and "Judahite" symbols—within a single royal system.

4. See Diringer 1949: 75–76. The prevalent view at this time was that the four-winged stamp-impression system preceded the two-winged system, the symbol of which was termed "Flying Scroll" (Watzinger 1933: 116; Diringer 1934: 155; 1949: 85–86; Albright 1943: 74; McCown 1947: 156; Lapp 1960: 21; Cross 1969: 20*–22*) or "Winged Sun Disc" (Sayce 1900; Diringer 1953: 342). This shift between the two symbols was attributed to Josiah, who abandoned the idolatrous symbol and preferred the abstract representation of the "Flying Scroll" (Diringer 1949: 75–76).

5. The first to accept the revised dating of the Level III destruction at Lachish to 701 BCE were Israeli scholars Y. Aharoni and R. Amiran (Aharoni and Amiran 1958: 182 and n. 42; Aharoni 1973: 5–6; 1975b: 15–16; Aharoni and Aharoni 1976), B. Mazar (1964: 295 and n. 18) and A.F. Rainey (1975). At this point most British and American scholars continued to support Starkey's attribution of the Level III destruction to the 597 BCE Babylonian campaign (Albright 1953: 46; 1958: 24; Buchanan 1954: 335–337; Kenyon 1957; Lapp 1960: 16–18; Wright 1965: 100–104; Cross 1969: 20*–21* and n. 4; Lance 1971: 321, 329; Holladay 1976: 266–267).

6. As noted by Ussishkin (2004c: 89, 92), this assumption was almost unanimously accepted. See, in particular, Ussishkin 1976; 1977: 57–59; Naʾaman 1979b; 1986; Vaughn 1999a; Fox 2000: 216–235; Hudon 2010.

manufactured and used during the rest of Hezekiah's reign (after the destruction) and in the period following his death (see, e.g., Ussishkin 1977: 56–57).

It was Naʾaman who attributed the *lmlk* stamp-impression system to Hezekiah's revolt and to his preparations for the 701 BCE Assyrian campaign (Naʾaman 1979b; 1986). Noting that most of the storage jars with *lmlk* stamp impressions were found on the western border of Judah, in the Shephelah, and on the northern border of the kingdom, he pointed out that these were the potential directions from which the anticipated Assyrian attack would come. Given the clear connection between the stamped storage jars and the destruction strata stemming from Sennacherib's campaign, Naʾaman concluded that the storage-jar system as a whole served in the context of the preparations for this campaign. In his opinion, the products stored in the royal storage jars were distributed to sites in the kingdom that were facing the threat of an Assyrian siege. On these grounds, he dated the appearance of the *lmlk* stamp impressions to the period following the outbreak of the revolt in 705 or 704 BCE, thus restricting the use of the stamped storage jars to a period of three or four years at most.[7]

Ussishkin projected this reasonable historical assumption onto the archaeological finds (Ussishkin 2004b: 2141–2142). However, while the presence of numerous sherds of storage jars in the Lachish Level III destruction layer provides a *terminus ante quem* for their use, it does not give any indication of their date of production. The claim that they were all manufactured in the three years prior to the destruction of Level III is a historical interpretation, not an archaeological fact.[8] Moreover, the findings in Ussishkin's excavations invalidated the stratigraphic-archaeological distinction between the four-winged and the two-winged stamp impressions: large quantities of all types of these stamp impressions were found sealed together beneath the Level III destruction layer (Vaughn 1999b: 85). The prevalent view had been that since four-winged stamp impressions were more prevalent in the Shephelah and their two-winged counterparts were more common in the hill country,[9] there must be a geographical distinction between the types. The scholarly assumption was that since all the different types of *lmlk* stamp impressions were found in the destruction level at Lachish, they must have all been produced at the same time.

Ussishkin's excavations at Lachish paved the way for a meticulous study of the types of stamp impressions found in Level III, which clearly belonged to a period preceding the Assyrian 701 BCE destruction (whether a few years or longer). In 1981 Lemaire presented his typology of *lmlk* stamp impressions, convincingly classifying numerous seals into four main groups. Unfortunately, no careful study was undertaken during the excavations or in the framework of the final report to determine which types were indeed uncovered in this Level III destruction layer and which were not, and Ussishkin made do with a general statement that all types of *lmlk* stamp impressions were found sealed beneath the Level III destruction layer (Ussishkin 1977: 56–57).

In recent years it has become clear that this claim was erroneous. A careful study of the various *lmlk* types defined by Lemaire has revealed that some types, represented by several hundred stamp impressions, were not, in fact, present in this destruction layer at Lachish or in any contemporaneous destruction layer.[10] Furthermore, handles stamped with these types have been

---

7. This view was extensively quoted, becoming almost axiomatic among scholars. See, e.g., Buchanan and Moorey 1988: 4; Mazar, Amit and Ilan 1996: 208–209; Mazar and Panitz-Cohen 2001: 97; Kletter 2002: 144; Ussishkin 2004b: 2142.

8. For criticism of Ussishkin's approach, see Lipschits 2012a: 6–9; Finkelstein 2012: 203–206. Because of the continuity between Levels IV and III in the 8th century BCE, the Lachish excavations cannot serve as a basis for determining when the *lmlk* stamp-impression system began to operate. The settlement gap following Sennacherib's destruction of Lachish means that the finds from the site cannot provide a basis for reconstructing the continued use of the system in the early 7th century BCE.

9. Indeed, many scholars have noted this; e.g., Buchanan and Moorey 1988: 5. Barkay and Vaughn (2004: 2167–2168) provide a summary of the various types.

10. Following several studies that examined the various types of stamp impressions, cross-referencing them with archaeological data (Lipschits, Sergi and Koch 2010; 2011), Ussishkin published a rejoinder (2011), in which he accepted the absence of several *lmlk* types from Lachish Level III and from corresponding strata in other sites destroyed in 701 BCE. Nevertheless, Ussishkin continues to contend that the archaeological finds do not prove that types absent from Lachish's Level III destruction layer were produced after 701 BCE.

found at sites dated to the 7th century BCE.[11] The dating of the beginning of the system has also been shown to be based on historical assumptions, with numerous problems. Once we consider the dating of the system of stamp impressions on storage jars from a broad perspective, free of preconceptions, we may reach a different historical reconstruction of the era when it began, of the circumstances that contributed to it, and of the purposes for which it was established.

The Inception of the
lmlk Stamp-Impression System

As aforementioned, the discovery of many *lmlk* storage jars in the Level III destruction layer in Lachish and in other destruction layers dated to the 701 BCE Assyrian campaign provides a *terminus ante quem* for this system. But does this help to determine when the storage jars were first produced and stamped?

There is no clear archaeological answer to the question how long the *lmlk*-stamped storage jars were in use prior to the 701 BCE destruction. Any proposal is mere historical speculation. The absence of such handles from settlement layers destroyed by the Assyrians at the beginning of the last third of the 8th century BCE offers no more than circumstantial evidence for determining the latest date when the *lmlk* stamp-impression system was not yet in use. In any case, most of the sites that were destroyed belonged to the Kingdom of Israel. Similarly, we cannot determine when the stamped storage jars were first manufactured on the basis of the finds from Lachish Level III, since this fortified city was probably established in the first half or the mid-8th century BCE and enjoyed a long duration until its destruction at the end of this century (Ussishkin 2004c: 82–83; Finkelstein and Piasetzky 2010). The fact that there were many different types of stamped storage jars and that the phenomenon continued for a period of 600 years shows that the system was not an *ad hoc* one, created for a specific purpose in

a specific period, but was a part of an evolving and long-lasting administrative system. While the pottery found sealed beneath a destruction layer should be attributed to the final stage of existence of that layer (Ussishkin 2011: 223), it does not provide any indication of the duration of this layer. Nor does it deal with the question of whether all types of pottery vessels have equal lifespans (whether storage jars, for example, share the same lifespan as cooking pots and bowls). Furthermore, Ussishkin's dating does not account for the fact that storage jars with *lmlk* stamp impressions were found in sites established in the second half of the 7th century BCE (Lipschits, Sergi and Koch 2010: 8; Lipschits 2012a: 7), more than fifty years after the production of this type of storage jar had, in his opinion, ceased.

While the notion that the *lmlk* stamp impressions reflect preparations to withstand Sennacherib's campaign is indeed a possible historical conjecture, it is not without challenges. The study of the storage jars points to a long tradition of production and a lengthy standardization process, leading to the development of certain types of storage jars. It is unlikely that this process took place in such a short time (see above, pp. 17–24). Furthermore, the sheer quantity of stamped handles and the large number of seals that were in use, reflecting a great variety of types, all represent a sophisticated administrative system. It is hard to imagine that such a complex system— involving the production of storage jars and the stamping of their handles at a single center, their distribution to agricultural estates to be filled with agricultural products, and their subsequent storage in royal centers—developed and was executed on such a broad scale during the brief period between Hezekiah's revolt and Sennacherib's campaign, a period of at most three years—if one assumes that preparations began immediately after the death of Sargon II. The large quantity of storage jars stamped with *lmlk* impressions, compared to the rosette-stamped storage jars, for example, also points to the long duration of this system. A close examination of the distribution of

---

11. For example, Mazar, Amit and Ilan (1996) uncovered a two-winged *lmlk* stamp impression at Ḥorvat Shilḥa (a short-lived single-period late 7th century BCE site, with no prior settlement). Handles with *lmlk* stamp impressions were found in similar contexts at Tel Batash, Khirbet es-Samrah, En-Gedi and ʿAroer (Mazar, Amit and Ilan 1996: 208–209). Consequently, Mazar suggested that *lmlk*-stamped storage jars continued to be used after Sennacherib's campaign, during the 7th century BCE. He stressed, however, that this does not constitute evidence for further storage-jar production and stamping, but merely for the continued use of existing stamped jars. In his opinion, storage jars from sites such as Jerusalem, which were not destroyed in 701 BCE, continued to be used throughout the kingdom in the 7th century BCE as well (Mazar, Amit and Ilan 1996: 209).

the various types suggests that some of the storage jars found in destruction layers attributed to Sennacherib's campaign had been filled and sent to royal centers more than once. Moreover, many storage jars bearing stamp impressions of the same types as those found sealed beneath 701 BCE destruction layers were uncovered in Judahite sites that were not involved in preparations for the Assyrian campaign; most of these sites continued to exist and develop during the 7th century BCE (Lipschits, Sergi and Koch 2010: 6–7; Lipschits 2012a: 6; see already Vaughn 1999b: 136–152). These finds are not in keeping with the notion that the entire system was established in preparation for the anticipated Assyrian attack. Furthermore, the claim that all the *lmlk* storage jars were part of these preparations does not take into account the existence of other systems of stamp impressions on storage-jar handles in Judah in the 7th century BCE and later in the Persian and Hellenistic province between the 6th and 2nd centuries BCE.

The possibility that Ramat Raḥel was established as an administrative center for the collection of agricultural produce under imperial guidance and supervision[12] is in keeping with our knowledge of the development of agricultural estates in the hill country—a process that presumably began in the late 8th century in the Rephaim Valley, around Moẓa and perhaps in other areas around Jerusalem.[13] In this period there were evidently technological changes and improvements in the agricultural production installations in Judah (Faust and Weiss 2005; Katz 2008: 55–59), and there were significant changes in its pottery production, with a shift from non-standardized and small-scale production in local

workshops to mass production and the widespread distribution of a small variety of uniform vessels (Mazar 1990: 509; Zimhoni 1997: 171–172; 2004b: 1705–1707; Katz 2008: 52–53, with further literature). This period also saw a move toward larger storage jars (Zimhoni 2004b: 1706). Standardization was also evident in the system of weights, which provided for greater governmental supervision of commerce and economy in Judah (Kletter 1998: 145–147; Katz 2008: 77–79, with further literature). All the above point to a centralized royal economy, with improved agricultural production output and delivery encouraged and promoted by the local authorities. While these changes have been noted by many scholars and their chronology has been established, the subjugation of Judah to Assyria has not yet been pinpointed as the catalyst driving these developments.[14]

The *lmlk* stamp impressions should, in my opinion, be viewed as part of the economic and administrative system introduced in Judah under Assyrian rule, with imperial encouragement and perhaps pressure to increase agricultural production in order to meet the annual tax quotas imposed by the empire upon its vassal kingdom.[15] This is supported by the evidence indicating the deliberate choice of a specific type of storage jar, which had been manufactured and widely used in the Shephelah for at least a century, and basing the system of agricultural collection on this type (Sergi *et al.* 2012; and see above, pp. 17–24). The high-quality production of this specific type of storage jar, with unprecedented uniformity, and the concentration of over 50% of the known storage jars of the late 8th century BCE in Lachish attest to the scope and

---

12. Lipschits *et al.* 2017: 36–56. For the establishment of the center in Ramat Raḥel, see also Naʾaman 2001: 270–274; Lipschits and Gadot 2008; cf. Lipschits *et al.* 2009a.

13. On the establishment of agricultural estates in the Rephaim Valley, see Lipschits and Gadot 2008; Gadot 2015; Finkelstein and Gadot 2015; around Moẓa, see De Groot and Greenhut 2002; Greenhut 2006; Greenhut and De Groot 2009; in other areas around Jerusalem, see Katz 2008: 169–178; Lipschits and Gadot 2008.

14. Maeir and Shai (2016: 324), for example, defined this change in Judah's administration and economy as follows: "The political-religious reforms that may have occurred in Judah in the 8th and 7th centuries BCE should be seen as attempts to impose a centralized authority on a very non-centralized kingdom." While they are aware of Assyria's role in shaping Judah's administration and economy (Maeir and Shai 2016: 330), they do not relate to the full impact and implications of its subjugation to Assyria.

15. Gitin noted (1995: 61–62), on the basis of his finds in Tel Miqne/Ekron, that the Assyrians had established "a new super-national system of political control in the eastern Mediterranean basin which produced the *Pax Assyriaca*, 70 years of unparalleled growth and development, and an international trading network which spanned the Mediterranean, stimulating Phoenician trade and colonization in the west." Schloen (2001: 146–147) and Faust (2011: 73), on the other hand, argued that the Assyrians were not interested in the economic development of their vassal kingdoms. For a well-structured and convincing critique of these views, see Younger 2015; cf. Lipschits 2018a.

operation of this system. The large number of *lmlk*-stamped jar handles—mainly late types dated to the early 7th century BCE—found at Ramat Raḥel indicates that this site functioned as an administrative center for the collection of storage jars containing agricultural products from the early 7th century through the end of the Persian period, long after Assyrian rule had come to an end and even after the destruction of the Kingdom of Judah.

The beginning of the *lmlk* stamp-impression system should therefore be dated to the period following the subjugation of Judah to Assyria—after King Ahaz traveled to Damascus in order to surrender to Tiglath-pileser III in 732 BCE, or shortly after Hezekiah ascended the throne (Lipschits 2018a)—and should be viewed as a response to the taxes imposed by Assyria.[16] The system developed in the course of a quarter of a century until Hezekiah's revolt (704 BCE) and Sennacherib's campaign (701 BCE). One may speculate that the choice of the four-winged scarab as the initial emblem of the system in Judah reflected Egyptian influence. Interestingly, Egyptian influence is evident in the administrative system of late 8th-century Judah in other contexts: in the *sheqel* mark engraved on weights, for example, and in the system of measurements used. This is not surprising, given the long years of contact with the nearby Egyptian empire and the fact that Assyrian presence in Judah had not yet been consolidated at this point.

The Chronology and Development of the Early *lmlk* Types

It is impossible on the basis of archaeology to determine the internal chronology—relative or absolute—or any gradual development among the various types of *lmlk* stamp impressions on handles found in or beneath destruction layers resulting from Sennacherib's campaign in Lachish and other sites in the Shephelah. This is an inherent limitation of archaeological research: while enabling us to capture the final moment of use of pottery vessels, it does not permit us to pinpoint the beginning

of the process or any intermediate stage prior to the destruction phase.

All the types of four-winged stamp impressions (Lemaire's Types Ia and Ib) and four sub-types of two-winged stamp impressions (Lemaire's Type IIa) clearly belong to the early stage of this system, as numerous handles bearing these stamp impressions were found in and beneath the destruction layer attributed to Sennacherib's campaign. The question arises whether there is any other evidence that could help determine the relative chronology and development processes among the various early types.

The notion that the four-winged scarab symbol was an early emblem was proposed by Lipschits, Sergi and Koch (2010: 17–18), who noted that all the stamp impressions of the various four-winged scarab types, as well as several types with the winged sun disk, appeared prior to the 701 BCE destruction, and that after the destruction, the two-winged emblem was the only one to be found. Moreover, far more handles with the four-winged emblem were found in the destruction layers than handles with the two-winged emblem: in Lachish Level III, 348 handles with the four-winged scarab were uncovered, as compared to 30 with the winged sun disk. From the early types of *lmlk* stamp impressions, most of the 552 handles with the four-winged scarab emblem found in excavations and surveys are related to destruction layers parallel to Lachish Level III, compared to some 171 handles with the winged sun disk (see above, pp. 40–48). It is therefore reasonable to assume that use of the four-winged symbol preceded use of the two-winged symbol and was discontinued prior to the Assyrian destruction of 701 BCE. While numerous storage jars with the four-winged emblem were still in use in sites destroyed in the Assyrian campaign, storage jars with the winged sun disk were already in use alongside them. These latter types began to be used shortly before the Assyrian campaign, and the number of storage jars stamped with these types was therefore smaller. After Sennacherib's onslaught, production of types with the new winged sun disk continued, while use of the early types of seals ceased.

---

16. Millard 2009: 29, 34; 2015: 118–119; Hudon 2010; Lipschits, Sergi and Koch 2010: 6–7; 2011: 6. For a detailed discussion of the historical circumstances and possible dates of Judah's subjugation to Assyria, see below, pp. 155–158.

The claim about the precedence of the four-winged scarab emblem, which can be substantiated today, now that the distinction between early and late *lmlk* stamp impressions has been established, was in fact prevalent in the past, when many scholars dated the entire *lmlk* stamp-impression system to the 7th century BCE and speculated that the four-winged scarab emblem of Egyptian origin was replaced with the "flying scroll" as part of a Judahite trend to eschew symbols relating to foreign ritual. Diringer linked this change to Josiah's reform, arguing that paleographically, too, the four-winged stamp impressions preceded the two-winged ones.[17] This distinction was abandoned following the Lachish excavation findings and in light of the sweeping determination that all the types of stamp impressions were found sealed beneath the Level III destruction,[18] and certainly after the strengthening of the historical notion that the entire *lmlk* stamp-impression system had been established in a short period of three or four years and discontinued after Sennacherib's campaign. However, this subject merits renewed scholarly debate in light of the new typological discussion of the *lmlk* stamp impressions and the distinction between the early types—located in or below Lachish Level III and other 701 BCE destruction layers—and the late types—which are entirely absent from these archaeological contexts (Lipschits, Sergi and Koch 2010; 2011).

The circumstantial evidence for the precedence of the four-winged scarab emblem is supported by glyptic studies, which have shown that the scarab symbol was prevalent already in the 9th and 8th centuries BCE. This symbol is identified with Egypt, which had a notable cultural influence on Israel and Judah prior to the subjugation to Assyria in the last third of the 8th century BCE (Sass 1993: 214; Keel and Uehlinger 1998: 276; Ornan 2005: 231–234). Ostensibly, this is supported by

Ussishkin's observation, as early as 1976, that "private" stamp impressions were found alongside two-winged stamp impressions, but were never found alongside four-winged stamp impressions on the same handle or on the same storage jar (Ussishkin 1976: 12; 2004b: 2142–2143; cf. Lipschits, Sergi and Koch 2010: 26, n. 45). This observation can now be updated, since the stamp impressions mentioned by Ussishkin were indeed of the two-winged types, but they all belong to the types that were defined above (pp. 40–48) as early (Lemaire's Type IIa) and were in use prior to the destruction of Lachish Level III. We do, however, know today of a jar handle found in Jerusalem stamped with a "private" impression alongside a four-winged *lmlk* stamp impression (Avigad and Barkay 2000: 248–249, No. 54). The main conclusion should be that while there is a chronological overlap between the "private" stamp impressions and the early types of *lmlk* stamp impressions—presumably toward the end of the early *lmlk* stamp-impression system on the eve of Sennacherib's campaign—this does not constitute proof of a chronological distinction between the four-winged scarab stamp impressions and the early types of the winged sun-disk emblem.

New paleo-magnetic research makes it possible to determine a relative chronology of the various four-winged types (Lemaire's Types Ia and Ib) and to point to the development between them.[19] The paleo-magnetic graph (Ben-Yosef *et al.* 2017) shows that Type Ib preceded Type Ia and means that the stamp impressions with the official (lapidary) script are earlier. These seals are larger and more skillfully engraved than the subsequent ones, and their uniformity suggests that they were produced as a series, probably by the same craftsman and at the same time. The system with the cursive script, which includes only three seals (as the place name Socoh is missing), replaced the earlier system, likely toward the end of the

---

17. Diringer 1949: 75–76, 85–86, followed by Lapp 1960: 21 and Cross 1969: 20*–22*. According to Tushingham (1970; 1971), the four-winged symbol was Israelite in origin and Josiah continued to use it alongside the two-winged symbol in an effort to "unite" Israel and Judah. Following the Lachish excavations and the dating of the Level III destruction layer to 701 BCE, Tushingham revised the dating of the system as a whole, but maintained his basic argument. He argued (1992) that it was Hezekiah, and not Josiah, who used the four-winged symbol in order to unite the Israelites and the Judahites. In his view, the winged sun symbol was Judahite and its use therefore continued in the 7th century BCE.

18. As early as 1960, Lapp argued that there is no stratigraphic evidence to support the distinction between the various types of stamp impressions, and he based the distinction between the four- and two-winged types solely on paleographic grounds. See Lapp 1960: 18; Lance 1971: 324.

19. The paleo-magnetic research is directed by Ron Shaar (Institute of Earth Sciences, the Hebrew University of Jerusalem) and Erez Ben-Yosef (Institute of Archaeology, Tel Aviv University). The discussion below is based on an M.A. thesis written by Michael Millman (2014) under Erez Ben-Yosef's and my guidance. For the comprehensive publication of this study, see Ben-Yosef *et al.* 2017.

8th century BCE, after the latter had been in use for many years, producing a wealth of stamp impressions on storage-jar handles. In view of the absence of the place name Socoh, we may speculate that the old seal remained in use, especially if it was kept in the storage-jar production center, which may also have been in Socoh.

This was later replaced by a system of four seals, similar in the quality of engraving of the symbol and script, but bearing the two-winged instead of four-winged emblem. The post-701 BCE *lmlk* stamp impressions bear a strong similarity to the earlier two-winged ones in quality and in components. It may be that only toward the end of the system of *lmlk* seals—probably in the first quarter of the 7th century BCE—there was a deterioration of the quality and script of the seals and a diminishing role of the text (one seal has no place name and three lack the word *lmlk* in the upper register). It is noteworthy that the place name Socoh is absent in this late system as well, with only three places mentioned—Hebron, Ziph and *mmšt*. Perhaps in this case, too, the earlier seal with the place name Socoh continued to be used at the site where the storage jars were manufactured and there was no need to replace it.

As for an absolute chronology for the early types of *lmlk* stamp impressions, the earliest among them—Lemaire's Type Ib—can be dated to the 720s, the end of Ahaz's rule. We may speculate that the transition to the late four-winged types (Lemaire's Type Ia) occurred around the time that Hezekiah came to power in 715 BCE. The transition to the two-winged system possibly took place only after the death of Sargon II. If this is the case, this system would have operated concurrently with that of the "private" stamp impressions, during the few years between the death of Sargon in battle and Sennacherib's campaign (705–701 BCE).

It should be stressed that while the relative chronology of the various *lmlk* stamp impressions presented here is well grounded, the absolute chronology posited is speculative.

lmlk Storage Jars Stamped with "Private" Impressions

There is a scholarly consensus about the date of the "private" stamp impressions. These impressions have always been identified as an integral part of the *lmlk* stamp-impression system, since the same type of storage jar served both systems (Ussishkin 1977: 57; 2004b: 2143). Mommsen, Perlman and Yellin (1984) showed that the storage jars with "private" stamp impressions were manufactured at the same place as the *lmlk* storage jars. Moreover, two storage-jar handles were uncovered with a *lmlk* and a "private" impression stamped side by side, one at Ramat Raḥel and the other at Umm Tuba,[20] and storage jars with "private" and *lmlk* impressions stamped on different handles were found at Lachish.[21]

As long as there was general scholarly agreement that the *lmlk* system was limited to a brief period preceding the 701 BCE Assyrian campaign, the "private" stamp impressions were attributed to that period as well. However, now that it appears that the stamping of *lmlk* impressions began after 732 BCE, as early as the 720s, and continued into the first quarter of the 7th century BCE, the question of the timespan of the "private" stamp-impression system is once again under debate. At present, some 260 handles have been found, stamped by 45 seals with private names. Of these, 183 handles originated from excavations and archaeological surveys carried out within the territory of the Kingdom of Judah. Not one of these was found in a secure archaeological context dated later than Lachish Level III (see already Vaughn 1999b: 95–98).

Of the 45 types of "private" stamp impressions known to date (= 45 seals), 22 were found at Lachish, mainly in

---

20. Aharoni 1962: 16, Fig. 14:2, Pl. 6:2. For another handle with a "private" stamp impression bearing an identical name (but not from the same seal) next to a *lmlk* stamp impression, see Deutsch and Heltzer 1994: 33–34. For the storage-jar handle from Umm Tuba stamped with both a "private" and a *lmlk* impression, see the Israel Antiquities Authority: http://www.antiquities.org.il/article_Item_ido.asp?sec_id =25andsubj_id=240andid=1495andmodule_id.

21. Diringer 1949: 71, 73, Figs. 2, 3; Ussishkin 1976: 1–3, 6, Figs. 1–4; 2004b: 2143. For the identification of one of these "private" stamp impressions, see Barkay and Vaughn 1995. For possible additional matches between handles with "private" and *lmlk* stamp impressions, see Garfinkel 1985: 108–109; Vaughn 1999b: 90–93. Garfinkel's reliance on finds of handles with *lmlk* and "private" stamp impressions in the same destruction layers is problematic, since this indicates that the use of the storage jars came to an end at the same time, but does not necessitate a similar production date.

the Level III destruction layer. Given the settlement gap following the 701 BCE destruction at the site, and given that no handles with "private" stamp impressions were found in Level II, it seems reasonable to assume that the few handles with "private" stamp impressions not found in a secure Level III context should be attributed to this layer and were produced and in use prior to 701 BCE.[22] To the handles with "private" stamp impressions found at Lachish we should add handles impressed by 14 additional seals found at other sites in the Shephelah destroyed in 701 BCE (Tel Goded, Tell Beit Mirsim, Beth Shemesh, Tell eṣ-Ṣafi, Azekah, Maresha, Tel Burna and Tel Batash; see above, Table 4.6). Like Lachish, these sites exhibit no evidence for renewed settlement in the first two decades of the 7th century BCE, even if there were some short-term reconstruction and resettlement efforts (Finkelstein and Naʾaman 2004; Dagan 2001: 207–212; Koch and Lipschits 2010: 19–21; and see discussion below). Only nine types of "private" stamp impressions were found at sites not destroyed by Sennacherib—all in the hill country. Five of them bear identical names (both of the seal's owner and his patronym) to stamp impressions found in Lachish Level III. Given the reasonable assumption that this name belongs to the same person, even the handles found at sites not destroyed in Sennacherib's campaign should be dated to the end of the 8th century BCE. Thus, it is only the four other types, which were found in the hill country and have no parallels in Lachish Level III or in other destruction layers in the Shephelah, that cannot be dated to before 701 BCE.[23] We may assume, therefore, that these are exceptional cases and that the "private" stamp-impression system as a whole should be dated to the

period preceding Sennacherib's campaign. Furthermore, we may assume that this system did not continue to exist after the Assyrian campaign.[24]

This assumption bears great significance for the function and place of the *lmlk* system in the economy and administration of the Kingdom of Judah prior to Hezekiah's revolt against Assyria. We have suggested that storage jars with "private" stamp impressions were produced and used within the framework of Judah's revolt against Assyria (705/704 to 701 BCE) and in the preparations to the Assyrian military campaign (Lipschits, Sergi and Koch 2010: 7). This system operated for a brief period, built onto the framework of the *lmlk* storage-jar system that had already been in use for some time, and operated in the same storage-jar production center alongside the *lmlk* system. It is even possible that the "private" stamp impressions replaced the *lmlk* stamp impressions for a short period during Judah's preparations for the revolt.[25]

The Continued Use of the *lmlk* System in the 7th Century BCE

The finds at Lachish and the claims by Tufnell, Lance, Ussishkin and Zimhoni led to the acceptance of the dating of the entire *lmlk* stamp-impression system (as well as the "private" stamp impressions) to the date of Level III at Lachish and the contemporaneous destruction layers in the Shephelah (Tell Beit Mirsim Stratum A, Tel Batash Stratum III, Beth Shemesh Stratum II, etc.).[26] Vaughn further substantiated this claim, pointing to the clear typological affinity between the storage-jar handles stamped with *lmlk* impressions and the ones stamped

---

22. Parallels to some of these handles were uncovered in Shephelah sites destroyed in 701 BCE; see above, pp. 50–52.

23. Four names (*hwš ʾm/ḥgy, ḥšy/ʾlšm ʾ, lṣmḥ/ʾlšm ʾ* and *ʾḥmlk/ʾmdyhw*) appear on stamped handles uncovered only at Ramat Raḥel, Jerusalem and Umm Tuba (Aharoni 1962: 18–19; Nadelman 1989: 131; Shoham 2000a: 82). These stamped handles are from fills with no clear stratigraphic context.

24. Scholars have noted this and have dated the "private" stamp impressions accordingly; see Vaughn 1999b: 95–98, 106; 1999a and further literature.

25. For an elaboration of this notion and for discussion of the characteristics of the "private" stamp impressions, the purposes of the storage-jar production and the circumstances that gave rise to this system alongside the *lmlk* stamp impressions, see below, pp. 186–187.

26. Tufnell 1953: 315; Lance 1971: 322–330; Ussishkin 1976; 1977: 54–57; 1978: 76–81; 2004c: 87; 2004b: 2141–2142; Zimhoni 2004a: 1799–1801. See also summaries in Vaughn 1999b: 93–95, 106–109; Barkay and Vaughn 2004: 2169. This claim, however, does not provide a sufficient response to Tushingham's criticism (1992) regarding the gap between Levels II and III at Lachish and the possibility that the *lmlk* stamp-impression system continued into the early 7th century BCE without any evidence for this at Lachish (and see Ussishkin's reservations in 2004b: 2142). Indeed, it is methodologically unsound to rely upon settlement layers that present a gap following 701 BCE to claim that storage-jar manufacture was discontinued at this stage (see further below), and on this, Tushingham's criticism is justified. See Finkelstein's criticism (2012) of Ussishkin's claims.

with "private" impressions (Vaughn 1999b: 93–110). As discussed above, handles with "private" stamp impressions were not found in any archaeological context later than Lachish Level III and were thus dated to the late 8th century BCE. "Private" seals bearing the name of an individual (presumably an official in the royal administration) were the private property of that person. According to Vaughn, since it is reasonable to expect an individual to serve in an official capacity for some 20 years, the maximum period of use of these seals would have spanned 20 years before and after Sennacherib's campaign. Determining the timespan for the "private" stamp impressions enabled him to determine the period of the *lmlk* system too. Vaugh believed that this system had a short timespan as well, concurrent with Hezekiah's reign in the late 8th/early 7th centuries BCE.[27]

Vaughn's conclusion regarding the timespan of one stamp-impression system, extrapolated from the data of another, is difficult to accept. Indeed, as discussed above, storage-jar handles with "private" stamp impressions are securely dated to the late 8th century BCE and it seems that the system did not continue after 701 BCE (or, to be more precise, very few remnants of the system were in use in the early 7th century BCE, with a very limited distribution). Vaughn's extrapolation from the data of the extremely limited "private" stamp-impression system to draw conclusions regarding the much larger and more widespread *lmlk* stamp impressions is methodologically unsound and unjustified.[28] The *lmlk* stamp impressions reflect a much broader phenomenon, handles impressed with these seals were found in more diverse archaeological contexts, and this system appears to have begun prior to

the "private" stamp-impression system and to have continued to exist into the 7th century BCE. Several types of *lmlk* stamp impressions have not been found in Assyrian destruction layers and thus appear to have been produced after 701 BCE; in addition, handles with various types of *lmlk* stamp impressions (some that were found sealed under the 701 BCE destruction layer and others that were not) have been uncovered in clear 7th-century BCE contexts.[29]

Indeed, most of the *lmlk* stamp impressions, which were found in a clear stratigraphic context in Shephelah sites, are from the destruction layers attributed to Sennacherib's campaign. In this area, we can clearly distinguish between 8th- and 7th-century strata. Even if we accept Finkelstein and Na'aman's view that there were temporary and unsuccessful efforts to rebuild Lachish and several other sites in the Shephelah in the early 7th century, shortly after the destruction of Sennacherib, in most of the sites the reconstruction took place long after the 7th century BCE, at a point when the *lmlk* stamp impressions had already ceased to exist.[30]

It is impossible to draw a distinction between 8th- and 7th-century BCE settlement layers in hill country sites (such as Jerusalem, Ramat Raḥel, Tell en-Naṣbeh and el-Jib), since these were not destroyed at the end of the 8th century, but continued to exist, without disruption, during the 7th century BCE.[31] Therefore, it is archae-ologically difficult to isolate the stamp-impression finds from these sites in order to determine the period during which the storage jars were used. In addition, even when a handle with a *lmlk* stamp impression is found in a clear archaeological context

---

27. Contra Vaughn, see Mazar, Amit and Ilan 1996: 206; Finkelstein and Na'aman 2004; Na'aman 2006: 417–419.

28. The ratio between the number of handles with "private" stamp impressions and those with *lmlk* stamp impressions is 1:7 (and see also Barkay and Vaughn 2004: 2171).

29. E.g., the stamp impressions uncovered at Ḥorvat Shilḥa (Mazar, Amit and Ilan 1996: 208) or from En-Gedi (Stern 2007c). *lmlk*-stamped handles were found in a similar context in Kenyon's City of David excavations (Steiner 2001: 76; Franken and Steiner 1990: 56, 129; Tushingham 1992: 62). Despite his awareness of these finds, Vaughn (1999b: 95–109) did not consider them evidence for the continued 7th-century BCE use of *lmlk* stamp impressions, and in each case he argued that the find had penetrated from earlier layers. As for the *lmlk*-stamped handles uncovered at Ḥorvat Shilḥa, where no "private" stamp impressions were found and which had no 8th-century BCE settlement layer, Vaughn considered it to be an exception and argued that it could not serve as a basis for the dating of the system (Vaughn 1999b: 109).

30. See, e.g., Finkelstein and Na'aman 2004; Finkelstein 2012: 205–206; Lipschits, Sergi and Koch 2011; and cf. Lipschits 2019a.

31. In these cases, it is impossible to determine archaeologically whether the *lmlk*-stamped handles belong to 8th- or 7th-century BCE contexts. Vaughn (1999b: 99–106; 2018) argued that all hill country *lmlk* storage jars should be dated to the 8th century BCE, on the basis of the finding of storage jars with "private" stamp impressions in the same archaeological contexts. As aforementioned, Vaughn argued that even if some stamped storage jars continued to be used in hill country sites that were not destroyed in the 701 BCE Assyrian campaign, this reflected the continued use of already existing storage jars and in any event, did not continue beyond the first two decades of the 7th century BCE.

attributed to the 7th century BCE, if it is an isolated find it could be argued that it is an intrusion from an earlier stratum. Furthermore, in all cases it may reflect the continued use of a storage jar produced before 701 BCE.

In the northern Judean Desert, on the other hand, *lmlk*-stamped handles were found at two sites that do not have 8th-century BCE settlement layers: En-Gedi (Stern 2007c) and Ḥorvat Shilḥa (Mazar, Amit and Ilan 1996: 208–209). In each of these sites, which are dated to the second half of the 7th century BCE, a jar handle was uncovered with a Type ZIIb *lmlk* stamp impression. The handle from En-Gedi also bore incised concentric circles. Since these incised circles are dated to the 7th century BCE (see below), this handle supports the claim that *lmlk* storage jars continued to be used in this period.[32] An additional *lmlk*-stamped handle was found at Khirbet es-Samrah, a site dated by Mazar, Amit, Ilan and Stern to the second half of the 7th century BCE.[33] Three additional *lmlk* handles were found in Tel Batash Stratum II, from the second half of the 7th century BCE (Mazar and Panitz-Cohen 2001: 194–195). Two were uncovered in a secure Level II context and the third in a mixed context that included finds from Level III, from the late 8th century BCE.[34]

In addition to the stamp impressions from the Judean Desert and from Tel Batash, two *lmlk* handles may have been found in a 7th-century BCE archaeological context—in the Ophel excavations in Jerusalem.[35] In the excavations of the extramural quarter in the southeastern part of the City of David, 61 *lmlk*-stamped storage-jar handles were found, sealed in a fill above the street floor exposed outside the Iron Age II city wall. Franken and Steiner dated the construction of the wall and the abutting street paving to 700 BCE. Of the stamped handles, 42 were found on the street pavement, 11 in a mud layer covering it and another eight in a layer of sand over the mud layer (Franken and Steiner 1990: 56, 129). All but two of these stamp impressions bear the two-winged sun disk, and stratigraphically, they should apparently be dated to the 7th century BCE. The stamp impressions themselves have not yet been published, precluding a discussion of their typology and its ramifications on the chronology of the royal stamp-impression system. In Lachish Level II, established in the second half of the 7th century BCE and destroyed in 586 BCE, 14 *lmlk*-stamped handles were found.[36] While most could be intrusions from previous settlement layers, two cases may indeed constitute evidence for the existence of late stamp impressions in a 7th-century BCE archaeological context: Handle 71 (Type SIIa), found on a floor securely attributed to Level II and unlikely to be intrusive, and Handle 68, stamped with an impression

---

32. For the continued use of *lmlk* storage jars in the 7th century BCE, see Mazar, Amit and Ilan 1996: 248–249; Finkelstein and Naʾaman 2004; Naʾaman 2006: 417–418.

33. For the site, see Cross and Milik 1956: 11 and Fig. 2; and for its dating, see Mazar, Amit and Ilan 1996: 249; Stern 2007c: 140. Although this dating is reasonable, there is still room for doubt: the partial publication of the finding from the site and Cross and Milik's (1956: 14–15) general assessment that the sites in the region are from the Iron II—"no earlier than the ninth century B.C., their abandonment toward the end of the seventh, or, more probably, in the early sixth century B.C."—do not rule out the possibility of an 8th-century BCE settlement layer at the site. Cf. Vaughn 1999b: 108. Nevertheless, the typology of the Khirbet es-Samrah *lmlk* stamp impression supports a dating of the site to the 7th century BCE.

34. For the former two, see Mazar and Panitz-Cohen 2001: 194, Photo 122, Pl. 51:12; 195, Photo 124, Pl. 61:13. For the third, see Mazar and Panitz-Cohen 2001: 194, Photo 123, Pl. 59:16. The handles were all broken, so it is theoretically conceivable that they penetrated from previous layers. However, as shown below, their typology links them to the 7th century BCE, not the 8th century.

35. The Ophel excavations revealed 21 *lmlk*-stamped handles, only two of which (of the four-winged SIb Type) are from a clear stratigraphic context (Nadelman 1989: 131–136), in Locus 23043, where two floors, one above the other, were exposed, the lower one on bedrock. Of the upper floor only a small section survived, but at its presumed location six cooking pots were found one on top of the other in the destruction layer alongside the two stamp impressions (Mazar and Mazar 1989: 21–23). The cooking pots (which could date from the 8th to the 6th century BCE) do not help narrow down the date of the later floor, but the fact that the lower floor precedes the upper one, with the destruction layer, makes it reasonable to conclude that the later floor—on which the handles were found—is from the 7th–6th centuries BCE. The type of stamp impression uncovered at the Ophel was also found in Lachish Level III (Ussishkin 2004b: 2136, Stamp Impression 43), further evidence that these stamp impressions continued to be used during the 7th century BCE.

36. Ussishkin 2004c: 91–92; 2004b: 2135–2141, Nos. 7, 8, 10, 11, 12, 33, 44, 46, 47, 50, 51, 54, 68, 71. These stamp impressions did not originate in a clear and sealed archaeological context, and most may, in fact, be late 8th-century intrusions.

that should be typologically ascribed to the 7th century BCE.[37]

The discovery of handles with *lmlk* stamp impressions in an archaeological context attributed to the 7th century BCE indicates that the administrative system continued to be used even after Sennacherib's campaign. This, however, does not necessarily mean that the manufacture and stamping of these storage jars continued. It is possible that some of the stamped storage jars in sites not destroyed by Sennacherib were manufactured previously and continued to be used in the 7th century BCE.[38] This is supported by the appearance of concentric circles incised on *lmlk* storage-jar handles in the 7th century BCE (see pp. 56–60) and the fact that the same types of storage jars upon which *lmlk* impressions had been stamped in the late 8th century BCE were stamped with rosette impressions in the late 7th century BCE.

The continuity observed both in the manufacture of the *lmlk* storage jars and in the use of royal emblems (concentric circle incisions and rosette stamp impressions) on their handles shows that the administrative-economic system associated with this practice continued at least until the destruction of the Kingdom of Judah in the early 6th century BCE. Since the concentric circle incisions and rosette stamp impressions are attributed to the 7th century BCE, the attempt to restrict the duration of use of the *lmlk* stamping system to the reign of Hezekiah is problematic: it requires the assumption of a hiatus of some 50 years (in the first half of the 7th century BCE) in the production of storage jars with royal emblems following Sennacherib's campaign. This hiatus is particularly difficult to explain against the backdrop of the reign of Manasseh, when Judah was being integrated into the Assyrian economy as a whole. On the contrary, the continuity evident in the manufacture of storage jars

and in the stamping of their handles necessitates the assumption of administrative continuity. Some of the storage jars in use in the 7th century had been stamped earlier, in the late 8th century BCE, and survived in sites not destroyed by Sennacherib (most notably, Jerusalem). Ultimately, concentric circle incisions and rosette stamp impressions replaced the *lmlk* stamp impressions in the second half of the 7th century BCE.[39]

The question that arises is: did the actual manufacture and stamping of storage jars continue after Sennacherib's campaign?

The Continued Manufacture and Stamping of *lmlk* Storage Jars in the Early 7th Century BCE

The distribution of the *lmlk* stamp impressions has been studied according to the symbols or place names appearing on them (e.g., Na'aman 1979b; 1986; Barkay and Vaughn 2004). Surprisingly, there has been no detailed study of the distribution of the various *lmlk* types in the different sites in Judah and their strata. The broad division into four-winged and two-winged types is insufficient because, as already shown by Lemaire in 1981, there is a wide range of types representing the many seals that were in use. Until now, scholars have made do with this general division in an effort to "prove" that all the four- or two-winged stamp impressions belong to the period represented by Level III at Lachish (e.g., Barkay and Vaughn 2004: 2169).

To the question whether all the types of *lmlk* seals were used at the same time we can most probably respond in the negative. In order to distinguish archaeologically between early and late types, one must conduct a meticulous examination of the appearance of the various types and sub-types in the destruction strata attributed to 701 BCE. Methodologically, two criteria enable us to

---

37. Ussishkin 2004b: 2137, No. 71, Pl. 29.15:7. For the attribution of this floor to Level II, see Ussishkin 2004a: 620. Another handle with this type of stamp impression was also found in Level III; see Ussishkin 2004b: No. 69.

38. This was Mazar, Amit and Ilan's assumption too (1996: 248–250 and n. 46).

39. Tushingham (1992) already claimed that storage jars stamped with two-winged scarab *lmlk* stamp impressions continued to be used after the days of Hezekiah and that this was not evident in Lachish because of the long gap between Strata III and II. For this gap, see Ussishkin 2004c: 90–91, with further literature. On the other hand, according to Tushingham, storage jars with four-winged scarab and two-winged sun-disc stamp impressions were not used concurrently in Jerusalem, and the latter went out of use only during the reign of Josiah. On the other hand, his criticism of the unequivocal reliance upon the Lachish finds and his exposition of the problematic nature of this interpretation because of the gap between Strata III and II have merit, in my opinion. Vaughn's attempt (1999b: 86) to attribute these differences to geographical differences pertaining to the development of Jerusalem is hard to accept.

determine the period of the *lmlk* types (each represented by a single seal):

1. Any *lmlk* type found sealed beneath a destruction layer dated to 701 BCE can be defined as early. The stratigraphic attribution of a handle found in Level III at Lachish or in any parallel stratum at another site points to its use prior to this period.

2. Any *lmlk* type of which not a single handle has been found in a 701 BCE destruction layer can be defined as late. Handles with these types have been uncovered only in sites displaying settlement continuity during the 8th–7th centuries BCE or in sites first established in the 7th century BCE. While this does not constitute positive proof that the storage jars bearing these stamp impressions were produced after 701 BCE, their total absence from 701 BCE destruction layers—layers that contained so many stamped handles—coupled with their appearance at sites that existed during the 7th century BCE, constitutes strong circumstantial evidence for assigning a late date to them.

   Furthermore, the fact that all the late types belong to specific groups of seals in which later development and, to some extent, even degeneration of some early features may be discerned gives this circumstantial evidence the strength of a reasonable conclusion: first, that these types were produced after Sennacherib's campaign, and second, that the practice of stamping *lmlk* impressions on storage-jar handles continued in the 7th century BCE as well. Obviously, if even a single handle bearing a "late" type is uncovered in a secure archaeological context of the 701 BCE destruction, that type can no longer be considered late.

On the basis of these premises, a detailed study was conducted in which the distribution and archaeological context of Lemaire's (1981) types of *lmlk* stamp impressions were examined (Lipschits, Sergi and Koch 2010; 2011; Lipschits 2012a; 2018b; 2019a). The study revealed that many types, with clear common denominators, were entirely absent from destruction layers in the Shephelah.

The first to consider the development of the *lmlk* storage jars to be part of a long process that began in the late 8th century BCE and continued until the destruction of the Kingdom of Judah was Ji, who also noted that while the use of the four-winged scarab emblem ceased after Sennacherib's campaign, the symbol of the two-winged sun disk continued to appear until the final third of the 7th century BCE (Ji 2001: 21). The division of the *lmlk* stamp impressions into "pre-Sennacherib" and "post-Sennacherib" types was proposed also by Grena, on the basis of 13 handles found in clear 7th-century BCE archaeological contexts—in Jerusalem, Arad, Lachish, Tel Batash and Ḥorvat Shilḥa (Grena 2004: 337; followed by van der Veen 2014: 26, n. 41).

Following is a synopsis of the data from Lipschits, Sergi and Koch's research:[40]

1. No Type IIb *lmlk*-stamped handle (with the two-winged scarab and a place name at the bottom, separated into two by the emblem) has been uncovered in any 701 BCE destruction layer. These handles are found only in hill country sites not destroyed in this campaign and in 7th-century BCE contexts; they therefore should be classified as "post-Sennacherib." This includes all subtypes of Type IIb:

   • Handles on which the place name Socoh appears at the bottom of the stamp impression, divided into two (Type SIIb). Twenty-five handles were uncovered at el-Jib, Tell en-Naṣbeh, Ramat Raḥel, Jerusalem, Jericho and Tel Batash.[41] The two stamped handles found at Tel Batash were attributed to Stratum II, dated to the 7th century

---

40. For a more detailed summary of the typological and archaeological data, see Lipschits, Sergi and Koch 2010.

41. Ten stamped handles of this type were found at el-Jib (Pritchard 1959: 24–25, Figs. 8a: 454, 9: 146, 409, 485). Pritchard identified only nine of them (Nos. 146, 293, 409, 415, 417, 454, 485, 532, 541), but it seems that another stamp impression (No. 216) should also be classified as Type SIIb. Four handles found at Tell en-Naṣbeh were assigned to this type (McCown 1947: 161), but only three of them actually belong to Type SIIb (according to Grena; see www.lmlk.com). Five stamped handles of this type were found at Ramat Raḥel (Aharoni 1962: 19, Fig. 15:8; 1964: 34, Pl. 39:4–5; Sergi 2016; forthcoming [b]). Four stamped handles of Type SIIb were found in Jerusalem: one in the Jewish Quarter excavations (Avigad and Barkay 2000: 252, Impression 23) and two presumably in the Ophel excavations. It seems that an additional stamped handle was found in Kenyon's City of David excavations, but has not yet been published; our information on it comes from Grena's website. Another one was apparently found at Jericho (Sellin and Watzinger 1913: 158, Pl. 42:h).

BCE.[42] No such stamped handle was found at any other Shephelah site—nor in the Lachish Level III destruction layer.

- Handles on which the place name Ziph appears at the bottom of the stamp impression, divided into two (Type ZIIb). Seventy-four handles were uncovered in Gibeon, Tell en-Naṣbeh, Ramat Raḥel, Beth-Zur and Jerusalem.[43] Two such handles were found in the Ḥorvat Shilḥa and En-Gedi settlement layers dating from the second half of the 7th century BCE. Another was identified at Lachish, but it was a surface find.[44]

- Handles on which the place name Hebron appears at the bottom of the impression, divided into two (Type HIIb). Some 78 handles of this type were found at el-Jib, Tell en-Naṣbeh, Tell el-Fûl, Ramat Raḥel, Jerusalem, Beth-Zur and Hebron,[45] all sites that existed without disruption in the 8th–7th centuries BCE. It seems that a single stamped handle of this type was uncovered at Khirbet es-Samrah, apparently in a 7th-century BCE settlement layer.[46] Several handles with this type of stamp impression were also uncovered in sites containing a destruction layer from Sennacherib's campaign, but in all cases, their attribution to that destruction is doubtful: three in Arad, but not in a clear stratigraphic context,[47] and two in Lachish—one in a locus that included mixed Levels III–II material[48] and the other a surface find. Here too, there is a high probability

---

42. Stamp impressions 12 and 13; see Mazar and Panitz-Cohen 2001: 194–195, Photos 123–124, Pls. 59:16, 61:13. Another stamped handle, possibly of this type (Impression 11), was uncovered in Stratum II (Mazar and Panitz-Cohen 2001: 194, Photo 122, Pl. 51:12), but the impression is eroded and illegible. It is more likely to belong to Type ZIIb.

43. Eleven stamped handles of this type were found at el-Jib. Eight were identified by Pritchard (1959: 25, Fig. 9:480, 490, Nos. 367, 480, 489, 490, 500, 507, 531, 540); three other two-winged stamp impressions, which Pritchard could not classify, may also belong to this type (Pritchard 1959: 25–26, Nos. 268, 355, 514). At least four handles of this type were found at Tell en-Naṣbeh (McCown 1947: 161, Pl. 56:2). In the Ramat Raḥel excavations, 35 were found (Aharoni 1962: 19–20, 47, Fig. 15:5; 1964: 34, 62–63, Pls. 38:10–12, 39:1–2; Sergi 2016; forthcoming [b]). One such handle was found at Beth-Zur (Sellers and Albright 1931: 8). Some 20 such handles were uncovered in Jerusalem: four or five in the Ophel excavations (Nadelman 1989: 134, Nos. 20–24, Photos 151–155), although Grena argues that Nos. 22 and 24 are in fact the same stamp impression (www.lmlk.com). An additional handle found in the Ophel excavations bears this type of impression, but was not identified with certainty by Nadelman (1989: No. 126, Photo 157). Six handles with this type were identified with certainty in Shiloh's City of David excavations, but there may be two more (Shoham 2000b: 76, Nos. 17–24, Pl. 79:17, 19, 20, 22, 23). Four handles bearing this type were found in the Jewish Quarter (Avigad and Barkay 2000: 252, Nos. 9–12), and Grena contends that five others were found in Kenyon's City of David excavations (www.lmlk.com).

44. For the Ḥorvat Shilḥa handle, see Mazar, Amit and Ilan 1996: 208–209. For the En-Gedi handle, see Stern 2007c: 140, Photo 4.7.1.1. For the surface find at Lachish, see Barkay and Vaughn 2004: 2152, No. 44. Three other handles stamped with two-winged *lmlk* impressions with the place name Ziph were uncovered at Lachish (Barkay and Vaughn 2004: 2151–2159, Nos. 3, 102, 274), but their type was not identified with certainty. All were surface finds. The fact that only one stamped handle from Lachish can be classified with certainty as Type ZIIb and, moreover, that it was found on the surface, reinforces the possibility that this handle does not belong to the 8th-century BCE corpus and that the type in general is late.

45. In el-Jib, 16 stamped handles of this type were found. Pritchard identified nine (1959: 24, Nos. 123, 356, 397, 416, 456, 457, 498, 555, 563, Fig. 8:456). Seven additional handles that he could not classify may belong to the same type (Pritchard 1959: 25–26, Nos. 118, 253, 318, 337, 411, 459, 488). In Tell en-Naṣbeh, five handles with two-winged Hebron stamp impressions were listed by McCown (1947: 161); they all appear to belong to Type HIIb, and Grena (www.lmlk.com) listed one more. In Ramat Raḥel, 18 handles of this type were uncovered (Aharoni 1962: 47, Fig. 15:6, Pl. 7:5; 1964: 62–63, Pl. 38:7–9; Sergi 2016; forthcoming [b]). Some 25 stamped handles of this type were found in Jerusalem. Eight were uncovered in Shiloh's City of David excavations (Shoham 2000b: 76, Nos. 8–15, Pl. 1:8–14), and two others from the City of David may also have been stamped with this type (Shoham 2000b: Nos. 29–30, Pl. 2:29–30). Seven stamped handles were found in the Jewish Quarter (Avigad and Barkay 2000: 252, Nos. 18–22, 30–31; 260, Photo 18; 261, Photos 9–22; 262, Photos 30–31). One was found in the Ophel excavations (Nadelman 1989: 134, No. 17; 139, No. 148). Three additional stamped handles were found in the Ophel excavations and published by Duncan (1931: 139). Three additional stamped handles uncovered in Kenyon's City of David excavations probably belong to this type; they were not published, but are cited by Grena (www.lmlk.com). A single handle with this impression type was found in the Tell el-Fûl excavations (Lapp 1981: 111, Pl. 28:4, Fig. 29:2). Two stamped handles were found at Beth-Zur (Sellers and Albright 1931: 8), and Grena added another. The handle from Hebron bearing this type of stamp impression is mentioned only by Grena (www.lmlk.com).

46. Cross and Milik 1956: 8, Fig. 2. The stamp impression cannot be identified with certainty and may be either Type HIIb or MIIb.

47. Aharoni 1981a: 126, Nos. 1–3; cf. Singer-Avitz 2002: 144. For a discussion of the handles with this type of impression found at Arad, see Vaughn 1999b: 106–108.

48. Ussishkin 2004b: 2137, No. 68, Fig. 15.29:7; Barkay and Vaughn 2004: 2152, No. 41. According to Ussishkin (2004a: 620), the handle was found in Locus 4343, which included material from the Lachish III destruction layer and was disturbed by a Level II foundation trench.

that these two handles are not from the Lachish III destruction layer.

- Handles on which the place name *mmšt* appears at the bottom of the stamp impression, divided into two (Type MIIb). Of this type, 47 handles were uncovered at Gibeon, Tell el-Fûl, Tell en-Naṣbeh, Jerusalem, Ramat Raḥel and Beth-Zur.[49] Additional handles with identical stamp impressions were found in the Shephelah, but not in any destruction layer from Sennacherib's campaign. One of these was found at Gezer, which, as mentioned above, was destroyed at the beginning of the final third of the 8th century BCE and became an Assyrian governmental center, which existed continuously throughout the 7th century BCE. Another handle with this stamp impression type was found at Lachish (Barkay and Vaughn 2004: 2158, No. 315). While its archaeological context is unclear, since it is an isolated find it probably did not originate in the Level III destruction layer.[50] Storage-jar handles with this type of impression were also recovered from Tel ʿErani (on the surface), Tel Jezreel and Kiryat Ata. The two latter sites are not within the borders of the Kingdom of Judah.[51]

2. No Type IIc handle (with the two-winged symbol, without the word *lmlk*, and with the place name at the top of the impression) was found in any 701 BCE destruction layer. Such handles were uncovered only in hill country sites that were not destroyed in this campaign or in 7th-century BCE contexts and should therefore be classified as "post-Sennacherib." This includes all IIc sub-types (as mentioned above, no Type IIc impressions with the place name Socoh have been found):

- Handles with the place name Hebron at the top of the stamp impression (Type HIIc). Four such handles have been found to date, in el-Jib, Tell en-Naṣbeh, Nebi Samwil and Hebron.[52] None have been found in the Shephelah.

- Handles with the place name *mmšt* at the top of the stamp impression (Type MIIc). Seven such handles were uncovered in the hill country: two in Jerusalem (one in the City of David and the other in the Jewish Quarter), two at Tell en-Naṣbeh and one each at Tell el-Fûl, Ramat Raḥel and Gezer.[53] With the exception of Gezer, an Assyrian administrative center in the late 8th century and the 7th century BCE, no such handles were found at any other Shephelah site.

- Handles with the place name Ziph at the top of the impression (Type ZIIc). Three handles of this type were found at el-Jib, and one handle was uncovered at Tell en-Naṣbeh, Jerusalem and Gezer.[54]

3. No Type XII handle (with a two-winged emblem and the word *lmlk* at the top of the impression, but without a place name), was found in the Shephelah

---

49. Seven stamped handles of this type were found at el-Jib. Pritchard identified six (1959: 24, Nos. 106, 486, 487, 499, 520, 522), and an additional handle (Pritchard 1959: 25, No. 105) may also belong to this type. One such handle was found at Tell el-Fûl (Lapp 1981: 111, Pl. 28:1–2, Fig. 29:1), and three were found at Tell en-Naṣbeh (McCown 1947: 161). McCown classified ten two-winged *lmlk* stamp impressions with the place name *mmšt*, but it seems that only three of them belong to Type MIIb (and see Grena, www.lmlk.com). A dozen stamped handles were found in Jerusalem: four in Shiloh's City of David excavations (Shoham 2000b: 76, Nos. 25–28, Pl. 2:25–27)., four in the Jewish Quarter (Avigad and Barkay 2000: 252, Nos. 13–16), and, according to Grena (www.lmlk.com), four others were found in Kenyon's City of David excavations and in Duncan and Macalister's Ophel excavations. In Ramat Raḥel, 20 stamped handles were uncovered (Aharoni 1962: 47; 1964: 63–65, Pl. 39:8–11; Sergi 2016; forthcoming [b]). Another handle with an identical stamp impression may have been found at Khirbet es-Samrah (Cross and Milik 1956: 8 and Photo 2).

50. Two additional handles with a two-winged *lmlk* stamp impression and the inscription *mmšt* were found at Lachish, but cannot be typologically classified with certainty, so it is unclear whether they belong to Type MIIb (Barkay and Vaughn 2004: 2156–2157, Nos. 231, 273). In any event, they are surface finds.

51. For additional information, see Grena (www.lmlk.com).

52. Pritchard 1959: 24, No. 145, Fig. 9:145; Magen 2008: 41. Additional information was compiled by Grena (www.lmlk.com).

53. Lapp 1981: 111, Pl. 28:8–9; McCown 1947: 161; Avigad and Barkay 2000: 252, 260, No. 17; Aharoni 1964: 62–63, Pl. 39:11. Grena presented an additional handle with this type of stamp impression found at Tell en-Naṣbeh (www.lmlk.com).

54. Pritchard 1959: 75, Nos. 79, 481, 501; McCown 1947: 161; Nadelman 1989: 131, 134, No. 26, Photo 156. For a handle with this impression type from Gezer, see Grena (www.lmlk.com).

or was linked to any destruction layer of Sennacherib's campaign.[55] In total, 42 or 43 handles of this type were found: 20 at Ramat Raḥel, nine at Tell en-Naṣbeh, six or seven in Jerusalem, six at el-Jib and one at Tell el-Fûl.[56]

From this distribution (Table 5.1), we can reasonably conclude that a series of seals was used for stamping impressions on storage-jar handles after 701 BCE. Not a single handle with these impression types is associated with 701 BCE destruction layers; all appear at sites that either existed continuously from the 8th to 7th century BCE or were first established only in the 7th century BCE.

The realization that there are chronological differences among the types makes it possible to discern the typological development of the *lmlk* stamp impressions. The most common type in the 7th century BCE (Type IIb, with 224 stamp impressions) continued the tradition of the 8th century, which included the word *lmlk* at the top of the seal, a two-winged symbol in its center and a place name at the bottom. The importance of the writing—both the place name and the word *lmlk*—gradually declined in the other 7th-century types: in Type IIc the word *lmlk* is absent and the place name is written at the top, and Type XII lacks the place name. The location of the royal symbol, in the center of the stamp impression, remained unchanged.

This trend continued during the 7th century BCE, when symbols alone were used in the concentric circle incisions and rosette stamp impressions. Writing was entirely absent from stamp impressions on storage-jar handles, reappearing only in the *mwṣh* stamp impressions of the 6th century BCE and in the *yhwd* stamp impressions from the beginning of the Persian period, when the influence of Aramaic writing was already notable.

The disappearance of the writing and the focus on a single central symbol may also support the chronological attribution of the late *lmlk* stamp impressions to the period following Sennacherib's campaign—the early 7th century BCE. It is in keeping with a dating of the concentric circle incisions to the mid-7th century BCE and with the attribution of the rosette stamp impressions to the end of the 7th and the early 6th centuries BCE (see below).

Conclusions

The above analysis points to two phases in the production and stamping of *lmlk* storage jars:

1.   Early *lmlk* stamp impressions were uncovered in the destruction layers attributed to 701 BCE. These

Table 5.1: Types of *lmlk* stamp impressions from the 7th century BCE and their distribution

Site	Type IIb					Type IIc					Type XII	Total
	Z	H	M	S	Total	Z	H	M	S	Total		
Jerusalem	20	25	12	4	61	1	0	1	0	2	7	70
Ramat Raḥel	34	22	19	5	80	0	1	1	0	2	18	100
Gibeon	11	16	7	10	44	3	0	1	0	4	4	52
Mizpah	4	5	3	3	15	1	1	1	0	3	9	27
Other sites	5	10	6	3	24	1	2	2	0	5	2	31
Total	74	78	47	25	224	6	4	6	0	16	40	280

55. One handle of this type was found at Ashdod (Dothan 1971: 83). However, as it was found beyond the borders of the Kingdom of Judah and in an unclear stratigraphic context, it has no real value for this discussion.

56. Aharoni 1964: 62–63; Sergi 2016; forthcoming (b); Pritchard 1959: 25, Nos. 75, 412, 414, 453; Sinclair 1960: 32, Pl. 166:3; Avigad and Barkay 2000: 252, 260, Nos. 24–26; Shoham 2000b: 76, Nos. 29–30, Pl. 2:29–30; for nine additional handles with an identical stamp impression, see the information compiled by Grena (www.lmlk.com), who also identified two additional ones from el-Jib, one from the Jewish Quarter (although this identification is uncertain), one from the Duncan and Macalister Ophel excavations (and Duncan 1931: 139) and an additional one excavated nearby by Kenyon.

storage jars were therefore manufactured and stamped and were in use before this event—presumably in the final third of the 8th century BCE.

2. Late *lmlk* stamp impressions were completely absent from the destruction layers of 701 BCE and were found only at sites (especially in the hill country) that existed continuously in the 8th and 7th centuries BCE or at sites first established in the 7th century BCE. The total absence of late *lmlk*-stamped handles from the 701 BCE destruction levels makes it reasonable to assume that they were manufactured and stamped and were in use after this event, probably in the first quarter of the 7th century BCE.

This has far-reaching consequences for an understanding of Judah's administrative and economic system in the late Iron Age, of the fate of the Shephelah, of Judah's development in the aftermath of Sennacherib's campaign, and, of course, of the role of Ramat Raḥel in this system. Furthermore, the conclusion that there were two groups of storage jars with *lmlk* stamp impressions, manufactured and stamped during two different time periods, makes them an important new *fossile directeur*, which may now assist in the dating of various settlement layers and serve as an important indicator for the existence of a settlement in the late 8th and/or early 7th century BCE. Since there are no destruction levels between the late 8th and the early 6th centuries in Judah, the early 7th century BCE was archaeologically almost "invisible." This tool sheds light upon this period, making it possible to pinpoint settlement layers more accurately and to delineate urban processes, especially the ones that occurred during the long reign of Manasseh. The distribution of late types of *lmlk* stamp impressions now offers an independent and reliable indicative tool for the settlement and demographic processes that Judah underwent after Sennacherib's campaign and the severe destruction of many regions in the kingdom, in particular the Shephelah (see Lipschits, Sergi and Koch 2011; Koch and Lipschits 2013; and see below, pp. 158–165).

The Chronology of the Concentric Circle Incisions

Concentric circles were incised on *lmlk* storage-jar handles after the firing of the vessels. In 143 of the 305 handles uncovered with such incisions (47%), the circles were engraved next to or even on top of the *lmlk* stamp impression (and in three cases near or on top of a "private" stamp impression).[57] These incisions are therefore clearly a function of the secondary use of these storage jars, added after the storage jars had been manufactured and stamped. The recovery of 162 storage-jar handles with concentric circle incisions, but without any *lmlk* or "private" stamp impression, indicates that the system was an independent one. A reasonable inference would therefore be that it cancelled or replaced the *lmlk* stamp-impression system or that it was adapted to it.

In 77 cases, concentric circles were incised next to late types of *lmlk* stamp impressions. Only in six cases were they incised alongside early types of *lmlk* stamp impressions, and in 57 cases they appear next to *lmlk* stamp impressions that are unidentifiable or for which insufficient data has been published, precluding an identification.[58] In three cases concentric circles were incised next to "private" stamp impressions, dated to the same pre-701 BCE period as the early *lmlk* types.[59]

Concentric circle incisions next to *lmlk* stamp impressions are known since Warren's excavations south of the Temple Mount (Wilson and Warren 1871: 152). Most of the incised handles were found in hill country sites, which escaped the late 8th century BCE destruction (see above, Table 4.16): 162 handles were uncovered in Jerusalem; 40 in Ramat Raḥel; 33 in el-Jib; 17 in Tell en-Naṣbeh; 15 in Khirbet el-Burj; five in Moẓa, and four each in Tell el-Fûl and Mordot Arnona. Seven incised handles were found in other sites in the area around Jerusalem, and in total, 287 out of the 305 incised handles (ca. 94%) were found in this region. Only ten incised handles were found in the Shephelah (ca. 3% of the total), four of these in Lachish (in unclear archaeological

---

57. Shoham 2000b: 75–77; Avigad and Barkay 2000: 246–248; Stern 2007c: 139–141; Lipschits, Sergi and Koch 2010: 9; 2011: 7–8, and see above, Table 4.9.

58. Only one instance is known of a concentric circle incision alongside a four-winged *lmlk* stamp impression—on a handle exposed in the Western Hill of Jerusalem; see Avigad and Barkay 2000: 258, No. 5.

59. Avigad and Barkay 2000: 247, No. 5; Shoham 2000a: 82, No. 2; 83, No. 5; Lipschits, Sergi and Koch 2011: 31, Table 3, literature on p. 35.

contexts) and four in Azekah (Lipschits, Sergi and Koch 2011: 7–8).

Since the concentric circles were incised after firing of the vessel, many scholars assumed that they were later than the *lmlk* stamp impressions, but there is no consensus regarding their dating. Even though no such incisions were uncovered in any destruction layer linked to the 701 BCE Assyrian campaign, several scholars suggested dating them to the late 8th–early 7th century BCE—the same period as the *lmlk* stamp impressions (Avigad and Barkay 2000: 246–247).[60] On the other hand, Yadin and Stern, to a large extent following Sinclair, suggested that the concentric circle incisions should be dated to the late 7th century BCE.[61]

In an attempt to date the concentric circle system, we should bear in mind that no handle with such incisions was found sealed beneath the Lachish Level III destruction layer or in any other destruction layer attributed to Sennacherib's campaign. This unequivocal archaeological fact means that 701 BCE must be the *terminus post quem* for this system and that there is no archaeological justification for dating the incisions to before the early 7th century BCE.[62] Moreover, the storage jars upon which the concentric circles were incised must have been readily available when there was a need or desire to incorporate them into the storage-jar administration. Rather than manufacturing new vessels, when there was sufficient supply to meet the needs of the administration, the existing storage jars were selected for the task and were marked with a different symbol. It is, therefore, reasonable to suggest that while the concentric circle incisions were later than the late types of *lmlk* storage jars, they were only slightly later. At this point in time, only a small number of older storage jars—produced before 701 BCE with the

early types of *lmlk* stamp impressions—would have remained in use. A similar number of concentric circle incisions appear on handles alongside "private" stamp impressions, which would also have been manufactured and stamped prior to the Assyrian destruction of 701 BCE, and so there would be fewer of them in stock. Most of the storage jars available for incision were newer, having been manufactured after 701 BCE and thus bearing later types of *lmlk* stamp impressions.

The concentric circle incisions should therefore be dated to the 7th century BCE—probably mid-century—subsequent to the late types of *lmlk* storage jars. The fact that a similar number of impressions have come to light from these two systems (as well as from the rosette-stamped jar system; see below) suggests that the three systems operated for similar lengths of time and under analogous geopolitical, administrative and economic conditions. The dating we propose is supported by the distribution of incised storage-jar handles, which bears a great similarity to the distribution of handles with late types of *lmlk* stamp impressions and differs significantly from the distributions of the early types of *lmlk* stamp impressions and of the rosette stamp impressions. The vast majority of the handles incised with concentric circles were uncovered in the Judean Hills, with only a few found in the Shephelah. This is indicative of the period in which the Shephelah lay in ruins, severed from the administrative system of Judah during most of the 7th century BCE. Nevertheless, the presence of handles with concentric circle incisions and their estimated date attest to the continuity of the royal stamp-impression system. This is further evident in the continued manufacture of royal storage jars in the main Shephelah production center,[63] and later, in the stamping of rosette impressions on royal

---

60. On the basis of the meager find of concentric circle incisions in Lachish Level II, built not before the last third of the 7th century BCE (Ussishkin 1977: 54), Barkay (1985: 408) understood that from the archaeological perspective, the system of concentric circle incisions should be dated to the period preceding the construction of this layer. Nevertheless, he continued to maintain the extremely early dating of this system, linking it to the end of the *lmlk* system, which, in his opinion, preceded the 701 BCE destruction, allowing for the possibility that it continued in Jerusalem and its environs for several additional years (Barkay 1985; Avigad and Barkay 2000: 247).

61. Sinclair (1960: 32) dated the concentric circle incisions to the late 7th–early 6th century BCE, concurrent with the rosette stamp impressions, mainly because he accepted the dating of two-winged stamp impressions, with concentric circles incised next to them, to this period (following Diringer 1941: 106; 1949: 85–86). See Yadin 1961a: 12. On the basis of his En-Gedi excavation findings, Stern assumed that the concentric circle incisions and rosette stamp impressions were contemporaneous systems and he dated them to the 7th and early 6th centuries BCE; see Stern 2001: 178; 2007c: 149–150.

62. Thus, Ussishkin's argument that all the concentric circles incised alongside *lmlk* stamp impressions pre-date the 701 BCE destruction (2011: 233–235) has no logic or archaeological basis; cf. Lipschits 2012a: 2, 9–10.

63. For the production site of the incised storage jars, see Mommsen, Perlman and Yellin 1984; Yellin and Cahill 2004.

storage jars in the late 7th century BCE. Therefore, the concentric circle incisions should be dated to the period preceding the use of the rosette stamp-impression system, i.e., before the final third of the 7th century BCE.[64] It is likely that these incisions were in use at the same time as or immediately after the *lmlk* stamp impressions from the early 7th century BCE—and thus, that they were in use in the second third of the 7th century BCE.[65]

The archaeological and chronological distinction between the system of concentric circle incisions and the subsequent rosette system was made by Ji on the basis of Aharoni's Ramat Raḥel excavation results and of the dating of Stratum Vb to the beginning or middle of the 7th century BCE and of Stratum Va to the second half of that century (Ji 2001: 14–17). Ji noticed that many *lmlk*-stamped handles were found in Stratum Vb, together with 24 concentric circle incisions, nine of them next to two-winged *lmlk* stamp impressions. In Stratum Va, on the other hand, 38 handles were uncovered with rosette stamp impressions, but not a single concentric circle incision was found. On the basis of this finding, Ji concluded that the concentric circle incisions preceded the rosette stamp impressions and that these two systems

did not overlap. The results from the new Ramat Raḥel excavations seem to corroborate this conclusion.

The Chronology of the Rosette Stamp Impressions

The dating of the rosette stamp-impression system relies upon a clear chronological boundary: the destruction layers of 586 BCE in Judah. In these layers, which provide the *terminus ante quem* for the system, 27 stamped handles were uncovered in sealed archaeological assemblages.[66] There is, however, no direct archaeological evidence to provide a precise dating of the commencement of the system. Since there are no 7th-century BCE destruction layers in Judah, the archaeological research does not offer sufficient data to identify chronological and ceramic stages in this century. Any attempt to reconstruct a more precise chronological framework for the establishment of the settlement strata in this period and for the onset of the political, economic and administrative systems in this period is by necessity based solely on historical considerations.[67]

---

64. Ji (2001: 14–17) reached a similar conclusion, albeit based on different considerations (see also Grena 2004: 314–315). Ji's dating was based on an analysis of all the symbols of the stamp-impression systems and on his understanding that they all represent different variations of divinity symbols adopted in Judah: the symbol on the *lmlk* stamp impressions was adopted by Hezekiah; the concentric circle incisions began under Hezekiah and continued under Manasseh, and the rosette symbol replaced it during the reign of Josiah. Ji's line of reasoning and conclusions are difficult to accept. Basing his argument on a concentric circle incision alongside a "private" stamp impression reading *lnry.b/n.šbnyhw* ("[belonging] to Neriah, the son of Shebnayahu") on a handle found in Jerusalem and an identical "private" stamp impression alongside a *lmlk* stamp impression on a handle excavated in Ramat Raḥel, coupled with the assumption that further "private" stamp impressions of Neriah were found at other sites in Judah, Ji postulated that Neriah was a royal official. He further surmised that the "private" stamp impression *lšbn/ˁ.šḥr* ("[belonging] to Shebna, the son of Shahar") found on a handle from Ramat Raḥel Stratum Vb and on a handle from Lachish Stratum II belonged to Shebna, Hezekiah's scribe (2 Kings 18:37; Isa. 22:15). If Neriah was indeed the son of Shebna, as suggested by Ji, Neriah might have been Manasseh's scribe, even if his royal service commenced earlier, in the days of Hezekiah. In Ji's opinion, this strengthens the dating of the concentric circle incisions to the reign of Manasseh, set in the early or mid-7th century BCE.

65. Yadin (1961a: 12), who noted the role of the concentric circle incisions as a link between the *lmlk* and rosette stamp-impression systems, argued that the concentric circle incisions accompanying the *lmlk* stamp impressions constitute an abstract form of the rosette and suggested that their lines are thicker because they were incised, rather than impressed with a delicate seal. He also believed that they served as a means to introduce the storage jars of the old *lmlk* system into the subsequent new system. Following Yadin, see Stern 2007c: 145–147.

66. Of these 27 stamp impressions from assemblages dated to the Iron Age, ten were excavated in the City of David, six in Tel Batash, four each in Tel ʿIra and Lachish, two in Tel Malḥata and one in En-Gedi. See Mazar, Dothan and Dunayevsky 1963: 48–50; 1966: 33; Aharoni 1964: 63; Cross 1969: 22*; Lapp 1981: 112; Naˀaman 1991b: 31–33; Cahill 1995: 247, 252; Stern 2001: 178.

67. This led many scholars to date the rosette stamp-impression system to the late First Temple period, without narrowing it down any further. Albright (1933: 10), for example, dated the rosette stamp impressions to the end of the Kingdom of Judah, which, he believed, was around the time that the *lmlk* stamp-impression system was in operation (following the dating of the *lmlk* stamp impressions to the days of Josiah, as was accepted at the time). Tufnell (1953: 55–58, 84–98) dated the Lachish Level III destruction to Sennacherib's campaign (701 BCE), thus determining the date of the numerous *lmlk* stamp impressions in this level. In the same report, however, Diringer (1953: 346) dated the rosette stamp impressions to this period as well, even though a few were uncovered in Level II assemblages (dated by Tufnell to the 7th century BCE). A late First Temple period date for the rosette stamp impressions was accepted by Lapp (1981: 112) and Yadin (1961a) too. Yadin later dated the zenith of the Judahite administrative system, including the system of royal stamp impressions, to the reign of Josiah. His approach, which was influenced by Aharoni, was later adopted by Mazar (Mazar, Dothan and Dunayevsky 1963: 48; 1966: 33) and Cross (1969: 20*).

Thus, for example, Ussishkin (1977: 52–53: 2004c: 110) argued that, like the *lmlk* storage jars on the eve of Sennacherib's campaign, the rosette storage jars were primarily part of the Kingdom of Judah's preparations for the punitive Babylonian onslaught.[68] This was based on his interpretation of the stamping system in general as a system of preparation and food storage in anticipation for the Assyrian campaign in 701 BCE (in the case of the *lmlk* stamp impressions) and for the Babylonian campaign (in the case of the rosette stamp impressions). It also relied on his assumption that pottery found in destruction layers reflects activities at the site shortly before the time of destruction and not much earlier. This general approach is fraught with problems. For one thing, there are many examples of pottery (especially storage jars) that were in use for longer periods than assumed by Ussishkin. For another, from the perspective of historical reconstruction, it is difficult to account for a hiatus of over 100 years between identical systems of stamp impressions on storage jars and to explain why the Kingdom of Judah would return to use the exact same method after such a long gap. Sufficient arguments have been raised above pointing to the use of the storage-jar stamp-impression system even before the revolt of Hezekiah against Assyria and to its continued existence after Sennacherib's campaign. The main argument against Ussishkin's view, however, lies in the continued presence of stamp impressions in Judah for hundreds of years after the Babylonian destruction in precisely the same format, on the same types of storage jars, and employing the same production, collection and management methods (as is evident from the lion, *yhwd* and *yršlm* stamp impressions; see above, Chapter 4).

Cahill expanded the time frame of the rosette system slightly beyond Ussishkin's, claiming that it began in the final decade of the 7th century BCE, i.e., the reign of Jehoiakim in Judah (Cahill 1995: 247–250; 1999: 363–364; 2001: 200). Drawing upon the biblical account of the conquest of Bethel by Josiah (2 Kings 23), Cahill concluded that since no rosette stamp impressions were found in Bethel, they must have appeared only after the reign of Josiah and therefore would have come into use only when the areas of southern Samaria were taken from Judah by Pharaoh Necho II (Cahill 1995: 248, n. 19). Archaeologically, she relied upon the finding of six rosette-stamped handles (all of the same type) in a sealed archaeological context in Tel Batash Stratum II—evidence, in her opinion, of Judahite aid to Philistine cities on the eve of Nebuchadnezzar's 604 BCE invasion (Cahill 2001: 197–201).

Cahill's reliance upon the absence of finds in Bethel is based upon her assumption that this site indeed belonged to Judah in the days of Josiah and that Judahite pottery should therefore be found in it, including the expected storage jars that would demonstrate an organized administration in this period. However, the finds at Bethel point to a small and sparsely populated village in the 7th century BCE (Finkelstein and Singer-Avitz 2009: 34–35, 39–41, 45). Even if one were to argue that the cultic site of Bethel was located near the spring, which lies in an unexcavated area beneath the modern town, nowhere in the site is there any evidence that Bethel served as part of the Judahite storage-jar administration, within which we should expect to find storage jars with rosette stamp impressions. Nor is there any extant information about the arrangements made by Pharaoh Necho in Judah following the death of Josiah and the exile of Jehoiakim. Therefore, this argument cannot be used as evidence for the earliest possible time of operation of the rosette stamp-impression system.

Nor can we accept Cahill's reliance on the six rosette stamp impressions uncovered at Tel Batash. It is methodologically unsound to rely upon six stamp impressions from a single site, located outside Judah, in order to date the rosette stamp-impression system. There is nothing to preclude the rosette storage jars from having begun earlier in Judah, even prior to the date determined by Cahill for the Tel Batash storage jars. Cahill's historical reconstructions, in fact, rely upon Ussishkin's interpretation of the storage jars as part of the activities in preparation for the siege. The attempt to use their presence or absence as grounds to determine when the system operated and to establish the chronology of the various rosette types does not withstand critical analysis.

---

68. Ussishkin (2004c: 92–93, 109–119) was relying upon findings from Lachish (including, in addition to the rosette stamp impressions, 14 unstamped storage jars; see Zimhoni 2004a: 1800–1801), from Tel 'Ira (including four rosette storage jars; see Cahill 1999: 360), from the City of David (14 rosette storage jars, one of them stamped; see Shiloh 1984: 18, Pl. 30:2; Cahill 2000b: 99) and from Tel Batash (Cahill 2001: 197–198).

Even if we accept Cahill's dating of the Tel Batash Stratum II destruction to 604 BCE,[69] her historical interpretation of the Tel Batash stamp impressions and of single stamp impressions found at Gezer, Tell eṣ-Ṣafi and Tel ʿErani (Cahill 1995: 248; 2001: 200)—which, she claimed, attest to the aid provided by Jehoiakim to neighboring Philistine kings in advance of the Babylonian onslaught—cannot be accepted. After the destruction of Samaria, Gezer served as an imperial center, whereas the Tel ʿErani settlement was probably part of Judah and was destroyed along with the rest of the Judahite cities and towns.[70] With regard to the finding of rosette stamp impressions at Shephelah sites close to the western border of the Kingdom of Judah, Naʾaman considered this to reflect Judahite influence on the material culture of its western neighbors and to be due to the geographical proximity of these sites to the pottery-production site. Naʾaman's view that these reflect normative long-term cultural influences of neighboring societies rather than indications of a single-event siege and war (1989: 43–45) is, in my opinion, preferable.

The proposal that the type of rosette stamp impression found at Tel Batash II (as well as at Gezer and Tel ʿErani) was earlier than other rosette stamp-impression types found at sites in the Negev (Tel ʿIra and Tel Malḥata)—sites that, in Cahill's opinion, were destroyed in 598 BCE, after the fall of Tel Batash Stratum II—is even more problematic.[71] Based on all the above, it is difficult to accept Cahill's historical reconstruction with regard to Jehoiakim's aid to the Philistine kings or to accept her assumption that the sites of Philistia were destroyed before the other stamp impression types came into use. The six Tel Batash handles can only offer information about the period of use of the type in question, but cannot provide a *terminus post quem* for it or give any insight into other types, either preceding or succeeding it. It thus seems that Cahill's arguments cannot provide any

evidence for the onset of the rosette stamp-impression system and that the chronological framework of this system should not be limited to the last decade of the 7th century BCE.

Naʾaman expanded the dating of the rosette stamp system to include the reign of Josiah, pointing to a correspondence between the distribution of these impressions and the biblical town lists of Judah and Benjamin (Josh 15:21–62, 18:21–28) (Naʾaman 1989: 42–45; 1991b: 31–33). He suggested that the town lists and the distribution of these stamp impressions are both in keeping with the dimensions and character of Josiah's kingdom, which, he argued, remained within its modest borders in the aftermath of Sennacherib's campaign and did not expand westward or northward (Naʾaman 1989: 45).[72]

Naʾaman's dating of the rosette stamp-impression system is supported by further archaeological data and historical considerations, which indicate that the rosette system had entered into use during the final third of the 7th century BCE, perhaps even at the beginning of this period (Koch 2008: 45–47; Koch and Lipschits 2010: 14–15). Two archaeological observations help determine when the rosette stamp-impression system began. Aharoni showed that not a single rosette stamp impression was found beneath the floors of the Ramat Raḥel Stratum VA building, dated to the late 7th century BCE, whereas numerous *lmlk* stamp impressions were exposed beneath these floors (Aharoni 1964: 35). This observation, further supported by the renewed excavations at Ramat Raḥel, indicates that rosette storage jars were not manufactured prior to the construction of the large palace at Ramat Raḥel (Aharoni's Stratum VA, the second building phase in the renewed excavations), probably early in the last third of the 7th century BCE (Lipschits *et al.* 2017: 65). This is the earliest possible date for the beginning of the rosette stamp-impression system. The

---

69. Mazar and Panitz-Cohen 2001: 282. Cf. Lipschits (2005: 64, n. 20 with further literature), who dated the Tel Batash Stratum II destruction to 601 BCE, and Ussishkin (2004c: 111), who dated it to 586 BCE.

70. Stern 2001: 146; Lipschits 2005: 164. Cf. Finkelstein and Naʾaman on the problems with the site's identification and its historical reconstructions (2004: 61, n. 1).

71. Cahill 1999: 364; 2001: 200. For a discussion of the date of destruction of the Negev sites, see Lipschits 2005: 141–146.

72. Other scholars have noted that the distribution of rosette stamp impressions does not correspond with the borders of Josiah's kingdom. Barkay (1985: 106–107), for example, considered rosette stamp impressions to be widespread only within the narrow borders of Judah, whereas, in his opinion, the kingdom expanded into the Coastal Plain and the northern Samaria region in the days of Josiah; on these grounds he concluded that the rosette stamp impressions must be later than the reign of Josiah.

second archaeological find is a single rosette-stamped handle uncovered in the City of David Area E1, attributed to Stratum XI (Reg. No. 14566), an interim 7th-century BCE layer under an archaeological assemblage of Stratum X, destroyed in 586 BCE and thus securely dated.[73] Taken in conjunction, these two archaeological findings indicate that the rosette stamp-impression system began before the final phase of the 7th century BCE.

This conclusion is further supported by the discussion above, which points to continuous use of stamped jars from the last third of the 8th century BCE until the rosette-stamped jars in the late 7th–early 6th centuries BCE. The continuity and overlap between the use of early and late types of *lmlk* stamp impressions are clear, as are the continuity and overlap between the (mainly) late types of *lmlk* stamp impressions and the concentric circle incisions. It is reasonable to expect continuity between the concentric circle incisions and the rosette stamp impressions as well, accompanied by typological development in storage-jar production (above, pp. 22–24) and the initiation of a new type of stamp impression. In this context, one might develop the notion suggested by Yadin that the concentric circle incisions constitute a schematic representation of the rosette symbol (see above, n. 65). One might view these circles as a "pre-rosette" symbol, linked on the one hand to the royal symbol of the winged sun disk and on the other hand to the rosette symbol, which preserves the circular motif and maintains the same tradition of a solitary round motif (without inscription) on the storage-jar handle (Yadin 1961b: 8; Koch 2008: 51). The rosette symbol thus continues the decline in the use of writing, a process that began with the late types of *lmlk* stamp impressions. Support for a long duration for the rosette stamp

impression system comes from a study by Koch, based on Cahill's research and slightly updating it; Koch found that at least 29 seals were used to stamp handles (2008: 27–33).[74] This runs counter to the position adopted by Ussishkin, and, to a certain extent, by Cahill, who argued for an extremely short duration of the rosette stamp-impression system.

The number of handles stamped by rosette seals (about 290) also indicates that the duration of this system was similar to that of the late types of *lmlk* stamp impressions (about 490 handles) and to that of the concentric circle incisions (about 305 handles).[75] It transpires that the number of *lmlk* stamp impressions of the late types, dated to the early 7th century BCE, is much less than double the number of concentric circle incisions from the mid-7th century BCE and that this number almost equals the number of rosette stamp impressions. We may conclude that the three 7th-century BCE Judahite administrative systems used a similar number of handles (and thus of storage jars). If one may extrapolate from this as to their duration, they are similar.

On the assumption that the stamp-impression system is part of an administrative system operating continuously from the last third of the 8th century through the 7th century and into the early 6th century BCE, all the evidence reviewed above leads to the conclusion that the rosette stamp-impression system began earlier than was generally believed. As a historical conjecture, one might date the beginning of this system to the 630s BCE, during the reign of Josiah.

In sum, on the basis of an analysis of all the currently available data, I propose that the rosette stamp-impression system started at the beginning of the last third of the 7th century BCE. As a historical conjecture—and in agreement with other scholars[76]—this date may be

---

73. See stratigraphic discussion in Shiloh 1984: 11–12. I do not accept Cahill's arguments (2000b: 98) against this dating.

74. To date, not a single excavated seal can be conclusively proven to have been used for stamping rosette impressions. However, a lead seal with a twelve-petalled rosette design was excavated at En-Gedi (Mazar and Dunayevsky 1964: 123; Stern 2007c: 156), and an eight-petalled rosette seal was discovered at Lachish (Tufnell 1953: 372, Pl. 45:137).

75. Ussishkin (2004c: 111), Cahill (1995: 247) and Kletter (1999: 37) compared this number of rosette stamp impressions to the number of *lmlk* stamp impressions—over five times as many—and concluded that the rosette system operated for an extremely short period. The new chronological classification of the *lmlk* stamp impressions, however, shows that most are from the stage preceding Sennacherib's campaign and that this large number of stamp impressions relates to the period when the Shephelah still served as the hub of the system and Judah had far greater production capabilities than it did after 701 BCE. It is also possible that the much-reduced area of the administrative system after 701 BCE also gave rise to more efficient storage-jar recycling, and this may also have contributed to the decline in the number of stamped handles in the various 7th-century BCE systems.

76. This is accepted by many scholars, from Albright (1928: 10), through Aharoni (1964: 35) and up to Na'aman (1989: 42–45; 1991b: 31–33).

associated with the rule of Josiah.[77] This administrative change could be linked to the decline of Assyria and its disappearance from the region or to the interval between the fall of Assyria and the rise of Babylon, when Judah was subjugated to Egypt (Naʾaman 1989: 51–53; Lipschits 2005: 38–47, with further literature).

Conclusions

The conclusion from this chapter is that the system whereby impressions were stamped on storage jars existed in the Kingdom of Judah from the last third of the 8th century BCE, when Judah became a vassal of Assyria, until the destruction of Jerusalem in the early 6th century BCE. The main conclusions regarding the chronology of the specific systems are as follows:

- The first stamp impressions to appear on storage jars in Judah were the four types of *lmlk* stamp impressions with the four-winged scarab symbol and official lapidary script (Lemaire's Type Ib). These are large stamp impressions, produced with high-quality seals. They bear the names of four sites in Judah: Hebron, Socoh, Ziph and *mmšt*. Their uniformity points to their production as a series, presumably by the same craftsman and at the same time. We may speculate—albeit without archae-ological corroboration—that this series came into use after 732 BCE, probably during the early 720s BCE, when Judah was subjugated to Assyria and began to adapt its administration and economy to the necessity of paying annual tribute as a vassal kingdom.

- A few years later, perhaps when Hezekiah came to power (715 BCE), the system was replaced by another system of *lmlk* seals, still with the four-winged scarab symbol but with cursive script. This series consisted of only three seals and lacked the place name Socoh. This suggests that the former seal of Socoh was still in use, especially if it was preserved at the site where the storage jars were produced—perhaps Socoh itself.

- This system was replaced by a set of four seals of similar quality and script, but with a two-winged symbol instead of the four-winged scarab. This system could not have been in use for more than a few years, as demonstrated by the scarcity of handles stamped with these impressions, uncovered in the destruction layers left by the Assyrian campaign of 701 BCE in Judah.

- It is possible that in the short period from the death of Sargon and the outbreak of the revolt in Judah (705 BCE) until Sennacherib's campaign and the renewed subjugation of Judah (701 BCE), the system of "private" stamp impressions operated in Judah. These impressions were stamped on the same types of storage jars as those used in the *lmlk* system—and in some cases, on the very same storage jars and even the same handles already bearing a *lmlk* stamp impression. This system served within the framework of the preparations for the Assyrian onslaught, and it ceased to exist after 701 BCE.

- The system of late types of *lmlk* stamp impressions, created after 701 BCE, consists of three series of seals. It may have been in existence during the first third of the 7th century BCE. The first series, consisting of four seals (Lemaire's Type IIb), is very similar in quality and components to the early two-winged series that operated for a brief period before 701 BCE. It continued the 8th-century BCE tradition of seals with the word *lmlk* at the top, a two-winged symbol in the center and a place name at the bottom. The script—both the place name and the word *lmlk*—gradually declined in importance in the two other series that were in use during the early 7th century BCE. In Type IIc, the word *lmlk* is absent and the place name appears at the top of the stamp impression. In Type XII, the place name is missing. The position of the royal symbol in the center of the stamp impression remained constant throughout this period. Interestingly, the place name Socoh is missing from this late system too. Again, perhaps the seal with the place name Socoh continued to be

---

77. This constitutes a kind of return to the theory proposed by Yadin (1961a), who argued that Josiah's reform exceeded the boundaries of religious activity and included an overhaul of the royal administration. Whereas Yadin linked the *lmlk* stamp impressions to this reform, the new dating of the stamp-impression systems suggests that the rosette stamp impressions should be associated with the reign of Josiah.

used at the site of manufacture of the storage jars and did not require replacement.

- The concentric circle incisions should most probably be dated to the second third of the 7th century BCE. This system immediately followed the late types of *lmlk* stamp impressions and preceded the rosette stamp impressions. The distribution of the incised handles is very similar to that of the late types of *lmlk* stamp impressions, reflecting the destruction of the Shephelah and its severance from the administrative system of Judah during most of the 7th century BCE. The system precedes the Assyrian withdrawal at the beginning of the last third of this century, when Judah regained its hold on the Shephelah and settlement in this area began to be restored.

- The rosette stamp impressions began to be used around the 630s BCE, replacing the system of concentric circle incisions. As mentioned above, this change presumably took place after the Assyrian withdrawal from the region, during the reign of Josiah, and thus it reflects the settlement revival that took place when Judah regained control over the Shephelah. This system continued to operate during the subsequent subjugation of Judah to Babylon and ended abruptly with the destruction of Jerusalem, when Judah was transformed from a vassal kingdom to a mere province.

6

The Function and *Modus Operandi* of the Stamped Storage-Jar System in the Kingdom of Judah

History of Research: Questions and Problems

Most of the research conducted on impressions stamped on storage jars in Judah focuses on the publication of finds from excavations and surveys (as well as finds of unknown provenance). More general studies have focused on specific groups and types, but without taking a broader view of the phenomenon as a whole, without drawing correlations between different types stamped on the same storage jars, and without considering the phenomenon as a whole and attempting to formulate a unified explanation for it.[1]

The *lmlk* Stamp Impressions

This group has traditionally been the focus of research because of the large quantity of finds and the scholarly consensus with regard to their dating and historical significance. The other groups, especially those dated to the Second Temple period (the lion, *mwṣh*, *yhwd* and *yršlm* stamp impressions), received little attention and have never been considered in conjunction with the First Temple period systems—certainly not with the *lmlk* stamp impressions. Nor was their function within the administrative system of their times given much consideration. The various types of stamp impressions and incisions received different, non-uniform, interpretations, which at times even ran counter to the interpretations offered for the *lmlk* stamp impressions.

From the beginning, most scholars assumed that the *lmlk* stamp impressions were part of the official royal administrative system. This was based on several factors: the appearance of the word *lmlk* at the top of all these stamp impressions (with the exception of one type, of which very few examples were found); the interpretation given to the symbols on these stamp impressions; and the fact that with only a few exceptions, the stamped

---

1. As early as 2001, Stern noted that a system of stamp impressions on storage jars was in operation for a long time at the end of the First Temple period, continuing into the Persian period (Stern 2001: 174–175). Although he repeated this notion in a comment in the En-Gedi excavation report (Stern 2007c: 140–141), indicating an awareness of the need for a comprehensive perspective on the phenomenon, he did not develop this idea further.

handles were recovered from within the borders of the Kingdom of Judah, particularly in the destruction layers of its central cities, most notably Lachish.[2] The interpretation of the function and characteristics of the system was derived from the interpretation of the place names appearing under the royal symbol: Hebron, Ziph, Socoh and *mmšt*. Diringer suggested that the sites mentioned were royal centers for storage-jar production and that the stamp impressions were marks guaranteeing the capacity of the storage jars or the quality of their contents, oil or wine (Diringer 1941: 108; 1949: 82). Yadin, Aharoni and others considered them to be the destinations of these royal storage jars after they were filled with agricultural products. Yadin argued that these were Judahite military centers, where a supply of wine and oil was stored in royal storage jars, while Aharoni interpreted them as royal administrative centers for the collection, storage and redistribution of tribute (Yadin 1961a; Aharoni 1987: 301–306).

These interpretations fail to account for the fact that very few stamped jar handles were found at Hebron and Ziph, whereas sites not mentioned on the stamp impressions, especially Lachish, yielded an abundance of stamped handles. It is therefore unlikely that the places mentioned served as collection centers for storage jars or were their destinations. Furthermore, excavations and surveys show that Hebron, Ziph and Socoh, three of the place names mentioned in the *lmlk* stamp impressions (if one discounts *mmšt*, the identification of which is uncertain; see below), were no more than rural settlements at the time, with no notable urban or military centers. On these grounds, and taking into account studies of the origin of the clay (see, especially, Mommsen, Perlman and Yellin 1984), many scholars considered it more likely that these sites were the destinations for the still empty storage jars, which had been manufactured at a single production center in the Shephelah, and that they were filled with agricultural products at these sites and then shipped to one or more collection centers.

Cross suggested that the stamp impressions were intended to guarantee the capacity of the storage jars and that the four place names identified royal wineries (Cross 1969: 21*). Rainey developed this idea further, arguing that these were centers for wine production in the Judean Hills and that the royal produce was distributed from there (Rainey 1982). They were followed by many scholars, who considered the four names to represent the places of origin of the agricultural produce, suggesting that Hebron, Ziph, Socoh and *mmšt* were royal estates or wineries, engaged in agricultural cultivation and in the production of wine and oil, in particular (Fox 2000: 226–235; Kletter 2002: 140, with further literature).

Na'aman provided an historical interpretation and a clear chronological and geographical context to these theories (Na'aman 1979b: 73–76, 85–86; 1986: 12), emphasizing that the main sites where *lmlk* stamp impressions were found (especially in the Shephelah) were in keeping with the historical sources that identified the Shephelah as the primary target of the Assyrian campaign. He concluded that Hezekiah, preparing for the Assyrian onslaught, selected several key sites in the Shephelah, fortified them and equipped them with provisions and food in anticipation of a siege. Na'aman claimed that the *lmlk* storage jars were manufactured in this period for this purpose and were shipped to the royal estates named in the stamp impressions, where they were filled with wine or oil and sent on to the border fortresses (Na'aman 1986: 12, 17). The interpretation of the storage-jar system as being part of Hezekiah's preparations for the Assyrian campaign was generally accepted, with a few variations.[3] This historical interpretation became the main rationale for the archaeological dating of all the *lmlk* storage jars to the short period between the outbreak of Hezekiah's revolt and Sennacherib's destruction of the Shephelah.

The main problem with Na'aman's suggested reconstruction is that it relies upon Ussishkin's erroneous attribution of all types of *lmlk* stamp impressions uncovered in Lachish to the Level III destruction layer. As previously stated, it is now clear that only some of the stamp impressions—those defined as "early types"— were found in the Sennacherib campaign destruction

---

2. When one considers the stamped storage jars to be part of a royal system, the iconographic change from the four-winged scarab to the two-winged "flying scroll" makes sense—it may be interpreted as evidence of Josiah's religious and cultic reforms. See, e.g., Albright 1943: 74; Diringer 1949: 74–76; and many others.

3. See, e.g., Rainey 1982; Ussishkin 1982: 47; 2004b: 2142; Garfinkel 1988: 69; Halpern 1991: 23; Kelm and Mazar 1995: 135.

layer.[4] Other similar storage jars, stamped by "late types" of *lmlk* stamp impressions, were manufactured only at a later stage, in the early 7th century BCE. Moreover, it now appears that stamped storage jars were produced even before Hezekiah's revolt against Assyria. Thus, the historical attribution of the *lmlk* storage-jar system to the revolt is no longer valid. As for Ussishkin's archaeological point of departure, since the Assyrian army targeted the Shephelah, destroying central sites there, many *lmlk* storage jars, along with other items in use just before the destruction, were buried beneath these destruction layers. While these sites, especially Lachish, undoubtedly held a large concentration of storage jars, we should bear in mind that Jerusalem, Ramat Raḥel and sites in the Benjamin region—all sites that were not destroyed in the Assyrian campaign—also yielded many jar sherds, including handles with early types of *lmlk* stamp impressions as well as handles bearing "private" stamp impressions. These were generally recovered from fills beneath construction layers from the late Iron Age or even later. The finding of *lmlk* storage jars at these sites— which continued in use in the 7th century BCE—further undermines the common association of the *lmlk* stamp impressions with the preparations for Hezekiah's revolt against Assyria.

Cracks in the theory that this was a short-lived system within the framework of the preparations against the Assyrian campaign emerged already in the 1980s and 1990s, when it transpired that all the *lmlk* storage jars— both the ones stamped with *lmlk* impressions and the ones that were left unstamped—were manufactured at a single production center in the Shephelah (Mommsen, Yellin and Perlman 1984) and that these storage jars enjoyed a long history of development, beginning in the late 9th century BCE.[5] It became clear that storage jars similar to the stamped type were manufactured in the 8th century BCE and that these storage jars, along with jars identical to the type that was stamped, were produced in the 7th century BCE. Scholars realized that the storage jars should be studied separately from the stamp impressions and that the stamp-impression system was part of a complex economy based on the manufacture of agricultural produce. Another factor important for understanding this administrative system was Ussishkin's finding that the storage jars did not all have the same capacity and that even among the stamped storage jars— the most uniform of all types of storage jars—variation reached at least 20% (Ussishkin 2004b: 2145; see also Sergi *et al.* 2012).

Vaughn, while accepting the commonly held date for the production of the *lmlk* storage jars, argued that the system that used stamped storage jars should not be restricted to the period of the revolt against Assyria and to the preparations for this campaign (1999b).[6] Arguing that many stamped storage jars were found at sites in the Shephelah and around Jerusalem that were not fortified in the late 8th century BCE and at sites that were not destroyed by the Assyrians, he suggested that the system was related to changes in the economy and administration of Judah in the days of Hezekiah. Consequently, Vaughn extended the duration of the system to a longer period within Hezekiah's reign (Vaughn 1999b: 138–157). Relying upon information that had accumulated regarding the development of the storage jars in the Shephelah, he posited a system of trade in wine and perhaps oil involving these storage jars—both the stamped and unstamped ones. Their distribution pointed, according to Vaughn, to a well-developed royal administration and large-scale trade, a system that, he claimed, was eventually channeled to meet the needs of the revolt—thus leading to the erroneous scholarly view that the entire system had been intended for these preparations (*ibid.*).

The thesis presented by Vaughn is methodologically unsound. His lack of distinction between the unstamped storage jars, the jars stamped with *lmlk* impressions and the ones stamped with "private" impressions blurs the distinction between the two systems of stamp impressions. It also obscures their connection with other storage jars in Judah—the ones produced before the late 8th century BCE, the ones produced at the same time as the jars stamped with *lmlk* and "private" impressions

---

4. Indeed, Ussishkin now concurs (2012).

5. Gitin 1990; Shai and Maeir 2003; Sergi *et al.* 2012, with further literature; see also above, pp. 17–24.

6. This is an adaptation of his Ph.D. dissertation, which focuses on the *lmlk* storage jars.

and the ones produced later in the 7th century BCE. Furthermore, Vaughn did not attempt to account for the emergence or disappearance of the phenomenon of the stamp impressions, and he did not deal with the plethora of questions arising from their features, such as: What do the four place names mentioned in the *lmlk* stamp impressions signify? What is the significance of the various types? Why is there such an exceptional use of iconography? Why do the stamp impressions display two symbols, and what relationship do they bear to one another? What is the significance of the word *lmlk* (which did not exist on stamp impressions before this period and did not continue afterward)? In addition, Vaughn did not distinguish between chronological groups within the *lmlk* stamp-impression system and did not link this system to the concentric circle incisions or to other stamp impressions on similar jar types, which continued in the 7th century BCE. Nor did he differentiate between the "*lmlk*-like," "pre-*lmlk*" and *lmlk* storage jars (both stamped and unstamped), and he did not realize that the latter are far more uniform in capacity and shape than other types of storage jars. Thus, despite Vaughn's pioneering work determining when production of these storage jars began, and although we can accept his insights regarding the locations where stamped storage jars were found—including sites in the hill country, sites that were not fortified and sites that were not destroyed in Sennacherib's campaign—his theory does not account for the economic and administrative system in which the jars were manufactured and the products collected, stored and shipped off.

The most important original study of the *lmlk* storage jars is perhaps Fox's comprehensive analysis of administration in the Kingdoms of Israel and Judah (Fox 2000: 216–235). Like Vaughn, she disassociated the storage jars from the revolt against Assyria and the preparations for Sennacherib's campaign, but she also reconstructed a complex administrative system in which these storage jars were manufactured, marked, filled and shipped off. Fox accepted the view that the *lmlk* storage jars were shipped from a central pottery workshop in the Shephelah to four royal estates, indicated in the stamp impressions. Her contribution to the research lies in her

reconstruction of the way the system operated from that time onward (Fox 2000: 227–235). She claims that the storage jars were shipped from these estates to members of the royal family. Some of the jars—the ones stamped with "private" impressions—were sent to individuals who were close to the monarchy and who received lands from the kings for fixed periods of time. Fox rejects the commonly accepted view that the names appearing on the "private" stamp impressions were the names of officials, considering them instead to represent distinguished individuals who received the products as royal payment.

The importance of Fox's theory lies in her proposal of a *modus operandi* for the storage-jar system, in which the economy was largely based on royal estates with wide-scale activities. Her distinction between the officials mentioned in the "private" stamp impressions and the *lmlk* system of stamp impressions is also very important. However, her assumption that the "private" stamp-impression system operated for only a short period prior to Sennacherib's campaign, with no later evidence for any activity of these "officials" in the running of the royal estates, makes it difficult to accept her reconstruction of the system's *modus operandi*. Furthermore, the absence of all the names appearing in the "private" stamp impressions from any other contemporaneous source (both epigraphic and biblical) also suggests that these were not, in fact, senior officials of the king or royal family members.

Surprisingly, despite the sophisticated and accurate typology developed by Lemaire in 1981 and the comprehensive corpus compiled by Grena (although not without methodological and practical problems),[7] for 30 years the research remained entrenched in the preconceptions and underlying assumptions based on the Lachish excavations and in the historical and chronological interpretation given to the findings at this site. The data was not reexamined and no comprehensive study was conducted to examine the relationship between the typology and the archaeology or to correlate the various types of stamp impressions with the stratigraphic and chronological information available for each type. Such a study could have served

---

7. Grena 2004; cf., especially, the comprehensive corpus on his website: www.lmlk.com.

as the basis for a reevaluation of the *modus operandi* of the *lmlk* stamp-impression system and its connection to the other systems of stamp impressions.

Given this lacuna in the research, Lipschits, Sergi and Koch introduced a new thesis in two articles published a decade ago (2010; 2011). They analyze the various types of *lmlk* stamp impressions according to their stratigraphy, dividing them into early and late *lmlk* types of stamp impressions on the basis of a careful examination of the entire corpus.[8] The conclusion that this system began early in the final third of the 8th century BCE and continued into the early 7th century BCE is not the main and most important conclusion of our work, and, as mentioned above, is not a new one. Its main importance lies in the comprehensive typological-chronological picture of the *lmlk* stamp impressions that it presents, in a way that this impacts our understanding of the storage-jar administration in Judah, enabling us to explain its aim, its historical, administrative and economic context, and its relation to the systems of stamp impressions that followed it. Also of importance is the understanding that this system is not a singular phenomenon, but is a part of an administrative method that operated for some 600 years, with a variety of types that continued to develop, both when Judah was a vassal kingdom and when it became a satrapy.

The "Private" Stamp Impressions

From early in the research, the "private" stamp impressions were associated with the *lmlk* stamp impressions and with the official royal storage-jar system in Judah, as both these kinds of stamp impressions were generally found in the same sites and in the same settlement layers. Both kinds were stamped on the same types of storage jars, and, as mentioned above, in three cases "private" and *lmlk* stamp impressions were found on the same handle, and in Lachish, two storage jars were uncovered bearing the two kinds of stamp impressions on different handles.

The names appearing on the "private" stamp impressions were initially thought to belong to the potters and to have been stamped on the vessel at the site of production. Diringer, on the basis of the limited distribution of the names on the "private" stamp impressions, associated these names with a small group of potters. On the assumption that the stamp impressions bear the name of the seal owner and his father, he created genealogical lists of families of potters (Diringer 1941: 89–91).[9] This view did not gain widespread scholarly support and is no longer valid.[10]

Most scholars considered the names in the "private" stamp impressions to refer to officials working in the royal administration, especially given the link between

---

8. As aforementioned, the notion of late *lmlk* stamp impressions, produced in the 7th century BCE, is not a novel one. Ji (2001) was the first to view *lmlk* storage jars as part of a long and continuous development, beginning in the late 8th century BCE and continuing until the destruction of the Kingdom of Judah. The distinction between "pre-Sennacherib" and "post-Sennacherib" *lmlk* stamp impressions was also proposed by Grena (2004: 337), who based his distinction on 13 handles found in clear 7th-century archaeological contexts (in Jerusalem, Arad, Lachish, Tel Batash and Ḥorvat Shilḥa). None of these studies, however, conducted a comprehensive analysis of the stamp impressions uncovered and a meticulous examination of the stratigraphy and chronology of the corpus as a whole. Following Grena, see van der Veen 2014: 26, n. 41.

9. Most of these names have since been found to be of different patronyms than those assigned by Diringer (Vaughn 1999b: 112). Diringer's interpretation was based upon an extremely small assemblage of stamp impressions, on an erroneous reading of some of them (see, e.g., Barkay and Vaughn 1996b) and on problematic points of departure for the interpretation of the administrative system as a whole.

10. Ussishkin (1983: 160–164; 1993: 909; 2004b: 2146) and, to some extent, Kelm and Mazar (1995: 133) are among the few scholars who supported the notion that the names belonged to the potters. Ussishkin argued that as all the *lmlk* storage jars were manufactured at a single production center and as, in a few cases, both *lmlk* and "private" impressions were stamped, often carelessly, onto the same storage jar, it should be concluded that these stamp impressions were not part of the administrative system, but were stamped by officials in these production centers or by the potters themselves. Furthermore, according to Ussishkin, the absence of a clear connection between the destination appearing on the *lmlk* stamp impressions and the find spot of the storage jars, coupled with the large concentration of officials in Lachish, undermine the proposals that link the stamping to the royal apparatus and support the connection between the storage-jar stamp impressions and the jars' place of manufacture. Ussishkin's conclusion does not withstand the test of criticism. It does not consider the possibility that these places were not the final destination of the storage jars, but could have been production centers of agricultural produce, to be transferred later on to specific collection and storage sites, especially Lachish. This notion has been linked to the rural nature of the areas in the three identifiable places mentioned in the stamp impressions (Hebrew, Socoh and Ziph). It further accounts for the recovery of a few storage-jar handles at locations that were clearly production sites for oil and wine, such as Rogem Gannim, on the outskirts of the Rephaim Valley—sites that not only operated within the framework of the *lmlk* storage-jar system, but also revealed a few handles incised with concentric circles, stamped with rosette impressions, and even—in the case of Rogem Gannim—stamped with *yhwd* impressions. For criticism of Ussishkin's proposals, see also Vaughn 1999b: 111–135.

"private" and *lmlk* stamp impressions.[11] However, none of the above suggestions offer a satisfactory explanation for the role of these officials in the stamp-impression system or for the connection between the relatively limited "private" stamp-impression system and the complex widespread system of *lmlk* stamp impressions. Fox (2000: 230–232) offered a different interpretation of the "private" stamp impressions, although not without its shortcomings.[12] As aforementioned, she rejected the accepted notion that the names referred to officials, interpreting them instead as notables who received agricultural produce from the king's lands as payment on behalf of the monarchy.

Nonetheless, after many years of study of the "private" stamp impressions and despite general agreement in the scholarly community regarding their date and their association with the *lmlk* stamp-impression system, there is still no satisfactory understanding of the nature of the relationship between the two systems, of the role of the individuals whose names appear in the impressions, and of the function and mode of operation of the system.

The Concentric Circle Incisions

The concentric circle incisions received even less attention in the research. At first it was suggested that they were potter's marks, but since they were engraved next to or on top of royal stamp impressions this approach was ruled out; the possibility that the incisions were decorative elements was similarly rejected (Pritchard 1959: 22). The function of these incisions was considered briefly between 1959–1961, and since then was hardly discussed. Pritchard was the first to offer three possible functions of the concentric circle incisions within the storage-jar system (Pritchard 1959: 22–23):

1. that the concentric circle incisions cancelled out the royal stamp impressions (based on six handles from Gibeon with circles engraved onto the royal stamp impression), thus annulling the association of these storage jars with the royal apparatus.

2. that the incisions served as confirmation that the addressee had received the freight, and were thus engraved upon reaching the destination.

3. that the incisions validated the storage jar's capacity. After firing, the jar was examined, and when its volume was confirmed to meet the standard requirements, the circles were engraved upon its handles.

While Pritchard's first suggestion was supported by Aharoni (1984: 323, n. 34) and Welten (1969: 189–190), Barkay correctly observed that only in a few cases the concentric circle incision was actually engraved on top of the stamp impression, and in most cases it appears next to it (Barkay 1985: 409). If it had indeed been intended to cancel the inclusion of these storage jars in the royal apparatus, the stamp impression could have simply been eroded or marked with a simple sign—and indeed, there are several cases of an X incised on the stamp impression (Wilson and Warren 1871: 369–370; Ussishkin 1983: 163, Pl. 43:1). Pritchard's second proposal did not receive support, presumably because many scholars realized that it was unlikely that there would be so few "confirmations of receipt," given the great quantity of stamped storage jars and the even greater quantity of unstamped ones. This proposal also does not provide a satisfactory explanation for why half the concentric circle incisions appear on storage-jar handles that bear no stamp impression. In all likelihood, the lack of support for Pritchard's third proposal stemmed from similar reasons.

---

11. Garfinkel 1985; Barkay 1985: 416; 1992a: 113–128; Vaughn 1999b: 90, 110. Garfinkel (1985) attempted to determine a hierarchy among the officials based on their geographical distribution, but as already demonstrated (Barkay and Vaughn 1995; 1996b; Vaughn 1999b: 110–135; Ussishkin 2004b: 2145–2146), this proposal is flawed and should be rejected. Vaughn (1999b: 112–136) showed differing levels of "formality" in the "private" stamp impressions and argued, contra Ussishkin, that several different craftsmen created the seals, that in some cases one individual possessed more than one seal, and that some seals mention the titles of the officials. He also argued that the seals were high-quality engravings on expensive raw materials. Cf. Deutsch and Heltzer (1995: 45–46), who contend that the seals were made of wood (although they rely upon a *lmlk* stamp impression that surfaced on the antiquities market, today in the Moussaieff collection).

12. The main problem with Fox's theory is that the storage jars were stamped during production and not while they were being filled prior to shipment or "payment" to royal beneficiaries. Moreover, the distribution of jars with the same stamp impression in different regions of the kingdom and the overall distribution of jars stamped with "private" impressions indicate that these jars were recycled and reused for many years. That being the case, it is unclear how effective it would be to stamp the storage jar during its manufacture and what connection the name on the stamp impression would bear to the recipient of the storage jar, who is supposedly receiving payment, and to its contents.

In this case too, it is unclear why the capacity of so few storage jars was confirmed, while there are many hundreds of storage jars with handles that were stamped before firing and a far greater number of storage jars that have no mark at all, yet are more or less identical in size and capacity to the jars with concentric circle incisions.

Around the time of publication of Pritchard's proposals, Lapp suggested that the incisions were an indication of the quality of the jar's contents or of the age of the stored liquid (wine?) (Lapp 1960: 22). This suggestion, which seems to have been prompted by practices of the modern wine industry, is also unlikely, given the discrepancy between the number of jars with incisions and the far greater quantity of unmarked jars. Another possibility introduced by Lapp—that this mark expresses a prohibition against reuse of the vessel (Lapp 1960: 22)—should be similarly questioned.

Yadin took a more comprehensive approach, considering the circular incisions to be an attempt to adapt the jars already in the Judahite system to the new stamp-impression system introduced in the late 7th century BCE—that of the rosette stamp impressions (Yadin 1961a: 12; see also Stern 2007c: 149). Yadin showed nicely that the concentric circle incisions could be seen as a schematic rosette symbol, its schematic nature stemming from the incision technique. Since he considered the system of concentric circle incisions to be identical to that of the rosette stamp impressions in chronology and function, he viewed all the incised and the rosette-stamped jars as part of the same system— some already in the system, and others first manufactured in this period. Generally speaking, this suggestion is in keeping with the characteristics of the stamp-impression system on storage jars in Judah, as shown below. Nonetheless, as pointed out above (pp. 114–116), a dating of the concentric circle incisions to such a late stage in the 7th century BCE is unlikely; this system does not

appear to have been in operation after the middle of the century. Thus, Yadin's explanation should be adapted to the chronology proposed here; the concentric circle incisions should be considered a mark intended to adapt the *lmlk* jars to the new system, which began to operate in the second third of the 7th century BCE and continued until the beginning of its final third, when the rosette stamp-impression system came into use.[13]

The Rosette Stamp Impressions

The rosette stamp impressions on storage-jar handles were also interpreted as potter's marks, from the discovery of the first handle in the late 19th century until the mid-20th century (Bliss and Macalister 1902: Pl. 56:35z– 43z; Mendelson 1940).[14] This notion was rejected following the finds of the Lachish excavation, when Diringer, on the basis of the affinity in shape between the *lmlk*- and rosette-stamped storage jars, postulated that the stamp impressions played a role in the royal administrative system of Judah (Diringer 1953: 345–346). Diringer's proposal was generally accepted, and, except for some discussions in the early 1960s, which provided further support, mainly on the basis of Aharoni's findings from Ramat Raḥel, the subject received little attention in subsequent decades.[15]

Following these studies, Ussishkin suggested that the rosette-stamped storage jars—like the *lmlk* storage jars that were used on the eve of Sennacherib's campaign— should be understood within the framework of the preparations of the Kingdom of Judah for the Babylonian onslaught (Ussishkin 1977: 52–53; 2004c: 92–93, 109–119). However, as mentioned above, it is unlikely that two different sophisticated and comprehensive systems were invented, using the same type of storage jars and the same method of stamping, in two periods about 115 years apart, with the goal of amassing supplies

---

13. Barkay 1985: 408–409. As mentioned above, Barkay dated the inception of this system to the late 8th or early 7th century BCE; see also Avigad and Barkay 2000: 247. Based on this dating, Barkay posited that the storage jars that survived Sennacherib's campaign were returned to the royal storerooms, where they were refilled and therefore incised with concentric circles.

14. Albright (1933: 10) also initially adopted this interpretation, but later, in an editorial comment to Mendelson's article about guilds in Judah (Mendelson 1940: 21, n. 51, with further literature), he claimed that the rosette symbol had royal significance.

15. In view of the excavation finds from Ramat Raḥel, Aharoni (1962: 21) concluded, following Diringer, that the rosette stamp-impression system was related to the royal system. Similarly, and as mentioned above, Yadin (1961b) supported this opinion; he argued that the concentric circle incisions were used as part of the rosette system, bringing the *lmlk* storage jars into the new system, which began to operate at the end of the 7th century BCE.

in the border towns. Furthermore, as shown above, the finds themselves, including the number of seals and stamped jars, the sophisticated system and its inner development, disprove this suggestion.

Taking a completely different approach—one that ran counter to the generally accepted scholarly opinion, Kletter suggested that the rosette stamp-impression system was not part of the royal administrative apparatus (Kletter 1999: 36–37). He argued that the absence of epigraphic features in the rosette stamp impressions was incongruous with the degree of literacy in the 7th century BCE, and he pointed out the absence of the rosette symbol on "private" seals of the period. Kletter proposed a longer duration for the rosette stamp-impression system than was generally accepted, claiming that the symbol was well known and widespread and that rosette-stamped handles were found from later periods in Judah as well. Kletter's two arguments are implausible: for one thing, there is no intrinsic relation between the degree of literacy and the emblem chosen to continue a certain administrative system, and for another, the lack of epigraphic content in the rosette stamp impressions is a continuation of a trend—the decline in the use of writing—already evident in the late types of *lmlk* impressions. Furthermore, the chronology of the rosette stamp impressions is securely dated, on the basis of archaeological finds from Judah, to the late 7th and early 6th centuries BCE. While some rosette stamp impressions from the Persian period have been found, after a long gap during the 6th and early 5th century BCE, this does not affect the dating of the early system. The later stamp impressions have different features, and they appear on handles that differ from those of the rosette stamp-impression system.[16]

In 2004, Yellin and Cahill showed that most of the rosette-stamped storage jars were manufactured at the same workshop in the Shephelah where the *lmlk* storage jars were previously produced. They also identified a limited production of rosette storage jars in the Jerusalem area.[17] This study strengthened the relationship between the rosette storage jars and the earlier stamped storage-jar systems and supported the view that they were part of the Judahite administrative system.[18] This was further established by additional studies dealing with the storage-jar system and with the history of Judah at the end of the First Temple period (e.g., Cahill 1995, with further literature; Fox 2000: 236–240). Na'aman's studies provide an important contribution to the debate. While he did not point to the precise use of the storage-jar system and did not define its function within the Judahite administrative system, he firmly established the connection between the rosette stamp-impression system and the Judahite administration by showing correlations between the distribution of these storage jars and the town-lists of Judah and Benjamin in the Book of Joshua (15:21–62, 18:21–28), which are customarily dated to the days of Josiah (Na'aman 1989: 42–45; 1991b: 31–33).

To sum up the research into the rosette stamp impressions, there is a near consensus that they are related to the administrative system in Judah, but hardly any actual proposals as to just what their function was. It has also been well established that this system is connected to the *lmlk* stamp-impression system, and it has been suggested that the concentric circle incisions served as a bridge between the earlier and later systems—although here also, no specific suggestions have been made regarding the use and function of this system in the economy and administration of the kingdom.[19]

The Purpose and Historical Context of the Storage-Jar System

The main thesis of this book is that the storage-jar administration developed in Judah when the kingdom was subjugated to Assyria in the early last third of the 8th century BCE, and that it continued to exist for some 600 years until after the Hasmonean revolt and the renewal of Judean independence in the second half of the 2nd century BCE. This was an innovative Judahite development of a simple and well-known technique,

---

16. For rosette stamp impressions from the Persian period, see Ras, Bocher and Koch 2016: 442–445.

17. Yellin and Cahill 2004: 192–198. For the identification of the site of production of the *lmlk* storage jars, see above; see also Mommsen, Perlman and Yellin 1984: 106–107.

18. For further literature, see Cahill 1995: 241–242.

19. Koch's 2008 study is therefore of great importance, as is Koch and Lipschits 2010.

already familiar throughout the ancient Near East, of stamping impressions on the handles or bodies of storage jars. For the first time in history, however, this technique was no longer used merely as a decorative device or a local response to a specific administrative, economic, or commercial need to mark a few vessels. The system invented and developed in Judah was large-scale, encompassing a broad geographical expanse, and involved numerous seals that were impressed on dozens, or even hundreds, of storage jars in the course of centuries. The need for this system arose as a result of the imperial taxes imposed upon Judah and the necessity to improve and strengthen the local economy for that purpose (Lipschits, Sergi and Koch 2010: 6–7; 2011: 6).

The swift development of the economy and administration of Judah at the end of the 8th century BCE is directly related to the Assyrian pressure, which, as aforementioned, imposed a sudden need for standardization and centralization upon the economic system (Lipschits 2018a; 2018b). The organization and economy of the Kingdom of Judah has been the subject of many biblical, anthropological[20] and archaeological studies.[21] Many scholars stressed the tribal, non-centralized and local characteristics of the society and economy in Judah and the importance of these features in the First Temple period.[22] All this changed suddenly and rapidly, in my view, in the first years of subjugation to Assyria, as an internal process within Judah led by the monarchy and the administration, which was under pressure to unify the economy and pay the high taxes demanded by Assyria.

In this early system, Lachish was chosen as the main collection center of storage jars in the Shephelah, while in the hill country, Ramat Raḥel was built as a royal administrative center for collecting agricultural products under Assyrian imperial direction and supervision.[23] This is in keeping with our knowledge of the development of agricultural estates, presumably royal estates—sites in the hill country and in the Shephelah that belonged to the Judahite monarchy, were relatively sparsely settled, and

did not undergo intensive agricultural cultivation. This development presumably began in the late 8th century BCE, after the subjugation to Assyria, in the Rephaim Valley (the biblical "Valley of the King"; Lipschits and Gadot 2008), in the vicinity of Moẓa (De Groot and Greenhut 2002; Greenhut 2006; Greenhut and De Groot 2009) and in more distant areas of the kingdom—Hebron, the Elah Valley, the southern Shephelah, and perhaps other areas around Jerusalem (Katz 2008: 169–178; Lipschits and Gadot 2008; Gadot 2015). The pottery culture of Judah underwent a drastic change, transitioning from small-scale, non-standardized production in local workshops to the mass production of a small selection of uniformly-shaped vessels for widespread distribution. The storage jars selected for production were of greater capacity than before (Mazar 1990: 509; Zimhoni 1997: 171–172; 2004b: 1705–1707; Katz 2008: 52–53, with further literature). Technological improvements in the agricultural production facilities in Judah should be attributed to this period, when the economy and administration of Judah as an Assyrian vassal kingdom, forced to pay heavy annual tribute, were undergoing change and consolidation (Faust and Weiss 2005; Katz 2008: 55–59). This increased the wine and oil production in these facilities. The economy underwent further change with the introduction of the *shekel* weights for use throughout the kingdom, a change that brought about uniformity of all the commercial measures and served as a catalyst for rapid commercial growth (Kletter 1998: 145–147; Katz 2008: 77–79, with further literature). These innovations and developments fostered the transition to a more centralized economy and improved the central government's ability to supervise commerce and govern the economic system as a whole.

The stamping of *lmlk* impressions on storage-jar handles should, therefore, be viewed as part of the new economic and administrative system that began in Judah under the rule of the Assyrians, with their encouragement and perhaps pressure to increase agricultural production in order to meet the annual quotas of tribute that it was

---

20. See, e.g., Lemche 1994; 1996; 2014; Chaney 2014; Boer 2015; Maeir and Shai 2016: 325, with further literature.

21. Stager 1985; 1998; 2003; Schloen 2001; 2016; Master 2001; Lipschits 2018a, with further literature.

22. See, e.g., Bendor 1986; Halpern 1991; 1996; Levine 2003; Lehmann 2004; Lehmann and Niemann 2006; Vanderhooft 2009; Faust 2012a; Maeir and Shai 2016.

23. Lipschits *et al.* 2017: 39–56; for Ramat Raḥel, see Naʾaman 2001: 270–274; Lipschits and Gadot 2008; Lipschits 2009a.

required to pay to the empire. The selection of a specific type of storage jar, which was produced and distributed in the Shephelah for at least a century, making it the standard for the collection of agricultural produts, lends further support to this view (Sergi *et al.* 2012; and see above, pp. 17–24). The high quality and unprecedented uniformity of this storage jar, on which the entire system was based, and the concentration of over 50% of the late 8th-century BCE storage jars at the main collection center in Lachish attest to the scope of this system in its early phase and to the way it operated. The establishment of Ramat Raḥel and its conversion into a major storage-jar collection center for hundreds of years, at first secondary to Lachish but with greater centrality after the destruction of Lachish and the loss of the Shephelah, demonstrate just how well established this administrative system was in Judah. After the destruction of Lachish, Ramat Raḥel became the undisputed center of storage-jar administration in the kingdom—and later, in the province, at least until the Seleucid period.

The main catalyst for the development of the complex storage-jar administrative system was the requirement that Judah, like the other Levantine kingdoms, pay annual tribute to Assyria in the form of precious metals and perhaps prestige and luxury objects (see, e.g., Fales and Postgate 1995: 33, lines 6–7; 57, line 1). It is therefore generally accepted that the Assyrian administration did not require the actual agricultural products of Judah, but their value in the form of silver, gold and prestige items.[24] Like other vassal kingdoms, Judah was required to pay certain quotas of valuable metals and of prestige and luxury items, and therefore, it can be assumed that its agricultural products were sold inside Judah, as well as to the Phoenicians and to the coastal cities that could use these products or export them overseas. Some or all of the metals and luxury items received in consideration for these products were paid as annual tribute to the Assyrian rulers.[25] It is also possible that some of the agricultural

products were sent to the Assyrian garrison forces based in various centers near Judah or were transferred to Judahite auxiliary forces in the service of the empire. In these cases, the Judahite storage jars would have remained in Lachish or Ramat Raḥel (to be recycled and reused in the system) and their contents would have been transferred to other vessels. Only on rare occasions were storage jars shipped beyond the borders of the Kingdom of Judah. There may have been limited trade in surplus products or in the storage jars paid or gifted by the royal household to officials, relatives, estate owners, or other functionaries close to the king.

This was not the lot of Judah alone—similar demands was presumably imposed upon the other small vassal kingdoms that survived under Assyrian rule in the empire's periphery. Moab, Ammon and Edom were also required to pay heavy tribute. Unlike Edom, which could have used the profits of the Arabian trade passing through its territory, Moab and Ammon were probably forced, like Judah, to convert agricultural produce into precious metals and prestige items to cover their payments. I suggest (see below, pp. 147–151) that administrative centers similar to Ramat Raḥel were built in Moab and Ammon, near the former capitals of these kingdoms. There too the economy developed with agricultural branches (perhaps animal husbandry, pasture, sheep, goats and cattle?) providing the basis for payment of tribute by the local governments.

Judah's main innovation, as opposed to its neighboring vassal kingdoms, was its development of the stamp-impression administrative system. This was due to the agricultural economy of Judah, which involved the production of valuable liquids, especially olive oil and wine. In Moab and Ammon, other administrative methods presumably developed, in keeping with their local agricultural branches and economy and with the way their products were converted to pay the imperial tribute. The provinces neighboring Judah to the north, especially

---

24. The payment of annual tribute to Assyria differs from provinces that were under direct Assyrian governance, whose economic potential was maximized by the Assyrian governors who were appointed for specific terms for this purpose. On the payment of annual tribute in the form of silver, gold and prestige items, see Byrne 2003: 21–22; Naʾaman 2003: 81–82; Thompson 2003: 93–94, with further literature. Hopkins (1996: 138) and Byrne (2003: 21) contended that the Kingdom of Israel paid tribute to Assyria in the form of agricultural produce until the days of Tiglath-pileser III. Cf. Liverani 1992: 158; Holladay 2006: 310.

25. There is biblical evidence for Judah's engagement in international commerce to obtain precious metals: gold and silver were shipped from distant lands—from Ophir (1 Kings 9:28; Job 28:16) and Tarshish (1 Kings 10:26)—and this is corroborated by archaeological research, which shows that silver originated in the western Mediterranean (Sherratt and Sherratt 1993: 366–369; Thompson 2003).

those within the borders of the former Kingdom of Israel, did not become vassal kingdoms required to pay tribute, and as provinces they were subject to direct imperial rule and to economic exploitation to the fullest by the officials appointed by the Assyrian rule. For these reasons, similar administrative systems did not develop there.

The main conclusion to be drawn from the archaeological finds in Judah in the early period of its subjugation to Assyria is that this subjugation served as the central catalyst driving the kingdom to develop and improve its administration and economy at an accelerated rate.[26] In Judah, as in other subjugated kingdoms, significant economic prosperity was the result of its integration within the imperial economic framework, in which Assyria encouraged the development of the economies of the small kingdoms. The pressure to pay fixed quotas of annual tribute also necessitated streamlining the local production system. A contributing factor was the stable security and political climate during the long period of *Pax Assyriaca* in the 7th century BCE, with new markets opening across the empire, which became a unified trade region (Fales 2008; Miller 2009: 128; Younger 2015). While the Assyrian goal was clearly to derive maximum profit from the vassal kingdoms and to amass wealth and prestige items in Assyria itself, this state of affairs also benefited the vassal kingdoms, offering great potential for stability and development, which had not been possible under the hegemony of the large territorial kingdoms that had controlled the region until the Assyrian takeover of the region in the 730s. These territorial kingdoms had dictated the economic and commercial arrangements, to a great extent limiting the ability of the small kingdoms in the Southern Levant and Transjordan to develop their potential.[27]

Some scholars opposed this view, with Elat arguing that it was not the Assyrians who were incentivizing the region's commerce and economy (Elat 1990: 87–88) and Stager claiming that Ekron (Tel Miqne) had prospered mainly under Egyptian rule (Stager 1996; cf. Gitin 2003). Faust claimed that this relative prosperity was due not to

Assyrian policy but to trade with the Phoenicians, who absorbed all the agricultural surplus produced inland (Faust 2011: 73–78; 2015; Faust and Weiss 2005; cf. Fales 2013: 59; Younger 2015: 189–197). Schloen (2001: 141–147) also argued that the Assyrians were not interested in the economic development of the areas they conquered, but only in what could be confiscated or taxed.[28]

The main flaw in these arguments is the lack of distinction between conquered kingdoms that became provinces and those that became vassals. The latter were integrated into the economy and commerce of the Assyrian empire, but suffered heavy taxes, prompting them to develop their economy and maximize their agricultural-commercial potential. Indeed, Younger suggested that the notion that the Assyrians did not seek to develop its vassal kingdoms stems, to a large degree, from the proponents of this view "falling victim to [the Assyrian] propaganda," evident mainly in royal inscriptions (Younger 2015: 181, with previous literature). Careful examination of administrative and economic texts elicits a completely different picture from the one that emerges from the royal inscriptions. There are many examples of Assyrian investment of effort and capital in the development of the economy, trade, improvement and protection of roads and agricultural areas, the establishment of commercial centers and fortified outposts and the taxation of all economic activities, especially commerce. Furthermore, the Assyrians were involved in commerce with Tyre, a vassal kingdom. These relations included full control over commercial activities, determination of their restrictions and regulations, taxation on cutting timber in the Lebanon Mountains, and the ability to prohibit the sale of timber to Egypt and the Philistine kingdoms. As shown by Naʾaman, the Assyrians appointed officials in the vassal kingdoms and took painstaking care to tax these kingdoms and take their share in maritime and inland commerce (Naʾaman 2001: 275). There is also evidence that Assyrian officials were present in Judah, as well as in the cities of Arwad, Byblos, Tyre, Ashdod and Gaza, and in the

---

26. For imperial taxation of vassal kingdoms as an incentive to develop their economies, see Frankenstein 1979: 273; Sherratt and Sherratt 1993: 366, 370; Hopkins 1997: 29; Bedford 2005: 72–73.

27. As aforementioned, Ekron best exemplifies the ability of a local kingdom to develop under Assyrian rule: it enjoyed unprecedented prosperity in the 7th century BCE under Assyrian control (Gitin 1995: 61–62).

28. For a review and critique of these ideas and for further literature, see Lipschits 2018a: 118–127.

kingdom of Edom. Among these officials there must have been a higher-level imperial representative (*qēpu*), whose job was to closely supervise the activities in these vassal kingdoms and to send reports to the royal court (Younger 2015: 193).

The reconstruction suggested above regarding the changes in economy and administration in Judah in the late 8th century BCE, mainly based on archaeological finds, can be compared to vassal kingdoms elsewhere in the Assyrian empire, where inscriptions were found. These were mainly letters between the Assyrian central administration and the local rulers, governors and officials, and they enable more detailed reconstructions of imperial methods of administration and control. Thus, for example, the kingdom of Kumme, close to the tributaries of the Khabur River north of the modern-day Iraqi–Turkish border, became an Assyrian vassal under Sargon II, several years after the subjugation of Judah (Parker 2001: 90–91; 2002). The kingdom had to pay tribute in the form of precious metals or stones and perhaps even agricultural produce.[29] Although Kumme was a vassal kingdom, an Assyrian supervisor was assigned to it; he resided in the capital and was responsible for its affairs, and the kingdom's rulers were required to report all their activities to him. On military affairs, Aššur-reṣūwa, an Assyrian official, reported directly to the crown prince about activities that took place beyond Kumme's border with the kingdom of Urartu.[30] With regard to administrative affairs, the Assyrian official was responsible for the tax shipments from Kumme to Assyria (Lanfranchi and Parpola 1990: 111, 117). His power stemmed from the presence of an Assyrian administration and military garrison in a province near Kumme, providing him with complete knowledge of the affairs of the kingdom and enabling him to supervise the economy and even to intervene in local politics (Lanfranchi and Parpola 1990: 106, lines 17–21; Dubovský 2006: 51–52).

This example of the kingdom of Kumme may provide insight into the situation in Judah, if we combine our knowledge of the Assyrian empire's methods of control and supervision over Kumme with the archaeological discoveries in Judah—especially with regard to the system of stamping impressions on storage jars and the establishment of the main storage-jar collection center at Ramat Raḥel. As discussed below, Ramat Raḥel may also have served as the place of residence of the *qēpu*, the direct representative of Assyrian rule.

To conclude this discussion, one should note additional taxation systems, local in nature, which operated in Judah in the 7th century BCE. The most notable of these is the system of fiscal bullae, evidently a royal taxation system operating during the reign of Manasseh or of Josiah, for which there is a growing number of archaeological finds. Avigad, the first to identify a fiscal bulla, coined this term for these finds (Avigad 1990: 262–265). Although almost all fiscal bullae surfaced on the antiquities market,[31] two bullae recovered by wet-sifting earth from the Temple Mount (Barkay 2011: 151–178; 2015) and one from the City of David (Reich 2012) support the authenticity of this phenomenon. It is therefore possible that these fiscal bullae represent a system that paralleled the system of storage jars and that it served to collect taxes from the various districts of the kingdom on behalf of the king (Millard 2009: 32–33; Barkay 2015: 44–46).

How the System Operated

The system of stamped storage jars was a highly complex system, which operated alongside the state economy and the administration of the royal household, but as a separate system. It consisted of three main components: a site where the vessels were manufactured and stamped; agricultural sites where the produce was manufactured; and one or more collection sites to which the storage jars were transported after they had been filled. From there the storage jars were shipped and replaced with silver, gold and luxury goods; the surplus may have been handed over to the close associates of the royal household and to official and army commanders

---

29. For the reporting requirement, see Lanfranchi and Parpola 1990: 106, l. 16. For paying tax in the form of valuable metals or precious stones, see *ibid.*, 284, l. 11; for the possibility that payment was made in agricultural produce, see *ibid.*, 98; Parker 2001: 91.

30. See, e.g., Parpola 1987: 29–31; Lanfranchi and Parpola 1990: 87–89, 95; Parker 2002: 383; Dubovský 2006: 51–52.

31. Deutsch 1997: 137–143; 2003a: 76–91; 2003b; 2011: 81–91; 2012; Deutsch and Heltzer 1999: 64–68.

at the various administrative and military centers operating in Judah. It is likely that the storage jars were sent to coastal cities, but there is no archaeological evidence of this, and the precise mechanism remains unclear. Unlike the many stamped storage jars—of all the different types—that were found within the borders of Judah, hardly any stamped storage jars or even jars of the type used for stamping have been found beyond the borders of the Kingdom of Judah, and hardly any coastal pottery was found within the Kingdom of Judah. Thus, the main weakness in the theory—pertaining to the collection of the agricultural products and their centralization—is related to this lacuna in our knowledge: we do not know the final destination of the products or the routes used.

It stands to reason that secondary administrative sites were established and storage jars containing agricultural surplus were sent there—as trade, as a gift by the central government, or as payment to officials and close associates of the royal family. We cannot determine whether the storage jars were sent to the secondary administrative sites directly from the central collection site(s), or whether all the surplus jars reached Jerusalem and were transported to the secondary sites from there. In my opinion—although this is speculative—all these jars were initially sent to Jerusalem. This would have enabled supervision over the system in the most efficient fashion; the royal family would have had full control over who would receive a share of these surplus storage jars. Some would have reached the private market too, perhaps stored in private homes or sold in private business transactions.

This theory places great significance on the additional places in Judah where storage jars were found, in small quantities and generally of different types. This suggests that they were given as gifts of solitary jars, ostensibly in order to support, encourage, reward or pay officials and military personnel residing in these secondary administrative centers.

The suggested *modus operandi* of the system is presented schematically in Fig. 6.1 (for the various stages, see below).

This system would, of course, have required a complex mechanism for transporting the empty and full storage jars

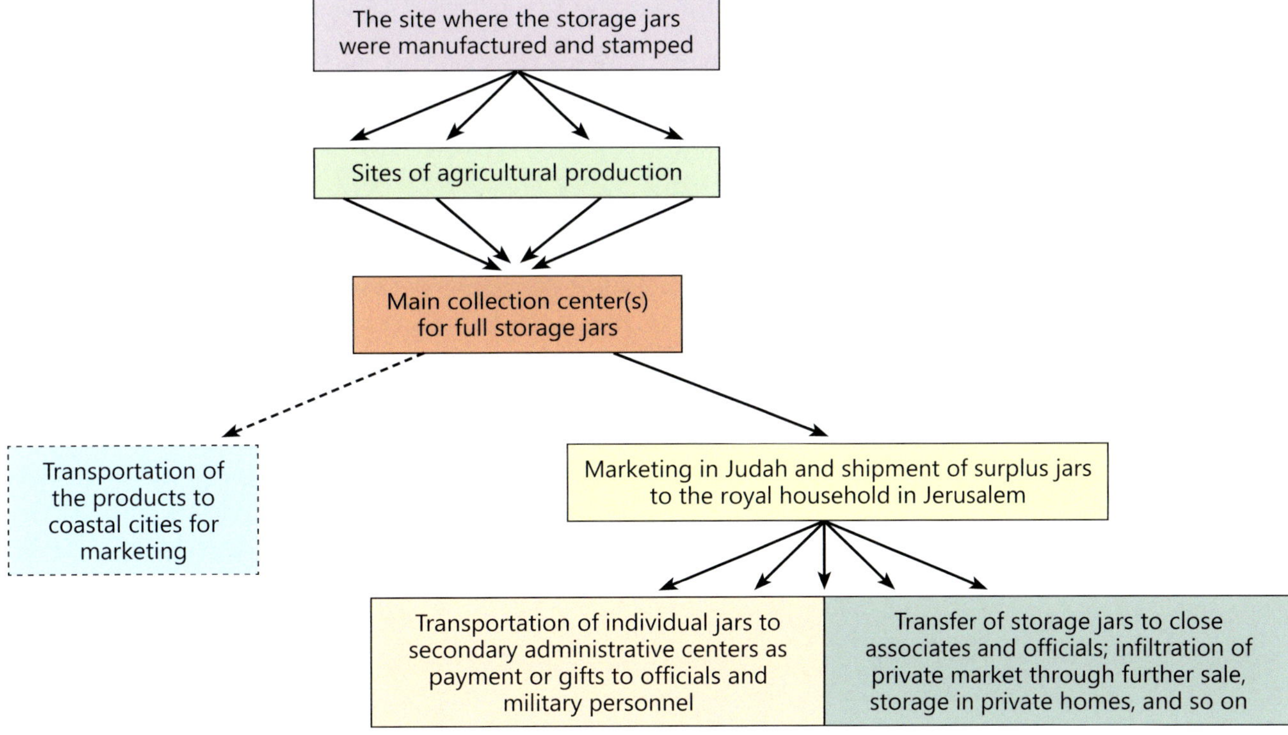

Fig. 6.1: The proposed *modus operandi* of the system

between the sites of production, administration and storage. The transportation of empty storage jars would not have been problematic, and there was no risk of losing freight in the event of breakage. The more expensive the product (wine, oil), the greater the loss from broken or cracked jars. Scholars assume that storage jars had a capacity of no more than 10–20 liters because larger vessels would have been more problematic to transport (Rice 1987: 240). However, Ussishkin examined nine storage jars from Lachish and found their maximum capacity to be 39–52 liters (Ussishkin 1983: 162). Storage jars with a similar capacity were found at Tel Batash too (Mazar and Panitz-Cohen 2001: 94–95). It is clear, therefore, that transporting such large and heavy storage jars would have required an entire system of transportation and of planning and development of an organized road system. In any event, the storage jars would have been transported over short or medium distances, and when full, the vessels would not have been sent over too great a distance.

Given these assumptions, one may speculate that a specific number of storage jars was used in the system, according to the required quantity of liquids. The jars were likely recycled after transporting the produce to meet the tax quotas, and they would have been reshipped back to the centers of agricultural produce for reuse. The number of jars that were lacking—either as a result of breakage at some point or because a few were delivered to individuals—could have been replaced at the pottery production site. Thus, a certain number of new storage jars would have had to have been manufactured every few years.

Following is our detailed reconstruction of the *modus operandi* of the system. Due to the incomplete nature of our knowledge, it includes many speculative components. The reconstruction is accompanied by explanations and justifications, and other possibilities are presented where appropriate.

Storage-Jar Production

The system relied upon the production of the jars themselves, the vessels in which these valuable liquids—the *raison d'être* of the system—were stored and transported. All the *lmlk*-type storage jars—both with and without stamped handles—were manufactured in a single central pottery workshop. Petrographic studies on the origin of the clay of storage jars stamped with early and late types of *lmlk* impressions, as well as with "private" impressions and with most of the rosette impressions, indicate that the production site of the vessels remained in the Shephelah, most likely in the Elah Valley. One of the prime candidates for this workshop is Tel Socoh, with its unusual concentration of handles with late *lmlk* and rosette, as well as early *lmlk* and "private" stamp impressions.[32] This indicates either that Tel Socoh continued to exist after Sennacherib's campaign or that it was quickly restored after 701 BCE (Lipschits and Amit 2011: 182–185). This is in contrast to all known sites in the Shephelah, including nearby Azekah, which was probably not resettled in the first half of the 7th century BCE, after its destruction by Sennacherib. The continuity evident at Tel Socoh is also remarkable compared to the southern Shephelah and the environs of Lachish, as well as the northern Shephelah and the Soreq Valley. Perhaps the exceptional continuity of the settlement at Socoh was due to its significance as the production center of *lmlk* storage jars and to the need to continue to manufacture storage jars for the kingdom's administration, in order to pay tribute to Assyria.

It is possible that royal officials came to Socoh, where they stamped the storage-jar handles during the production process. We cannot determine any consistency or clear method in the stamping. Among the complete storage jars restored from the Lachish excavations are some with one stamped handle, some with two, and some with three or four. Among the storage jars that were stamped with both *lmlk* and "private" impressions, no clear method could be discerned either (Ussishkin 2004b: 2143). As aforementioned, two storage-jar handles were uncovered at Ramat Raḥel and two at Umm Tuba with both types of impressions stamped on each (Aharoni 1962: 16, Fig. 14:2, Pl. 6:2).

Following Kelm and Mazar and the recovery of storage jars at Tel Batash, scholars assumed that only

---

32. See above, p. 43. Noteworthy are the 11 handles stamped with late *lmlk* impressions (compared to only four in Lachish and 20 in all Shephelah sites) and five stamped with rosettes—mainly random surface finds in a site excavated for a single limited season. No handles with concentric circle incisions have yet been found at Socoh, suggesting that these incisions were not made at the site of production of the storage jars.

a small percentage of storage jars from each series was stamped (Kelm and Mazar 1985: 105; 1995: 135). Ussishkin noted a similar pattern between stamped and unstamped storage jars in Storeroom 4014, Area GE, at Lachish: out of 18 *lmlk* storage jars, the handles of only three (or perhaps four) vessels were stamped (Ussishkin 2004b: 2144). Since each storage jar has four handles and only rarely were they all stamped, the working premise should be that if on average, two handles of each storage jar designated for marking were stamped, this would represent approximately 10% of the handles (cf., e.g., Ussishkin 2004b: 2144, Fig. 29.17). The *lmlk*-stamped handles were not counted methodically in Ramat Raḥel, and furthermore, most of the material was from fills. However, given that all the handles were cleaned and examined, a ratio of 1:10 jars (1:20 to 1:40 handles) seems to be the minimal reasonable ratio of stamped handles out of the total number of storage-jar handles found.

As mentioned above, the finds have been interpreted as indicating that in each series of storage jars produced, the handles of a specific number of vessels were marked. This relies upon the assumptions that all the storage jars were manufactured during a short period before Sennacherib's campaign as preparation for the onslaught and that the findings in the Level III destruction layer at Lachish accurately reflect the number of jars that were manufactured and the ones that were stamped. If, however, this was not the case—and storage jars were produced and stamped for decades before Sennacherib's campaign and continued to be produced for centuries after it—we may conclude that the finding in the Lachish III destruction layer reflects the limited organization prior to the campaign and the gathering of provisions from any source available in Judah at the time, but does not enlighten us with regard to storage-jar production or with regard to the ratio of stamped to unstamped storage jars in any given series of production.

Alternatively, we may assume that throughout its existence, the storage-jar administrative system required a certain number of storage jars for collecting agricultural produce during the late summer and early winter season—the harvest time of grapes and olives. In each system, with the exception of the early types of *lmlk* stamp impressions,[33] the total number of handles ranges between 250 and 500. The difference in the number of handles may stem mainly from the difference in the duration of the various systems. Even though the number of handles uncovered presumably represents only a (small?) percentage of all the storage jars used in the system, it means that 10,000–20,000 liters of liquids were involved—a considerable amount, which could certainly have been a significant component of the economy of Judah, providing the means for payment of tribute to the empires governing it.

This also leads to the assumption that the stamped storage jars were intended to serve the liquid-production and collection system for many years. Whenever there was a shortage of storage jars, it would have been necessary to manufacture new ones. This is probably why several seals were involved in the stamping of the same types of impressions in various systems and why in some cases, the number of handles stamped by a seal was very small—presumably in an effort to complete the inventory of storage jars necessary for the system's smooth operation. When there was a transition, in particular to the rosette, lion and *yhwd* stamp-impression systems, and new series of storage jars had to be manufactured, a specific quantity of storage jars would have been reproduced in the production center (presumably, as mentioned above, at Tel Socoh, and later in the area of Jerusalem). From then on, it was only necessary to refresh the number of storage jars in circulation when it declined below the minimum required for the system's operation.

Stamping the Handles

The stamp impressions on the handles were generally of low quality and often illegible. Moreover, the smoothing of the juncture between handle and body often partially, or even completely, obliterated the stamp impression. Following Naᵓaman (1979b; 1986), Kelm and Mazar (1995: 135) surmised that this was because the stamping had been executed hastily within the framework of preparations for

---

33. The early *lmlk* stamp-impression system, in which the Shephelah was the main production source, required many more storage jars, as it had much more agricultural land. After Sennacherib's campaign this area was cut off from Judah.

Sennacherib's campaign. Ussishkin, however, who also linked the production of the storage jars to the preparations for Sennacherib's attack, justifiably rejected this view (Ussishkin 2004b: 2144). The low quality of the impression is in stark contrast to the quality of production of the storage jars, their symmetry and uniformity of size. Ussishkin showed that in some cases, the impression itself was of good quality, but the seal was held upside-down—indicating that what was important was the actual stamping of a certain number of jars of each production series, rather than its quality.

In my opinion, the stamping of the royal impression was intended to mark the destination of the storage jar—to one of the king's estates, where it would be filled with wine or oil. This would explain why the various royal estates yielded different quantities of stamped handles. There is a clear preference for the name Hebron among the early types of stamp impressions, especially among the ones that were brought to Lachish; the name Hebron features on more than double all the other place names uncovered at Lachish.

Nonetheless, most of the storage jars were "recycled" and in some cases were in use for many years. Thus, it was not necessary to manufacture the same number of storage jars every year, and it is possible that the various types of stamped storage jars ended up mixed together, perhaps even entering the storage and transportation cycle of the private economy in different ways. This may account for why most of the private storerooms and buildings in Jerusalem and other cities of Judah have yielded a variety of types of stamped handles. Indeed, only in specific cases, when the number of handles of certain types uncovered is abnormally high or low, can we try to point to trends characteristic of specific sites and specific settlement layers (see below).

Shipping the Empty Jars to the Agricultural Production Centers

The next stage was the shipping of the empty storage jars from the single, central pottery workshop to the royal estates, where they were filled with oil or wine. We have suggested above that the place names appearing in the *lmlk* stamp impressions are the centers of royal estates where the storage jars were filled (see below).

In the various stamp-impression systems—including that of the *lmlk* stamp impressions, but especially in the later systems, in particular during the Second Temple period—small centers producing wine and olive oil operated in the royal estates that received the empty storage jars. The main evidence for this is the recovery of a few handles of a variety of types and periods at these sites, indicating that the agricultural centers functioned for long periods of time, sometimes throughout the 600 years of operation of this stamp-impression system.

Shipping the Full Jars to the Central Collection Center(s)

The full storage jars were then collected at one or two major centers. At first, this was at Lachish in the Shephelah and Ramat Raḥel in the hill country, and following the destruction of Lachish and the Shephelah, Ramat Raḥel became the main collection center (see below).

In the various systems there were secondary administrative centers, to which a few storage jars were transferred—probably surplus jars to be traded after the vessels were collected at the main collection centers. This would account for the prevalence of storage jars at central sites, generally around Jerusalem and Ramat Raḥel (especially sites in the Benjamin region) and in the eastern periphery (Jericho and En-Gedi), and this is most likely the reason for the numerous storage jars found in Jerusalem itself.

Identification of the Place Names on the *lmlk* Stamp Impressions and Their Importance for a Historical Reconstruction

Diringer suggested that the sites mentioned in the *lmlk* stamp impressions were royal centers for production of the storage jars. The impressions themselves were, in his opinion, royal stamps intended to guarantee the quality or quantity of the liquids in the storage jar (Diringer 1941: 108; 1949: 82). Cross concurred that the stamp impressions served as a royal guarantee for the quantity of liquid in the storage jar, but believed that the place names indicated royal wineries (Cross 1969:

21*). Contrary to these views, it is clear today that the royal storage jars were manufactured at a single center in the Shephelah and that they were not identical in capacity (Mommsen, Yellin and Perlman 1984; Ussishkin 2004b: 2145).

Yadin and Aharoni suggested that the place names referred to the destination sites of the royal storage jars.[34] Aharoni claimed these names represented four district towns used to collect and store tax in kind, while Yadin suggested that they represented four military, administrative district towns that received the supply of wine and oil in royal storage jars. However, the paucity of finds in Hebron, Ziph and Socoh makes it unlikely that the royal storage jars were collected at these places (cf. Fox 2000: 224–225). Naʾaman suggested that the names represent four districts (not necessarily cities) in the Judean Hills and the Shephelah and that supplies were sent to the fortified cities in these districts in preparation for Sennacherib's campaign, thus accounting for the numerous stamp impressions found around Jerusalem and the Shephelah (Naʾaman 1986). However, as previously discussed, the attribution of the impressions exclusively to the period of preparations for Sennacherib's campaign can no longer be accepted.

As mentioned above, the most likely explanation is that the names on the stamp impressions did not represent the destination sites, but the sites of origin of the agricultural products that would fill the storage jars. Since these are royal stamps, many scholars believe these sites to be royal wineries or royal estates.[35] That Socoh (both the Socoh in the hill country and the one in the Shephelah), Ziph, Hebron and *mmšt* are not fortified sites or administrative centers supports this hypothesis. Thus, it is reasonable to assume that the storage jars were manufactured at a royal center in the Shephelah, where they were also stamped with the royal seal, prior to being shipped off to the designated royal estate (Ziph, Hebron, or *mmšt*; Socoh may have served both functions, and in this case, a certain number of jars were left at the site), where they were filled with oil or wine. These products were then sent to the main collection centers (Lachish and Ramat Raḥel, in particular).

Yadin and Aharoni suggested identifying Ziph in the Negev (Yadin 1961b: 9; Aharoni 1987: 305), allowing them to contend that the site names represent four districts in the Kingdom of Judah. Thus, Ziph would represent the Negev (the Beersheba–Arad Valleys), Socoh would represent the Shephelah, Hebron would represent Judah and *mmšt* would represent Jerusalem. The identification of *mmšt* in Jerusalem relies upon a suggestion made by Ginsberg that the place name should read ממש[ל]ת (*mmš(l)t*) (Ginsberg 1948). It is, however, unlikely that the *lamed* would be missing; furthermore, there is no evidence for Jerusalem ever having been called this. The identification of Ziph in the Negev is also quite problematic (Fox 2000: 224). Today, the place is generally identified at Tel Ziph, ca. 7 km south of Hebron, mainly on the basis of a reference in Joshua 15:55 (Kletter 2002: 137, with further literature). Naʾaman suggested identifying *mmšt* (*mmš[i]t*) in the Jerusalem area, in view of the numerous stamp impressions with this place name in this area (Naʾaman 1986: 17; Kletter 2002: 138). While this suggestion appears at first glance reasonable, it is no longer valid, as the distribution of the stamp impressions does not correspond with the place names appearing on them. Most of the Hebron stamp impressions, for example, were found at Lachish. Since both Ziph and Hebron are located in the Judean Hills and since the place names, in any case, do not refer to large fortified cities, it is likely that *mmšt* should be identified in the hill country as well (as also argued in Kletter 2002: 138).

If, indeed, the four names mentioned in the *lmlk* stamp impressions referred to royal estates or wineries, where agricultural products were produced, and the storage jars were filled there and gathered at one main location, a central candidate for the identification of *mmšt* would be the village of Khirbet er-Ras in the middle of the modern-day Rephaim Valley (the "Valley of the King" of the late First Temple period) at the foot of Ramat Raḥel.[36] However, *mmšt*, which is not mentioned in the town-list

---

34. Yadin 1961b; Aharoni 1987: 305. Aharoni based his theory on Clermont-Ganneau (1900) and Albright (1925: 44–54).

35. See, e.g., Galling 1977: 339; Tufnell 1953; Lapp 1960: 22; Cross 1969: 21*; Rainey 1982; Fox 2000: 226–235; Kletter 2002: 140.

36. Lipschits, Sergi and Koch 2010: 21. On the location of Khirbet er-Ras and its characteristics, see Gadot 2015, with further literature.

in the Book of Joshua or in any other biblical source indicating the settlements in Judah at the end of the First Temple period, could, alternatively, be located in any of the other districts of Judah.[37]

In our efforts to identify Socoh, we may draw support from the characteristics of the *lmlk* stamp-impression system and from the place of Tel Socoh in the Elah Valley within this system.[38] The multitude of storage jars found there is not a decisive factor, since in contrast to Ramat Raḥel, which was the main collection center for stamped storage jars, in Hebron and Ziph only a few stamped handles were uncovered. Far more significant is the continuity of settlement in Tel Socoh in the 7th century BCE, in contrast to all the other sites in the Shephelah, and its identification as a possible site for the production of *lmlk* storage jars.

It may be assumed, therefore, that in addition to the two sites used as rural royal estates in the southern hill country (Ziph and Hebron), Socoh and *mmšt* were chosen not only because they were at the center of the king's estates (the Elah and Rephaim Valleys), but because they also served crucial functions in the stamp impression system: Socoh was the site where the storage jars were produced, and *mmšt*—if its identification at Khirbet er-Ras is accepted—was at the center of the king's estate, ruled from Ramat Raḥel, the main gathering point for all the storage jars.

One further factor relating to the history of the royal estates in Judah and their connection to the Davidic line and its legacies should be added. The connection between the Davidic line and Hebron has been well established. According to the traditions relating to the early reign of David, he ruled in Hebron, his first capital (cf., e.g., 2 Sam 2:1–4, 11; 3:1–5; 5:1–5), next to which there was a place of worship related to the dynasty, at least as seen by Absalom's request as a

pretext for his desire to rebel against the king (2 Sam 15:7).

The connection between the dynasty and the environs of Bethlehem, Ramat Raḥel and the Rephaim Valley— "the Valley of the King"—is also well established.[39] "The Valley of Shaveh, which is the Valley of the King" is mentioned as a place to where the king of Sodom came with "the kings who were with him" to meet Abraham when he returned from the war against Chedorlaomer (Gen 14:17). "Shaveh" (*šāwê*) means "plain"; thus, the Valley of Shaveh is "the Valley of the Plain," with the addition of the word "Shaveh" pointing to the uniqueness of the valley located in the mountainous region (Lipschits and Naʾaman 2011: 75). "The Valley of the King" is also mentioned as the place where Absalom placed his tombstone. While several scholars identified the place at the foot of the City of David, Lipschits and Naʾaman have suggested that it referred to the Rephaim Valley of today, in the western part of modern-day Jerusalem, and that its name stems from the prevalence of royal agricultural estates established there from the end of the 8th century BCE, contemporaneously with the establishment of the site of Ramat Raḥel.[40] The connection of the Davidic line to this area is linked to stories about the early days of David, as well as to another place— Baal-Perazim, south of Jerusalem. According to 2 Samuel 23:13–14, the Philistines attacked David immediately after he was crowned over all of Israel and conquered Jerusalem: "while a band of Philistines was encamped in the valley of Rephaim. David was then in the stronghold; and the garrison of the Philistines was then at Bethlehem." After organizing his forces, David made a surprise attack on the Philistines (2 Sam 5:20): "So David came to Baal-Perazim, and David defeated them there. He said, 'The Lord has burst forth against my enemies before me, like a bursting flood.' Therefore, that

---

37. The centrality and magnificence of Ramat Raḥel, as well as the large number of storage-jar handles with *lmlk* stamp impressions found there, led Barkay (2006: 43) to identify the site as *mmšt*. Relying upon Ginsberg's (1948) reading of the name *mmšt* as *mmš(l)t* (see above), Barkay argued that the size and significance of this place should have been identical to the three other centers (Hebron, Socoh and Ziph) and that it should have been populated during Hezekiah's reign. This suggestion encounters three problems: the fact that *mmš(l)t* is an unreasonable reading; the reliance upon the quantity of stamped handles uncovered; and the comparison to the other settlements—Hebron, Ziph and Socoh. Contra Barkay's proposal, see Lipschits and Naʾaman 2011: 71–72.

38. For the identification of the Socoh mentioned in the *lmlk* stamp impressions with Tel Socoh in the Elah Valley, see Naʾaman 1986: 17.

39. For the ancient source that probably served as the basis for these stories, see Naʾaman 1996, and further literature.

40. Lipschits and Naʾaman 2011: 75, with further literature. In that publication they also discuss the possibility that the narrative about Absalom, who during his lifetime placed a monument in the King's Valley, refers to one of the tumuli in the area—perhaps Rogem Gannim, the largest.

place is called Baal-Perazim."[41] Several scholars suggested that "Baal-Perazim" was a fortress controlling the Rephaim Valley, to which David arrived to prepare for battle, and they raised several hypotheses regarding its precise location.[42] Contra these views, Lipschits and Naʾaman suggested that "Baal-Perazim" was not a settlement but the name of a mountain, probably linked to the rite of Baal, and that this was the ancient name of the mountain upon which the palace called "Beth-hakkerem," identified in the Ramat Raḥel site, was built in the late 8th or early 7th century BCE.[43] We cannot determine whether a cultic site existed somewhere on the hill, although it is possible. It is not unreasonable that because of traditions associated with this cultic site no settlement was erected on the hilltop until much later.

David's connection to Ziph and its environs is also described in stories about him prior to his ascension to the throne in Jerusalem. According to 1 Samuel 23:14, "David remained in the strongholds in the wilderness, in the hill country of the Wilderness of Ziph"; and Saul also came there to look for him (1 Sam 26:2). Socoh is also mentioned in the stories about David, and the story of the battle between David and Goliath is introduced in 1 Samuel 17:1 with the description: "Now the Philistines gathered their armies for battle; they were gathered at Socoh, which belongs to Judah, and encamped between Socoh and Azekah, in Ephes-dammim."

All this makes it likely that within the new economic-administrative system that was instituted in Judah upon its subjugation to Assyria, new areas were developed that belonged or were related to the royal family in Jerusalem. These became royal estates with the purpose of supplying the products necessary to pay the annual tribute to the empire. These areas were relatively unsettled, and the agricultural development consisted mainly of planting vines and olive orchards and establishing the agricultural installations necessary to produce oil and wine.

Given this understanding of the place names mentioned in the stamp impressions, the word *lmlk* ("[belonging] to the King") at the top of the stamp impressions is better understood: this word can now be seen to emphasize and express the royal family's ownership of the goods produced in these estates.

As for the functioning of the jar-stamping system, we may posit that the storage jars were manufactured at a central production site (probably Socoh) and were shipped empty to the royal estates of Hebron, Ziph and *mmšt*, with some remaining in the estate of the Elah Valley, near the pottery workshop at Socoh. The storage jars would then be filled with oil and wine and shipped off to the central collection site. At first, these central sites were at Lachish in the Shephelah, where products from Socoh, Hebron and Ziph were gathered, and at Ramat Raḥel, the destination for the production in the Rephaim Valley. Later, after the 701 BCE Assyrian military campaign and the destruction of Lachish and the Shephelah, a single collection site remained—in Ramat Raḥel, above the royal estate of the King's Valley, with *mmšt* at its center, if the identification suggested here of Khirbet er-Ras is correct.

At this stage, in the early 7th century BCE, the writing on the stamp impressions gradually declined in importance. Hebron and Ziph became less important in the *lmlk* storage-jar administrative system, and after the destruction of the Shephelah, the system became centered around Jerusalem—at Ramat Raḥel and the Rephaim Valley area, south of the city, and in the Benjamin region to its north. The main production was transferred from the traditional royal estates to small production sites that developed in the areas south and north of Jerusalem. The attribution of these sites to the royal family is no longer so clear, and neither are the estate names. Therefore, use of the traditional seals gradually diminished, and the word *lmlk* at the top of the seal and the name of the estate

---

41. Kallai 1954: 290; Naʾaman 1999: 148. This victory is also implied in Isa 28:21; where the place, however, is called "Mount Perazim," with a deliberate omission of the "Baal" component

42. The following suggestions have been made for the identification of Mount Perazim: Procksch (1909: 70) and Dalman (1924: 21–23): around the ridge upon which the Mar Elias monastery was built; Alt (1927: 16): on the Shuʿafat ridge; Kallai (1954: 290): at Jebel Deir Abu Tor; and Mazar (1980: 28–29; 1981): on the Gilo ridge. See also Naʾaman 1999: 148; Elitzur 2009: 327, 431, with further literature. Maisler (1935: 9–10) distinguished between Baal-Perazim, which he viewed as an ancient cultic site located near the Kathisma Well, and Mount Perazim, which he located on the Ramat Raḥel hilltop. Aharoni (1955: 149 and n. 4), on the other hand, argued that the commanding position of Ramat Raḥel reinforces its identification with Baal-Perazim.

43. Lipschits and Naʾaman 2011: 77–79. Name places with the component "Baal" are usually located at an elevated point of the mountain region. Therefore, Baal-Perazim should be sought on a high hill located near the Rephaim Valley, whose name the author cited to indicate the battle site. For this subject see already Naʾaman 1999: 140–141, 144–147.

below the symbol disappeared. This was probably a gradual process, reflecting the adaptation of the storage-jar administration system to the reality that prevailed after Sennacherib's campaign.

Lachish: The Main Collection Center prior to Sennacherib's Campaign

At the time of Judah's subjugation to Assyria, Lachish appears to have been the main tax-collection center, where the produce of three royal estates—Hebron, Ziph and Socoh—was gathered. This is evident in the many handles found in Lachish stamped with early *lmlk* impressions bearing the name Hebron, the relatively large number of such handles with the name Ziph, and the proximity of Lachish to Socoh, the main royal estate in the Shephelah. Lachish's proximity to the port cities in the southern coastal area presumably enabled convenient transport of produce to these cities and the receipt of silver, gold and luxury products in exchange, which were then used to pay the taxes to Assyria.

The proposal that Lachish was central to the storage-jar administrative system in its early stage, prior to Sennacherib's campaign, would account for the many *lmlk* storage jars found in Level III, where over 50% of all the stamped handles of the early types were found (378 out of 723). It would also account for the special importance attached to Lachish by the Assyrians, manifest in the relief depicting the city's conquest that adorns the throne room of Sennacherib's palace in Nineveh (Ussishkin 1980; 1982; 2003: 207; 2004c: 89–90; Uehlinger 2003: 292). The relief depicts the force of the siege, the conquest and plundering of the city, the deportation of its residents and the killing of its leaders (Ussishkin 2003: 209–214; Uehlinger 2003: 282–284). While Lachish, the secondary capital of the Kingdom of Judah, was indeed of strategic importance (Ussishkin 2006: 353), and its conquest compensated, to some extent, for the failure to conquer Jerusalem, the Assyrians' choice of Lachish as their prime target, the effort they invested in its conquest, and the new arrangements they

later installed in the Shephelah have not received a satisfactory explanation.[44]

In my view, the main reason for the systematic destruction of Lachish was its function as the Judahite administrative center within the Assyrian taxation system. The destruction of the city, the exiling of its population, the transfer of large areas from the Shephelah to neighboring kingdoms, and the fact that Lachish and the entire Shephelah remained desolate throughout the period of Assyrian rule in the Southern Levant demonstrate that this was punitive action taken by Assyria against the Kingdom of Judah, specifically targeting the administrative system that handled the collection of the agricultural products and their transportation to the coastal cities in the west. Indeed, these Assyrian arrangements tore away the most important and fertile areas of Judah, forcing the debilitated kingdom to develop its mountainous areas, especially around Jerusalem and including the Benjamin region, in order to meet the heavy annual tax quotas. The agricultural products developed for this purpose were gathered at Ramat Raḥel, which now remained the sole collection center.

Ekron (Tel Miqne), an important oil-production center, profited the most from the harsh blow delivered to Judah. Its prosperity under Assyrian rule in the 7th century BCE is directly related to the weakening of the Judahite kingdom and the loss of its lands in the Shephelah,[45] when the Assyrians centralized production in the single large industrialized center of Ekron and moved away from the system of many small oil-production sites with a central collection center at Lachish.

When Assyria withdrew from the region in the early 630s BCE, Egypt took over (Naʾaman 1989: 45–56), and, perhaps as a lesson learned from its battles against Assyria in the first half of the 7th century BCE, immediately consolidated its control over Philistia. Egypt maintained its control for about a quarter of a century, until it was forced out by Nebuchadnezzar's military forces (605/604 BCE), and the small kingdoms in Philistia maintained their loyalty to it even in the early days of Babylonian rule in the area. It seems that the wine and the oil were of great importance in the Egyptian

---

44. These arrangements also included the targeted punishment of the local Lachish elite; see Ussishkin 1982: 67–82; 2003.

45. Dothan and Gitin 1994: 18–25; Gitin 1997; 1998: 274–278; Mazar 1994: 260–263, and cf. Lipschits 2018a: 126–127, with further literature.

economy.[46] Therefore we see continuity in the storage-jar administrative system as well as a certain recovery in Shephelah sites, which once again became part of Judah's administrative and economic system (for further discussion, see below, pp. 165–172).

Ramat Raḥel: The Administrative Center of the Jar-Stamping System

The History of the Site in Light of the Excavations

On the hilltop where the ancient site of Ramat Raḥel was situated, archaeological remains were described by visitors and researchers as early as the 19th century.[47] In August 1954, a salvage excavation was conducted by Aharoni, prior to the building of a water reservoir for the Ramat Raḥel kibbutz (Aharoni 1955: 147–174). Due to surprising discoveries, including a monumental structure and many stamped jar handles from the First and Second Temple periods, Aharoni conducted four extensive excavation seasons from 1959 to 1962.[48] Excavations were

renewed in 2004, and a large-scale excavation project was carried out at Ramat Raḥel until 2010.[49]

The results of the renewed excavations, combined with earlier excavations, provide a clear picture of the history of the site and the settlement around it over the course of its 2,000-year existence. The hill was not settled until the late 8th century BCE; it might have earlier been called "Baal-Perazim" or "Mount Perazim," and may have featured a ritual site dedicated to Baal (Lipschits and Na'aman 2011: 77–79; see also discussion above). At that point a magnificent administrative center was built at the top of the hill.[50] Most of the finds from this layer were discovered in the fills of later structures, but it is clear that in its construction quality and architectural features, the monumental building is unparalleled throughout the Kingdom of Judah. These architectural items include the decorated stone capitals and the small stone balustrades adorning windows, alongside other elements. The numerous storage-jar handles uncovered bearing *lmlk* and "private" stamp impressions point to the site having been an important Judahite center for the collection of agricultural products from the outset (Lipschits *et al.*

---

46. Contra Stager (1996: 70*–71*) and Vanderhooft (1999: 64–70), who claimed that prosperity in the region began under Egyptian rule, Gitin argued for a decline in the status and output of the large oil- and wine-production centers in Ashkelon and Ekron, which had prospered under Assyrian rule (Gitin 1997: 99–100 and n. 65, with bibliography). Strategically, the coastal area and the western part of the lowland are considered Egypt's "safety zone"—the only gateway to Egypt from the north, which served as a necessary holding point for whoever sought to cross the desert and invade the inner land. It required Egyptian presence in the area and strict governmental control along the Via Maris leading northward. This was also the central—in fact, only—route for whoever wished to move military forces toward Egypt. In addition, it seems that the route and the ports along it were extremely important for transferring Egyptian military forces toward the Euphrates. On this, see Redford 1992: 444 and literature in n. 57.

47. Several scholars who explored the area also described the finds at the site. For a description of the finds and a review of the literature, see Lipschits *et al.* 2017: 19–21; Lipschits, Oeming and Gadot 2020: 14–17, with further literature. The first salvage excavation of a burial cave found by chance on the periphery of the tel, ca. 200 m from its peak, was carried out by Maisler and Stekelis in late 1930 and early 1931; Maisler 1935; Stekelis 1935.

48. Aharoni published several interim reports and two volumes (Aharoni 1962; 1964), in which he presented a detailed picture of the architectural remains and the finds. The full results of Aharoni's excavations were published in a final report; see Lipschits, Gadot and Freud 2016. A limited excavation was conducted in 1984 on behalf of the Institute of Archaeology of Tel Aviv University, Israel Exploration Society and the Israel Antiquities Authority, led by Gabriel Barkay; for a preliminary and partial publication of the finds, see Barkay 2006. Between 2000–2002, Gideon Solimany conducted small-scale salvage excavations on behalf of the Israel Antiquities Authority; for a preliminary publication, see Solimany and Barzel 2008; 2016.

49. The renewed excavations at Ramat Raḥel were the fruit of cooperation between the Institute of Archaeology of Tel Aviv University and the Faculty of Theology in Heidelberg University, Germany. For the first season, see Lipschits *et al.* 2006; for the second and third seasons, see Lipschits *et al.* 2009b: 7–28. For a comprehensive summary of the excavation results, see Lipschits *et al.* 2017; Lipschits, Oeming and Gadot 2020. The finds of the renewed excavations will be published by Lipschits *et al.* (forthcoming).

50. Aharoni's proposal, made after the second excavation season, that the Ramat Raḥel palace should be identified with Uzziah's "Beit Hahofshit" ("The House of the Dead," "The House of Lepers"), mentioned in 2 Kings 15:2 (Aharoni 1961: 115–116), should clearly be rejected, given the dating of the building to the late 8th or early 7th century BCE. After completing his excavation at Ramat Raḥel, Aharoni himself reached this conclusion, proposing instead that the Ramat Raḥel fortress should be identified as Jehoiakim's palace, according to the description in Jer 22:13–19 (Aharoni 1971a; 1971b: 183–189). Yadin harshly criticized Aharoni's suggestion, demonstrating numerous difficulties (Yadin 1973), but his suggestion that Ramat Raḥel was the "House of Baal" built by Athaliah in Judah cannot be accepted, as there is no evidence for construction in the 9th century BCE at the site.

2017: 36–56). The site continued to develop throughout the 7th century BCE and even after the destruction of the Kingdom of Judah in the early 6th century BCE, when Judah became a Babylonian province, reaching its peak during the rule of the Persian empire in the 5th and 4th centuries BCE (Lipschits *et al.* 2017: 57–94). This continuity supports the view that Ramat Raḥel served from its very inception as a Judahite administrative center under imperial supervision, where tax was collected for the Assyrian empire.

The second phase of construction, from the second half of the 7th century BCE, gave the site its monumental character. This was manifest not only in the continued use of decorative architectural elements from the first phase, but also in the emergence of a comprehensive and complex vision, evident in the quality of construction and in the extensive infrastructure that completely changed the appearance of the hill. Along its western side a royal garden, at least five dunams (0.5 hectare) in size, was developed. The garden surrounded the palace on a lower level, achieved by removing the upper layer of *nari* caliche rock, leveling the lower layer of soft chalk and laying down a fill of dark garden soil taken from the nearby valley, spread evenly to a depth of some 40 cm.

Within this uniform area, agricultural plots and rows were planted, integrated into a water system that included pools, channels and drainpipes. The enormous quantity of quarrying waste was used as fill on the eastern side of the hill, and on this elevated and carefully leveled layer the extended palace, with its courtyards and walls, was built. The extensive work required to adjust the natural outline of the spur to the design attests to the magnificence, the might and the royal involvement in the second construction phase of the palace (Lipschits *et al.* 2017: 39–43, cf. Lipschits, Gadot and Langgut 2012).

There is nothing to suggest that the building was destroyed in the early 6th century BCE. On the contrary, there is evidence for its continued existence throughout the period when Judah was a Babylonian province, its affairs managed by a satrap residing in Mizpah, in northern Benjamin (Lipschits 2015: 238–242, 255–259; 2019c: 196–208). During the Persian period the status of the administrative center at Ramat Raḥel grew further, and the palace was expanded at the expense of the northern part of the garden (Fig. 6.2). Many 5th- and 4th-century finds were uncovered in the excavation, including a vast quantity of stamped storage-jar handles. It can thus be determined that Ramat Raḥel was, at that

Fig. 6.2: Three-dimensional reconstruction of the Persian period palace at Ramat Raḥel (imaging: Roy Albag)

time, one of the centers of power—perhaps the most important—in which the taxes exacted from the province's residents were collected, to be sent on to the central government. Persian involvement is evident in the intensive construction carried out, particularly in the addition of a northwestern wing, in a style and momentum unparalleled in the hill country in general, and in Judah in particular (Lipschits *et al.* 2017: 98–116).

In the early Hellenistic period, the site apparently declined in importance and a few of its walls were robbed. During the 3rd and early 2nd centuries BCE, it became the administrative center of the province once again, as is evident from the distribution of handles with administrative stamp impressions, continuing the tradition of the late First Temple period and the Persian period (Lipschits *et al.* 2017: 114–118). This was the "swan song" of Ramat Raḥel, which had earlier served as the fortified imperial administrative center for the Kingdom of Judah and its successor, the satrapy of Yehud. During the second half of the 2nd century BCE, under Hasmonean rule, the palace and the garden were completely eradicated, with the walls demolished down to their foundation courses and with an earthen fill covering the garden (Lipschits *et al.* 2017: 117–121). For the first time in the site's history, a rural village sprang up on the hilltop, and it continued to exist and to fluctuate in response to the circumstances until its final destruction and abandonment in the Abbasid period.[51]

The Role of Ramat Raḥel in Light of the *lmlk* Stamp Impressions

At Ramat Raḥel, 224 handles with *lmlk* stamp impressions were found, 164 of them in Aharoni's excavations in 1954, 1956 and 1959–1962. Another 60 handles were uncovered in the renewed Ramat Raḥel excavations, conducted by Tel Aviv and Heidelberg Universities.[52] Ramat Raḥel is thus the third most important center in the administration, after Lachish with 413 stamped handles and Jerusalem with some 302.[53]

Of the 224 *lmlk*-stamped handles found at Ramat Raḥel, 46 are of the early types—24 of these bear the four-winged emblem (Types Ia and Ib) and 22 are the early two-winged-type impressions (Type IIa). Another 133 handles bear late types of *lmlk* stamp impressions, dated to the early 7th century BCE. Of these, 100 stamp impressions bear the two-winged emblem with the place name beneath the symbol divided into two (Type IIb), and 33 display the two-winged emblem without the word *lmlk* and with the place name appearing at the top (Type

---

51. Upon the ruins of the early administrative center, a Jewish village developed in the late Hellenistic and Early Roman periods (late 2nd–1st centuries BCE until the First Jewish Revolt in the 1st century CE). Many remains of this settlement were uncovered, including ritual baths, columbaria, pottery, stone vessels and coins. Like other rural settlements in the Jerusalem region, this village ceased to exist after the suppression of the revolt and the destruction of Jerusalem in 70 CE (Lipschits *et al.* 2017: 119–128). Following a short period of abandonment, it was resettled in the 2nd century CE, with a marked change in its ethnic composition—the formerly Jewish settlement was now Roman in character. In subsequent centuries the site underwent changes of a religious and cultural character, but remained rural throughout. In the late Byzantine period (the 6th and perhaps 7th centuries BCE), a church was built in the northeastern part of the site, with additional buildings. In the early Islamic period, under Umayyad rule, community life continued, including use of the church, without interruptions except for local repairs and additions. There is evidence of collapse and conflagration in several places in the site in the 8th century CE, and the settlement may have been destroyed in the January 18, 749 earthquake (Lipschits *et al.* 2017: 130–139). The rural Christian village did not recover from its damage. A farmstead, with adjacent agricultural installations, was built here during the Umayyad period; it continued to exist in the Abbasid period and was destroyed in the 10th or 11th century CE. From subsequent centuries surface finds have been recovered, including coins, pottery sherds and even installations on the hilltop, but there is no evidence of a permanent settlement after the 11th century CE (Lipschits *et al.* 2017: 139–148).

52. In the preliminary excavation reports, Aharoni (1962: 19–21, 45–48; 1964: 33–35, 61–63) reported on 145 *lmlk* stamp impressions, only 46 of which were fully published, with an illustration or photograph of the impression (Aharoni 1962: Figs. 14:2, 15:1–8, 31:4–9, Pls. 6:2, 7:1–6, 29:1–12, 30:1–4; 1964: Pls. 38:1–12, 39:1–11). In the course of the work of the Tel Aviv–Heidelberg University expedition on the complete scientific publication of Aharoni's excavations, we discovered documentation of 19 additional stamp impressions in the registration card index, in the photo albums and the antiquities warehouses (of the Hebrew University of Jerusalem, the Israel Antiquities Authority, Tel Aviv University, Israel Museum and La Sapienza University in Rome). On these impressions, see Sergi 2016. For stamp impressions found in the renewed excavations, see Sergi, forthcoming (b).

53. Surprisingly, despite the numerous stamp impressions uncovered, very few sherds of *lmlk* storage jars were found, in stark contrast to the large number of holemouth jars found all over the site. How is it possible that stamped handles were found throughout the site, while the storage jars themselves are absent? We have no satisfactory explanation for this enigma. We should, however, consider the fact that Ramat Raḥel was populated for a long time during and after the Iron Age, without any severe destructions. In the absence of clear destruction layers, which "freeze" the material culture of the destruction period in time, it is likely that the *lmlk* storage jars at the site were reused time and again until they broke and their sherds scattered.

IIc) or without a place name (Type XII). The stamp impression on the remaining 45 handles are unidentifiable. It can generally be determined whether they bear the two- or four-winged emblem, but since the writing style is indecipherable, they cannot be dated.

Ramat Raḥel's rise in status is therefore reflected in the finds: the number of late types of *lmlk* handles uncovered (133) is three times the number of early types (45). Assuming, furthermore, that some of the handles with early types of *lmlk* stamp impressions continued to be used in the early 7th century BCE, they attest to the undisputed status of Ramat Raḥel in the early 7th century BCE, host to more than 25% of all late *lmlk* types found to date.

Most of the *lmlk*-stamped handles were found out of context, usually in late fills, and some were surface finds. Only a quarter of the handles were uncovered in clear archaeological contexts, generally sealed beneath floors and installations from the second construction phase of the site, making these handles central for the dating of this phase. Most of the *lmlk* handles were found beneath the central courtyard of the royal enclosure, underneath the northern building excavated by Aharoni and under the external courtyard to the northwest of the enclosure. These handles include the entire spectrum of *lmlk* stamp impressions—from the early types of the late 8th century BCE to the late types of the early 7th century BCE. Furthermore, the few handles incised with concentric circles found in clear and sealed archaeological contexts were found alongside the handles stamped with late *lmlk* stamp impressions, beneath floors of the second construction phase (Lipschits *et al.* 2017: 44–48; Sergi 2016; forthcoming [a]).

The importance of this find for the chronology of the Ramat Raḥel royal complex is two-fold. First, the finding of late types of *lmlk*-stamped handles, from the first third of the 7th century BCE, and handles with concentric circle incisions, from the second third of that century, in the very same contexts under floors of the second construction phase provides strong support for a *terminus post quem* for the construction of this phase. In conjunction with other evidence, these finds show that the second phase was constructed no earlier than the 630s BCE and probably even slightly later. Furthermore, the recovery of the entire chronological spectrum of *lmlk*

stamp impressions, along with the concentric circle incisions—which replaced the *lmlk* stamp impressions in the mid-7th century BCE—beneath floors of the second construction phase shows that these stamp impressions were in use during the first construction phase of the site. Thus, despite the absence of clear-cut stratigraphic evidence for the first construction phase at Ramat Raḥel, the numerous *lmlk* stamp impressions leave no doubt that the site functioned as an important administrative center even before the construction of the royal compound and the garden—that is, from the establishment of the site in the late 8th century BCE, and especially in the early 7th century BCE, immediately after Sennacherib's campaign.

In order to determine the role played by Ramat Raḥel as an administrative center in the Kingdom of Judah, we must compare for each period the quantity of stamped and incised handles found there to finds from other sites. The underlying assumption is that a site that yielded many such handles served as a collection and distribution center of agricultural products or as a secondary administrative center receiving surplus jars. The main methodological problem lies in the comparison of finds from sites with destruction layers with finds from sites that escaped destruction. In the former, the destruction layers "freeze" the material culture in time, whereas in the latter, continuity of use would lead to a gradual disappearance of the earlier vessels as they broke and were replaced. A smaller quantity of finds in the latter is, thus, only to be expected, and is not necessarily a reflection of the actual state of affairs during the time period in question.

This methodological problem accounts for the discovery of plenty of handles with early types of *lmlk* stamp impressions at Lachish and other sites in the Shephelah (ca. 70% of all such finds), while only a relatively small percentage of these handles were uncovered at sites around Jerusalem, Ramat Raḥel and the Benjamin region (ca. 27%). The findings indicate that already at this stage, the hill country in general, and Jerusalem and Ramat Raḥel in particular (together with Mizpah and Gibeon in the Benjamin region), were important centers in the storage-jar administration in Judah. They further suggest that Ramat Raḥel was the most central and important collection center serving the royal estate located below, in the "Valley of the King." This is the only administrative center in the hill country. Unlike other sites, such as Jerusalem and Lachish, which were relatively large settlements, or even fortified cities, Ramat Raḥel was merely a local fortress, recently erected at the end of the 8th century BCE. Nevertheless, more stamped storage-jar handles have been found at Ramat Raḥel than any other site in Judah, reflecting a period of some 600 years. Even though the centrality of Ramat Raḥel is not reflected in the numbers when it comes to the *lmlk* stamp impressions, this may be due to the methodological problem described above and should not detract from the broader picture, which suggests that Ramat Raḥel served a central role in this administrative system from the very beginning.

It is unlikely that storage jars were shipped straight from the sites of agricultural production to the various collection sites and that the destination of each oil or wine jar was known in advance. While this is not impossible, it is more likely, in my opinion, that all the storage jars were filled in the production sites and then gathered at collection centers. Until 701 BCE, there would have been two such centers: one operating in the Shephelah (Lachish) and one in the hill country (Ramat Raḥel). Once Lachish fell and most of the production centers in the Shephelah were destroyed, production would have been restricted to the hill country, with Ramat Raḥel as the sole collection center. It is, of course, possible that individual jars filled at production sites in the Benjamin region were shipped directly to the secondary sites in this region (Mizpah and Gibeon, in particular), but in my opinion, it is more likely that the trade, gifting and shipment of surplus containers took place after the necessary tax quotas had been met and all the products had been gathered at the central collection site. Thus, the relatively large number of *lmlk*-stamped handles found in Jerusalem may be viewed as surplus jars sent from Ramat Raḥel, once the requisite number of storage jars had been collected for imperial tax payments.

The Role of Ramat Raḥel in Light of Parallel Administrative Centers in Moab and Ammon

The Iron Age volute capitals (the so-called "Proto-Aeolic" or "Proto-Ionian" capitals) are among the most impressive and special finds discovered in archaeological excavations in Israel. The size of the capitals, their weight, the quality of their carving and their impressive design point to their function in the gates and palaces of the ancient kingdoms of Israel and Judah.

Twenty-seven decorated stone capitals have been discovered in the central cities of the Kingdom of Israel: in Samaria (seven capitals), Megiddo (12), Hazor (two) and Dan (three), as well as three capitals of unknown origin (perhaps from Shechem) found on Mount Gerizim (Lipschits 2011e: 205–207, with further literature). These capitals, apparently from the mid-9th century BCE, are presumably remains of the large-scale construction in the kingdom in the reign of the Omride dynasty (Finkelstein 2000: 120–121; Lipschits 2011e: 205–208).

The most outstanding architectural features in the Ramat Raḥel palace are the decorated stone capitals (e.g., Fig. 6.3) that adorned its gates and courtyard already in the first construction phase (Lipschits 2011e: 209–212; Lipschits *et al.* 2017: 53–56). These capitals are not a common find in structures in the Kingdom of Judah and are rare even in Jerusalem.[54] That these decorated stone capitals were a symbol of the exalted status of Ramat Raḥel can be seen in a decorated stone capital relief discovered at the entrance to a large spring in the Rephaim Valley (ʿAin Joweizeh) (Ein Mor and Ron 2013; 2016), serving as a proclamation that the irrigation system beginning at this spring belonged to "the Valley of the King," over which the Ramat Raḥel palace rises and dominates.

Decorated stone capitals are rare in the architecture of the Transjordanian kingdoms as well: they have been found in only one building in Moab—at Khirbet el-Mudeibiʿ, a fortress or administrative building located about 21 km southeast of el-Kerak, the capital of Moab,

---

54. More than ten decorated stone capitals, some complete and others broken and in secondary use, were uncovered at Ramat Raḥel, whereas only two fragments of a single decorated stone capital were found in Kathleen Kenyon's City of David excavations. On this, see Lipschits 2011e: 212–213, with further literature.

Fig. 6.3: Capital from Ramat Raḥel (photo by the author)

which served a similar function as Ramat Raḥel in Judah.[55] The el-Mudeibi‘ fortress is made of basalt stones, although both the outer and inner gates were made of limestone, and so were the five volute capitals that probably formed part of the entrance complex (Fig. 6.4:3; Drinkard 1997; Mattingly and Pace 2007; Lipschits 2011e: 213–216, with further literature). These stone capitals bear a strong resemblance to the Ramat Raḥel capitals and appear to have been built according to the same principle, but with slightly different proportions and emphases. There is no unequivocal archaeological evidence to determine the date of the el-Mudeibi‘ fortress (Lipschits 2011e: 213–216, with the various scholarly views and updated literature). Typological parallels to the decorated stone capitals and architectural comparisons regarding the structure and the features of the fortress point, in my opinion, to a date no earlier than the late 8th–early 7th centuries BCE. The layout of the fortress, the great investment in the quality of construction and the decorated stone capitals are all indications of the exceptional nature of this fortress in Moabite construction. Furthermore, they make it possible to associate the construction at this site with the emergence of the Assyrians in the region and with their activities in the peripheral areas of southern Levant. As in Moab, decorated stone capitals are rare in Ammon too: they appear only in the remains of the fortress at Rabbat Ammon, where two fragments of two separate capitals of unclear origin were found (Fig. 6.4:4; Lipschits 2011e: 216–217, with details and further literature).[56]

There are significant typological differences between the capitals found in the Kingdom of Israel (Fig. 6.5) and the ones uncovered in the Kingdoms of Judah, Moab and Ammon (Fig. 6.4), and it is likely that there is a chronological gap between them, with the southern group emerging in Judah and Moab only after the destruction of the major cities in Israel. While many scholars have discussed the typological differences between the Israelite types and the Judahite types from Ramat Raḥel and Jerusalem, as well as a capital known from the 1930s from Moab, they did not sufficiently highlight the chronological differences between the various groups of capitals or the connection between the Israelite capitals and the ones from Judah and Moab (Lipschits 2011e: 217–219, with further literature). They did not refer to the anomalous nature

---

55. The citadel at Khirbet el-Mudeibi‘ is located between the "Kings Highway" and the desert road, at a point dominating a central wadi (Fajj al-‘Usaykir), which connects these two main routes (Lipschits 2011e: 213, with further literature).

56. Prag attempted to identify elements of window balustrades at Ammon, and connected them to the architectural style of the phase of the decorated capitals with an image of a woman's head chiseled in limestone. The woman's head was found in secondary use embedded in the Hellenistic construction of the citadel of Amman, and was dated to the 8th or 7th century BCE (Prag 1987: 122–123).

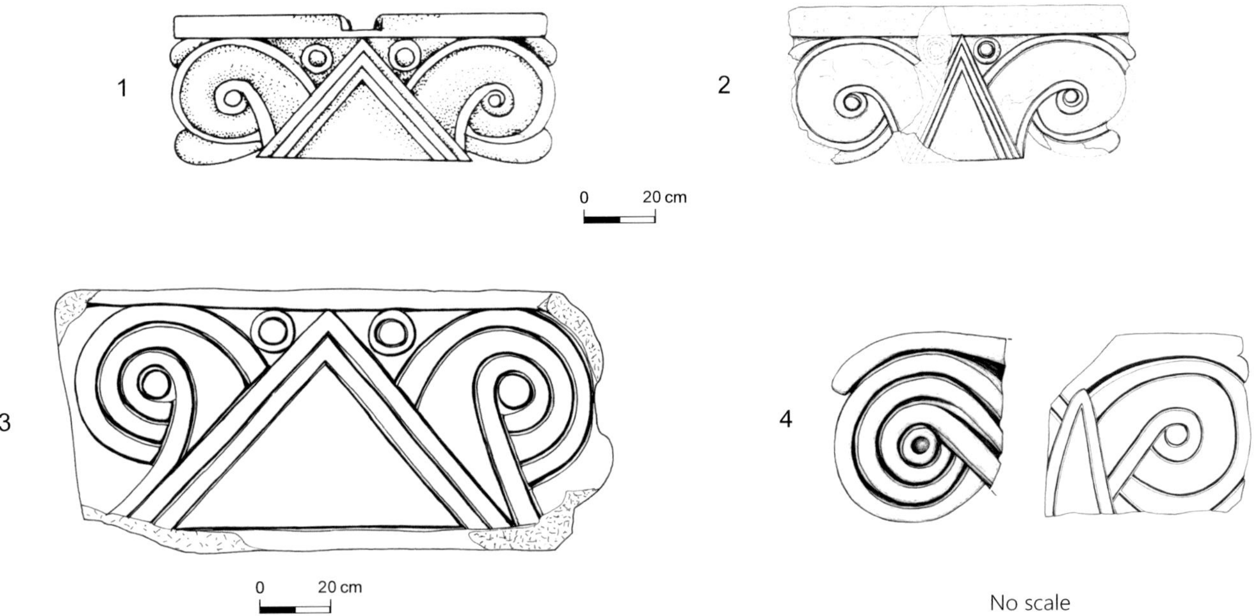

Fig. 6.4: Decorated stone capitals from Judah, Moab and Ammon:
1) Ramat Raḥel; 2) City of David; 3) Khirbet el-Mudeibiʿ; 4) Rabbat Ammon

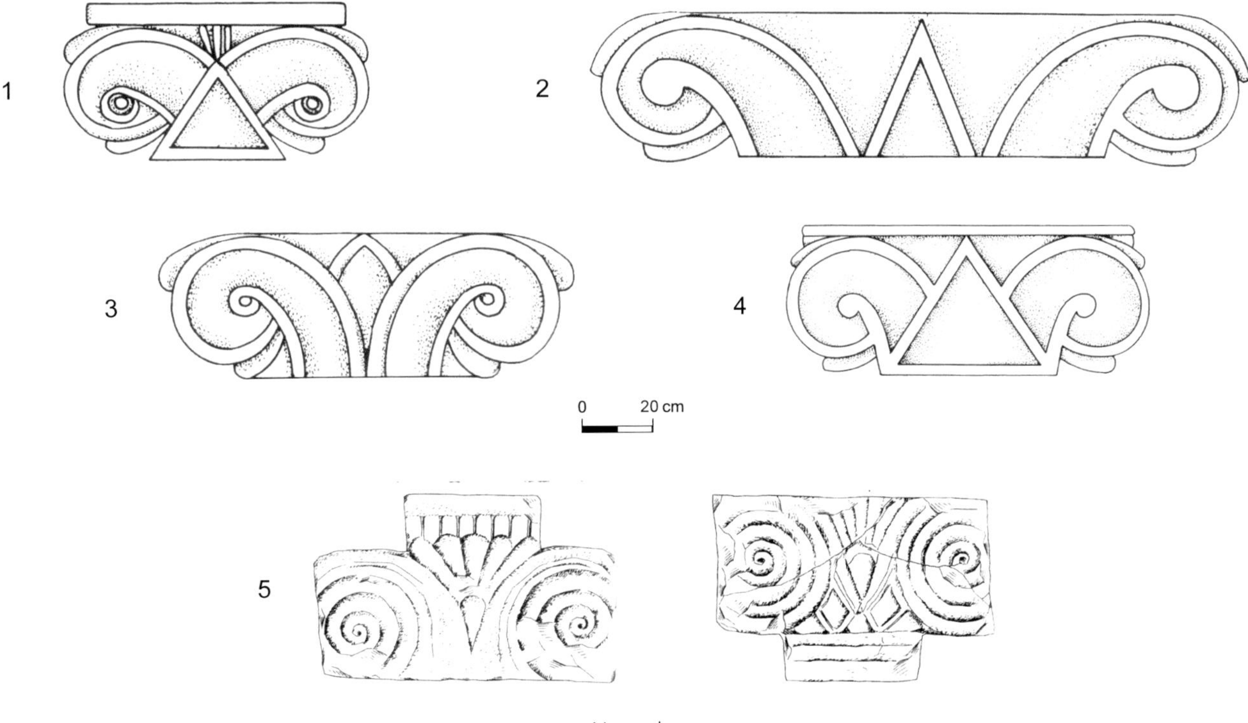

Fig. 6.5: Decorated stone capitals from the Kingdom of Israel:
1-2) Megiddo; 3) Hazor; 4) Megiddo and Samaria; 5) Mount Gerizim

of these capitals in the local architecture of the Kingdoms of Judah, Moab and Ammon; they have no precedent in the architecture of these kingdoms and no continuation after this period. These decorative features appeared mainly in structures that can be interpreted as fortresses, royal centers, or administrative centers, and they rarely appear in the capital cities of these local kingdoms. Moreover, scholars did not draw any chronological connection between the appearance of these decorated capitals and the Assyrian arrival in the region.

Based on the above, I have suggested that the appearance of the decorated stone capitals in Judah, Moab and Ammon is related to the Assyrian subjugation of these kingdoms. When the Assyrians conquered the Kingdom of Israel, they saw its decorated stone capitals—a unique architectural phenomenon that had begun over a century earlier (there was no evidence for a similar phenomenon during the same period in other kingdoms in the region)—and were captivated by their unique style, size, aesthetics and quality, as well as their location in the gates and the royal palaces. These capitals gained prestige with the Assyrian destruction of the Kingdom of Israel, and the Assyrian rulers, known for their propensity for integrating artistic and architectural elements into their local traditions, adopted the Israelite capitals in an unusual manner and for a limited period. Such capitals appeared in reliefs decorating Sargon's palace in his new city of Dur-Sharrukin (Khorsabad), as well as in Sennacherib's palace in Nineveh.[57] At the same time, they were placed in palaces, fortresses and formal buildings that served the Assyrian administration in the vassal kingdoms of Judah, Moab and Ammon, probably with Assyrian encouragement or patronage. Of particular importance is a stone relief (Fig. 6.6), discovered in a palace at Dur-Sharrukin (Khorsabad),[58] which was built during the period between the destruction of the Israelite cities that featured stone capitals and the emergence of such capitals in Ramat Raḥel (and perhaps also in Jerusalem, Moab and Ammon). In a relief in Room H in Ashurbanipal's palace in Nineveh, the gardens of Sennacherib were described some 50 years after their creation (Fig. 6.7).[59] The unusual phenomenon of reliefs depicting stone columns topped by stone capitals may reflect the influence of Israelite architecture on Assyrian architecture. They may also express war booty, offerings, or the induction of Israelite architects to serve in Assyrian construction enterprises. As mentioned above, this phenomenon has no other manifestation in Assyrian architecture and appears to be limited in time and scope.

The two Assyrian reliefs discussed above portray the royal gardens attached to Assyrian palaces. It may be assumed that the Assyrians, during whose reign the Ramat Raḥel palace was built as an administrative and economic center (as well as perhaps the el-Mudeibi‘ fortress and possibly also the Amman citadel), were the ones who brought the decorated stone capitals to these

---

57. As is well known in Assyrian architectural studies, stone columns are unusual in Assyrian buildings and palaces. While there are early examples of stone columns in Mesopotamia, they disappeared in later periods. They had no lasting place in Mesopotamian architecture and were never a component of a specific type of construction or architecture, even at the peak of imperial rule in the 9th–7th centuries BCE. They remained a foreign element, used mainly as decorative elements in parts of buildings with symbolic value, usually without any functional use, or in the second floors of palaces. The proposal that the use of stone columns was for symbolic purposes, expressing conquest of the West, is, in my view, likely. Only in the 7th century BCE did columns also feature in private architecture in Assyria, in contexts similar to their uses in public constructions; in such cases, they may be interpreted as a status symbol. See Lipschits 2011e: 219–222.

58. This relief was found in Room 7 of the northwestern palace, and in the 12th plate of the hunting scene a square structure on a high podium is depicted and the front entrance of the building is decorated with two columns, standing on round bases. The columns are smooth and round, with an upper ornament of three perpendicular rings, topped by a decorated stone capital. A stone block lies above the upper frame at the top of the capitals; its narrow part is on top of the capitals, and its broad side carries the large lintel, decorated with crenellations, holding the building's roof. The building is at the edge of the royal garden, with a stream flowing at its foot; above the building there is a large wooded hill with an additional structure like an altar above it. For literature on this subject, see Lipschits 2011e: 220–221.

59. This relief depicts a large garden on a high hill, with various types of trees. An aqueduct leads to the garden, and the water flows from it in channels throughout the garden. At the top of the hill there is a structure, next to a royal stele, and an altar stands on the slope. The building is supported by four columns—two front and two rear ones, probably an attempt to give it a dimension of depth. All four columns are smooth and round, and the two rear ones stand upon decorated bases. The columns are topped by decorated stone capitals, which bear the crenellated roof beams. An additional stone block lies at the top of the two rear capitals, its narrow side upon the capital and its broad side carrying the lintel. For literature on this subject, see Lipschits 2009b: 23.

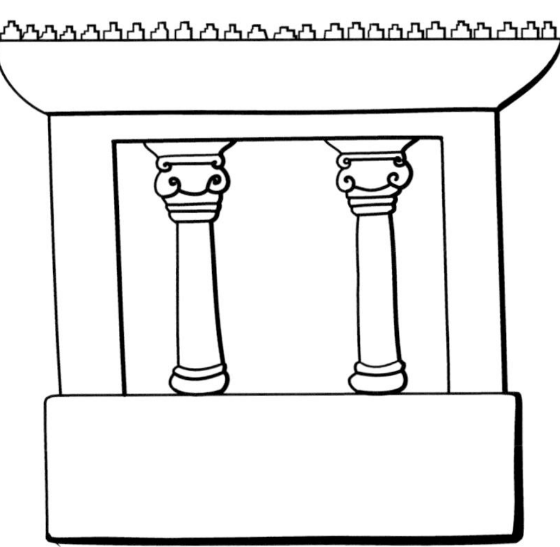

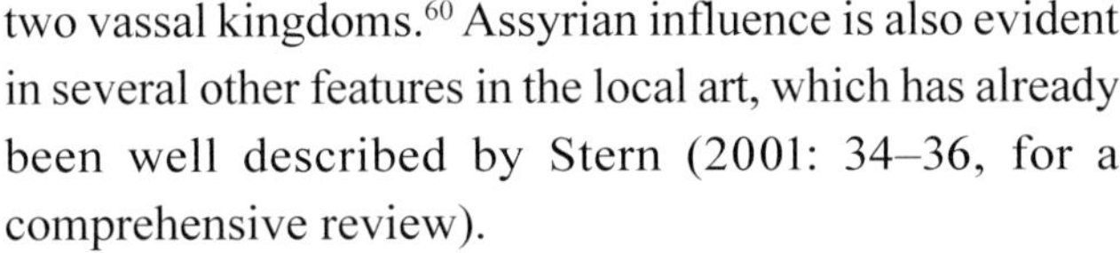

Fig. 6.6: Drawing of part of the 12th plate of the relief in Room 7 of the northeastern palace at Dur-Sharrukin (Khorsabad)

Fig. 6.7: Drawing of part of the 8th plate in the left part of Panel WA124939, Room H of Ashurbanipal's palace at Nineveh

two vassal kingdoms.[60] Assyrian influence is also evident in several other features in the local art, which has already been well described by Stern (2001: 34–36, for a comprehensive review).

All the above supports the possibility that the Ramat Raḥel fortress was built under the influence, if not direct command, of the Assyrian empire, which had ruled the region since the days of Tiglath-pileser III, and with even more force since Sargon. The el-Mudeibiʿ fortress and perhaps the palace or fortress at Amman were probably built in a similar way. All these may be viewed as part of the building projects that the small vassal kingdoms were forced to execute in the late 8th or early 7th century BCE. These fortresses, which do not reflect local building traditions in quality, in components, or in general layout, must have served the imperial administration. Perhaps the Assyrian *qēpu* resided there, temporarily or permanently, and small garrison forces placed in key strategic locations may have encamped in them. The architecture of these buildings is a singular combination of local and foreign elements, some familiar from earlier periods in the region and others completely foreign. Such

a combination has no precedent in the local architecture and should be viewed as yet another feature of this unique and formative period in the history of the land, which began with the *Pax Assyriaca* in the ancient Near East.

The Role of Ramat Raḥel after Sennacherib's Campaign as Reflected in the Late *lmlk* Stamp Impressions

The ravages of the Assyrian campaign and its disastrous consequences for the Kingdom of Judah are reflected in the late *lmlk* finds, dating from the early 7th century BCE. As mentioned above, the Shephelah completely declined in importance, with the exception of Socoh, which apparently continued to serve as the site of manufacture of *lmlk* jars. Thus, 11 handles stamped with late *lmlk* types were found there, from surveys and small-scale excavations alone. From all the other Shephelah sites together, only nine handles with late types were found, four of these at Lachish. These handles were generally found in unclear stratigraphic contexts or in contexts dated to the late 7th century BCE. Most of the handles

---

60. This proposal was raised by Naʾaman (2001), who presented numerous parallels for the construction of the Assyrian administrative centers in the vassal kingdoms.

with late *lmlk* stamp impressions were found in the hill country. In sum, the distribution of late types of *lmlk* stamp impressions points to the Shephelah—especially Lachish—completely losing its role in the royal administrative system of Judah following its fall in the Assyrian campaign.

Following the loss of the Shephelah, Ramat Raḥel became much more important in the system of stamped jars. Of the late types of *lmlk* stamp impressions, 133 handles out of a total of 486 were found in this site—ca. 27% of all such handles. Furthermore, as stated above, this system continued to operate for many decades, even after the *lmlk* stamp-impression system was replaced by new systems. This would suggest that these handles were mainly fragments that broke at the site and were discarded and that many hundreds of storage jars passed through the gates of the magnificent compound at Ramat Raḥel over its centuries of existence.

In Jerusalem, the estimation is that 180 handles were found with late types of *lmlk* stamp impressions—ca. 37% of all such finds. The number of such handles found at Gibeon (63), Mizpah (38), Khirbet al-Burj (15) and Tell el-Fûl (5)—a total of 25% of the finds—points to the Benjamin region growing in importance in the first third of the 7th century BCE, and shows that this region became part of the storage-jar administration, probably in compensation for the loss of the Shephelah. In total ca. 90% of the handles with late types of *lmlk* stamp impressions were found at Ramat Raḥel, Jerusalem and sites in the Benjamin region.

The distribution of handles with concentric circle incisions reflects a similar situation. In Jerusalem, 146 of these handles were found, out of a total of some 282 handles—ca. 52% of these finds. Another 40 were found at Ramat Raḥel (ca. 14%), and 70 were uncovered at sites in the Benjamin region (ca. 25%), mainly at Gibeon (33 handles), Mizpah (17) and Khirbet al-Burj (15). This demonstrates that the distribution of incised handles closely follows the trend of the late *lmlk* stamp impressions, with approximately 91% of the handles with concentric circle incisions found in Jerusalem, Ramat Raḥel and Benjamin region sites. The absence of handles with concentric circle incisions in the Shephelah shows that in the mid-7th century BCE Judah's rule had not yet been renewed over areas lost in Sennacherib's campaign.

To conclude, Sennacherib inflicted a devastating blow upon the Kingdom of Judah, from which it struggled to recover during the years of Assyrian imperial rule, at least until the last third of the 7th century BCE. Almost all the handles with 7th-century stamp impressions and concentric circle incisions were found between the Benjamin settlements north of Jerusalem and Ramat Raḥel to its south, indicating that during this period the administrative-economic system of Judah was concentrated in Jerusalem and its environs alone. With this in mind, the status of Ramat Raḥel is even more remarkable: some 25% of the storage jars of the royal administrative system from the early and mid-7th century BCE were concentrated in Ramat Raḥel, a figure that represents one-third of the stamp impressions found in Jerusalem. Thus, even though Ramat Raḥel was a small governmental center, it played an extremely important role in the economic and administrative system of Judah under Assyrian imperial rule, and its importance only grew in the course of the centuries to come.

The Role of Ramat Raḥel in Light of the Rosette Stamp Impressions

In Ramat Raḥel, 57 rosette-stamped handles were uncovered—constituting ca. 23% of the total 290 handles. This is a similar proportion for Ramat Raḥel as that seen in its *lmlk* stamp impressions and concentric circle incisions. From Jerusalem, 108 handles were recovered (ca. 37% of all the rosette-stamped handles). As for the distribution of finds in the Benjamin region, a clear decline is evident, with only 19 rosette stamped handles (ca. 6.5%), consisting of isolated handles found in a variety of sites, with no concentration at any specific site. Thus, a total of 66% of the rosette-stamped handles came from the Jerusalem area and the Benjamin region. When one compares this to the handles stamped with late *lmlk* impressions and the those incised with concentric circles (ca. 90% in both cases), it transpires that Jerusalem and its environs declined in importance and that the Benjamin region suffered an even greater decline, after a long period in which it appeared to play a significant role in the storage-jar administration. The main explanation for this appears to be the renewed activity of the Shephelah in the administration, evident in the find of 71 rosette-stamped handles (ca. 24.5% of all the finds), mainly in Tel Azekah (30 stamped handles) and Lachish (24), but also in Tel Batash (six) and Tel Socoh (five).

In my opinion, the number of rosette-stamped handles is not an indication that the Shephelah regained the level of wine and oil production that it had demonstrated in the late 8th century BCE, before Sennacherib laid waste to the area. Instead, it points to Lachish, as well as several other sites to a lesser degree, regaining some importance as secondary administrative centers. These centers would have received surplus products as payment, logistic support, or gifts from the central administration to officials or military personnel stationed there. Like these Shephelah sites, the eastern periphery now emerges, for the first time in the history of Judah, as playing a role in the stamped-jar administration, represented by 11 rosette-stamped handles found at En-Gedi. It appears that En-Gedi, like Lachish and Azekah, was a secondary center, receiving surplus jars from the central seat of power. Ten rosette-stamped handles were uncovered at sites in the Beersheba–Arad Valleys too, suggesting that these two served as secondary administrative centers.

Archaeological research shows that in the last third of the 7th century BCE, following Assyria's withdrawal from the region, Judah was partly rehabilitated from the devastation it suffered in 701 BCE. The main reconstruction is expressed in a renewed settlement system reestablished in areas beyond the hill country. During this period, there were major changes in the administration of the Kingdom of Judah: a second monumental phase of construction took place at the administrative center of Ramat Raḥel, which evidently became the core of a new administrative system, involving storage jars stamped with rosette impressions.

The distribution of the rosette stamp impressions shows the expansion of the Judahite administrative system into areas that had been blocked to Judah during the Assyrian rule. The reconstruction of the Shephelah began with a center established at Lachish, with additional Judahite centers probably built at Tel Azekah and Tel Batash after the fall of Ekron. Judahite administration was renewed in the Beersheba–Arad Valleys with the construction of Tel ʿIra as a center and the fortress network across the valley; in the eastern part of the kingdom, the Dead Sea area was settled and its natural resources utilized via new bases established in En-Gedi and Jericho. Dozens of campsites and forts were erected along routes connecting this lower eastern region to Jerusalem in the hill country.

Throughout all this development in Judah, Ramat Raḥel continued to serve as the collection center for the storage-jar administration. We do not know what its status was in the interim period when Egypt ruled Judah, before Babylon's subjugation of the entire area and of Judah in 604 BCE. We do know, however, that during the last third of the 7th century BCE, the second phase of construction took place at Ramat Raḥel and the rosette stamp-impression system began; thus, it is likely that the storage-jar administration continued here under Egyptian rule. We cannot be sure whether annual taxes were paid to Egypt in the form of agricultural produce or whether these were sold and converted into silver and luxury products. In any case, the continued existence of the system under Babylonian rule, even after Jerusalem was destroyed and the Kingdom of Judah reduced to a Babylonian province, coupled with Ramat Raḥel's continued central role in the system, indeed suggest that the storage-jar administrative system continued to operate under Egyptian rule.

7

The Stamped Storage-Jar Systems in Their Chronological, Historical and Archaeological Contexts

Judah as an Assyrian Vassal Kingdom and the Beginning of the Stamped Storage-Jar System

Judah's subjugation to Assyria at the beginning of the final third of the 8th century BCE is undisputed, and most scholars agree that with the exception of a brief period when Hezekiah rebelled against Assyria—after Sargon's death (in 705 BCE) until Sennacherib's campaign (in 701 BCE)—Judah maintained its loyalty to Assyria. Judah remained a vassal kingdom until Assyria's withdrawal from the region at the beginning of the final third of the 7th century BCE. Furthermore, there is a consensus regarding the significance of this subjugation to Assyria. It would seem, however, that biblical historiography displays a certain disregard for the subjugation to Assyria, with many scholars downplaying its significance and implications. Many scholars dealing with the history of Judah from the period of Ahaz and Hezekiah until the reigns of Manasseh and Josiah do not even consider its status as a vassal kingdom.

Assyria gained a presence in the region around the Kingdom of Judah in the 730s BCE and rapidly consolidated its control there. Tiglath-pileser III, who ruled Assyria between 745–727 BCE, led an unprecedented campaign of conquests and within a few years had reshaped the geopolitical arena in accordance with the economic, military and strategic interests of Assyria. Most of the kingdoms in the area "across the river"—from the Euphrates to the Mediterranean coast and all the way to Egypt—were wiped out, large populations were deported and other populations brought in from far-flung areas of the empire. The lands of these kingdoms were annexed to Assyria, and they became provinces. A few kingdoms, particularly the ones populating the Mediterranean coast, the Southern Levant and Transjordan, became Assyrian vassals. Under constant supervision, they were forced to pay heavy tribute and were integrated into the economic system of the Assyrian Empire.

After Tiglath-pileser III's conquest of northern Syria in 740 and 738 BCE, an anti-Assyrian alliance formed in the Southern Levant, headed by Aram-Damascus, along with the Kingdom of Israel, and with the participation of Tyre, the Philistine kingdoms and the Arabian tribes—an alliance that perhaps enjoyed Egyptian support. The Bible relates that Ahaz, who had just come to power in Judah in 734 BCE, was attacked by the kings of Israel and Aram-Damascus for his refusal to join the anti-Assyrian alliance. According to 2 Kings 16:7–8, Ahaz did not capitulate: "Ahaz sent messengers to King Tiglath-pileser of Assyria, saying, 'I am your servant and your son. Come up, and rescue me from the hand of the king of Aram and from the hand of the king of Israel, who are attacking me.' Ahaz also took the silver and gold found in the house of the Lord and in the treasures of the king's house, and sent a present to the king of Assyria."[1] According to this description, Ahaz voluntarily surrendered to Assyria; in retrospect, this appears to have been a sound policy, the bitter fate suffered by the other kingdoms only highlighting the danger Judah faced. With the support of the prophet Isaiah, Ahaz stood his ground against those who favored joining the anti-Assyrian alliance (Isa 8:6): "Because this people has refused the waters of Shiloah that flow gently, and melt in fear before Rezin and the son of Remaliah."[2] This policy, deeply rooted in Judahite history,[3] suggests that the kings of Judah were aware of the kingdom's frailty and preferred a policy of voluntary submission over a military campaign that might destroy it. Thus, until the days of Hezekiah, Judah remained loyal to the Assyrian Empire, paying annual tribute and refraining from joining the frequent rebellions against it. In a summary inscription, Tiglath-Pileser III mentions Ahaz—whom he calls "Jehoahaz of the land of Judah"—as one of the kings

who paid him tribute (Tadmor and Yamada 2011: 122–123, lines 6b–13), and in the Assyrian inscription describing the revolt of Ashdod (711 BCE), Judah is presented as a loyal vassal kingdom that paid tribute (Fuchs 1994: 457–458; 1998: 83–85).

Until the final destruction of the Kingdom of Israel (722–720 BCE), Judah did not share a border with Assyria: the Kingdom of Israel served as a buffer between the Assyrian army and the northern border of Judah. Within ten years, however, the Kingdom of Israel was vanquished. At first, the Galilee, the northern valleys and the Coastal Plain were conquered (732 BCE), their settlements suffering heavy destruction and much of their population exiled.[4] The borders of the Kingdom of Israel were greatly diminished to include only the Samaria region, and ultimately, its final vestiges were conquered, presumably by Shalmaneser V (727–722 BCE). Its conquest, destruction and annexation were completed in the early days of Sargon II (722–705 BCE); the conquest of the city of Samaria (720 BCE) was accompanied by heavy destruction of the main cities of the Samaria hills. The lands of the kingdom were annexed to Assyria and the province of Samaria (Samerina) was established (Tadmor 1973: 69–72; for further literature, see Na'aman 1993: 107, n. 3), which included the Samaria hill country, the eastern Sharon and the northern Shephelah (Aphek and Gezer included).[5] Many were deported from

---

1. Hayes and Hooker 1988: 59; Irvine 1990; Na'aman 1991a: 91–94; 1994b, with further literature. It is unclear how much importance the Assyrians placed on Ahaz's plea to Tiglath-pileser, but that same year Tiglath-pileser conducted a military campaign along the Philistine coast and conquered Gaza. The Assyrian goal was presumably to control Gaza's port and the Arabian trade passing through it, as well as to prevent the Egyptian army from coming to the aid of the local kingdoms. This subject has been dealt with extensively; see Tadmor 1966: 89–90; Elat 1977: 130–135; 1978: 26–30; Otzen 1979: 255–256; Na'aman 1979a: 83–86; 1995: 113; Eph'al 1982: 14–17; Edens and Bawden 1989; Finkelstein 1992; 1995: 146–149; Parpola 2003: 103–104; Jasmin 2006; Siddal 2009. In 733 BCE, Tiglath-pileser attacked and conquered the kingdom of Damascus, destroying its capital, deporting many captives, annexing it and establishing three provinces: the province of Qarnaim, which included the Bashan and the Hauran, the province of Damascus, which included the area east of the Anti-Lebanon ridge, and the province of Ṣubat/Ṣubite (Ṣôbâ), which extended over the northern Beqa' of Lebanon and the Anti-Lebanon Mountains (Lipschits 2005: 5–6, with further literature).

2. For differing views about when the description of Isaiah's involvement and support for Ahaz was written, see Reventlow 2008; Kostamo 2012.

3. According to the biblical account, Rehoboam paid tribute to Shoshenq, Asa sent gifts to Ben-Hadad king of Aram, and Jehoash paid tribute to Hazael king of Aram-Damascus.

4. Many central cities were destroyed and never rebuilt, whereas others were resettled, but in most cases sparsely and with no evidence of fortifications; Stern 2001: 46–49. The provisions made by Tiglath-pileser III for these areas continued until the Babylonian and Persian rules and included the establishment of two provinces: Dor (Du'ru), in the narrow Carmel coastal area, extending to the Yarkon River in the south, and Megiddo (Magidû), in Upper and Lower Galilee, the Beth Shean Valley and the Jezreel Valley. See Stern 1990a; 1990b; 2001: 46–49; Na'aman 1995: 106–107, with further literature; Gilboa 1996. Following Alt (1945: 128–146), most scholars believe that Tiglath-pileser III established an additional province—the province of Gilead—in Transjordan; see literature in Na'aman 1995: 107. However, given the reservations of Oded (1970) and Na'aman (1995: 107), there does not seem to be solid evidence for an array of Assyrian provinces in northern Transjordan.

5. Na'aman 1993: 106–107 and Fig. 1 on p. 105. During the 7th century BCE the region of Samaria slowly recovered, including gradual renewal of rural settlement. However, there was no urban renewal in the Samaria hill country throughout the Assyrian rule, and with the exception of the capital of the province, there is no evidence of any fortifications. For a summary of the data from surveys, see Zertal 1990. The claim made by several scholars that Josiah annexed the province of Samaria after the Assyrian withdrawal from the region (e.g., Redford 1992: 445) is untenable. See Tadmor 1973: 70–71; Stern 2001: 49–50.

the city of Samaria and its environs, to be replaced by deportees from distant places.

The Kingdom of Judah now had a direct border with Assyria. In the west, it bordered on vassal kingdoms and Assyrian provinces, since the Assyrian arrangements in the Philistine Shephelah were also established in the late 8th century, during the reigns of Sargon II and Sennacherib:[6] Ashdod was an isolated Assyrian province amid vassal kingdoms, ruled by a local king, alongside an Assyrian governor.[7] The vassal kingdoms of Ashkelon, Ekron and Gaza continued to exist to the north and south of Ashdod and had grown territorially and economically stronger under Assyrian rule,[8] presumably because of Philistia's strategic and economic importance as a gateway to Egypt (Elat 1978: 30–34; 1990; Oded 1979: 168). Ashkelon was a central port and commercial center, with a flourishing wine industry.[9] Ekron, a major center for olive-oil production and, evidently, textiles (Gitin 1997: 87–93), profited the most from the harsh blow suffered by Judah in Sennacherib's campaign. Its prosperity under Assyrian rule during the 7th century BCE was a direct consequence of the weakening of the Kingdom of Judah and the loss of its lands in the Shephelah (Dothan and Gitin 1994: 18–25; Gitin 1997; 1998: 274–278; Mazar 1994: 260–263). Gaza was the southernmost city of Philistia, and its port served as the main outlet for the Arabian trade route; consequently, it was the focus of the Assyrian efforts during the reign of

Tiglath-pileser III and early in the reign of Sargon II. It is not surprising, therefore, that it remained a loyal Assyrian vassal from the days of Sargon II until the final collapse of Assyrian rule in this region (Tadmor 1964: 271; Katzenstein 1994: 37–38).

Judah remained the only vassal kingdom in the hill country, while the Kingdoms of Ammon, Moab and Edom to its east were subjugated. Assyria remained dominant in the Southern Levant, and it seems that the vassal kingdoms—Judah included—had little room to maneuver.[10] They were forced to keep their fealty, pay annual tribute and obey the orders of the Assyrian king, as conveyed through his representatives in the area.

In an inscription dated 717 BCE, Sargon II is termed "the subduer of the land of Judah which lies far away" (Winckler 1889: 188, lines 28, 36; Tadmor 1958: 38, n. 146; Na'aman 1994c). This appellation should be connected to the rebellion of 720 BCE, when, according to Sargon II's inscriptions, he conducted a large-scale campaign to the west, captured Samaria, deported many of its inhabitants, and annexed it to Assyria (cf. 2 Kings 17:5–6). At the same time, he also conquered the entire coast of Philistia. The phrase "which lies far away" and the fact that Judah is not mentioned in any inscription relating the events of 720 BCE indicates that Judah did not take part in this revolt (Na'aman 1994b: 235–250, with further literature). Ahaz was presumably still reigning in Judah, which maintained its loyalty to Assyria,

---

6. These arrangements were in effect until the death of Ashurbanipal and the outbreak of the rebellion in Babylon in 627 BCE. Historical reconstructions that suggest that widespread changes took place in the region even earlier—whether after the Scythian invasion or due to Egypt's early advances into the Southern Levant—are untenable.

7. From a Sargon II inscription we know that an Assyrian governor was appointed in Ashdod (probably in 712 BCE), and that a governor of the city of Ashdod served as the eponym in 669 BCE. The province of Ashdod continued to exist under Persian rule and presumably under Babylonian rule prior to this. It seems, therefore, that the arrangements established by Sargon II and by Sennacherib remained intact throughout the period of Assyrian rule and served as the territorial and administrative basis for Babylonian and Persian rule. On the other hand, in the days of Sennacherib, Ashdod had a king. For an account of this exceptional duality, see Tadmor 1964: 272–276. For a critique of Tadmor and an alternative suggestion, see Na'aman 1979a: 72; 1994a: 9–11, with further literature.

8. During Sennacherib's reign, part of the territory of Judah was transferred to these three Philistine kingdoms, most likely to solidify and strengthen them. This served a dual purpose: the Assyrians consolidated control of the empire's southwestern border, near Egypt, and enjoyed economic profits from the prosperity of these royal cities and integration of their ports in the Arabian trade network. For further literature, see Gitin 1997: 99–100.

9. At the end of the 8th century BCE, prior to Sennacherib's campaign, Ashkelon had an enclave around Jaffa. There is no evidence that this changed at any point under Assyrian rule, although it is likely that at some point the enclave was brought under the rule of the adjacent Ekron. See Stager 1996; Gitin 1997: 84; Na'aman 1998: 222–223; Lipschits 2018a: 126–127, with further literature.

10. After the destruction of Samaria, Sargon conducted another campaign southward in Syria and the Southern Levant. Assyrian inscriptions indicate that he fought Gaza, which was aided by the Egyptian army, and reached Raphia. Sargon intended to gain control over the outlets of Arabian commerce in the Mediterranean ports and over part of its routes by establishing economic centers, building custom collection posts and a network of fortresses in key positions. He attempted to establish regional control through exiles brought from distant places and through agreements signed with local tribal leaders. See Na'aman 1979a; 1993; 2001; Na'aman and Zadok 1988; 2000.

and the empire was continuing to consolidate its power in the region and to develop its economic interests. In a letter (2765 ND) from the days of Sargon, written prior to 712 BCE (Deller 1985: 330; 1987: 219), and perhaps even ca. 715 BCE (Weippert 2010: 349, with further literature), the governor of Nimrud reported to King Sargon on the arrival of a delegation of representatives from kingdoms in the west, including a messenger from Judah. In another, apparently contemporaneous, document, representatives from Judah are mentioned in a list of wine recipients (Deller 1985: 328–329; Weippert 2010: 349–350, with further literature). This indicates that Judah remained loyal to Assyria and continued to pay tribute.

From the above, we may conclude that Judah was a loyal Assyrian vassal until the sudden death of Sargon II in the 705 BCE campaign. This loyalty was expressed in regular payments of tribute and obedience to the orders of the Assyrian king, conveyed through his representatives in the region. The possibility suggested above—that the changes in the administration and economy of Judah, enabling it to meet its payments of tribute to Assyria, took place immediately after its subjugation—seems, therefore, a reasonable one (Lipschits, Sergi and Koch 2010: 6–7; 2011: 6; Lipschits 2018b). On the basis of the Judean king's early submission to the Assyrian Empire— even before the fall of Gaza and before the conquest of the northern region of the Kingdom of Israel (733– 732 BCE)—it seems likely that immediately after the Assyrians had established a presence to the north and west of Judah, the latter began to adapt its economy and administration in an effort to adjust to the new reality. It was Ahaz who initiated this activity, which apparently gained momentum after the accession of Hezekiah to the throne in 715 BCE.[11] The activities in the royal estates and the development of the storage-jar administration were part of this process. Thus, the beginning of the final third of the 8th century BCE may have been a critical point in the establishment of this system. As a general

historical hypothesis, we propose that the storage-jar system commenced around 730 BCE, during the reign of Ahaz, and that the transition from the early series of *lmlk* stamp impressions with the four-winged scarab emblem (Type Ib) to the later series of four-winged stamp impressions (Type Ia) took place in 715 BCE, when Hezekiah gained the throne.

The activities of the royal estates and the storage-jar administration, in which agricultural products were amassed in Lachish and Ramat Raḥel, continued as long as Judah was subjugated to Assyria and was part of its imperial network. The stamp-impression system and Ramat Raḥel, which served as the main collection center from the destruction of Lachish in 701 BCE, were the tangible symbols of subjugation to Assyria, while in Jerusalem itself the kings from the Davidic dynasty continued to reign as before.

The *lmlk* Stamp Impressions and the Concentric Circle Incisions: Judah's Economic and Demographic Crisis following Sennacherib's Campaign

Towards the end of the 8th century BCE, Judah was a highly developed and mature kingdom. It included a relatively dense settlement network of farms and villages, small towns and major cities, which covered the entire territory of the kingdom. The Shephelah was the most populated and fertile region, with Lachish serving as a secondary capital. Jerusalem was undoubtedly the largest and most important center of government, the place of residence of the king and his family, the priests and much of the elite. In this period Jerusalem expanded beyond the narrow southeastern spur known as the City of David to the Western Hill, its population grew tenfold within a few decades, and strong fortifications and a sophisticated water system were built. There is a notable rise in the number of finds attesting to script and writing, to an administration and its officials, and an unprecedented

---

11.   The chronology of Hezekiah's reign has long been the subject of scholarly dispute. Some, relying on 2 Kings 18:1, 9–10, which refers to Hezekiah's accession to the throne in the third regnal year of Hosea in Samaria, date his reign to 727–698 BCE. Others, relying mainly on 2 Kings 18:13 (cf. also Isa 36:1), according to which Sennacherib's campaign against Judah took place in Hezekiah's 14th year, date his reign to 715/714–686 BCE. This later date is also in keeping with the account of Hezekiah's miraculous recovery from illness prior to the Assyrian attack on Jerusalem and God's message that he would reign for another 15 years (2 Kings 20:1–11). Na'aman's arguments in favor of the later dating for Hezekiah's reign (1994b: 236–239, with further literature) are convincing.

wealth of material finds. This sophisticated settlement and administration was the culmination of a long process of development that took place in the 9th and 8th centuries BCE. Judah enjoyed many years of tranquility, especially in the second half of the reign of Ahaz (734–715 BCE) and in the first decade of Hezekiah's rule (715–686 BCE).

In 705 BCE, Sargon was killed in battle in eastern Anatolia, when the Assyrian army suffered a severe defeat. Sargon's body was not returned to Assyria for burial, and revolts broke out across the empire. In Babylon, Marduk-apla-iddina II (Merodach-baladan in 2 Kings 20:12–19) was crowned as king again (703 BCE, after reigning between 722–710 BCE), with the support of the king of Elam (cf. 2 Kings 20:12–19), and at the far end of the empire a coalition of kingdoms, led by Hezekiah and supported by Egypt, revolted. In 704–701 BCE, Judah and its neighbors, aware that the Assyrian army would soon come to crush the rebellion, focused on building fortifications and preparing the army. A coup was carried out in Ekron, its king, Padi, was delivered to Hezekiah, and the city was fortified and became part of the rebelling coalition. In Ashkelon too, Rukibtu, loyal to Assyria, was removed from the throne and was replaced by Ṣidqa, a member of the royal dynasty who supported the revolt.[12]

The Assyrian military campaign was not long in coming. The rebelling coalition soon collapsed, the Egyptian army, which had come to their aid, was driven back, and Sennacherib executed a policy of systematic destruction of the Shephelah, the Negev and perhaps other areas in the kingdom, leaving the kingdom desolate. The destruction of "all the fortified cities of Judah" (2 Kings 18:13)—a total of 46 cities according to Sennacherib's prism inscription—and the wholesale deportation of their populations gave rise to the greatest demographic crisis in the history of Judah.[13] In addition to Lachish, all the cities of the Shephelah were destroyed: Beth Shemesh (Bunimovitz and Lederman 1997a; 1997b; 2003; Lipschits 2019a), Tel Batash (Mazar 1994: 258–260), Tell Beit Mirsim (Dagan 2001: 184–185;

Finkelstein and Naʾaman 2004: 61–64), Tel Goded (Gibson 1994: 230; Dagan 1992: 41–45; 2001: 91–93), Tel Ḥalif (Finkelstein and Naʾaman 2004: 64 with further literature), Maresha (Dagan 1992: 45–47; Kloner 1993; Kloner and Eshel 1999: 150) and Tel ʿEton (Ayalon 1985; Zimhoni 1985; Faust 2008; Katz and Faust 2012: 43–44). The wealthiest and most important region of the kingdom—which had experienced prosperity and development in the 9th and 8th centuries BCE, had been densely populated and had become the economic and administrative center of the Kingdom of Judah—was now destroyed, abandoned for years to come, and it never fully recovered (Naʾaman 2000a: 623; Dagan 2001: 210).

The administrative and economic infrastructure of the kingdom was also demolished. Judah had to pay a heavy tax to Assyria, in addition to the annual tribute, and these were a great burden on its economy. The independent and prosperous kingdom of the late 8th century BCE, which was not damaged by war from the 10th century BCE until the days of Hezekiah, now suffered devastation and a decline in its population. It seems that Sennacherib's main goal was to weaken the Kingdom of Judah, which remained a strong buffer between the areas controlled by Assyria and those ruled by Egypt. The Assyrians wanted to avoid any coalescence of power that had the potential to undermine their hegemony in the buffer zone with Egypt. Assyrian officials probably monitored the situation in Judah more closely now, and, following Naʾaman (1994b: 239), we may surmise that after the surrender of Hezekiah, Sennacherib appointed Manasseh, Hezekiah's young son, as the kingdom's regent. Ramat Raḥel presumably expanded at this stage, becoming the main— or perhaps the only—center for collection of agricultural produce, now near Jerusalem and relying upon new agricultural areas that were cultivated in the hill country (Lipschits and Gadot 2008; Lipschits *et al.* 2017: 36–43; Gadot 2015).

Tens of thousands were deported from Judah following Sennacherib's campaign, and many refugees must have fled from the Shephelah and perhaps the southern hill country and the Beersheba–Arad Valleys before, during

---

12. For a general review, see Eshel 1991; Grabbe 2003.

13. Ungnad 1942–43: 199–202; Millard 1991: 221–222; Naʾaman 1993: 117–120, with further literature; Younger 2003: 254, n. 65, with literature. For a review of the research, see Grabbe 2003: 20–36.

and following the Assyrian campaign. They would have taken refuge in Jerusalem and in the northern Judean hills, leading to rapid growth of the population of Jerusalem and probably serving as the basis for new arrangements in other sites in the Judean hills and the Benjamin region, areas that were unharmed in that campaign.[14]

Following the Assyrian campaign and the destruction of the Shephelah, Judah, like the entire Southern Levant, enjoyed several decades of tranquility—a period known as *Pax Assyriaca*. Until the 630s BCE, Assyria had complete dominion over the entire region, and this brought about a long period of domestic and external stability to all the Assyrian provinces and vassal kingdoms, a period when commerce was strengthened, the political, cultural and religious borders were opened, and Assyrian influence on the kingdoms' domestic affairs increased (Finkelstein 1994; Finkelstein and Na'aman 2004; Knauf 2005). This period of peace and stability in the early 7th century BCE apparently enabled the rehabilitation of the areas destroyed in Sennacherib's campaign. Refugees could settle in Jerusalem and its environs,[15] and for a short period some may have tried to return to the Shephelah.[16]

As long as Assyria controlled the region, Judah presumably could not regain its status in the Shephelah. This stems in part from the development of the Kingdom of Ekron, which for most of the Iron Age II had been a small kingdom in the shadow of its strong western and eastern neighbors. Ekron was the greatest beneficiary of the destruction of the Shephelah. The city was apparently not severely damaged in the Assyrian campaign, and it made a rapid recovery. Padi was restored to his throne, and the city's loyalty to Assyria during the campaign was rewarded by the Assyrians in its aftermath. The small kingdom received large areas taken from Judah and gained a rich agricultural hinterland, and the size of its built-up area rapidly grew to ca. 200 dunams (50 acres).

Ekron may also have received refugees from Judah, although their numbers cannot be determined. The economy of Ekron relied upon olive-oil production from the many orchards in the northern Shephelah,[17] and a large part of this production apparently served to pay tribute to Assyria.

The distribution of the early and late types of *lmlk* stamp impressions could shed new light upon the history of Judah in the period under discussion and provide additional insights. Before examining this distribution, two methodological remarks are warranted:

1. The general distribution of the *lmlk* stamp impressions does not reflect the borders of the kingdom and does not represent the economy or commerce in the various periods. It reflects only the storage-jar administration, which operated in a "closed cycle" between the jar-production center, the centers of agricultural production and the central collection site(s). The only point of contact between this administration and other components of the kingdom's society, administration and economy was the transportation of a large number of jars of all types to Jerusalem, probably to be exchanged with silver, gold and other goods needed for the annual tribute and paid by the local elite. From there jars were apparently delivered to sites defined above as "secondary administrative sites"—central sites in Judah where a handful of storage jars of different types were found, probably representing payment or gifts of the central government to officials or other individuals close to the royal circle.

2. When we draw a distinction between storage jars stamped with early and late types of *lmlk* impressions, we must be careful to avoid a bias stemming from the nature of archaeological research. Sennacherib's heavy destruction of sites in the Shephelah led to the sealing beneath the destruction layers of a wealth

---

14. Na'aman (2006) counters suggestions that the growth in the population of Jerusalem and the other Judahite cities in the late 8th century BCE was due to the influx of thousands (and perhaps tens of thousands) of refugees from the Ephraim hills after the Assyrian conquest of 720 BCE. On the archaeology of the 7th century, see Lipschits 2019b.

15. On the growth of population around Jerusalem during the 7th century BCE, see Gadot 2015. Jerusalem seems to have undergone a gradual decline in population during the 7th century BCE; see Geva 2006.

16. For unsuccessful attempts to resettle a few of the devastated Shephelah cities and their rapid abandonment, see Finkelstein and Na'aman 2004.

17. See Gitin 1989: 48–51; 1996; 1997; Kelm and Mazar 1996. The extent of Assyria's active involvement in the economic growth of Ekron is the subject of scholarly debate; see Na'aman 1993: 106; 2003: 85–88; Gitin 1995: 61–63; 1997: 82; Master 2003: 50; cf. Lipschits 2018a: 126–127.

of finds, representing the material culture that prevailed prior to the campaign. Clearly, the large number of marked and unmarked storage jars accurately reflects the numerous storage jars that were in use at these sites during the late 8th century BCE. However, in sites *not* destroyed by Sennacherib's campaign—especially in the hill country—the number of marked and unmarked storage jars that were in use cannot be determined. In these sites, storage jars continued to be used by the storage-jar administrative system for many years to come. Transported from the sites of agricultural production to the main collection site (Ramat Raḥel), and from there to Jerusalem and to the secondary administrative sites, they would, in the course of time, have been broken and discarded or otherwise gone out of use and would have been replaced by later types of storage jars. In view of the above, the storage jars with early *lmlk* stamp impressions uncovered in sites *not* destroyed by Sennacherib's campaign (especially in the hill country) should be assumed to reflect only a small percentage of the jars that were in use at these sites in the late 8th century BCE. Methodologically, one should not compare the finding of the storage jars with the early types of *lmlk* stamp impressions in the Shephelah to the ones uncovered in the hill country.[18]

Given these methodological comments, the distribution of the early types of *lmlk* stamp impressions in the various sites in Judah suggests that the eastern and southern peripheral areas were never real components of the system. It is not surprising that no handles bearing early *lmlk* stamp impressions were found in the eastern periphery, as these sites were probably only built in the 7th century BCE and perhaps only in the middle or second half of the century (see below). However, hardly any handles with late *lmlk* types were found in this area either. Only a single handle was uncovered at Jericho,

one at En-Gedi, two at Qumran and one at Khirbet es-Samrah, attesting to the insignificance of this area in the storage-jar system. The situation was no different in the mid-7th century BCE: only four handles with concentric circle incisions were found in this area—one at Jericho and three at En-Gedi. We may conclude that the sites in the eastern periphery were not directly connected to the Judahite storage-jar administration and that even in the middle or second half of the 7th century BCE, the kingdom's rulers did not feel it necessary to support officials or military personnel residing in Jericho and En-Gedi with surplus storage jars from the *lmlk* storage-jar administration.

The Beersheba and Arad Valleys too, despite the prosperity of the late 8th century BCE, did not play a significant role in the storage-jar administration.[19] Eight handles with early *lmlk* stamp impressions were found in this area, along with four handles with late types and five handles stamped with types that are unidentifiable. Approximately half of these handles were found at the fortress in Tel Arad; these storage jars were presumably brought there as payment or as gifts to the fortress commanders or officials. The fact that only one handle incised with concentric circles was found throughout the region indicates that the storage-jar administration did not operate there in this period; perhaps this is a continuation of the decline from the period prior to Sennacherib's campaign (eight handles) to its aftermath (four handles). This is in keeping with the general picture of the development and recovery of the Negev in the early 7th century BCE, following the severe blow inflicted by Sennacherib (Lipschits, Sergi and Koch 2011: 19): ʿAroer Stratum II and Tel Malḥata Stratum III were built during this period (Thareani-Sussely 2007a), while Tel ʿIra Stratum VI was constructed according to the layout of the previous stratum (VII), with clear evidence of continuity between the two strata.[20] The greatest change in this area is the destruction

---

18. For similar methodological remarks, see Naʾaman 2007; 2009a; Finkelstein 2012; Gadot 2015: 7–8.

19. Lipschits, Sergi and Koch 2011: 14–15, with further literature and discussion of the circumstances that led to the Judahite administration not being part of the prosperity of the Negev sites.

20. Beit-Arieh 1999b: 176–177. For the date of destruction of Stratum VII, see Singer-Avitz and Eshet 1999: 56; Thareani-Sussely 2007b: 71–72; cf. Beit-Arieh 1999b: 171–173; Freud 1999: 194–214. Clear traces of the Stratum VII destruction are evident mainly in the northeastern part of the fortifications; see Finkelstein and Beit-Arieh 1999: 76, 81. For the reconstruction of the city and the Stratum VII–VI continuity, see Finkelstein and Beit-Arieh 1999: 82; Beit-Arieh and Bunimovitz 1999: 20; Beit-Arieh and Negbi 1999: 29.

of the two Judahite fortresses at Tel Beersheba and Arad. While the Tel Beersheba fortress was never rebuilt, the fortress at Arad was reconstructed (Strata VII–VI), apparently during the second half of the 7th century BCE. We may conclude that some of the settlements in the Beersheba–Arad Valleys were reconstructed and renewed shortly after Sennacherib's campaign, in the early 7th century BCE, whereas the sites of the Judahite administration in this area were built only at a later stage, probably not before the middle of the century. The distribution of the stamp impressions is in keeping with this scenario. The historical conclusion to be drawn is that the prosperity in the Negev sites was not initiated or encouraged by the Kingdom of Judah. It is likely that in their efforts to punish Judah, the Assyrians destroyed the Beersheba and Arad fortresses and they also encouraged the rapid reconstruction of the trade routes (for extensive discussion, see Lipschits, Sergi and Koch 2011: 19–20; see further below). Thareani has suggested (2009: 184) that in the 8th century BCE the Beersheba–Arad area was governed by elite Judahite families, who were directly subject to Assyrian rule. In light of the above, Lipschits, Sergi and Koch (2011: 20) claim that this reality is more in keeping with the early 7th century BCE and that it took the Kingdom of Judah much longer to regain its control in this region.

In contrast to the peripheral areas in the east and south of the kingdom, it is clear that the Shephelah in general and Lachish in particular were the central component in the early system of *lmlk* storage jars (Lipschits, Sergi and Koch 2011: 11–12). In total, 506 handles bearing *lmlk* stamp impressions of the early types were found at sites in the Shephelah (ca. 70% of some 723 such handles). Lachish was clearly a central collection site at this stage, as indicated by the 378 handles with these types of stamp impressions found there (ca. 52% of all such finds), and the other major cities in the Shephelah also served an important role in the system—probably as secondary administrative cities, where officials and associates received individual storage jars from the various types of stamp impressions.

The fact that almost all the storage jars were found at sites in the northern and central Shephelah, with Lachish the southernmost city in the region where such finds were uncovered, has not been sufficiently dealt with. Stamped handles are very rare in the southern Shephelah, with four handles uncovered at Tell Beit Mirsim, one at Tel Ḥalif and two at Khirbet Qeʿilah. Thus, the absence of *lmlk* handles at Tel ʿEton should not be a factor that plays a role in dating destruction layers at this site (contra Katz and Faust 2012: 43–44).[21]

Ramat Raḥel played an important role in the storage-jar administration and the *lmlk* stamp-impression system from its early stages (Lipschits, Sergi and Koch 2011: 15; Lipschits *et al*. 2017: 44–49). The edifice, which was constructed around the time that the stamped storage-jar system first emerged and was presumably meant to serve it, was an important collection center in these early days. Although the 46 stamped handles found there, mostly from the early phase of construction, constitute only ca. 6.5% of the total number of handles with early *lmlk* types, the site exhibited centuries of continuous existence, with no destruction layer—not even from the early 6th century BCE. It is not surprising, therefore, that a similar number of handles incised with concentric circles (40) and handles stamped with rosette impressions (57) were found here. These apparently reflect the rate of jars that were damaged or broken and discarded over the many years that Ramat Raḥel served as a collection site and storage facility; they thus constitute a small percentage of the total number of storage jars gathered here at any stage of the system's duration through successive historical periods. The 133 stamped handles with late *lmlk* types (27% of the 490 handles of these late *lmlk* types) may be an important indication of the change that occurred in the administrative system after the destruction of the Shephelah, as well as a clear indication for the longer period of time that the storage-jar system continued

---

21. Katz and Faust describe the destruction of Tel ʿEton at the end of the 8th century BCE, its partial reconstruction and subsequent second destruction, leading to a long period of abandonment. Noting the absence of *lmlk*-stamped handles (Katz and Faust 2012: 44–48), they proposed that the site was destroyed before these handles first appeared, though they continued to support the accepted date of Sennacherib's campaign (701 BCE). Finkelstein (2012: 204) suggested that the site was destroyed before the Assyrian campaign. However, as stated here, the paucity of stamped handles throughout the southern region precludes drawing any conclusions from the absence of finds at Tel ʿEton; moreover, one cannot rule out the possibility that early *lmlk* handles will be recovered from its destruction levels in the future.

to operate after Sennacherib's campaign rather than before it.

Many handles stamped with early *lmlk* types were uncovered in Jerusalem too; the total of ca. 90 constitutes ca. 12.5% of all such finds. As mentioned above, Jerusalem was probably the most important secondary center, to which much of the produce was sent on a regular basis in exchange for silver, gold and other goods needed to be paid as tribute to the Assyrians. These storage jars, received by Jerusalem notables, members of the royal household, the priesthood and governmental officials, might have remained within the private economy and never been recycled back into the storage-jar administrative system. This would account for the relatively numerous storage jars uncovered in the city, even though it was not destroyed in Sennacherib's campaign.

As for late types of *lmlk* stamp impressions, Jerusalem, like Ramat Raḥel, exhibits a large number of such handles, which, as aforementioned, were dated to the early 7th century BCE: some 180 handles (ca. 37% of the 490 handles of these late *lmlk* types). These numbers further substantiate the claims made above regarding: 1) the importance of Ramat Raḥel as the only collection center following the destruction of Lachish; and 2) the importance of these storage jars to the economy of Jerusalem in the early 7th century BCE. These large numbers likely reflect two changes that took place in the storage-jar system after Sennacherib's campaign (Lipschits, Sergi and Koch 2010: 13; 2011: 15–16):

1. The focus of operations in the hill country— particularly around Jerusalem and Ramat Raḥel—along with increased agricultural activity in the Rephaim Valley and its environs,[22] was presumably concurrent with the decline of activity in the Elah Valley, around Socoh. Although the central production of storage jars probably continued at Socoh, agricultural and industrial operations in this area were damaged along with the entire Shephelah, and this would have impacted the concentration of agricultural activity and industry in the hill country. Most of the

agricultural produce in the Shephelah presumably moved in this period to Ekron.

2. The storage-jar system probably continued to operate for a longer time after Sennacherib's campaign than before it, apparently at least through the first quarter, if not the first third, of the 7th century BCE. This would have greatly impacted both the number of storage jars that were damaged, broken and discarded at the main collection center of Ramat Raḥel and the number of jars sent on to Jerusalem, transferred to secondary administrative centers, and sold or delivered to officials as gifts or as payment, thus entering the private market.

Against this backdrop, the collapse of the storage-jar administration in the Shephelah following the destruction of the region and the loss of most of Judah's territory is all the more striking (Lipschits, Sergi and Koch 2011: 16–17). The distribution of storage jars rules out Fantalkin's argument for short-term renewal of the settlement in Beth Shemesh within the framework of collaboration between Judah and Ekron (Fantalkin 2004: 255) and shows that there is no evidence for Judahite royal involvement in this process (Lipschits 2019a).[23] The only site in the Shephelah that continued to exist in the early 7th century was, as previously mentioned, Tel Socoh—and if it was destroyed, it was rapidly restored, and probably resumed its activity as the storage-jar production center. Of the 21 handles with late *lmlk* stamp impressions found in the Shephelah, 11 were recovered from Tel Socoh; these were mainly surface finds, discovered before wide-scale excavations were conducted there.

Nevertheless, there was a sharp decline in the number of stamped handles bearing the name Socoh, clearly reflecting the reduced production ability of the royal estate around Socoh—presumably the estate that processed the agricultural products of the Elah Valley. Whereas Socoh was the most common place name after Hebron in the early *lmlk* types, prior to Sennacherib's campaign in the late 8th century BCE, it becomes the least common in the late types (SIIb), dating

---

22. For the prosperity of the rural hinterland of Jerusalem in the 7th century, see Gadot 2015.

23. See Lipschits, Sergi and Koch 2011: 17, where it is also argued that the Assyrians transferred the entire Soreq Valley area to the Kingdom of Ekron.

from the early 7th century BCE, disappearing entirely in the third and final system (the IIc types).[24]

The great drop in the overall number of stamped storage jars—from 723 to 490—is an indication of the severity of the blow inflicted by Sennacherib on Judah's ability to manufacture agricultural products (mainly olive oil and wine), presumably mainly in the Elah Valley area. On these grounds, we suggest that the origin of the storage jars ceased to be of importance in the 7th century BCE— perhaps because they continued to be produced only in the hill country and consequently, stamping the name of the royal estate became redundant and was discontinued. This is evident first in the Type XII *lmlk* stamp impressions and later in the concentric circle incisions and the rosette stamp impressions. We may also surmise that accelerated development of the agricultural areas in the environs of Jerusalem—the Rephaim Valley, on the one hand, and the Benjamin region, on the other—compensated to some extent for the loss of the lands of the Shephelah and necessitated a change to the infrastructure, which until then had been based upon the four traditional royal estates.

The finds from the Benjamin region complete the picture of the changes that took place in the storage-jar administration and the significance of the system in the history of Judah. Of the early types of *lmlk* stamp impressions, 45 handles (ca. 6%) were found in the Benjamin region, mainly in Mizpah (27 handles) and Gibeon (17 handles), with one handle recovered from Khirbet al-Burj. Mizpah and Gibeon were therefore two administrative sites of importance north of Jerusalem; they would have received jars from the main collection sites, either directly or via Jerusalem, in a secondary distribution of storage jars that reached the capital. In contrast, of the late types of *lmlk* stamp impressions, ca. 25% were found in the Benjamin region (124 handles). Along with a significant rise in the importance of Gibeon (where 63 handles with late types were found, compared to 17 with early types) and a certain growth in the importance of Mizpah (38 handles with late types, compared to 17 with early types), Khirbet al-Burj now occupies a central position (15 handles with late types), as well as Tell el-Fûl

(five handles with late types). The same pattern is evident in the mid-7th century BCE as well, with ca. 25% of the handles incised with concentric circles appearing in sites in the Benjamin region (75 handles), the same percentage as late *lmlk* types. In this period too, Gibeon continues to be the central city in the Benjamin region (with 33 incised handles), followed by Mizpah (17 handles), Khirbet al-Burj (15) and Tell el-Fûl (four). These four settlements were therefore the central and most important administrative centers in the Benjamin region, an area that served as a critical resource for the economy of Judah, especially after the loss of the Shephelah, when Judah was in need of new agricultural areas in the hill country and near Jerusalem.

The general picture arising from the archaeological findings pertaining to Judah in the late 8th and early 7th centuries BCE, including the distribution of the early and late types of *lmlk*-stamped handles, is one of a severe demographic crisis, resulting from the loss of major areas and a mortal blow to the economy. In an effort to find creative ways to deal with this crisis, the Kingdom of Judah resorted to the development of agriculture in the hilly regions to the north and south of Jerusalem, relying as never before on the settlement in the Benjamin area. The storage-jar administration continued to operate as it did prior to Sennacherib's campaign, mainly in the region of Jerusalem, but on a much smaller scale.

These conclusions run counter to earlier scholarly suggestions that downplayed the damage inflicted by Sennacherib's campaign upon Judah.[25] The importance of the Shephelah within the settlement network of Judah prior to the Assyrian campaign should be reiterated. Its fertile soil and climatic conditions conducive to the cultivation of grains, coupled with its olive groves and vineyards, make the Shephelah the most important economic center in Judah, with an agricultural potential second to none in a mountainous kingdom with limited agricultural potential (Dagan 2006: 9*–13*). It is, therefore, clear why most of the fortified cities of Judah in the late 8th century BCE were located in the Shephelah, along with the operational center of the storage-jar administration. For this reason, the loss of these areas was a harsh blow to the administration,

---

24. See details in Lipschits, Sergi and Koch 2010: 17.

25. E.g., Faust (2008), who claims that all the excavations in Judah, except in the Shephelah, point to an increased density in settlement in the 7th century BCE, compared to the 8th century BCE.

economy, settlements and demography of Judah, from which it never fully recovered (Lipschits, Sergi and Koch 2011: 23–24).

Moreover, while claims about the density of the Judahite settlements in the 7th century BCE are correct, they reflect only the second half of this century, showing that Judah's recovery from the destructive blow dealt by the Assyrians was a long, gradual and continuous process.[26] As described above, there are no grounds for claims of any recovery in the Shephelah or in the Beersheba–Arad Valleys before the last third of the 7th century BCE, and Judah never regained its demographic strength or realized the economic potential of the Shephelah in the late 8th century BCE. There is no evidence to suggest that the grains cultivated in the Beersheba–Arad Valleys could compensate for the loss of the crops grown in the Shephelah. In any event, it seems that in the first half of the 7th century BCE, the Judahite administration did not play any role in the developments that took place in this region (cf. Faust 2008: 171–172; see also Master 2009: 308–311).

The Rosette Stamp Impressions: The "Archaeology of the Days of Josiah"

The Assyrian arrangements instated after Sennacherib's campaign remained in place until the withdrawal of Assyria from the region early in the 630s BCE. This did not create a geopolitical void, as Egypt replaced Assyria, probably as a "successor state" (Na᾿aman 1989: 45–56). Egypt ruled the region for 25 years, until it was driven back by Nebuchadnezzar's army (605/604 BCE). Throughout this period, the Egyptians' main economic interests lay along the Phoenician coast, due to the economic importance of its ports and of the cedars from the Lebanon Mountains. It is therefore clear why the Egyptians attached great importance to the Via Maris, which made it possible to maintain land trade with the Southern Levant (Redford 1992: 435), and they consolidated their rule mainly between Tyre and Arwad (Katzenstein 1973: 299, n. 24, 313, n. 100; Redford 1992: 442; Schipper 2010: 200–204).

Perhaps drawing a lesson from their battles against Assyria in the early 7th century BCE, the Egyptians established their hold in Philistia immediately after the withdrawal of the Assyrian army.[27] According to Herodotus (B 157), the Egyptians besieged Ashdod for 29 years until the city fell.[28] There is no information about the rest of the coastal cities in Philistia,[29] but it is reasonable to assume that during the *Pax Assyriaca* they maintained close ties with Egypt and that they were the first to recognize its status as a successor kingdom.[30] In any event, Egypt rapidly consolidated its rule in

---

26. As is well known, pinpointing the dating of ceramic assemblages of Judah within the 7th century BCE is problematic. Such assemblages generally occur in settlement strata that parallel Lachish Level II, dated to the late 7th–early 6th centuries BCE (Zimhoni 2004a). It is unknown, however, when Level II began, and it is unclear when the gradual transition took place from late 8th-century ceramic assemblages—especially in the destruction layers that parallel Lachish Level III—to the assemblages known from strata contemporaneous with Lachish Level II. Clearly, in light of the above, any appraisal of the settlement and demographic development in Judah in the 7th century BCE should rely upon additional stratigraphic and historical considerations. The Lachish model can no longer serve as the basis for generalizations: the long settlement gap—at least through the first half and perhaps even the first two thirds of the 7th century BCE—at Lachish, and probably at most Shephelah sites, did not occur in sites elsewhere in Judah, particularly in the hill country north and south of Jerusalem. For the arguments dating most of the 7th-century BCE sites to late within this century, see Lipschits, Sergi and Koch 2011: 25–27. For a general discussion of this problem, see Lipschits 2019b.

27. Katzenstein (1973: 298, 302) argued that there was no true Egyptian rule in the area throughout this period, but it seems that the prevailing scholarly view, according to which Egypt had already consolidated its rule in the region at this stage, should be accepted. See Kienitz 1953: 20; Spalinger 1976; Redford 1992: 444–448; Schipper 2010.

28. We can assume that the lengthy period of Assyrian rule meant that Ashdod was less attached to Egypt, and upon the Assyrian retreat, it attempted to establish its independence. Tadmor (1966: 102; Cogan and Tadmor 1988: 300) suggested interpreting the number 29 as referring to the 29th year of Psammetichus I, i.e., 635 BCE, concluding that this was the year of the Assyrian withdrawal. Na᾿aman (1989: 52), however, suggests that this is chronological speculation on the part of Herodotus, based upon the 28-year period of Scythian rule in Asia. See also Malamat 1983: 231–232; James 1991: 714; Redford 1992: 441–442, with literature in n. 44. For the archaeological evidence of the Egyptian conquest, see the viewpoint of the excavators (Dothan and Freedman 1967: 11, n. 46; Dothan 1971: 115; Dothan and Porath 1982: 57–58); cf. Vanderhooft 1999: 71–72.

29. See Redford 1992: 442. We know that Ekron suffered decline from its floruit under Assyrian rule at the end of the 7th century BCE (Dothan and Gitin 1994: 23–25), but we cannot determine whether this decline took place before, during, or at the end of the period when Egypt gained control over the area.

30. Evidence of ties between the coastal cities and Egypt can be found in the letter of Adon, King of Ekron, to the king of Egypt on the eve of the Babylonian conquest; see Porten 1981.

Philistia, and the kingdoms of Philistia maintained their loyalty to it even in the early days of Babylonian rule. Philistia served as a "gateway" to Egypt, and indeed, this sheds light upon the existence of the Egyptian fortress at Meṣad Ḥashavyahu and the evidence for the presence of Egyptian personnel in Stratum VIIIb at Yavne-Yam, as well as at Ashkelon, Ekron and Timnah, much like the Egyptian fortresses existing at that time in Migdol and Dafna.[31]

It is unclear to what extent the Egyptians were interested in the hinterland and how much effort they invested in consolidating their rule there. However, the presence of Pharaoh Necho in Megiddo and the killing of Josiah there (2 Kings 23:29), the later removal of Jehoahaz from the throne in Jerusalem (2 Kings 23:33) and the appointment of Eliakim-Jehoiakim as king (2 Kings 23:34) attest to the Egyptians' intention to establish their rule over Judah, as well as over all the vassal kingdoms, Phoenician and Philistine cities and the previously Assyrian provinces in the region. The geopolitical events and the biblical evidence suggest that Judah was under Egyptian patronage at the time and could not conduct an independent foreign policy, certainly not with regard to the Shephelah and Coastal Plain (Naʾaman 1989: 45–71).

In the first two years of Nebuchadnezzar's reign (605–604 BCE), Babylon gained control over Ḥatti-land, including Greater Syria and the Southern Levant. The crucial battle that enabled the Babylonian army to conquer the entire region took place in Carchemish in the early summer of King Nabopolassar's last regnal year (May–July 605 BCE). The army of Nebuchadnezzar, the Babylonian successor to the throne, crossed the Euphrates, routed the Egyptian army encamped in Carchemish and broke through into Syria. The remnants of the Egyptian army withdrew south and, according to the Babylonian Chronicle, were pursued by Nebuchadnezzar's army to the region of Hamath, where they were delivered a crushing blow. Nebuchadnezzar returned to northern Syria after the death of his father (late 605–early 604 BCE), probably in order to consolidate his hold over this area in preparation for the subsequent year's campaign (Lipschits 2005: 32–42, with further literature). It seems that by early 604 BCE, the Babylonians had established their control all the way to the Orontes River in northern Syria and had made Riblah their major administrative and military center in Ḥatti-land. It is unlikely that at this stage, any changes took place in the political arrangements in central and northern Syria. These were already well established, in some cases since the late 8th century BCE, and there were no polities or populations with a national identity upon which to rely for instating any alternative arrangements.

The remaining areas of Ḥatti-land, including southern Syria, Phoenicia, Philistia and the hinterland region, on both sides of the Jordan, were captured by the Babylonians between the months of Simanu and Šabaṭu (between June 604 BCE and January/February 603 BCE). During this campaign, "[Nebuchadnezzar] marched about victoriously. … All the kings of Ḥatti-land came before him and he received their vast tribute" (for a reconstruction of the events, see Lipschits 2005: 39–42). The king of Ashkelon was the only local king who dared to stand up to Nebuchadnezzar.[32] The Babylonians dealt a resounding blow to the city, and its fate served as an example to the other kingdoms in the region: Ashkelon was conquered

---

31. Naveh (1962: 99) was the first to attribute the construction of Meṣad Ḥashavyahu to Psammetichus I's mercenaries, prior to its conquest by Josiah. He later changed his position (1993: 586) and supported Tadmor's (1966: 102, n. 59) and Strange's proposal (1966: 138) to attribute the Greek mercenaries there to Josiah (cf. also Cross's previous suggestion [1962: 42]). This proposal was generally accepted, although a few scholars returned to Naveh's original suggestion and supported the existence of two separate phases for the site (Eshel 1986–87: 236). The inclination today to return to Naveh's original viewpoint seems more reasonable based on the site history and on the analysis of the archaeological finds. For a comprehensive discussion of the material finds at Meṣad Ḥashavyahu, the characteristics of the site, and its comparison to other coastal sites, see Fantalkin 2000: esp. 66–70; 2001: esp. 128–147; Schipper 2010. On the importance of mercenaries in Egypt during Psammetichus' reign and the Meṣad Ḥashavyahu fortress in this framework, see Redford 1992: 443–444; see also Miller and Hayes 1986: 389; Naʾaman 1989: 56–60; Finkelstein 1995: 148; Vanderhooft 1999: 78–80; Kletter 1999: 42; Schipper 2010. For a comparison between the population at Meṣad Ḥashavyahu and at contemporaneous Egyptian border fortresses (Migdol and Dafna), see Naʾaman 1989: 57–58. In view of these findings, Wenning's minority view (1989) that the site was first built as late as the reign of Jehoiakim should not be accepted; it seems that by his fifth year (604 BCE) it was already destroyed (Naʾaman 1989: 58).

32. The proximity of Ashkelon to the Egyptian border and the long period of Egyptian rule were, in all likelihood, factors that led its king to continue to rely upon Egyptian assistance. Not understanding the changes that had taken place in the international balance of power, he refused to capitulate to Babylon.

in the month of Kislev (November/December 604 BCE);[33] its king was taken into captivity, it was severely plundered, many prisoners were seized and the city was razed to the ground.[34] It is possible that this is when the territory of Ashkelon was annexed to Ashdod; if so, this is the only known geopolitical change made by the Babylonians in the Southern Levant.[35] One may assume that the fate of Ashkelon was exceptional, that the Babylonians quickly gained control over Ḫatti-land in its entirety, and that following Ashkelon's defeat, all the other kingdoms in the region, including the Kingdom of Judah, surrendered to Nebuchadnezzar.

The swiftness of the Babylonian conquest points to the weakness of the small kingdoms in the region and to the void left after the Egyptian withdrawal. There is no evidence of Babylonian activity in the hill country or in Transjordan during these years. It seems that all the kings of the Phoenician coast, Philistia and Transjordan surrendered to Nebuchadnezzar in the second half of 604 BCE, and this was presumably when Judah was subjugated to Babylon as well (Lipschits 2005: 42–49, with further literature). The Babylonians probably assumed that they could rely upon the loyalty of the small kingdoms in the hinterland on both sides of the Jordan and thus they left intact the administrative organization that they found when they arrived on the scene. This policy was manifest, most notably, in the fact that Jehoiakim, king of Judah, was left on the throne even though he had been appointed by the Egyptians only five years earlier. It is hard to accept Albright's suggestion (1956: 31) that Nebuchadnezzar met with the staunch opposition of the local population and kings, who were

allied with Egypt, necessitating his recurrent campaigns in subsequent years. There is no evidence of such opposition in the Babylonian Chronicles or in any reconstruction of the history of the region in the years of Babylonian rule. It is more likely that the initial campaigns (605–604 BCE) were designed to establish Babylonian rule in the region and that the subsequent campaigns (602–601 BCE) were intended to prepare the ground for an invasion of Egypt (Lipschits 2005: 45–49). It was only the failure of the 601 BCE invasion of Egypt that prompted a temporary wave of anti-Babylonian unrest amongst the kingdoms of the Southern Levant, motivated by a hope for the imminent return of Egypt.[36]

In 601 BCE, three years into Babylonian rule (cf. 2 Kings 24:1), Babylonian imperial control was undermined throughout the region when Nebuchadnezzar failed in his attempt to invade and conquer Egypt (cf. also Jer 46:13–28).[37] The renewed Egyptian rule was short-lived, and after the Babylonians reestablished their control over the region in 598 BCE, they set out to consolidate their rule over Judah, too, waging war against Jerusalem following Jehoiakim's rebellion. Jehoiakim died during the Babylonian siege, and his son Jehoiachin came to power. The only act of Jehoiachin during his three months of reign—which coincided with the three months of the Babylonian campaign—was to surrender to Babylon and exit the gates of besieged Jerusalem together with his mother, his ministers and his kingdom's elite. Nebuchadnezzar, following his pragmatic policy of appeasement, accepted his surrender and did not punish Jerusalem and the Davidic dynasty for their lack of loyalty. He appointed Jehoiachin's uncle Mataniah as

---

33. The date of Ashkelon's conquest in the month of Kislev should be linked to the emergency convention held in Jerusalem "in the fifth year of Jehoiakim, son of Josiah, King of Judah, in the ninth month" (Jer 36:9); see Lipschits 2005: 40–42.

34. For a detailed discussion on 7th-century BCE Ashkelon and the 604 BCE destruction, see Stager, Master and Schloen 2011. There is clear archaeological evidence of the Babylonian destruction of Ashkelon (Stager 1996; Master 2003: 61; 2009: 312). The excavations point to a direct connection between Ashkelon and Egypt, perhaps even an Egyptian presence in the city (Stager 1996: 68*–69*). The city lay in ruins throughout the 6th century BCE and was rebuilt only in the Persian period (Katzenstein 1994: 41).

35. At the beginning of the Persian period Ashkelon was part of the province of Ashdod. Although there is no explicit information about this, the political situation in the Persian period was likely a continuation of the administrative structure instated by Nebuchadnezzar after the conquest of the city. However, one may assume that the historical reality of the Persian period was the product of gradual geopolitical processes about which we have no information, but which were not based on official Babylonian practice.

36. This shows Nebuchadnezzar's practical approach and his reasonable premise that anybody who was wise enough to remain loyal to Egypt would continue to be realistic and would shift their loyalty to Babylonian rule. See the reconstruction of the events of these years in Lipschits 2005: 45–62.

37. The Egyptians probably sought to reestablish their power throughout the entire Southern Levant, and Jehoiakim, king of Judah, who began his reign as an Egyptian vassal, presumably also transferred his loyalty back to Egypt. Cf. to Lipschits 2005: 49–55.

king of Judah, changing his name to Zedekiah, and deported Jehoiachin himself, along with his courtiers, leaders and nobility, to Babylon (2 Kings 24). Thus, Nebuchadnezzar hoped to achieve stability in Jerusalem and guarantee its loyalty.[38]

However, the final 11 years of the Kingdom of Judah under Zedekiah's reign were years of turbulence and political instability. The unwavering belief that was prevalent in Judah, that Jerusalem is the place that God has chosen and the place that received an eternal promise, led to a reckless policy that coincided with Egyptian efforts to undermine the stability of the small kingdoms in the Southern Levant, especially along the Mediterranean coast. The continuous instability and recurrent rebellions led Nebuchadnezzar, in 588 BCE, to change his policy from indirect rule over semi-independent kingdoms to direct rule over provinces (Lipschits 2005: 62–67). The result was the systematic destruction of the local kingdoms that had survived the Assyrian expansion to the Southern Levant, and the annexation to Babylon by the establishment of a network of provinces under direct Babylonian rule. Judah was the first kingdom to be conquered and annexed (587/6 BCE), and a new chapter in its history thus began (for a detailed description, see Lipschits 2005: 62–84).

A review of these events suggests that the Babylonian kingdom, which had developed within a few short years into a tremendous empire, lacked experience in ruling wide expanses of territories far from the urban centers in Babylon. Moreover, the Babylonians presumably had limited familiarity with the political structure in Ḫatti-land. There is no evidence that Nebuchadnezzar attempted to develop the area or to defend it. It seems that his policy was to intervene as little as possible, to invest the minimal effort necessary to maintain his rule and to continue the arrangements instated earlier during Assyrian and Egyptian rule (see Lipschits 1999b).

The system of rosette stamp impressions is a useful tool for a reconstruction of the changes that took place in the storage-jar administration in Judah after the Assyrian withdrawal from the region in the late 7th century BCE. The distribution of the rosette-stamped handles, their stratigraphic contexts and their dating shed light upon the historical processes that the Kingdom of Judah underwent in the transition from Assyrian to Egyptian and then Babylonian rule. It also illuminates the resulting changes in Judah's administration, economy and settlement structure (Koch and Lipschits 2013). The rosette stamp-impression system is of particular importance for determining when the change in the settlement structure in the various regions of the kingdom took place. The understanding that the rosette stamp impressions should be viewed as a continuation of the late types of *lmlk* stamp impressions and of the concentric circle incisions enables us to date these changes to the reign of Josiah and his successors, following the Assyrian withdrawal from the region, and to the period of Egyptian rule in Judah (see above, pp. 116–120).[39]

In the 7th century BCE, the Judahite settlement was concentrated mainly in the hill country, and most of the handles stamped with late *lmlk* stamp impressions or incised with concentric circles were found around Jerusalem and in the Benjamin region (Lipschits, Sergi and Koch 2011, and see above, pp. 105–116). A similar picture is evident in the late 7th century BCE: most of the rosette-stamped handles were found in hill country sites around Jerusalem (172 handles out of the 290 rosette-stamped handles = 59.5%), a decline compared to the number of handles with concentric circle incisions (212 handles out of 305 = ca. 69.5%) and an even greater decline compared to handles bearing late types of *lmlk* stamp impressions (319 handles out of 490 = 65%). The main decline is in Jerusalem—from ca. 180 handles bearing late *lmlk* stamp impressions to 162 handles incised with concentric circles and 108 rosette-stamped handles. This may suggest a drop in the number of storage jars taken out of circulation and given or sold to dignitaries in Jerusalem. In Ramat Raḥel, an increase is evident in the number of rosette-stamped handles (57 handles = ca. 20% of all such finds), compared to 40 handles with concentric circle incisions (ca. 13%).

---

38. For a reconstruction of the events of these years, see Lipschits 2001; 2005: 49–62, with further literature.

39. This runs counter to scholarly views linking these changes to the *Pax Assyriaca* during the reign of King Manasseh and to the Judahite need to compensate for the loss of areas destroyed in Sennacherib's campaign; see Finkelstein 1994. For the new analysis based on this approach, see Koch and Lipschits 2013; Lipschits 2019b.

At first glance, this seems to reflect continuity from the previous administrative systems, but in fact, a notable change took place in the hill country. The renewed Ramat Raḥel excavations have shown that the second phase of the administrative center was established no earlier than the late 7th century BCE and that this phase completely transformed the overall appearance of the site. A citadel with a courtyard and a royal garden were added onto the previous buildings, most notably the western tower overlooking the Rephaim Valley (Lipschits *et al.* 2017: 60–94). As mentioned above, not a single rosette stamp impression was found in the fill beneath the fortress and palace floors, but this fill yielded finds dated to the second half of the century—mainly pottery sherds contemporaneous with Lachish Level II, handles with late types of *lmlk* stamp impressions and handles with concentric circle incisions. This indicates that the second phase of the center at Ramat Raḥel was built before the rosette stamp-impression system had begun. Nonetheless, it can still be suggested that the construction of the center and the initiation of the new system were part of the same administrative stage in the history of Judah.

The most notable change that took place in the Judahite administrative system in the late 7th century BCE is the reemergence of the Shephelah and its cities. After the devastation of the region in 701 BCE, the Judahite hold on it was weakened and only in the second half of the 7th century BCE was Lachish reestablished.[40] We may assume that other secondary centers were built in the Shephelah at the time, most notably Tel Azekah (the third most important city in the rosette system, with 30 rosette-stamped handles = ca. 10.5% of the finds), Timnah (Tel Batash) with six stamped handles and Socoh with five. In Lachish, 24 handles with rosette stamp impressions were found (ca. 8% of all these finds). Like at Ramat Raḥel, no rosette handles were found under the floors of Level II, but,

unlike at Ramat Raḥel, and due to the long settlement gap between Level III and Level II at Lachish, no other type of handle (with *lmlk* stamp impressions or with concentric circle incisions) was found in a clear context under the Level II floors either (Ussishkin 2004c: 90–91). It seems, therefore, that just like the construction of the second phase of the Ramat Raḥel administrative center, Lachish Level II was built when the rosette stamp-impression system came into use—at the beginning of the last third of the 7th century BCE. One should stress, however, that despite the reemergence of Lachish, the administrative center of Level II was apparently no more than a shadow of its predecessor. The archaeological finds suggest that it was a small and poorly constructed city, compared to the previous phase (Ussishkin 2004c: 91–92), and the stamp impressions give rise to the same conclusion: whereas Lachish Level III, of the late 8th century BCE, produced 52% of all the early types of *lmlk* handles, Level II yielded only 8% of all the rosette stamp impressions. This difference reflects a major change in the status of Lachish: at the end of the 7th century BCE it was no longer a main collection center as in the previous century, but only a secondary administrative center. Most of the storage jars found at Lachish were probably delivered to officials or military personnel stationed there, within the framework of the central authority's efforts to strength the site.

The 30 stamped handles discovered at Tel Azekah[41] are an indication that the central authority wished to encourage resettlement at this site, a major border city in the Shephelah, and may even signify the renewal of activities in the Elah Valley, in an attempt to exploit once again the agricultural potential of this fertile area. The discovery of six rosette-stamped handles at Tel Batash/Timnah may—like at Azekah—suggest a phase during which the central authority in Jerusalem delivered storage jars to officials or officers residing there. In my view, contrary to the opinion of the excavators (Mazar

---

40. Naʾaman 1989: 70; Ussishkin 2004c: 90–92; Katz 2008: 124; Dagan 2001: 207–210.

41. The unique status of the center at Azekah is evident from the finds from Bliss and Macalister's excavation, which include handles stamped with four types of impressions that are unique to this site. While the depiction of rosettes with a unique number of petals may be due to faulty documentation, these finds may, alternatively, be compared to the discovery of an impression with a unique number of petals (seven) during Macalister's excavation in Gezer. Just a few years ago it was shown that the drawing of the stamp impression (which has since been lost) was accurate, since a similar stamp impression was found at Khirbet er-Ras (Koch 2008: 35–36).

and Panitz-Cohen 2001: 181), the city was not part of the Kingdom of Ekron at this stage.[42] It seems plausible that upon the destruction of Ekron in 604 BCE (Naʾaman 2003: 85, n. 9), Judah—whose king, Jehoiakim, was still loyal to Babylon—gained control over the eastern lands of its neighbor, which was punished for its loyalty to Egypt, and secured Tel Batash/Timnah for itself.[43] The suggestion that Tel Batash was a Judahite city in the early 6th century BCE is based on the destruction of Ekron, on the Judahite material culture found in Tel Batash, including Judahite pottery vessels, weights, figurines and loom weights,[44] on the rosette-stamped handles, and on the absence of any such handles in Ekron itself.

In conclusion, the archaeological data, including the rosette stamp impressions, support the currently accepted historical reconstruction of the setting and dating of the reconstruction of the Shephelah, as well as its limited scope.[45] In the first half of the 7th century BCE, the Shephelah was, to a large extent, abandoned. Even after the beginning of its reconstruction—probably in the final third of the 7th century BCE—it was a mere shadow of what it had achieved a century earlier in the size of its population, the intensity of its urbanization, the might of its fortifications and the strength of its economy. Compared to the strength of the region in the 8th century BCE, the settlement in the Shephelah of the late 7th century BCE consisted of solitary administrative and military centers, and significant sites such as Beth Shemesh, Tel Goded and Tell Beit Mirsim were never resettled.[46]

The development of the Benjamin region and its incorporation into Judah's storage-jar administration in the 7th century BCE compensated to a large extent for the loss of the Shephelah. A total of 124 handles with late *lmlk* stamp impressions (ca. 25% of all such finds) was uncovered in the Benjamin region, as well as 75 handles with concentric circle incisions (ca. 25% of these finds). In this period the settlement in the Benjamin region flourished (Lipschits 1999a), but archaeologically, one cannot distinguish sub-phases in the 7th century BCE or determine whether changes occurred. In terms of the role this region played in the Judahite storage-jar administration, however, a sharp change is evident at the end of the 7th century: as the Shephelah regained its place in the rosette stamp-impression system, with 24.5% of all the rosette-stamped handles uncovered there, the number of such handles found in the Benjamin region dropped to only 19 (6.5%). As we are not aware of any demographic decline or change in this region, this drop in percentage presumably stemmed from the recovery of the Shephelah and the need to support the resettlement of this area, which once again had become an important source of agricultural produce in Judah. As a result, the Benjamin region returned to its previous modest role in the storage-jar administrative system of Judah, and perhaps in the Judahite administration in general.[47]

---

42. Cahill (2001: 199–200) argued that the six rosette stamp impressions are evidence of an emergency shipment from Jerusalem to the Kingdom of Ekron on the eve of Nebuchadnezzar's campaign in the late 7th century BCE. This argument is implausible: it is based upon Cahill's opinion that the rosette stamp-impression system came into use within the framework of the pro-Egyptian Jehoiakim's preparations for the Babylonian onslaught—a view that is based on the now disproven hypothesis that the *lmlk* stamp-impression system was created as part of Hezekiah's preparations before the anticipated Assyrian campaign. Moreover, Cahill's argument is based on her hypothesis that Tel Batash was destroyed in the Babylonian campaign in the late 7th century BCE, along with Ekron. However, there is no scholarly agreement on the timing of the destruction of Tel Batash or of the destruction of Ekron and on the connection between the two events. See Lipschits 2005: 40–42 and nn. 18–19; Ussishkin 2004c: 111.

43. See, albeit with slight reservations, already Mazar 1985: 321; 1994: 262–263. See also Ussishkin 2004c: 111. For the pro-Egyptian policy of the Philistine kingdoms, see Naʾaman 1989: 62. The failed attempt to settle Beth Shemesh may also attest to Ekron's blocking of the Shephelah until the late 7th century BCE. On this, see Bunimovitz and Lederman 2003: 17–23; cf. Fantalkin 2004.

44. Mazar and Panitz-Cohen 2001: 160–161, 208–210, 238–241. Cf. Naʾaman (1987: 14 and n. 21), who claims that Judahite findings could have arrived at Tel Batash during the *Pax Assyriaca* and that their distribution would, therefore, not be indicative of Judah's borders.

45. Naʾaman 1989: 70; 1994b: 248; Dagan 2001: 201–207; Faust 2008: 173. For literature dating Judah's expansion westward to the reign of Manasseh, see Finkelstein 1994: 181.

46. For the destruction of Beth Shemesh in 701 BCE, see Bunimovitz and Lederman 2009: 139–140; for the destruction of Tel Goded, see Gibson 1994: 229; for the destruction of Tell Beit Mirsim, see Zimhoni 1985: 82–83. To complete the archaeological picture, see Dagan 2004: 2681–2682. For a summary of the unsuccessful attempts at settlement in the early 7th century BCE, see Finkelstein and Naʾaman 2004.

47. Naʾaman (2009b: 116) suggested that this decline in the administrative importance of the Benjamin region should be linked to the claim that the area declined in importance in the wake of the destruction of the altar in Gibeon under Josiah's cultic reform (2 Kings 23).

In several sites in the Beersheba–Arad Valleys, ceramic assemblages paralleling Lachish Level II (the late 7th century BCE) were uncovered. These include: four sites (from west to east): Bir es-Sebaʿ, ʿAroer, Tel ʿIra (probably the regional administrative town) and Tel Malḥata;[48] several fortresses, most notably, Ḥorvat ʿAnim, Ḥorvat ʿUza, Ḥorvat Ṭov, Ḥorvat Radum and Tel Arad;[49] and unwalled settlements, including Tel Masos, Tel Shoket, Mount Yattir, Khirbet Yiten, Khirbet Hur and Naḥal ʿAnim.[50] Here too, it is archaeologically impossible to discern sub-phases within the 7th century BCE and to determine at what point in this century these settlement processes began—whether in the first half, the middle, or the latter half of the century. Nevertheless, the prevalent view in recent years is that this settlement network in the Beersheba–Arad Valleys developed during the reign of Manasseh within the framework of the *Pax Assyriaca*. It was also out of Judah's need to compensate for the loss of the fertile Shephelah.[51] The rosette finds may shed light on this subject from another direction and point to the date when the storage-jar administration returned to the Beersheba–Arad Valleys—even if only in terms of shipments to officials and military personnel stationed there. In this respect the picture is clear. Compared to only four handles stamped with late types of *lmlk* stamp impressions and one handle incised with concentric circles, sites in the Beersheba–Arad Valleys yielded ten handles with rosette stamp impressions—the largest number of stamped handles of any type to be found in this region. Indeed, like the finds from Ramat Raḥel and from Lachish Level II, all rosette-stamped handles from this area uncovered in clear stratigraphic contexts were found on floors and are thus contemporary with or later than the time of construction of the sites. Despite the small number of handles recovered, it would seem to represent evidence for the time that the Judahite storage-jar administration renewed its interest in the Beersheba–Arad Valleys and perhaps even supported officials there. This activity consisted mainly of construction of the center at Tel ʿIra, along with an entire network of fortresses. The return of the Judahite administration to the Beersheba–Arad Valleys only late in the 7th century makes one question to what extent Judah ruled the region from Sennacherib's campaign until the final third of the 7th century, especially in light of the settlement strata from early in this century in Tel Malḥata and ʿAroer[52] and given the Edomite material culture, which had become very dominant during this century.[53]

A dozen handles with rosette stamp impressions found in the eastern periphery of Judah indicate that the area was sparsely populated in the late 7th century BCE too, and point to its importance to the Judahite

---

48. For comprehensive literature about these sites, see Koch and Lipschits 2013: 59–60, and nn. 11, 16.

49. For the fortresses, see Beit-Arieh 2007; Thareani-Sussely 2002: 49–70.

50. For details and literature, see Thareani-Sussely 2002: 81–84.

51. Beit-Arieh 1985; Naʾaman 1987: 11; Biran 1987: 32; Finkelstein 1994: 165; Tatum 1991; Thareani-Sussely 2002: 145; Knauf 2005: 171–180.

52. These facts, coupled with the possibility that the Assyrians gained control over the Arabian trade in the Beersheba–Arad Valleys by granting autonomy to local elites (Thareani-Sussely 2002: 184–191), may suggest that this area was administered by the local population under Assyrian protection in the last third of the 8th century and throughout most of the 7th century BCE. In this case too, the change, including the resumption of Judahite control, may have occurred only after Assyrian withdrawal from the region.

53. "Edomite" pottery vessels were exposed in most settlement strata in the Beersheba–Arad Valleys from the 7th century BCE (Singer-Avitz and Eshet 1999: 30–38; Thareani-Sussely 2002: 100–101), but primarily in Tel Malḥata (Singer-Avitz and Eshet 1999: 56–57; Beit-Arieh 1999b: 18–19) and perhaps also in ʿAroer (Singer-Avitz and Eshet 1999: 56). The "Edomite" finds in the Beersheba–Arad Valleys should perhaps be considered as evidence for the local material culture, rather than for Edomites taking control of the area. Alongside 8th-century BCE pottery, numerous 7th-century BCE finds were uncovered, such as the seal and ostracon from ʿAroer (Biran and Cohen 1981: 264 and Pl. 49:5; Thareani-Sussely 2002: 222–224); the ostracon from Ḥorvat ʿUza featuring two Edomite names (Beit-Arieh 2007: 133–137), and perhaps the seal from that site (Beit-Arieh 2007: 178–179); Arad Letters Nos. 3, 21 and 40 (Aharoni 1981b: 17–18, 42–43, 70–74) and the temple at Ḥorvat Qitmit (Beit-Arieh 1995). This finding points to local Edomites residing in the Beersheba–Arad Valleys during the 8th–7th centuries BCE, rather than to the conquest of the area by kings residing in Buṣeirah. This would account for the reference to Edomites in the Arad letters and the inclusion of Edomite officials in the Ḥorvat ʿUza ostracon, as locals integrated into the Judahite administration (the Ḥorvat ʿUza ostracon was apparently written by an Edomite residing in the Beersheba–Arad Valleys and was not sent from Edom). See Lipschits 2015: 224–232; also Finkelstein 1994: 159; Naʾaman 1999a: 408–409; Naʾaman and Thareani-Sussely 2006. In light of these findings, we should reject the historical reconstruction that suggested that tribes invaded the Beersheba–Arad Valleys from the Negev in the late 7th century BCE (see, e.g., Ephʿal 1982: 81–169; Malamat 1983: 184–185; Rainey 1987: 25; Beit-Arieh 1987: 35; 2007: 2).

administration. There were two main settlements in this area at the time: Jericho and En-Gedi.[54] According to the excavators of En-Gedi, on the basis of ceramic parallels to Lachish Level II, Tel Goren Stratum V was established in the late 7th century BCE (Yezerski 2007) and served as a site for the production of perfumes and other products from the natural resources of the Dead Sea (Mazar, Dothan and Dunayevsky 1966: 38; Katz 2008: 45–47; Lipschits 2000). Fortresses and some hamlets and few other small settlements were built around En-Gedi and Jericho, and at least ten fortresses and several dozen camp sites were established along the roads descending from the hill country down toward the Dead Sea area (Lipschits 2000: 317–326, with further literature; Faust 2008: 170). The settlement in the eastern periphery was also dated by several scholars to the early 7th century BCE (Finkelstein, in Finkelstein and Magen 1993: 177–178; Faust 2008: 181), but in this case too, a reexamination of the data suggests that in most cases the prosperity of the region should be dated later, to the end of the century. In any event, only after the Assyrian withdrawal could Judah have expanded to the Jericho region, which until then had belonged to the province of Samaria (Naʾaman 1989; Stern 1994: 400).

All the rosette-stamped handles uncovered at En-Gedi were found on—and not beneath—floors, and the three handles incised with concentric circles were found in mixed assemblages (Stern 2007c). It seems, therefore, that like the administrative centers in Ramat Raḥel and Lachish and, as in the Shephelah and the Beersheba–Arad Valleys, the centers in the eastern periphery (including the network of fortresses and camp sites) were established during the time of operation of the rosette stamp-impression system and not earlier. The 12 handles with rosette stamp impressions uncovered may be interpreted as support given to officials and military personnel stationed at En-Gedi in the form of storage-jar shipments.

To conclude, the dating of the rosette stamp-impression system to the last third of the 7th century BCE, considered in conjunction with the analysis of the distribution and stratigraphic contexts of these handles,

as well as the archaeological data gathered in recent years, all point to a return to the accepted dating of Judah's re-expansion to the last third of the 7th century BCE, following the blow dealt by Assyria at the end of the 8th century BCE. We must, therefore, reject the term "archaeology of the days of Manasseh" as defining the development of the settlement in Judah in the first half of the 7th century BCE under the rule of Manasseh (Finkelstein 1994). It seems that during Manasseh's long reign, Judah continued to be a loyal Assyrian vassal, operating within the restrictions imposed upon it after Sennacherib's campaign, and that its administrative system did not extend to those areas located beyond the hill country. Perhaps, then, we should prefer the term "archaeology of the days of Josiah" and conclude that during his reign, Judah enjoyed relative prosperity and expanded its activities southward and eastward to areas impacted by Sennacherib's campaign; this would be for the last time in the history of Judah, only a few decades before its destruction (Koch and Lipschits 2013). The distribution of the rosette stamp impressions reflects the expansion of the Judahite administration into areas where it could not have operated as long as Assyria ruled the Southern Levant. After the Assyrian withdrawal early in the last third of the 7th century BCE, reconstruction of the Shephelah began along with the establishment of the administrative and military centers at Lachish and Azekah. The Judahite administration was restored in the Beersheba–Arad Valleys with the establishment of both the center at Tel ʿIra and the network of fortresses across the valley. In the eastern areas, the Dead Sea region was repopulated and its natural resources utilized with the establishment of centers at En-Gedi and Jericho. Along the roads descending to the east from Jerusalem, dozens of camp sites and fortresses were built.

The Lion Stamp Impressions: The "Myth of the Empty Land"

The Babylonian onslaught against Judah between 588–586 BCE was a focused campaign, aimed at

---

54. For Jericho, see Weippert and Weippert 1976; Stern 1994: 400; Naʾaman 1989: 36–37. For En-Gedi, see Mazar, Dothan and Dunayevsky 1966; Stern 1994: 404; Stern and Matskevich 2007a; 2007b; Lipschits 2000.

unseating from power the Davidic dynasty, which had repeatedly been disloyal, and at destroying Jerusalem and the Temple, the focal point of anti-Babylonian unrest. On their way to Jerusalem, the Babylonians destroyed the cities of the Shephelah. According to the biblical description (2 Kings 25:1–21), the Babylonian army then besieged the capital, until severe famine led to its surrender. Zedekiah, who tried to flee, was captured and brought before Nebuchadnezzar. His punishment was severe: his sons were slaughtered before his eyes and he was blinded immediately afterwards. The walls of Jerusalem were torn down, and all its buildings, including the city's important symbols—the palace and temple—destroyed by fire.[55]

Judah's western border was attacked and its urban, administrative and military centers destroyed and abandoned. In a more protracted process, the peripheral areas of the kingdom—in the Negev, the Judean Desert, the Jordan Valley and along the Dead Sea shore—presumably collapsed. The small kingdom suffered a severe demographic crisis. Many Judahites, especially the elite and the residents of Jerusalem, were deported to Babylon, while the others suffered the severe consequences of the war campaign and the presence of Babylonian military forces in Judah. Tens of thousands died or were exiled; others decided to abandon Judah or were forced to leave their homes and their lands. The small kingdom, which had existed for 400 years, became a province. This new period in the history of Judah began with greatly reduced borders, with a sparse population, and with the elite and the religious and societal leaders now dwelling in Babylon.[56]

Those who remained in Judah were concentrated in the Benjamin area, north of Jerusalem, and in Ramat Raḥel, the Rephaim Valley, and the area between Bethlehem and Beth-Zur, south of Jerusalem. Gedaliah, a son of Ahikam and a member of an elite and prominent Jerusalemite family (2 Kings 25:22–26; Jer 40–41), was appointed as their leader (Lipschits 2005:

84–97). The center of the new Babylonian government was established at Mizpah, the capital of the province of Judah, where it remained for some 50 years, until Babylon fell to the Persian king Cyrus in 539 BCE. Mizpah continued to be the capital of the Judean province even at the beginning of the Persian period and the reestablishment of Jerusalem as the place of the temple, at least until the mid-5th century BCE (Lipschits 2005: 109–112).

On the basis of the biblical narrative and the archaeological findings from the main Judahite cities destroyed in the Babylonian campaign, many scholars have depicted a scenario of wide-scale destruction and total exile throughout Judah, portraying it as a land bereft of its population (e.g., Stern 2000; Faust 2007; 2012b). However, new finds from the 6th century BCE and new studies, pointing to continuity in the material culture of Judah in the 7th–5th centuries BCE, suggest a different picture. The 65-year period of Babylonian rule, which began in 604 BCE, was a period of continuity in the province's administration, economy and material culture, despite the severe consequences of the war, the settlement crisis (mainly in the urban centers), the disastrous impact on the demography and the destruction of the ancient system of rule in Judah. This is evident particularly in areas to the north of Jerusalem, in the Benjamin region, and to the south of Jerusalem, in the areas of Ramat Raḥel and the Rephaim Valley—and presumably in Jerusalem itself.[57]

The heavy crisis notwithstanding, this period is notable as a bridge linking the material culture of the First Temple period to that of the Second Temple period. Not only did the local material culture continue to exist, but the storage-jar administration continued to function, along with the collection of agricultural produce, as tribute still had to be paid to the ruling empire. This administration could not have existed without continuity in the network of rural settlements—and indeed, it seems that continuity in rural settlements can be identified both to the north and the south of

---

55. For a detailed reconstruction of these events, see Lipschits 2005: 68–84.

56. On the demographic crisis in Judah, see Lipschits 2003; 2005: 258–271.

57. Lipschits 1999a; 2003; 2004; 2005: 185–271; 2007; 2011e.

Jerusalem.[58] This administrative continuity—persisting through the destruction of the First Temple to the period when Judah became first a Babylonian and then a Persian province—is nowhere more evident than in: 1) the continued manufacture of the same type of storage jars as the ones used prior to the Babylonian destruction;[59] 2) the continued stamping of impressions on jars; 3) the continued collection of the jars at the same central center; and 4) even the continued practice of transferring jars to secondary administrative centers, especially to Jerusalem. Throughout this period, the administrative center at Ramat Raḥel continued to function the same way as it did prior to the destruction of Jerusalem, and no change or crisis is evident from the archaeological finds. The second building phase at the site continued to operate in this period without any notable change.[60]

Indeed, the continuation of the administrative system into the 6th century BCE is evident from an assemblage of storage jars recently excavated in a pit at Ramat Raḥel with 6th-century BCE "private" and lion stamp impressions on their bodies, alongside identical storage jars with early types of *yhwd* stamp impressions on their handles (see above, p. 79), all of which resemble the rosette-stamped jars of the late Iron Age. A petrographic study of the clay of these storage jars shows that the central production center had moved from the Shephelah to the environs of Jerusalem. These findings indicate that the storage jars continued to be manufactured in Judah in the 6th century as well—within the framework of the regular vessel production system and as an inseparable component of the stamped storage-jar administrative system.[61]

Much fewer sites and agricultural settlements were involved in the storage-jar administrative system now, compared to before Sennacherib's destruction. The Hebron district was no longer part of the province, and the Elah Valley, now on the province's border, was of lesser importance in the administration and economy of Judah. The province consisted of the small area north of Jerusalem, the Benjamin region, to its south the "Valley of the King" at the foot of Ramat Raḥel, and probably also from the northern Judean Hills until the border of the province at Beth-Zur.[62] The biblical account of the fate of the Benjamin region before, during and after the Babylonian campaign, the archaeological excavations in the central sites of this area, and the information gathered in archaeological surveys all indicate that settlement continued here in the 6th century BCE. A reasonable historical conclusion is, therefore, that even before the destruction of Jerusalem, the Babylonians had selected Mizpah to be the capital of the province and had appointed Gedaliah son of Ahikam as the first governor (Lipschits 2005: 102–118; 2015: 237–246).

The area south of Jerusalem, with the "Valley of the King" (the Rephaim Valley) at its center, probably suffered a similar fate as the Benjamin region. This valley, with its rich alluvium soil and its moderate terraces on the surrounding hill slopes, had been for many years one of the most flourishing regions around Jerusalem and one of the most essential for its existence. The archaeological finds from this valley and its environs,

---

58. On this, see Lipschits 2011f: 68–71; 2015: 238–240; Lipschits and Gadot 2008. Gadot provided an in-depth analysis of the archaeological data from the Jerusalem hinterland (2015). Almost all the rural settlements of the Persian period continued to exist from the Iron Age, showing clear evidence of 6th-century BCE continuity. While some settlements may have been temporarily abandoned in the years prior to the destruction, and some of their residents may have found refuge in Jerusalem during the siege, the continuity in rural settlement nevertheless seems clearer and better established today.

59. The most notable example of continuity in material culture is the production of the storage jars known from the 6th century into the 5th and 4th centuries BCE. These jars are characterized by an oval or sack-shaped body, a convex base, a narrow neck, rounded shoulders, a thick everted rim and four rounded ear-shaped handles extending from the shoulder to the body. They thus exhibit features of the late Iron Age jars, some of which bore rosette stamp impressions on their handles. The storage jars manufactured between the 6th and 4th centuries BCE—Type A in Stern's typology (Stern 1982: 103; Lipschits 2005: 199)—continued the local production tradition and were found only within the province of Yehud.

60. Contrary to Aharoni (1964: 120), no evidence was found at Ramat Raḥel for the destruction of the second building phase in the administrative center, which continued to function in the early 6th century BCE, and there is no evidence for a settlement gap during this period. For the conclusions from the renewed study of Aharoni's excavation findings and the renewed excavation project, which make it clear that the site continued to exist in the 6th century BCE, see Lipschits 1999b: 473–476; Lipschits, Gadot and Freud 2016; Lipschits *et al.* 2017: 81–82.

61. For a detailed summary of the Babylonian–Persian Pit and its contents, see Lipschits *et al.* 2021.

62. For the districts in the province of Judah in the Babylonian and Persian periods, see Lipschits 2017.

consisting mainly of numerous agricultural installations, confirm that its periods of prosperity parallel the periods of activity at Ramat Raḥel—from the late Iron Age through the late Persian and early Hellenistic periods, with no evidence of interruption of activities (Lipschits and Gadot 2008; Gadot 2015).

Rogem Gannim was the main production site in the "Valley of the King" (Greenberg and Cinamon 2006). The site, situated at the western end of the valley, ca. 7 km west of Ramat Raḥel, consists of a large tumulus (9 m high; 40 m in length) with a wine press, storage caves and plastered installations exposed nearby, but not a single structure. This points to an agricultural industry, presumably part of the royal estate in the valley. The pottery excavated here consisted mainly of storage jars, most of which were dated to the late Iron Age and the Persian period (Greenberg and Cinamon 2006: 229). The new conclusions from the study of lion stamp impressions and their dating to the 6th century BCE suggest that the site was active in the Babylonian period as well.[63] It seems that this important production site was situated close to Ramat Raḥel in order to operate in coordination with the administrative center there (Greenberg and Cinamon 2006: 229, 233–235; Lipschits and Gadot 2008; Lipschits and Vanderhooft 2011: 49–50).

Khirbet er-Ras, on a slope in the northern part of the valley, is the only site in which residential buildings were exposed alongside agricultural installations. The finds include pottery dating from the late Iron Age and the Persian period, as well as a few finds from the Middle Bronze Age and the Early Roman period (Gadot 2015: 8–13 and further literature). Edelstein's excavations uncovered a handle with a late *lmlk* stamp impression (Edelstein 2000: 47 and Fig. 12:6), and another handle with a late *lmlk* type was found in Nurit Feig and Omar Abd Rabu's excavations, alongside two lion-stamped handles.[64] Yuval Gadot's excavations revealed two

additional handles with late types of *lmlk* stamp impressions, alongside two rosette handles (Gadot 2015: 11). Analysis of the pottery and these stamp impressions led him to conclude that Khirbet er-Ras was settled mainly in the 7th century BCE (Gadot 2015: 11–13); additional ceramic finds, along with the lion stamp impressions, point to the continued settlement of er-Ras even after the destruction of Jerusalem, in the 6th century BCE (Lipschits 2011f: 62–63; 2015: 238–240; Lipschits and Gadot 2008). Many agricultural installations were found throughout the valley near Khirbet er-Ras— especially wine and oil presses, all containing late Iron Age and Persian period pottery (Greenberg and Cinamon 2006: 223). In addition to the farmstead at Khirbet er-Ras (Feig 1996; Edelstein 2000), there was another farmstead(?) along with wine presses at Beit Ṣafafa (Feig 2003), a residential cave near the Holyland Hotel (Ben-Arieh 2000), and apparently installations and farms in the modern Jerusalem neighborhoods of Manaḥat, Givʿat Massuʾa and several other small sites.[65]

Even though these small sites do not exhibit stratigraphic continuity, Greenberg and Cinamon suggested, on the basis of the chronology of the stamp impressions, that the Rephaim Valley served as the southwestern wine region of Jerusalem from the late 8th to the 5th century BCE (2006: 236–238). Like earlier scholars, they associated the development in the Rephaim Valley in the late 8th century BCE to the development of Jerusalem in that period. Following Naʾaman (2001) and on the basis of the detailed discussion of Lipschits and Gadot (2008), Lipschits and Vanderhooft suggested that the development of the Rephaim Valley was related to the establishment of the administrative center at Ramat Raḥel under Assyrian imperial rule and was not part of Jerusalem's independent development (2011: 49–50).[66] This is based on the assumption that the development in the Rephaim Valley was related to the Kingdom of

---

63. Four storage-jar handles with *lmlk* stamp impressions were uncovered at Rogem Gannim, alongside three handles incised with concentric circles and three others stamped with rosette impressions. Three handles stamped with lion impressions, two with early types of *yhwd* impressions and five with intermediate *yhwd* types were also uncovered. See Greenberg and Cinamon 2006: 231–233, Fig. 3 and 234, 240.

64. Feig and Abd Rabu 1996. The handles have not been published properly and are therefore not included in the corpus presented here.

65. Greenberg and Cinamon (2006: 234–236 and Table 2) mention 35 wine presses (eight in Rogem Gannim, 16 near Manaḥat, five at Givʿat Massuʾa, four at Beit Ṣafafa and two at Khirbet er-Ras), along with numerous plastered installations, such as collection pits and storage caves. The absence of silos, like the ones exposed in Moẓa, and the absence of animal pens known from throughout the Judean Hills also point to a large area that was used as a royal estate and specialized in groves for oil and wine production. See also Faust 2003.

66. See, earlier, the proposal of Greenberg and Cinamon (2006: 238–239).

Judah's system of royal estates in the late 8th and early 7th centuries BCE and apparently took place after Judah had become an Assyrian vassal kingdom. It seems that the valley developed into a royal estate (perhaps the *mmšt* of the *lmlk* seals?) in order to supply oil and wine to the local administration. This would account for the concentration of wine-production installations away from settlements, for wine production and storage, and for the function of Ramat Raḥel as an administrative center throughout the long period of agricultural activity in the valley. The administrative and economic character of the Rephaim Valley, its relation with the Ramat Raḥel administrative center, and the archaeological evidence for continued production and other activities here until the early Hellenistic period point clearly to this area having operated under Babylonian rule as well, like the Benjamin region north of Jerusalem.[67]

A consideration of the data regarding the lion stamp impressions within the broader historical and archaeological context shows that the stamp-impression system and the central collection center at Ramat Raḥel were not related to the royal dynasty in Jerusalem or to the kingdom's administrative system, since these had already been destroyed. When the lion stamp-impression system is viewed as following on the heels of systems that were in operation from the late 8th century BCE through the 7th century and into the early 6th century BCE, and when the role of Ramat Raḥel in the system in the same periods is considered, it becomes evident that their source of authority was the empire ruling Judah— the constant focal point of power, with consistent interests and needs, both before and after the destruction of Jerusalem. The continuity evident in the storage-jar administration thus provides further evidence for the desire of the Babylonian empire to maintain stability in the rural settlements, in the agricultural production around Jerusalem and in the administrative system based in Ramat Raḥel, even after Jerusalem was destroyed and Judah was reduced to a mere province.

The quantitative data regarding the lion stamp impressions further support this picture: the total number of handles bearing lion impressions uncovered at Ramat Raḥel—73 handles, representing ca. 54% of all the lion-stamped handles found—is unprecedented both in terms of number and percentage. The large number of lion-stamped jar handles found in the City of David (31, ca. 23% of all the handles) indicates that, contrary to previous scholarly opinion, the capital had not been completely abandoned. A small number of storage jars continued to reach Jerusalem, and the decline in importance of the secondary administrative sites further suggests that this was their intended destination. Since Jerusalem was no longer the seat of the royal household or the temple, one may surmise that members of the elite, perhaps related to the royal family or to the governmental apparatus, remained in the city, as well as perhaps priests and others who continued to guard the remains of the temple and to preserve its memory and worship. These storage jars were probably intended for them.

A major change took place in the Benjamin region: Nebi Samwil, already prominent alongside Khirbet el-Burj by the end of the First Temple period, now became the sole secondary administrative center in the region, with a relatively large number of storage jars bearing lion stamp impressions sent there—13 such handles were found (9.5% of all the lion stamp impressions uncovered). While a few storage jars also made their way to Mizpah (where five were uncovered) and to Gibeon (two), it seems that a parallel system—that of the *mwṣh* stamp impressions—designed for different purposes was operating at these two sites during the 6th century BCE (and see below, pp. 185–187).

As for the eastern periphery, five handles bearing lion stamp impressions were discovered at En-Gedi, indicating that this site continued to operate in the 6th century BCE and was extremely important for the administration of the Babylonian province. Jericho was traditionally less important for Judah's central administration, and it seems that the single storage jar that was uncovered there, as well as the two jars with early types of *yhwd* stamp impressions, are a clear indication of this. As aforementioned, the system of lion stamp impressions is not represented in the Shephelah at all. Indeed, this is in keeping with the archaeological information we have

---

67. It is not clear on what data Faust bases his view (which he propounds in a series of publications—2003; 2004; 2007; 2012b) that the Rephaim Valley sites were abandoned in the early 6th century BCE and resettled in the Persian period, a view on the basis of which he develops a theory about a crisis in rural settlement in Judah.

regarding the destruction of the main cities in this area during the Babylonian campaign to Jerusalem. The area, which did not manage to recover and regain a central position in the economy of Judah in the late 7th and early 6th century BCE, was, at this stage, a mere shadow of the strong and well-established settlement of the late 8th century BCE.

From the above data it seems that the system of lion stamp impressions reflects the survival of the province of Judah after the severe blow dealt to the kingdom by the Babylonians and manifests its adaptation to the new reality. Both qualitatively and quantitatively, the system is meager compared to the systems prior to the destruction. Technologically, the storage jars and the stamp impressions are of poor quality; in terms of numbers, only half the number of storage jars bearing rosette stamp impressions and concentric circle incisions were found with lion stamp impressions. In terms of the secondary administrative centers and the general distribution—the distribution of lion-stamped handles is on a far smaller scale than that of any of the other systems and is focused mainly in Nebi Samwil, Jerusalem and Ramat Raḥel. Ramat Raḥel was the focal point of the system, as is evident not only by the exceptional concentration at the site of ca. 54% of all the finds, but also by the fact that the finds from Ramat Raḥel represent all the types and sub-types in the system, almost always in large proportions (see above, pp. 68–74).

The *yhwd* Stamp Impressions: The Storage-Jar Administration in the Persian and Hellenistic Periods

The 205 years of Persian rule—from 539/8 to 333 BCE—constitute a well-defined historical period, beginning with the conquest of Babylon by Cyrus, King of Persia, and concluding with the fall of the Persian Empire to Alexander the Great. In the Old Testament, the Persian period begins with the Edict of Cyrus, permitting exiles to return from Babylon and rebuild the Temple in Jerusalem. It is the beginning of the Second Temple period in Judah, defined in the Book of Ezra and

Nehemiah by three central events: the return from Babylon, the rebuilding of the Temple and the restoration of the walls of Jerusalem. This notion is well rooted in the biblical descriptions, as well as in many reconstructions of the history of Judah. This period is considered by many scholars to be crucial—a period in which many of the biblical books were written and redacted and which witnessed spiritual, religious, ritual and social developments that shaped the Judaism of the Second Temple period. It is therefore surprising how little we know of the material culture of this period, even in comparison to earlier periods and certainly in comparison to later ones.

Our understanding of the material culture of the Persian period is impacted by two main factors. First, this is a long interim period in which there were no kings in Judah and consequently no finances, no desire and no permission to carry out large-scale construction projects that would glorify Jerusalem and Judah. There was no army or apparatus that could build border towns and administrative centers, and indeed, the imperial ruler may have tried to downplay any such efforts. Presumably, in the absence of finances and demand, the quality of craftsmen was poorer, and no professional builders, artisans, engravers, or stonemasons could be found in Judah. According to 2 Kings 24:16, in the exile of Jehoiachin, "the king of Babylon brought captive to Babylon all the men of valor, seven thousand, the artisans and the smiths, one thousand, all of them strong and fit for war." This, in my view, is why the timespan between the destruction of the First Temple and the Hasmonean period is characterized by sparse construction, poor material culture and low-quality pottery and seals.[68] Ramat Raḥel is exceptional in its quality of construction and its magnificence, presumably because of its status as the representative of imperial rule and because it served as the collection site for the agricultural produce required as tribute (Lipschits *et al.* 2017: 95–118).

Second, it should be borne in mind that the Persian period is a part of an extremely long timespan between the Babylonian destruction of 586 BCE and the Hasmonean wars in the mid-2nd century BCE, without any destruction or other notable event that

---

68. For a detailed review on the material culture of this period in Judah, see Lipschits 2011d.

could serve as a chronological anchor to determine stages in the development of the material culture. Such chronological anchors could help illuminate the material culture by "freezing" a given stage. In such a long period of continuity, early finds are generally recovered from refuse pits, from fills under later construction projects or on the periphery of settlements. Thus, in the sites that continued to exist throughout the Persian and Hellenistic periods, we can expect only meager Persian period finds (Lipschits 2011d: 188–194).[69]

Given the above, it is clear why no signs have been found in the material culture to point to changes taking place in the transition from Babylonian to Persian Achaemenid rule. Thus, we have no clear markers distinguishing the two centuries of Persian rule as a separate archaeological period and no data enabling us to further distinguish sub-phases within the Persian period. Any division of the Persian period is based upon a projection of our historical knowledge onto the archaeological finds and generally involves a conservative and insufficiently critical interpretation of the biblical texts. Scholars dealing with this period in Judah and its environs had a clear view of the region and the processes it underwent between the 6th and

the 3rd centuries BCE: the periods known as "exilic" and "post-exilic" with Judah characterized as being an "empty land" prior to the Persian period and witnessing a "mass return" at its inception, with a demographic peak in the days of Ezra and Nehemiah (even if a few scholars placed Nehemiah before Ezra or viewed Ezra as an imaginary figure), and clear continuity within the Persian period—from the 5th to the 3rd century BCE, when the Hellenistic period began.

Regarding the material culture of the Persian period, it seems that, with the exception of Ramat Raḥel, discussed below, and the small but important site of En-Gedi,[70] no well-defined stratum with a clear Persian period assemblage has been discerned anywhere in Judah. Even in Jerusalem, the main Persian period finds are isolated sherds and small finds (most notably *yhwd* stamp impressions).[71] In the Persian and the early Hellenistic periods, settlement was concentrated in the City of David, at the upper part of the spur, and most of the archaeological excavations did not take place here.[72] Within the settled area, numerous Persian period sherds and many stamp impressions were found, as is evident in the excavations of R.A.S. Macalister and of Eilat Mazar; here too, however, most of the finds were recovered from late fills

---

69. Albright and Kenyon argued that the archaeological finds point to a cessation of urban settlement in Judah and a focus on rural settlement; see Albright 1960: 142; Kenyon 1965: 296–297, 302. Aharoni (1956: 108; 1964: 120) and Kelso (1968: 38) argued that during the Persian period, the domiciles were outside the cities of the previous period and that this is why they were not exposed in the archaeological excavations. Stern (2001: 461–462) suggested—correctly, in my view—that the meager finds do not necessarily reflect the historical reality of the Persian period, but stem from the abandonment of settlements in this period; since they were never rebuilt, the upper layer became degraded. Furthermore, the extensive construction in the late Hellenistic and the Roman period, in many cases with fortifications and major architectural complexes, may have damaged the earlier Persian period remains.

70. One of the most characteristic Persian period settlements in Judah is En-Gedi Stratum IV; for comprehensive review, see Stern and Matskevich 2007c. Mazar and Dunayevsky (1966: 188–189; 1967: 137–138) dated the Persian settlement at this site to the late 6th or early 5th century BCE, and its end to the late 5th or early 4th century BCE. Today, however, it is clear, especially in light of the Attic pottery recovered from the site, that it continued to exist until the mid-4th century BCE (Stern 2007a: 230). An exceptional wealth of material finds was exposed in this layer, including stamp impressions, local vessels characteristic of the 5th century BCE and Attic pottery; see Mazar, Dothan and Dunayevsky 1963: 59; Pls. D:2, E:2, G:1–2; 1966: 38–39. The renewed study of *yhwd* stamp impressions supports these conclusions; see Stern, Lipschits and Vanderhooft 2007; Lipschits and Vanderhooft 2011: 760–762; and discussion below. The discovery of five handles with lion stamp impressions at En-Gedi indicates, as noted above, that the site continued to exist at least during part of the 6th century BCE.

71. Lipschits 2009a; 2011c; Lipschits and Vanderhooft 2007a; Finkelstein 2008b; 2010. Many Persian period finds were uncovered in the northern part of the City of David spur, mainly in fills under later buildings, presumably built before the late Hellenistic period.

72. These include Kenyon's excavations in Areas A, F, O, W, K and N (not to mention Areas B, D and E on the eastern slope of the southwestern hill), the Shiloh excavations in Areas B, D, E and G, and Reich and Shukrun's excavations in Areas A and B; see Lipschits 2009a: 12–13. Apart from the City of David, and as already shown by Avigad, the entire southwestern hill was abandoned from the end of the Iron Age to the early Hellenistic period. Only a few sherds and small finds from the Persian period were exposed, generally in fills from the Hellenistic and especially the Roman periods, without any stratigraphic context; see Avigad 1972a; 1974; 1983: 61–63; cf. Geva 2000b: 24; 2003b: 524. Many scholars accept this; see Kenyon 1974: 188–255; Tsafrir 1977: 36; Geva 1983; 1994; 2000a: 158; Geva and Reich 2000: 42; Geva and Avigad 2000: 218; Shiloh 1984: 23; Tushingham 1985: 85; Broshi and Gibson 1994; Finkielsztejn 1999: 28; Lipschits 2005: 212–213; Lipschits and Vanderhooft 2007a: 108–112.

and lack any stratigraphic or architectural context.[73] In all other sites in Judah there are only meager Persian period finds. See, for example, Tell es-Sultan (Jericho),[74] Stratum I in Tell en-Naṣbeh (Mizpah)[75] and Bethany;[76] in other Judahite sites the Persian period is hardly represented. These sites include central settlements, described as district centers (Beth-Zur),[77] or central sites in the Benjamin region, such as Gibeon, Tell el-Fûl and Bethel.[78]

73. In Shiloh's City of David excavation report, Stratum IX was attributed to the Persian period, but it does not appear in all the excavation areas (Shiloh 1984: 4, Table 2)—only in Areas D1, D2 and G. Finds from Area E1 and from fills in Area H (west of the Siloam Pool, on the slopes of Mount Zion) were also attributed by Shiloh to this stratum. Persian period sherds and typical stamp impressions were found in Reich and Shukrun's excavations in Areas A and B, above the Kidron Valley, 200–250 m south of the spring (Reich and Shukrun 1998; 2007), presumably originating from the settlement above the spur. De Groot argued that most of the Persian period finds were exposed in Area E, where three Stratum 9 phases were observed (De Groot 2001: 77; 2004: 15; Cahill 1992: 191–198, Fig. 14). At the early stage (9c), dated to the late 6th and early 5th century BCE (De Groot 2001: 78; 2004: 14), there is evidence of secondary use of a large Iron Age building, destroyed, along with the entire city, in 586 BCE (De Groot 2001: 77–78). A level of quarry waste was attributed to the second phase (9b), from the 5th century BCE. De Groot and Ariel associated this phase with the city's reconstruction in the days of Nehemiah, mid-5th century BCE (De Groot 2001: 78; 2004: 15; 2005: 82). A similar quarried surface, exposed in Area D1, ca. 500 m south of Area E, was attributed to Stratum IX (Ariel, Hirschfeld and Savir 2000: 59; Shiloh 1984: 7; De Groot 2001: 78). Additional quarrying activities were noted in the eastern City of David, documented by Bliss and Dickie (1898) and Weil (1920), and in Area K (Ariel and Magness 1992). It thus seems that there was wide-scale construction in Jerusalem in the 5th century BCE. The excavators attributed several terrace walls and a few floors with *tabun*s to the late phase (9a).

74. Sellin and Watzinger exposed the remains of a small village in Tell es-Sultan (Jericho), dated to the 5th and 4th centuries BCE. The ceramic assemblage includes a few imported Attic vessels, local Persian period decorated ceramic sherds, as well as ten *yhwd* stamp impressions and one lion stamp impression; Sellin and Watzinger 1913: 79–82, 147–148, Fig. 186, Pls. 1, 3, 42. See also Stern's re-dating of the pottery of the period (1982: 38). Garstang's 1930–1936 excavations and Kenyon's 1952–1958 excavations added only meager data about the Persian period; see Kenyon 1974: 201. The most important find recovered was a stamp impression reading *yhwd/orio* (Hammond 1957a; Vanderhooft and Lipschits 2007: 16–17; Lipschits and Vanderhooft 2011: 107–111). Following Stern (1982: 38), we attribute the settlement here to the 5th–4th centuries BCE, but the meager ceramic finds preclude any conclusions about Judah's material culture.

75. The excavations at Tell en-Naṣbeh revealed many Persian period finds, mostly from cisterns throughout the site. The finds include a bronze coin, dated by Albright and Boyce to 406–393 BCE (McCown 1947: 229) and re-dated by Bellinger to the 5th and 4th centuries BCE (Stern 1982: 32); various types of stamp impressions (including *yhwd* ones); and a limestone incense altar fragment. See McCown 1947: 154–155, 164–172, 174, 227, 236–237, 259, 275, Pls. 1:102, 14:56–57, 84; and Stern 1982: 31–32; 2001: 432–433). Scholars noted two pits with homogeneous Persian period assemblages (Stern 1982: 31–32): Pit 304, dated to 600–450 BCE and Pit 361, dated to the late 5th–early 4th centuries BCE. The former contained an ostracon with six letters, dated by Albright and Torrey to the 8th–7th centuries BCE (McCown 1947: 31–32, n. 9) and by Wampler to the 7th century (1941: 31). An amphora, dated to 540–520 BCE, and two kylix sherds, 490–420 BCE, were also recovered from this cistern (Wampler 1941: 31). For the finds from this cistern, see Wampler 1941: 31–36; McCown 1947: 135, and for the finds from the second cistern, see Wampler 1941: 36–43; McCown 1947: 137. Two Greek sherds were dated to 530–500 BCE (Stern 1982: 206). A *mwṣh* stamp impression and another stamp impression, not detailed, were uncovered (Wampler 1941: 36). Two additional cisterns, No. 183, the second phase of which was dated to 450–200 BCE (McCown 1947: 132–133), and No. 191 (McCown 1947: 133–134), included Persian period finds. Notable are several "second-rate East Greek ware" and Attic vessels dated to 500–420 BCE and a Clazomenian sherd, dated to 540–530 BCE (McCown 1947: 175–178, 304, Tables 59–60). Due to the Attic vessels dated to 540–420 BCE and a bronze coin, an Athenian tetradrachm imitation from 406–393 BCE (Stern 2001: 432), found alongside middle types of *yhwd* stamp impressions, the site appears to have existed throughout most of the Persian period. However, this was a period of decline (Lipschits 1999a: 156–170).

76. In contrast to Tell en-Naṣbeh, the Persian period finds at Bethany—pottery and stamp impressions—were recovered mainly from a fill from the Middle Ages (Locus 65), and not in an archaeological assemblage or architectural context; see Saller 1957: 222, 237; cf. Barkay 1985: 303.

77. The Beth-Zur excavators did not define a settlement layer from the Persian period, and because the site is terraced, most of the pottery was unstratified (Sellers and Albright 1931: 4; Sellers 1933: 10, 32). Contra Sellers and Albright (1931: 8–9; see also Sellers 1933: 43; Sellers *et al.* 1968: 28, 54), who argued for a settlement gap between the 6th–2nd centuries BCE, P.W. Lapp (1970: 185) dated the Hoard 44 pottery to the last quarter of the 6th century BCE, a dating supported by N. Lapp (1981: 86–87). Reich (1992) suggested that the Beth-Zur fortress was the regional governor's residence in the Persian period. However, it is unlikely that settlement was renewed in the early 6th century BCE and that the gap between the Iron Age and the Persian period is narrower than presumed by the excavators, as this relies on a small ceramic assemblage, not represented in other areas of the site. See Carter 1999: 154–155.

78. El-Jib/Gibeon shows evidence of 6th-century activity (Stern 1982: 32–33; 2001: 433; Lipschits 1999a: 167–171; Edelman 2003: 157), but excavations did not expose typical Persian period vessels or yhwd stamp impressions (Lipschits and Vanderhooft 2011: 57, Finkelstein 2008a: 13). Pritchard noted only minimal evidence from the late 6th–early 5th century BCE, but nevertheless argued for a settlement here in this period (Pritchard 1962: 163; 1993: 513). The finds support Stern's claim (1982: 32–33; 2001: 433) for late 6th–early 5th century BCE activity. See also Edelman 2003: 163–164; Lipschits 2005: 243–245. Tell el-Fûl was also sparsely settled in the late 6th–early 5th century BCE (Lipschits 1999a: 177–178), remaining desolate until the Hellenistic period. N. Lapp (1981: 39, 59) associated the site's abandonment to the restoration of Jerusalem and migration there in the early Persian period. See Stern 2001: 321–322. 80. At least part of the Bethel site was settled in the 6th century BCE (Stern 2001: 432), as is evident from some pottery finds (Kelso 1968: Pl. 67:8) and a Babylonian seal purchased in the nearby village of Beitin (Kelso 1968: 37; Stern 1982: 31). Kelso (1968: 37, 38) suggested that the site was destroyed in the latter half of the 6th century BCE (and see Lipschits 1999a: 171–172; Stern 2001: 432). No yhwd-stamped handles or any Persian period settlement layer was uncovered. However, excavations were not conducted in the village of Beitin, next to the spring (Kelso 1968: 38). Finkelstein and Singer-Avitz (2009: 42) claim that the site was at most sparsely settled in the Persian period, but cf. Lipschits 2017.

The main conclusion to be drawn from the archaeological finds from Judah is that during the Persian period, there was a decline in the urban settlements, a process that began in the Assyrian period and continued into the Babylonian period. This phenomenon is in marked contrast to the continuity noted in rural sites, particularly in the northern Judean Hills and in the Benjamin region.[79] In most of these small sites, pottery and other Persian period finds were recovered, but usually in small quantities and not in a clean assemblage.[80]

Given the nature of the Persian period finds from sites in Judah, it is clear why the Ramat Raḥel excavation finds are so important and unique for understanding the material culture of the province of Judah in this period. This is true even though this site is not a typical Judahite settlement and, due to its hilly terrain, it has a very complex and problematic stratigraphy. As aforementioned, the first building phase at the site was dated to the late 8th or early 7th century BCE, when Judah was a vassal kingdom under the rule of the Assyrian Empire. The site was presumably originally built as a Judahite administrative center where agricultural products— mainly storage jars filled with olive oil and wine—were gathered. Even in this early stage, it was the most magnificent structure in Judah, built of hewn stones and adorned with stone capitals, decorated window balustrades, crenellations lining its roofs and other stone ornaments (Lipschits *et al.* 2017: 36–56).

The monumentality of the site and its place in the landscape were designed in the second building phase, probably during the latter half of the 7th century BCE. At this stage the complex was surrounded by a magnificent garden, built on leveled bedrock, with large pools, open and covered water canals and other water installations. There is no evidence of destruction or of any settlement gap in the early 6th century BCE, when Jerusalem was destroyed and Judah became a Babylonian province (Lipschits *et al.* 2017: 57–94). The magnificent complex and royal garden continued to exist throughout the 6th century BCE and was even extended in the Persian period with a square annex (600 m²; 20 × 30 m) attached to its

northwestern corner, near the large northern pool of the second building phase. This appears to have been planned as an expansion of the existing compound—an extension of the western tower overlooking the Rephaim Valley— rather than as a separate building. The structure was built on a lower level than the tower and may have been just as high. This might account for the massive nature of the foundation trenches, which reached a depth of 2–3 m and a width of ca 2.5 m. The sections of the walls preserved at the bottom of the foundation trenches show a unique building technique, unknown in the region before the Roman period. In this technique, which could be called "half casting," the large *nari* stones were placed in front of the wall in high and equal courses. The face of the stone was cut smoothly while the rest of the stone was turned toward the inside of the wall. The mass of masonry inside the wall turned into a strong solid unit onto which a grey bonding mixture, rich with ash and quicklime, was poured, affording it an unusual strength and the quality of concrete casting. Only one floor section, also unique in construction method, has been exposed to date. It was set onto a concrete layer, 15 cm thick, over a foundation of dressed limestones (Lipschits *et al.* 2017: 98–105).

There is clear evidence for dating this building phase to a time between the late 6th and the late 4th centuries BCE, with two sub-phases. The unparalleled building technique and strength of the structure suggest Persian imperial involvement.[81] Furthermore, a study of the garden identified rare plants, as well as plants appearing in the Levant for the first time (Lipschits, Gadot and Langgut 2012; Langgut *et al.* 2013; Lipschits *et al.* 2017: 108–111), including the first appearance of citron and walnut trees in the Levant. The cedar of Lebanon, not generally found in the dry hilly region of Jerusalem, must have been imported from afar and planted in the garden, as well as willow and birch, which usually grow in the region, but in stream beds rather than semi-arid lands. Evidence was also found for water plants such as water lilies and for the more common flora of the region, such as myrtle, grapevine, fig and pomegranate.

---

79. See Carter 1994; 1999: 137–166; Lipschits 1999a; 2003: 326–355; 2005: 240–261; Milevski 1996–97.

80. A most instructive example of this was recently presented by Gadot (2015).

81. See Lipschits *et al.* 2009a: 70–72; 2017: 104–105; Lipschits, Gadot and Langgut 2012: 68–75.

As aforementioned, in the southeastern corner of the site a large pit was exposed with hundreds of pottery vessels, including dozens of storage jars, some with handles bearing early types of *yhwd* stamp impressions and a few with "private" stamp impressions from the 6th century BCE, along with lion stamp impressions on storage-jar bodies. These finds, together with some 500 Persian and Hellenistic stamp impressions uncovered at the site, constitute the strongest evidence that Ramat Raḥel was the main center of the storage-jar administration system. It also suggests that the Persian period system was a continuation of the *lmlk* and rosette systems from the late Iron Age, as well as of the lion stamp-impression system from the Babylonian period.

The other vessels uncovered in the pit also attest to continuity from the 6th to the 5th centuries BCE, and demonstrate that there was no real change from the "exilic period" to the early Persian period. On the contrary, the pottery of Ramat Raḥel shows continuity in the local pottery tradition from the late Iron Age and to the Persian period—a tradition of potters in Judah that continued uninterrupted from the 9th–8th until the 4th–3rd centuries BCE (Fig. 7.1; Lipschits 2005: 192–206; 2011f; Lipschits *et al.* 2017: 98–100). To date, the Ramat Raḥel ceramic assemblage is the only one that fills the missing 150 years between the late Iron Age and the Persian period, supporting the theoretical assumption that the local ceramic traditions continued to exist in the 6th century BCE (Lipschits 2005: 192–210). These traditions include the Persian period storage jar (Stern's Type A) (Stern 1982: 103; see also Lipschits 2005: 199), with features resembling the late Iron Age "rosette storage jars" in Judah. A jar of this type was uncovered at Ramat Raḥel bearing a "private" stamp impression alongside a lion stamp impression, together with storage jars bearing early *yhwd* stamp impressions—all similar to the "rosette storage jars" in size and proportions. This is a clear indication that these storage jars continued to be manufactured in Judah in the 6th and early 5th centuries BCE and that only later, in the 5th–4th centuries BCE, did they develop into the "classic" Persian storage jar (Stern's Types B and C; Stern 1982: 103–104, see also Lipschits 2005). On many of these storage jar handles there were middle types of *yhwd* stamp impressions, as well as later ones.

The same is true of other pottery vessels from the Persian period, which were manufactured continuously from the late Iron Age, through the 6th and until the early 5th century BCE. In the 5th century BCE, new features appeared in the jar's shape and decoration and in its

Fig. 7.1: Various types of stamped storage jars:
1) *lmlk* storage jar from Tel Azekah
2) rosette storage jar from Tel Malḥata
3) early *yhwd* storage jar, typologically similar to the lion storage jar from Ramat Raḥel
4) *yhwd* storage jar from Ramat Raḥel

production techniques and material, which is probably due to foreign influences and gradual developments, interaction with neighboring regions and cultures, as well as with the Babylonian and Persian cultures and later with the Hellenistic culture. The features typical of almost all Persian period vessels—a thick rim inclining outward, a convex base or elevated disc base, an oval or sack body, and elevated or suspended handles—emerged only in the 5th century BCE (Lipschits 2005: 192–210).

In the southern part of the garden of the second building phase at Ramat Raḥel, three storage jars, a juglet and several other vessels were found on a floor beneath a destruction layer. This assemblage dates the destruction and abandonment of the building to the end of the Persian period, in the 4th century BCE. This small late Persian/ early Hellenistic assemblage completes the early Babylonian–Persian assemblage. These two new ceramic assemblages from Ramat Raḥel contribute to our knowledge about the chronology and typology of Persian period vessels. A continuous development may be discerned from the early Persian period (late 6th–early 5th century BCE) to the "classical" pottery vessels of the mid-5th century BCE, and to the well-known vessels from the late Persian and early Hellenistic periods (4th century BCE). The discovery of stamp impression types, which are securely dated, facilitates the dating of such assemblages, and makes it easier to identify them in other sites, including small and rural ones, which yield very few Persian period ceramic vessels. This serves as the basis for a revised dating of the various sites and for drawing up a map of the sites for each of the different phases of the 200-year Persian period.

In recent years, with advances in the research of stamp impressions on storage-jar handles, these impressions have become a new archaeological tool for dating settlement layers and finds from the Persian period. Not only are they key to dating the various stages between the 6th century and the first half of the 2nd century BCE, but they are also important for understanding the general economic and administrative structure in these periods. We note continuity in all these aspects from the late Iron Age to the Hellenistic period. The cataloguing of the many types of

yhwd stamp impressions (Lipschits and Vanderhooft 2011) has led to the typological and chronological differentiation among the early types (from the late 6th–5th centuries BCE), the middle types (from the 4th–3rd centuries BCE) and the late types (from the 2nd century BCE). It is the main tool for understanding how the system developed in Judah and for interpreting Judah's administrative, economic and historical significance. The *yhwd* stamp impressions are one of the only tools at our disposal to sub-divide the Persian period and to determine the development processes that took place within the era— during the 200 years of Persian imperial rule and the first 200 years of the Hellenistic period.

In Ramat Raḥel, 57.5% of the handles with *yhwd* stamp impressions were uncovered—372 out of the 647 stamp impressions included in the current corpus. With regard to the early types of *yhwd* stamp impressions, 127 were found at Ramat Raḥel (77% of the 165 finds). The percentage at Ramat Raḥel declines to ca. 63% for the middle types (212 stamped handles out of 338 were found at this site), and further drops to 23% for the late types (33 stamped handles out of a total of 144).

Jerusalem played only a peripheral role in the administrative system of the *yhwd* stamp impressions, especially in its early stages. When we combine the data from all the excavation areas around the city, including the Western Hill, within the boundaries of 2nd-century BCE Jerusalem, 162 handles of the various *yhwd* types have been uncovered (25% of the entire corpus). Most of these were found in the City of David (135 handles; ca. 83% of the Jerusalem finds), with only 27, all of the late group, found in the Western Hill.[82] Of all the finds from Jerusalem, only 17 handles were stamped with early *yhwd* impressions (ca. 10% of the early types), demonstrating the city's insignificance in the stamp-impression system of the late 6th–5th centuries BCE. The 59 handles stamped with middle types of *yhwd* impressions were also uncovered solely in the City of David (ca. 17.5% of the middle types; note further that most of them—40 handles—bore the same type of stamp impression, indicating that a single seal was used). This means that Jerusalem did not play a significant role in

---

82. This number is in keeping with the paucity of Persian period pottery finds in the Western Hill. See summary in Lipschits and Vanderhooft 2007a; cf. Lipschits 2011c; 2012b. The scarcity of such finds in the Western Hill and their late dating to the 2nd century BCE further supports the generally accepted view that the Western Hill was devoid of settlement throughout the Persian period.

the *yhwd* stamp-impression system in the 4th and 3rd centuries BCE either. Of the 86 stamp impressions of the late types found in Jerusalem (ca. 60% of the 144 stamped handles attributed to these types), 27 appear for the first time beyond the City of David spur—in the Western Hill and its environs. This means that the Western Hill began to develop and became a significant part of the city during the 2nd century BCE, perhaps "as an accelerated spontaneous-organic process, in which the settlement in Jerusalem expanded westward from the traditional residential area in the City of David up the slope of the southwestern hill" (Geva 1985: 29). The percentage of *yhwd* stamp impressions is much higher than that of the Rhodian ones, of which only ca. 5% were found on the Western Hill. It is unlikely that this discrepancy points to the different populations living in the two areas of the city prior to the 141 BCE destruction of the Acra by Simon (1 Macc 13:49–51);[83] a more likely explanation would be that the first settlement of the Western Hill took place at a later date, when there was a sharp decline in Rhodian wine imports (Ariel 1990: 21–25; 2000: 267–269).

If we consider the *yhwd* stamp-impression system as a whole, it should be emphasized that 82.5% of all the stamp impressions were uncovered in Ramat Raḥel and Jerusalem (534 out of 647). The origin of 13 additional *yhwd*-stamped handles is unknown. Thus, ca. 15.5% of the corpus (100 stamped handles in total) originated from other sites. In most of the sites that yielded a significant number of *yhwd*-stamped handles, these belong to the early or middle types. This is in keeping with the broader archaeological picture of Judah and the changes it underwent during the Hellenistic period—especially in the 2nd century BCE—but can also inform us about changes in material culture in the various districts of Judah during the two centuries of the Persian period.

Significantly, in all the sites that yielded many *yhwd*-stamped handles, not a single handle was uncovered with a late type; the vast majority belong to the middle types and a few are of the early types.[84]

The early group of *yhwd* stamp impressions is characterized by its great diversity, with 12 types,[85] suggesting that the administrative method had not yet been firmly established. This group may be divided into two sub-groups. One includes six types that yielded a great number of stamp impressions (Types 1, 4, 6, 7, 10, 12). They have been uncovered mainly in Ramat Raḥel and Jerusalem: of a total of 150 handles, 125 were uncovered at Ramat Raḥel (ca. 83%), 14 in the City of David (ca. 9%) and only 12 (ca. 8%) were found elsewhere. The second sub-group includes the other six types, of which very few stamp impressions were found—of a total of 14, only three were uncovered in the City of David and two in Ramat Raḥel. If we disregard these types—considering them *ad hoc* types, of which only a few jars were stamped with a distribution mainly in sites far from Ramat Raḥel and Jerusalem (Gezer, Jericho, Tel Ḥarasim, Ṣuba, Mizpah, Nebi Samwil, Moẓa, Tel Nimrin in Transjordan and one in the city of Babylon)—the dominance of Ramat Raḥel and the relative insignificance of the City of David in the administrative system of the early *yhwd* stamp impressions becomes even more marked (Fig. 7.2). Furthermore, if we consider that the City of David is mainly represented by one type (Type 1: אחיב/פחוא, *'ḥyb / pḥw'* (see above, Fig. 4.26); with nine stamped handles uncovered in the City of David out of a total of 18 handles), the insignificance of Jerusalem stands out even more. As for the other types of stamp impressions, four types did not yield any stamp impressions in the City of David; five types yielded a

---

83. See Finkielsztejn 1999: 28–31, with further literature. Cf. Ariel 1990: 25; 2000: 269, 276–280; and see also Geva 2003a: 115–116 on the conservative nature of the traditional agrarian society.

84. This is true of Tell en-Naṣbeh, where of the 19 stamped handles (ca. 3% of the *yhwd* corpus), only one belongs to the early group and 18 to the middle types—and not a single handle was found with a late type of *yhwd* stamp impression; of Nebi Samwil, where 16 handles were recovered (ca. 3%), only three from the early group and 13 from the middle types; of Jericho, where 18 stamped handles were found (ca. 3%), only two belonging to the early group and 16 to a middle type; of En-Gedi, where of the ten handles recovered (ca. 1.7%), three belonged to the early group and seven to middle types; and of Rogem Gannim, one of the small and important agricultural production centers where *yhwd*-stamped storage jars were filled—there seven such handles were found (ca. 1%), two with early types and five with middle types. In Gezer, far from the center of Judah, the picture was slightly different: of the eight handles recovered, two bore early types of *yhwd* stamp impressions, one belonged to a middle type and five were stamped with late types.

85. One early type has yielded only one stamp impression; three types have yielded two; one type—three, one type—four; one type—five; one type—six; two types—11; one type—16; and from one type only we know of a significant number of 37 stamp impressions.

Fig. 7.2: The distribution of the early types of *yhwd* stamp impressions

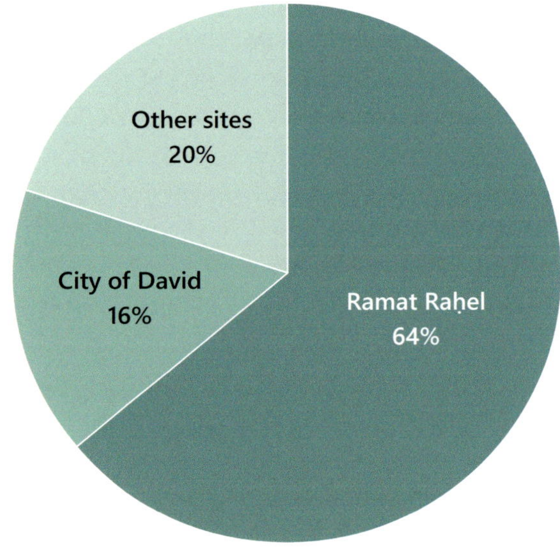

single stamp impression there; and two types yielded two in Jerusalem.

Furthermore, Type 1 is exceptional, even within the group of early types, in terms of its inscription, the many stamp impressions produced with a single seal, the distribution of the stamp impressions in two centers, and the archaeological and paleographic evidence for the early nature of this type (Lipschits and Vanderhooft 2011: 83–87; cf. Naveh 1970: 59–60; Ariel and Shoham 2000: 138). We may conclude from this (contra Ariel and Shoham 2000: 138) that Jerusalem is poorly represented in the administration that employed the early types of *yhwd* stamp impressions. The centrality of Ramat Raḥel, on the other hand, is striking. Interestingly, three types of stamp impressions that were not found at Ramat Raḥel are not present in Jerusalem either. As for two other types that were not found at Ramat Raḥel, a single stamp impression was uncovered in the City of David; both of these early types appear to have a limited distribution.

The most significant change in the *yhwd* stamp-impression system occurred during the Persian period, probably in the late 5th or early 4th century BCE: the shape, style, paleography and orthography of the stamp impressions changed, apparently due to the growing importance of the Southern Levant to the Persian Empire after it lost its hold over Egypt (Lipschits and Vanderhooft

2007b). The unification in the forms of the stamp impression in Judah was one of the many changes in the Southern Levant. The Achaemenid rule strengthened its control over the peripheral parts of the empire, as indicated by the Aramaic epigraphic finds from the southern Shephelah, from the establishment of the administrative center at Lachish (Fantalkin and Tal 2006), and apparently from the construction of forts in Judean hills, the Shephelah and the Negev. The Persian army had a need for agricultural products, such as grain, wine and oil, when Persian soldiers and officials settled in the area within the framework of preparations for military campaigns to Egypt or defensive battles against the Egyptian army and its allies (Lipschits and Vanderhooft 2007b).

The changes that occurred at this stage were due to the tighter Persian control, manifest in the distribution of the stamp impressions with the name or abbreviation of the province becoming the only information appearing on them. The name of the local ruler became of no importance, leaving only the origin of the produce—the name of the province. Additional regional centers were built, and along with the 212 handles stamped with middle types of *yhwd* impressions uncovered at Ramat Raḥel, and 59 such handles found in the City of David, 67 handles with these stamp impressions were exposed in another nine sites: 18 at Tell en-Naṣbeh, 16 at Jericho, 13 at Nebi Samwil, seven at En-Gedi and five at Rogem Gannim (Fig. 7.3).[86]

The system that used the middle types of *yhwd* stamp impressions operated for a long period during the 4th and 3rd centuries BCE, apparently continuing into the early 2nd century BCE. This reflects the continuity of the administration from the end of the Persian period to the Ptolemaic period, with no notable change in material finds. Similar continuity was observed in the local coins from this period (Meshorer 2001: 11), and in both cases paleo-Hebrew and the lapidary Aramaic script were used simultaneously. This is also evident in the coins of Samaria (Meshorer 2001: 22).

The next change in the *yhwd* stamp-impression system occurred only under Hasmonean rule, and even then continuity is evident in the transition from the middle-type to the late-type system. In the latter, only the name of the province appears, abbreviated to יה (*yh*) or in the paleo-Hebrew script with the sign ט (*t*). At this point, the secondary centers that existed in the middle-type system—probably evidence of bonuses or payments in storage jars, in order to get the gold, silver and other goods for the annual tribute payments—disappeared.[87]

Jerusalem, where 60% of the finds were uncovered, became the only administrative center. With the exception of Ramat Raḥel, which was probably abandoned during part of this period, no other site except for Gezer and Bethany yielded more than a single stamped handle (Fig. 7.4). This is an indication of the total concentration of storage jars at Jerusalem during the establishment of Hasmonean rule. These were joined by new types of storage jars marked with *yršlm* stamp impressions, whose purpose was also apparently to help consolidate the government in the new capital of the Hasmonean dynasty.

The Short-Lived *Ad Hoc* Systems: Their Significance for an Understanding of the History of Judah

In the course of the six centuries in which storage jars were systematically stamped, three systems were in operation for brief periods. These systems—involving "private," *mwṣ* and *yršlm* stamp impressions—are designated as *ad hoc*, as they appear to have operated for a brief period concurrently with one of the regular

Fig. 7.3: The distribution of the middle types of *yhwd* stamp impressions

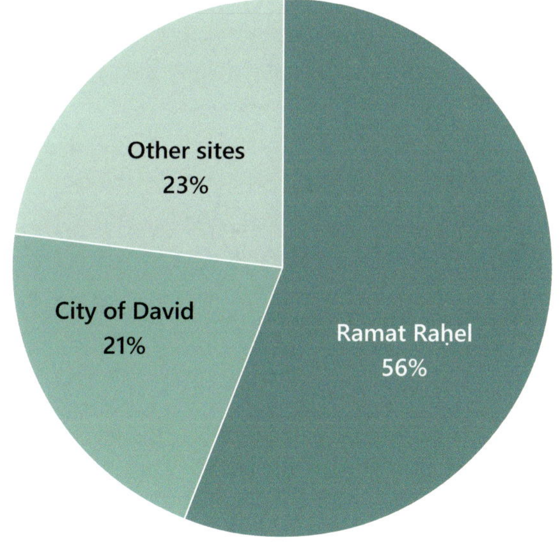

---

86. A single handle was found in each of four sites beyond the borders of Judah—Gezer, Khirbet Nisya, Kadesh-Barnea and Tell Jemmeh—and the origin of four additional handles is unknown.

87. Along with Ramat Raḥel's 33 handles and Jerusalem's 86 handles (including the City of David and the Western Hill), only 16 stamped handles were exposed at 11 sites: five at Gezer, two at Bethany and nine handles from nine sites; the origin of eight additional handles is unknown.

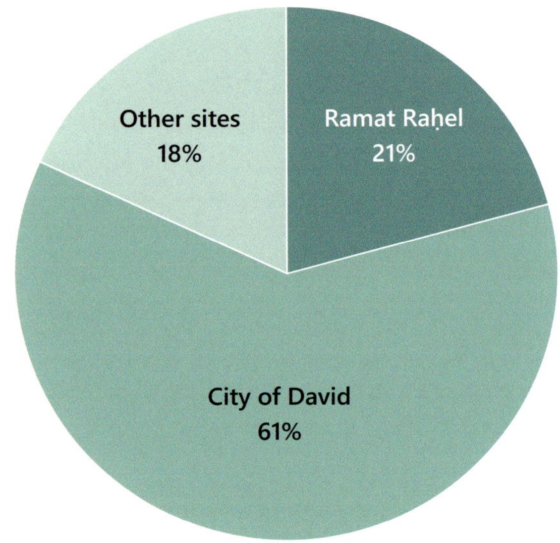

Fig. 7.4: The distribution of the late types of *yhwd* stamp impressions

storage-jar administrative systems, and they apparently served a specific purpose. The common denominator of these systems is that they are represented by very small numbers, compared to the regular systems, and their main collection centers were not at Ramat Raḥel: Lachish was presumably the center for the "private" stamp impressions, Mizpah for the *mwṣh* stamp impressions and Jerusalem for the *yršlm* stamp impressions. The concentration of the stamped jars at these three centers is exceptional in scope, and these systems do not exhibit the regular pattern in which stamped jars were collected at one center and sent from there to secondary administrative centers.

Our historical conjecture is that these systems functioned in conjunction with the regular storage-jar administrative systems during three separate periods when a localized need for a supply of oil and wine arose. In order to meet this need, exceptional use was made of the familiar system of stamped storage jars—perhaps concurrently with that system.

The "Private" Stamp Impressions

In the case of the "private" stamp impressions, it was the need to amass food reserves in the main fortifications of the Shephelah in advance of Sennacherib's campaign; as stated above, this system began to operate a few years before that campaign and likely did not continue after 701 BCE. The "private" stamp-impression system is much more restricted in scope than the *lmlk* system,[88] and the distribution of such handles is more limited than the *lmlk* stamp impressions. Nevertheless, in contrast to the *lmlk*-stamped handles, whose distribution was more or less the same in the Shephelah and in the Jerusalem region (northern Judean Hills and Benjamin), most of the "private" stamp impressions were centered in the Shephelah.[89] If we take into account that the "private" stamp impressions were used for a much shorter time than the *lmlk* stamp impressions, we may conclude that the "private" stamp-impression system reflects a short period in which the *lmlk* system was mobilized for Hezekiah's preparations for Sennacherib's campaign. The storage jars continued to be manufactured in the same site in the Shephelah, and some were even stamped with both *lmlk* and "private" seals. It is possible that in preparation for the revolt, further seals were added, denoting the recipient of the royal estate's products, who was responsible for a known quantity of supplies for the fortified cities and military warehouses.

---

88. Only 183 handles with "private" stamp impressions were uncovered in archaeological excavations and surveys, compared to some 1,500 handles with *lmlk* stamp impressions—a ratio of approximately 1:7. See also Barkay and Vaughn 2004: 2171.

89. Of the 183 handles of known provenance with "private" stamp impressions, 125 were recovered from the Shephelah. In Jerusalem, on the other hand, only 13 handles bore "private" stamp impressions, in Ramat Raḥel 19, and in all the sites of the region of Benjamin 11.

This would account for the significant concentration of the "private" stamp impressions in the Shephelah (ca. 70% of the finds)—since it served as the western boundary of Judah, and since this was Judah's most important region, it was anticipated that the Assyrians would attack from that direction.

This interpretation of the data concerning the "private" stamp-impression system seems likely—contra Naʾaman (1986), who attributed the entire *lmlk* system to the preparations for the Assyrian onslaught—as this system is the only one that fits the time and place of this campaign. The *lmlk* stamp-impression system, which had already developed for a brief period in order to meet the need to pay heavy taxes to the Assyrian Empire, was harnessed to this purpose for a short period. As discussed above, the system dealt with transporting royal produce to royal office holders, who received the supplies and were responsible for their distribution. After Sennacherib's campaign, with the reestablishment of the Assyrian Empire in the region in general and in Judah in particular, the "private" stamp impression system disappeared; in contrast, the *lmlk* stamp-impression system, a component of Judah's economic and administrative organization under Assyrian rule, continued to function for a few decades.

The *mwṣh* Stamp Impressions

The *mwṣh* system also appeared for only a brief and well-defined period. Only 43 *mwṣh* stamp impressions are known, mainly stamped by the same seal. Most of these impressions (30; ca. 70%) were found at one center—Tell en-Naṣbeh (Mizpah), the capital of the new province that was established after the fall of Jerusalem—and only one was found at Ramat Raḥel. Four stamped handles were found in Jerusalem, four in Gibeon (near Tell en-Naṣbeh) and two in Jericho.[90] Given the fact that the lion stamp-impression system was in operation during this same period—a system that in many ways continued

the rosette system and was later replaced by the early *yhwd* system in the Persian period—it appears that the *mwṣh* stamp impressions constituted an *ad hoc* system, established for a specific need and functioning alongside the regular stamp-impression system of the time. Given the geographical distribution of the *mwṣh*-stamped handles and the assumption that Moẓa was an agricultural estate integrated into the kingdom and provincial administrative system, it is reasonable to suggest that the *mwṣh* system was intended to fulfill the needs of the new governor dwelling in Mizpah. He would have needed a source of supply for himself and his people without making demands on the agricultural collection system intended for imperial tax payments. The Moẓa estate might have originally belonged to the royal dynasty in Jerusalem, but it is not unlikely that after the destruction and exile, the Babylonians transferred it to the governor for use as a source of income and supply for himself and his people. We may further postulate that within a few years, after the province's administrative system had been set up, the governor found his own sources of income and no longer required the "governor's bread" (cf. Neh 5:14); thus, the *mwṣh* stamp-impression system went out of use.

The *yršlm* Stamp Impressions

The *yršlm* system operated alongside the system of the late *yhwd* stamp impressions. As in the case of the other two *ad hoc* systems, only a few *yršlm* stamp impressions were found; furthermore, they contain a symbol, after centuries in which the regular seals contained script alone. Fifty-eight *yršlm* stamp impressions were found within Jerusalem (ca. 56% of the finds), a clear indication of the status of the renewed place of the independent Judean leaders.[91] The *yršlm* stamp-impression system is also unique in its use of vessels other than storage jars.[92]

During the Hasmonean period, despite the gradual disappearance of the *yhwd* stamp impressions and the

---

90. One additional *mwṣh* handle was found at Ṣuba, probably a production center for wine or oil, and one came from an unknown location.

91. The distribution of the *yršlm* stamp impressions in the City of David and in the Ophel (43 handles) and in the Western Hill (ten handles) points to a rise in the significance of the Western Hill during the 2nd century BCE; see also Reich 2003: 259. A similar phenomenon was noted by Lipschits and Vanderhooft (2007c) with respect to the late types of *yhwd* stamp impressions; see above, pp. 82–88.

92. Thus, for example, one *yršlm* stamp impression was found on a cooking pot from Tel Yarmouth, and four on jugs from the City of David and the Jewish Quarter.

sharp decline in the status of Ramat Raḥel, agricultural products apparently continued to be collected in storage jars; thus, quite a lot of storage jars were uncovered at Ramat Raḥel—some 33 handles were found with *yršlm* stamp impressions (ca. 32% of the *yršlm* stamp impressions). Interestingly, there were hardly any other sites where *yršlm* stamp impressions were found and none in which more than one handle was uncovered.

It is likely that upon the establishment of Hasmonean rule, there was a strong need to strengthen the status of Jerusalem and to gather more supplies there, and indeed, part of the late *yhwd* stamp-impression system may have been geared toward this end. Nevertheless, it seems this was the goal of the *yršlm* system, with its special symbol: the letters of the name of the capital interspersed between the points of the pentagram. At the same time, the use of storage jars stamped with late types of *yhwd* impressions gradually declined and came to an end.[93]

The distribution of the *yršlm*-stamped handles corroborates our archaeological and historical knowledge about the sharp decline in the status of Ramat Raḥel: the magnificent administrative center that had existed from the late 8th century BCE was obliterated, along with all its splendid buildings and the royal garden. A Jewish village was established above its ruins, as is evident from the numerous finds exposed here, such as many ritual baths and the columbaria. A Hasmonean fortress may have stood next to the village (see Lipschits *et al.* 2011: 37; 2017: 119–128).

Summary

The existence of these three stamp-impression systems as *ad hoc* mechanisms, designed for short periods of time, in different periods and for different needs, shows that the idea arose out of the regular jar-stamping system in operation at the time—a mechanism that was used for 600 years. These short-term systems prove that in terms of the various governmental mechanisms operating in Judah, the storage-jar administration was a fact of daily life. It was a mechanism that could be imitated and duplicated for specific needs, with full confidence that the purpose for which it was duplicated would be achieved.

---

93. Ariel and Shoham (2000: 161) argued that the appearance of the name of the city for the first time in the *yršlm* stamp impressions, rather than the name of the province, suggests that the jars were stamped in or on behalf of Jerusalem. Geva (2007: 101) argued that the limited geographical area in which *yršlm*-stamped handles were found points to an administrative function in the vicinity of Jerusalem within the context of the Hasmonean revolt and the region's new-found independence. The appearance on these stamp impressions of the name of the capital and the paleo-Hebrew script of the First Temple period are, in his view, symbolic of the revival of Jerusalem, as in its Iron Age zenith.

8

Conclusions

The main thesis of this book is that the seal impressions stamped on storage-jar handles in Judah over a period of some 600 years should be viewed as a single administrative phenomenon, operating without interruption throughout the centuries when Judah was ruled by the regional superpowers. We should no longer accept explanations that consider the various types of stamp impressions to be separate phenomena fixed within limited timespans and serving a specific purpose.

This leads to the conclusion that the jar-stamping system was not related to a particular empire. It did not depend upon the status of Judah as a vassal kingdom or as a province or upon the status of Jerusalem as capital of the kingdom or as the center of the province. Furthermore, it was not related to the presence (or non-presence) of the Temple. It began to operate when Judah was a vassal kingdom—first under Assyria, then under Egypt and later under Babylon—with Jerusalem as its capital and the Temple at its center. It continued to operate when Judah became a Babylonian province, with its capital transferred to Mizpah in the Benjaminite territory and its temple in ruins. It persisted in the Second Temple period, when Judah was successively a Persian, Ptolemaic and Seleucid province, at which time Jerusalem's status as capital was restored and the Second Temple became the undisputed ritual center of the people. Throughout this period Ramat Raḥel was the heart of the system, as manifest by the great number of stamp impressions uncovered at the site, dating from all the periods in which the system operated—from the end of the 8th to the end of the 2nd century BCE.

The storage-jar administration was not a technological, economic, or administrative innovation of Judah, but a Judahite development of a simple technique, familiar throughout the ancient Near East. For the first time in history, this technique became a method that functioned in a large area and in great numbers, supported by an abundance of seals stamped onto thousands of storage jars over centuries. Alongside the development of the storage-jar administration and the selection of main collection centers, the rapid development of the economy included the accelerated construction and expansion of agricultural estates—presumably royal estates in relatively sparsely populated and uncultivated areas. These estates were: the Rephaim Valley (the biblical "Valley of the King"), with the village of Khirbet er-Ras—which I have suggested identifying with the name *mmšt* (Mamsh[i]t) on *lmlk* stamp impressions—in its center; the Elah Valley (with Socoh in its center), as well as the region around Hebron and the area around Ziph. These administrative and organizational changes under Assyrian rule impacted other areas of economy and administration as well and included an abrupt change in the ceramic culture: a transition from non-standardized, small-scale production in local workshops to mass production of a small selection of uniform vessels of a greater capacity, which gained wide distribution. Other changes included technological improvements in agricultural installations and the introduction of the shekel weights. These developments and innovations attest to the transition to a more centralized, state-organized economy, which could be supervised and controlled by the central authority and above it by the imperial government.

The *lmlk* stamp impressions were, in my opinion, part of the economic and administrative system that began to operate in Judah under Assyrian rule and with Assyrian encouragement and perhaps pressure to increase agricultural production as part of the annual tribute required of the Kingdom of Judah. For this purpose, a specific type of storage jar—manufactured and prevalent in the Shephelah for over a century—was selected to become the vessel upon which the system was based. The high-quality and unprecedented uniform production of this specific type of storage jar, upon which the entire system of *lmlk* stamp impressions relied, and the discovery of over 50% of the storage jars from the late 8th century BCE at a single collection center (Lachish), attest to the scope and *modus operandi* of this system. The collection center at Ramat Raḥel was established as an auxiliary to Lachish, and later—perhaps from the early stage of the Assyrian subjugation of Judah, but certainly after the destruction of Lachish and the loss of the Shephelah—it became the undisputed center of the storage-jar administration in Judah until the Seleucid period.

The catalyst for the development of this complex administrative system was the Assyrian requirement that Judah, like the other vassal kingdoms of the Levant, deliver annual tribute to Assyria in the form of precious metals and perhaps prestige and luxury items. While the Assyrian administration probably did not need the agricultural produce of Judah for its own consumption, this may have been the only way that Judah could reach the necessary quotas imposed upon it. The products were probably sold to the Judean elite in Jerusalem and in the various main sites in the kingdom (which became "secondary administrative centers" in this system), as well as to the Phoenicians and the coastal cities that could export them overseas. Some jars may have been sent to Assyrian garrison forces stationed at centers near Judah or to Judahite auxiliary forces in the service of the empire. In the latter case, the storage jars would have remained at Lachish to be "recycled" in the system and their contents transferred to other vessels. Only rarely were storage jars sent beyond the borders of the Kingdom of Judah, and it is possible that limited trade took place with the surplus products or storage jars received by officials, members of the royal household and estate owners as payment or gifts.

The processes described here of adaptation to the exigencies of Assyrian rule were not unique to Judah. The other small vassal kingdoms in the periphery of the Assyrian Empire presumably faced similar challenges. What was unique to Judah was the development of the storage-jar administration as a response to these challenges. This was due to the specific characteristics of its agriculture and economy, which enabled the production of expensive liquids—in particular, olive oil and wine—along with cereal crops. Moab, Ammon and Edom were also taxed heavily by the Assyrian Empire. While Edom could pay its tribute from the profits of the Arabian trade passing through its territory, one might surmise that Moab and Ammon, whose economies relied heavily on sheep and cattle husbandry, developed other methods of administration conducive to their own branches of agriculture. Perhaps they converted the derivative products of agricultural and animal husbandry into valuable metals and prestige items in order to meet their annual tribute quotas. In order to supervise and manage their own administrative systems, centers identical to the one at Ramat Raḥel were built in Moab and Ammon, near the ancient capitals of these vassal kingdoms. There too, agricultural branches were developed in order to enable the local governments to pay their tribute. In contrast to the kingdoms in the peripheral mountainous regions of the Assyrian Empire and to the coastal cities in Phoenicia and Philistia, whose main advantage for the empire lay in their inland and maritime trade possibilities, the large and strong territorial kingdoms of the Southern Levant were swiftly destroyed and reduced to provinces and, as such, were subject to direct imperial rule and to maximum economic exploitation by its officials.

All this supports the hypothesis that the Ramat Raḥel edifice was constructed by the king of Judah under the influence—if not direct command—of the Assyrian Empire, which ruled the region since Tiglath-pileser III, and with even greater force in the days of Sargon II. The fortress at Khirbet el-Mudeibiʿ and perhaps the edifice or fortress at Rabbat Ammon were presumably built in similar fashion—part of the construction enterprises imposed upon the small vassal kingdoms in the late 8th century BCE. Indeed, the quality, general layout and specific features of these fortresses do not reflect local building traditions; they therefore must have served the imperial administration, perhaps with the Assyrian supervisor (*qēpu*) residing in them, on a temporary or permanent basis, while small garrison forces stationed at key strategic points might have encamped there. The architecture of these buildings—an unprecedented and unique integration of local and foreign features, some familiar from earlier periods and others completely new in the region—should therefore be viewed as an additional feature of this special formative period in the history of the land of Israel in the early days of *Pax Assyriaca* in the ancient Near East.

Despite being no more than a local citadel, built only in the late 8th century BCE, and although there were larger, fortified, settlements, Ramat Raḥel became the storage-jar "capital" for a period of some 600 years, as evidenced by the sheer number of stamp impressions uncovered there—more than at any other site in Judah. This supports the notion that from its inception, Ramat Raḥel was linked to the royal administration and economy. Even if the actual number of early *lmlk*-stamped handles discovered at this site does not suggest that it was central to the system, the broader picture demonstrates its importance from the very beginning.

The main conclusion to be derived from the archaeological finds from the early days of Judah's subjugation to Assyria is that this subjugation was a key factor in the drive to develop the kingdom's administration and economy. Great economic prosperity is evident in Judah, as in other vassal kingdoms that were integrated into the imperial economic system, within the framework of which Assyria encouraged their development. The need to meet annual tax quotas necessitated the streamlining of local production systems in order to promote efficiency. This was supported by the political stability enjoyed during the long period of *Pax Assyriaca* in the 7th century BCE and the opening up of new markets throughout the empire, which became a huge single economic and commercial zone. While the aim of the Assyrians was to gain maximum profit from the vassal kingdoms, bringing wealth into Assyria proper, this state of affairs offered the vassal kingdoms great potential for stability and development, impossible under the hegemony of the large territorial kingdoms that had ruled the region until the early 730s—kingdoms that had dictated the economic and commercial order and, to a large extent, had limited the abilities of the small kingdoms in the Southern Levant and in Transjordan to develop their own potential.

Much of this book is concerned with establishing the chronology of the stamp impression system and the chronological sequence of its types. Precisely when the system began is largely a matter of conjecture. Due to the nature of archaeological research, it is often possible to determine when processes came to an end, especially in the event of destructions, but their onset is much more difficult to pinpoint. As a reasonable historical postulation, I would suggest that the systematic stamping of storage-jar handles in Judah began in the early final third of the 8th century BCE, when Judah became a vassal kingdom to Assyria. The first stamp-impression system included the series of the four *lmlk* stamp impressions with a four-winged scarab and written in the official lapidary script (Lemaire's Type Ib). Use of this series probably began after Judah had been subjugated to Assyria and began adjusting its administration and economy to pay the annual tribute required of it. A historical conjecture is that 715 BCE is the transition point between the early series of seals with the four-winged scarab, belonging to the reign of

Ahaz, when the storage-jar administration began, and the late series of seals with the four-winged scarab, which operated in the first half of the reign of Hezekiah. This system, which employs cursive script (Lemaire's Type Ia), consists of only three seals; the place name Socoh—which was probably, in addition to being one of the sites of agricultural production, also the main site of storage-jar production—is absent. Perhaps the old seal was retained in the workshop and used over and over again. This system of stamp impressions with the four-winged emblem was later replaced by another system of four seals, comparable in the quality of engraving, but bearing a two-winged symbol (Lemaire's Type IIa). This system did not last for more than a few years, as discerned from the small number of handles bearing this type of impression uncovered in the destruction layers left by Sennacherib's campaign.

We may posit that the short period that elapsed from the death of Sargon II and the outbreak of the revolt in Judah (705 BCE) to Sennacherib's campaign and the re-subjugation of Judah (701 BCE) is when the first of three *ad hoc* systems operated. This system—that of "private" stamp impressions—was employed when the need arose to concentrate supplies at specific sites, mainly in the Shephelah, within the framework of preparations to withstand the anticipated Assyrian military campaign. The "private" impressions were stamped on the same types of storage jar—and in some cases on the same storage jar and even the same handle—as the *lmlk* stamp impressions. This system ceased to exist after 701 BCE.

The later *lmlk* stamp impressions, dating after 701 BCE, include three different series; this system probably existed in the first third of the 7th century BCE. The first series of four seals (Lemaire's Type IIb) appears to resemble the early two-winged series—which operated shortly before 701 BCE—in quality and features. The writing (the place name and the word *lmlk*) gradually declined in importance in the two other 7th-century series: in Type IIc the word *lmlk* is absent and the place name is inscribed at the top of the seal, while in Type XII the place name is absent. The royal symbol retained its position on all seals from this period. Interestingly, the name Socoh is missing from this series too. Perhaps in this case, too, the earlier seal with the place name Socoh

(SIIb) survived at the storage-jar production site and there was no need to replace it.

The concentric circle incisions should be dated, in all probability, to the second third of the 7th century BCE. This system followed the late *lmlk* stamp impressions and preceded the rosette stamp impressions. It may be seen as an attempt to adapt the storage jars in the system to the new method of marking. We cannot determine whether this included the production of new storage jars, incised with concentric circles after firing. The distribution of the incised handles is very similar to that of the late types of *lmlk* stamp impressions, reflecting the period when the Shephelah was destroyed and disconnected from the administrative system of Judah during most of the 7th century BCE. It precedes the Assyrian withdrawal in the early 630s.

Rosette stamp impressions began to be used at the beginning of the last third of the 7th century BCE, replacing the system of concentric circle incisions. On the assumption that this occurred after Assyrian withdrawal from the region, in the days of Josiah, it took place when Judah was regaining its hold over the Shephelah and resettlement was beginning. This system continued to operate in the years of Judah's subjugation to Babylon and ended abruptly with the destruction of Jerusalem and the shift in the status of Judah from vassal kingdom to province.

After the Babylonian destruction, a new system of stamp impressions, with the lion symbol in the center, began to operate in Judah. The same types of storage jars continued to be stamped at the same centers, with the bulk of the production gradually shifting from the Shephelah to the vicinity of Jerusalem and with most storage jars collected in the Ramat Raḥel administrative center. Once again—as was the case with the rosette seals from before the Babylonian destruction—a royal symbol, well known in the Babylonian world, adorned the center of the seal. The change in the selected emblem reflects a new era, in which Judah was greatly reduced in size and no longer included the Beersheba–Arad Valleys, the southern hill country, or the Shephelah, and the Benjamin region also declined in status. The main historical significance of this administrative system is that it points to administrative and economic continuity between the First and Second Temple periods and leads to the conclusion that the period of the Babylonian exile served as a link between the material cultures, administrations and economies of the 7th and the 5th centuries BCE.

Another system of stamp impressions, operating alongside the lion seals, was that of the *mwṣh* stamp impressions. Unlike the other systems, very few handles bearing *mwṣh* impressions were uncovered, with a limited distribution, presumably reflecting a very small number of seals and a short duration. This system was presumably a response to a specific need. These impressions do not bear any symbol that could be interpreted as representing the deity or monarchy; there is no reference to the highest authority in the kingdom (*lmlk*) or to the name of the province (*yhwd*) or governor. The only name appearing on the seal was the place name *mwṣh*, apparently referring to a royal estate—evidence that this system served a different function. It was presumably an *ad hoc* system, created in order to bring supplies to the Babylonian governor residing in Mizpah, perhaps in the early days of the province, before the provincial system under Babylonian rule had been firmly established. In this respect, the *mwṣh* stamp-impression system bears a strong resemblance to the system of "private" stamp impressions, used in conjunction with the *lmlk* stamp impressions during the short period of preparation for Sennacherib's onslaught. The distribution of the *mwṣh* stamp impressions shows that they were collected at one site, Tell en-Naṣbeh—a site that did not play an important role in any of the previous systems. Only a few handles bearing *mwṣh* stamp impressions were recovered from Jerusalem and Ramat Raḥel, which had served as the main collection sites in all the systems operating before and after the destruction of the First Temple, including that of the lion stamp impressions.

From the 8th to the 6th centuries BCE, there is a clear decline in the importance of writing on the seals. In all the early types of *lmlk* stamp impressions, from the late 8th century BCE, as well as in Type IIb of the early 7th century BCE, the seals bore the word *lmlk* at the top, a four- or two-winged symbol in the center and a place name at the bottom. In the late *lmlk* types of the early 7th century BCE, the writing becomes less important: Type IIc lacks the word *lmlk* and Type XII has no place name. The place of the royal symbol on the stamp impression remains constant in all types from this period. This trend continued in the mid-7th century, when only symbols

were stamped (rosettes) or incised (concentric circles). Writing was entirely absent, including on the lion stamp impressions from the 6th century BCE. The one exception is the *mwṣh* stamp-impression system, which operated for a short time in the Benjamin region and displayed writing only, with no symbol. The most significant change occurred at the beginning of the Persian period, when the *yhwd* stamp-impression system, which went on to operate for centuries, employed only writing on its seals, at first with notable influence of the lapidary Aramaic script and later with a return to the tradition of paleo-Hebrew. This is the only discernable change in material culture evident in the transition from the period of the Babylonian exile to the era of the "Return" and Persian rule in Judah.

The system of *yhwd* stamp impressions consisted of 17 main types stamped with many dozens of seals, which operated for some 400 years from the end of the 6th century BCE to the second half of the 2nd century BCE. This system can be divided into three main chronological groups. The early group, dated to the end of the 6th and the 5th centuries BCE, consists of 12 types, stamped by 14 seals. This group displays great diversity, attesting to an administrative method that had not yet become permanent and well established. The group also bears much resemblance to the stamp impressions of the late First Temple period, including the appearance of private names (and, in one case, the name of the individual's father too) and a line (usually single, but sometimes double) separating the two rows of text. All the seals of this early group are round or oval, and most employ Aramaic lapidary script. In nine types the name of the province *yhwd* appears in plene spelling, three types contain the title *phw'* (Aramaic for "the governor"), and two governors are mentioned by name: *'ḥyb* and *yhw'zr*.

The middle group, dating from the 4th and 3rd centuries BCE, consists of three types, stamped by 16 seals, displaying great uniformity. Private names and titles are completely absent. The letter *waw* is missing in the spelling from the name of the province, and from this point on it is written with defective spelling—with three letters (*yhd*) or only two (*yh*). Most of the *yhd* impressions are rectangular with rounded corners, and the *yh* impressions are round and enclosed within a frame. There are paleographical changes too, apparently influenced by paleo-Hebrew script. This group of *yhwd* stamp impressions is crucial for an understanding of the administration in Judah in the Persian, Ptolemaic and early Seleucid rules, as it continued throughout, regardless of the changes in imperial rule. The characteristics of the storage-jar administration in the early 4th century BCE continued until the 2nd century BCE. This, too, is evidence that the arrangements implemented in Judah when it became a vassal of Assyria continued to operate despite the geopolitical and administrative changes. Throughout the rule of foreign superpowers in Judah, the storage-jar administrative system continued to exist.

The late group of *yhwd* stamp impressions consists of two main types, stamped by at least 21 seals. Most stamped handles were uncovered in archaeological contexts dated to the 2nd century BCE—perhaps even to the second half of this century—and were found in the same contexts as *yršlm* stamp impressions. An examination of their contexts suggests that the *yhwd* stamp impressions went out of use in the second half of the 2nd century BCE, at the same time or slightly before the *yršlm* stamp impression system ceased to exist.

Only 104 *yršlm*-stamped handles were uncovered, exhibiting a very small number of types (= seals). This system probably existed for a very short period. All the stamp impressions are rounded, and their most notable aspect is the reemergence of iconography: they display a pentagram with five paleo-Hebrew letters between its points, forming the name *yršlm*. Almost all the handles were uncovered in Jerusalem and Ramat Raḥel; their distribution clearly shows that Ramat Raḥel had become less important in the administrative system and was now secondary to Jerusalem.

The *yršlm* stamp-impression system is the final stage in the 600 years in which storage jars were stamped in Judah. The system is securely dated to the beginning of the Hasmonean period, probably to the days of Simon, who came to power after the death of his brother Jonathan and was engaged in consolidating and strengthening the kingdom. It may be viewed as the final *ad hoc* system, intended to strengthen the status of the city by ensuring the delivery of regular supplies to it. The selection of the Hellenistic symbol protecting the capital city is a conscious choice of integration with the West, while the return to paleo-Hebrew script symbolizes the nationalism

that was prevalent in those days, reflecting the desire to restore the kingdom to its erstwhile grandeur.

Following my efforts to define the time period in which the administration that stamped impressions on storage jars functioned in Judah (Chapter 5), I have sought to reconstruct in as great detail as possible the role and *modus operandi* of the system (Chapter 6). I have suggested that the extremely complex system had three core components: a site for the manufacture and stamping of storage jars, sites where the agricultural goods were produced, and one or more collection sites to which the filled storage jars were transported.

The system relied upon the manufacture of storage jars, the receptacles for the valuable liquids that were the *raison d'être* of the system. All the *lmlk*-type storage jars—both the stamped vessels and those that were not stamped—were manufactured at a single central workshop. Petrographic tests of the clay of both early- and late-type *lmlk*-stamped handles, as well as handles stamped with "private" impressions and most of the rosette-stamped handles, indicate that the place of production was always in the Shephelah—apparently in the Elah Valley, with a preference for the central site of Tel Socoh. According to my reconstruction, administrative officials would come to Socoh and would stamp the storage-jar handles with the seals.

The storage-jar administrative system would have required a certain number of storage jars for the purpose of collecting agricultural products in the summer and during the grape- and olive-harvesting seasons. The number of stamped handles uncovered for each of the systems, with the exception of the early types of *lmlk* stamp impressions, ranges from 250 to 500. It would seem that the difference between the numbers uncovered for the various systems is a function of their different durations. Although this number represents only a (small?) part of all the storage jars that were used in each system, this translates into 10,000–20,000 liters of liquids. This is a considerable quantity, which would have played an important role in the economy of Judah and in obtaining the means to pay the requisite tribute to the governing empires.

It seems, therefore, that in order to ensure the running of the system, a specific number of storage jars were produced and some of them were stamped; these served as receptacles for the liquids for many years. Whenever there was a shortage of storage jars, new vessels had to be manufactured. This would perhaps account for the different seals used in the same period. The fact that for some types, the number of stamped handles uncovered was very small may suggest that some seals were produced in order to "top up" the number of storage jars in the event of a shortage.

Whenever the historical circumstances required reorganization of the system—especially in the transition to the rosette stamp-impression system (after the Assyrian withdrawal from the region, and perhaps in the early years of the reign of Josiah?), in the transition to the lion stamp-impression system (after the destruction of Jerusalem when Judah became a province) and in the transition to the *yhwd* stamp-impression system (at the beginning of Persian rule)—a specific quantity of storage jars was again manufactured at the production center in order to create a full series according to the quantity required for the smooth running of the administration. From that moment on, it would only have been necessary to update the inventory of storage jars when the quantity fell below the minimum required.

As discussed above, the empty storage jars were shipped to the royal estates, where they were filled with oil or wine. Upon its subjugation to Assyria, a new administrative-economic system was instated in Judah, and areas that belonged or were connected to the royal dynasty were developed and turned into royal estates. These were intended to provide the products upon which the royal dynasty relied for payment of its annual tribute to the empire. These areas were relatively sparsely settled, and the main development was the establishment of agricultural installations to extract oil and wine. Along with the two rural royal estates in the southern hill country (Ziph and Hebron), Socoh and *mmšt* (probably Mamsh[i]t) served as the two "terminus" points of the storage-jar administrative system. Socoh was apparently the site of production of the storage jars, and *mmšt*—if, indeed, it can be identified as Khirbet er-Ras, in the center of the royal estate of the "Valley of the King" controlled from Ramat Raḥel—would have been the main collection center of the storage jars. If this is the case, the word *lmlk* appearing on the seals would denote the royal ownership of the goods produced in the estates.

It is suggested that most of the storage jars manufactured at Socoh were shipped empty to the three royal estates in Hebron, Ziph and *mmšt*, with some remaining in the royal estate in the Elah Valley, near the production site at Socoh. The storage jars were then filled with oil and wine and shipped off to the central collection center. At the time of Judah's subjugation to Assyria, Lachish apparently served as this main collection center, where the produce of three royal estates—Hebron, Ziph and Socoh—was concentrated. This is evidenced by the vast quantity of handles uncovered at Lachish bearing early types of *lmlk* stamp impressions with the name Hebron and the relatively large number of such handles with the name Ziph. It is further supported by the close proximity of Lachish to Socoh, the main royal estate in the Shephelah. Lachish's proximity to the port cities in the southern coastal area would presumably have facilitated transport of the goods to these cities, where they would have been exchanged for silver, gold and prestige items.

Given the large number of *lmlk* stamp impressions uncovered at Ramat Raḥel and despite the lack of unequivocal stratigraphic evidence for the first building phase, there is no doubt that Ramat Raḥel served as an important administrative system since the first building phase of the royal complex at the end of the 8th century—and certainly immediately after Sennacherib's campaign in the early 7th century BCE. The products from the "Valley of the King" were probably gathered at Ramat Raḥel, and it remained the sole collection center of storage jars after the destruction of Lachish and the Shephelah sites.

At this stage in the 7th century BCE, the writing on the stamp impressions was in gradual decline. Hebron and Ziph were now less important to the *lmlk* storage-jar administration, and after the destruction of the Shephelah, production took place in the environs of Jerusalem: in the vicinity of Ramat Raḥel and the Rephaim Valley south of the city and apparently in the Benjaminite region to its north as well. The main agricultural production was transferred from the royal estates to small production sites developed in the area north and south of Jerusalem. The association of these sites with the royal dynasty was no longer clear, and nor were the names of the estates. Thus, the use of the traditional seals declined, and the word *lmlk* above the symbol and the estate name below it disappeared. This was apparently a gradual process reflecting the adaptation of the storage-jar administration to the new reality following Sennacherib's campaign.

The system gave rise to another type of site: secondary administrative sites, to where storage jars with agricultural produce were brought, in varying quantities . Jerusalem was probably the main destination for these shipments, and the local elite, members of the royal household, ministers, priests and others in the city could receive the valuable liquids in exchange for precious metals and other goods. It might be that this need for payment in metals was the reason behind the development of the system of the *shekel* weights.

In other administrative and military sites too, as well as in central sites in the kingdom, where other members of the Judahite elite, close associates of the royal family, government officials or military personnel were residing, a certain amount of jars could be shipped and were exchanged with precious metals. It might be that all the surplus jars—the excess beyond the quota required for the annual tribute—were transferred to Jerusalem in storage jars and delivered to the royal dynasty. From there a few storage jars would have been transferred to other secondary administrative sites throughout the kingdom as bonuses, support, or perhaps payment. Some surplus jars may have been delivered to people residing in Jerusalem itself, and thus, they would also have been introduced into the private market—stored in private homes, sold, or further passed on. We cannot determine whether the surplus jars were transferred to secondary sites directly from the central collection site, or whether they were first shipped to Jerusalem—along with the surplus jars for which Jerusalem was the final destination—and from there transferred to the secondary administrative sites. In my opinion (although this is purely speculative), it is more likely that all the storage jars—those intended as tribute along with all the surplus—were gathered at the central collection site of the kingdom and from there sent to Jerusalem. The royal dynasty could thus monitor the number of active storage jars and have complete control over who would receive the surplus.

Since the jar-stamping system operated according to the same format and method for 600 years, it may shed light upon the administration and economy of Judah under the rule of successive empires. It may also contribute to an understanding of the history of Judah at the end of the First Temple period and throughout most of the Second Temple period. The first insight it offers pertains to the central position and role of the Shephelah in the economy and administration of the Kingdom of Judah, as well as to its demography in the late 8th century BCE. The centrality of Lachish in this period is reflected in its place in the storage-jar administration. This would explain why the Assyrians delivered such a harsh blow to the region in general and to Lachish in particular in their 701 BCE campaign. The glorification of the conquest of Lachish in Sennacherib's royal inscriptions and in his palace reliefs was not merely "compensation" for the failure to conquer Jerusalem. The targeting of Lachish and the massive effort invested in its conquest reflect the city's function as the administrative center of Judah in the Assyrian taxation system. The destruction of the city, the deportation of its residents, the ripping of large areas from the Shephelah and their transfer to neighboring kingdoms are all manifestations of Assyria's punitive retaliation against the Kingdom of Judah. Lachish and the entire Shephelah were left desolate throughout the years of Assyrian rule in the southern Levant. Indeed, Assyria placed special emphasis on targeting the heart of the administration that handled the collection of agricultural products and their transfer to the coastal cities in the west. The result was that the most fertile areas of the Kingdom of Judah were torn from it, forcing the debilitated kingdom to develop the hill country, particularly around Jerusalem, including Benjamin, and these areas suffered the consequences.

Ekron, the important center of oil production, was the main beneficiary of the harsh blow suffered by Judah. Its prosperity in the 7th century BCE is directly related to the weakening of Judah and to the Assyrian decision to move away from the method of numerous small production centers of oil, and to a lesser extent, of wine, with a central collection center at Lachish, and instead, to focus production in a single large industrial center at Ekron, to which all produce was gathered from most of the fields and orchards of the Shephelah.

The distribution of storage jars stamped with early and late types of *lmlk* impressions clearly shows that the peripheral areas to the east and to the south were never intrinsic to the system. While the sites in the Jordan Valley and the Dead Sea area were apparently established during the 7th century BCE, perhaps even in the middle or second half of the century, even the Beersheba–Arad Valleys, which flourished in the late 8th century BCE, did not play a significant role in the storage-jar administration. The storage-jar finds support the assumption that the prosperity of the Negev sites was not initiated or encouraged by the kings of Judah. The Assyrians apparently destroyed the Beersheba and Arad fortresses, which represented the power and presence of Judah in the region, and they encouraged rapid reconstruction of the southern trade routes, perhaps through their control of elite Judahite families who were directly subject to their rule.

The Shephelah was at the epicenter of the system of early types of *lmlk* stamp impressions. This region completely disappeared from the system after Sennacherib's campaign, with the storage-jar administration now focused in the hill country, mainly around Jerusalem and Ramat Raḥel, with increased activity in the Rephaim Valley and its environs, presumably at the same time as the decline in activity in Socoh and its environs. The center of storage-jar production probably remained at Socoh, which, even if destroyed in the 701 BCE Assyrian military campaign, quickly resumed its activities and returned to function once again as the production center of storage jars. Nevertheless, the decline in the production capabilities of the royal estate around Socoh, where the agricultural produce of the Elah Valley was processed, is evident in the sharp decline in the number of handles uncovered bearing impressions with the name Socoh. While this place name was the most common name after Hebron in the early types of *lmlk* stamp impressions, it became the least common name in the late types from the early 7th century BCE, disappearing completely in the third and final system of *lmlk* stamp impressions, probably from the end of the first quarter of the 7th century BCE.

The sharp decline in the overall number of storage jars bearing stamp impressions attests to the severe blow to the agricultural capabilities of Judah, in particular its ability to produce olive oil and wine, as a result of the damage to the Shephelah. In the hill country, the Benjamin region developed as a substitute for the loss of the Shephelah. The finds support the historical reconstruction according to which Sennacherib's 701 BCE campaign caused a severe crisis in settlement and demography, including the loss of significant areas and a mortal blow to the economy. The Kingdom of Judah was forced to find creative ways to deal with this crisis, and it did so mainly by developing agriculture in the mountainous areas to the north and south of Jerusalem, with an unprecedented reliance on the settlement in the Benjamin region. The storage-jar administration continued to operate in the same manner as prior to Sennacherib's campaign, especially in the environs of Jerusalem, but on a much smaller scale.

In the first half of the 7th century BCE, the Shephelah was largely abandoned. Even after its reconstruction began in the last third of the 7th century BCE—a lengthy gradual process, which could take place only after the Assyrian withdrawal from the region—its recovery was only partial. Its population was greatly reduced compared to its heyday a century earlier, and its fortifications and economy were weaker. In sharp contrast to the region's strength in the 8th century BCE, in the late 7th century its settlement consisted of solitary administrative and military centers. Important sites, such as Beth Shemesh, Tel Goded and Tell Beit Mirsim, were not resettled.[1] Lachish was no longer the main collection center of the system; it was merely a secondary administrative center, where officials or officers would occasionally receive one or two rosette-stamped storage jars as part of the collection of the royal payment or the central government's support of its reconstruction. Another city in the Shephelah that received storage jars with rosette stamp impressions was Azekah; this constituted evidence for the desire of the central government to encourage resettlement in a formerly important frontier city in the Shephelah. Perhaps it even points to a renewal of activities in the Elah Valley and at least a partial return to realizing the agricultural potential of this fertile area.

---

1. The salvage excavations to the east of Tel Beth Shemesh suggest that a village existed in this area during the 7th century, but precise details have not yet been published; see Lipschits 2019a.

Just as the development and integration of the Benjamin region into Judah's storage-jar administration in the 7th century BCE to a large extent counter-balanced the loss of the Shephelah, when reconstruction—albeit limited—began in the Shephelah at the end of the 7th century, the Benjamin region played a lesser role in the rosette stamp-impression system. The discovery of a few rosette-stamped handles in the Beersheba–Arad Valleys points to the very late date when the storage-jar administration in Judah was once again involved here. Perhaps this system supported the Judahite officials and administration in this region, as well as in the sites in the eastern periphery—Jericho and En-Gedi, to where Judah expanded apparently only after the Assyrian withdrawal, in the 630s BCE.

The dating of the rosette stamp-impression system to the last third of the 7th century BCE, leads to the conclusion that the term "archaeology of the days of Manasseh" should be abandoned. During this king's long reign, it seems that Judah continued to be a loyal Assyrian vassal, greatly reduced in size and suffering various restrictions imposed upon it following Sennacherib's campaign, and its administrative system did not extend beyond the hill country. To my mind, the term "archaeology of the days of Josiah" is to be preferred: during Josiah reign, Judah enjoyed relative prosperity, expanded its activities and its borders to areas afflicted by Sennacherib's campaign, and in the final decades before its destruction, also expanded its activities southward and eastward.

After the crushing blow of the Babylonians, the lion stamp impressions reflect the adaptation of the province of Judah to its new reality. This system was a mere shadow of the systems that operated prior to the destruction. Technologically, the storage jars and stamp impressions were of low quality. Quantitatively, the number of lion-stamped handles uncovered is only about half the total number of rosette-stamped storage jars and jars incised with concentric circles. In terms of the secondary administrative centers and the overall distribution, the distribution of the lion-stamped storage jars is much smaller than any of the other systems and was centered mainly in Nebi Samwil, Jerusalem and Ramat Raḥel.

Ramat Raḥel was the undisputed center of this system: an unprecedented concentration of over 50% of all the lion-stamped handles has been uncovered there. The discovery of such handles in the City of David indicates that the capital of the kingdom was not completely abandoned, as formerly believed. A small number of storage jars continued to reach Jerusalem, and the decline in significance of the secondary administrative sites further supports the possibility that Jerusalem was the final destination of these surpluses. Various individuals related to the royal dynasty or connected to the government apparatus probably remained in the city after the destruction, perhaps along with priests and others who guarded the ruins of the temple and preserved its memory and the rites that used to be conducted there. The Benjamin region continued to be part of the storage-jar administrative system, and Nebi Samwil, which was prominent in the system by the end of the First Temple period alongside Khirbet el-Burj, became the only secondary administrative center in Benjamin and received a relatively large quantity of the lion-stamped storage jars. The discovery of five handles with lion stamp impressions at En-Gedi indicates that this site continued to exist in the 6th century BCE and was extremely important to the Babylonian provincial administration. No lion stamp impressions whatsoever were uncovered in the Shephelah, and this is in keeping with our archaeological knowledge of the destruction of its main cities during the Babylonian campaign against Jerusalem. The Shephelah, which had not fully recovered in the late 7th and early 6th centuries and had not regained a central position in the economy of Judah, could not continue to survive after the destruction inflicted by the Babylonians on the region.

In the early Persian period, the *yhwd* stamp impressions came into use. The early *yhwd* stamp impressions demonstrate full continuity of the administration and economy at least until the mid-5th century BCE. Ramat Raḥel continued to be central in this stage too. Noteworthy is the marginal status of Jerusalem, indicating that the city and its temple were not crucial to the storage-jar administration. What is most striking about the early types of *yhwd* stamp impressions is the great diversity demonstrated by its 12 types, pointing to an administrative system that had not become fully standardized.

The main development in the *yhwd* stamp-impression system presumably occurred in the late 5th or early 4th century BCE, with major changes evident in shape, style, paleography and orthography, evidently influenced by the growing importance of the southern Levant for the Persian empire after it lost its grip on Egypt. The increased conformity in stamping practices in the province of Judah was one of the many changes that took place in the southern Levant as the Achaemenids strengthened their control over the periphery of the empire. The middle types of *yhwd* stamp impressions were used in the 4th and 3rd centuries BCE and probably continued in the early 2nd century BCE. This system reflects the administrative continuity between the end of the Persian period and the Ptolemaic period, with no notable change in the material culture.

The *yhwd* stamp-impression system underwent change only under Hasmonean rule, and even then, there is much continuity in the transition from the system employing middle types to the system using late types of *yhwd* stamp impressions. The most notable change is the disappearance of the secondary centers, with Jerusalem remaining the sole administrative center. Ramat Raḥel was abandoned, at least for some time, and no more than one stamped handle was uncovered at any other site. This points to the concentration of all the storage jars in Jerusalem in the period of consolidation of Hasmonean rule, as is also evident by the new types of impressions stamped by *yršlm* seals, also presumably intended to help consolidate the new rule in the capital. With the establishment of the Hasmonean kingdom and Judah's regaining full political independence after 600 years of subjugation, Ramat Raḥel was destroyed to its foundations and the jar-stamping system ceased to exist. An administrative method that accompanied Judah throughout the end of the First Temple period and most of the Second Temple period disappeared forever, buried, like Ramat Raḥel, under layers of rocks and stones.

In this book, I have sought to collect the vast data on the full range of stamp-impression systems and to present them as a single entity—reflecting a continuous administration that existed in Judah, languishing under the yoke of successive imperial rules. I have presented the data and drawn conclusions about the dating of each system and the role of the different regions within the kingdom in each, in an effort to establish a unified theory that will account for the diverse finds. Many of the explanations offered for the *modus operandi* of the storage-jar administration are based on hypotheses and what I consider to be reasonable proposals. In all likelihood, the suggestions and solutions proposed here do not constitute the final word on the subject.

It is my hope that future studies and new archaeological discoveries will shed further light on the modes of operation of the storage-jar system and illuminate the history of Judah in its long epoch under the rule of the great empires.

Bibliography

Abel, F.M. 1938. *Géographie de la Palestine* II: *Géographie Politique. Les Villes*. Paris.

Aharoni, M. 1981a. Inscribed Weights and Royal Seals. In: Aharoni, Y., ed. *Arad Inscriptions*. Jerusalem: 126–127.

Aharoni, M. and Aharoni, Y. 1976. The Stratification of Judahite Sites in the 8th and 7th Centuries B.C.E. *Bulletin of the American Schools of Oriental Research* 224: 73–90.

Aharoni, Y. 1955. Excavations at Ramat Rachel. *Yediʿot: Bulletin of the Israel Exploration Society* 19: 147–174 (Hebrew).

Aharoni, Y. 1956. Excavations at Ramath Raḥel: Preliminary Report. *Israel Exploration Journal* 6: 102–111, 137–157.

Aharoni, Y. 1958. The Negeb of Judah. *Israel Exploration Journal* 8: 26–38.

Aharoni, Y. 1959. Some More YHWD Stamps. *Israel Exploration Journal* 9: 55–56.

Aharoni, Y. 1960. Hebrew Jar-Stamps from Ramat Raḥel. *Eretz-Israel* 6: 56–60 (Hebrew), 28* (English summary).

Aharoni, Y. 1961. Excavations at Ramat Rahel. *The Biblical Archaeologist* 24: 97–118.

Aharoni, Y. 1962. *Excavations at Ramat-Rahel, Seasons 1959 and 1960*. Rome.

Aharoni, Y. 1964. *Excavations at Ramat-Rahel, Seasons 1961 and 1962*. Rome.

Aharoni, Y. 1971a. *Paths and Sites*. Tel Aviv (Hebrew).

Aharoni, Y. 1971b. "Woe unto him that buildeth his house by unrighteousness". In: *Studies in the Book of Jeremiah* II. Givatayim: 55–76.

Aharoni, Y. 1973. *Beer-sheba* I: *Excavations at Tel Beer-sheba, 1969–1971 Seasons* (Publications of the Institute of Archaeology of Tel Aviv University 2). Tel Aviv.

Aharoni, Y. 1975a. Excavations at Tel Beer-Sheba: Preliminary Report of the Fifth and Sixth Seasons, 1973–1974. *Tel Aviv* 2: 146–168.

Aharoni, Y. 1975b. *Investigations at Lachish: The Sanctuary and the Residency (Lachish V)* (Publications of the Institute of Archaeology of Tel Aviv University 4). Tel Aviv.

Aharoni, Y. 1981b. *Arad Inscriptions* (Judean Desert Studies). Jerusalem.

Aharoni, Y. 1984. *The Land of Israel in Biblical Times: A Historical Geography* (rev. ed.). Jerusalem.

Aharoni, Y. 1987. *The Land of the Bible: A Historical Geography* (2nd rev. ed.). Philadelphia.

Aharoni, Y. and Amiran, R. 1958. A New Scheme for the Sub-Division of the Iron Age in Palestine. *Israel Exploration Journal* 8: 171–184.

Aḥituv, S. 2005. *Ha-Ketav Ve-Hamiktav—Handbook of Ancient Inscriptions from the Land of Israel and the Kingdoms Beyond the Jordan from the Period of the First Commonwealth*. Jerusalem.

Albright, W.F. 1923. The Site of Mizpah in Benjamin. *Journal of the Palestine Oriental Society* 3: 110–121.

Albright, W.F. 1925. The Administrative Divisions of Israel and Judah. *Journal of the Palestine Oriental Society* 5: 17–54.

Albright, W.F. 1926. Notes on Early Hebrew and Aramaic Epigraphy. *Journal of the Palestine Oriental Society* 6: 75–102.

Albright, W.F. 1928. The Second Campaign at Tell Beit Mirsim (Kiriath-Sepher). *Bulletin of the American Schools of Oriental Research* 31: 1–11.

Albright, W.F. 1932a. *The Excavation of Tell Beit Mirsim in Palestine* I: *The Pottery of the First Three Campaigns* (Annual of the American Schools of Oriental Research 12). New Haven.

Albright, W.F. 1932b. The Seal of Eliakim and the Latest Preëxilic History of Judah, with Some Observations on Ezekiel. *Journal of Biblical Literature* 51: 77–106.

Albright, W.F. 1933. A New Campaign of Excavation at Gibeah of Saul. *Bulletin of the American Schools of Oriental Research* 52: 6–12.

Albright, W.F. 1943. *The Excavation of Tell Beit Mirsim* III: *The Iron Age* (Annual of the American Schools of Oriental Research 21–22). New Haven.

Albright, W.F. 1953. Some Recent Publications. *Bulletin of the American Schools of Oriental Research* 132: 46–47.

Albright, W.F. 1956. The Nebuchadnezzar and Neriglissar Chronicles. *Bulletin of the American Schools of Oriental Research* 143: 28–33.

Albright, W.F. 1957. The Seal Inscription from Jericho and the Treasures of the Second Temple. *Bulletin of the American Schools of Oriental Research* 148: 28–30.

Albright, W.F. 1958. Recent Progress in Palestinian Archaeology: Samaria-Sebaste III and Hazor I. *Bulletin of the American Schools of Oriental Research* 150: 21–25.

Albright, W.F. 1960. *The Archaeology of Palestine*. Harmondsworth.

Alt, A. 1927. Das Institut im Jahre 1926. *Palästinajahrbuch des Deutschen Evangelischen Instituts für Altertumswissenschaft des Heiligen Landes zu Jerusalem* 23: 5–51.

Alt, A. 1945. Neue assyrische Nachrichten über Palästina und Syrien. *Zeitschrift des Deutschen Palastina-Vereins* 67: 128–159.

Amiet, P. 1996. Les sceaux et empreintes de sceaux de Tell el-Farʿah. In: Amiet, P., Briend, J., Courtois, L. and Doumortier, J.-B, *Tell El-Farʿah: Historie, glyptique et céramologie, sous la direction de Henri de Contenson

(Orbis Biblicus et Orientalis 14). Fribourg and Göttingen: 15–30.

Amiran, R. and Eitan, A. 1973. Excavations in the Citadel, Jerusalem, 1968–1969 (Preliminary Report). *Eretz-Israel* 11: 213–218 (Hebrew), 29* (English summary).

Amit, D. 2009. Water Supply to the Upper City of Jerusalem during the First and Second Temple Periods in Light of the Mamilla Excavations. In: Amit, D., Stiebel, G.D. and Peleg-Barakat, O., eds. *New Studies in the Archaeology of Jerusalem and Its Region* III. Jerusalem: 94–108 (Hebrew).

Archi, A. 1999. The Steward and His Jar. *Iraq* 61: 147–158.

Ariel, D.T. 1990. Imported Stamped Amphora Handles. In: Ariel, D.T., ed. *Excavations at the City of David 1978–1985 Directed by Yigal Shiloh* II: *Imported Stamped Amphora Handles, Coins, Worked Bone and Ivory, and Glass* (Qedem 30). Jerusalem: 13–98.

Ariel, D.T. 2000. Imported Greek Stamped Amphora Handles. In: Geva, H., ed. *Jewish Quarter Excavations in the Old City of Jerusalem, Conducted by Nahman Avigad, 1969–1982* I: *Architecture and Stratigraphy: Areas A, W and X-2, Final Report*. Jerusalem: 267–283.

Ariel, D.T., Hirschfeld, H. and Savir, N. 2000. Area D1: Stratigraphic Report. In: Ariel, D.T., ed. *Excavations at the City of David 1978–1985 Directed by Yigal Shiloh* V: *Extramural Areas* (Qedem 40). Jerusalem: 33–72.

Ariel, D.T. and Magness, J. 1992. Area K. In: De Groot, A. and Ariel, D. T., eds. *Excavations at the City of David 1978–1985 Directed by Yigal Shiloh* III: *Stratigraphical, Environmental, and Other Reports* (Qedem 33). Jerusalem: 63–97.

Ariel, D.T. and Shoham, Y. 2000. Locally Stamped Handles and Associated Body Fragments of the Persian and Hellenistic Periods. In: Ariel, D.T., ed. *Excavations at the City of David 1978–1985 Directed by Yigal Shiloh* VI: *Inscriptions* (Qedem 41). Jerusalem: 137–171.

Aruz, J. 1992. The Stamp Seals from Tell Esh Sheikh. *Anatolian Studies* 42: 15–28.

Åström, P. 1966. *Excavations at Kalapsidha and Ayios Iakovos in Cyprus*. Lund.

Avigad, N. 1953. Another *bat le-melekh* Inscription. *Israel Exploration Journal* 3: 121–122.

Avigad, N. 1958a. A New Class of Yehud Stamps. *Yediʿot: Bulletin of the Israel Exploration Society* 22: 3–10 (Hebrew).

Avigad, N. 1958b. New Light on the MṢH Seal Impressions. *Yediʿot: Bulletin of the Israel Exploration Society* 22: 126–133 (Hebrew).

Avigad, N. 1959. Some Notes on the Hebrew Inscriptions from Gibeon. *Israel Exploration Journal* 9: 130–133.

Avigad, N. 1960. Yehûd or Haʿîr? *Bulletin of the American Schools of Oriental Research* 158: 23–27.

Avigad, N. 1961. Some Unpublished Ancient Seals. *Yediʿot: Bulletin of the Israel Exploration Society* 25: 239–244 (Hebrew).

Avigad, N. 1963. Two Newly Found Hebrew Seals. *Israel Exploration Journal* 13: 322–324.

Avigad, N. 1964. Seals and Sealings. *Israel Exploration Journal* 14: 190–194.

Avigad, N. 1965. Seals of Exiles. *Israel Exploration Journal* 15: 222–232.

Avigad, N. 1969. A Group of Hebrew Seals. *Eretz-Israel* 9: 1–9 (Hebrew), 134 (English summary).

Avigad, N. 1970. Ammonite and Moabite Seals. In: Sanders, J.A., ed. *Near Eastern Archaeology in the Twentieth Century*. New York: 284–295.

Avigad, N. 1972a. Excavations in the Jewish Quarter of the Old City of Jerusalem, 1971. *Israel Exploration Journal* 22: 193–200.

Avigad, N. 1972b. Two Hebrew Inscriptions on Wine Jars. *Israel Exploration Journal* 22: 1–9.

Avigad, N. 1974. More Evidence on the Judean Post-Exilic Stamps. *Israel Exploration Journal* 24: 52–58.

Avigad, N. 1975. New Names on Hebrew Seals. *Eretz-Israel* 12: 66–71 (Hebrew), 120*–121* (English summary).

Avigad, N. 1976a. *Bullae and Seals from a Post-Exilic Judean Archive* (Qedem 4). Jerusalem.

Avigad, N. 1976b. New Light on the Naʿar Seals. In: Cross, F.M., Lemke, W.E. and Miller, P.D., eds. *Magnalia Dei: The Mighty Acts of God. Essays on the Bible and Archaeology in Memory of G. Ernest Wright*. New York: 294–300.

Avigad, N. 1978a. Baruch the Scribe and Jerahmeel the King's Son. *Israel Exploration Journal* 28: 52–56.

Avigad, N. 1978b. The Seal of Seraiah (Son of) Neriah. *Eretz-Israel* 14: 86–87 (Hebrew), 125* (English summary).

Avigad, N. 1979. A Group of Hebrew Seals from the Hecht Collection. In: *Festschrift: Rëuben R. Hecht*. Jerusalem: 119–126.

Avigad, N. 1980. *The Upper City of Jerusalem*. Jerusalem (Hebrew).

Avigad, N. 1983. *Discovering Jerusalem*. Nashville.

Avigad, N. 1986a. *Hebrew Bullae from the Time of Jeremiah: Remnants of a Burnt Archive*. Jerusalem.

Avigad, N. 1986b. Three Ancient Seals. *The Biblical Archaeologist*: 49: 51–53.

Avigad, N. 1987. The Contribution of Hebrew Seals to an Understanding of Israelite Religion and Society. In: Miller, P.D., Hanson, P.D. and McBride, S.D., eds. *Ancient Israelite Religion*. Philadelphia: 195–208.

Avigad, N. 1990. Two Hebrew "Fiscal" Bullae. *Israel Exploration Journal* 40: 262–266.

Avigad, N. 1992. A New Seal Depicting a Lion. *Michmanim*: 6: 33–36.

Avigad, N. and Barkay, G. 2000. The *lmlk* and Related Seal Impressions. In: Geva, H., ed. *Jewish Quarter Excavations in the Old City of Jerusalem, Conducted by Nahman Avigad, 1969–1982* I: *Architecture and Stratigraphy: Areas A, W and X-2, Final Report*. Jerusalem: 243–266.

Avigad, N. and Sass, B. 1997. *Corpus of West Semitic Stamp Seals*. Jerusalem.

Ayalon, E. 1985. Trial Excavation of Two Iron Age Strata at Tel ʿEton. *Tel Aviv* 12: 54–62.

Aznar, C.A. 2005. *Exchange Network in the Southern Levant during the Iron Age II: A Study of Pottery Origin and Distribution* (Ph.D. dissertation, Harvard University). Cambridge, MA.

Badè, W.F. 1932. A Jar Handle Stamp from Tell en-Nasbeh. *Zeitschrift für die Alttestamentliche Wissenschaft* 50: 89–90.

Badè, W.F. 1933. The Seal of Jaazaniah. *Zeitschrift für die Alttestamentliche Wissenschaft* 51: 150–156.

Barag, D. 1986–87. A Silver Coin of Yohanan the High Priest and the Coinage of Judea in the Fourth Century B.C. *Israel Numismatic Journal* 9: 4–21.

Barag, D. 1999. Owners of Multiple Seals in Judea during the Eighth–Early Sixth Century BCE. *Eretz-Israel* 26: 35–38 (Hebrew), 227*–228* (English summary).

Barkay, G. 1985. Northern and Western Jerusalem in the End of the Iron Age (Ph.D. dissertation, Tel Aviv University). Tel Aviv (Hebrew), I–XXXII (English summary).

Barkay, G. 1992a. A Group of Stamped Handles from Judah. *Eretz-Israel* 23: 113–128, 150*–151* (English summary).

Barkay, G. 1992b. "The Prancing Horse"—An Official Seal Impression from Judah of the 8th Century B.C.E. *Tel Aviv* 19: 124–129.

Barkay, G. 1995. The King of Babylonia or a Judaean Official? *Israel Exploration Journal* 45: 41–47.

Barkay, G. 2006. Royal Palace, Royal Portrait? The Tantalizing Possibilities of Ramat Rahel. *Biblical Archaeology Review* 32(5): 34–44.

Barkay, G. 2011. A Fiscal Bulla from the Slopes of the Temple Mount—Evidence for the Taxation System of the Judean Kingdom. In: Baruch, E. and Faust, A., eds. *New Studies on Jerusalem* 17. Ramat Gan: 151–178 (Hebrew).

Barkay, G. 2015. Evidence of the Taxation System of the Judean Kingdom—A Fiscal Bulla from the Slopes of the Temple Mount and the Phenomenon of Fiscal Bullae. In: Lubetski, M. and Lubetski, E., eds. *Recording New Epigraphic Evidence: Essays in Honor of Robert Deutsch*. Jerusalem: 17–50.

Barkay, G. and Vaughn, A.G. 1995. An Official Seal Impression from Lachish Reconsidered. *Tel Aviv* 22: 94–97.

Barkay, G. and Vaughn, A.G. 1996a. LMLK and Official Seal Impressions from Tel Lachish. *Tel Aviv* 23: 61–74.

Barkay, G. and Vaughn, A.G. 1996b. New Readings of Hezekian Official Seal Impressions. *Bulletin of the American Schools of Oriental Research* 304: 29–54.

Barkay, G. and Vaughn, A.G. 2004. The Royal and Official Seal Impressions from Lachish. In: Ussishkin, D., ed. *The Renewed Archaeological Excavations at Lachish (1973–1994)*, IV (Monograph Series of the Institute of Archaeology of Tel Aviv University 22). Tel Aviv: 2148–2173.

Barrois, A.G. 1931. La métrologie dans la bible. *Revue Biblique* 40: 185–213.

Bartlett, J.R. 1982. Iron Age and Hellenistic Stamped Jar Handles from Tell es-Sultan. In: Kenyon, K.M. and Holland, T.A. *Excavations at Jericho* IV: *The Pottery Type Series and Other Finds*. London: 537–545.

Beck, P. 2004. Section B: Cylinder Seals. In: Ussishkin, D., ed. *The Renewed Archaeological Excavations at Lachish (1973–1994)* (Monograph Series of the Institute of Archaeology of Tel Aviv University 22). Tel Aviv: 1525–1536.

Bedford, P.R. 2005. The Economy of the Near East in the First Millennium BC. In: Manning, J.G. and Morris, I., eds. *The Ancient Economy: Evidence and Models*. Stanford: 58–83.

Beit-Arieh, I. 1985. Tel ʿIra—A Fortified City of the Kingdom of Judah. *Qadmoniot* 69/70: 17–25 (Hebrew).

Beit-Arieh, I. 1987. Tel-ʿIra and Horvat ʿUza: Negev Sites in the Late Israelite Period. *Cathedra* 42: 34–38 (Hebrew).

Beit-Arieh, I. 1995. *Horvat Qitmit: An Edomite Shrine in the Biblical Negev* (Monograph Series of the Institute of Archaeology of Tel Aviv University 11). Tel Aviv.

Beit-Arieh, I. 1999a. עשרת Ostracon from Horvat ʿUza. *Eretz-Israel* 26: 30–34 (Hebrew), 227* (English summary).

Beit-Arieh, I. 1999b. *Tel ʿIra: A Stronghold in the Biblical Negev* (Monograph Series of the Institute of Archaeology of Tel Aviv University 15). Tel Aviv.

Beit-Arieh, I. 2007. *Horvat ʿUza and Horvat Radum: Two Fortresses in the Biblical Negev* (Monograph Series of the Institute of Archaeology of Tel Aviv University 25). Tel Aviv.

Beit-Arieh, I. and Bunimovitz, S. 1999. Area A. In: Beit-Arieh, I., ed. *Tel ʿIra: A Stronghold in the Biblical Negev* (Monograph Series of the Institute of Archaeology of Tel Aviv University 15). Tel Aviv: 17–23.

Beit-Arieh, I. and Negbi, O. 1999. Area B. In: Beit-Arieh, I., ed. *Tel ʿIra: A Stronghold in the Biblical Negev* (Monograph Series of the Institute of Archaeology of Tel Aviv University 15). Tel Aviv: 24–39.

Ben-Arieh, S. 2000. Salvage Excavations near the Holyland Hotel, Jerusalem. *ʿAtiqot* 40: 1–24.

Ben-Dor, I. 1946. A Hebrew Seal from Samaria. *Quarterly of the Department of Antiquities in Palestine* 12: 77–83.

Ben-Dor, I. 1948. Two Hebrew Seals. *Quarterly of the Department of Antiquities in Palestine* 13: 64–68.

Bendor, S. 1986. *The Social Structure of Ancient Israel: The Institution of the Family (Beitʾab) from the Settlement to the End of the Monarchy*. Jerusalem (Hebrew).

Ben-Dov, M. 1982. *The Dig at the Temple Mount*. Jerusalem (Hebrew).

Benenson, I. 2009. Response to Kletter. *Journal for Archaeological Method Theory* 16: 366–367.

Bennett, C.-M. 1966. Umm el-Biyara. *Revue Biblique* 73: 400–401.

Bennett, C.-M. 1975. Excavations at Buseirah, Southern Jordan, 1973: Third Preliminary Report. *Levant* 7: 1–19.

Ben-Tor, A. 1978. *Cylinder Seals of Third Millennium Palestine* (Bulletin of the American Schools of Oriental Research Supplement Series 22). Cambridge, MA.

Ben-Yosef, E., Millman, M., Shaar, R., Tauxe, L. and Lipschits, O. 2017. Six Centuries of Geomagnetic Intensity Variations Recorded by Royal Judean Stamped Jar Handles. *Proceedings of the National Academy of Sciences* 114: 2160–2165. https://doi.org/10.1073/pnas.1615797114.

Bikaki, A.H. 1984. *Ayia Irini: The Potters' Marks*. Mainz.

Biran, A. 1980. Tell Dan: Five Years Later. *The Biblical Archaeologist* 43: 168–182.

Biran, A. 1987. Tel-ʿIra and ʿAroʿer Towards the End of the Judean Monarchy. *Cathedra* 42: 26–33 (Hebrew).

Biran, A. 1988. A Mace-Head and the Office of Amadiyo at Dan. *Qadmoniot* 81/82: 11–17 (Hebrew).

Biran, A. 1994. *Biblical Dan*. Jerusalem.

Biran, A. 1995. Tel Dan—1991. *Excavations and Surveys in Israel* 13: 8–11.

Biran, A. and Cohen, R. 1981. Aroer in the Negev. *Eretz-Israel* 15: 250–273 (Hebrew), 84* (English summary).

Bliss, F.J. 1899a. First Report on the Excavations at Tell Zakariya. *Palestine Exploration Fund Quarterly Statement*: 10–25.

Bliss, F.J. 1899b. Second Report on the Excavations at Tell Zakariya. *Palestine Exploration Fund Quarterly Statement*: 89–111.

Bliss, F.J. 1899c. Third Report on the Excavations at Tell Zakariya. *Palestine Exploration Fund Quarterly Statement*: 170–187.

Bliss, F.J. 1900a. First Report on the Excavations at Tell Ej-Judeideh. *Palestine Exploration Fund Quarterly Statement* 32: 87–101.

Bliss, F.J. 1900b. Fourth Report on the Excavations at Tell Zakarîya. *Palestine Exploration Fund Quarterly Statement* 32: 7–16.

Bliss, F.J. 1900c. Second Reports on the Excavations at Tell Ej-Judeideh. *Palestine Exploration Fund Quarterly Statement* 32: 199–222.

Bliss, F.J. and Dickie, A.C. 1898. *Excavations at Jerusalem 1894–1897*. London.

Bliss, F.J. and Macalister, R.A.S. 1902. *Excavations in Palestine During the Years 1898–1900*. London.

Block, D.I. 1998. *The Book of Ezekiel: Chapters 25–48* (The New International Commentary on the Old Testament). Grand Rapids.

Boardman, J. 1972. *Greek Gems and Finger Rings, Early Bronze Age to Late Classical*. London.

Boaz, A., Maeir, A. and Schneider, T. 1998. Tel Ẓafit. *Ḥadashot Arkheologiot* 108: 156 (Hebrew).

Bocher, E. 2012. The *yršlm* Stamp Impressions from the Early Hellenistic Period (M.A. thesis, Tel Aviv University). Tel Aviv (Hebrew).

Bocher, E. 2016. *yršlm* Stamp Impressions. In: Lipschits, O., Gadot, Y. and Freud, L. 2016. *Ramat Raḥel III: Final Publication of Yohanan Aharoni's Excavations (1954, 1959–1962)* (Monograph Series of the Institute of Archaeology of Tel Aviv University 35). Tel Aviv and Winona Lake: 447–457.

Bocher, E. Forthcoming. *yršlm* Stamp Impressions. In: Lipschits, O., Oeming, M., Freud, L. and Gadot, Y., eds. *Ramat Raḥel V: The Renewed Excavations by the Tel Aviv–Heidelberg Expedition (2005–2010): The Finds* (Monograph Series of the Institute of Archaeology of Tel Aviv University). Tel Aviv and University Park, PA.

Bocher, E. and Koch, I. 2016. Persian Period Stamp Impressions. In: Lipschits, O., Gadot, Y. and Freud, L., eds. *Ramat Raḥel III: Final Publication of Yohanan Aharoni's Excavations (1954, 1959–1962)* (Monograph Series of the Institute of Archaeology of Tel Aviv University 35). Tel Aviv and Winona Lake: 437–446.

Bocher, E. and Lipschits, O. 2011. First Conclusions from the Study of the *yršlm* Stamp Impressions on Jar Handles. In: Baruch, E. and Faust, A., eds. *New Studies on Jerusalem* 17. Ramat Gan: 199–218 (Hebrew), 55*–56* (English summary).

Bocher, E. and Lipschits, O. 2013. The *yršlm* Stamp Impressions on Jar Handles: Distribution, Chronology, Iconography and Function. *Tel Aviv* 40: 99–116.

Boer, R. 2015. *The Sacred Economy of Ancient Israel* (Library of Ancient Israel). Louisville.

Brandl, B. 1993. Scarabs and Other Glyptic Finds. In: Finkelstein, I. Bunimovitz, S. and Lederman, Z., eds. *Shiloh: The Archaeology of a Biblical Site* (Monograph Series of the Institute of Archaeology of Tel Aviv University 10). Tel Aviv: 203–222.

Brandl, B. 2002. Two Stamped Jar Handles. In: Finkelstein, I., Ussishkin, D. and Halpern, B. *Megiddo IV: The 1998–2002 Seasons* (Monograph Series of the Institute of Archaeology of Tel Aviv University 24). Tel Aviv: 426–429.

Broshi, M. and Gibson, S. 1994. Excavations along the Western and Southern Walls of the Old City of Jerusalem. In: Geva, H., ed. *Ancient Jerusalem Revealed*. Jerusalem: 147–155.

Buchanan, B. 1954. Review of Tufnell, O. 1953. *Lachish III (Tell ed-Duweir): The Iron Age. American Journal of Archaeology* 58: 335–339.

Buchanan, B. 1967. The Prehistoric Stamp Seal: A Reconsideration of Some Old Excavations. *Journal of the American Oriental Society* 87: 265–279, 525–540.

Buchanan, B. and Moorey, P.R.S. 1984. *Catalogue of Ancient Near Eastern Seals in the Ashmolean Museum* II: *The Prehistoric Stamp Seals*. Oxford.

Buchanan, B. and Moorey, P.R.S. 1988. *Catalogue of Ancient Near Eastern Seals in the Ashmolean Museum* III: *The Iron Age Stamp Seals (c. 1200–350 BC)*. Oxford.

Bunimovitz, S. and Lederman, Z. 1997a. Beth-Shemesh: Culture Conflict on Judah's Frontier. *Biblical Archaeology Review* 23(1): 42–49, 75–77.

Bunimovitz, S. and Lederman, Z. 1997b. Six Seasons of Excavation in Tel Beth-Shemesh—A Border Town in Judah. *Qadmoniot* 113: 22–37 (Hebrew).

Bunimovitz, S., and Lederman, Z. 2003. The Final Destruction of Beth Shemesh and the *Pax Assyriaca* in the Judean Shephelah. *Tel Aviv* 30: 3–26.

Bunimovitz, S. and Lederman, Z. 2009. The Archaeology of Border Communities: Renewed Excavations at Tel Beth-Shemesh, Part 1: The Iron Age. *Near Eastern Archaeology* 72: 114–142.

Busink, T.A. 1970. *Der Tempel von Jerusalem von Salomo bis Herodes: eine archäologisch-historische Studie unter Berücksichtigung des westsemitischen Tempelbaus I der Tempel Salomos* (Studia Francisci Scholten memoriae dicata 3). Leiden.

Byl, J. 1998. On the Capacity of Solomon's Molten Sea. *Vetus Testamentum* 48: 309–314.

Byrne, R. 2003. Early Assyrian Contacts with Arabs and the Impact on Levantine Vassal Tribute. *Bulletin of the American Schools of Oriental Research* 331: 11–25.

Cahill, J.M. 1992. The Chalk Assemblages of the Persian/Hellenistic and Early Roman Periods. In: De Groot, A. and Ariel, D.T., eds. *Excavations at the City of David 1978–1985 Directed by Yigal Shiloh* III: *Stratigraphical, Environmental, and Other Reports* (Qedem 33). Jerusalem: 190–274.

Cahill, J.M. 1995. Rosette Stamp Seal Impressions from Ancient Judah. *Israel Exploration Journal* 45: 230–252.

Cahill, J.M 1997. Royal Rosettes Fit for a King. *Biblical Archaeology Review* 23(5): 48–57, 68–69.

Cahill, J.M. 1999. Rosette Stamp Seal Impressions from Ancient Judah. In: Beit-Arieh, I., ed. *Tel ʿIra: A Stronghold in the Biblical Negev* (Monograph Series of the Institute of Archaeology of Tel Aviv University 15). Tel Aviv: 360–373.

Cahill, J.M. 2000a. Rosette-Stamped Handle. *ʿAtiqot* 40: 54–56.

Cahill, J.M. 2000b. Rosette-Stamped Handles. In: Ariel, D.T., ed. *Excavations at the City of David 1978–1985 Directed by Yigal Shiloh* VI: *Inscriptions* (Qedem 41). Jerusalem: 85–108.

Cahill, J.M. 2001. Rosette Stamp Seal Impressions. In: Mazar, A. and Panitz-Cohen, N., eds. *Timnah (Tel Batash) II: The Finds from the First Millennium BCE. Text* (Qedem 42). Jerusalem: 197–202.

Cahill, J.M. 2003. Rosette Stamp Seal Impressions. In: Geva, H., ed. *Jewish Quarter Excavations in the Old City of Jerusalem, Conducted by Nahman Avigad, 1969–1982 II: The Finds: Areas A, W and X-2, Final Report*. Jerusalem: 85–98.

Campbell, E.F., Jr. and Wright, G.R.H. 2002. *Shechem III: The Stratigraphy and Architecture of Shechem/Tell Balâṭah* (American Schools of Oriental Research Archaeological Reports 6). Boston.

Carter, C.E. 1994. The Province of Yehud in the Post-Exilic Period: Soundings in Site Distribution and Demography. In: Eskenazi, T.C. and Richards, K.H., eds. *Second Temple Studies, 2: Temple and Community in the Persian Period* (Journal for the Study of the Old Testament Supplement Series 175). Sheffield: 106–145.

Carter, C.E. 1999. *The Emergence of Yehud in the Persian Period: A Social and Demographic Study* (Journal for the Study of the Old Testament Supplement Series 294). Sheffield.

Chambon, A. 1984. *Tell el-Farʿah* I: *l'âge du fer* (Editions Recherche sur les Civilisations, Memoire 31). Paris.

Chaney, M.L. 2014. The Political Economy of Peasant Poverty: What the Eighth-Century Prophets Presumed but Did Not State. *Supplement Series for the Journal of Religion & Society Supplement Series* 10: 34–60.

Christoph, J.R. 1993. *The Yehud Stamped Jar Handle Corpus: Implications for the History of Postexilic Palestine* (Ph.D. dissertation, Duke University). Durham.

Clermont-Ganneau, C. 1900. Inscribed Jar-Handles of Palestine. *Palestine Exploration Fund Quarterly Statement* 32: 251–253.

Cogan, M. 2001. *I Kings: New Translation with Introduction and Commentary* (The Anchor Bible 10). New York.

Cogan, M. and Tadmor, H. 1988. *II Kings: New Translation with Introduction and Commentary* (The Anchor Bible 11). Garden City.

Cohen, H.R. 1975. *Biblical Hapax Legomena in the Light of Akkadian and Ugaritic* (Ph.D. dissertation, Colombia University). New York.

Cook, S.A. 1925. Inscribed Jar Handels. *Palestine Exploration Fund Quarterly Statement* 57: 91–95.

Cooke, G.A. 1936. *A Critical and Exegetical Commentary on the Book of Ezekiel* (International Critical Commentary). Edinburgh.

Cross, F.M. 1962. Epigraphic Notes on Hebrew Documents of the Eighth-Sixth Centuries B.C.: II: The Murabbaʿât Papyrus and the Letter Found near Yabneh-yam. *Bulletin of the American Schools of Oriental Research* 165: 34–46.

Cross, F.M. 1968. Jar Inscriptions from Shiqmona. *Israel Exploration Journal* 18: 226–233.

Cross, F.M. 1969. Judean Stamps. *Eretz-Israel* 9: 20*–27*.

Cross, F.M. 1975. A Reconstruction of the Judean Restoration. *Journal of Biblical Literature* 94: 4–18.

Cross, F.M. 1981. An Aramaic Ostracon of the Third Century B.C.E. from Excavations in Jerusalem. *Eretz-Israel* 15: 67*–69*.

Cross, F.M. 2008. Inscriptions in Phoenician and Other Scripts. In: Stager, L.E., Schloen, J.D., and Master, D.M., eds. *Ashkelon* I: *Introduction and Overview (1985–2006)*. Winona Lake: 333–372.

Cross, F.M. and Milik, J.T. 1956. Explorations in the Judaean Buqêʿah. *Bulletin of the American Schools of Oriental Research* 142: 5–17.

Cross, F.M. and Stager, L. 2006. Cypro-Minoan Inscriptions Found in Ashkelon. *Israel Exploration Journal* 56: 129–159.

Crowfoot, J.W., Crowfoot, G.M. and Kenyon, K.M. 1957. *The Objects from Samaria* (Samaria-Sebaste: Reports of the Work of the Joint Expedition in 1931–1933 and of the British Expedition in 1935, 3) London.

Crowfoot, J.W. and Fitzgerald, G.M. 1929. *Excavations in the Tyropoeon Valley, Jerusalem, 1927.* Manchester.

Dagan, Y. 1992. The Shephelah during the Period of the Monarchy in Light of Archaeological Excavations and Surveys (M.A. thesis, Tel Aviv University). Tel Aviv (Hebrew).

Dagan, Y. 2001. *The Settlement in the Judean Shephelah in the Second and First Millennium BCE: A Test-case of Settlement Processes in a Geographic Region* (Ph.D. dissertation, Tel Aviv University). Tel Aviv (Hebrew).

Dagan, Y. 2004. Results of the Survey: Settlements Patterns in the Lachish Region. In: Ussishkin, D., ed. *The Renewed Archaeological Excavations at Lachish (1973–1994)*, V (Monograph Series of the Institute of Archaeology of Tel Aviv University 22). Tel Aviv: 2672–2690.

Dagan, Y. 2006. *Map of Amayza (109)* 1: *The Northern Sector* (Archaeological Survey of Israel). Jerusalem.

Dalman, G. 1924. *Orte und Wege Jesu* (3rd ed.), Gütersloh.

De Groot, A. 2001. Jerusalem during the Persian Period. In: Faust, A. and Baruch, E., eds. *New Studies on Jerusalem, Proceedings of the Seventh Conference*. Ramat Gan: 77–81 (Hebrew).

De Groot, A. 2004. Jerusalem in the Early Hellenistic Period. In: Baruch, E. and Faust, A., eds. *New Studies on Jerusalem* 10. Ramat Gan: 67–70 (Hebrew).

De Groot, A. 2005. Excavations in the South of the City of David— Reinterpretation of Former Excavations. *Qadmoniot* 130: 81–86 (Hebrew).

De Groot, A. and Ariel, D.T. 2005. The *yhwd* Stamp Impressions from Shiloh's Excavations in the City of David. In: Lipschits, O., ed. *New Studies on the* yhwd *Stamp Impressions—Booklet of Abstracts*. Tel Aviv: 15 (Hebrew).

De Groot, A. and Greenhut, Z. 2002. Moza—A Judahite Administrative Center Near Jerusalem. In: Faust, A. and Baruch, E., eds. *New Studies on Jerusalem* 8: 7–14 (Hebrew).

Deller, K. 1985. SAG.DU UR.MAH, Löwenkopfsitula, Löwenkopfbecher. *Baghdader Mitteilungen* 16: 327–346.

Deller, K. 1987. SAG.DU.UR.MAH: Eine Nachlese. *Baghdader Mitteilungen* 18: 219–220.

Derin, Z. 1999. Potters' Mark of Ayanis Citadel, Van. *Anatolian Studies* 49: 81–100.

Deutsch, R. 1997. The Corpus of the Hebrew Bullae: First Temple Period, 750–586 (M.A. thesis, Tel Aviv University). Tel Aviv (Hebrew).

Deutsch, R. 1999. *Messages from the Past. Hebrew Bullae from the Time of Isaiah through the Destruction of the First Temple*. Tel Aviv.

Deutsch, R. 2003a. *Biblical Period Hebrew Bullae, The Josef Chaim Kaufman Collection*. Tel Aviv.

Deutsch, R. 2003b. A Hoard of Fifty Hebrew Clay Bullae from the Time of Hezekiah. In: Deutsch, R., ed. *Shlomo: Studies in Epigraphy, Iconography, History and Archaeology in Honor of Shlomo Moussaieff*. Tel Aviv: 45–98.

Deutsch, R. 2011. *Biblical Period Epigraphy. The Josef Chaim Kaufman Collection: Seals, Bullae, Handles*. Jerusalem.

Deutsch, R. 2012. Six Hebrew Fiscal Bullae from the Time of Hezekiah. In: Lubetski, M. and Lubetski, E., eds. *New Inscriptions and Seals Relating to the Biblical World* (Archaeology and Biblical Studies 19). Atlanta: 59–67.

Deutsch, R. and Heltzer, M. 1994. *Forty New Ancient West Semitic Inscriptions*. Tel Aviv.

Deutsch, R., and Heltzer, M. 1995. *New Epigraphic Evidence from the Biblical Period*. Tel Aviv.

Deutsch, R. and Heltzer, M. 1999. *West Semitic Epigraphic News of the 1st Millennium BCE*. Tel Aviv: 66–68.

Dever, W.G. 1998. *Gezer: A Crossroad in Ancient Israel*. Tel Aviv (Hebrew).

Dever, W.G., Lance, D.H., Bullard, R.G., Cole, D.P. and Seger, J.D. 1974. *Gezer* II: *Report of the 1967–70 Seasons in Fields I and II* (Annual of the Nelson Glueck School of Biblical Archaeology 2). Jerusalem.

Dever, W.G., Lance, H.D. and Bullard, R.G. 1986. *Gezer* IV: *The 1969–71 Seasons in Field VI, "The Acropolis"* (Annual of the Nelson Glueck School of Biblical Archaeology 4). Jerusalem.

Diringer, D. 1934. *Le iscrizioni antico-ebraiche Palestinesi*. Firenze.

Diringer, D. 1941. On Ancient Hebrew Inscriptions Discovered at Tell ed-Duweir (Lachish)—I and II. *Palestine Exploration Quarterly* 73: 38–56, 89–109.

Diringer, D. 1943. On Ancient Hebrew Inscriptions Discovered at Tell ed-Duweir (Lachish)—III. *Palestine Exploration Quarterly* 75: 89–99.

Diringer, D. 1949. The Royal Jar Handle Stamps of Ancient Judah. *The Biblical Archaeologist* 12: 70–86.

Diringer, D. 1950. Three Early Hebrew Seals. *Archiv Orientální* 18: 65–69.

Diringer, D. 1953. Early Hebrew Inscriptions. In: Tufnell, O., ed. *Lachish* III *(Tell ed-Duweir): The Iron Age*. London, New York and Toronto: 331–359.

Dobbs-Allsopp, F.W., Roberts, J.J.M., Seow, C.L. and Whitaker, R.E. 2004. *Hebrew Inscriptions: Texts from the Biblical Period of the Monarchy with Concordance*. New Haven and London.

Donnan, C.B. 1971. Ancient Peruvian Potters' Marks and Their Interpretation through Ethnographic Analogy. *American Antiquity* 36: 460–466.

Dothan, M. 1971. *Ashdod* II–III: *The Second and Third Seasons of Excavations 1963, 1965. Soundings in 1967* (ʿAtiqot 9–10, English Series). Jerusalem.

Dothan, M. and Freedman, D.N. 1967. *Ashdod* I: *The First Season of Excavations 1962* (ʿAtiqot 7, English Series). Jerusalem.

Dothan, M. and Porath, Y. 1982. *Ashdod* IV: *Excavation of Area M—The Fortifications of the Lower City* (ʿAtiqot 15, English Series). Jerusalem.

Dothan, T. and Gitin, S. 1994. Tel Miqne/Ekron—The Rise and Fall of a Philistine City. *Qadmoniot* 105/106: 2–28 (Hebrew).

Drinkard, J.F. 1997. New Volute Capital Discovered. *The Biblical Archaeologist* 60: 249–250.

Dubovský, P. 2006. Tiglath-Pileser III's Campaigns in 734–732 B.C.: Historical Background of Isa 7, 2 Kgs 15–16 and 2 Chr 27–28. *Biblica* 87: 153–170.

Duncan, J.G. 1931. *Digging Up Biblical History: Recent Archaeology in Palestine and Its Bearing on the Old Testament Historical Narratives* (2 vols.). London.

Edelman, D.V. 2003. Gibeon and the Gibeonites Revisited. In: Lipschits, O. and Blenkinsopp, J. (eds.). *Judah and the Judeans in the Neo-Babylonian Period*. Winona Lake: 153–167.

Edelstein, G. 2000. A Terraced Farm at Er-Ras. ʿ*Atiqot* 40: 39–63.

Edelstein, G., Milevski, I. and Aurant, S. 1999. *Villages, Terraces and Stone Mounds: Excavations at Manahat, Jerusalem, 1987–1989* (IAA Reports 3). Jerusalem.

Edens, C. and Bawden, G. 1989. History of Taymaʾ and Hejazi Trade during the First Millennium B.C. *Journal of the Economic and Social History of the Orient* 32: 48–103.

Eggler, J., Herr, L.G. and Root, R. 2002. Seals and Seal Impressions from Excavation Seasons 1984–2000. In: Herr, L.G., Clark, D.R., Geraty, L.T., Younker, R.W. and LaBianca, O.S., eds. *Madaba Plains Project* 5: *The 1994 Season at Tall al-ʿUmayri and Subsequent Studies*. Berrien Springs: 234–304.

Eggler, J. and Keel, O. 2006. *Corpus der Siegel-Amulette aus Jordanien: vom Neolithikum bis zur Perserzeit*. Fribourg.

Ein Mor, D. and Ron, Z. 2013. "Golat Hakoteret": A Royal Spring Tunnel from the Iron Age in the Naḥal Refaim Area. In: Stiebel, G.D., Peleg-Barakat, O., Ben-Ami, D., Weksler-Bdolah, S. and Gadot, Y. eds. *New Studies in the Archaeology of Jerusalem and Its Region* 7. Jerusalem: 85–109 (Hebrew).

Ein Mor, D and Ron, Z. 2016. ʿAin Joweizeh: An Iron Age Royal Rock-Cut Spring System in the Naḥal Refaʾim Valley, near Jerusalem. *Tel Aviv* 43: 127–146.

Elat, M. 1977. *Economic Relations in the Land of the Bible (c. 1000–539 B.C.)*. Jerusalem (Hebrew).

Elat, M. 1978. The Economic Relations of the Neo-Assyrian Empire with Egypt. *Journal of the American Oriental Society* 98: 20–34.

Elat, M. 1990. International Commerce in Palestine under Assyrian Rule. In: Kedar, B.Z., Dothan, T. and Safrai, S., eds. *Commerce in Palestine Throughout the Ages*. Jerusalem: 67–88 (Hebrew).

Elitzur, Y. 2009. *Ancient Toponyms in the Land of Israel: Preservation and History*. Jerusalem (Hebrew).

Ellenbogen, M. 1962. *Foreign Words in the Old Testament: Their Origin and Etymology*. London.

Emberling, G., and McDonald, H. 2003. Excavations at Tell Brak 2001–2002: Preliminary Report. *Iraq*: 65: 1–75.

Ephʿal, I. 1982. *The Ancient Arabs: Nomads on the Borders of the Fertile Crescent 9th–5th Centuries B.C.* Jerusalem and Leiden.

Ephʿal, I. and Naveh, J. 1993. The Jar of the Gate. *Bulletin of the American Schools of Oriental Research* 289: 59–65.

Eshel, H. 1991. Sennacherib's Campaign to Jerusalem. In: Amit, D. and Gonen, R., eds. *Jerusalem in the First Temple Period*. Jerusalem: 143–156 (Hebrew).

Eshel, Y. 1986–87. *The Chronology of Selected Pottery Assemblages from the Late Iron Age in Judah Based on the Excavations of Tel Laḥish and Meṣad Ḥashavyahu* (Ph.D. dissertation, Tel Aviv University). Tel Aviv (Hebrew).

Fales, F.M. 2008. On Pax Assyriaca in the Eighth–Seventh Centuries BCE and Its Implications. In: Cohen, R. and Westbrook, R., eds. *Isaiah's Vision of Peace in Biblical and Modern International Relations: Swords into Plowshares*. New York: 17–35.

Fales, F.M. 2013. Ethnicity in the Assyrian Empire: A View from the *Nisbe* (I): Foreigners and "Special" Inner Communities. In: Vanderhooft, D.S. and Winitzer, A., eds. *Literature as Politics, Politics as Literature. Essays on the Ancient Near East in Honor of Peter Machinist*. Winona Lake: 47–73.

Fales, F.M. and Postgate, J.N. 1995. *Imperial Administrative Records* II: *Provincial and Military Administration* (State Archives of Assyria 11). Helsinki.

Fantalkin, A. 2000. Mezad Hashavyahu: Analysis of the Material Culture and Its Contribution to Historical Reconstruction at the End of the Iron Age (M.A. thesis, Tel Aviv University). Tel Aviv (Hebrew).

Fantalkin, A. 2001. Mezad Hashavyahu: Its Material Culture and Historical Background. *Tel Aviv* 28: 3–166.

Fantalkin, A. 2004. The Final Destruction of Beth Shemesh and the *Pax Assyriaca* in the Judahite Shephelah: An Alternative View. *Tel Aviv* 31: 245–261.

Fantalkin, A. and Tal, O. 2006. Redating Lachish Level I: Identifying Achaemenid Imperial Policy at the Southern Frontier of the Fifth Satrapy. In: Lipschits, O. and Oeming, M., eds. *Judah and the Judeans in the Persian Period*. Winona Lake: 167–197.

Farhi, Y. 2001. A Stamped Handle from Naḥal Yarmut. *Ḥadashot Arkheologiyot—Excavations and Surveys in Israel* 113: 176 (Hebrew), 124*–125* (English summary).

Faust, A. 2003. Judah in the Sixth Century B.C.E.: A Rural Perspective. *Palestine Exploration Quarterly* 135: 37–53.

Faust, A. 2004. Social and Cultural Changes in Judah during the Sixth Century B.C.E. and Their Implications for Our Understanding of the Nature of the Neo-Babylonian Period. *Ugarit-Forschungen* 36: 157–176

Faust, A. 2007. Settlement Dynamics and Demographic Fluctuations in Judah from the Late Iron Age to the Hellenistic Period and the Archaeology of Persian Period Yehud. In: Levin, Y, ed. *A Time of Change: Judah and Its Neighbors during the Persian and Early Hellenistic Periods*. London: 23–51.

Faust, A. 2008. Settlement and Demography in Seventh-Century Judah and the Extent and Intensity of Sennacherib's Campaign. *Palestine Exploration Quarterly* 140: 168–194.

Faust, A. 2011. The Interests of the Assyrian Empire in the West: Olive Oil Production as a Test-Case. *Journal of the Economic and Social History of the Orient* 54: 62–86.

Faust, A. 2012a. *The Archaeology of Israelite Society in Iron Age II*. Winona Lake.

Faust, A. 2012b. *Judah in the Neo-Babylonian Period: The Archaeology of Desolation* (Archaeology and Biblical Studies 18). Atlanta.

Faust, A. 2015. Settlement, Economy, and Demography under Assyrian Rule in the West: The Territories of the Former Kingdom of Israel as a Test Case. *Journal of the American Oriental Society* 135: 765–789.

Faust, A. and Weiss, E. 2005. Judah, Philistia, and the Mediterranean World: Reconstructing the Economic System of the Seventh Century BCE. *Bulletin of the American Schools of Oriental Research* 338: 71–92.

Faust, A. and Weiss, E. 2011. Between Assyria and the Mediterranean World: The Prosperity of Judah and Philistia in the Seventh Century B.C.E in Context. In: Wilkinson, T., Sherratt, S. and Bennet, J., eds. *Interweaving Worlds: Systemic Interaction in Eurasia: 7th to 1st Millennia BC*. Oxford: 189–204.

Feig, N. 1996. New Discoveries in the Rephaim Valley, Jerusalem. *Palestine Exploration Quarterly* 128: 3–7.

Feig, N. 2003. Excavations at Beit Ṣafafa: Iron Age II and Byzantine Agricultural Installations South of Jerusalem. *'Atiqot* 44: 191–238.

Feig, N. and Abd Rabu, O. 1996. Jerusalem, Khirbet er-Ras. *Excavations and Surveys in Israel* 15: 74–75.

Finkelstein, I. 1992. Ḥorvat Qiṭmīt and the Southern Trade in the Late Iron Age II. *Zeitschrift des Deutschen Palästina-Vereins* 108: 156–170.

Finkelstein, I. 1994. The Archaeology of the Days of Manasseh. In: Coogan, M.D., Exum, J.C. and Stager, L.E., eds. *Scripture and Other Artifacts: Essays on the Bible and Archaeology in Honor of Philip J. King*. Louisville: 169–187.

Finkelstein, I. 1995. *Living on the Fringe: The Archaeology and History of the Negev, Sinai and Neighbouring Regions in the Bronze and Iron Ages*. Sheffield.

Finkelstein, I. 2000. Omride Architecture. *Zeitschrift des Deutschen Palästina-Vereins* 116: 114–138.

Finkelstein, I. 2002. Gezer Revisited and Revised. *Tel Aviv* 29: 262–296.

Finkelstein, I. 2008a. Archaeology and the List of Returnees in the Books of Ezra and Nehemiah. *Palestine Exploration Quarterly* 140: 7–16.

Finkelstein, I. 2008b. Jerusalem in the Persian (and Early Hellenistic) Period and the Wall of Nehemiah. *Journal for the Study of the Old Testament* 32: 501–520.

Finkelstein, I. 2009. Persian Period Jerusalem and Yehud: A Rejoinder. *The Journal of Hebrew Scriptures* 9. http://www.jhsonline.org/Articles/article_126.pdf.

Finkelstein, I. 2012. Comments on the Date of Late-Monarchic Judahite Seal Impressions. *Tel Aviv* 39: 203–211.

Finkelstein, I. and Beit-Arieh, I. 1999. Area E. In: Beit-Arieh, I., ed. *Tel 'Ira: A Stronghold in the Biblical Negev* (Monograph Series of the Institute of Archaeology of Tel Aviv University 15). Tel Aviv: 67–96.

Finkelstein, I. and Gadot, Y. 2015. Mozah, Nephtoah and Royal Estates in the Jerusalem Highlands. *Semitica et Classica* 8: 227–234.

Finkelstein, I. and Magen, Y., eds. 1993. *Archaeological Surveys in the Hill Country of Benjamin*. Jerusalem.

Finkelstein, I. and Naʾaman, N. 2004. The Judahite Shephelah in the Late 8th and Early 7th Centuries BCE. *Tel Aviv* 31: 60–79.

Finkelstein, I. and Piasetzky, E. 2010. Radiocarbon Dating the Iron Age in the Levant: A Bayesian Model for Six Ceramic Phases and Six Transitions. *Antiquity* 84: 374–385.

Finkelstein, I. and Singer-Avitz, L. 2001. Ashdod Revisited. *Tel Aviv* 28: 231–259.

Finkelstein, I., and Singer-Avitz, L. 2009. Reevaluating Bethel. *Zeitschrift des Deutschen Palästina-Vereins* 125: 33–48.

Finkelstein, I. and Ussishkin, D. 2000. Archaeological and Historical Conclusions. In: Finkelstein, I., Ussishkin, D. and Halpern, B., eds. *Megiddo* III: *The 1992–1996 Seasons* (Monograph Series of the Institute of Archaeology of Tel Aviv University 18). Tel Aviv: 576–605.

Finkielsztejn, G. 1999. Hellenistic Jerusalem: The Evidence of the Rhodian Amphora Stamps. In: Faust, A. and Baruch, E., eds. *New Studies on Jerusalem. Proceedings of the Fifth Conference*. Ramat Gan: 21–36.

Finkielsztejn, G. and Gibson, S. 2007. The Retrograde-F-Shaped *yh(d)* Monogram: Epigraphy and Dating. *Tel Aviv* 34: 104–113.

Finkielsztejn, G. and Gorzalczany, A. 2010. ʿEn Tut: Preliminary Report. *Ḥadashot Arkheologiyot—Excavations and Surveys in Israel* 122. http://www.hadashot-esi.org.il/Report_Detail_Eng.aspx?id=1412&mag_id=117.

Fischer, P.M. 1998. Tall Abū al-Kharaz: The Swedish Jordan Expedition 1997, Eighth Season. Preliminary Excavations Report. *Annual of the Department of Antiquities of Jordan* 42: 213–223.

Fox, N.S. 2000. *In the Service of the King: Officialdom in Ancient Israel and Judah* (Monographs of the Hebrew Union College 23). Cincinnati.

Frankel, D. 1975. The Pot Marks of Vounous: Simple Clustering Techniques, Their Problems and Potential. *Opuscula Atheniensia* 11: 37–51.

Franken, H.J. 1989. Deir ʿAlla (Tell). In: Homès-Fredericq, D. and Hennessy, J., eds. *Archaeology of Jordan* II.1: *Field Reports, Surveys and Sites A–K*. Leuven: 201–205.

Franken, H.J. and Ibrahim, M.M. 1977–78. Two Seasons of Excavations at Tell Deir ʿAlla, 1976–1978. *Annual of the Department of Antiquities of Jordan* 22: 57–80.

Franken, H.J. and Steiner, M.L. 1990. *Excavation in Jerusalem 1961–1967* II: *The Iron Age Extramural Quarter on the South-East Hill* (British Academy Monographs in Archaeology 2). Oxford.

Frankenstein, S. 1979. The Phoenicians in the Far West: A Function of Neo-Assyrian Imperialism. In: Larsen, M.T., ed. *Power and Propaganda: A Symposium on Ancient Empires*. Copenhagen: 263–294.

Frankfort, H. 1939. *Cylinder Seals: A Documentary Essay on the Art and Religion of the Ancient Near East*. London.

Freud, L. 1999. Pottery: Iron Age. In: Beit-Arieh, I., ed. *Tel ʿIra: A Stronghold in the Biblical Negev* (Monograph Series of the Institute of Archaeology of Tel Aviv University 15). Tel Aviv: 189–289.

Fritz, V. 1996. *Das erste Buch der Könige* (Zürcher Bibelkommentare Altes: Testament 10:1). Zürich.

Fuchs, A. 1994. *Die Inschriften Sargons II aus Khorsabad*. Göttingen.

Fuchs, A. 1998. *Die Annalen des Jahres 711 v. Chr.: Nach Prismenfragmenten aus Ninive und Assur* (State Archives of Assyria Studies 8). Helsinki.

Gadot, Y. 2010. The Lion Stamp Impressions from Ramat Raḥel: Stratigraphy, Chronology and Contexts. In: Lipschits, O. and Koch, I., eds. *New Studies on the Lion Stamp Impressions from Judah (Abstracts of a Symposium, 14 January 2010, Tel Aviv University)*. Tel Aviv: 8–10 (Hebrew).

Gadot, Y. 2015. In the Valley of the King: Jerusalem's Rural Hinterland in the 8th–4th Centuries BCE. *Tel Aviv* 42: 3–26.

Galling, K. 1977. *Biblisches Reallexikon* (Handbuch zum Alten Testament 1) (2nd ed.). Tübingen.

Garbini, G. 1962. The Dating of Post-Exilic Stamps. In: Aharoni, Y., ed. *Excavations at Ramat Rahel: Seasons 1959 and 1960*. Rome: 61–68.

Garfinkel, Y. 1984. The Distribution of Identical Seal Impressions and the Settlement Pattern in Judea before Sennacherib's Campaign. *Cathedra* 32: 35–53 (Hebrew).

Garfinkel, Y. 1985. A Hierarchic Pattern in the Private Seal-Impressions on the "lmlk" Jar-Handles. *Eretz-Israel* 18: 108–115 (Hebrew), 69* (English summary).

Garfinkel, Y. 1987. The City-List, Epigraphic Evidence and the Administrative Division in the Kingdom of Judah. *Zion* 52: 489–494 (Hebrew), XVII (English summary).

Garfinkel, Y. 1988. 2 Chr 11:5–10 Fortified Cities List and the *lmlk* Stamps—Reply to Nadav Naʾaman. *Bulletin of the American Schools of Oriental Research* 271: 69–73.

Garfinkel, Y. 1990. The Eliakim Naʿar Yokan Seal Impressions: Sixty Years of Confusion in Biblical Archaeological Research. *The Biblical Archaeologist* 53: 74–79.

Germer-Durand, E.P. 1909–10. Mesures de capacité des Hébreux. In: *Conférences de Saint-Étienne* (École pratique d'études bibliques). Paris.

Geva, H. 1983. Excavations in the Citadel of Jerusalem, 1979–1980: Preliminary Report. *Israel Exploration Journal* 33: 55–71.

Geva, H. 1985. The "First Wall" of Jerusalem during the Second Temple Period. An Architectural-Chronological Note. *Eretz-Israel* 18: 21–39 (Hebrew), 65* (English summary).

Geva, H. 1994. Excavations at the Citadel of Jerusalem, 1976–1980. In: Geva, H., ed. *Ancient Jerusalem Revealed*. Jerusalem: 156–167.

Geva, H. 2000a. Excavations at the Citadel of Jerusalem, 1976–1980. In: Geva, H., ed. *Ancient Jerusalem Revealed* (reprinted and expanded edition). Jerusalem: 156–167.

Geva, H. 2000b. General Introduction to the Excavations in the Jewish Quarter. In: Geva, H., ed. *Jewish Quarter Excavations in the Old City of Jerusalem, Conducted by Nahman Avigad, 1969–1982* I: *Architecture and Stratigraphy: Areas A, W and X-2, Final Report*. Jerusalem: 1–31.

Geva, H. 2003a. Hellenistic Pottery from Areas W and X-2. In: Geva, H., ed. *Jewish Quarter Excavations in the Old City of Jerusalem, Conducted by Nahman Avigad, 1969–1982* II: *The Finds: Areas A, W and X-2, Final Report*. Jerusalem: 113–175.

Geva, H. 2003b. Summary and Discussion of Findings from Areas A, W and X-2. In: Geva, H., ed. *Jewish Quarter Excavations in the Old City of Jerusalem, Conducted by Nahman Avigad,*

1969–1982 II: *The Finds: Areas A, W and X-2, Final Report.* Jerusalem: 501–552.

Geva, H. 2005. The Excavations of the Jewish Quarter: New Chronological Conclusions on the Dating of the Late *yhwd* Stamp Impressions. In: Lipschits, O., ed. *New Studies on the* yhwd *Stamp Impressions—Booklet of Abstracts.* Tel Aviv: 16 (Hebrew).

Geva, H. 2006. The Settlement on the Southwestern Hill of Jerusalem at the End of the Iron Age: A Reconstruction Based on the Archaeological Evidence. *Zeitschrift des Deutschen Palästina-Vereins* 122: 140–150.

Geva, H. 2007. A Chronological Reevaluation of Yehud Stamp Impressions in Palaeo-Hebrew Script, Based on Finds from Excavations in the Jewish Quarter of the Old City of Jerusalem. *Tel Aviv* 34: 92–103.

Geva, H. and Avigad, N. 2000. Area X2—Stratigraphy and Architecture. In: Geva, H., ed. *Jewish Quarter Excavations in the Old City of Jerusalem, Conducted by Nahman Avigad, 1969–1982* I: *Architecture and Stratigraphy: Areas A, W and X-2, Final Report.* Jerusalem: 199–240.

Geva, H. and Reich, R. 2000. Area A—Stratigraphy and Architecture IIa: Introduction. In: Geva, H., ed. *Jewish Quarter Excavations in the Old City of Jerusalem, Conducted by Nahman Avigad, 1969–1982* I: *Architecture and Stratigraphy: Areas A, W and X-2, Final Report.* Jerusalem: 37–43.

Gibson, J.C.L. 1971. *Textbook of Syrian Semitic Inscriptions* I: *Hebrew and Moabite Inscriptions.* Oxford.

Gibson, M. and Biggs, R.D. 1977. *Seals and Sealings in the Ancient Near East* (Bibliotheca Mesopotamica 6). Malibu.

Gibson, S. 1994. The Tell ej-Judeideh (Tel Goded) Excavations: A Re-appraisal Based on Archival Records in the Palestine Exploration Fund. *Tel Aviv* 21: 194–234.

Gilboa, A. 1996. Assyrian-type Pottery at Dor and the Status of the Town during the Assyrian Occupation Period. *Eretz-Israel* 25: 122–135 (Hebrew), 92* (English summary).

Gilboa, A., Karasik, A., Sharon, I. and Smilansky, U. 2004. Towards Computerized Typology and Classification of Ceramics. *Journal of Archaeological Science* 31: 681–694.

Ginsberg, H.L. 1948. MMŠT and MṢH. *Bulletin of the American Schools of Oriental Research* 109: 20–22.

Gitin, S. 1989. Tel Miqne-Ekron: A Type-Site for the Inner Coastal Plain in the Iron Age II Period. In: Gitin, S. and Dever, W.G., eds. *Recent Excavations in Israel: Studies in Iron Age Archaeology* (Annual of the American Schools of Oriental Research 49). Winona Lake: 23–58.

Gitin, S. 1990. *Gezer* III: *A Ceramic Typology of the Late Iron II, Persian and Hellenistic Periods at Tell Gezer.* Jerusalem.

Gitin, S. 1995. Tel Miqne-Ekron in the 7th Century B.C.E.: The Impact of Economic Innovation and Foreign Cultural Influences on a Neo-Assyrian Vassal City-State. In: Gitin, S., ed. *Recent Excavations in Israel: A View to the West, Reports on Kabri, Nami, Miqne-Ekron, Dor, and Ashkelon* (Archaeological Institute of America Colloquia and Conference Papers 1). Dubuque: 61–79.

Gitin, S. 1996. Tel Miqne-Ekron in the 7th Century B.C.: City Plan Development and The Oil Industry. In: Eitam, D. and Heltzer, M., eds. *Olive Oil in Antiquity: Israel and Neighboring Countries from the Neolithic to the Early Arab Period* (History of the Ancient Near East Studies 7). Padova: 219–242.

Gitin, S. 1997. The Neo-Assyrian Empire and Its Western Periphery: The Levant, with a Focus on Philistine Ekron. In: Parpola, S. and Whiting, R.M., eds. *Assyria, 1995. Proceedings of the 10th Anniversary Symposium of the Neo-Assyrian Text Corpus Project, Helsinki, September 7–11, 1995.* Helsinki: 77–103.

Gitin, S. 1998. The Philistines in the Prophetic Texts: An Archaeological Perspective. In: Magness, J. and Gitin, S., eds. *Hesed ve-Emet: Studies in Honor of Ernest S. Frerichs* (Brown Judaic Studies 320). Atlanta: 273–290.

Gitin, S. 2003. Neo-Assyrian and Egyptian Hegemony over Ekron in the Seventh Century BCE: A Response to Lawrence E. Stager. *Eretz-Israel* 27: 55*–61*.

Gitin, S. 2006. The *lmlk* Jar-Form Redefined: A New Class of Iron Age II Oval Shaped Storage Jar. In: Maeir, A.M. and de Miroschedji, P., eds. *"I Will Speak the Riddles of Ancient Times": Archaeological and Historical Studies in Honor of Amihai Mazar on the Occasion of His Sixtieth Birthday.* Winona Lake: 505–524.

Goren, Y. and Halperin, N. 2004. Selected Petrographic Analyses. In: Ussishkin, D., ed. *The Renewed Archaeological Excavations at Lachish (1973–1994)*, V (Monograph Series of the Institute of Archaeology of Tel Aviv University 22). Tel Aviv: 2553–2569.

Grabbe, L.L., ed. 2003. *"Like a Bird in a Cage": The Invasion of Sennacherib in 701 BCE* (Journal for the Study of the Old Testament, Supplement Series 363). London and New York.

Graham, J.N. 1984. Enigmatic Bible Passages: "Vinedressers and Plowmen": 2 Kings 25:12 and Jeremiah 52:16. *The Biblical Archaeologist* 47: 55–58.

Grant, E. and Wright, G.E. 1939. *Ain Shems Excavations (Palestine)* V: *Text* (Biblical and Kindred Studies 8). Haverford.

Greenberg, M. 1983. *Ezekiel 1–20: A New Translation with Introduction and Commentary* (The Anchor Bible 22). Garden City.

Greenberg, R. and Cinamon, G. 2006. Stamped and Incised Jar Handles from Rogem Gannim and Their Implications for the Political Economy of Jerusalem, Late 8th–Early 4th Centuries BCE. *Tel Aviv* 33: 229–243.

Greenhut, Z. 2006. *Production, Storage and Distribution of Grain during the Iron Age and Their Linkage to the Socio-Economic Organization of the Settlement in Israel* (Ph.D. dissertation, Tel Aviv University). Tel Aviv (Hebrew).

Greenhut, Z. and De Groot, A. 2002. Moẓa—A Bronze and Iron Age Village West of Jerusalem. *Qadmoniot* 123: 12–17.

Greenhut, Z. and De Groot, A. 2009. *Salvage Excavations at Tel Moza: The Bronze and Iron Age Settlements and Later Occupations* (IAA Reports 39). Jerusalem.

Grena, G.M. 2004. *LMLK—A Mystery Belonging to the King.* Redondo Beach.

Gross, B. and Goren, Y. 2010. A Technological Research of the Lion Stamp Impressions: Preliminary Results. In: Lipschits, O. and Koch, I., eds. *New Studies on the Lion Stamp Impressions from Judah (Abstracts of a Symposium, 14 January 2010, Tel Aviv University).* Tel Aviv: 11–12 (Hebrew).

Gunneweg, J., Perlman, I. and Meshel, Z. 1985. The Origin of the Pottery of Kuntillet ʿAjrud. *Israel Exploration Journal* 35: 270–283.

Gurvin, S. 2010. Technology and Function of Judean Bullae from the First Temple Period (M.A. thesis, Tel Aviv University). Tel Aviv (Hebrew).

Hadas, G. 1983. Naḥal ʿArugot, Seal Impression. *Excavations and Surveys in Israel* 2: 77.

Halpern, B. 1991. Jerusalem and the Lineages in the Seventh Century BCE: Kinship and the Rise of Individual Moral Liability. In: Halpern, B. and Hobson, D.W., eds. *Law and Ideology in Monarchic Israel* (Journal for the Study of the Old Testament Supplement Series 124). Sheffield: 11–107.

Halpern, B. 1996. Sybil, or the Two Nations? Archaism, Kinship, Alienation, and the Elite Redefinition of Traditional Culture in Judah in the 8th–7th Centuries BCE. In: Cooper, J.S. and Schwartz, G.M., eds. *The Study of the Ancient Near East in the Twenty-First Century: The William Foxwell Albright Centennial Conference.* Winona Lake: 291–338.

Hammond, P.C. 1957a. A Note on a Seal Impression from Tell es-Sultân. *Bulletin of the American Schools of Oriental Research* 147: 37–39.

Hammond, P.C. 1957b. A Note on Two Seal Impressions from Tell Es-Sulṭan. *Palestine Exploration Quarterly* 89: 68–69.

Haran, M. 1979. The Law Code of Ezekiel XL–XLVIII and Its Relation to the Priestly School. *Hebrew Union College Annual* 50: 45–71.

Harding, G.L. 1943. *Guide to Lachish, Tell ed-Duweir.* Jerusalem.

Hayes, J.H. and Hooker, P.K. 1988. *A New Chronology for the Kings of Israel and Judah and Its Implication for Biblical History and Literature.* Atlanta.

Heltzer, M. 1983. The Ugaritic *ltḥ* and the Biblical *ʿiśśārōn. Shnaton: An Annual for Biblical and Ancient Near Eastern Studies* 7/8: 159–161 (Hebrew), IX (English summary).

Heltzer, M. 1989. Some Questions of the Ugaritic Metrology and Its Parallels in Judah, Phoenicia, Mesopotamia and Greece. *Ugarit-Forschungen* 21: 195–208.

Heltzer, M. 2008. A New look at the nēbel Measure. In: Bar, S., ed. *In the Hill-Country, and in the Shephelah, and in the Arabah (Joshua 12, 8): Studies and Researches Presented to Adam Zertal in the Thirtieth Anniversary of the Manasseh Hill-Country Survey.* Jerusalem: 70*–74*.

Herzog, Z., Aharoni, M., Rainey, A.F. and Moshkovitz, S. 1984. The Israelite Fortress at Arad. *Bulletin of the American Schools of Oriental Research* 254: 1–34.

Herzog, Z. and Singer-Avitz, L. 2004. Redefining the Centre: The Emergence of State in Judah. *Tel Aviv* 31: 209–244.

Hestrin, R. and Dayagi-Mendels, M. 1979. *Inscribed Seals: First Temple Period, Hebrew, Ammonite, Moabite, Phoenician and Aramaic, from the Collections of the Israel Museum and the Israel Department of Antiquities and Museums.* Jerusalem.

Hestrin, R., Israeli, Y., Meshorer, Y. and Eitan, A. 1972. *Inscriptions Reveal: Documents from the Time of the Bible, the Mishna and the Talmud.* Jerusalem.

Hirschfeld, N. 2008. How and Why Potmarks Matter. *Near Eastern Archaeology* 71: 120–129.

Hizmi, H. and Shabbtai, Z. 1991. Khirbet Qeila, Seal Impression. *Excavations and Surveys in Israel* 10: 170.

Hoftijzer, J. and van der Kooij, G. 1976. *Aramaic Text from Deir ʿAlla* (Documenta et Monumenta Orientis Antiqui 19). Leiden.

Hognesius, K. 1994. The Capacity of the Molten Sea in 2 Chronicles IV 5: A Suggestion. *Vetus Testamentum* 24: 349–358.

Holladay, J.S., Jr. 1976. Of Sherds and Strata: Contributions toward an Understanding of the Archaeology of the Divided Monarchy. In: Cross, F.M., Lemke, W.E. and Miller, P.D., eds. *Magnalia Dei: The Mighty Acts of God. Essays on the Bible and Archaeology in Memory of G. Ernest Wright.* New York: 253–293.

Holladay, J.S., Jr. 2006. Hezekiah's Tribute, Long-Distance Trade, and the Wealth of Nations ca. 1000-600 BC: A New Perspective. In: Gitin, S., Wright, J.E. and Dessel, J.P., eds. *Confronting the Past: Archaeological and Historical Essays on Ancient Israel in Honor of William G. Dever.* Winona Lake: 309–332.

Hopkins, D.C. 1996. Bare Bones: Putting Flesh on the Economics of Ancient Israel. In: Fritz, V. and Davies, P., eds. *The Origins of the Ancient Israelite States* (Journal for the Study of the Old Testament Supplement Series 228). Sheffield: 121–139.

Hopkins, D.C. 1997. Agriculture. In: Meyers, E.M., ed. *The Oxford Encyclopedia of Archaeology in the Near East.* Oxford: 22–30.

Hudon, J.P. 2010. The *LMLK* Storage Jars and the Reign of Uzziah: Towards a Mid-Eighth Century B.C. *Terminus a Quo* for the Royal Jars of the Kingdom of Judah. *Near East Archaeological Society Bulletin* 55: 27–44.

Ibrahim, M.M. 1978. The Collared-Rim Jars of the Early Iron Age. In: Moorey, R. and Parr, P., eds. *Archaeology in the Levant: Essays for Kathleen Kenyon.* Warminster: 116–126.

Ibrahim, M.M. 1983. Siegel und Siegelabdrücke aus Saḥāb. *Zeitschrift des Deutschen Palästina-Vereins* 99: 43–53.

Inge, C. H. 1938. Excavations at Tell ed-Duweir: The Wellcome Marston Archaeological Research Expedition to the Near East. *Palestine Exploration Quarterly* 70: 240–256.

Inge, C.H. 1941. Post-Scriptum. *Palestine Exploration Quarterly* 73: 106–109.

Irvine, S.A. 1990. *Isaiah, Ahaz, and the Syro-Ephraimite Crisis* (Society of Biblical Literature Dissertation Series 123). Atlanta.

James, T.G.H. 1991. Egypt: The Twenty-Fifth and Twenty-Sixth Dynasties. In: Boardman, J., Edwards, I.E.S., Sollberger, E. and Hammond, N.G.L., eds. *The Assyrian and Babylonian Empires and Other States of the Near East, from the Eighth to the Sixth Centuries B.C.* (Cambridge Ancient History 3.2). Cambridge, U.K.: 677–747.

Janssen, J.J. 1975. *Commodity Prices from the Ramesside Period: An Economic Study of the Village of Necropolis Workmen at Thebes.* Leiden.

Janssen, J.J. 1988. On Prices and Wages in Ancient Egypt. *Altorientalische Forschungen* 15: 10–23.

Jasmin, M. 2006. The Emergence and First Development of the Arabian Trade Across the Wadi Arabah. In: Bienkowski, P. and Galor, K., eds. *Crossing the Rift: Resources, Settlement Patterns and Interaction in the Wadi Arabah* (Levant Supplementary Series 3). Oxford: 143–150.

Ji, C.-H.C. 2001. Judean Jar Handles Bearing Concentric Circles. *Near East Archaeological Society Bulletin* 46: 1–24.

Kallai, Z. 1954. Baal-Perazim. *Encyclopaedia Biblica* 2. Jerusalem: 290–291 (Hebrew).

Kang, H. and Garfinkel, Y. 2015. Finger-Impressed Jar Handles at Khirbet Qeiyafa: New Light on Administration in the Kingdom of Judah. *Levant* 47: 186–205.

Karasik, A. and Smilansky, U. 2006. Computation of the Capacity of Pottery Vessels Based on Drawn Profiles. In: Mazar, A., ed. *Excavations at Tel Beth Shean 1989–1996*, I: *From the Late Bronze Age IIB to the Medieval Period.* Jerusalem: 392–394.

Karasik, A. and Smilansky, U. 2008. 3D Scanning Technology as a Standard Archaeological Tool for Pottery Analysis: Practice and Theory. *Journal of Archaeological Science* 35: 1148–1168.

Karasik, A. and Smilansky, U. 2011. Computerized Morphological Classification of Ceramics. *Journal of Archaeological Science* 38: 2644–2657.

Karasik, A., Smilansky, U. and Beit-Arieh, I. 2005. New Typological Analyses of Early Bronze Age Holemouth Jars from Tel Arad and Southern Sinai. *Tel Aviv* 32: 20–31.

Katz, H. 2008. *"A Land of Grain and Wine ... a Land of Olive Oil and Honey": The Economy of the Kingdom of Judah.* Jerusalem (Hebrew).

Katz, H. and Faust, A. 2012. The Assyrian Destruction Layer at Tel ʿEton. *Israel Exploration Journal* 62: 22–53.

Katzenstein, H.J. 1973. *The History of Tyre: From the Beginning of the Second Millenium B.C.E. until the Fall of the Neo-Babylonian Empire in 538 B.C.E.* Jerusalem.

Katzenstein, H.J. 1994. Gaza in the Neo-Babylonian Period (626–539 B.C.E.). *Transeuphratène* 7: 35–49.

Keel, O. 1995. *Corpus der Stempelsiegel-Amulette aus Palästina/Israel: Von den Anfangen bis zur Perserzeit: Einteilung* (Orbis Biblicus et Orientalis 10). Fribourg.

Keel, O. 1997. *Corpus der Stempelsiegel-Amulette aus Palästina/Israel: Von den Anfängen bis zur Perserzeit* I: *Von Tell Abu Farağ bis ʿAtlit* (Orbis Biblicus et Orientalis 13). Fribourg.

Keel, O. 2004. Scarabs, Stamp Seal-Amulets and Impressions. In: Ussishkin, D., ed. *The Renewed Archaeological Excavations at Lachish (1973–1994)*, III (Monograph Series of the Institute of Archaeology of Tel Aviv University 22). Tel Aviv: 1537–1571.

Keel, O. 2010a. *Corpus der Stempelsiegel-Amulette aus Palästina/Israel*, II: *Von Bahan bis Tel Eton* (Orbis Biblicus et Orientalis 29). Fribourg.

Keel, O. 2010b. *Corpus der Stempelsiegel-Amulette aus Palästina/Israel*, III: *Von Tell el-Farʿa Nord bis Tell el-Fir* (Orbis Biblicus et Orientalis 31). Fribourg.

Keel, O. and Mazar, A. 2009. Iron Age Seals and Seal Impressions from Tel Reḥov. *Eretz-Israel* 29: 57*–69*.

Keel, O. and Uehlinger, C. 1998. *Gods, Goddesses and Images of God in Ancient Israel.* Minneapolis (trans. by T.H. Trapp from the German edition, 1992). Minneapolis.

Kelm, G.L. and Mazar, A. 1985. Tel Batash (Timnah) Excavations: Second Preliminary Report (1981–1983). In: Rast, W.E., ed. *Preliminary Reports of ASOR-Sponsored Excavations 1981–83* (Bulletin of the American Schools of Archaeological Research Supplement 23). Winona Lake: 93–120.

Kelm, G.L. and Mazar, A. 1995. *Timnah: A Biblical City in the Sorek Valley.* Winona Lake.

Kelm, G.L. and Mazar, A. 1996. 7th Century B.C. Oil Presses at Tel Batash, Biblical Timnah. In: Eitam, D. and Heltzer, M., eds. *Olive Oil in Antiquity: Israel and Neighboring Countries from the Neolithic to the Early Arab Period* (History of the Ancient Near East Studies 7). Padova: 243–248.

Kelso, J.L. 1968. *The Excavation of Bethel 1934–1960* (Annual of the American Schools of Oriental Research 39). Cambridge, MA.

Kenyon, K.M. 1957. The Evidence of the Samaria Pottery and Its Bearing on Finds at Other Sites. In: Crowfoot, J.W., Crowfoot, G.M. and Kenyon, K.M., eds. *The Objects from Samaria* (Samaria-Sebaste: Reports of the Work of the Joint Expedition in 1931–1933 and of the British Expedition in 1935, 3). London: 198–209.

Kenyon, K.M., 1965. *Archaeology in the Holy Land* (2nd ed.). London.

Kenyon, K.M. 1974. *Digging Up Jerusalem*. London.

Kenyon, K.M. and Holland, T.A. 1982. *Excavations at Jericho* IV: *The Pottery Type Series and Other Finds*. London.

Kienitz, F.K. 1953. *Die politische Geschichte Ägyptens vom 7. Bis zum 4. Jarhundert von der Zeitwende*. Berlin.

Kletter, R. 1995. *Selected Material Remains of Judah at the End of the Iron Age in Relation to Its Political Borders* (Ph.D. dissertation, Tel Aviv University). Tel Aviv (Hebrew).

Kletter, R. 1998. *Economic Keystones: The Weight System of the Kingdom of Judah* (Journal for the Study of the Old Testament Supplement Series 276). Sheffield.

Kletter, R. 1999. Pots and Polities: Material Remains of Late Iron Age Judah in Relation to Its Political Borders. *Bulletin of the American Schools of Oriental Research* 314: 19–54.

Kletter, R. 2002. Temptation to Identify: Jerusalem, *mmšt*, and the *lmlk* Jar Stamps. *Zeitschrift des Deutschen Palästina-Vereins* 118: 136–149.

Kletter, R. 2009. Comment: Computational Intelligence, *Lmlk* Storage Jars and the Bath Unit in Iron Age Judah. *Journal of Archaeological Method and Theory* 16: 357–365.

Kletter, R. 2014. Vessels and Measures: The Biblical Liquid Capacity System. *Israel Exploration Journal* 64: 22–37.

Kloner, A. 1993. Maresha (Marisa). In: Stern, E., ed. *The New Encyclopedia of Archaeological Excavations in the Holy Land* 3. Jerusalem: 948–957.

Kloner, A. and Eshel, E. 1999. A Seventh-Century BCE List of Names from Maresha. *Eretz-Israel* 26: 147–150 (Hebrew), 233*–234* (English summary).

Knauf, E.A. 1995. Edom: The Social and Economic History. In: Edelman, D.V., ed. *"You Shall Not Abhor an Edomite for He Is Your Brother": Edom and Seir in History and Tradition* (Archaeology and Biblical Studies 3). Atlanta: 93–117.

Knauf, E.A. 2005. The Glorious Days of Manasseh. In: Grabbe, L.L., ed. *Good Kings and Bad Kings: The Kingdom of Judah in the Seventh Century BCE* (Journal for the Study of the Old Testament Supplement Series 393). London: 164–188.

Koch, I. 2008. Rosette Stamp Impressions of Jar Handles from Ancient Judah (M.A. thesis, Tel Aviv University). Tel Aviv (Hebrew).

Koch, I. 2016. Rosette Stamp Impressions. In: Lipschits, O., Gadot, Y. and Freud, L., eds. *Ramat Raḥel* III: *Final Publication of Yohanan Aharoni's Excavations (1954, 1959–1962)* (Monograph Series of the Institute of Archaeology of Tel Aviv University 35). Tel Aviv and Winona Lake: 371–388.

Koch, I. Forthcoming. Rosette Stamp Impressions. In: Lipschits, O., Oeming, M., Freud, L. and Gadot, Y., eds. *Ramat Raḥel V: The Renewed Excavations by the Tel Aviv–Heidelberg Expedition (2005–2010): The Finds* (Monograph Series of the Institute of Archaeology of Tel Aviv University). Tel Aviv and University Park, PA.

Koch, I. and Lipschits, O. 2010. The Final Days of the Kingdom of Judah in Light of the Rosette-Stamped Jar Handles. *Cathedra* 137: 7–26 (Hebrew).

Koch, I. and Lipschits, O. 2013. The Rosette Stamped Jar Handle System and the Kingdom of Judah at the End of the First Temple Period. *Zeitschrift des Deutschen Palästina-Vereins* 129: 55–78.

Kochavi, M. 1970. The First Season of Excavations at Tell Malhata. *Qadmoniot* 9: 22–24 (Hebrew).

Kochavi, M. 1974. Khirbet Rabûd = Debir. *Tel Aviv* 1: 2–33.

Kostamo, S. 2012. Remembering Interactions Between Ahaz and Isaiah in the Late Persian Period. In: Ben Zvi, E. and Levin, C., eds. *Remembering and Forgetting in Early Second Temple Judah* (Forschungen zum Alten Testament 85). Tübingen: 55–72.

KTU = Dietrich, M., Loretz, O. and Sanmartín, J. 2013. *Die keilalphabetischen Texte aus Ugarit, Ras Ibn Hani und anderen Orten* (3rd ed.) (Alter Orient und Altes Testament 360). Münster.

Laato, A. 1992. *Josiah and David Redivivus: The Historical Josiah and the Messianic Expectations of Exilic and Postexilic Times* (Coniectanea biblica, Old Testament Series 33). Stockholm.

Lance, H.D. 1971. The Royal Stamps and the Kingdom of Josiah. *The Harvard Theological Review* 64: 315–332.

Lanfranchi, G.B. and Parpola, S. 1990. *The Correspondence of Sargon II 2: Letters from the Northern Provinces* (State Archives of Assyria 5). Helsinki.

Langgut, D., Gadot, Y., Porat, N. and Lipschits, O. 2013. Trapped Pollen Reveals the Secrets of Royal Persian Garden at Ramat Rahel, Jerusalem. *Palynology* 37: 115–129. http://dx.doi.org/10.1080/01916122.2012.736418.

Lapp, N.L. 1981. *The Third Campaign at Tell el-Fûl: The Excavations of 1964* (Annual of the American Schools of Oriental Research 45). Cambridge, MA.

Lapp, N.L. 1989. Cylinder Seals and Impressions of the Third Millennium B.C. from the Dead Sea Plain. *Bulletin of the American Schools of Oriental Research* 273: 1–15.

Lapp, P.W. 1960. Late Royal Seals from Judah. *Bulletin of the American Schools of Oriental Research* 158: 11–22.

Lapp, P.W. 1963. Ptolemaic Stamped Handles from Judah. *Bulletin of the American Schools of Oriental Research* 172: 22–35.

Lapp, P.W. 1968. The Excavation of Field II. In: Sellers, O.R., Funk, R.W., McKenzie, J.L., Lapp, P. and Lapp, N. *The 1957 Excavation at Beth-Zur* (Annual of the American Schools of Oriental Research 38). Cambridge, MA: 26–34.

Lapp, P.W. 1970. The Pottery of Palestine in the Persian Period. In: Kuschke, D.A. and Kutsch, E., eds. *Archäologie und Altes Testament. Festschrift für Kurt Galling*. Tübingen: 179–197.

Lawal, M.L. 2000. Graffiti, Wine Selling, and the Reuse of Amphoras in the Athenian Agora, ca. 430 to 400 B.C. *Hesperia* 69: 3–90.

Layton, S.C. 1991. A New Interpretation of an Edomite Seal Impression. *Journal of Near Eastern Studies* 50: 37–43.

Lehmann, G. 2004. Reconstructing the Social Landscape of Early Israel: Rural Marriage Alliances in the Central Hill Country. *Tel Aviv* 31: 141–193.

Lehmann, G. and Niemann, H.M. 2006. Klanstruktur und charismatische Herrschaft: Juda und Jerusalem 1200– 900 v. Chr. *Theologische Quartalschrift* 186: 134–159.

Lemaire, A. 1975a. Mmšt = Amwas, vers la solution d'une énigme de l'épigraphie Hébraïque. *Revue Biblique* 82: 15–23.

Lemaire, A. 1975b. Note on an Edomite Seal Impressions from Buseirah. *Levant* 7: 18.

Lemaire, A. 1975c. Remarques sur la datation des estampilles "Lmlk." *Vetus Testamentum* 25: 678–682.

Lemaire, A. 1977. *Inscriptions hébraïques* I: *Les ostraca*. Paris.

Lemaire, A. 1978. Les ostraca paléo-hébreux des fouilles de l'Ophel. *Levant* 10: 156–161.

Lemaire, A. 1979. Nouveau sceau north-ouest sémitique avec un lion rugissant. *Semitica* 29: 67–69.

Lemaire, A. 1981. Classification des estampilles royale Judéennes. *Eretz-Israel* 15: 54*–60*.

Lemaire, A. 1990. Trois sceaux inscrits inedits avec lion rugissant. *Semitica* 39: 13–21.

Lemaire, A. 1991. Le royaume de Tyre dans le second moitie du IV av. J.C. In: Acquaro, E. ed. *Atti del II Congresso internazionale di studi fenici e punici: Roma, 9–14 novembre 1987* (Collezione di studi fenici 30) Rome: 132–149.

Lemaire, A. 1995. Épigraphie Palestinienne: nouveaux documents II—décennie 1985–1995. *Henoch* 17: 209–242.

Lemaire, A. 2007. New Inscribed Hebrew Seals and Seal Impressions. In: Lubetski, M., ed. *New Seals and Inscriptions, Hebrew, Idumean and Cuneiform* (Hebrew Bible Monographs 8) Sheffield: 9–22.

Lemche, N.P. 1994. Kings and Clients: On Loyalty between the Ruler and the Ruled in Ancient "Israel." *Semeia* 66: 119–132.

Lemche, N.P. 1996. From Patronage Society to Patronage Society. In: Fritz, V. and Davies, P.R., eds. *The Origins of the Ancient Israelite States* (Journal for the Study of the Old Testament Supplement Series 228). Sheffield: 106–120.

Lemche, N.P. 2014. *Biblical Studies and the Failure of History* (Changing Perspectives 3). London and New York.

Levine, B.A. 2003. The Clan-Based Economy of Biblical Israel. In: Dever, W.G. and Gitin, S., eds. *Symbiosis, Symbolism, and the Power of the Past: Canaan, Ancient Israel and Their Neighbors from the Late Bronze Age through Roman Palestina (Proceedings of the Centennial Symposium W. F. Albright Institute of Oriental Research and American Schools of Oriental Research, May 29–31, 2000)*. Winona Lake: 445–453.

Levy, S. and Edelstein, G. 1972. Cinq années de fouilles à Tel ʿAmal (Nir David). *Revue Biblique* 79: 325–367.

Lipschits, O. 1999a. The History of the Benjaminite Region under Babylonian Rule. *Tel Aviv* 26: 155–190.

Lipschits, O. 1999b. Nebuchadrezzar's Policy in "Ḥattu-Land" and the Fate of the Kingdom of Judah. *Ugarit-Forschungen* 30: 467–487.

Lipschits, O. 2000. Was There a Royal Estate in Ein-Gedi by the End of the Iron Age and During the Persian Period? In: Schwartz, J., Amar, Z. and Ziffer, I., eds. *Jerusalem and Eretz Israel (Arie Kindler Volume)*. Tel Aviv: 31–42 (Hebrew).

Lipschits, O. 2001. Judah, Jerusalem and the Temple, 586–539 B.C. *Transeuphratène* 22: 129–142.

Lipschits, O. 2003. Demographic Changes in Judah between the Seventh and the Fifth Centuries B.C.E. In: Lipschits, O. and Blenkinsopp, J., eds. *Judah and the Judeans in the Neo-Babylonian Period*. Winona Lake: 323–376.

Lipschits, O. 2004. The Rural Settlement in Judah in the Sixth Century BCE: A Rejoinder. *Palestine Exploration Quarterly* 136: 99–107.

Lipschits, O. 2005. *The Fall and Rise of Jerusalem: Judah under Babylonian Rule*. Winona Lake.

Lipschits, O. 2007. The Babylonian Period in Judah: In Search of the Half Full Cup. In: Vanderhooft, D., ed. In Conversation with Oded Lipschits, *The Fall and Rise of Jerusalem. The Journal of Hebrew Scriptures* 7: 40–49. http://www.jhsonline.org/Articles/article_63.pdf.

Lipschits, O. 2008. Ein Privatsiegelabdruck aus Ramat Raḥel. In: Kottsieper, I., Schmitt, R. and Wörle, J., eds. *Berührungspunkte. Studien zur Sozial- und Religionsgeschichte Israels und seiner Umwelt. Festschrift für Rainer Albertz zu seinem 65. Geburtstag* (Alter Orient und Altes Testament 350). Münster: 491–498.

Lipschits, O. 2009a. Persian Period Finds from Jerusalem: Facts and Interpretations. *The Journal of Hebrew Scriptures* 9. http://www.jhsonline.org/Articles/article_122.pdf.

Lipschits, O. 2009b. The Time and Origin of the Volute-Capitals from Judah, Moab, and Ammon. *Cathedra* 131: 5–24 (Hebrew).

Lipschits, O. 2010. First Thoughts Following the Corpus of the Lion Stamp Impressions. In: Lipschits, O. and Koch, I., eds. *New Studies on the Lion Stamp Impressions from Judah (Abstracts of a Symposium, 14 January 2010, Tel Aviv University)*. Tel Aviv: 17–19 (Hebrew).

Lipschits, O. 2011a. "Here is a man whose name is Ṣemaḥ" (Zechariah 6:12). *Eretz-Israel* 30: 283–289 (Hebrew), 153*–154* (English summary).

Lipschits, O. 2011b. The Ivory Seal of *šlm* (Son of) *klkl*, Discovered at Ramat Raḥel. *Israel Exploration Journal* 61: 162–170.

Lipschits, O. 2011c. Jerusalem between Two Periods of Greatness: The Size and Status of Jerusalem in the Babylonian, Persian and Early Hellenistic Periods. In: Grabbe, L.L. and Lipschits, O., eds. *Judah Between East and West: The Transition from Persian to Greek Rule (ca. 400–200 BCE)*. London: 163–175.

Lipschits, O. 2011d. A New Look on the Archaeology of Persian Period Judah. In: Jonker, L., ed. *Texts, Contexts and Readings in Postexilic Literature*: *Explorations into Historiography and Identity Negotiation in Hebrew Bible and Related Texts* (Forschungen zum Alten Testament II, 53). Tübingen: 187–211.

Lipschits, O. 2011e. The Origin and Date of the Volute Capitals from the Levant. In: Finkelstein, I. and Naʾaman, N. eds. *The Fire Signals of Lachish: Studies in the Archaeology and History of Israel in the Late Bronze Age, Iron Age, and Persian Period in Honor of David Ussishkin*. Winona Lake: 203–225.

Lipschits, O. 2011f. Shedding New Light on the Dark Years of the "Exilic Period": New Studies, Further Elucidation, and Some Questions Regarding the Archaeology of Judah as an "Empty Land". In: Kelle, B.E., Ames, F.R. and Wright, J.L., eds. *Interpreting Exile: Interdisciplinary Studies of Displacement and Deportation in Biblical and Modern Contexts* (Ancient Israel and Its Literature 10). Atlanta: 57–90.

Lipschits, O. 2012a. Archaeological Facts, Historical Speculations and the Date of the *LMLK* Storage Jars: A Rejoinder to David Ussishkin. *The Journal of Hebrew Scriptures* 12. http://www.jhsonline.org/Articles/article_166.pdf.

Lipschits, O. 2012b. Between Archaeology and Text: A Reevaluation of the Development Process of Jerusalem in the Persian Period. In: Nissinen, M., ed. *Congress Volume, Helsinki 2010* (Supplements to Vetus Testamentum 148). Leiden and Boston: 145–165.

Lipschits, O. 2015. The Rural Economy of Judah during the Persian Period and the Settlement History of the District System. In: Miller, M.L., Ben Zvi, E. and Knoppers, G.N., eds. *The Economy of Ancient Judah in Its Historical Context*. Winona Lake: 237–264.

Lipschits, O. 2017. Bethel Revisited. In: Lipschits, O., Gadot, Y. and Adams, M.J., eds. *Rethinking Israel: Studies in the History and Archaeology of Ancient Israel in Honor of Israel Finkelstein*. Winona Lake: 233–246.

Lipschits, O. 2018a. The Changing Faces of Kingship in Judah under Assyrian Rule. In: Gianto, A. and Dubovský, P., eds. *Changing Faces of Kingship in Syria-Palestine 1500–500 BCE* (Alter Orient und Altes Testament 459). Münster: 115–138.

Lipschits, O. 2018b. Judah under Assyrian Rule and the Early Phase of Stamping Jar Handles. In: Farber, Z.I. and Wright, J.L., eds. *Archaeology and History of Eighth-Century Judah* (Ancient Near East Monographs 23). Atlanta: 337–355.

Lipschits, O. 2019a. The *lmlk* and 'Private' Stamp Impressions from Tel Beth-Shemesh: An Added Dimension to the Late 8th and Early 7th Century BCE History of the Site. *Tel Aviv* 46: 102–107.

Lipschits, O. 2019b. The Long Seventh Century BCE: Archaeological and Historical Perspectives. In: Čapek, F. and Lipschits, O., eds. *The Last Century in the History of Judah: The Seventh Century BCE in Archaeological, Historical, and Biblical Perspectives* (Ancient Israel and Its Literature 37). Atlanta: 9–44.

Lipschits, O. 2019c. Materialkultur, Verwaltung und Wirtschaft in Juda während der Perserzeit und die Rolle des Jerusalemer Tempels. In: Achenbach, R., ed. *Persische Reichspolitik und lokale Heiligtümer, Beiträge einer Tagung des Exzellenzclusters "Religion und Politik in Vormoderne und Moderne" vom 24.–26. Februar 2016 in Münster* (Beihefte zur Zeitschrift für altorientalische und biblische Rechtsgeschichte 25). Wiesbaden: 185–208.

Lipschits, O. Forthcoming. Lion Stamp Impressions. In: Lipschits, O., Oeming, M., Freud, L. and Gadot, Y., eds. *Ramat Raḥel V: The Renewed Excavations by the Tel Aviv–Heidelberg Expedition (2005–2010): The Finds* (Monograph Series of the Institute of Archaeology of Tel Aviv University). Tel Aviv and University Park, PA.

Lipschits, O. and Amit, D. 2011. 18 Unpublished Stamped Jar Handles. In: Baruch, E., Levy, A. and Faust, A., eds. *New Studies on Jerusalem* 17. Ramat Gan: 179–198 (Hebrew), 54*–55* (English summary).

Lipschits, O., Freud, L., Oeming, M. and Gadot, Y., eds. 2021. *Ramat Raḥel VI: The Renewed Excavations by the Tel Aviv–Heidelberg Expedition (2005–2010). The Babylonian-Persian Pit* (Monograph Series of the Institute of Archaeology of Tel Aviv University 40). Tel Aviv and University Park, PA.

Lipschits, O. and Gadot, Y. 2008. Ramat Raḥel and the Emeq Rephaim Sites—Links and Interpretations. In: Amit, D. and Stiebel, G.D., eds. *New Studies in the Archaeology of Jerusalem and Its Region, Collected Papers* 2. Jerusalem: 88–96 (Hebrew).

Lipschits, O., Gadot, Y. Arubas, B. and Oeming, M. 2009a. Ramat Raḥel and Its Secrets. *Qadmoniot* 138: 58–77 (Hebrew).

Lipschits, O., Gadot, Y., Arubas, B. and Oeming, M. 2011. Palace and Village, Paradise and Oblivion: Unraveling the Riddles of Ramat Raḥel. *Near Eastern Archaeology* 74: 1–49.

Lipschits, O., Gadot, Y. Arubas, B. and Oeming, M. 2017. *What Are the Stones Whispering? 3000 Years of Forgotten History at Ramat Raḥel*. Winona Lake.

Lipschits, O., Gadot, Y. and Freud, L. 2016. *Ramat Raḥel III: Final Publication of Yohanan Aharoni's Excavations (1954, 1959–1962)* (Monograph Series of the Institute of Archaeology of Tel Aviv University 35). Tel Aviv and Winona Lake.

Lipschits, O., Gadot, Y. and Langgut, D. 2012. The Riddle of Ramat Raḥel: The Archaeology of a Royal Persian Period Edifice. *Transeuphratène* 41: 57–79.

Lipschits, O. and Koch, I., eds. 2010. *New Studies on the Lion Stamp Impressions from Judah (Abstracts of a Symposium, 14 January 2010, Tel Aviv University)*. Tel Aviv.

Lipschits, O. and Koch, I. 2016. Lion Stamp Impressions. In: Lipschits, O., Gadot, Y. and Freud, L., eds. *Ramat Raḥel III: Final Publication of Yohanan Aharoni's Excavations (1954, 1959–1962)* (Monograph Series of the Institute of Archaeology of Tel Aviv University 35). Tel Aviv and Winona Lake: 389–408.

Lipschits, O. and Koch, I. 2020. Lion Stamp Impressions. In: Lipschits, O., Oeming, M. and Gadot, Y., eds. *Ramat Raḥel IV: The Renewed Excavations by the Tel Aviv–Heidelberg Expedition (2005–2010): Stratigraphy and Architecture* (Monograph Series of the Institute of Archaeology of Tel Aviv University 39). Tel Aviv and University Park, PA.

Lipschits, O. and Koch, I. 2021. Lion Stamp Impressions from the Babylonian Period. In: Lipschits, O., Freud, L., Oeming, M. and Gadot, Y., eds. *Ramat Raḥel VI: The Renewed Excavations by the Tel Aviv–Heidelberg Expedition (2005–2010). The Babylonian-Persian Pit* (Monograph Series of the Institute of Archaeology of Tel Aviv University 40). Tel Aviv and University Park, PA: 76–80.

Lipschits, O., Koch, I., Shaus, A. and Guil, S. 2010. The Enigma of the Biblical Bath, and the System of Liquid Volume Measurement during the First Temple Period. *Ugarit-Forschungen* 42: 453–478.

Lipschits, O. and Naʾaman, N. 2011. From "Baal Perazim" to "Beth-Haccerem": Further Thoughts on the Ancient Name of Ramat Raḥel. *Beit Mikra* 86–65 :56 (Hebrew).

Lipschits, O., Oeming, M. and Gadot, Y. 2020. *Ramat Raḥel IV: The Renewed Excavations of the Tel Aviv–Heidelberg Expedition (2005–2010): Stratigraphy and Architecture* (Monograph Series of the Institute of Archaeology of Tel Aviv University 39). Tel Aviv and University Park, PA.

Lipschits, O., Oeming, M., Gadot, Y., Arubas, B. and Cinamon, G. 2006. Ramat Raḥel 2005. Notes and News. *Israel Exploration Journal* 56: 227–235.

Lipschits, O., Oeming, M., Gadot, Y. and Vanderhooft, D. 2007. Seventeen Newly-Excavated Yehud Stamp Impressions from Ramat Raḥel. *Tel Aviv* 34: 74–89.

Lipschits, O. and Ornan, T. 2010. Introduction: On the State of Research of the Judean Lion Stamp Impressions and the Sources of the Lion in the Judean Stamp Impressions. In: Lipschits, O. and Koch, I., eds. *New Studies on the Lion Stamp Impressions from Judah (Abstracts of a Symposium, 14 January 2010, Tel Aviv University)*. Tel Aviv: 1–5 (Hebrew).

Lipschits, O., Sergi, O. and Koch, I. 2010. Royal Judahite Jar Handles: Reconsidering the Chronology of the *lmlk* Stamp Impressions. *Tel Aviv* 37: 3–32.

Lipschits, O., Sergi, O. and Koch, I. 2011. Judahite Stamped and Incised Jar Handles: A Tool for the Study of the History of Late Monarchic Judah. *Tel Aviv* 38: 5–41.

Lipschits, O. and Vanderhooft, D.S. 2007a. Jerusalem in the Persian and Hellenistic Periods in Light of the *Yehud* Stamp Impressions. *Eretz-Israel* 28: 106–115 (Hebrew), 12*–13* (English summary).

Lipschits, O. and Vanderhooft, D.S. 2007b. Yehud Stamp Impressions of the Fourth Century B.C.E.: A Time of Administrative Consolidation? In: Lipschits, O., Knoppers, G.N. and Albertz, R., eds. *Judah and the Judeans in the Fourth Century B.C.E.* Winona Lake: 75–94.

Lipschits, O. and Vanderhooft, D.S. 2007c. Yehud Stamp Impressions: History of Discovery and Newly-Published Items. *Tel Aviv* 34: 3–11.

Lipschits, O. and Vanderhooft, D.S. 2009. 40 Unpublished *Yehud* Stamp Impressions from Aharoni's Excavations at Ramat Raḥel. *Eretz-Israel* 29: 248–269 (Hebrew), 291* (English summary).

Lipschits, O. and Vanderhooft, D.S. 2011. *Yehud Stamp Impressions: A Corpus of Inscribed Stamp Impressions from the Persian and Hellenistic Periods in Judah.* Winona Lake.

Lipschits, O. and Vanderhooft, D.S. 2014. Continuity and Change in the Persian Period Judahite Stamped Jar Administration. In: Frevel, C., Pyschny, K. and Cornelius, I., eds. *Jewish "Material" Otherness? Studies in the Formation of Persian Period Judaism(s)* (Orbis Biblicus et Orientalis 264). Fribourg: 43–66.

Lipschits, O. and Vanderhooft, D.S. 2020. Yehud Stamp Impressions from Ramat-Raḥel: An Updated Tabulation. *Bulletin of the American Schools of Oriental Research* 384: 191–209.

Lipschits, O. and Vanderhooft, D.S. 2021. *yhwd* Stamp Impressions. In: Lipschits, O., Freud, L., Oeming, M. and Gadot, Y., eds. *Ramat Raḥel VI: The Renewed Excavations by the Tel Aviv–Heidelberg Expedition (2005–2010). The Babylonian-Persian Pit* (Monograph Series of the Institute of Archaeology of Tel Aviv University 40). Tel Aviv and University Park, PA: 96–116.

Lipschits, O. and Vanderhooft, D.S. Forthcoming. *yhwd* Stamp Impressions. In: Lipschits, O., Freud, L., Oeming, M. and Gadot, Y., eds. *Ramat Raḥel V: The Renewed Excavations by the Tel Aviv–Heidelberg Expedition (2005–2010): The Finds* (Monograph Series of the Institute of Archaeology of Tel Aviv University). Tel Aviv and University Park, PA.

Lipschits, O., Vanderhooft, D.S., Gadot, Y. and Oeming, M. 2008. Twenty-Four New *Yehud* Stamp Impressions from the 2007 Excavation Season at Ramat-Raḥel. *Maarav* 15: 7–25.

Lipschits, O., Vanderhooft, D.S., Gadot, Y. and Oeming, M. 2009b. Twenty-Seven New *Yehud* Stamp Impressions from the 2008 Excavation Season at Ramat- Raḥel. *Maarav* 16: 7–28.

Liverani, M. 1992. *Studies on the Annals of Ashurnasirpal II 2: Topographical Analysis*. Rome.

Loud, G. 1948. *Megiddo* II: *Seasons of 1935–1939: Text and Plates* (Oriental Institute Publications 62). Chicago.

Lubetski, M. 2000. Beetlemania of Bygone Times. *Journal for the Study of the Old Testament* 91: 3–26.

Lux, U. 1972. Vorläufiger Bericht über die Ausgrabung unter der Erlöserkirche im Muristan in der Altstadt von Jerusalem in den Jahren 1970 und 1971. *Zeitschrift des Deutschen Palästina-Vereins* 88: 185–201.

Macalister, R.A.S. 1907. Fifteenth Quarterly Report on the Excavation at Gezer. *Palestine Exploration Fund Quarterly Statement*: 254–268.

Macalister, R.A.S. 1912. *The Excavation of Gezer, 1902–1905 and 1907–1909* II. London.

Macalister, R.A.S. and Duncan, J.G. 1926. *Excavations on the Hill of the Ophel, Jerusalem, 1923–1925: Being the Joint expedition of the Palestine Exploration Fund and the "Daily Telegraph"* (Palestine Exploration Fund Annual 4). London.

Maeir, A.M. 2004. The Historical Background and Dating of Amos VI 2: An Archaeological Perspective from Tell eṣ-Ṣâfî/Gath. *Vetus Testamentum* 54: 319–334.

Maeir, A.M. 2008. Ẓafit, Tel. In: Stern, E., ed. *The New Encyclopedia of Archaeological Excavations in the Holy Land* 5: *Supplementary Volume*. Jerusalem: 2079–2081.

Maeir, A.M. 2010. "And brought in the offerings and the tithes and the dedicated things faithfully" (2 Chron. 31:12): On the Meaning and Function of the Late Iron Age Judahite "Incised Handle Cooking Pots." *Journal of the American Oriental Society* 130: 43–62.

Maeir, A.M. 2012. *Tell es-Safi/Gath* I: *Report on the 1996–2005 Seasons* (Ägypten und altes Testament 69). Wiesbaden.

Maeir, A.M. and Shai, I. 2016. Reassessing the Character of the Judahite Kingdom: Archaeological Evidence for Non-Centralized, Kinship-Based Components. In: Ganor, S., Kreimerman, I., Streit, K. and Mumcouglu, M., eds. *From Shaʿar Hagolan to Shaaraim: Essays in Honor of Prof. Yosef Garfinkel*. Jerusalem: 323–340.

Magen, Y. 2008. Nebi-Samuel: Where Samuel Crowned Israel's First King. *Biblical Archeology Review* 34(3): 36–54.

Magen, Y. and Dadon, M. 1999. Nebi Samwil (Shmuel Hanavi– Har Hasimha). *Qadmoniot* 118: 62–77 (Hebrew).

Magen, I. and Har-Even, B. 2007. Persian Period Seal Impressions from Nebi Samwil. *Tel Aviv* 34: 38–58.

Magen, Y. and Peleg, Y. 2007. *The Qumran Excavations 1993– 2004: Preliminary Report* (Judea and Samaria Publications 6). Jerusalem.

Maisler, B. 1935. Ramat Rachel and Kh. Salah. *Qobetz* 3: 4–18 (Hebrew).

Maisler, B. 1950–51. The Excavations at Tell Qasîle: Preliminary Report. *Israel Exploration Journal* 1: 194–218.

Maisler, B. 1951. Two Ostraca from Tell Qasîle. *Journal of Near Eastern Studies* 10: 265–267.

Malamat, A. 1983. *Israel in Biblical Times: Historical Essays*. Jerusalem (Hebrew).

Master, D.M. 2001. State Formation Theory and the Kingdom of Ancient Israel. *Journal of Near Eastern Studies* 60: 117–131.

Master, D.M. 2003. Trade and Politics: Ashkelon's Balancing Act in the Seventh Century B.C.E. *Bulletin of the American Schools of Oriental Research* 330: 47–64.

Master, D.M. 2009. From the Buqêʿah to Ashkelon. In: Schloen, J.D., ed. *Exploring the Longue Durée: Essays in Honor of Lawrence E. Stager*. Winona Lake: 305–317.

Mattingly, G.L. and Pace, J.H. 2007. Crossing Jordan: By Way of the Karak Plateau. In: Levy, T.E., Daviau, P.M.M., Younker, R.W. and Shaer, M., eds. *Crossing Jordan: North American Contributions to the Archaeology of Jordan.* London and Oakville: 153–159.

Mazar, A. 1980. An Early Israeli Site near Jerusalem. *Qadmoniot* 49/50: 34–39 (Hebrew).

Mazar, A. 1981. A Response to the Remarks by A. Kempinski. *Qadmoniot* 53/54: 64 (Hebrew).

Mazar, A. 1985. Between Judah and Philistia: Timnah (Tel Batash) in the Iron Age II. *Eretz-Israel* 18: 300–324 (Hebrew), 75*– 76* (English summary).

Mazar, A. 1990. *Archaeology of the Land of the Bible 10,000–586 B.C.E.* (The Anchor Bible Reference Library). New York.

Mazar, A. 1994. The Northern Shephelah in the Iron Age: Some Issues in Biblical History and Archaeology. In: Coogan, M.D., Exum, J.C. and Stager, L.E., eds. *Scripture and Other Artifacts: Essays on the Bible and Archaeology in Honor of Philip J. King*. Louisville: 247–267.

Mazar, A., Amit, D. and Ilan, Z. 1996. Hurvat Shilhah: An Iron Age Site in the Judean Desert. In: Seger, J.D., ed. *Retrieving the Past: Essays on Oriental Research and Methodology in Honor of Gus W. Van Beek*. Winona Lake: 193–211.

Mazar, A. and Panitz-Cohen, N. 2001. *Timnah (Tel Batash)* II: *The Finds from the First Millennium BCE, Text* (Qedem 42). Jerusalem.

Mazar, B. 1964. Sennacherib's Campaign to Judah. In: Liver, J., ed. *The Military History of the Land of Israel in Biblical Times*. Tel Aviv: 286–295 (Hebrew).

Mazar, B., Dothan, T. and Dunayevsky, I. 1963. ʿEin-Gedi: Archaeological Excavations 1961–1962. *Yediʿot: Bulletin of the Israel Exploration Society* 27: 1–134 (Hebrew).

Mazar, B., Dothan, T. and Dunayevsky, I. 1966. *En-Gedi: The First and Second Seasons of Excavations 1961–1962* (ʿAtiqot 5, English Series). Jerusalem.

Mazar, B. and Dunayevsky, I. 1964. En-Gedi: Third Season of Excavations. *Israel Exploration Journal* 14: 121–130.

Mazar, B. and Dunayevsky, I. 1966. The Fourth and Fifth Seasons of Excavations at En-Gedi. *Yedi'ot: Bulletin of the Israel Exploration Society* 30: 183–194 (Hebrew).

Mazar, B. and Dunayevsky, I. 1967. En-Gedi: The Fourth and Fifth Season of Excavations Preliminary Report. *Israel Exploration Journal* 17: 133–143.

Mazar, E. and Mazar, B. 1989. *Excavations in the South of the Temple Mount: The Ophel of Biblical Jerusalem* (Qedem 29). Jerusalem.

Mazzoni, S. 1984. Seal Impressions on Jars from Ebla in the Late Early Bronze Age. *American Journal of Archaeology* 88: 488–489.

Mazzoni, S. 2000. Syria and the Periodization of the Iron Age: A Cross-Cultural Prespective. In: Bunnens, G., ed. *Essays on Syria in the Iron Age* (Ancient Near Eastern Studies, Supplement 7). Louvain, Paris and Sterling, VA: 31–59.

McCown, C.C. 1947. *Tell En-Naṣbeh: Excavated under the Direction of the Late William Frederic Badè* 1: *Archaeological and Historical Results*. Berkeley and New Haven.

Mendelson, I. 1940. Guilds in Ancient Palestine. *Bulletin of the American Schools of Oriental Research* 80: 17–21.

Meshorer, Y. 1982. *Ancient Jewish Coinage* (2 vols.). New York.

Meshorer, Y. 2001. *A Treasury of Jewish Coins from the Persian Period to Bar Kochba.* Jerusalem.

Meshorer, Y. and Qedar, S. 1991. *The Coinage of Samaria in the Fourth Century BCE.* Jerusalem.

Meshorer, Y. and Qedar, S. 1999. *Samarian Coinage* (Numismatic Studies and Researches 9). Jerusalem.

Meyers, E.M. and Meyers, C.L. 1990. *Excavations at the Ancient Synagogue of Gush Ḥalav.* Winona Lake.

Milevski, I. 1996–97. Settlement Patterns in Northern Judah during the Achaemenid Period, According to the Hill Country of Benjamin and Jerusalem Surveys. *Bulletin of the Anglo-Israel Archaeological Society* 15: 7–29.

Milevski, I. 2005. The Hebrew Ostraca from Site 94/21, Cave A-2, at Ramat Bet Shemesh. *'Atiqot* 50: 19–25.

Milgrom, J. 1991. *Leviticus 1–16: New Translation with Introduction and Commentary* (The Anchor Bible 3). New York.

Millard, A.R. 1972. An Israelite Royal Seal? *Bulletin of the American Schools of Oriental Research* 208: 5–9.

Millard, A.R. 1991. Large Numbers in the Assyrian Royal Inscriptions. In: Cogan, M. and Eph'al, I., eds. *Ah, Assyria...: Studies in Assyrian History and Ancient Near Eastern Historiography Presented to Hayim Tadmor* (Scripta Hierosolymitana 33). Jerusalem: 213–222.

Millard, A.R. 2009. Administration in Ancient Judah. In: Davies, P.R., Ramos, J.A. and Valdez, M.A.T., eds. *From Antiquity to the Present: The 2008 European Association of Biblical Studies Lisbon Meeting.* Lisbon: 29–37.

Millard, A.R. 2015. Aramaic in Nebuchadnezzar's Babylon— Stamps on Bricks from Babylon and Stamps on Jar Handles from Judah. In: Lubetski, M. and Lubetski, E., eds. *Recording New Epigraphic Evidence: Essays in Honor of Robert Deutsch.* Jerusalem: 113–122.

Miller, D.R. 2009. Objectives and Consequences of the Neo-Assyrian Imperial Exercise. *Religion and Theology* 16: 124–149.

Miller, J.M. and Hayes, J.H. 1986. *A History of Ancient Israel and Judah.* Philadelphia.

Millman, M. 2014. Archaeomagnetic Constraints on the Chronology of the Judean Stamped Jar Handles (M.A. thesis, Tel Aviv University). Tel Aviv.

Mitchell, T.C. and Searight, A. 2008. *Catalogue of Western Asiatic Seals in the British Museum, Stamp Seals* III: *Impressions of Stamp Seals on Cuneiform Tablets, Clay Bullae, and Jar Handles.* Leiden and Boston.

Mittmann, S. 1991. "Königliches bat" und "ṭēt-Symbol": Mit einem Beitrag zu Micha 1,14b und 1 Chronik 4,21–23. *Zeitschrift des Deutschen Palästina-Vereins* 57: 59–76.

Mittmann, S. 1993. "Gib den Kittäern 3 b(at) Wein": Mengen und Güter in den Arad-Briefen. *Zeitschrift des Deutschen Palästina-Vereins* 109: 39–48.

Mommsen, H., Perlman, I. and Yellin, J. 1984. The Provenience of the *lmlk* Jars. *Israel Exploration Journal* 34: 89–113.

Montgomery, J.A. 1951. *A Critical and Exegetical Commentary on the Books of Kings* (The International Critical Commentary). Edinburgh.

Moore, M.S. 1985. The Judean *lmlk* Stamps: Some Unresolved Issues. *Restoration Quarterly* 28: 17–26.

Muchiki, Y. 1999. *Egyptian Proper Names and Loanwords in North-West Semitic* (Society of Biblical Literature Dissertation Series 173). Atlanta.

Muilenburg, J. 1954. A Hyksos Scarab Jar Handle from Bethel. *Bulletin of the American Schools of Oriental Research* 136: 20–21.

Mulder, J.M. 1998. *1 Kings* I: *1 Kings 1–11* (Historical Commentary on the Old Testament). Leuven.

Musche, B. 1994. Zur altorientalischen Rosette; ihr botanisches Vorbild und dessen pharmazeutische Verwertung. *Mesopotamia* 29: 49–71.

Mussell, M.-L. 1989. The Seal Impression from Dhiban. In: Dearman, A., ed. *Studies in the Mesha Inscription and Moab* (Archaeology and Biblical Studies 2). Atlanta: 247–251.

Na'aman, N. 1979a. The Brook of Egypt and Assyrian Policy on the Border of Egypt. *Tel Aviv* 6: 68–90.

Na'aman, N. 1979b. Sennacherib's Campaign to Judah and the Date of the *lmlk* Stamps. *Vetus Testamentum* 29: 61–86.

Na'aman, N. 1981. Royal Estates in the Jezreel Valley in the Late Bronze Age and under the Israelite Monarchy. *Eretz-Israel* 15: 140–144 (Hebrew), 81* (English summary).

Na'aman, N. 1986. Hezekiah's Fortified Cities and the "LMLK" Stamps. *Bulletin of the American Schools of Oriental Research* 261: 5–21.

Na'aman, N. 1987. The Negev in the Last Century of the Kingdom of Judah. *Cathedra* 42: 4–15 (Hebrew).

Na'aman, N. 1989. The Town-Lists of Judah and Benjamin and the Kingdom of Judah in the Days of Josiah. *Zion* 54: 17–71 (Hebrew), I–II (English summary).

Na'aman, N. 1991a. Forced Participation in Alliances in the Course of the Assyrian Campaigns to the West. In: Cogan, M. and Eph'al, I., eds. *Ah, Assyria...: Studies in Assyrian History and Ancient Near Eastern Historiography Presented to Hayim Tadmor* (Scripta Hierosolymitana 33). Jerusalem: 80–98.

Na'aman, N. 1991b. The Kingdom of Judah under Josiah. *Tel Aviv* 18: 3–71.

Na'aman, N. 1993. Population Changes in Palestine Following Assyrian Deportations. *Tel Aviv* 20: 104–124.

Na'aman, N. 1994a. Ahaz's and Hezekiah's Policy Toward Assyria in the Days of Sargon II and Sennacherib's Early Years. *Zion* 59: 5–30 (Hebrew), V (English summary).

Na'aman, N. 1994b. Hezekiah and the Kings of Assyria. *Tel Aviv* 21: 235–254.

Na'aman, N. 1994c. The Historical Portion of Sargon II's Nimrud Inscription. *State Archives of Assyria Bulletin* 8: 17–20.

Na'aman, N. 1995. Province System and Settlement Pattern in Southern Syria and Palestine in the Neo-Assyrian Period. In: Liverani, M., ed. *Neo-Assyrian Geography* (Quaderni di Geografia Storica 5). Rome: 103–115.

Na'aman, N. 1996. Sources and Composition in the History of David. In: Fritz, V. and Davies, P.R., eds. *The Origins of the Ancient Israelite States* (Journal for the Study of the Old Testament Supplement Series 228). Sheffield: 170–186.

Na'aman, N. 1998. Two Notes on the History of Ashkelon and Ekron in the Late Eighth–Seventh Centuries B.C.E. *Tel Aviv* 25: 219–227.

Na'aman, N. 1999. Baal Toponyms; Baal-Gad; Baal Hamon; Baal Hazor; Baal Hermon; Baal Judah; Baal Meon; Baal-Perazim; Baal-Shalisha; Baal-Tamar. In: van der Toorn, K., Becking, B. and van der Horst, P.W., eds. *Dictionary of Deities and Demons in the Bible*. Leiden: 140–141, 144–147, 148–149, 151–152.

Na'aman, N. 2000a. Ḫabiru-like Bands in the Assyrian Empire and Bands in Biblical Historiography. *Journal of the American Oriental Society* 120: 621–624.

Na'aman, N. 2000b. No Anthropomorphic Graven Image: Notes on the Assumed Anthropomorphic Cult Statues in the Temples of *YHWH* in the Pre-Exilic Period. *Ugarit-Forschungen* 31: 391–415.

Na'aman, N. 2001. An Assyrian Residence at Ramat Raḥel? *Tel Aviv* 28: 260–280.

Na'aman, N. 2003. Ekron under the Assyrian and Egyptian Empires. *Bulletin of the American Schools of Oriental Research* 332: 81–91.

Na'aman, N. 2004. The Boundary System and Political Status of Gaza under the Assyrian Empire. *Zeitschrift des Deutschen Palästina-Vereins* 120: 55–72.

Na'aman, N. 2006. The Rise of Jerusalem as the Kingdom of Judah's Premier City in the 8th–7th Centuries BCE. *Zion* 71: 411–456 (Hebrew), XXVI (English summary).

Na'aman, N. 2007. When and How Did Jerusalem Become a Great City? The Rise of Jerusalem as Judah's Premier City in the Eighth–Seventh Centuries B.C.E. *Bulletin of the American Schools of Oriental Research* 347: 21–56.

Na'aman, N. 2009a. The Growth and Development of Judah and Jerusalem in the Eighth Century BCE: A Rejoinder. *Revue Biblique* 116: 321–335.

Na'aman, N. 2009b. The Sanctuary of the Gibeonites Revisited. *Journal of Ancient Near Eastern Religions* 9: 101–124.

Na'aman, N. and Thareani-Sussely, Y. 2006. Dating the Appearance of Imitations of Assyrian Ware in Southern Palestine. *Tel Aviv* 33: 61–82.

Na'aman, N. and Zadok, R. 1988. Sargon II's Deportations to Israel and Philistia (716–708 B.C.). *Journal of Cuneiform Studies* 40: 36–46.

Na'aman, N. and Zadok, R. 2000. Assyrian Deportations to the Province of Samerina in the Light of Two Cuneiform Tablets from Tel Hadid. *Tel Aviv* 27: 159–188.

Nadelman, Y. 1989. Hebrew Inscriptions, Seal Impressions, and Marking of the Iron Age II. In: Mazar, E. and Mazar, B., eds. *Excavations in the South of the Temple Mount: The Ophel of Biblical Jerusalem* (Qedem 29). Jerusalem: 128–141.

Naveh, J. 1962. The Excavations at Meṣad Ḥashavyahu: Preliminary Report. *Israel Exploration Journal* 12: 89–113.

Naveh, J. 1970. *The Development of the Aramaic Script* (Proceedings of the Israel Academy of Sciences and Humanities V). Jerusalem.

Naveh, J. 1992. The Numbers of *Bat* in the Arad Ostraca. *Israel Exploration Journal* 42: 52–54.

Naveh, J. 1993. Ḥashavyahu, Meẓad. In: Stern, E., ed. *The New Encyclopedia of Archaeological Excavations in the Holy Land* 2. Jerusalem: 585–586.

Naveh, J. 1996. Gleanings of Some Pottery Inscriptions. *Israel Exploration Journal* 46: 44–51.

Naveh, J. 1998. Scripts and Inscriptions in Ancient Samaria. *Israel Exploration Journal* 48: 91–100.

Nordquist, G.C. 1987. *A Middle Helladic Village: Asine in the Argolid* (Boreas: Uppsala Studies in Ancient Mediterranean and Near Eastern Civilizations 16). Uppsala.

Noth, M. 1966. *Exodus: A Commentary*. London (originally published in German, *Das zweite Buch Mose, Exodus*, 1959).

Noth, M. 1974. *Leviticus: A Commentary*. Philadelphia (originally published in German, *Das dritte Buch Mose, Leviticus*, 1962).

Oded, B. 1970. Observations on Methods of Assyrian Rule in Transjordan after the Palestinian Campaign of Tiglath-Pileser III. *Journal of Near Eastern Studies* 29: 177–186.

Oded, B. 1979. Israel's Neighbours on the East. In: Malamat, A., ed. *The Age of the Monarchies: Political History* (World History of the Jewish People 4). Jerusalem: 152–170, 273–274 (Hebrew).

Ofer, A. 1986. Tel Rumeideh (Hebron)—1985. *Excavations and Surveys in Israel* 5: 92–93.

Ofer, A. 1988. Tel Rumeideh (Hebron) —1986. *Ḥadashot Arkheologiyot* 90: 47–48 (Hebrew).

Ofer, A. 1993. *The Highland of Judah during the Biblical Period* (Ph.D. dissertation, Tel Aviv University). Tel Aviv (Hebrew).

Ornan, T. 2004. Idols and Symbols: Divine Representation in First Millennium Mesopotamian Art and Its Bearing on the Second Commandment. *Tel Aviv* 31: 90–121.

Ornan, T. 2005. A Complex System of Religious Symbols: The Case of the Winged-disc in First-Millennium Near Eastern Imagery. In: Suter, C.E. and Uehlinger, C., eds. *Crafts and Images in Contact: Studies on Eastern Mediterranean Minor Art of the 1st Millennium BCE* (Orbis Biblicus et Orientalis 210). Fribourg and Göttingen: 207–241.

Ornan, T. 2009. The Winged Disc as an Emblem of Major Deities in the Neo-Assyrian Period. In: Ephʿal, I. and Naʾaman, N., eds. *Royal Assyrian Inscriptions—History, Historiography and Ideology: A Conference in Honor of Hayim Tadmor on the Occasion of His Eightieth Birthday, 20 November 2003*. Jerusalem: 70–96.

Ornan, T. 2010. The Sources of the Lion in the Judean Stamp Impressions. In: Lipschits, O. and Koch, I., eds. New *Studies on the Lion Stamp Impressions from Judah (Abstracts of a Symposium, 14 January 2010, Tel Aviv University)*. Tel Aviv: 15–16 (Hebrew).

Ornan, T., and Lipschits, O. Forthcoming (a). *Lions of Judah: Late Babylonian and Early Persian Period Stamped Seal Impressions from Judah* (Mosaics: Studies on Ancient Israel). Tel Aviv and University Park, PA.

Ornan, T. and Lipschits, O. Forthcoming (b). The Lion Stamp Impressions from Judah: Typology, Distribution, Iconography, and Historical Implications. A Preliminary Report. *Semitica*.

Ornan, T., Weksler-Bdolah, S., Greenhut, Z., Sass, B. and Goren, Y. 2008. Four Hebrew Seals, One Depicting an Assyrian-like Archer, from the Western Wall Plaza Excavations. Jerusalem. ʿ*Atiqot* 60: 115–129.

Otzen, T. 1979. Israel under the Assyrians. In: Larsen, M.T., ed. *Power and Propaganda: A Symposium on Ancient Empires* (Mesopotamia 7). Copenhagen: 251–261.

Palaima, T.G. 1990. *Aegean Seals, Sealings and Administration* (Aegaeum 5). Liège.

Papadopoulos, J.K. 1994. Early Iron Age Potter's Marks in the Aegean. *Hesperia* 63: 437–507.

Parayre, D. 1993. À propos des sceaux ouest-sémitiques: Le rôle de l'iconographie dans l'attribution d'un sceau à une aire culturelle et à un atelier. In: Sass, B. and Uehlinger, C., eds. *Studies in the Iconography of Northwest Semitic Inscribed Seals* (Orbis Biblicus et Orientalis 125). Fribourg and Göttingen: 27–51.

Pardee, D. 1978. Letters from Tel Arad. *Ugarit-Forschungen* 10: 289–336.

Pardee, D. 1982. *Handbook of Ancient Hebrew Letters: A Study Edition*. Chico.

Parker, B.J. 2001. *The Mechanics of Empire: The Northern Frontier of Assyria as a Case Study in Imperial Dynamics.* Helsinki.

Parker, B.J. 2002. At the Edge of Empire: Conceptualizing Assyria's Anatolian Frontier ca. 700 BC. *Journal of Anthropological Archaeology* 21: 371–395.

Parpola, S. 1987. *The Correspondence of Sargon II*, 1: *Letters from Assyria and the West* (State Archives of Assyria 1). Helsinki.

Parpola, S. 2003. Assyria's Expansion in the 8th and 7th Centuries and Its Long-Term Repercussions in the West. In: Dever, W.G. and Gitin, S., eds. *Symbiosis, Symbolism, and the Power of the Past: Canaan, Ancient Israel and Their Neighbors from the Late Bronze Age through Roman Palestina (Proceedings of the Centennial Symposium W.F. Albright Institute of Oriental Research and American Schools of Oriental Research, May 29–31, 2000)*. Winona Lake: 99–111.

Porten, B. 1981. The Identity of King Adon. *The Biblical Archaeologist* 44: 36–52.

Postgate, J.N. 1992. The Land of Assur and the Yoke of Assur. *World Archaeology* 23: 247–263.

Powell, M. 1992. Weights and Measures. In: Freedman, D.N., ed. *The Anchor Bible Dictionary* 6. New York: 897–908.

Prag, K. 1987. Decorative Architecture in Ammon, Moab and Judah. *Levant* 19: 121–127.

Pritchard, J.B. 1959. *Hebrew Inscriptions and Stamps from Gibeon*. Philadelphia.

Pritchard, J.B. 1961. *The Water System of Gibeon* (University of Pennsylvania Museum Monographs 22). Philadelphia.

Pritchard, J.B. 1962. *Gibeon, Where the Sun Stood Still: The Discovery of the Biblical City* (Princeton Studies on the Near East). Princeton.

Pritchard, J.B. 1964. *Winery, Defenses, and Soundings at Gibeon* (University of Pennsylvania Museum Monographs 26). Philadelphia.

Pritchard, J.B. 1993. Gibeon. In: Stern, E., ed. *The New Encyclopedia of Archaeological Excavations in the Holy Land* 2. Jerusalem: 511–514.

Procksch, O. 1909. Der Schauplatz der Geschichte Davids. *Palästinajahrbuch des Deutschen Evangelischen Instituts für Altertumswissenschaft des Heiligen Landes zu Jerusalem* 5: 58–80.

Propp, W.C. 2006. *Exodus 19–40: A New Translation with Introduction and Commentary* (The Anchor Bible 2). New York.

Puech, E. 1977. Documents Epigraphiques De Buseirah. *Levant* 9: 11–20.

Pullen, D.J. 1994. A Lead Seal from Tsoungiza, Ancient Nemea, and Early Bronze Age Aegean Sealing Systems. *American Journal of Archaeology* 98: 35–52.

Rahmani, L.I. 1969. Notes on Some Acquisitions. *'Atiqot* 5 (Hebrew Series): 81–83 (Hebrew), 10–11 (English summary).

Rainey, A.F. 1975. The Fate of Lachish during the Campaigns of Sennacherib and Nebuchadrezzar. In: Aharoni, Y., ed. *Investigations at Lachish: The Sanctuary and the Residency (Lachish V)* (Publications of the Institute of Archaeology of Tel Aviv University 4). Tel Aviv: 47–60.

Rainey, A.F. 1982. Wine from the Royal Vineyards. *Bulletin of the American Schools of Oriental Research* 245: 57–62.

Rainey, A.F. 1987. Arad in the Latter Days of the Judean Monarchy. *Cathedra* 42: 16–25 (Hebrew).

Rappaport, U. 1995. The History of the Hasmonaean State—from Jonathan to Antigonos. In: Eshel, H. and Amit, D., eds. *The Hasmonean Period*. Jerusalem: 61–76 (Hebrew).

Rattray, S. 1991. The Biblical Measures of Capacity. In: Milgrom, J. *Leviticus 1–16: New Translation with Introduction and Commentary* (The Anchor Bible 3). New York: 890–901.

Redford, D.B. 1992. *Egypt, Canaan, and Israel in Ancient Times*. Princeton.

Redpath, H.A. 1907. *The Book of the Prophet Ezekiel* (Westminster Commentaries). London.

Reich, R. 1992. The Beth-Zur Citadel II—A Persian Residency? *Eretz-Israel* 23: 247–252 (Hebrew), 154* (English summary).

Reich, R. 2003. Local Seal Impressions of the Hellenistic Period. In: Geva, H., ed. *Jewish Quarter Excavations in the Old City of Jerusalem, Conducted by Nahman Avigad, 1969–1982* II: *The Finds: Areas A, W and X-2, Final Report*. Jerusalem: 256–262.

Reich, R. 2012. A Fiscal Bulla from the City of David, Jerusalem. *Israel Exploration Journal* 62: 200–205.

Reich, R. and Brandl, B. 1985. Gezer under Assyrian Rule. *Palestine Exploration Quarterly* 117: 41–54.

Reich, R. and Shukron, E. 1998. Jerusalem: City of David. *Excavations and Surveys in Israel* 18: 91–92.

Reich, R. and Shukron, E. 2007. Some New Insights and Notes on the Cutting of the Siloam Tunnel. In: Meiron, E., ed. *City of David—Studies of Ancient Jerusalem (The 8th Annual Conference)*. Jerusalem: 133–161 (Hebrew).

Renfrew, C. 1972. *The Emergence of Civilisation: The Cyclades in the Third Millennium B.C.* London.

Reventlow, H. 2008. A Religious Alternative to a Political Response to a Severe Political Crisis: King Ahaz and the Prophet Isaiah. In: Reventlow, H. and Hoffman, Y., eds. *Religious Responses to Political Crisis in Jewish and Christian Tradition* (Library of Hebrew Bible/Old Testament Studies 444). New York and London: 36–51.

Rice, P.M. 1987. *Pottery Analysis—A Sourcebook*. Chicago.

Richardson, H.N. 1968. A Stamped Handle from Khirbet Yarmuk. *Bulletin of the American Schools of Oriental Research* 192: 12–16.

Rowe, A. 1936. *A Catalogue of Egyptian Scarabs, Scaraboids, Seals and Amulets in the Palestine Archaeological Museum*. Cairo.

Saller, S.J. 1953. Stamped Impression on the Pottery of Bethany. *Studii Biblici Franciscani Liber Annuus* 3: 5–36.

Saller, S.J. 1957. *Excavations at Bethany (1949–1953)*. Jerusalem.

Sass, B. 1993. The Pre-Exilic Hebrew Seals: Iconism vs. Anicinism. In: Sass, B. and Uehlinger, C., eds. *Studies in the Iconography of Northwest Semitic Inscribed Seals* (Orbis Biblicus et Orientalis 125). Fribourg and Göttingen: 194–256.

Sass, B. 2000. The Small Finds. In: Finkelstein, I., Ussishkin, D. and Halpern, B., eds. *Megiddo* III: *The 1992–1996 Seasons* (Monograph Series of the Institute of Archaeology of Tel Aviv University 18). Tel Aviv: 349–423.

Sass, B. 2005. *The Alphabet at the Turn of the Millennium: The West Semitic Alphabet ca. 1150–850 BCE; The Antiquity of the Arabian, Greek and Phrygian Alphabets* (Occasional Publications of the Institute of Archaeology of Tel Aviv University 4). Tel Aviv.

Sass, B. 2010. Lion Stamps from Babylon in the Sixth Century BCE and Their Connection to the Lion Stamps from Judah. In: Lipschits, O. and Koch, I., eds. *New Studies on the Lion Stamp Impressions from Judah (Abstracts of a Symposium, 14 January 2010, Tel Aviv University)*. Tel Aviv: 13–14 (Hebrew).

Sayce, A.H. 1893. The Cuneiform and Other Inscriptions Found at Lachish and Elsewhere in the South of Palestine. *Palestine Exploration Fund Quarterly Statement*: 25: 25–32.

Sayce, A.H. 1900. The Age of the Inscribed Jar-Handles from Palestine. *Palestine Exploration Fund Quarterly Statement* 32: 66–69.

Schipper, B.U. 2010. Egypt and the Kingdom of Judah under Josiah and Jehoiakim. *Tel Aviv* 37: 200–226.

Schloen, J.D. 2001. *The House of the Father as Fact and Symbol: Patrimonialism in Ugarit and the Ancient Near East* (Studies in the Archaeology and History of the Levant 2). Winona Lake.

Schloen, J.D. 2016. Economy and Society in Iron Age Israel and Judah: An Archaeological Perspective. In: Niditch, S., ed. *The Wiley Blackwell Companion to Ancient Israel*. Chichester: 433–453.

Scott, R.B.Y. 1958. The Hebrew Cubit. *Journal of Biblical Literature* 77: 205–214.

Scott, R.B.Y. 1970. Weights and Measurements of the Bible. *Biblical Archaeology Review* 3: 345–358.

Segrè, A. 1945. A Documentary Analysis of Ancient Palestinian Units of Measure. *Journal of Biblical Literature* 64: 357–375.

Sellers, O.R. 1933. *The Citadel of Beth-Zur; A Preliminary Report of the First Excavation Conducted by the Presbyterian Theological Seminary, Chicago, and the American School of Oriental Research, Jerusalem, in 1931 at Khirbat et Tubeiqa*. Philadelphia.

Sellers, O.R. and Albright, W.F. 1931. The First Campaign of Excavation at Beth-Zur. *Bulletin of the American Schools of Oriental Research* 43: 2–13.

Sellers, O.R., Funk, R.W., McKenzie, J.L., Lapp, P. and Lapp, N. 1968. *The 1957 Excavation at Beth-Zur* (Annual of the American Schools of Oriental Research 38). Cambridge, MA.

Sellin, E. and Watzinger, C. 1913. *Jericho: Die Ergebnisse der Ausgrabungen* (Wissenschaftliche Veröffentlichungen der Deutsche Orientgesellschaft 22). Leipzig.

Sergi, O. 2016. *lmlk* Stamp Impressions. In: Lipschits, O., Gadot, Y. and Freud, L., eds. *Ramat Raḥel III: Final Publication of Yohanan Aharoni's Excavations (1954, 1959–1962)* (Monograph Series of the Institute of Archaeology of Tel Aviv University 35). Tel Aviv and Winona Lake: 287–341.

Sergi, O. Forthcoming (a). Concentric Incised Circles. In: Lipschits, O., Oeming, M., Freud, L. and Gadot, Y., eds. *Ramat Raḥel V: The Renewed Excavations by the Tel Aviv–Heidelberg Expedition (2005–2010): The Finds* (Monograph Series of the Institute of Archaeology of Tel Aviv University). Tel Aviv and University Park, PA.

Sergi, O. Forthcoming (b). *LMLK* Stamp Impressions. In: Lipschits, O., Freud, L., Oeming, M. and Gadot, Y., eds. *Ramat Raḥel V: The Renewed Excavations by the Tel Aviv–Heidelberg Expedition (2005–2010): The Finds* (Monograph Series of the Institute of Archaeology of Tel Aviv University). Tel Aviv and University Park, PA.

Sergi, O., Karasik, A., Gadot, Y. and Lipschits, O. 2012. The Royal Judahite Storage Jar: A Computer-Generated Typology and Its Archaeological and Historical Implications. *Tel Aviv* 39: 64–92.

Shai, I., Ben-Shlomo, D. and Maeir, A.M. 2012. Late Iron Age Judean Cooking Pots with Impressed Handles: A New Class of Stamp Impressions from the Kingdom of Judah. In: Maeir, A.M., Magness, J. and Schiffman, L.H., eds. *"Go Out and Study the Land" (Judges 18:2): Archaeological, Historical and Textual Studies in Honor of Hanan Eshel* (Supplements to the Journal for the Study of Judaism 148). Leiden: 225–244.

Shai, I., Dagan, A., Reihl, S., Orendi, A., Uziel, J. and Suriano, M. 2014. A Private Stamped Seal Handle from *Tell Bornāṭ/ Tēl Burnā*, Israel. *Zeitschrift des Deutschen Palästina-Vereins* 130: 121–137.

Shai, I. and Maeir, A.M. 2003. Pre-*lmlk* Jars: A New Class of Iron Age IIA Storage Jars. *Tel Aviv* 30: 108–123.

Sherratt, S. and Sherratt, A. 1993. The Growth of the Mediterranean Economy in the Early First Millennium BC. *World Archaeology* 24: 361–378.

Shiloh, Y. 1984. *Excavations in the City of David*, I: *1978–1982 Interim Report of the First Five Seasons* (Qedem 19). Jerusalem.

Shiloh, Y. 1986. A Group of Hebrew Bullae from the City of David. *Israel Exploration Journal* 36: 16–38.

Shoham, Y. 2000a. A Hebrew Seal and Seal Impressions. In: Ariel, D.T., ed. *Excavations at the City of David 1978–1985 Directed by Yigal Shiloh* VI: *Inscriptions* (Qedem 41). Jerusalem: 81–84.

Shoham, Y. 2000b. *Lmlk* Seal Impressions and Concentric Circles. In: Ariel, D.T., ed. *Excavations at the City of David 1978– 1985 Directed by Yigal Shiloh* VI: *Inscriptions* (Qedem 41). Jerusalem: 75–80.

Siddal, L.R. 2009. Tiglath-Pileser III's Aid to Ahaz: A New Look at Problems of the Biblical Accounts in Light of the Assyrian Sources. *Ancient Near Eastern Studies* 46: 93–106.

Sinclair, L.A. 1960. *An Archaeological Study of Gibeah (Tell el-Fûl)* (Annual of the American Schools of Oriental Research 34–35). New Haven.

Singer-Avitz, L. 2002. Arad: The Iron Age Pottery Assemblages. *Tel Aviv* 29: 110–214.

Singer-Avitz, L. and Eshet, Y. 1999. Beersheba—A Gateway Community in Southern Arabian Long-Distance Trade in the Eighth Century B.C.E. *Tel Aviv* 26: 3–75.

Skinner, J. 1895. *The Book of Ezekiel*. London.

Solimany, G. and Barzel, V. 2008. Ramat Raḥel. *Ḥadashot Arkheologiyot—Excavations and Surveys in Israel* 120. http://www.hadashot-esi.org.il/report_detail_eng .aspx?id=793&mag_id=114.

Solimany, G. and Barzel, V. 2016. Salvage Excavations 2000– 2002. In: Lipschits, O., Gadot, Y. and Freud, L., eds. *Ramat Raḥel III: Final Publication of Yohanan Aharoni's Excavations (1954, 1959–1962)* (Monograph Series of the Institute of Archaeology of Tel Aviv University 35). Tel Aviv and Winona Lake: 679–701.

Spalinger, A. 1976. Psammetichus, King of Egypt: I. *Journal of the American Research Center in Egypt* 13: 133–147.

Stager, L.E. 1985. The Archaeology of the Family in Ancient Israel. *Bulletin of the American Schools of Oriental Research* 260: 1–35.

Stager, L.E. 1996. Ashkelon and the Archaeology of Destruction: Kislev 604 BCE. *Eretz-Israel* 25: 61*–74*.

Stager, L.E. 1998. Forging an Identity: The Emergence of Ancient Israel. In: Coogan, M.D., ed. *The Oxford History of the Biblical World*. New York: 123–175.

Stager, L.E. 2003. The Patrimonial Kingdom of Solomon. In: Dever, W.G. and Gitin, S., eds. *Symbiosis, Symbolism and the Power of the Past: Canaan, Ancient Israel and Their Neighbors from the Late Bronze Age through Roman Palestina (Proceedings of the Centennial Symposium W.F. Albright Institute of Oriental Research and American Schools of Oriental Research, May 29–31, 2000)*. Winona Lake: 63–74.

Stager, L.E., Master, D.M. and Schloen, J.D. 2011. *Ashkelon 3: The Seventh Century B.C.* (Final Reports of the Leon Levy Expedition to Ashkelon). Winona Lake.

Starkey, J.L. 1937a. Excavations at Tell Ed Duweir: The Wellcome Marston Archaeological Research Expedition to the Near East. *Palestine Exploration Quarterly* 69: 228–241.

Starkey, J.L. 1937b. Lachish as Illustrating Bible History. *Palestine Exploration Quarterly* 69: 171–179.

Steiner, M.L. 2001. *Excavations by Kathleen M. Kenyon in Jerusalem 1961–1967* III: *The Settlement in the Bronze and the Iron Ages*. London and New York.

Stekelis, M. 1935. A Jewish Tomb-Cave at Ramat Rachel. *Qobetz* 3: 19–40.

Stern, E. 1962. Measures and Weights. *Encyclopedia Biblica* 4: 846–878 (Hebrew).

Stern, E. 1971a. Achemenid Lion-Stamps from the Satrapy of Judah. *Eretz-Israel* 10: 268–273 (Hebrew), xix (English summary).

Stern, E. 1971b. Seal-Impressions in the Achaemenid Style in the Province of Judah. *Bulletin of the American Schools of Oriental Research* 202: 6–16.

Stern, E. 1982. *Material Culture of the Land of the Bible in the Persian Period 538–332 B.C.* Warminster.

Stern, E. 1984. The Archeology of Persian Palestine. In: Davies, W.D. and Finkelstein, L., eds. *Cambridge History of Judaism* I. Cambridge, U.K.: 88–114.

Stern, E. 1990a. The Dor Province in the Persian Period in the Light of the Recent Excavations at Dor. *Transeuphratène* 2: 147–155.

Stern, E. 1990b. Hazor, Dor and Megiddo in the Time of Ahab and under Assyrian Rule. *Israel Exploration Journal* 40: 12–30.

Stern, E. 1994. The Eastern Border of the Kingdom of Judah in Its Last Days. In: Coogan, M.D., Exum, J.C. and Stager, L.E., eds. *Scripture and Other Artifacts: Essays on the Bible and Archaeology in Honor of Philip J. King*. Louisville: 399–409.

Stern, E. 2000. The Babylonian Gap. *Biblical Archeology Review* 26(6): 45–51, 76.

Stern, E. 2001. *Archaeology of the Land of the Bible* II: *The Assyrian, Babylonian, and Persian Periods (732–332 BCE)* (The Anchor Yale Bible Reference Library). New York, London, Toronto, Sydney and Auckland.

Stern, E. 2007a. Stratum IV—The Persian Period. In: Stern, E., ed. *En-Gedi Excavations* I: *Conducted by B. Mazar and I. Dunayevsky. Final Report (1961–1965)*. Jerusalem: 193–270.

Stern, E. 2007b. Stratum IV—The Persian Period: Handles with Lion Seal Impressions. In: Stern, E., ed. *En-Gedi Excavations* I: *Conducted by B. Mazar and I. Dunayevsky. Final Report (1961–1965)*. Jerusalem: 253–255.

Stern, E. 2007c. Stratum V—The Late Judean Period: Impressions of the Kingdom of Judah. In: Stern, E., ed. *En-Gedi Excavations* I: *Conducted by B. Mazar and I. Dunayevsky. Final Report (1961–1965)*. Jerusalem: 139–156.

Stern, E. 2007d. Stratum V—The Late Judean Period: Prancing Horse Impression. In: Stern, E., ed. *En-Gedi Excavations* I: *Conducted by B. Mazar and I. Dunayevsky. Final Report (1961–1965)*. Jerusalem: 163–164.

Stern, E. 2007e. Stratum V—The Late Judean Period: Seal Impression of Nera'. In: Stern, E., ed. *En-Gedi Excavations* I: *Conducted by B. Mazar and I. Dunayevsky. Final Report (1961–1965)*. Jerusalem: 161–162.

Stern, E., Lipschits, O. and Vanderhooft, D.S. 2007. New Yehud Stamp Impressions from En Gedi. *Tel Aviv* 34: 66–73.

Stern, E. and Matskevich, S. 2007a. Stratigraphy of the Excavated Areas. In: Stern, E., ed. *En-Gedi Excavations* I: *Conducted by B. Mazar and I. Dunayevsky. Final Report (1961–1965)*. Jerusalem: 69–75.

Stern, E. and Matskevich, S. 2007b. Stratum V—The Late Judean Period: Stratigraphy of Stratum V. In: Stern, E., ed. *En-Gedi Excavations* I: *Conducted by B. Mazar and I. Dunayevsky. Final Report (1961–1965)*. Jerusalem: 77–85.

Stern, E. and Matskevich, S. 2007c. Stratum IV—The Persian Period: Stratigraphy of Stratum IV. In: Stern, E., ed. *En-Gedi Excavations* I: *Conducted by B. Mazar and I. Dunayevsky. Final Report (1961–1965)*. Jerusalem: 193–197.

Stewart, S.T. 1988. Bureaucracy and Packaging at Lerna: Evidence from the Clay Sealings in the House of the Tiles. *American Journal of Archaeology* 92: 253.

Strange, J. 1966. The Inheritance of Dan. *Studia Theologica* 20: 120–139.

Strawn, B.A. 2005. *What Is Stronger than a Lion? Leonine Image and Metaphor in the Hebrew Bible and the Ancient Near East* (Orbis Biblicus et Orientalis 212). Fribourg and Göttingen.

Sukenik, E.L. 1933. The "Jerusalem" and "The City" Stamps on Jar Handles. *Journal of the Palestine Oriental Society* 13: 226–231.

Sukenik, E.L. 1933–34. Enigmas in Hebrew Epigraphy. *Bulletin of the Israel Exploration Society* 2: 5–7 (Hebrew).

Swanson, K. 2002. A Reassessment of Hezekiah's Reform in Light of Jar Handles and Iconographic Evidence. *Catholic Bible Quarterly* 64: 460–469.

Tadmor, H. 1958. The Campaigns of Sargon II of Assur: A Chronological-Historical Study. *Journal of Cuneiform Studies* 12: 22–40, 77–100.

Tadmor, H. 1964. The Assyrian Campaigns to Philistia. In: Liver, J., ed. *The Military History of the Land of Israel in Biblical Times.* Tel Aviv: 261–285 (Hebrew).

Tadmor, H. 1966. Philistia under Assyrian Rule. *The Biblical Archaeologist* 29: 86–102.

Tadmor, H. 1973. On the History of Samaria in the Biblical Period. In: Aviram, J., ed. *Eretz Shomron: The Thirtieth Archaeological Convention, September 1972.* Jerusalem: 67–74 (Hebrew), xv (English summary).

Tadmor, H. 1975. Assyria and the West: The Ninth Century and its Aftermath. In: Goedicke, H. and Roberts, J.J.M., eds. *Unity and Diversity: Essays in the History, Literature, and Religion of the Ancient Near East.* Baltimore and London: 36–48.

Tadmor, H., ed. 1983. *The History of the People of Israel, First Series: From the Beginning to the Bar-Kochvah Revolt; The Returning to Zion: The Period of Persian Rule.* Jerusalem (Hebrew).

Tadmor, H. and Yamada, S. 2011. *The Royal Inscriptions of Tiglath-Pileser III (744–727 BC) and Shalmaneser V (726–722 BC), Kings of Assyria* (Royal Inscriptions of the Neo-Assyrian Period 1). Winona Lake.

Tal, O. 2006. *The Archaeology of Hellenistic Palestine: Between Tradition and Renewal.* Jerusalem (Hebrew).

Tatum, L. 1991. King Manasseh and the Royal Fortress at Ḥorvart ʿUsa. *The Biblical Archaeologist* 54: 136–145.

Thareani, Y. 2009. In the Service of the Empire: Local Elites and "*Pax Assyriaca*" in the Negev. *Eretz-Israel* 29: 184–191 (Hebrew), 288* (English summary).

Thareani, Y. 2010. *Towns in the Desert: Geographical, Economic and Sociopolitical Perspectives* (Ph.D. dissertation, Tel Aviv University). Tel Aviv (Hebrew with English summary).

Thareani-Sussely, Y. 2002. Center and Periphery—A Case Study: The Arad–Beersheba Valley at the End of the Iron Age (M.A. thesis, Tel Aviv University). Tel Aviv (Hebrew).

Thareani-Sussely, Y. 2007a. Ancient Caravanserais: An Archaeological View from ʿAroer. *Levant* 39: 123–141.

Thareani-Sussely, Y. 2007b. The 'Archaeology of the Days of Manasseh' Reconsidered in the Light of Evidence from the Beersheba Valley. *Palestine Exploration Quarterly* 139: 69–77.

Thompson, C.M. 2003. Sealed Silver in Iron Age Cisjordan and the "Invention" of Coinage. *Oxford Journal of Archaeology* 22: 67–107.

Thompson, J.A. 1942. On Some Stamps and a Seal from Lachish. *Bulletin of the American Schools of Oriental Research* 86: 24–27.

Torgë, H. and Gendelman, P. 2008. Khirbat Burnat. *Ḥadashot Arkheologiyot—Excavations and Surveys in Israel* 120. http://www.hadashot-esi.org.il/Report_Detail_Eng.aspx?id=923&mag_id=114.

Torrey, C.C. 1970. *Pseudo-Ezekiel and the Original Prophecy.* New York.

Tsafrir, Y. 1977. The Walls of Jerusalem in the Period of Nehemiah. *Cathedra* 4: 31–42 (Hebrew).

Tsur, Y. 2015. Tel Socoh in Light of Archaeological Survey (M.A. thesis, Tel Aviv University). Tel Aviv (Hebrew).

Tuell, S.S. 1992. *The Law of the Temple in Ezekiel 40–48* (Harvard Semitic Monographs 49). Atlanta.

Tufnell, O. 1950. Excavations at Tell ed-Duweir, Palestine, Directed by the Late J. L. Starkey, 1932–1938: Some Results and Reflections. *Palestine Exploration Quarterly* 82: 65–80.

Tufnell, O. 1953. *Lachish* III *(Tell ed-Duweir): The Iron Age.* London, New York and Toronto.

Tufnell, O. 1959. Hazor, Samaria and Lachish: A Synthesis. *Palestine Exploration Quarterly* 91: 90–105.

Tushingham, A.D. 1970. A Royal Israelite Seal (?) and the Royal Jar Handle Stamps (Part One). *Bulletin of the American Schools of Oriental Research* 200: 71–78.

Tushingham, A.D. 1971. A Royal Israelite Seal (?) and the Royal Jar Handle Stamps (Part Two). *Bulletin of the American Schools of Oriental Research* 201: 23–35.

Tushingham, A.D., ed. 1985. *Excavations in Jerusalem 1961–1967* I. Toronto.

Tushingham, A.D. 1992. New Evidence Bearing on the Two-Winged *LMLK* Stamp. *Bulletin of the American Schools of Oriental Research* 287: 61–65.

Uehlinger, C. 1993. Northwest Semitic Inscribed Seals, Iconography and Syro-Palestinian Religions of Iron Age II: Some Afterthoughts and Conclusions. In: Sass, B. and Uehlinger, C., eds. *Studies in the Iconography of Northwest Semitic Inscribed Seals* (Orbis Biblicus et Orientalis 125). Fribourg and Göttingen: 257–288.

Uehlinger, C. 1997. Figurative Policy, Propaganda und Prophetie. In: Emerton, J.A., ed. *Congress Volume Cambridge 1995* (Supplements to Vetus Testamentum 66). Leiden: 297–349.

Uehlinger, C. 1999. "Powerful Persianisms" in Glyptic Iconography of Persian Period Palestine. In: Becking, B. and Korpel, M.C.A., eds. *The Crisis of Israelite Religion: Transformation of Religious Tradition in Exilic and Post-Exilic Times* (Oudtestamentische Studiën 42). Leiden: 134–182.

Uehlinger, C. 2003. Clio in a World of Pictures—Another Look at the Lachish Reliefs from Sennacherib's Southwest Palace at Nineveh. In: Grabbe, L.L., ed. *"Like a Bird in a Cage": The Invasion of Sennacherib in 701 BCE* (Journal for the Study of the Old Testament, Supplement Series 363). London and New York: 221–305.

Ungnad, A. 1942–43. Die Zahl der von Sanherib deportierten Judäer. *Zeitschrift für die Alttestamentliche Wissenschaft* 59: 199–202.

Ussishkin, D. 1976. Royal Judean Storage Jars and Private Seal Impressions. *Bulletin of the American Schools of Oriental Research* 223: 1–13.

Ussishkin, D. 1977. The Destruction of Lachish by Sennacherib and the Dating of the Royal Judean Storage Jars. *Tel Aviv* 4: 28–60.

Ussishkin, D. 1978. Excavations at Tell Lachish, 1973–1977 Preliminary Report. *Tel Aviv* 5: 1–97.

Ussishkin, D. 1980. The "Lachish Reliefs" and the City of Lachish. *Israel Exploration Journal* 30: 174–195.

Ussishkin, D. 1982. *The Conquest of Lachish by Sennacherib* (Publications of the Institute of Archaeology of Tel Aviv University 6). Tel Aviv.

Ussishkin, D. 1983. Excavations at Tell Lachish 1978–1983: Second Preliminary Report. *Tel Aviv* 10: 97–175.

Ussishkin, D. 1993. Lachish. In: Stern, E., ed. *The New Encyclopedia of Archaeological Excavations in the Holy Land* 3. Jerusalem: 897–911.

Ussishkin, D. 1996. Excavations and Restoration Work at Tel Lachish 1985–1994: Third Preliminary Report. *Tel Aviv* 23: 3–60.

Ussishkin, D. 2003. Symbols of Conquest in Sennacharib's Reliefs of Lachish: Impaled Prisoners and Booty. In: Potts, T., Roaf, M. and Stein, D., eds. *Culture Through Objects: Ancient Near Eastern Studies in Honour of P.R.S. Moorey*. Oxford: 207–217.

Ussishkin, D. 2004a. Area GW: The Outer City-Gate. In: Ussishkin, D., ed. *The Renewed Archaeological Excavations at Lachish (1973–1994)* II (Monograph Series of the Institute of Archaeology of Tel Aviv University 22). Tel Aviv: 535–623.

Ussishkin, D. 2004b. The Royal Judean Storage Jars and Seal Impressions from the Renewed Excavations. In: Ussishkin, D., ed. *The Renewed Archaeological Excavations at Lachish (1973–1994)* IV (Monograph Series of the Institute of Archaeology of Tel Aviv University 22). Tel Aviv: 2133–2147.

Ussishkin, D. 2004c. A Synopsis of the Stratigraphical, Chronological and Historical Issues. In: Ussishkin, D., ed. *The Renewed Archaeological Excavations at Lachish (1973–1994)* I (Monograph Series of the Institute of Archaeology of Tel Aviv University 22). Tel Aviv: 50–119.

Ussishkin, D. 2006. Sennacherib's Campaign to Philistia and Judah: Ekron, Lachish and Jerusalem. In: Amit, Y., Ben Zvi, E., Finkelstein, I. and Lipschits, O., eds. *Essays on Ancient Israel in Its Near Eastern Context: A Tribute to Nadav Na'aman*. Winona Lake: 339–358.

Ussishkin, D. 2011. The Dating of the *lmlk* Storage Jars and Its Implications: Rejoinder to Lipschits, Sergi and Koch. *Tel Aviv* 38: 220–240.

Ussishkin, D. 2012. *Lmlk* Seal Impressions Once Again: A Second Rejoinder to Oded Lipschits. *Antiguo Oriente* 10: 13–23.

Van Buren, E.D. 1939. The Rosette in Mesopotamian Art. *Zeitschrift für Assyriologie* 45: 99–107.

Vanderhooft, D.S. 1995. The Edomite Dialect and Script: A Review of the Evidence. In: Edelman, D.V., ed. *You Shall Not Abhor an Edomite for He Is Your Brother: Edom and Seir in History and Tradition* (Archaeology and Biblical Studies 3). Atlanta: 137–157.

Vanderhooft, D.S. 1999. *The Neo-Babylonian Empire and Babylon in the Latter Prophets* (Harvard Semitic Museum Monographs 59). Atlanta.

Vanderhooft, D.S. 2009. The Israelite *mišpāḥâ*, the Priestly Writings, and Changing Valences in Israel's Kinship Terminology: An Archaeologist's View. In: Schloen, J.D., ed. *Exploring the Longue Durée: Essays in Honor of Lawrence E. Stager*. Winona Lake: 485–496.

Vanderhooft, D.S. 2011. ʾel-mĕdînâ ûmĕdînâ kiktābāh: Scribes and Scripts in Yehud and in Achaemenid Transeuphratene. In: Lipschits, O., Knoppers, G.N. and Oeming, M., eds. *Judah and the Judeans in the Achaemenid Period: Negotiating Identity in an International Context*. Winona Lake: 529–544.

Vanderhooft, D.S. and Lipschits, O. 2007. A New Typology of the Yehud Stamp Impressions. *Tel Aviv* 34: 12–37.

Vanderhooft, D.S., Richey, M. and Lipschits, O. 2019. A New Type of *Yehud* Stamp Impression: *yhwd/gdlyh*. *Israel Exploration Journal* 69: 54–59.

Vaughn, A.G. 1999a. Palaeographic Dating of Judaean Seals and Its Significance for Biblical Research. *Bulletin of the American Schools of Oriental Research* 313: 43–64.

Vaughn, A.G. 1999b. *Theology, History and Archaeology in the Chronicler's Account of Hezekiah*. Atlanta, GA.

Vaughn, A.G. 2016. *lmlk* and Official Seal Impressions. In: Bunimovitz, S. and Lederman, Z., eds. *Tel Beth-Shemesh: A Border Community in Judah. Renewed Excavations 1990-2000: The Iron Age* (Monograph Series of the Institute of Archaeology of Tel Aviv University 34). Winona Lake: 480–501.

Vaughn, A.G. 2018. Should All of the LMLK Jars Still Be Attributed to Hezekiah? Yes! In: Farber, Z. and Wright, J.L., eds. *Archaeology and History of Eighth-Century Judah*. Atlanta: 351–356.

de Vaux, R. 1961. *Ancient Israel: Its Life and Institutions*. New York.

de Vaux, R. 1973. *Archaeology and the Dead Sea Scrolls*. Oxford.

van der Veen, P.G. 2014. *The Final Phase of Iron Age II in Judah, Ammon and Edom: A Study of Provenanced Official Seals and Bullae as Chronological Markers* (Alter Orient und Altes Testament 415) Münster.

Vieweger, D. and Häser, J. 2007. Tall Ziraʿa: Five Thousand Years of Palestinian History on a Single-Settlement Mound. *Near Eastern Archaeology* 70: 147–167.

Vincent, L.H. 1956. *Jerusalem de l'ancien testament: recherches d'archéologie et d'histoire* II: *Archéologie du temple-—Evolution historique de la ville.* Paris.

Vitelli, K.D. 1977. Neolithic Potter's Marks from Lerna and the Franchthi Cave. *The Journal of the Walters Art Gallery* 36: 17–30.

Wagenaar, J.A. 2003. Post-Exilic Calendar Innovations. The First Month of the Year and the Date of Passover and the Festival of Unleavened Bread. *Zeitschrift für die Alttestamentliche Wissenschaft* 115: 3–24.

Walsh, C.E. 2000. *The Fruit of the Vine*: *Viticulture in Ancient Israel* (Harvard Semitic Monographs 60). Winona Lake.

Wampler, J.C. 1941. Three Cistern Groups from Tell en-Naṣbeh. *Bulletin of the American Schools of Oriental Research* 82: 25–43.

Wampler, J.C. 1947. *Tell en-Naṣbeh Excavated under the Direction of the Late William Frederic Badè* II: *The Pottery.* Berkeley and New Haven.

Ward, W.A. 1968. The Four-Winged Serpent on Hebrew Seals. *Revisita degli Studi Orientali* 43: 135–143.

Warren, C. and Conder, C.R. 1884. *The Survey of Western Palestine: Jerusalem.* London.

Watzinger, C. 1933. *Denkmäler Palästinas: eine Einführung in die Archäologie des Heiligen Landes* I: *Von den Anfängen bis zum schen Königszeit.* Leipzig.

Weil, R. 1920. *La Cité de David: compte rendu des fouilles exécutées à Jérusalem, sur le site de la ville primitive: campagne de 1913–1914.* Paris.

Weinberger-Stern, M. 2015. Khirbet el-Burj and Jerusalem Surroundings in the Late Iron Age and the Persian Period (M.A. thesis, Tel Aviv University). Tel Aviv (Hebrew).

Weippert, H. and Weippert, M. 1976. Jericho in der Eisenzeit. *Zeitschrift des Deutschen Palästina-Vereins* 92: 105–148.

Weippert, M. 2010. *Historisches Textbuch zum Alten Testament.* Göttingen.

Welten, P. 1969. *Die Königs-Stempel. Ein Beitrag zur Militärpolitik Judas unter Hiskia and Josia* (Abhandlungen des Deutschen Palästinavereins 1). Wiesbaden.

Wenning, R. 1989. Mesad Hasavyahu: Ein Stützpunkt des Jojakim? In: Hossfeld, F.L., ed. *Vom Sinai zum Horeb: Stationen alttestamentlicher Glaubensgechichte.* Würzburg: 169–196.

Wevers, J.W. 1950. Exegetical Principles Underlying the Septuagint Text of I Kings ii 12–xxi 43. *Oudtestamentische Studiën* 8: 300–322.

Wiencke, M. 1969. Further Seals and Sealings from Lerna. *Hesperia* 38: 500–521.

Williamson, H.G.M. 1988. The Governors of Judah under the Persians. *Tyndale Bulletin* 39: 59–82.

Wilson, C. and Warren, C. 1871. *The Recovery of Jerusalem: A Narrative of Exploration and Discovery in the City and the Holy Land.* London.

Winckler, H. 1889. *Die Keilschrifttexte Sargons nach den Papierabklatschen und Originalen neu herausgegeben.* Berlin.

Winn Leith, M.J. 1997. *Wadi Daliyeh: The Wadi Daliyeh Seal Impressions* (Discoveries in the Judaean Desert 24). Oxford.

Winter, I.J. 2000. Le Palais imaginaire: Scale and Meaning on the Iconography of Neo-Assyrian Cylinder Seals. In: Uehlinger, C., ed. *Images as Media, Sources for the Cultural History of the Near East and the Eastern Mediterranean (1st Millennium BCE)* (Orbis Biblicus et Orientalis 175). Fribourg and Göttingen: 51–87.

Wood, B.G. 1990. *Sociology of Pottery in Ancient Palestine: The Ceramic Industry and the Diffusion of Ceramic Style in the Bronze and Iron Ages* (Journal for the Study of the Old Testament Supplement Series 103). Sheffield.

Wright, G.E. 1965. *Shechem: A Biography of a Biblical City.* New York and Toronto.

Yadin, Y. 1961a. Ancient Judean Weights and the Date of the Samaria Ostraca. *Scripta Hierosolymitana* 8: 9–25.

Yadin, Y. 1961b. The Fourfold Division of Judah. *Bulletin of the American Schools of Oriental Research* 163: 6–12.

Yadin, Y. 1973. The "House of Baal" in Samaria and in Judah. In: Aviram, J., ed. *Eretz Shomron: The Thirtieth Archaeological Convention, September 1972.* Jerusalem: 52–66 (Hebrew).

Yadin, Y., Aharoni, Y., Amiran, R., Ben-Tor, A., Dothan, M., Dothan, T., Dunayevsky, I., Geva, S. and Stern, E. 1961. *Hazor* III–IV: *An Account of the Third and Fourth Seasons of Excavations, 1957–1958. Plates.* Jerusalem.

Yadin, Y., Aharoni, Y., Amiran, R., Dothan, T., Dunayevsky, I. and Perrot, J. 1960. *Hazor* II: *An Account of the Second Season of Excavations, 1956.* Jerusalem.

Yeivin, S. 1959. Tell Gath (Tell Sheikh el-ʿAreini). Notes and News. *Israel Exploration Journal* 9: 269–271.

Yeivin, S. 1961. *First Preliminary Report of the Excavations at Tel "Gat" (Tell Sheykh ʾAhmed el-ʿAreiny): Seasons 1956–1958.* Jerusalem.

Yellin, J. and Cahill, J.M. 2003. Provenance of the Rosette-Stamped Seal Impressions. In: Geva, H., ed. *Jewish Quarter Excavations in the Old City of Jerusalem, Conducted by Nahman Avigad, 1969–1982* II: *The Finds: Areas A, W and X-2, Final Report.* Jerusalem: 99–106.

Yellin, J. and Cahill, J.M. 2004. Rosette-Stamped Handles: Instrumental Neutron Activation Analysis. *Israel Exploration Journal* 54: 191–213.

Yezerski, I. 2007. Stratum V—The Late Judean Period: Pottery of Stratum V. In: Stern, E., ed. *En-Gedi Excavations* I: *Final Report (1961–1965).* Jerusalem: 86–129.

Younger, K.L., Jr. 2003. Assyrian Involvement in the Southern Levant at the End of the Eighth Century B.C.E. In: Vaughn, A.G. and Killebrew, A.E., eds. *Jerusalem in Bible and Archaeology: The First Temple Period* (Society of Biblical

Literature Symposium Series 18). Leiden and Boston: 235–263.

Younger, K.L., Jr. 2015. The Assyrian Economic Impact on the Southern Levant in the Light of Recent Study. *Israel Exploration Journal* 65: 179–204.

Younker, R.W. 1985. Israel, Judah and Ammon and the Motifs on the Baalis Seal from Tell el-ʿUmeiri. *The Biblical Archaeologist* 48: 173–180.

Zapassky, E., Finkelstein, I. and Benenson, I. 2006. Ancient Standards of Volume: Negevite Iron Age Pottery (Israel) as a Case Study in 3D Modeling. *Journal of Archaeological Science* 33: 1734–1743.

Zapassky, E., Finkelstein, I. and Benenson, I. 2009. Computing Abilities in Antiquity: The Royal Judahite Storage Jars as a Case-Study. *Journal for Archaeological Method Theory* 16: 51–67.

Zerner, C. 1986. Middle Helladic and Late Helladic Pottery from Lerna. *Hydra* 2: 58–74.

Zertal, A. 1990. The Pahwah of Samaria (Northern Israel) during the Persian Period: Types of Settlement, Economy, History and New Discoveries. *Transeuphratène* 3: 9–30.

Zimhoni, O. 1985. The Iron Age Pottery of Tel ʿEton and its Relation to the Lachish, Tell Beit Mirsim and Arad Assemblages. *Tel Aviv* 12: 63–90.

Zimhoni, O. 1997. *Studies in the Iron Age Pottery of Israel: Typological, Archaeological, and Chronological Aspects* (Occasional Publications of the Institute of Archaeology of Tel Aviv University 2). Tel Aviv.

Zimhoni, O. 2004a. *The Pottery of Levels III and II.* In: Ussishkin, D., ed. *The Renewed Archaeological Excavations at Lachish (1973–1994)* IV (Monograph Series of the Institute of Archaeology of Tel Aviv University 22). Tel Aviv: 1789–1899.

Zimhoni, O. 2004b. *The Pottery of Levels V and IV and Its Archaeological and Chronological Implications.* In: Ussishkin, D., ed. *The Renewed Archaeological Excavations at Lachish (1973–1994)* IV (Monograph Series of the Institute of Archaeology of Tel Aviv University 22). Tel Aviv: 1643–1788.

Zorn, J.R. 1994. Two Rosette Stamp Impressions from Tell en-Nasbeh. *Bulletin of the American Schools of Oriental Research* 293: 81–82.

Zorn, J.R. 1995. Three Cross-Shaped "Tet" Stamp Impressions from Tell en-Nasbeh, *Tel Aviv* 22: 98–106.

Zorn, J.R., Yellin, J. and Hayes, J. 1994. The *m(w)ṣh* Stamp Impressions and the Neo-Babylonian Period, *Israel Exploration Journal* 44: 161–183.

Index of Geographic Names

Index of Historical Figures

Index of Modern Authors